Charles Hodge

Charles Hodge

Guardian of American Orthodoxy

Paul C. Gutjahr

OXFORD
UNIVERSITY PRESS

Oxford University Press, Inc., publishes works that further
Oxford University's objective of excellence
in research, scholarship, and education.

Oxford   New York
Auckland   Cape Town   Dar es Salaam   Hong Kong   Karachi
Kuala Lumpur   Madrid   Melbourne   Mexico City   Nairobi
New Delhi   Shanghai   Taipei   Toronto

With offices in
Argentina   Austria   Brazil   Chile   Czech Republic   France   Greece
Guatemala   Hungary   Italy   Japan   Poland   Portugal   Singapore
South Korea   Switzerland   Thailand   Turkey   Ukraine   Vietnam

Published by Oxford University Press, Inc.
198 Madison Avenue, New York, New York 10016

www.oup.com

Oxford is a registered trademark of Oxford University Press

Library of Congress Cataloging-in-Publication Data
Gutjahr, Paul C.
Charles Hodge : guardian of American orthodoxy / Paul C. Gutjahr.
p.   cm.
Includes bibliographical references and index.
ISBN 978-0-19-974042-0 (hardback : alk. paper) 1. Hodge, Charles, 1797–1878. I. Title.
BX9225.H6G88   2011
230′.51092—dc22
[B]
2010014509

1 3 5 7 9 8 6 4 2

Printed in the United States of America
on acid-free paper

For
Isaac and Jeremiah
Beloved sons and treasured friends

ACKNOWLEDGMENTS

A wonderfully kind man started me down the road to writing this book. William Harris, formerly the head special-collections librarian at Princeton Theological Seminary, first introduced me to the massive, and largely untouched, collection of Charles Hodge papers. That chance meeting with Bill Harris has been the source of much gratitude and much turmoil in my life, as it has taken me a decade to bring to completion a work that has been at different times exhilarating, enervating, and educational. I have learned many things in the course of this biography, but one of the central lessons remains: if you are going to undertake a biography, pick a subject who dies young. In this particular regard, I chose poorly. Hodge lived an abnormally long and prolific life. When people reach their seventies, they often think their work is done. Not so with Hodge. His last years were among his most productive as he sat ensconced in his study, wielding his favorite pen to compose literally thousands of manuscript pages, which would eventually become his monumental *Systematic Theology* and his incisive *What is Darwinism?* Many an evening as I poured over his seemingly endless *Systematic*, I wondered what possessed me to yield to Bill Harris's siren song of the unexplored Hodge papers.

Ten years is a long time to dedicate to any project, and each of those years stands as a vibrant testimony to the fact that scholarship is not a solo endeavor. A number of funding sources helped me bring this project to completion. I wish to express my gratitude to the Center for the Study of Religion at Princeton University under the directorship of Robert Wuthnow for a yearlong fellowship that allowed me to embark on this project. The Christian Scholars Foundation under the directorship of Bernard Draper, the Princeton Library Research Fund, a visiting summer Presidential Fellowship at Princeton Theological Seminary, the Ballsy-Whitmore Fund for Research of Tenured Faculty in the Indiana University English Department, the Presidential Arts and Humanities Initiative at Indiana University, the Grant-in-Aid Fellowship fund from Indiana University, and Indiana University's Arts and Humanities Institute have all provided funding to see this project completed. Princeton Theological Seminary's library also helped greatly when they waived the permission fees to reprint images from their collections.

Countless individuals have also offered valuable commentary and insights as the work progressed. Mark Noll, Jim Moorhead, David Morgan, Leigh Schmidt, Steve Stein, and John Stewart were constant sounding boards for all things Hodge, often offering archival tidbits and research insights at crucial moments. Many of my colleagues at Indiana University were tireless in their willingness to lend a hand or offer a listening ear during my struggles with Hodge. I remain truly grateful in these regards to Jonathan Elmer, Mary Favret, Ray Hedin, George Hutchinson, Christoph Irmscher, Josh Kates, Andrew Miller, Jesse Molesworth, Richard Nash and Nick Williams. Bob Brown went above and beyond all calls of friendship in reading and commenting on large portions of the manuscript. Cary Curry stood as the living embodiment of the kindness and generosity that so marked Hodge's life. My friend Alex Van Riesen kept things light by constantly leaving me voice mail messages from Hodge spurring me on to complete the work. A typical message might run (always employing a suitably ghostlike voice): "Paul... Charles Hodge here. Where are you? Why aren't you in your office working on my biography? History awaits."

My wife, Cathy, proved to be my smartest critic as she worked her way (sometimes multiple times) through the manuscript, constantly pointing out how I might sharpen my thinking and trim my chubby prose. I will never forget the day she returned the first one hundred pages of my manuscript, having reduced it to a mere forty pages through her editing. If readers find themselves bored with what follows, they need only imagine what bloated beast might have awaited them if my wife had not constantly intervened.

Over the years, others have come alongside to shepherd this work to completion. I have had the pleasure to have worked with many excellent research assistants. Steve Davis, Heather Love, Andrew Longeman, and Laura Robinson retrieved articles, spent endless hours at microfilm machines, and ferreted out old books to help bring Charles Hodge to life. Each of them did yeoman's service, and the entire project is stronger for their efforts. Librarians such as AnnaLee Pauls in the Special Collections at Princeton University's Firestone Library, as well as Steve Crocco and Ken Henke at Princeton Theological Seminary's library offered invaluable aid. Madeleine Gonin and Cordah Pearce were helpful beyond measure as I prepared the book's illustrations. Bruce Van Patter did a marvelous job with the thumbnail sketches of key individuals in Hodge's life. I also had a wonderful and supportive editor in Cynthia Read. I was unbelievably fortunate to have her as both a guide and a sponsor. The anonymous readers of the manuscript for the press were also outstanding, and this book is much stronger for the countless insights they offered.

In the end, as always, I reserve my sincerest gratitude for my family, who have forever stood as the bedrock foundation of this—and every—project I undertake. The unconditional love and amazing generosity of my parents and sister Karen are a constant source of wonder for me. My physician father-in-law, Richard Freeman, allowed me to spend too much time recounting various ailments Hodge and his family suffered as I forced him to try to puzzle out what this or that disease might have been. My wife, Cathy, continues to be the best thing that ever happened to me, and my sons were understanding enough with my biographical obsession that when we finally decided to get a dog, they let me name it "Hodge."

It is to my sons, Isaac and Jeremiah, that I dedicate this volume. When I started this project, my oldest son had barely entered preschool. Now they are teenagers and have been forced to wonder for far too long both if their father would ever finish this book and who might actually want to read it if he did. At one particularly memorable dinner, Isaac calculated that while I had begun working on Hodge in my thirties, at my current rate of speed I would be well into my fifties before I finished. He then mused aloud whether Hodge might, in fact, outlive me even though he was already dead. He got a good chuckle out of that one. So much humor in one so young. And yet, it is the love (and humor) of my sons that has enriched my life beyond measure. As I leave this project behind, I find myself wishing that their lives might be filled with the joy that so marked Hodge's life. He was a man who not only loved his Lord, but who loved to laugh. On some deep, profoundly spiritual level Hodge understood that where there is no laughter, there is no Gospel. May God grant Isaac and Jeremiah lives rich in both.

TABLE OF CONTENTS

Part VIII 1870s: Systematic Theologian and Scientist

ILLUSTRATIONS

KEY EVENTS

IN HODGE'S LIFE

Engraved by W. G. Armstrong.

Thus saith the LORD; Behold, I set before you the WAY of LIFE.
Jer. XXI. 8.

Figure 0.1 *Way of Life* frontispiece: Frontispiece illustration from Hodge's popular devotional, *The Way of Life* (1841) [*Library of the Author*]

CHRONOLOGY

1797 December 27, Hodge is born in Philadelphia.

1810 Attends the Classical Academy in Somerville, New Jersey, with his brother.

1812 Moves with family to study at the College of New Jersey (Princeton College).
Princeton Theological Seminary founded.

1815 Professes personal faith and joins Presbyterian Church in Princeton.
September, Graduates from Princeton College.

1816 July, Visits Silver Lake, Pennsylvania, and decides to attend seminary.
October, accompanies Dr. Alexander in a tour through Virginia.
November, enters Princeton Seminary.

1819 September, graduates from Princeton Seminary.

1820 May, appointed to a one-year position at Princeton Seminary as instructor of Greek and Hebrew.
June, arrives at Princeton to live with Dr. Alexander and take up teaching post.
October, visits Boston with Benjamin Wiser; meets Moses Stuart of Andover Seminary and Nathaniel W. Taylor of the Yale Divinity School.

1821 November, ordained by the Presbytery of New Brunswick.

1822 Produces his first publication: "A Dissertation on the Importance of Biblical Literature."
May, appointed Professor of Oriental and Biblical Literature.
June 17, marries Sarah Bache, the great-granddaughter of Benjamin Franklin.

1823 June 18, Archibald (Archie) Alexander Hodge born.

1824 Builds house where he will reside the rest of his life.

1825 Founds journal which will eventually be named the *Biblical Repertory and Princeton Review* (BRPR).
August 31, Mary Elizabeth Hodge born.

1826 October, leaves Princeton for two-year study leave in Europe.

1828 May 7, Hugh Hodge marries Margaret Elizabeth Aspinwall.
September, returns to Princeton.

1830 February 21, Caspar Wistar Hodge Sr. born.

1832 March 22, Charles Hodge Jr. born.
April, mother dies in Philadelphia.

1833 Crippled, begins teaching in his home's study.

1834	May 1, John Bayard Hodge born.
1835	Publishes commentary on Romans.
	Joseph Addison Alexander formally appointed to the seminary's faculty.
1836	August 30, Catharine Bache Hodge born.
	Resumes teaching outside of his home.
1836	Publishes "Slavery" article in *BRPR*.
1837	Schism of the Old and New School Presbyterians.
1838	October 24, Francis Blanchard Hodge born.
1839	Publishes first volume of *The Constitutional History of the Presbyterian Church in America*.
1840	Appointed Professor of Exegetical and Didactic Theology.
	Publishes second volume of *The Constitutional History of the Presbyterian Church in America*.
	December 23, Sarah Bache Hodge born.
1841	Publishes *The Way of Life*.
1845	July, publishes first extended discussion on "Romish Baptism" in *BRPR*.
	November 20, Albert Dod dies.
1846	Elected the moderator of the Old School General Assembly.
1847	June 17, Archibald Alexander Hodge marries Elizabeth Holliday.
	September 9, Mary Hodge marries William M. Scott.
	Archibald Alexander Hodge and his wife leave to become missionaries in India.
1848	May 19, Ashbel Green dies.
1849	Christmas Day, his wife Sarah, dies.
1850	January 7, Samuel Miller dies.
	Embarks on intellectual battle with Edwards Amasa Park over biblical language.
	Becomes a trustee of the Princeton College.
	Archibald Alexander Hodge and family return from India.
1851	October 22, Archibald Alexander dies.
1852	July 8, marries second wife, Mary Hunter Stockton.
1856	Publishes commentary on Ephesians.
	Buys farm on the Millstone River.
1857	Publishes commentary on 1 Corinthians.
1859	Publishes commentary on 2 Corinthians.
1860	January, Publishes "The State of the Country" in *BRPR*.
	January 28, Joseph Addison Alexander dies.
1861	His daughter, Mary Hodge Scott, moves back to Princeton with her family.
	December, Presbyterian Church of the Confederate States of America founded.
	December 22, his son-in-law, William M. Scott, dies.

1866	Publishes revision of his commentary on Romans.
1869	Old and New School Presbyterians Reunite.
1872	Publishes the first and second volumes of his *Systematic Theology*.
	April 24, Semi-Centennial Celebration of his Professorship.
1873	Publishes the third volume of his *Systematic Theology*.
	February 26, his brother Hugh dies.
1874	Publishes *What is Darwinism?*
1876	April 5, John Johns, his college roommate and longtime friend, dies.
	July 31, his son Charles Jr. dies.
1877	Archibald Alexander Hodge appointed as a Seminary faculty member intended to replace his father.
1878	May 16, as his last public act, Hodge offers a prayer at funeral of Joseph Henry in Washington, D.C.
	June 19, dies in Princeton.

KEY FIGURES

IN HODGE'S LIFE

Figure 0.2 *Hodge and his brother*: Hodge and his brother, Hugh, were best friends their entire lives. [*Special Collections, Princeton Theological Seminary Libraries*]

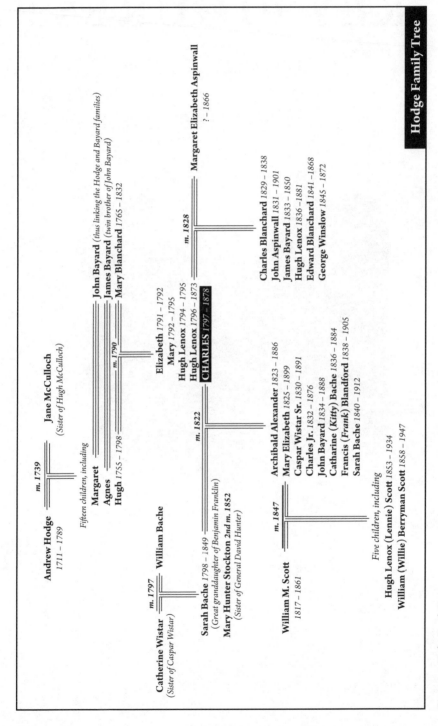

Figure 0.3 *Hodge Family Tree*

Archibald Alexander (1772–1851) was the founding faculty member of Princeton Theological Seminary. Outside of his immediate family, Alexander was the single most important influence on Hodge's life.

James Waddel Alexander (1804–1859) was the eldest son of Archibald Alexander. Following in his father's footsteps, he served as a Presbyterian pastor and a professor both in college and seminary settings. He also became one of the most famous American Presbyterian preachers of his generation.

Joseph Addison Alexander (1809–1860), commonly called "Addison," was the third son of Archibald Alexander. He was a gifted linguist and served as a faculty member at Princeton Theological Seminary from 1838 until his death. Hodge said of him: "incomparably the greatest man I ever knew, incomparably the greatest man our church has ever produced."

Margaret Aspinwall (1804–1873) married Charles Hodge's brother, Hugh, in 1828, thereby linking the Hodges to one of the wealthiest merchant families in New York City. Hugh and Margaret had seven boys, the first of which they named "Charles."

Lyman Atwater (1813–1883) served as a professor both at Princeton College and Princeton Theological Seminary. He wrote extensively for the *Biblical Repertory and Princeton Review* and became one of the journal's lead editors when Hodge stepped down in 1872.

Albert Barnes (1798–1870) was the much-beloved pastor of First Presbyterian Church in Philadelphia. An important leader among New School Presbyterians, he stood against slavery and wrote an immensely popular New Testament commentary series.

John Bayard Jr. was Charles Hodge's cousin. An influential merchant and businessman, he encouraged Hodge and his brother to come to his hometown of Somerville to attend school, and he took the role of Hodge's surrogate father for a time.

Henry A. Boardman (1808–1880) was an 1833 graduate of Princeton Theological Seminary. He served but one church, the Tenth Presbyterian Church of Philadelphia, for his entire career (1833–1876) and became one of Hodge's closest friends as he served on the seminary's board of directors.

John Breckinridge (1797–1841) was Hodge's classmate both at Princeton College and Princeton Theological Seminary. He joined the seminary faculty for a short time as its Professor of Pastoral Theology and Missionary Instruction before becoming the denomination's National Secretary of Foreign Missions.

Robert Jefferson Breckinridge (1800–1871) was one of the great champions of Old School Presbyterianism. Hodge disliked Breckinridge's factionalism, which helped lead to the denomination's 1837 split, but later found the Kentuckian a valuable pro-Union ally during the Civil War.

Horace Bushnell (1802–1876) graduated from Yale and served for over twenty-six years as the pastor of North Congregational Church in Hartford, Connecticut. Due to poor health, he resigned his pastorate in 1859 and spent the rest of his life writing and occasionally preaching. His romantic theories on language troubled Hodge.

William Cunningham (1805–1861) stood alongside Thomas Chalmers as one of the great leaders in the movement to establish the Free Church of Scotland. He became fast friends with Hodge when he visited Princeton in 1843, and his work in establishing common funds to support clergy greatly inspired Hodge.

Albert Baldwin Dod (1805–1845) attended Princeton Theology Seminary, but after his ordination decided to become a mathematics professor at Princeton College. He became one of Hodge's closest friends, and Hodge considered him "one of the most gifted men of the Church."

Edward Everett (1794–1865) was the first American to receive a European Ph.D. He taught at Harvard for a short time before entering politics, where he served both as a United States congressman and senator.

Charles Finney (1792–1875) was one of the most famous revivalist preachers of his day. He later became a faculty member at Oberlin College in Ohio. Hodge strongly disagreed with his mechanist approach to revivalism and Arminian-inflected theological stances.

Theodore Frelinghuysen (1787–1862) became lifelong friends with Hodge when they were both students at Somerville Academy. Frelinghuysen went on to become a United States senator, a Whig vice presidential candidate on Henry Clay's ticket, and finally the president of Rutgers College.

Ashbel Green (1762–1848) served as a pastor, Princeton College's president, and then editor of the conservative Presbyterian periodical, *The Christian Advocate*. He was a key player in founding Princeton Theological Seminary in 1812 and served on the seminary's board for over three decades. Hodge grew apart from him over the years on account of Green's radically conservative and reactionary Old School views.

William Henry Green (1825–1900) was first Hodge's student and then his colleague on the seminary's faculty. They became close personal friends, and Hodge felt forever indebted to him for being the principal initiator and organizer of his teaching jubilee in 1872.

Arnold Henry Guyot (1807–1884) was a Swiss-born geologist and geographer who joined Princeton College's faculty in 1854. His theories on the development of the solar system influenced Hodge's reading of Genesis and his views on evolution.

John Haviland (1792–1852) was one of antebellum Philadelphia's premier architects. Responsible for designing a number of churches and government buildings, he drew up plans for Charles Hodge's house in 1822. Later, he gained an international reputation as a designer of penitentiaries.

Ernst Wilhem Hengstenberg (1802–1869), a onetime student of August Tholuck, distinguished himself in the study of Middle Eastern languages. Hodge became good friends with him while he was in Berlin and attended his lectures on the Old Testament there. Hengstensberg became the editor of the highly influential, conservative evangelical periodical *Evangelische Kirchenzeitung*, which Hodge read whenever he had the opportunity.

Joseph Henry (1797–1878) was a professor at Princeton College and mentor to Archibald Alexander Hodge before taking the position of founding president of the Smithsonian Institution. Offering the prayer at Henry's funeral was Charles Hodge's last public act.

Andrew Hodge (1711–1790), Hodge's paternal grandfather, had settled in Philadelphia in the 1730s. He made a sizeable fortune in international trade and became one of the city's wealthiest and most politically active citizens.

Archibald Alexander Hodge (1823–1886), nicknamed "Archie," was Hodge's eldest son. After serving as a missionary in India, he returned to the United States, where he took a Virginia pastorate and eventually replaced his father at Princeton Theological Seminary. Following his father's death, he wrote Hodge's only biography.

Caspar Wistar Hodge Sr. (1830–1891) was the second son of Charles Hodge and became Professor of New Testament Literature and Greek Exegesis at Princeton Theological Seminary in 1860, a post he held until his death. His son, Caspar Wistar Hodge Jr., became the last Hodge to sit on the Seminary's faculty.

Hugh Hodge Sr. (1755–1798), the eldest son of Andrew Hodge, was Hodge's father. Educated at Princeton College, he pursued both merchant and medical careers in Philadelphia. He died from repeated exposure to yellow fever when Hodge was just six months old.

Hugh Lenox Hodge (1796–1873) was Hodge's older brother. He became one of Philadelphia's most eminent physicians and helped establish the specialized practices of gynecology and obstetrics in the United States.

Mary Blanchard Hodge (1765–1832), Hodge's mother, was born in Boston and remembered vividly many of the events of the American Revolution that took place there. A woman of keen intellect and indomitable will, she moved to join her brother in Philadelphia in 1785, where she met and married Hugh Hodge.

Mary Elizabeth Hodge (1825–1899) was Charles Hodge's first and favorite daughter. She married William M. Scott, who died in 1861, leaving Mary and her three young sons to return to live in Hodge's own home. Her son, William Berryman Scott, became a great favorite of Hodge's.

Mary Hunter Stockton Hodge (1807–1880) married Hodge in 1852. A widow, she had two children from a previous marriage. She was a member of the great Stockton family who had deeded land for the founding both of the Princeton College and Princeton Theological Seminary.

Sarah Bache Hodge (1798–1849), a great-granddaughter of Benjamin Franklin, married Charles Hodge in 1822. Together they had eight children.

David Hunter (1802–1886), Mary Stockton's brother, was a Union General during the Civil War. He became a hated figure throughout the South, earning the nickname "Black Dave Hunter" for actions which included emancipating slaves in three states without Lincoln's permission and burning the Virginia Military Institute to the ground. He later served as the lead judge in the John Wilkes Booth conspiracy trail.

John Johns (1796–1876) was Charles Hodge's roommate at Princeton Theological Seminary and dear lifelong friend. He turned down Archibald Alexander's offer to become the Seminary's third professor, and thus opened the way for Hodge to take the position. He ultimately became an influential bishop in the Episcopalian Church in Virginia.

John Maclean Jr. (1800–1886) was Hodge's classmate both at Princeton College and Princeton Theological Seminary. Eventually, he became the tenth president of Princeton College (1854–1868), during which time Hodge served on the College's board of trustees.

Marie-Joseph Paul Marquis de Lafayette (1757–1834) was a French nobleman who became friends with George Washington and other prominent Americans during the Revolutionary War. He made a special point to hear Hodge preach in Paris and later invited Hodge to his home, where Hodge was first introduced to Alexander Von Humboldt.

Samuel Miller (1765–1850) served as a pastor in New York City before becoming Princeton Theological Seminary's second professor. An immensely learned man, he was acknowledged by all as the Presbyterian Church's foremost expert on church polity and governance.

Guillaume "Billy" Monod (1800–1896) was the most fiery member of the celebrated French revivalist Monod family. He shared a boarding house with Hodge while they were both in Berlin. He and Hodge went out on several ministry excursions together.

Adolphe Monod (1802–1856) was Billy's younger brother and the most famous French revivalist preacher of his era. He was a professor at the seminary at Montauban, France.

George Müller (1805–1898) served as Charles Hodge's German-language tutor while Hodge was in Halle. He later moved to Bristol, England, and became a world-famous evangelist and crusader for the proper care of orphans.

Johann Neander (1789–1850) made his reputation as a German theologian and church historian. Hodge met and befriended him while in Europe. Neander had a profound influence on John Williamson Nevin, Philip Schaff, and their Mercersburg Theology.

John Williamson Nevin (1803–1886), a onetime student of Hodge's and then his teaching replacement at Princeton Theological Seminary while Hodge studied in Europe, was responsible for helping to formulate the Mercersburg Theology, a school of Reformed thought that Hodge battled for nearly thirty years.

Andrews Norton (1783–1860) became known as the "Unitarian Pope" after composing several influential pieces on Unitarian biblical interpretation. As Transcendentalism fractured New England Unitarianism, Norton became an unlikely ally of Hodge as both men attempted to stem the rising tide of German Idealist thought in American theology.

 **Edwards Amasa Park** (1808–1900) was a professor at Andover Seminary and edited its influential periodical *Bibliotecha Sacra*. In 1850, he entered into a titanic battle with Hodge over biblical language and its interpretation.

 **Edward Robinson** (1794–1863) became the first American biblical scholar to gain an international reputation. A professor at Andover Seminary, he distinguished himself as a biblical geographer, becoming the father of biblical archaeological studies. Hodge shared boarding houses with him in Halle and then again in Berlin when they both studied in Europe.

 **Robert Rose** was a prominent Pennsylvania physician who married one of Hodge's aunts. In 1809, he bought 100,000 acres in northern Pennsylvania that he named "Hibernia." It was during a summer visit to Hibernia that Hodge made his final decision to enter the ministry.

 **Benjamin Rush** (1745–1813) was prominent as a Philadelphia physician and a colonial patriot. He signed both the Declaration of Independence and the Constitution. He also became an implacable foe of Hodge's father when they disagreed on how best to treat Philadelphia's various yellow-fever epidemics in the 1790s.

Sylvestre de Sacy (1758–1838) was the foremost Western expert on Middle Eastern languages when Hodge went to study with him in Paris in 1826. He tutored Hodge in Arabic, Syriac, and Hebrew, and was renowned for the sympathetic care with which he treated his American pupils.

Philip Schaff (1819–1893) was a Swiss theologian who taught first in Berlin and then immigrated to Pennsylvania to join John Williamson Nevin at the German Reformed Theological Seminary in Mercersburg. He became a world-renowned church historian and a crucial influence in the development of the Mercersburg Theology.

Friedrich Schleiermacher (1768–1834) was one of the most important German theologians of the early nineteenth century. Hodge met and heard him preach while he studied in Europe but found his theology too emotional and obscure.

Hugh Lenox Scott (1853–1934) was Hodge's grandson and came to live with Hodge after the death of his father, William M. Scott. He had a distinguished military career after graduating from West Point in 1876. He was the Army's Chief of Staff when the United States entered the First World War.

William Berryman Scott (1858–1947) was the youngest son of Hodge's daughter Mary and Hodge's favorite grandson. After the death of his father, he lived with Hodge for the next seventeen years. He later became a professor at Princeton University and one of the nation's leading paleontologists.

William McKendree Scott (1817–1861) graduated from Princeton Seminary in 1846, having fallen in love with Hodge's daughter Mary while studying there. He and Mary wed in 1849. He experienced success as a teacher both at Centre College in Danville, Kentucky, and later at the Theological Seminary of the Northwest in Chicago. He and Mary had five children, two of whom survived into adulthood.

Henry Boynton Smith (1815–1877) was one of the great leaders of New School Presbyterianism and the principle advocate for reuniting the Old and New School wings of American Presbyterianism after the Civil War. He taught both church history and systematic theology at Union Theological Seminary in New York City.

Samuel Stanhope Smith (1751–1819) was the founding president of Virginia's Hampden-Sydney College and the seventh president of Princeton College. He was also John Witherspoon's son-in-law. A progressive thinker, Smith enjoyed early success in his tenure at Princeton, but was eventually forced to resign as the College's trustees lost faith in his educational vision and administrative abilities.

Phillip Stapfer (1766–1873) was closely associated with the French revival activities of the Monods. He was a Professor of Literature and Philosophy at the University of Paris and befriended Hodge during his time in Europe.

Moses Stuart (1780–1852) was a professor at Andover Theological Seminary and an important early influence on Hodge's own study of ancient languages. He encouraged Hodge to study in Europe. One of the country's leading conservative biblical scholars, he later wrote an influential commentary on the book of Romans. Hodge disagreed with his tendency to stress human ability over the Calvinist doctrine of total depravity.

Nathaniel Taylor (1786–1858) was a Congregational minister who became the first professor of Yale's Divinity School. While at Yale, he developed the influential New Haven Theology, which gained wide popularity among New School Presbyterians. Hodge felt that he put too much emphasis on human agency in the process of conversion and sanctification.

Gilbert Tennent (1703–1764) was trained by his father, William, in the Log College. He was one of the First Great Awakening's most famous revivalist preachers, and he later became the founding pastor of Philadelphia's Second Presbyterian Church, where Hodge's ancestors worshiped.

Friedrich August Tholuck (1799–1877) was a renowned scholar of theology and languages and served as a professor at the University of Berlin. He became Hodge's best European friend.

James Thornwell (1812–1862) was one of the most prominent leaders of Southern Presbyterians in the years leading up to the Civil War. Hodge disagreed with his views on the church and slavery.

Francis Turretin (1623–1687) was a Swiss reformed theologian whose massive three-volume *Institutes of Elenctic Theology* was highly prized by Hodge. The *Institutes* were used as a standard textbook at Princeton Theological Seminary until it was replaced by Hodge's own *Systematic Theology* in the 1870s.

Ludwig Von Gerlach (1795–1877) was a prominent Prussian judge and politician who befriended Hodge in Berlin. Hodge said that he "excited more love and respect" in him than any man he met in Europe.

Otto Von Gerlach (1801–1849) was a conservative Prussian theologian who taught at the University of Berlin, where Hodge first met him. He was deeply committed to missions and known as "The Wesley of Berlin."

Alexander Von Humboldt (1769–1859) was an internationally famous German naturalist and explorer who provided important letters of introduction for Hodge during his European tour. When Humboldt offered a long series of lectures in Berlin, Hodge studiously attended them.

Benjamin Breckinridge Warfield (1851–1921) was one of Hodge's last students. He returned to teach at Princeton Theological Seminary after the death of A. A. Hodge, taking the faculty position held first by Hodge and then his son. A brilliant theologian, he became one of the Seminary's greatest defenders of conservative, confessional doctrine.

George Whitefield (1714–1770) was a minister in the Church of England and became the most popular evangelist during the First Great Awakening. His revivalist activity catalyzed the Old Side/New Side split in eighteenth-century American Presbyterianism.

Mark Wilks (?–1854) was an English Independent clergyman who traveled to France in 1815 to serve as a Protestant missionary. He became an important figure in the *Réveil* (France's Protestant Revival). While he studied in Paris, Hodge became friends with Wilks and preached several times for the English-speaking congregation Wilks had founded there.

Benjamin Wisner (1794–1835) was an early and lasting friend of Hodge. They traveled to Boston together soon after Wisner's graduation from Princeton Theological Seminary. Wisner became an influential leader of the American Board of Commissioners for Foreign Missions, where he encouraged American missionaries to go to France and played a role in Archibald Alexander Hodge's decision to go to India.

Caspar Wistar (1761–1818) was a friend of both the Hodge and Bache families and the man who principally trained Hodge's brother, Hugh, in medicine. So great was Charles and Sarah Hodge's esteem for the man that they named one of their sons after him. Even though it was misspelled, the botanical genus "Wisteria" was also named in his honor.

John Witherspoon (1723–1794) was a Scottish clergyman who immigrated to the colonies to take over the presidency of Princeton College. He played a pivotal role in bringing Scottish Common Sense Realist philosophy to America.

Charles Hodge

PROLOGUE

THE POPE OF PRESBYTERIANISM

Figure 0.4 *Alexander Hall*: A building which clearly echoed the design and functionality of Nassau Hall, the Seminary's main building (later named Alexander Hall) was completed in 1818. It contained living quarters, classrooms, libraries, and dining facilities capable of accommodating one hundred students. [*Special Collections, Princeton Theological Seminary Libraries*]

On a brisk April morning in 1872, over five hundred former students, family, friends, and colleagues congregated to honor Charles Hodge on his fiftieth teaching anniversary at Princeton Theological Seminary.[1] Some had traveled from as far away as California, Texas, and Ireland to attend the event. As the throngs packed into the pews and crowded to obtain standing room in Princeton's First Presbyterian Church, speaker after speaker praised the seventy-five-year-old Hodge, paying tribute to a man already widely acknowledged as the Pope of Presbyterianism and the "Nestor" of American theology.[2] With one voice they anointed him the greatest Reformed theologian their country had ever produced.

Hodge's semicentennial celebration offers but a glimpse of the immense influence he exercised over nineteenth-century American Protestantism. During his fifty-six-year career at Princeton, he taught over three thousand seminarians. No American professor had taught more graduate students. He extended his influence through his aggressive and savvy use of the country's growing print culture by founding the *Biblical Repertory and Princeton Review* in 1825, a quarterly theological journal he directed for nearly five decades. By editing over one hundred and twenty issues and contributing more than two hundred articles to its pages, Hodge established himself as a major voice in the most important religious controversies of his day. By the time he left the journal to others in 1872, it stood as the second oldest quarterly publication in the United States and enjoyed so great an international reputation that the *British Quarterly Review* called it "beyond all question the greatest purely theological Review that has ever been published in the English tongue."[3]

In addition to his articles for the *Repertory*, Hodge completed several longer book-length works: commentaries on four New Testament books including a world-renowned volume on Romans, the first extended critical analysis of Transcendentalism, a major history of the American Presbyterian Church, a landmark critique of Darwinism, the immensely popular devotional *The Way of Life*, and his magnum opus, a three-volume *Systematic Theology*. Almost all these works are still in print today, and his *Systematic Theology* remains a foundational text in the study of American systematic theology.

While Hodge towered in the theological circles of his day, his fame has dimmed as the years have passed. When the great men of nineteenth-century American Christianity are named, figures such as Charles Finney, Ralph Waldo Emerson, Horace Bushnell, Joseph Smith Jr., Henry Ward Beecher and D.L. Moody come quickly to mind. Charles Hodge does not. Biographies are but one indicator of who perseveres in the American religious imagination. In the past fifty years, three biographies of Bushnell have appeared, five of Emerson, six of Finney, and a staggering seven of Joseph Smith Jr. Only a single biography exists on Hodge, completed just two years after his death in 1878 by his son Archibald Alexander Hodge. No one has deemed Hodge worthy of his own biography for more than one hundred and thirty years.

Within this biographical lacuna, opinions have varied as to Hodge's importance. Some have claimed him as America's greatest theologian, while others see him as little more than a derivative thinker who simply taught and disseminated the ideas of others.[4] Still others have sounded darker notes, believing him to be a pro-slavery racist whose every trace should be erased.[5] Whatever judgments exist, the truth remains that in the life of Charles Hodge one finds a stunning panoramic view of nineteenth-century Protestantism. His story touches many, if not all, of the most critical developments in the American Christianity of his era, and whether one admires or despises Hodge, there is no denying that he exercised a profound influence in his day with lasting consequences after his death. As one historian has noted, without Hodge

"American Presbyterianism and American Calvinism would have received an entirely different shape."[6]

Through his heartfelt personal piety, encyclopedic intellect, and position of influence at the country's most important Presbyterian seminary, Hodge spent his nearly-sixty-year career crafting a uniquely American strain of Reformed theology. Mainly through his writings in the *Repertory*, but in numerous other venues as well, he brought his confessional beliefs to bear on issues as diverse as slavery, temperance, presidential politics, war, international diplomacy, advances in science, educational reform, and domestic and foreign missions.[10] He firmly believed in the rational faculties and that no realm of creation stood beyond the reach and essential insights offered by the Bible and theology. His tender heart offered a sympathetic and optimistic, yet thoroughly conservative, type of Calvinism, which encouraged the cultivation of personal piety and eschewed such harsh doctrines as infant damnation. He believed the world was improving and that God wanted to save more people than he damned. Convinced that there was only a single human species, Hodge's sympathy extended across cultural and racial divides, making every person equally capable of enjoying Christ's promise of salvation.

While many today may be unaware of Hodge and the enduring influence of his theological legacy, his ghost lingers throughout contemporary American Christianity. This biography is based on the simple premise that few Americans can match the depth, breadth, and longevity of Hodge's theological influence, and perhaps no single figure is better able to help one appreciate the immensely powerful and hugely complex nature of conservative American Protestantism in the nineteenth, twentieth, and twenty-first centuries than the deeply pious, keenly intelligent, and yet largely forgotten Charles Hodge.

PART I

1730–1810
The Hodges of Philadelphia

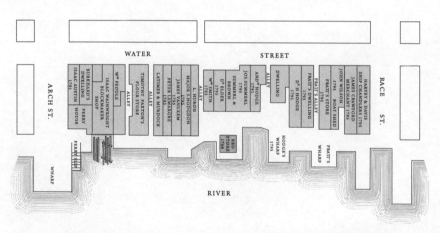

Figure 1.1 *Hodge's Wharf*: Andrew Hodge and his brothers built an international shipping business and were able to gain control of one of Philadelphia's much coveted riverside wharves, which Philadelphians called "Hodge's Wharf" until the 1840s. By the time of Charles Hodge's birth, Philadelphia stood only behind Boston and New York in commercial importance. [*Herman B Wells Library, Indiana University*]

1

ANDREW HODGE, FAMILY PATRIARCH

When Charles Hodge was born two days after Christmas 1797, he became a member of one of Philadelphia's most respected and distinguished families. By the time of his birth, however, the once mighty Hodges of Philadelphia were in decline. Not only were the best days of their international shipping business behind them, but the repeated yellow fever outbreaks that wracked the city in the 1790s decimated the once proud and powerful Scotch-Irish clan, killing not only two of Hodge's siblings, but his father as well. Hodge's early years were marked by the expectations, but not the resources, which accompanied bearing the name of one of Philadelphia's elite families.

The power, influence, and dynastic aura of the Hodge family stemmed principally from one man, Hodge's grandfather Andrew Hodge. Andrew Hodge had arrived in Philadelphia along with his two brothers, William and Hugh, in the early 1730s as they joined the throngs of Scotch-Irish immigrants who flooded the American colonies in the opening decades of eighteenth century. These years saw thousands of Scotch-Irish leave Ireland for America as England persecuted dissenting Protestants who refused to bow to the Anglican Church and enacted a series of devastating Irish taxation policies. By the middle of the century, some thirty thousand Scotch-Irish had made their home in Pennsylvania, and by the time of the Revolution, the Scotch-Irish became the colonies' largest non-English ethnic group.[1]

Among these immigrants, Andrew Hodge proved to be a man of exceptional vision and determination. With the help of his brothers, he gathered what capital he could and quickly became successful as an international merchant. Within a decade, the Hodge brothers owned three ships and were trading regularly with Jamaica and Europe.[2] By the 1760s, the Hodges owned in whole or in part a merchant fleet of six ships.[3] With their armada, Andrew Hodge and his brothers traded widely in flour, wheat, sugar, and rum, among other products.

Flour and wheat were the most important staples of much of Philadelphia's trade.[4] So intimate was the city's ties to farm production and seaborne commerce that the Philadelphia seal (adopted in 1791) pictured both a sheaf of wheat and a sailing ship.[5] Wheat and the sea had made Philadelphia a great city, and this same combination had made the Hodges a great family. Andrew became one of the city's leading flour merchants and then moved to augment his fortune by operating several bakeries in the city, which provisioned countless Philadelphia ships.[6] As his various business enterprises grew in both size and scope, Andrew Hodge became one of the city's most powerful men, and as Andrew and his brothers had children, their sons entered the family businesses.[7] Some became merchants; others became sea captains.

In 1762, Andrew purchased one of Philadelphia's twenty-six main wharfs, which lined the Delaware River along with accompanying buildings on Water Street, a street running parallel to the river's waterfront. The value of owning one of these wharves is difficult to imagine today; it might be likened to owning a seat on the New York Stock Exchange, the advantages for one's business were so great. Andrew turned his newly acquired properties into his family's home, a warehouse, and a store. His already substantial foothold in Philadelphia trade was now enhanced by how his wharf quite literally brought business to his doorstep. He had also centralized his businesses so that he could receive, send, store, and sell his goods in one place. The dock would be known as "Hodge's Wharf" well into the 1830s, long after the Hodges were no longer a force in the city's mercantile enterprises.[8]

Like the other buildings on this part of Water Street, Andrew's various properties were built out of sturdy red brick, an expensive and lasting material that signified his house and his neighborhood were filled with "very respectable residents, none more so in the city."[9] Andrew was a man never slow to display the trappings of his success. In the early 1750s, he owned Philadelphia's only six-horse carriage, a sign of remarkable wealth for the time. He kept carriages throughout his life, and by the time of the American Revolution he continued to mark himself as a leading citizen by operating one of only eighty-two carriages to be found amid Philadelphia's twenty thousand inhabitants.[10]

Andrew and his brothers also distinguished themselves beyond the realm of business. All of them became active in the political affairs of Philadelphia. Both Andrew and his brother William signed a 1756 petition addressed "To the King's most Excellent Majesty," arguing that Philadelphia was constantly threatened by the region's Native American population and the Quaker-dominated Assembly failed in every regard to counteract the threat. Almost every prominent non-Quaker citizen of the city signed this petition, and the document serves as an early glimpse of the Hodges' sense of political action and civic responsibility.

In the coming years, Andrew Hodge, along with many of his contemporaries, made the slow turn from trusting the king of England to protect them to seeing that same "most Excellent Majesty" as a threat. Even though he was in his sixties when the American Revolution began, Andrew's anti-English, Scotch-Irish sympathies were reignited through his adopted country's conflict with England. It did not help that Britain's policy of taxing certain types of trade hit merchants such as the Hodges particularly hard. Too old to serve in the armed forces, Andrew offered four of his sons to the cause. One of them, William, served as a secret agent in Paris, where he worked with his connections at Dunkirk and Best to outfit ships with arms and ammunition for the colonial cause.[11] William's patriotic activities eventually landed him in the Bastille.

The war touched the Hodges in devastating ways. Andrew's home was burned to the ground during the British occupation of the city in 1777, but far more tragic was the loss of two sons.[12] Through it all, Andrew never ceased to give his full support to the colonial fight for independence, even going so far as to lend great sums of money to the cause. In 1780, he joined a host of fellow Philadelphia patriots in underwriting the Pennsylvania bank by giving the impressive amount of 2,000 pounds in currency to buy supplies for the Continental Army.[13]

Andrew Hodge married Jane McCulloch in 1739. To get some sense of just how tight-knit Philadelphia's elite community was at this time, it is interesting to note that Jane McCulloch was a sister to William Hodge's first wife. Two Hodge brothers had married two McCulloch sisters. Andrew's family grew to include fifteen children, seven of whom survived to adulthood. Just like their parents, two of the daughters made marriage into a family affair, marrying a set of twin brothers from the socially prominent Bayard clan.[14]

Marriage into the Bayard family sealed the Hodges to one of the most important political dynasties of the nineteenth century. One of Andrew's grandsons, James Bayard Jr., became one of the most respected congressmen of his generation, serving multiple terms in both the House of Representatives and in the Senate. Perhaps his greatest political legacy came when he cast the deciding vote in the presidential election of 1800, after a split in electoral votes left the presidential election up to the House of Representatives. In a move of tremendous political courage, Bayard moved against his own Federalist Party to choose Thomas Jefferson over Aaron Burr, reasoning that Jefferson had received a greater share of the popular vote. Bayard believed it unsafe for the young country's democracy to have the small body of Congress overturn what he saw as the will of people. James Jr. became the fountainhead of two more generations of national politicians. His sons Richard Henry Bayard and James Ashton Bayard were contemporaries of Charles Hodge, and both sat in the United States Senate, as did James Jr.'s grandson Thomas F. Bayard. The Bayards remained so active in national politics throughout the century that Thomas was nominated no less than three times by the Democratic Party as its presidential candidate in the 1870s and 1880s.

Hodge's own connection to the Bayard clan started early as several Bayards came alongside Mary Hodge to help watch over her sons, Charles and Hugh, after the loss of their father. Hodge's own lifelong interest in politics was deeply rooted not only in his grandfather's patriotism, but his close connection to the politically powerful Bayard clan. These relationships did much to mold a high sense of civic duty in Hodge.

2

PRESBYTERIAN HERITAGE

The Hodge brothers were not solely interested in Philadelphia's business and politics. Following the same religious convictions they had held in Ireland, they quickly established themselves as among the city's most important Presbyterian laymen. One of the brothers, Hugh, formally linked the Hodges to Philadelphia's nascent Presbyterian population by marrying Hannah Harkum, whose grandfather had been a founding member of the city's first Presbyterian church in 1695.[1] Hannah did not die until 1805, becoming one of the city's most venerable Presbyterian matriarchs. Charles Hodge remembered her fondly from his youth as a model of Christian piety.

Hannah not only linked the Hodges to the most established circles of Presbyterianism in the city, but her own conversion marked some of the most important religious events to touch the city in the eighteenth century. Although a lifelong church attender, Hannah attributed her true spiritual awakening to the preaching ministry of the dynamic English evangelist, George Whitefield. Whitefield first visited Philadelphia in 1739 and arrived in the city as an international celebrity. In England, his combined preaching tours had gathered over eighty thousand listeners, making him one of the greatest open-air orators of his day.[2] Americans also flocked to him. Not put off by his "infant childish" appearance or his crossed-eyes, crowds as large as twenty-five thousand gathered to hear him preach.[3] Whitefield's popularity was so immense that Philadelphians joined together in 1740 to build a special "high and lofty hall" in the heart of the city with the express purpose of being able to hold the crowds that clamored to hear him speak.[4] "Whitefield's Hall," as it commonly came to be known, was the city's largest structure when it was built, exceeding even the size of the city's grand State House.

Whitefield blended passionate exhortation, tears of entreaty, and a unique ability to dramatize biblical stories as he traveled the colonies, speaking in town squares, barns, churches and open fields. The spiritual enthusiasm he created led one observer to comment that "[r]eligion is become the subject of most conversation. No books are in request but those of piety and devotion, and instead of idle songs and ballads the people are everywhere entertaining themselves with psalms, hymns, and spiritual songs."[5]

Even the skeptical Benjamin Franklin found himself moved by Whitefield's eloquence. Determined to see the celebrity for himself, Franklin went to hear Whitefield having "silently resolved he should get nothing form me. I had in my Pocket a Handful of Copper Money, three or four silver Dollars, and five Pistoles in Gold. As he proceeded I began to soften, and concluded to give the Coppers. Another Stroke of his Oratory made me asham'd of that, and determin'd to give the Silver, and he finish'd so admirably that I empty'd my Pocket wholly into the Collector's Dish, Gold and all."[6] Whitefield's preaching laid the foundation for a new style of pulpit oratory in the colonies, and his evangelistic fervor provided the spark that set ablaze a series of Protestant revivals in the colonies, which only later came to be known as the First Great Awakening.

While Whitefield had numerous supporters in the city, there were many who shunned his emotionality and what they perceived as too great an emphasis on human agency in the conversion process. Presbyterians found themselves divided over his theological thinking and evangelistic methods, splitting into two rival factions known as the Old and New Sides. Those of the New Side were seen as "proselytes to the well known Whitefield."[7] They promoted revivalism and prized the emotional aspects of religious experience. Over the years, they became known as the party which favored heartfelt personal piety in their ministers over formal training. Those belonging to the Old Side, on the other hand, were skeptical of Whitefield's ministry and its fruits. They favored a more reasoned approach to the Christian faith, and put a high premium on established ritual and sound Calvinist doctrine.[8] They expected their ministers to have the best formal training available so that they might rightly preach the word of God.

This division became particularly important for the Hodge family when the formerly unified First—and only—Presbyterian Church of Philadelphia split in 1743 under the pressure of the New/Old Side tensions.[9] The Hodges joined some one hundred and forty people who left the First Presbyterian Church to begin holding meetings in Whitefield's Hall. Eventually, this group formed the Second Presbyterian Church.

Among those who joined the Hodges was Hugh McCulloch, Andrew Hodge's brother-in-law. Known to everyone as the most stubborn and outspoken of men, Hugh McCulloch proved invaluable as he stood against the Old Side Presbyterians in helping organize the city's first New Side congregation.[10] Hugh McCulloch's strong will and obstinacy became legendary among the Hodges. Charles Hodge often smiled as he told the story of how his Uncle Hugh "would never consent to the assertion that the earth moves: maintaining that it was contrary alike to his own observation and to Bible authority, as Joshua commanded not the earth, but the sun to stand still." Among the Hodges, anyone characterized by an ability to hold and advocate an unshakeable opinion came to be called an "Uncle M'Culloch."[11]

Andrew Hodge and Hugh McCulloch saw to it that the Second Presbyterian Church building was a regal affair. Located in the middle of the city, it was adorned with large stone columns at its entrance and built of solid brick. The structure also boasted a towering steeple, an ornament usually reserved for Episcopal and Catholic churches of the period. The city's Episcopalians found the steeple so unbecoming on a Presbyterian church that they freely circulated a humorous poem about edifice:

> The Presbyterians built a church,
>   And fain would build a steeple:
> We think it may become the church,
>   But not become the people.[12]

In the end, the steeple became a short-lived ornament. It had been added after the building's construction, largely by the efforts of Andrew Hodge, who wished his church to literally stand above its First Presbyterian Church counterpart.[13] The steeple ended up being a grand addition, but also a dangerously unstable one that needed to be removed just a few years after it had been erected.

The Second Presbyterian Church became famous in its early years not only for its towering wooden steeple, but also as the home of one of the city's most provocative pastors. The church's founding pastor was the fire-breathing revivalist preacher, Gilbert Tennent. Tennent was the son of William Tennent, whose rustic Log College seminary located just twenty miles north of Philadelphia would serve as a model in the founding of the College of New Jersey (hereafter referred to as "Princeton College"). More important than even his religious pedigree was Gilbert Tennent's unique and powerful speaking ability. Standing over six feet tall with piercing grey eyes, Tennent had made a name for himself as a painfully blunt, no-holds-barred evangelist.[14] Reportedly when he visited Yale in 1740, students flocked before his preaching to profess their faith, and his speaking tours in New England attracted thousands of listeners.[15] As his funeral eulogist, Samuel Finley, would later say, Tennent's life was marked by absolute conviction and unquenchable energy. "What he did, he did with all his might."[16] Plain, forthright language marked both his sermons and his everyday conversation, and he was known to all for his quick temper and passionate nature. He once wrote to his brother William: "Let us come out for God as Flames of Fire, and say with gallant *Luther, Madness is better than mildness in the cause of God*."[17] Whitefield

Figure 2.1 *Ashbel Green*: Ashbel Green had a long and special relationship with Hodge's family. He served as the family's pastor in Philadelphia where he catechized a young Charles Hodge. He was president of Princeton College while Hodge was an undergraduate student there, and he married and buried both Hodge's parents. [*Library of the Author*]

nicknamed him a "Son of Thunder" and characterized him as a man who did "not fear the faces of men."[18] Others, who did not like him as well, had another nickname for him: "Hell-fire Tennent."[19]

Tennent was a natural choice to become the first pastor of Philadelphia's Second Presbyterian Church. He was a close personal friend of Whitefield, and he seamlessly fit into the church his friend had inspired.[20] Until his death in 1764, Tennent served as

Second Presbyterian's head pastor, and upon his death, his congregation were so over-whelmed with grief that they chose to honor their universally beloved pastor by burying his remains under the church's central aisle.

In 1769, James Sproat—a man who had been converted by one of Gilbert Ten-nent's sermons and then studied under Jonathan Edwards—became pastor of Second Presbyterian Church.[21] Known as a man of abundant "charity and tenderness . . . on all occasions," Sproat became a much-loved figure both to his own congregation and to Philadelphia more generally.[22] Sproat had taken over Second Presbyterian at the not-so-tender age of forty-seven years, and as his health began to deteriorate noticeably in the late 1780s, members of the Second Presbyterian Church decided to call a prom-ising twenty-five-year-old associate pastor by the name of Ashbel Green to help their aging pastor with the burdens of his ministry.

Ashbel Green had his own genealogical roots in revivalism. His father, both a cler-gyman and a physician, had been yet one more convert through George Whitefield's preaching. He had wished Ashbel to become a farmer, but the boy showed an early talent for study. His father thus allowed Ashbel a more scholarly vocation by letting him attend Princeton College. In 1783, Green graduated and soon took ordination at Philadelphia's Second Presbyterian Church where he worked alongside and eventu-ally succeeded Reverend Sproat.

Green became one of the most persistent figures in Charles Hodge's life, and their decades-long, not always congenial, relationship dated back to Green's first pastorate in Philadelphia. Green married Hodge's parents. He also presided over each of their funerals. He baptized and catechized both Charles and his brother Hugh, and he stood as Princeton College's newly appointed president when Hodge began his studies there in 1812. Even as Green aged, he remained a trustee of Princeton Seminary and as such had contact with Hodge until his death in 1848.

Considering his family's profound ties to Philadelphia's Second Presbyterian Church and its New Side roots, Hodge remained true to the New Side's respect for Calvinist doctrine but spent much of his life distancing himself from its association with emotional revivalism.[23] Hodge went so far as to denounce many of Whitefield's activities and attribute much of eighteenth-century revivalism to nervous disorders and mass hysteria.[24] Although his own life was marked by profound personal piety and an openness to well-ordered revival activity, Hodge remained ever wary of revivalism that too greatly stressed human agency and too highly prized religious enthusiasm over a more reasoned assent to the truths of scripture. The reactionary Presbyterian-ism of the early Hodges became much more conservative and staid in Charles Hodge's hands.

3

HODGE'S PARENTS

Charles was just six months old when his father, Hugh Hodge, died. Having lived through four devastating outbreaks of yellow fever, Hodge's father finally succumbed to the disease in 1798. His prolonged exposure to it had so crippled his body that the final years of his life were filled with dreadful pain, characterized by "frequent attacks of jaundice and other lymphatic complaints."[1] In many ways, his death came as a merciful end to his chronic physical suffering.

Hugh Hodge had enjoyed every advantage that being the son of Andrew Hodge could afford. Due to his father's affluence and religious leanings, he had been able to attend the newly established, New Light–oriented Princeton College, where he studied with such distinction that he gave the valedictory address at his class's graduation.[2] After college, he went to study medicine with Dr. Thomas Cadwalader in Philadelphia, one of the city's most distinguished physicians.[3] Andrew Hodge's ability to attach his son Hugh to such a man did much to establish Hugh as one of the city's most promising young doctors. Cadwalader trained Hugh and then helped him get appointed as an army surgeon to the Continental Army during the Revolutionary War.[4] Hugh was later captured by the British and only gained his freedom when George Washington himself interceded on his behalf.

After Hugh Hodge was freed, he returned to Philadelphia and moved into one of his father's houses on Water Street near Hodge's wharf. Disillusioned by the harsh realities of battlefield medicine, Hugh abandoned his medical practice and attempted to become a merchant like his father. For the next several years, he made frequent trips to the West Indies, but in the end, he found that he enjoyed being a physician more than being a businessman.[5] After his father's death in 1790, Hugh decided to return to the practice of medicine.

Soon after returning to medicine, Hugh was forced to revisit the horrors of mass sickness and death. In the early summer of 1793, a number of ships arrived in Philadelphia from the West Indies and delivered over two thousand refugees into city's notoriously hot and unsanitary streets. Many of these refugees came from Santo Domingo, where slave revolts had ravaged the island's sugar plantations. Refugees poured forth from their ships with tales not only of the plantation burnings and murders, but of a deadly fever spreading throughout the Caribbean Islands. The disease of which they spoke was yellow fever, and within weeks it became clear that they had brought it to Philadelphia.

Germ theory was still decades away in the 1790s, as doctors entertained different theories about the bodily humors and how fluids worked in a hydraulic-like fashion to keep the body functioning. If the fluids were corrupted or got out of balance, sickness resulted. The widespread practice of putting leeches on a patient was rooted in the belief that leeches could both extract toxins from the body and potentially recalibrate a body's fluid composition. Not one of Philadelphia's eighty physicians knew that mosquitoes were responsible for spreading yellow fever through their contact with infected human blood.[6]

The mosquito proved to be a terribly efficient and aggressive carrier of the disease. Each time an infected mosquito fed on another human host—something which happened approximately every three days—the infection spread. Normally five people a day would die in Philadelphia in the late eighteenth century. The yellow fever epidemic of 1793 increased this mortality rate by a factor of ten. In September, 1,500 Philadelphians died of the fever. At the epidemic's height in October, one hundred Philadelphians were dying each day. Before the fever tapered off with the first frosts of late November, nearly half of Philadelphia's fifty-five thousand residents had fled the city while another ten thousand lay dead.

Hugh's own engagement with Philadelphia's first yellow fever epidemic was tragically personal. In August of 1793, he called his friend the renowned Benjamin Rush to the bedside of his sick three-and-a-half-year-old daughter, Elizabeth. Rush arrived to find a feverish, yellow-skinned little girl wasting away. She died two days later. Within two weeks, five more people who lived near Hodge's Water Street home died of the fever. So began the deadly 1793 yellow fever epidemic, and its first victim had been a Hodge.[7] As events unfolded, Water Street became the epicenter of the city's most severe eighteenth-century epidemic.

The friendship that Hugh Hodge and Benjamin Rush enjoyed in the late summer of 1793 did not outlive the epidemic. As people continued to fall sick, Hodge and Rush ended up advocating diametrically opposed treatments for the disease. Following the advice found in an old manuscript given to him by Benjamin Franklin on a 1741 yellow fever epidemic in Virginia, Rush believed the best way to fight the disease was to make patients swallow large doses of mercury to induce vomiting while also draining up to a quart of their blood.[8] Rush became convinced that such aggressive treatment was the only way to fight the fever. Nature must not be allowed to run its course; it must be dominated. The more aggressive the treatment the better. What now seems a ghastly course of action capable of killing even healthy patients, became immensely popular throughout the city due to Rush's prestige and relentless promotion of it.

Not everyone, however, was convinced that Rush was correct in his treatment of the fever, and no one took a stronger stand against his high-dosage mercurial cure than Hugh Hodge. Hugh advocated moderation in treating the fever, counseling that little blood be taken and purges be mild in form and infrequent in application. At every turn, he advised his patients to fight the fever by drinking clean water and eating healthy food. He encouraged brandy be administered, even to the extent of taking baths in the alcohol. Because the stakes of the epidemic were so high, Hodge and Rush soon found themselves in open conflict that threatened to come to blows. Rush described Hugh as a beast of a man, "*nearly* as large as Goliath of Gath," and "vauntful and malignant" in proportion to his enormous size.[9] Hugh responded by ridiculing Rush for proscribing mercurial dosages more fit for horses than humans, and threatened at one point to flog Rush for the way he was abusing his patients with his savage cures.[10]

Rush believed himself vindicated when the Second Presbyterian Church's much-beloved Reverend James Sproat died in Hugh Hodge's care. Although countless Philadelphia clergy fled the city when it became clear that the fever respected neither class nor occupation, the seventy-two-year-old Sproat refused to leave. Instead, he made the entire his city his congregation, visiting the sick and burying the dead. His acts of mercy, however, came at a terrible cost as he succumbed to the disease along with his son and younger daughter. In a city where public funerals had all but disappeared because of the overwhelming death rate and peoples' fears about being near the sick and the dead lest they too fall ill, over one hundred people attended Reverend Sproat's funeral. In blaming Sproat's death on Hodge's treatment of the fever, Rush declared: "It is truly distressing to think of the desolation which has followed the footsteps of this man."[11]

Elizabeth was not the only child Hugh and his wife, Mary, lost to disease. His next two children, a daughter and a son, fell victims to measles. Only with their next child, Hugh Lenox Hodge, did the couple see one of their children survive infancy. Eighteen months after the younger Hugh's birth, Mary gave birth to her last child, Charles, around midnight on December 27, 1797. At least one relative called Charles that "strange named child" because "Charles" was a new name for the Hodge family.[12] The joy of another child was short-lived. Hugh Hodge died only six months after Charles's birth. With no father, the two boys faced the oncoming nineteenth century fully dependent on relatives, family friends, and most of all their mother, Mary, a woman who turned out to be no less formidable than her husband.

A twenty-year-old Mary Blanchard had arrived in Philadelphia from Boston after the death of her parents led her to join the household of her brother, a Philadelphia merchant.[13] By all reports, Mary was breathtakingly beautiful. Even though he was ten years her senior, it was love at first sight for Hugh.[14] They courted in the midst of Hugh's frequent business trips to the West Indies and finally wed in 1790 just before Hugh decided to return to medicine.[15]

Little is known about Mary before her marriage to Hugh. She was descended from Huguenots, Calvinist French Protestants who left France after Protestantism was outlawed in 1685. As a girl, she possessed an uncommonly sharp mind, often stealing away by herself to read books. Remembered for her great love of reading, Charles Hodge and his brother had vivid memories of her penchant to recite lines from Dryden and Pope.[16] Her own love of learning formed the cornerstone for her fervent commitment to her sons' educations.

In the year before Hugh died, the Hodges decided to move with their two sons from the deadly Water Street to the more centrally located Arch Street as new variations of yellow fever continued to ravage the dockside neighborhoods almost every summer. The city had grown considerably since Andrew Hodge had purchased the Water Street properties in the 1760s. Where once Water Street had housed the city's most distinguished families, by the turn of the nineteenth century many of these families had moved to large homes further inland.[17] The yellow fever epidemics of 1790s only hastened the departure of Water Street's more affluent inhabitants.[18]

Hugh Hodge's death not only left the family without a husband and father, but it left them without a stable means of income. Charles Hodge's uncle Colonel Hodgdon became administrator of the estate upon Hugh's death, but the estate proved to be small, amounting to a small number of uncollected physician's fees. Added to these fees stood the income Mary collected from the property Andrew Hodge had willed his son. She was entitled to some income from the store on Water Street along with one-third of the proceeds from the wharf, but these sources of revenue proved so small that Mary found herself forced to rent out portions of her home to boarders.[19]

Only months after his birth, Charles Hodge's birthright consisted mainly of considerable social standing but precious little economic means. With the outbreak of war again with Britain in 1812 and its accompanying trade embargoes, Mary Hodge found herself in ever-more-desperate economic straights. Only two years after Charles's birth, she was forced to sell her furniture and occupy only the front room of her Arch Street home's third floor.[20] The rest of the house she gave over to her brother-in-law Andrew Hodge Jr. and his family.

In 1803, Mary decided to escape her one-room home and another humid Philadelphia summer by leaving on an extended tour of her relatives. After spending several months first in Norfolk, Virginia, and then in Wenham, Massachusetts, Mary returned to Philadelphia convinced that she needed more than a single room as a home.[21] In the next few years, Mary Hodge moved several times with her two boys, each time continuing to supplement her income by taking in boarders.[22] One cannot help but wonder whether Hodge's extreme aversion to change, which became one of his defining characteristics, had its roots in the instability that characterized his earliest years. His family's nomadic life coupled with the stresses brought on by poverty may well have helped form Hodge's strong attachment to rituals and ideologies that were based on time-honored traditions and provided various forms of stability.

The reduced circumstances of his youth probably also laid the groundwork for Hodge's lifelong commitments to hospitality and generosity. Throughout his life, Hodge opened his home to needy relatives and family friends, reminiscent of a charity that had been daily modeled for him in his youth by his mother. Mary Hodge had been one of the founding members of one of Philadelphia's first philanthropic organizations, known as the "Female Association." This society gathered food and clothing for the relief of widows and poor single women.[23] Countless meetings of the Female Association's leadership were held in Mary's home, and Mary herself spearheaded the establishment of a soup kitchen to serve the impoverished women of the city.

Hodge's own early history was marked by a complicated relationship to charity. As he grew older and his mother became ever poorer, he had no choice but to rely heavily on the kindness of relatives and family friends as he pursued his education. He continued to enjoy the benefits of the Hodge name as he moved in respected and elite social circles, but he was painfully aware that he was frequently the object of charity. He keenly felt his own poverty as he struggled with things so mundane as attempting to keep himself in presentable clothes.

PART II

The 1810s

Student Years

Figure 4.1 *Nassau Hall*: After students and tutors took residence in Nassau Hall in 1756, the entire life of the college was contained within its walls. Students ate, slept, attended classes and church services all under its roof. [*Princeton University Library*]

4

THE BEGINNINGS OF SELF

As Charles Hodge grew old enough to attend school, he entered a Philadelphia educational system that was little more than a loose confederation of private instructors who ran small schools or offered tutorial arrangements. Benjamin Franklin had attempted to set up a more centralized public academy in the 1750s and had even taken over Whitefield's Hall for the purpose, but by the end of the century, schools remained largely decentralized one-room affairs.[1] Hodge attended a string of schools in Philadelphia, his first memory being of a small room full of boys and girls presided over by an elderly matron. This school was sponsored by his church, and after he grew too old for it, he began to attend a school run by Andrew Brown, a respected elder at Second Presbyterian Church.

After Brown's school, Hodge went to study with a gentleman named Taylor who he fondly remembered as an enthusiast, a Swedenborgian who taught in a manner calculated to inspire educational passion in his students. Rather than making his students memorize endless facts and figures, Taylor gave energetic lectures on European politics, history, and culture. He was particularly good at recounting—and often vibrantly reenacting—famous American and European battles. Hodge not only remembered Taylor's teaching method, which his own passion in the classroom later imitated, but he also recalled the names of many of his classmates nearly seventy years later.[2]

Reading, writing, and arithmetic were not the only subjects Hodge studied in his formative Philadelphia years. His mother emphasized religious training as well. She regularly brought Hodge and his older brother to her pastor, Ashbel Green, to be drilled in the memorization and recitation of the Westminster Shorter Catechism. Such recitations were a common tradition among Scottish Presbyterians. On a regular basis, Hodge presented himself ramrod straight before Ashbel Green and answered his pastor's queries from the catechism.

Mastery of the catechism was central to Hodge's early theological development. Composed between 1642–1647, the Westminster Longer and Shorter Catechisms were designed to teach the key points of Christian doctrine as they were laid out in the Westminster Confession of Faith. This confession had been written to expound Calvinist doctrine in response to the challenges posed by Arminianism, a school of thought first developed by the Dutch theologian Jacob Arminius. Arminianism first spread in the Netherlands in the early seventeenth century as a precursor to later Enlightenment thought. Although it shared several doctrinal points with Calvinism, it differed in its belief that humans could play a role in attaining their own salvation. Such a belief was diametrically opposed to Calvin's teaching on total human depravity. God alone could bring about salvation; humans could only receive his gift. Armininianism's high view of human ability helped lead to the creation of the Westminster Confession, which laid a pronounced stress on God's absolute sovereignty, an emphasis which made the Westminster Confession different from earlier statements of faith such as the Belgic Confession (1561) and the Heidelberg Catechism (1563), which had not been written to refute Arminianism's rising power.[3] Thus, from his earliest religious training, Hodge was thoroughly indoctrinated in theological views that stood solidly against any notion that humans could play a significant role in their own redemption.

Hodge became familiar with traditional Calvinism through the Westminster Shorter Catechism, which was only "short" in relationship to its longer counterpart. The Shorter Catechism came to be widely used with children because of its relative brevity. Brevity, however, did not mean it was easy to master. It contained one hundred and seven questions and answers. Children were expected to memorize the entire catechism word for word. Questions ranged widely, including general topics such as "What is the chief end of man?" to the more specific "What is the reason annexed to the fifth commandment?" Answers differed in complexity and type, varying from just a few words to several sentences. Learning and reciting the catechism was an intensely rigorous ordeal, but those who had mastered it in their youth often proudly recited its contents well into their old age. It was a highly formalized and structured way of teaching that Presbyterians made great use of throughout the eighteenth and early nineteenth centuries. Hodge learned his lessons well, and the doctrines he memorized as a boy provided the foundation for the theological views he held his entire life.

In fact, it is nearly impossible to overstate the importance of the Westminster Confession on Hodge's thought. Throughout his later theological development, no single intellectual commitment ever rivaled his allegiance to the truths set forth in the confession. Although he would inflect traditional Calvinism in minor ways as he applied it to his American setting and combined it with the epistemology of Scottish Common Sense Realism, this confession provided the line to all Hodge's thinking. His later contributions to American theology largely consist of carefully reasoned defenses of the confession's most central stances on the absolute supremacy of God and his sole pre-rogative to save only those he wished, the absolute nature of human sinfulness inher-ited from Adam, the absolute culpability of all humanity for Adam's first disobedience, the absolute inability of humans to pursue their salvation without first being touched by God's mercy, and the absolute efficacy of Christ's work on the cross as the only means of paying the penalty humanity had incurred in rebelling against God. These absolutist beliefs comprised the core of Hodge's theology.[4] They were first formed through his early exposure to the Westminster Shorter Catechism and then nurtured by a long series of mentors equally committed to the catechism's confessional beliefs.

Mary also enrolled her sons in drawing school. A genteel activity, which reflected the elite social circles in which Mary expected her sons to move, the study and mastery of drawing was a marker of cultural refinement. Until his death, Hodge proudly dis-played a landscape scene in his study that he had painted while at this school. He was fond of telling visitors that this little painting was his greatest achievement in the finer arts, and laughed along with his listeners when he recounted that the master of this drawing school, an Englishman named Cox, often stood over his shoulder offering such criticisms as "Charles, I think I could spit paint better than that."[5] Although he never again picked up an artistic paint brush, Hodge enjoyed working with his hands throughout his life. Just years before his death he spent endless hours cutting and then polishing a glass inkwell. When it was finally done, he declared that he was more proud of it than his massive three-volume *Systematic Theology*.

In the spring of 1810, Mary Hodge made the difficult decision to send her sons away from Philadelphia for school. Compelled largely by her growing poverty, Mary accepted an offer from one of her relatives, John M. Bayard, to have her boys attend the local classical academy near Bayard's home in Somerville, New Jersey, where her boys could obtain an excellent education for a price far more reasonable than any she could obtain in Philadelphia.[6]

When Charles and Hugh Hodge arrived in Somerville, it was a tiny village of roughly two dozen dwellings.[7] Its central New Jersey location and rich farmland, how-ever, made it the home of a number of wealthy families, who had pooled their resources to start a classical academy to train their sons.[8] Bayard had made his money by owning several mills and had been politically active for a time in the region.[9] He along with his neighbors had invested such great resources into Somerville Academy that it had become one of the premier schools in the region, established expressly to teach "Eng-lish grammar, various languages, the arts and sciences, and public speaking."[10] The academy was particularly strong in teaching the classical languages, and it was during his time in Somerville that Hodge developed his linguistic aptitude. Hodge dove into the study of Latin and enjoyed it so much that many days he arrived early at school to complete his lessons.[11] He then picked up French before finally studying ancient Greek.

During his two years in Somerville, Hodge lived with two of the region's most wealthy and influential Dutch families: the Vandeveres and the Strykers.[12] He also became a frequent visitor to the Frelinghuysen home. Like the Bayards, the Frelinghuysens were political and service-minded. In the coming years, Frelinghuysens became important United States senators and military officers. Hodge's familiarity with all these families underscored the reality that although he was relatively poor, he still moved in the highest social circles.

Hodge became good friends with Theodore Frelinghuysen, a young man ten years his senior. Frelinghuysen showed immense aptitude in the areas of leadership and politics.[13] Moving from Federalist to National Republican to Whig parties, he served in a number of important government posts and was chosen as Henry Clay's running mate in the presidential election of 1845. Frelinghuysen's and Hodge's friendship was built on a host of common interests. A pious Presbyterian his whole life, Frelinghuysen served as the president of both the American Bible Society and American Tract Society, as well as standing as an officer of a number of other benevolent organizations including the American Colonization Society. He also thought seriously about studying for the ministry after politics had lost its allure, but instead took education positions, first as chancellor of New York University and then as president of Rutgers University in New Jersey. Rutgers' proximity to Princeton, as well as their common commitment to the religious aspects of education, kept Frelinghuysen and Hodge friends for over fifty years.

While in Somerville, Hodge kept in constant contact with his mother through letters. Their correspondence provides an instructive window into Mary's strong desire to put her stamp on Hodge's character. Mary writes constantly to Hodge and his brother of her high expectations for them, stating that she has the "greatest mortification" ("mortification" is one of her favorite words) that they might prove "only *common* characters such as the mass of mankind are."[14] She expects them to work extremely hard not only for her sake, but for the sake of the God who has allowed them a situation so "favourable for improvement," and who offered the warning: "To whom much is given, much will be required."[15]

Mary drives into her sons certain values that undergird her own life. She tells them that "nothing truly valuable can be obtained without labour & perseverance" directing them to develop the disciplines of patience, hard work, and self-denial.[16] Mary does everything within her power to nurture in them an appreciation for hard work and structure. She writes that developing proper work habits makes any arduous activity "not only easy but agreeable."[17] She instructs them to plan out their weeks and then give her an accounting of how they spend each day, preaching a work ethic that fixes "a particular hour for every thing."[18] With such attention to structure and scheduling, she tells them that they will have more than enough time to succeed in all that they undertake—including writing her weekly.

With echoes of Benjamin Franklin—whose educational strategies she fondly references in her letters—Mary tells her sons that they must turn their attention to cultivating good personal qualities.[19] She tells them that one of the best ways to pursue virtue is to study figures from classical works who provide "perfect" models worthy of emulation.[20] As she makes suggestions for researching potentially helpful historical figures, Mary reveals an impressive knowledge of Cicero, Telemachus, Virgil, Solon, Aeneas, and Cyrus.[21] She tells her boys not to be overawed by such great figures, but to examine their lives looking for both their good and bad attributes.[22]

Mary's encouragement to find role models extends to more personal levels as well. She exhorts her sons to make themselves known to their teachers so that such men might take a greater interest in them. She tells them to read the letters of Lord Chesterfield so that they might better be able to attract attention of superior men through their proper behavior and knowledge of genteel etiquette.[23] She gives them myriad rules on how best to behave in public settings, including everything from how to make proper eye contact during introductions to what distinguishes a person in casual conversation.[24] Underlying all her advice is Mary's keen awareness of her sons' semi-orphaned state. She takes great care in recommending to her sons ways of getting to know older male figures who might be able to help them as they lack a father who is able to so.[25]

In all her advice, Mary stresses regulation and systemization and this extends even to how they are to process the knowledge they are learning in the classroom. She tells her sons that "altho we may collect a large store of facts & observations" yet they are worth nothing if not "properly systemized" in a manner that allows them to be put into connection with larger truths and readily accessed for use in any number of settings.[26] Hodge's own love of habit and systemization in both his personal behavior and theological writings clearly has its roots in the lessons his mother repeated to him throughout his youth.

At the root of his mother's correspondence lay her profound commitment to the character formation of her sons. Whether physically present or not, Mary Hodge never lost an opportunity to instruct her sons in ways intended to form within them a virtuous personal identity stemming from a proper and controlled notion of self. She wished them to be a particular type of young man and taught them to pursue this ideal by showing them how to order their lives, address the world, and structure their desires.[27] Clearly committed to her social caste's republican ideals of industry, duty, and communal service, Mary did all in her power to produce sons who could take their place as productive citizens in a country whose very survival depended on the good character of its citizens and where personal success was closely correlated to personal achievement.[28]

To an uncanny decree, Hodge learned these lessons and inculcated them into the fabric of his life and his patterns of intellectual thought. As he grew into a teenager,

Hodge committed himself to a rigorous work ethic, which he maintained his entire life. He ordered his days through the use of personal rituals and carefully maintained schedules to maximize his productivity. His life became a testimony to how much work might be done if one sets goals and then systematically pursues them. He also trained himself to delay personal gratification, and in his personal writings most often pointed to a concept of duty as the main motivation behind his actions. He postponed his first marriage until he had a job that produced a steady income, and he later took the position of Professor of Didactic Theology against his own ardent wishes because he felt his personal desires weighed as nothing against the need to serve the greater good. With his mother's words seemingly forever in his mind, Hodge judged his life by taking stock of his accomplishments. Soon after his election as the moderator of his denomination's General Assembly, a position many considered a crowning career achievement, Hodge wrote his brother bemoaning the fact that "the years that remain must be few" and that he had "a painful feeling of having accomplished so little."[29] These marked tendencies toward hard work, self-denial, and personal achievement became as central to Hodge's character as the Westminster Confession was to his theological thinking, and these traits can be traced all the way back to his mother's influence.

One of Hodge's greatest struggles in Somerville involved a nagging self-consciousness about his poverty. His mother encouraged him to strive to become a refined gentleman, but he keenly felt the lack of a gentleman's resources as he moved amid the most distinguished circles in Somerville. He turned down chances to socialize because he was ashamed of his constant lack of presentable clothes at social occasions. His mother attempts to nudge him out of this stance, but it is clear that he regrets his dependent, fatherless status among his relatives and such affluent families as the Vandeveres, Strykers, and Frelinghuysens.[30] The ways in which Hodge had to negotiate the intricacies of social status and poverty in his youth profoundly influenced the accents of his later theological thinking concerning slavery and property rights. Hodge proved loathe to redistribute wealth without paying the most exacting attention to both biblical and civic laws, and in all areas of his own property management, Hodge remained mindful of the relationship between one's wealth and one's place in society.

Hodge's feelings of social and financial awkwardness met with new challenges when his brother Hugh moved away from Somerville in the fall of 1811 to pursue the final stages of college preparation in New Brunswick.[31] Bereft now for the first time in his life of both mother and brother, Hodge took tentative steps to establish his own personality by exploring new activities.[32] He began singing lessons and took new interest in a small debating society he had helped found called the "Debatents."[33] Although he still struggled with his poverty, his brother's absence forced him to take more advantage of the distinguished social circles around him. Hodge gained confidence as he moved from behind his brother's shadow and found himself well-liked and with a true gift for forming deep and lasting friendships.

In the early part of 1812, Hodge moved to Princeton to be reunited with his family. Mary had enrolled Hugh at the Princeton College, and she had decided to gather her family there partly in recognition that Hodge would also soon embark on his own college career. Princeton College had long been a staple among the Hodges. Hodge's father was a graduate of the class of 1773, and countless other Hodge relations had attended the distinctly New Side school, including: Andrew Hodge Jr. (1772), Hugh Hodge Jr. (1774) James Ashton Bayard (1777), Andrew Bayard (1779), James Asheton Bayard (1784), Nicholas Bayard (1792), Lewis Pintard Bayard (1809), and Richard Henry Bayard (1814). Mary rented a house on Witherspoon Street, just two blocks from the College's main building, Nassau Hall. Little did Hodge suspect as he took up residence once again with his mother and brother that aside from a two-year study leave in Europe, Princeton would serve as his home for the next sixty-six years.

5

PRINCE'S TOWN

Located halfway between New York City and Philadelphia, the small town of Princeton, New Jersey, bustled with activity in the opening years of the nineteenth century. Hundreds of horses and wagons daily filled its streets as nearly a dozen stagecoach and freight lines used the town as a principal relay station between the nation's two largest cities.[1] In the summer months, great clouds of dust engulfed pedestrians as they tried to negotiate the narrow sidewalks running alongside the roads, and in the winter deep ruts cut by wagon wheels made many of the streets impassable.[2] Even with its reputation as one of the region's premier marketplaces, Princeton managed to keep its small-borough feeling for decades, and when the railroad decided in the 1850s to bypass using the town as a major hub, Princeton's destiny as an intellectual rather than commercial center was set.

When Mary reunited with her sons in Princeton, the small town of seven hundred inhabitants had existed for almost a century. Its original settlers had been Quakers, and William Penn himself had once held title to the land upon which the town was built. In the early eighteenth century, there had been many variations on its name: "Prince's Town," "Princetown" and "Princeton." Neighboring towns like Kingston and Queenston hint that "Princeton" was simply an extension of the regal naming tradition of the region.

Its future as the setting for one of the country's great colleges was tied to its central location coupled with the resources of large local landowners like John Stockton who enabled the town to win the charter of Princeton College in 1754.[3] The idea for a college in New Jersey originated with a small band of Presbyterian ministers and laymen who included two of the College's first presidents: Jonathan Dickinson and Aaron Burr Sr., father of the famous duelist.[4] Dissatisfied that only three colleges existed in the colonies—Harvard in Massachusetts (1636), William and Mary in Virginia (1693), and Yale in Connecticut (1701)—Dickinson and Burr led a group of like-minded New Side Presbyterians to create a more centrally located college in the middle colonies.

New Side Presbyterians had also become disillusioned with the anti-revival leanings of both Harvard and Yale. Legend has it that Yale's expulsion in 1742 of David Brainerd, a New Side ministerial candidate, ultimately galvanized Dickinson, Burr, and others to establish a Presbyterian college. Yale's president had expelled Brainerd for his willful disobedience of school rules in attending pro-revival meetings and his lack of respect for his teachers. (Reportedly, Brainerd had told one of his friends that he believed his tutor had "no more grace than the chair I am leaning upon."[5]) A delegation of prominent Presbyterians outraged by the expulsion deputized Burr to make the arduous, yet ultimately fruitless, journey from Newark to New Haven to plead Brainerd's case. The incident totally soured an already-deteriorating relationship between New Side Presbyterians and Yale. Burr later commented: "if it had not been for the treatment received by Mr. Brainerd at Yale College, New Jersey College never would have been erected."[6]

In the wake of the Brainerd affair, Dickinson and Burr set about their dream of founding a new college with a vengeance. Although firmly committed to creating a school characterized by their own theological beliefs, the New Side ministers were savvy enough to know that if they remained too narrow in their theological proclamations, more moderate Presbyterians would not join their cause. In order to build a bridge between Old and New Side Presbyterians, as well as run the gauntlet of the New Jersey state government, which was heavily predisposed toward the Church of England, the founders of the College built into their charter certain tenets of religious freedom that welcomed men from all denominations.[7] Even with these concessions to religious tolerance, the New Side Presbyterians kept a firm hand on the institution once it had been approved by the New Jersey legislature. The College's distinctly Presbyterian flavor remained for the next century, as its first eleven presidents were all ardent Presbyterians.

In 1747, the College's initial classes began to meet in the home of the school's first president, Jonathan Dickinson. It was not until the completion of the College's first building, Nassau Hall, in 1756 that students finally moved into a more formal educational space.[8] Both Gilbert Tennent and Andrew Hodge played important roles in soliciting funds to build Nassau Hall, which had been named in honor of King William III, a member of the royal house of Nassau.[9] The hall soon became synonymous not only with the College but with the town itself.[10]

As Princeton College slowly grew in both size and prestige, the town of Princeton distinguished itself in other ways. During the College's earliest years, Princeton came to be known more for the role it played in the American Revolution than for its newly established institution of higher learning. On January 3, 1777, George Washington personally led a force in what would later be called the Battle of Princeton. The battle was of pivotal importance for Washington because it gave him an undisputed victory over British forces when the American army was severely demoralized and upon the point of collapse. A confrontation which started in a field outside of town quickly moved into the streets of Princeton. Nassau Hall became a locus of fighting with British cannonballs flying against its walls and through its windows. One legendary ball penetrated the College's library, embedding itself in a full-length portrait of George III, decapitating the portrait's figure. After the war, Washington visited Princeton and offered a gift of money to the College. The trustees quickly voted to use the money to prepare a full-length portrait of Washington to replace the now-headless George III. Thus, the ornaments of Nassau Hall reflected the larger political realities of the country as one George replaced another.

The Revolution turned out to be but a precursor to yet another conflict between the United States and Britain, the War of 1812. During her wars with Revolutionary and then Napoleonic France, Britain blockaded a great deal of American trade and impressed some six thousand American sailors into the British navy. The United States attempted several strategies to right these wrongs, including embargo acts in both 1807 and 1809 that halted all trade with Great Britain, but Britain failed to respond to these embargos and war was eventually declared. So, although the War of 1812 officially lasted only three years, the actual conflict had begun five years earlier. For eight years, American sea trade with Europe was brought to a virtual standstill, a state of affairs that had dire consequences for Mary Hodge, whose personal finances were intimately tied to international trade through the revenue that was generated—or not generated in this case—by the Hodge family wharf in Philadelphia. At first, she coped with her severely reduced income by taking boarders into her home, but by 1812, with no end of the conflict in sight, she had decided to leave the more expensive urban environment of Philadelphia and settle her family in Princeton.[11]

Mary's relocation to Princeton proved difficult. In order to support her family and pay for her sons' schooling, she rented a house large enough to take in four additional boys as boarders. All of her boarders were relatives, and her life was suddenly filled with the challenges of managing the daily routines of six boys.[12] The additional rent money proved to be insufficient for Mary's needs, and to supplement her income further she was forced to do laundry for those in the neighborhood.

Hugh Hodge remembered the sacrifices his mother made for his education. Sobered by their poverty, Hugh attacked his schoolwork, seeing his education as his best chance at a better life. Convinced that he must "either study or starve," Hugh entered the sophomore class at Princeton College in the Spring of 1812, while Charles finished secondary school at Princeton Academy, a small grammar school informally attached to the College and located only a few hundred feet from the front entrance of Nassau Hall.[13] The Academy had sprung up in 1790 as a place where Princeton's elite young men might prepare for future collegiate education.

Hodge attended Princeton Academy for six months before entering the sophomore class at Princeton College in September 1812.[14] Along with honing his skills in Latin, rhetoric, mathematics, and science, Hodge used his time at Princeton Academy to become good friends with a number of his classmates, including James W. Alexander, the eldest son of the founding professor of Princeton Seminary. James became a lifelong friend, and for a brief time, a colleague on the faculty at Princeton Seminary.

6

WITHERSPOON'S COMMON SENSE

When Hodge began his studies at Princeton College, the school was in crisis. The student body had shrunk by nearly half over the previous six years, and this decrease forced the release of some of the school's best instructors. In the midst of the turmoil, the College's trustees had turned to Hodge's childhood pastor, Ashbel Green, to occupy the recently vacated position of president in an attempt to stabilize the affairs of the school. Green reluctantly took the job.

To understand the roots of the school's crisis, it is necessary to consider the policies and personalities of the presidents who preceded Green in his new post. By the time Green became its head, Princeton College had run through seven presidents in its sixty-six-year history. While Aaron Burr Sr. had done much to lay the pivotal foundations for the College in the 1750s, the position ultimately drove him to exhaustion and death in 1757. Jonathan Edwards next held the presidency, but he held the position for barely two months before dying from the effects of a smallpox vaccine in 1758. Samuel Davies followed Edwards, but he too was dead after only two years due to extreme exhaustion and fever. Samuel Finley was next. He ascended the presidency in 1761 only to die five years later of sickness brought on by excessive fatigue. In less than a decade, the College had ground through four presidents.

Just four months after Finley's death, the College's trustees found themselves facing yet another presidential search. They approached John Witherspoon of Scotland to become the school's next president because of his international reputation as a writer, preacher, and vocal champion of orthodoxy. Witherspoon was also an attractive candidate because he was an outsider to the American Presbyterian Old and New Side schism. A descendant of Presbyterianism's founder John Knox, Witherspoon had the requisite orthodoxy for Old Siders and passion enough to satisfy the New Side.

Figure 6.1 *John Witherspoon*: John Witherspoon – minister, educator and patriot – brought Scottish Common Sense Realism to Princeton College. Scottish Realism and Calvinism formed the two central pillars of Hodge's theological thinking. [*Princeton University Library*]

Playing upon the links between American and Scottish Presbyterianism, the trustees implored Witherspoon to take the post using such rhetorical flourishes as: "The Young Daughter of the Church of Scotland, helpless and exposed in this foreign land, cries to her tender and powerful parent for relief."[1] Only after much soul-searching, and against the wishes of his wife, did Witherspoon accept the position in 1767.

When Witherspoon's ship arrived in Philadelphia a year later, he disembarked with his wife, five children, and a library of three hundred books.[2] He was met on the dock by none other than Andrew Hodge, who served as his host during his first few days in the American colonies.[3] When Witherspoon traveled to Princeton nearly a week later, the entire town turned out to line the streets and escort him to Nassau Hall. The first Sunday after his arrival, he preached a sermon at the First Presbyterian Church entitled "The Union of Piety and Science." The sermon's topic proved to be a significant foretaste of the direction in which he would steer the College over the next quarter of a century. His was to be a presidency committed to the melding orthodox religion with the scientific and philosophical advances of the age.

Prior to Witherspoon's arrival, Princeton College had focused on training ministerial candidates, and it had done so with considerable success. In the College's first twenty years, it sent out 158 ministers, nearly half of its graduating classes.[4] Witherspoon took the College in a new direction, desiring to broaden the educational mandate of the school to engage a wider array of professional endeavors. By the time Witherspoon's presidency ended with his death in 1794, Princeton College had shifted from primarily training ministerial candidates to an emphasis on preparing young men for the realms of law, politics, education, medicine, and business.[5] Witherspoon's quarter century as president witnessed a sharp decline in the number of students entering the ministry. During the last decade of his presidency, only 13 percent of the graduating classes entered the ministry, a far cry from the 47 percent boasted by the five presidents who had preceded him.[6] Even Ashbel Green in his usually glowing biography of Witherspoon admitted that many thought Witherspoon's own commitment to politics during the American Revolution had taken precedent over his fervor for training ministers.[7]

This shift away from training young men for the ministry was in large part due to how Witherspoon expanded the College's curriculum to reach beyond training in classical languages, English composition, oratory, and theology. He himself was an accomplished linguist, and he introduced the study of modern languages to the College. He also worked hard to develop the mathematical and scientific components of the curriculum. He created faculty positions in the sciences and bought expensive scientific equipment such as David Rittenhouse's celebrated orrery, an unique instrument which showed the movement of the planets around the sun.[8] Witherspoon's commitment to scientific inquiry and his desire to put religion and science into meaningful dialogue set the course for the College's approach to learning for decades to come.

Even more importantly, Witherspoon brought a new philosophical orientation to the College. Led by Witherspoon, the College became infused with a profound commitment to Scottish Common Sense Realism.[9] Witherspoon became the great champion of this intellectual paradigm in American higher education, an intellectual school of thought which permeated not only most of American intellectual thinking up to the Civil War, but also became a defining characteristic of Hodge's own theological thinking.[10]

Founded on the writings of Francis Hutcheson and Thomas Reid, Scottish Common Sense Realism was a multifaceted system of belief that attempted to take serious account of new Enlightenment developments in science, but not lose sight of science's connections to religious belief.[11] At its core, Scottish Common Sense held out three central truths.[12] First, it taught that some basic truths were self-evident. Being a careful and patient observer made truth accessible to anyone through one's ordinary, "common" senses, and thus the senses could be trusted to provide a sound basis for all scientific, philosophical, and theological endeavors. The idea that all people held these senses in common, and thus shared an ability to perceive the world accurately, was particularly important in matters of religion. For those who believed in Common Sense Realism, all of God's manifold work and his very presence in the world was a fact available and verifiable to all thoughtful observers. Second, Scottish Realism contained a pronounced ethical dimension; it taught that all people in addition to their five senses had a common moral sense that allowed them to distinguish between good and evil. Third, Scottish Realism advocated a methodology refined and popularized by the seventeenth-century scientist and natural philosopher, Francis Bacon. Bacon taught that the pursuit of all intellectual inquiries must be built upon strict methods of inductively investigating all irreducible facts offered through experience.

So central was Common Sense Realism to Witherspoon's view of the world that he used it as the organizing principle of his year-long capstone senior seminar on moral philosophy.[13] As a consequence, the crowning seminar of a student's career was focused on integrating the lessons they had learned in their previous College courses into a coherent whole, synthesized through the lens of Scottish Realism. In this way, no student left Princeton without a firm grounding in the basic tenets of Common Sense Realism and the ethical imperative of revealing God's accessible truth to all.

What is easy to miss in considering Witherspoon's immense role in the spread of Scottish Common Sense Realism in America is the way in which this philosophical system stood in uneasy relationship with Calvinism. Just ten years prior to his arrival in New Jersey, Witherspoon had looked askance at Common Sense Realism largely because of its views on a common moral sentiment. Such thinking was diametrically opposed to earlier Reformed thinking which reserved the practice of true virtue only for God's elect, while teaching that the unregenerate were hopelessly lost and their every action evil. Such towering Puritan figures as Cotton Mather and Jonathan Edwards had balked at Europe's rising enchantment with notions of a universal moral philosophy, considering it a vile form of paganism offensive to God's sovereignty because of the stress it laid on human moral ability.[14] One of Princeton College's beloved founding fathers, Jonathan Dickinson, summarized this early American Protestant feeling against a universal moral sentiment when he stated: "you can't trust too little your selves; nor too much to" God.[15]

Witherspoon had held views much closer to those of Mather, Edwards, and Dickinson while in Scotland. Once in the colonies, however, he underwent a marked transformation, becoming a critically important agent in the American Protestant embracement of notions of moral philosophy that only a generation earlier had been held as anathema by staunch American Calvinists.[16] The causes both for Witherspoon's conversion to supporting Scottish Common Sense in particular and the conversion of American Protestantism to this philosophical system more generally are complex. What does become clear, however, in studying the intellectual currents swirling around the American Revolution is that Scottish Common Sense provided a much-needed system of understanding virtue in a country which had set upon an unprecedented course of rebellion against its mother country to establish a broad-based form of democratic governance. American Protestants found themselves desperately wishing to hold to traditional religious beliefs and values, but they could no longer depend on the means that had supported those values such as a rich sense of history, ecclesiastical traditions, social hierarchies, and inherited forms of political and church governance.[17]

The country's radically new course demanded a new way of understanding the human condition, and so Protestants found themselves embracing notions of moral philosophy that posited that the possibility of virtue was embedded in every man and woman. Paths toward personal goodness and social stability resided not only in the exterior rituals and institutions so exalted in the past; they could be found in the human heart. The librarian and historian Norman Fiering, a careful student of the intellectual currents of eighteenth-century America, has argued that the new moral philosophy became a perfect fit for "an era still strongly committed to traditional religious values and yet searching for alternative modes of justification for those values."[18] Scottish Common Sense Realism allowed American Protestants to join their fellow citizens in embracing a more expansive conception of moral reasoning and behavior not solely confined to God's elect. Instead, Scottish Realism held out the possibility that every person had at least the potential for virtuous behavior planted deeply within them, a crucial prerequisite for the virtuous behavior so necessary for the survival of a democracy where acting rightly was the most fundamental building block for effective political governance and amiable social stability.

The thorough acceptance of Scottish Realism's moral reasoning at Princeton College had a profound effect on Hodge's own theological thinking. Although rigorously tied to the Calvinist beliefs of the Westminster Confession, Hodge came to offer Americans a unique strain of Reformed theological thinking largely based on a notion of a universal moral sentiment. His stands against the damnation of infants and that God intended to save the majority of humanity had their roots in the moral philosophy of Witherspoon's Scottish Realism. Witherspoon's belief in a common moral

Figure 6.2 *Samuel Stanhope Smith*: Samuel Stanhope Smith married the daughter of John Witherspoon and succeeded him as the president of Princeton College in 1795. [*Princeton University Library*]

sense laid the groundwork for Hodge's slightly more hopeful view of the human condition. His own theology became a complex and conflicted mix of Calvinist notions of total depravity leavened with the conviction that every human held within themselves a moral sense capable of detecting virtue. Ultimately, a thin current of humanistic optimism surfaces at times in the usually hard-edged and conservative Calvinism Hodge offered Americans. The hellfire predictions of damnation that so marked the careers of Cotton Mather and Jonathan Edwards found a lighter touch in the Calvinism of Hodge.

Princeton College's commitment to Common Sense Realism may have begun with Witherspoon, but it did not end when he died in 1794. Witherspoon's son-in-law and successor, Samuel Stanhope Smith, first held the College's chair in moral philosophy and eventually became the College's president. Smith built upon Witherspoon's work in two ways. He broadened the school's curriculum by appointing faculty members in the languages, theology, mathematics, astronomy, and chemistry, as well as by purchasing the latest scientific equipment available.[19] He also made Witherspoon's treasured Scottish Common Sense Realism the basis of his entire educational vision, systematically applying it to the theories and teaching of theology, science, politics and the humanities.[20]

Smith's presidency lasted seventeen years. While the early years of his tenure were marked by prosperity, his latter years were troubled. During his presidency, the student body grew to number nearly two hundred, and Smith accommodated this growth by adding both professors and tutors to the College's faculty.[21] Discontent, however, grew along with the school's size. Students who had been brought up in the aftermath of the Revolution were a new breed of young men, acquainted with concepts of individual rights and free thinking that stood against the age-old hierarchical and religious bent of traditional higher education. Such young men felt belittled and constrained by an educational paradigm of top-down authority and religious rigidity so prevalent at Princeton College.

Just how much tension existed beneath the surface of Smith's presidency became clear in 1807 when the College experienced the worst student revolt in its history. The trouble started innocently enough with the suspension of three students, one for being in a tavern where he had gotten drunk and two for insolence toward College faculty members. These suspensions led to a committee of ten students approaching the faculty with a written petition, signed by a large portion of the student body, which all but demanded that the three students be reinstated.[22] The faculty who read the statement were dumbfounded. Not only was their authority being questioned, there was a rule against forming "combinations" to resist the authority of the College's faculty or trustees. Immediately, the faculty met with the only trustee then in town, Richard Stockton Jr., to decide on a course of action.

The resulting decision lacked finesse. The faculty called the student body into Prayer Hall and declared that the students who refused to retract their names from the petition would be suspended immediately. Such a threat did nothing but fan the flames of student anger.[23] One hundred and twenty-five students stormed out of the Hall while roughly forty remained. Those who left proceeded to barricade themselves in Nassau Hall. Smith and Stockton had the local militia called out, but when the militia attempted to enter Nassau Hall they were repelled by students throwing stones and wielding all manner of weapons including stairway banisters that had been ripped from the walls.[24] Finally, President Smith had to admit that the crisis had gotten out of control. He dismissed the whole college for five weeks until the next meeting of the board of trustees was scheduled to meet.

When the board met in April, they supported the faculty but great damage had been done to both the reputation of the College and to President Smith. A number of students eventually retracted their names from the petition and returned to school, but over fifty did not. In many ways, the rebellion of 1807 marked the end of President Smith's effectiveness as the College's leader. Even before the riot, the College's trustees had become weary of Smith's educational vision. Many of them were older Presbyterian stalwarts who bemoaned the fact that by 1806, barely 9 percent of the College's graduates were entering the ministry, down from the already low 13 percent of Witherspoon's last years.[25] The student unrest just confirmed in their eyes that Smith had lost his ability to lead.[26] Student enrollment decreased dramatically after the riot. Just months after the confrontation at Nassau Hall, the College's student population dropped nearly in half to 112 students. By 1810, the College had fewer than one hundred students.[27]

More than prestige and goodwill were lost in these decreasing numbers. The primary source of income for the College was tuition, and as fewer students chose to come to Princeton, the College's operating budget shrank. The years of work Smith had dedicated to building up the faculty and expanding the College's curriculum were washed away by the 1807 riot and its aftermath. In the face of the precipitous drop in enrollment, Smith released treasured faculty members. By 1810, the College that had once boasted four professors, three tutors and an instructor in French was now whittled down to only two faculty members (President Smith and Professor John Maclean Sr.) and two tutors.[28] Princeton College now entered the worst decade of its existence.

Two years later, Professor Maclean accepted a position at William and Mary, and Smith resigned after the trustees made it clear that they wanted someone new to take the helm. Smith became the College's first president to step down, a sign of the extreme tension that existed between him and the College's board of trustees. Into this troubled climate stepped a reluctant Ashbel Green, who became the College's eighth president in 1812, well aware that the task before him was not one for the faint of heart.[29]

7

"CLASSICK LEARNING"

Ashbel Green had deep and heartfelt connections to Princeton College. His father had acted as the school's interim vice president between the tenures of Jonathan Edwards and Samuel Davies, and he had graduated with distinction from the institution in 1783.[1] Two years after his graduation, Green married Elizabeth Stockton, one of the daughters of Princeton's powerful scion Richard Stockton.[2] Green, like Smith, had also been a devoted student of Witherspoon's. In fact, Green held his former teacher in such high esteem that upon Witherspoon's death he wrote a biography of the man, commenting that he owed to him more "than to all other men, and perhaps to all the books he has ever read."[3]

When Green was approached to take over the College's presidency, he was serving on the school's board of trustees. On the board, he had come to lead a powerful clerical faction which found fault with Smith's broader educational vision and wished the College to return to its religious roots. Green felt a certain degree of vindication for his views in March 1802 when Nassau Hall was burned to the ground. No one was ever charged, but Green and several other trustees believed the arsonists to be students who had given themselves over to "vice and irreligion."[4]

The loss of Nassau Hall required Smith to make a national tour to solicit funds to rebuild the Hall. During his absence in 1802–1803, Green took over the College's presidency on an interim basis. Green's actions during his brief tenure highlighted his differences with Smith. During Smith's absence, Green lost no time correcting what he saw as Smith's mistakes. He instituted a much-stricter code of student conduct, and he promised both the students and their parents that obedience to this code would be scrupulously enforced.[5] He also made several curricular changes that put greater emphasis on religious training. He instituted Sunday Bible instruction, catechism classes, and made William Paley's *A View of the Evidences of Christianity* required reading for all seniors.[6] Upon his return, Smith once again attempted to enact his own educational vision, but his deteriorating relationship with his trustees and the loss of students after the riot of 1807 ultimately doomed his attempts to establish a more progressive curriculum at Princeton.

When Green ascended to the presidency in 1812, he considered the College to be in "a most deplorable state," and entered upon his formidable duties "with the resolution to reform" the College "or to fall under the attempt."[7] After a single semester as president, Green found himself more convinced than ever of the College's pitiful state. To summarize his thoughts, he wrote the trustees a ninety-six-page report detailing the school's every deficiency. According to Green, "classick learning" had decayed to such a degree that undergraduates could not translate their own diplomas from the Latin in which they were written. He lamented that the school's "state of religion & morals . . . were completely prostate" and the quality of its religious instruction was "disastrous & discouraging."[8]

Armed with his report, Green wasted no time in making changes. He quickly sought to reform both the College's student discipline and its curriculum. He made the laws of the college even stricter than the code he had introduced in 1802: tutors were assigned to check on students by entering their rooms three times a day; Sabbath activities were constricted; and special permission was needed to rent horses or go on such extracurricular activities as sleigh rides. Green even began the practice of writing each student's parents offering a detailed review of personal conduct and academic progress.[9] He bolstered the Latin and Greek language requirements, made the study of the Bible a required course for the first time in the College's history, and mandated the study of William Paley's writings on natural theology. Perhaps most importantly, he returned to Witherspoon's lectures in moral philosophy, lectures that had changed under Smith, who had developed his own (sometimes controversial) philosophical positions on moral thought and action.[10] Green had little interest in pursuing an educational vision more in step with a new age and a new kind of American student. He shunned curriculums that offered a greater choice of courses and more flexibility on graduation requirements. Students needed to adapt to Green's conservative notions of pious education or find another school.[11]

Green's every presidential action grew from his desire to raise up pious young men for the good of the country and God's kingdom. John Maclean Jr., one of Green's students and a later president of the College, wrote of Green: "In every way that he could, officially and unofficially, in public and in private, he labored to promote the spiritual welfare of his pupils; and he never lost sight of the great object for which the College was founded."[12] Green instituted a weekly religious lecture, which was well attended throughout his tenure.[13] He also worked closely with Princeton's fledgling seminary to provide students from both institutions with opportunities to become involved in a variety of voluntary organizations, which concerned themselves with everything from literacy education to foreign missions.

Green's commitment to offering his students a religiously based education even reached into the ranks of the College's tutors. During his presidency, almost all the tutors were either Princeton Seminary students or recent Seminary graduates. Tutors may have occupied a lower rung on the faculty ladder at colleges, but they were often the most important authority figures in the lives of undergraduates. Tutors spent more time with the students than did the faculty members and were more responsible for shepherding them through their daily educational exercises. Green's choice of seminary-trained tutors, rather than simply Princeton College graduates, was but another attempt to saturate the College with Presbyterian piety from top to bottom. Green became famous for the way in which he saw himself as the College's father figure who daily prayed for his children, asking that God might "pour out His Spirit" and make the school all that "its pious founders intended it to be."[14]

Into this setting of turmoil and reformation stepped the fourteen-year-old Charles Hodge, who joined an incoming class of roughly thirty students in the fall of 1812. He was on the young side of his entering class. The average first-year college student was fourteen or fifteen years of age, and such youth helped account for the high degree of paternal control exercised by college faculties of the day.[15] Hodge's class helped to swell the College's population to nearly one hundred students.[16] He entered as a sophomore, having passed through the requisite language and general knowledge examinations that made him able to forego his freshmen year.

Hodge's days as an undergraduate were both rigorous and regimented. Every morning aside from the Sabbath, Nassau Hall's bell rang at six o'clock to rouse students from their sleep. Because the bell often did not prove forceful enough, a small group of hand-picked students also ran through the corridors blowing trumpets to waken the laggards. Students then immediately left for morning prayers in the unheated chapel followed by a short time to review their day's recitation before breakfast at seven thirty. At nine o'clock, juniors and seniors retired to their rooms to study, but freshmen and sophomores were required to go to the recitation room where they either recited or studied until noon. At one o'clock, lunch was served and often students met in the dining room to study until the time the meal was served. Hodge and other underclassmen then traveled once again to the recitation room at two o'clock, where they remained until five when they were dismissed for evening prayers and dinner. The remainder of the evening was then used to study, hold meetings, or enjoy a brief outing. Beginning at nine o'clock, the College's tutors began making their rounds to make sure that students were indeed present in the hall and either preparing for bed or for their next day's classes.[17]

The studies Hodge pursued during these years centered on science, classical literature, rhetoric, and theology.[18] Prior to Green's tenure, Smith had done much to loosen some of the College's early moorings to biblical and classical education, but Green moved decisively in the opposite direction. While Smith had largely limited the study of Latin to the freshman year, Green mandated that students study Latin and Greek every year. Green put a great emphasis on using these languages in biblical study and recitation work. To this end, students were assigned to study in either Latin or Greek five chapters of the Bible each week. They were also expected to memorize—in Latin—the catechism of their parents' church.

Hodge's college years may have had a pronounced religious and classical emphasis, but he was expected to become proficient in a number of other subjects as well. As a sophomore, he studied English composition, rhetoric, geography, arithmetic, and algebra. As a junior, he moved from algebra to the study of geometry, trigonometry, conic sections, surveying, navigation, mechanics, fluxions, and mensuration. He also spent his junior year studying natural philosophy, astronomy, belles lettres (the study of literature that concentrated on its imaginative rather than informative or didactic qualities), composition, history, and moral philosophy—including the study of Locke on human understanding. As a senior, Hodge continued his work in composition, belles lettres, history, mathematics, mechanics, and natural philosophy, but he added courses in chemistry, natural theology (with special attention to William Paley's *Natural Theology*), and moral philosophy.[19]

Clearly, Green's curriculum was reactionary for its time. Under Witherspoon and Smith, the course of study at the College had begun to grow in the more practical and commerce-friendly areas of science, modern languages, and mathematics. While Green kept elements of these curriculums, the emphasis he placed on the Bible and on classical-language texts inevitably took student time and institutional focus away from his predecessors' more modernizing curricular moves. Green pursued a course that largely resembled American college curriculums almost a century earlier. Hodge entered Princeton at this moment of renewed conservatism, and Green's traditionalism proved absolutely pivotal in the development of his own intellectual life and his lifelong commitment to cultivating a religious ethos at the College.

Alongside the College's formal classes, there were two literary societies—the American Whig and Cliosophic—connected with the school that proved critical to the educational and social development of a large number of the College's students.[20] Both societies had been founded during the presidency of Samuel Davies. Davies enjoyed a substantial reputation for his considerable oratorical skill, and his own commitment to rhetoric and the art of persuasion inspired him to make sure his students regularly practiced their public speaking.[21] Eventually, this emphasis on rhetoric spawned a number of literary societies, but the ones that enjoyed the greatest prestige, power and longevity were the American Whig Society (1769) and the Cliosophic Society (1770).

Hodge's father, Hugh, had been present at the inception of these clubs, helping to establish the Whig Society alongside such luminaries as James Madison, Samuel Stanhope Smith, Philip Freneau, and future Virginia governor Henry Lee.[22] Because of the great emphasis put on genealogical ties in these societies, it was a foregone conclusion that both Hodge brothers were destined to become "Whigs."[23] To have joined the "Clios," or to have not joined a society at all, would have been a slap in the face to the family's school loyalties.

The rivalry between the two clubs was intense. Members faced off against each other with an unremitting sense of no-holds-barred competition, which took endless forms: grades in daily class assignments, the production of literary works, formal debates, and honors accrued by members at graduation. The rivalry seeped into everyday life at the College. A Whig would never think of rooming with a Clio, and vice versa. Pranks between the societies were common, as were the epithets hurled from one society to the other. A Whig thought nothing of writing of a Clio that he was "A heap of mud, vile unmeaning lump/ Shot by the devile from his full charged Rump."[24] Clios, in turn, gave as good as they got.

Because these societies proved to be an important nexus between the College's social and intellectual realms, they often became the single most important element of a student's life at Princeton. They provided a forum for meaningful intellectual interchange, as well as a place to live out passionate allegiances and form lifelong friendships. Although no formal relationship existed between faculty members and these clubs, instructors often turned to these societies in matters of discipline, finding that even loafers and pranksters could be brought into line by their society brothers. Students repeatedly pointed to their membership in these societies as the best part of their college education, and many a young man chose to attend Princeton College because of the unique role these clubs played at the school.[25]

Hodge and his brother became Whigs within months of arriving in Princeton.[26] While a Whig, Hodge wrote a number of essays on a wide variety of topics. Underclassmen were expected to write such essays about once a month, and Hodge dutifully churned out works throughout 1814 on topics such as: Happiness, Ambition, Education of Youth, Envy, Love of Liberty, Monastaries, and Firmness & Decision of Character.[27] He also participated in the periodic debates held by the society. His diverse interests become evident through the debate topics he chose. Surprisingly, Hodge favored debating political and scientific topics rather than religious issues. Twice in 1814, he debated topics surrounding European political structures, and in 1815 he poured himself into addressing the question: "Do Brutes Contain Reason?"[28]

Both brothers also served in almost every society office. At one point, Hodge was elected to the post of censor, a position second only to the society's moderator in importance. According to the society's constitution, censors were tasked with inspecting the "morals and conduct of the members and by their advice, and with the consent privately to admonish, publickly to ensure or report, who are deficient in study and scholarship, who are guilty of any immorality, irregularity, indecency or any violation of the laws of the College or this society."[29] During Hodge's time at the College, being a censor was a particularly prickly business because various Whigs were in constant trouble with the College's administration. So pronounced was the problem that the Whig historian for 1815 recorded in his yearly summary that the year bore witness to "the humiliating fact" that instances of College discipline fell "chiefly on the members of this hall."[30] Out of the roughly fifty members of the society, Hodge and his brother steered clear of serious disciplinary problems. Occasionally, one of them was leveled with a small fine for laughing during a meeting or tardiness, but it is clear from the records that they both behaved in an exemplary fashion compared to their troublesome fellow Whigs.

Their good behavior in the society was but a mirror of their college behavior as a whole. While faculty records note that Hodge's peers were often visiting taverns, insulting tutors, dueling with canes, scraping their feet during prayers, lighting firecrackers in College buildings, becoming intoxicated, sneaking women into Nassau Hall after hours, and showing disrespect toward townspeople, Hodge and his brother were never cited for a single infraction by the College's administration. No doubt their clean records were largely due to the fact that both boys lived with their mother and were personally accountable to her. It no doubt helped Mary's stabilizing influence that Ashbel Green, a man she had known for over two decades, frequently stopped by the Hodge home to share a cup of afternoon tea.[31]

As the student turmoil under Smith's tenure shows, discipline was a constant concern for the College's faculty. Complicating the faculty's desire that students lead peaceful, studious, and well-ordered lives was the fact that their daily schedules did not include any forms of sanctioned physical activity. It is not hard to imagine the problems that might arise from housing ninety young boys in the same structure and expecting them to do nothing but study. The faculty scheduled no athletic events or exercises for the boys, and they even discouraged unstructured outdoor physical activity because it was thought to be unhealthy and lead to a number of both minor and major illnesses.

The stresses caused by such inactivity usually reached their height each year in the frigid winter months when even such innocent physical activities as taking walks were curtailed. Thus, wintertime became a classic time of student unrest in Princeton. In February 1813, one of Hodge's classmates was brought before the faculty for breaking into Nassau Hall's prayer hall and slicing a cavity into the pages of the pulpit Bible in such a way as to insert "a pack of playing cards" with one of the cards inscribed "with a sentence of the most horrible profanity."[32] Unfortunately for the perpetrator, he had failed to disguise his handwriting, and Green—who had just recently reviewed a paper of his—quickly identified him. Green's penchant for harsh discipline sprang forth. Not only did Green expel the student, but he demanded that he clear his things out of Nassau Hall by three P.M. that same day.

The following winter saw one of the greatest displays of student frivolity ever seen at the College. As a prelude to what turned out to be the main event, the "privy of the college was discovered on fire," at about three o'clock in the morning on January 8, 1814.[33] The fire was arson, but no students were charged. But on the evening of the following day, an event which came to be known as "the big cracker" literally shook the foundations of Nassau Hall.[34] Princeton students had long used gunpowder in various forms to make firecrackers, which they then set off on the College grounds. It was a harmless, if largely irritating practice, which always brought some sort of administrative censure. Hodge's classmates, however, took playing with firecrackers to a whole new level by creating the largest firecracker ever seen in Princeton.

Somewhere around a dozen students worked together to pack a hollow log with two pounds of gunpowder, which they then leaned against one of the central doors of Nassau Hall. The resulting earth-shattering explosion demolished the doors to the Hall, broke numerous windows, hurled wood fragments in all directions, and even cracked a significant portion of the masonry surrounding the doorway. Ashbel Green commented that it was a miracle that the bomb had not severed the "limbs of several students, as well as the tutors of the college who had passed near it only a few minutes before."[35] Once again, all were reminded of the student unrest of the previous decade. The trustees were severely shaken as they paused to reflect upon whether they had elected a president capable of reversing the College's seemingly unstoppable downward slide. It was only in the great religious revival that swept through the College the following winter that their growing fears about Green's ability to lead were at least momentarily relieved.

8

ENLISTING UNDER THE BANNER OF KING JESUS

As Hodge entered his senior year, he found himself once again without the comforting companionship of brother Hugh. Hugh had graduated in the fall of 1814 and had moved back to Philadelphia to study medicine. Caspar Wistar, an old family friend, had agreed to take on Hugh as an apprentice in his medical practice.[1] Now largely retired, Wistar had been one of Philadelphia's most prominent physicians and had also served as the president of the American Philosophical Society. So close were the Hodge and Wistar families that Catherine Bache, Wistar's sister, was boarding in Mary's Princeton home along with her three children when Hugh left for Philadelphia.[2]

As Hodge entered his senior year, he also was planning to pursue a medical career. In just a few months, however, his plans radically changed. Beginning in mid-January 1815, a great religious revival visited Princeton College. Green described its advent by writing the College's trustees that a "divine influence seemed to descend like the silent dew of heaven; and in about four weeks there were very few individuals in the College who were not deeply impressed with a sense of the importance of spiritual and eternal things."[3] These winter months became the highwater mark of Green's presidency. For a short time, everyone believed that his strict sense of discipline and his curricular emphasis on religion was paying dividends.

Interestingly, it was another act of discipline that set the revival in motion. A student who had been dismissed for bad behavior was "almost immediately seized with a remorse of conscience and anguish of mind that were very affecting."[4] Out of this one student's deep regret sprang a fountain of introspection and spiritual reflection that touched the entire student body. In the weeks that followed, Green and the new Seminary's founding professor, Archibald Alexander, spent countless hours counseling students who were in anguish over the state of their souls. Seminary students joined with the College's tutors to advise students who were struggling with issues like the primacy of God in their own lives, their love of their fellow men, the vanity of certain amusements, and the trustworthiness of the Bible.[5] Nightly prayer meetings sprang up in Nassau Hall, and Dr. Green and Dr. Alexander shared teaching responsibilities in offering Tuesday and Friday evening lectures on religion and Sunday Bible lessons. Throughout the winter, a religious energy coursed through the College which made almost every student mindful of their sinfulness and need for God's salvation.[6]

The revival of 1815 lasted well into the spring. By mid-April, some forty students had made a public confession of faith while fifteen more seriously considered making such a profession. Of the one hundred and five students currently at the College, the revival had seen roughly one-third of them converted. Counting those who were already "professors of religion," Green proudly declared that by the summer a "majority" of the College's students were professing Christians.[7] He rejoiced in how his prayers for the spiritual welfare of his school were being answered.

The sense of community which sprang from this revival was intense and lasting. As Green examined each of the new converts "individually and carefully," he was forcibly struck with the fact that they seemed to feel that they along with their classmates had been set apart by God for a special purpose.[8] The students of the 1815 revival came to view themselves as a special remnant, a chosen people of the Lord. Many of these students went on to take influentially pious roles in both church and civil offices, including two governors, a senator, a Speaker of the House of Representatives, two bishops in the Episcopal Church, seven pastors, one secretary of the American Board of Commissioners for Foreign Missions, and one missionary to Hawaii.[9]

Hodge had been raised in the Presbyterian Church, and later commented that his childhood was the time he "came nearer to conforming to the apostle's injunction: 'Pray without ceasing,' than in any other period" of his life.[10] As far back as he could remember, he had practiced "the habit of thanking God for everything."[11] So marked by a religious sensibility was his youth that he could only recall a single time that he uttered a profane word.[12] Even with his tendency toward piety, the events of the 1815 revival shook Hodge to his core. He began asking himself just how seriously he took the Presbyterian-laced beliefs of his youth, and he began to wonder if he was truly converted. As the revival activities of 1815 gathered momentum, Hodge came to the conclusion that his faith was indeed genuine, and he wished to make a public profession to that effect. On January 15, 1815, he stood before the congregation of Princeton's Presbyterian Church to profess his faith publically and become a member of the congregation. By so doing, Hodge became one of the 1815 revival's first "converts."

When Hodge's friend, Edward Allen, happened upon John Maclean, Jr., another classmate, near Nassau Hall, he proudly proclaimed that "Hodge had enlisted." This announcement made Maclean pause because the War of 1812 was not yet over, and there was at the moment an enlisting sergeant in Princeton's main square attempting to recruit young men. Puzzled, Maclean asked Allen why Hodge joined the army. Smiling at his own wit, Allen told Maclean that Hodge had "enlisted under the banner of King Jesus!"[13]

As Hodge publicly committed himself to Jesus, he became less committed to his studies. He increasingly gave himself over to a variety of religious activities and meetings as the winter months progressed. At the same time, his health deteriorated as a chest ailment became progressively worse. He began losing significant weight and suffered from a severe cough and frequent chest pains. In April, he passed his midterm examinations with the highest honors, but by the time he took his final examinations in August, he had slipped down among the ranks of those awarded second honors in his class.[14]

Weak and emaciated, Hodge found himself barely able to attend the College's graduation ceremony in September 1815.[15] Noticeably thin and unsteady on his feet, Hodge offered his class's valedictory address, an honor awarded by drawing lots. His oration was titled "On the Translations & Diffusion of the Holy Scriptures," and it served as an early indication of his growing interest in the serious study of biblical languages. By the time of his graduation, Hodge had changed his plans from medicine to ministry. His mother was not excited about the decision, but she knew better than to try to change Hodge's mind. She commented to Hugh that Hodge had Uncle McColloch stubbornness, which made all appeals useless once his mind had been made up. She was never able "to throw a straw" in the way of any decision he had ever firmly made.[16]

Pursing a ministry career necessitated that Hodge undertake further studies at Princeton's new seminary. He did not begin such studies immediately, however, for although Mary could not turn Hodge from his purpose, she did demand that he take some time off before he continued his education. Mary was seriously worried about her son's health, and in the end his feeble state forced him to submit to her wishes. After graduation, Hodge returned with his mother to Philadelphia to convalesce with the added benefit of once again being near his brother.

9

HAPPY JAUNTS AND THE "MAN OF MEN"

Hodge passed the winter months upon his return to Philadelphia in a course of general reading, but contrary to his mother's best-laid plans, his health grew worse during the city's cold winter months. His condition became so troubling that Mary decided that Hodge needed a change of setting. So as spring approached, she decided to send him out of the city to visit relatives. He first spent several months with his cousin Mrs. Harrison Smith in her home outside Washington, D.C., where Hodge later attributed the beginning of his recuperation to a new drink that Mrs. Smith gave him regularly, a mixture of fresh milk and honey. Whether it was this drink or his new environs, he began to improve.

That same summer, Hodge decided to make the four-day journey to northern Pennsylvania to visit relatives. Here he stayed with his cousin Jane Rose, the eldest daughter of his uncle, Andrew Hodge Jr. Jane had married the well-to-do physician Robert Hutchinson Rose. Rose was a Scotsman of such considerable wealth that he had purchased over ninety-nine thousand acres of land in 1809 near a group of lakes on the border between Pennsylvania and New York. He named his vast land holdings "Hibernia" in honor of his Scottish roots.

On the shore of Silver Lake, Hibernia's most scenic body of water, Rose had constructed an imposing wooden mansion which included a large library, conservatories, an impressive collection of art, and extensive gardens.[1] It was also capable of hosting as many as thirty overnight guests at a time. Hodge enjoyed his time at Silver Lake immensely, spending many of his days fishing on the lake in an old canoe. As his health improved, he gained both strength and weight. Dr. Rose continually asked him to spend the rest of the summer with them, but Hodge wrote his mother that he felt it necessary to keep his visit short for "want of clothes."[2]

Figure 9.1 *Rose Country Manor*: Robert Rose's manor house was the center of his northern Pennsylvania estate. This mansion rivaled any private residence in the state and contained a massive library of 2000 volumes, an impressive art collection, and enough rooms to accommodate thirty house guests at time. [*From the Collection of the Susquehanna County Historical Society as found in History of Susquehanna County Pennsylvania by Emily C. Blackman, 1873*]

It was during his time at Silver Lake that Hodge once again felt a call to the ministry. He wrote his mother that although a ministerial career contained "the least prospect of earthly happiness, since there are so many deprivations and inconveniences to which those who embrace it must submit," yet he so clearly saw it as "the path of my duty" that no other course held even the slightest allure.[3] He went on to write that he believed another year out of school would be time "even worse than lost."[4] He pleaded with his mother to allow him to attend Princeton's seminary in the coming fall, arguing that it was the best possible place to enjoy the fellowship of like-minded divinity students, as well as be trained by godly men.

Mary was slow to give her blessing. Aside from her desire to not be separated again from her youngest son, she worried about his return to the rigors of the academic regimen. His health was still tenuous in her mind. In the end, however, she found herself unable to stand against Hodge's ardent desire to get back to school. She resigned herself to his strong will and gave him permission to return to Princeton. Before leaving for seminary in November, however, Hodge took one more trip. It turned out to be one of the most memorable of his life, a journey he would later recount innumerable times to his children. In October, Dr. Archibald Alexander asked Hodge if he would accompany him on an extended tour through Virginia.

Dr. Alexander had actually known Hodge for more than three years. Both had arrived in Princeton nearly simultaneously in 1812: Alexander as the founding faculty

Figure 9.2 *Archibald Alexander:* Archibald Alexander was Princeton Theological Seminary's first faculty member. After meeting him while an undergraduate student at Princeton College and then training under him at the Seminary, Hodge came to consider Alexander a surrogate father figure and named his first son after him. [*Special Collections, Princeton Theological Seminary Libraries*]

member of the town's new seminary and Hodge as a precollegiate student at Princeton Academy. It was in a classroom at the academy where they first met. One day Alexander happened upon Hodge "stammering over a verse in the Greek Testament."[5] He stopped and took notice of the fourteen-year-old boy in the midst of his troubles and even asked him a clarifying question about the verse. Hodge found himself unable to answer the question, but from that moment forward a friendship between the two grew into a cord that, in Hodge's own words, was "never broken."[6]

When Alexander arrived at the Seminary, he was a man in the prime of life. Nearly forty years in age, Alexander had already accomplished a great deal before he agreed to take the reins of Princeton Seminary. Standing only five and a half feet tall, the brown-haired Alexander had an impish build and sprightly gait. He also had dark, penetrating eyes and a wonderful sense of humor. His frequent loud, clear laugh was considered a trademark of his personality.[7]

Born in Virginia, Alexander had grown up in a frontier settlement. He had been raised in a Presbyterian family but showed no special interest in religion until his seventeenth year. Then, while reading to an elderly neighbor lady one Sunday evening from the writings of the seventeenth-century English Presbyterian John Flavel, he was suddenly impressed that every word he read seemed to apply to him. Before he could finish, he was overcome with "emotions . . . too strong for restraint."[8] He fled to an isolated spot, dropped on his knees and poured out his heart in prayer. In the next few moments, he was "overwhelmed with a flood of joy," an experience so profound that he was vividly able to recall it the rest of his life.[9] Alexander's conversion experience bore many of the marks of the revivalist activity that had begun sweeping the country in the mid-eighteenth century. It was an experience that gave him a lifelong sympathy for revivals, although he was not always supportive of every means they employed.

Alexander quickly built upon his conversion experience with the decision to pursue the ministry. His natural abilities insured that he rose quickly in a variety of pastoral and academic settings. Ordained at nineteen, by the age of twenty-four he was the president of Hampden-Sydney College near Richmond, Virginia. From there he moved to become the head pastor of Third Presbyterian Church in Philadelphia and at the age of thirty-five was elected as a remarkably young general moderator of the Presbyterian Church in America. He excelled in everything he did.

In 1812, when the Presbyterian Church was looking for the inaugural faculty member of its first seminary, Alexander was the logical choice. He had pastoral, administrative, and teaching experience. He possessed a rare mix of piety, oratorical and interpersonal skills which made him almost universally popular and respected.[10] His pastoral heart also made him a wonderful mentor. Throughout his life, he took students under his wing as both their teacher and their benefactor. So, it was not unique that Alexander never failed to notice Hodge when their paths crossed after their initial meeting. Their friendship blossomed, and soon Alexander regularly asked Hodge to accompany him in his small horse-drawn buggy when he went out into the countryside to preach at various churches and religious gatherings.

His trip with the then nineteen-year-old Hodge involved several weeks of travel by steamboat, stage, and horseback to cover over twelve hundred miles in a total of five different states. Wherever they went, Alexander was thronged by old friends and parishioners. In many places, he was so moved by the affection of those who came to see him that he needed to fight back tears with a nervous laugh. During their time together, Hodge witnessed Alexander preach countless "excellent and affecting sermons."[11] Using an extemporaneous style, Alexander's sermons took on a lively, dramatic nature reminiscent of the high theatrics and emotional solicitude found in George Whitefield's preaching. Hodge recalled that Alexander's oratorical skill was so great that his listeners would often involuntarily find themselves becoming a part of the sermon. Once, when speaking of the return of the Son of Man, Alexander pictured the happening in such graphic detail that the entire congregation "by one impulse, rose, and bent to the windows, that they might" actually see Christ coming down out of the clouds.[12] Hodge stood in awe of his mentor, who he described in one of his letters to his mother as *the man of men.*"[13]

It is worth noticing that once again Hodge was plagued by money worries as he traveled with Alexander. During the trip, he often had trouble sleeping as he fretted over the state of his traveling funds.[14] But he continually met with stunning generosity and kindness wherever he went. As it turned out, he may have been deeply self-conscious about his poverty, but he was never put to serious discomfort because of it. His journey into seminary studies at Princeton really began with his "very happy . . . jaunt" with Alexander, who had already started to become the most influential male figure in Hodge's life, quickly taking the role of the father he had never known.[15]

10

"GIVE US MINISTERS!"

Ashbel Green was not the only minister disturbed by the declining number of College graduates choosing the ministry as their vocation. A general alarm was slowly spreading throughout the entire denomination. The 1810 Presbyterian General Assembly reported over four hundred pastoral vacancies while less than 10 percent of Princeton College's graduates were entering the pastorate.[1] As demand rose, supply dwindled. Green gave the clearest voice to the sense of raising panic: "'Give us ministers,' is the cry of the missionary regions;—'Give us ministers,' is the importunate entreaty of our numerous and increasing vacancies—'Give us ministers,' is the demand of many large and important congregations in our most populous cities and towns.'"[2]

The nation's exploding population added to the urgency of the situation. By 1810, there were seven million Americans, roughly double the figure just twenty years earlier. The trickle of ministers trained at Princeton College could not hope to meet the ministerial needs created by such growth. The country's frontier regions experienced particularly striking population increases. For example, Kentucky had grown from 70,000 inhabitants in 1790 to over 410,000 in 1810.[3] While Baptists and Methodists, whose ideas of ministerial training and ordination were far less rigorous than Presbyterians, flooded states like Kentucky with circuit riders and itinerant ministers to establish dozens of vibrant congregations, Presbyterians struggled to send even a handful of trained ministers into these regions.[4] As the country's population expanded at an unprecedented rate, Presbyterians found themselves in the midst of a profound clergy crisis.

Complicating this crisis were events at Princeton like the riot of 1807, which did little to assure those in the denomination that the College was going to produce a greater number of ministers any time soon.[5] In fact, many supporters of the College believed the riot to be a sign of how the school was succumbing to the same revolutionary impulses and moral decadence that had wrought so much havoc in Europe and, in the words of one frightened College trustee, threatened to extend "its baleful ravages throughout the civilized world."[6] The election of Thomas Jefferson, who many a Calvinist considered to be little better than an atheist, only underlined these fears. More than ever, Presbyterian leaders felt the weight of what they saw as their denomination's pivotal role in providing trained ministers capable of performing the key religious and civic duties absolutely essential to helping steer an increasingly unmanageable democracy in the right direction.[7] It was this sense of urgency and the firm belief that an educated clergy was absolutely essential to the health and survival of the nation that helped Archibald Alexander, Ashbel Green, and others push for the establishment of a Presbyterian seminary that would not only help bring salvation to individual Americans, but to the nation as a whole.[8]

Stanhope Smith was by no means ignorant of the pressing need for Presbyterian ministers and his college's historic role in training clergy. In 1803, he appointed one of his favorite former students, the twenty-five-year-old Henry Kollock, to the post of Professor of Theology with the specific mandate to equip students interested in the ministry. Kollock barely lasted three years, seeing his "labors of little consequence" because so few students offered themselves as ministerial candidates.[9] His departure only fueled those agitating for a change at the College. Presbyterian leaders began to formulate ideas for a new ministry school, and they showed little interest in associating such a school with Princeton College. Samuel Miller, one of the College's trustees and later a professor of the Seminary, captured this sentiment when he argued that a new Presbyterian divinity school was sorely needed, but it was essential that it should stay "uncontaminated by the college" and "have its government unfettered, and its orthodoxy and purity perpetual."[10]

Soon after the 1807 riot at Princeton, Miller joined forces with Archibald Alexander and Ashbel Green to maneuver a plan through the General Assembly to establish a single, centrally located seminary for the denomination.[11] As these three men spearheaded plans for a new Presbyterian seminary, Stanhope Smith experienced a growing sense of dread. He was well aware of the trustees' unhappiness with the College, and he feared that a new seminary would reduce, or even cut off, denominational aid to the College. Once Smith became certain that a seminary would be built, he moved quickly to convince the General Assembly that there was no better place for such a school than Princeton. Linked together, the College and a seminary could benefit each other and better husband the denomination's resources. Smith made exorbitant concessions in order to see the Seminary brought to Princeton. He agreed to share the College's every resource with the new school—buildings, dormitories, eating facilities, classrooms and even faculty—with no expectation of having any power of governance over the Seminary.

Events moved quickly after the 1811 General Assembly approved the establishment of the Seminary. Richard Stockton offered four acres of land for the school, and a board of directors was selected. In 1812, the same year he became president of the College,

Figure 10.1 *Samuel Miller*: Witty and urbane, Samuel Miller was a gifted preacher and the Presbyterian Church's leading scholar on issues of church government. [*Special Collections, Princeton Theological Seminary Libraries*]

Ashbel Green was named the first president of the Seminary's board. With such an action, tremulous Presbyterians were assured that the College and the Seminary would work together. By the summer of 1812, Alexander was training the school's first three students in his new home, which stood but a few blocks from Nassau Hall. By the following spring, another nine students had arrived.

Within a year, Alexander found that he was teaching more students than he could handle. The original plan for the Seminary had called for an eventual faculty of three professors: one responsible for teaching divinity, one for oriental and biblical languages, and one for ecclesiastical history and church government. During the Seminary's first year, Alexander taught every subject, but as the student body grew the General Assembly proceeded in 1813 to give the school a second professor. It named Samuel Miller to the post of Professor of Ecclesiastical History and Church Government.

Having played a key role in helping to establish the Seminary, Miller proved to be an ideal addition to its faculty. From the school's inception, he had shared its vision, and he brought a great deal of knowledge and skill to his area of study. He was also a perfect complement to Archibald Alexander. While they were similar in their theological convictions, they were distinct opposites in their backgrounds and personalities. Alexander had grown up a thorough Southerner, while Miller had been born in Delaware and could trace his ancestry all the back to the *Mayflower*.[12] Alexander was emotional, gregarious and personable. Miller was aristocratic, systematic and reserved.

Although his earlier life had many of the marks of a freer spirit, by the time Miller arrived at age forty-four in Princeton, he had committed himself to a life of rigorous order and discipline. Princetonians joked that they could set their clocks according to the regular times he passed their homes or shops on his afternoon walks. His son remembered him by noting: "He was punctual to a minute, in doors and out. . . . His personal habits fell into undeviating routine—so his use of cold water ablution, his attention to the temperature of his study, his caution against cold and rain. He kept, for years, a record of the state of the thermometer at a certain hour, to which he constantly referred with pleasure to compare the seasons."[13] Miller encapsulated the unchanging and ever-dependable nature of the Seminary and the Calvinist orthodoxy it taught.

Miller had come from pastoring the most prestigious Presbyterian church in New York City, a metropolis that exposed him to some of the most progressive thinking of his age. During his time in New York, he had been an active member of the literary-scientific circle known as the "Friendly Club," which included among others a playwright, two professors from Columbia, and the novelist Charles Brockden Brown.[14] His wide-ranging interests and formidable intellect ultimately led him to write an encyclopedic two-volume work entitled *A Brief Retrospect of the Eighteenth Century* (1803). In it, he surveyed the major accomplishments of the past century, a study that ranged across fields as diverse as mechanical philosophy (with specialized topics including electricity, pneumatics, hydraulics, and optics), physiognomy, medicine, chemistry, geography, navigation, agriculture, literature, and the arts. Widely acclaimed on both sides of the Atlantic, *A Brief Retrospect* earned him honorary degrees from two colleges and memberships in several learned societies.

Aside from his early scientific and literary interests, Miller was also interested in politics. Although he became a staunch Whig later in life, Miller had supported Jefferson and his more liberal democratic ideals while in New York. Miller also had political ties stemming from his marriage to Sarah Sergeant in 1801. Not only did Sarah enjoy a distinguished Presbyterian heritage—her great-grandfather had been Jonathan Dickinson, the founding president of Princeton College—but her father was John Dickinson, a former member of the Continental Congress and one of the signers of the Constitution.

By the time Miller was inaugurated as the second professor of the Seminary in September 1813, the color of his life had come to take on a more rigorously religious hue. Having just recovered from a nearly fatal bout of typhoid just months after his brother Edward had died of the disease, Miller took up his duties in Princeton reborn. His brother's death had thrown Miller into a profound period of self-reflection. He could not escape the haunting thought that he was "now the only surviving son of seven born to my parents. . . . Solemn situation! When shall I be called to give an account of my stewardship?"[15] Praying that the Lord might "make me thankful for this privilege [of life]," Miller reconsecrated his life "unreservedly to his glory!" and wrote "Oh for grace to improve this solemn dispensation of his providence."[16] In coming to Princeton, Miller had determined to be a blessing both to his colleague and his students. As a consequence, he ruthlessly reoriented his life to focus on things almost exclusively religious. Where once novel reading and dancing had been acceptable activities, Miller now devoted himself to cultivating his own inner spiritual life, writing on religious topics, and training young men for the ministry.[17]

With two professors in place, the next order of business became constructing a seminary building. As early as September 1813, Alexander reported to the Seminary's board of directors that the College's student body was once again growing and that many of the Seminary students had to be moved out of Nassau Hall to lodgings in town to be comfortably accommodated.[18] He asked the board to consider erecting at least one building for the Seminary. Two years passed before the board was able to start such a building program.

The General Assembly of 1815 finally approved funds to buy an additional seven acres of land from Richard Stockton and provide $15,000 to begin constructing a large building to be dedicated to the Seminary's sole use. By September, the cornerstone had been laid for what would eventually be called "Alexander Hall." At considerable cost, the Seminary enlisted the renowned American architect John McComb Jr. to design the building. McComb had made a name for himself designing several prominent buildings including the recently completed New York City Hall. For the Seminary, McComb designed a massive structure in the standard Greek revival style similar to that of Nassau Hall and popular in colleges across the Northeast. The building was 150 feet long and 50 feet wide and included all of the Seminary's public rooms (dining room, library, kitchen, and lecture hall), as well as enough rooms to lodge one hundred students. By May 1816, building began in earnest, but it would not be until the winter of 1818 that students actually took up residency in the hall, even though some rooms were in use earlier for teaching, common meals, and meetings. With one of the largest buildings dedicated purely to theological studies in the country, Princeton Seminary was on its way to becoming a vital force in nineteenth-century American Protestantism.

11

STUDENT YEARS AT THE SEMINARY

In early November 1816, at the age of eighteen, Hodge returned to Princeton to begin his studies at the Seminary. He entered along with twenty-five other students, the Seminary's largest class to date.[1] Eight of his classmates had attended Princeton College with him.[2] Ashbel Green's concerted efforts to see more young men from the College pursue ministry careers were apparently being fruit.

Because the Seminary's main building was not yet finished, Hodge spent his first seminary year boarding at the home of a family friend, Mrs. Catharine Bache. As soon as the Seminary building opened, however, he took up residence there and roomed with John Johns, a close friend from his undergraduate days. Hodge and Johns drew extremely well in the room lottery, and they thrilled to be able to choose one of the warmest rooms in the building due to its location directly over the kitchen.[3] During the long winter months ahead, they frequently congratulated themselves for their choice.

The Seminary's school year was broken into two terms. The first began in early November and consisted of six months followed by a six-week vacation. The second, or summer, session commenced in late June and went through late September, once again followed by a six-week vacation. Students might enter at any time, but they were encouraged to begin their studies in the fall, so that they might properly join classes when they began their cycles. Hodge dove into his first term, taking full advantage of everything the Seminary had to offer. He wrote his mother that he was "up before sunrise, and not to bed ever much before twelve."[4] Four evenings a week, he attended various meetings until nine and then retired to his room to study until midnight. It is remarkable that his health remained robust considering the intensity of his schedule, but he suffered no relapse of the prior year's chest complaint.

When Hodge embarked on his seminary studies his first-year courses covered seven basic areas: the original language of the Scriptures (this meant Greek more than Hebrew since Hebraic study was still in its infancy), sacred chronology, sacred geography, connecting biblical and profane history, Jewish antiquities, biblical studies, and the rudiments of interpretative practice called "exegetical theology." His middle year was dedicated primarily to biblical criticism, ecclesiastical history, and didactic theology, which explored the biblical basis for different church doctrines. The final year continued with the study of didactic theology and church history with an added course in polemic theology (the biblical texts that focused on preaching and teaching). So scholastic was the Seminary's training that only the final three-month summer session was given over to practical courses such as homiletics and pastoral care.

In the Seminary's first decade, the basic contours of the curriculum followed what Archibald Alexander had set in place upon his arrival. The fact that Alexander was the guiding light of the school's early curriculum makes an appreciation of his own theological training vitally important. He trained others as he had been trained. Of particular note were his own early studies under William Graham.[5] Graham was an active pastor and the founder of Liberty Hall Academy in Mt. Pleasant, Virginia. He immersed Alexander in two crucial strains of thought. First, primarily using the works of Swiss Reformed theologian Francis Turretin, he trained Alexander in the basic tenets of Calvinism and Calvinist apologetics. Second, Graham indoctrinated Alexander in Scottish Common Sense Realism through the writings of Hugh Blair, Thomas Reid, and John Witherspoon (whom he had studied under at Princeton).[6]

Alexander became the Seminary's founding faculty member just as European Enlightenment rationalism was beginning to make significant inroads into American theological thought. As a consequence, Alexander emphasized rational thinking and the importance of analyzing both scientific and historical evidence to support theological claims. In this regard, he was influenced by the work of the English politician and writer Soame Jenyns and the English Presbyterian Puritan John Flavel. Both men argued that the biblical and natural evidence supporting the Christian faith could be verified through an examination of human nature itself. Such thinkers helped Alexander approach proving the verity of Christianity through a synthetic examination of objective evidence in conjunction with more subjective personal experience.[7] Throughout his life, Alexander remained a man with ties to both the intellectual and emotional aspects of religion. Such a combination makes any easy characterization of his thinking difficult. He was not entirely systematic and consistent in all of his theological stances.

At the heart of the Seminary's rigorous intellectual training was a conservative brand of Calvinism whose tap-root was the Westminster Confession (1646). Later, this particular confessional strain of conservative Reformed theology as it was filtered through particular American cultural pressures came to be known as the "Princeton Theology," named for its sponsoring school much like the Andover Theology taught at Andover Seminary or the Oberlin Theology of Oberlin College. When Hodge began to take classes at Princeton Seminary, however, it would be misleading to say that he was immersed in a well-formulated and unique system which could be denominated as the "Princeton Theology." Both Alexander and Miller were just taking up their duties during Hodge's early years, and their educational strategies and the consequent theological emphases were still emerging in the 1810s.

That said, Alexander and Miller did set the theological trajectory of the Seminary from their earliest days by advocating a narrowly defined type of Reformed, Calvinist theology that placed a premium on exalting God's glory by stressing his omnipotence and absolute sovereignty.[8] Central to their thinking was the conviction that God orchestrated every aspect of his creation and that he, not human beings, was the pivotal agent in human salvation. Alexander and Miller also carefully shaped their teaching by paying special attention to certain key Reformed confessional statements widely accepted by Presbyterians alongside the Westminster Confession, including the Second Helvetic Confession (1566) and the Canons of Dort (1619). They then interpreted these statements using the intellectual legacies of certain seventeenth-century Reformed theologians, most notably Francis Turretin, and Witherspoon's brand of Scottish Common Sense Realism.[9]

The Seminary's pronounced theological conservatism can be partially traced to Alexander's travels through New England during the last decade of the eighteenth century. During these journeys, Alexander had met such theological luminaries as Samuel Hopkins, Nathanael Emmons, and Jedidiah Morse. These meetings, and others like them, deeply impressed upon him the growing diversity of American theological opinion and how attempts to accommodate theological differences had done great harm to orthodox Calvinist beliefs. As a result, Alexander arrived at Princeton firmly committed to teaching what he believed to be traditional, confessional Presbyterianism. From its beginning, Alexander's seminary teaching was characterized by a "strong doctrinal exclusivism" that quickly became a lasting trademark of the theology taught at Princeton.[10]

This exclusivism was reinforced by developments in early nineteenth-century American Presbyterianism. By 1810, it was becoming clear that the denomination was fracturing due to theological and methodological disputes arising from the revival activity sweeping the nation. Widespread revivalism helped give birth to the Cumberland Presbyterians and Alexander Campbell's Christian Movement, both of which attracted hundreds of Presbyterians, and the General Assembly grew vexed as it saw its ranks split apart.[11] The plan for founding a single denominational seminary in Princeton was partly based on the General Assembly's hope that a single school might help unify the denomination and forestall further defections. Such a dream ultimately proved futile as Presbyterian fissures continued to appear even after the Seminary's founding. By 1838, there were twelve Presbyterian seminaries, spanning a theological spectrum from conservative Calvinism to Arminian-inflected views of human agency.[12] While Princeton Seminary remained the largest and most influential of these schools, no hope any longer existed that every Presbyterian minister might be trained in a single strain of Reformed orthodoxy.

The personal nature of the seminary education of the day cannot be overestimated. Unlike seminaries and colleges today, which have large faculties teaching narrowly defined fields of specialty, Hodge's entire theological education was intimately guided by Archibald Alexander, and to a lesser extent by Samuel Miller. Hodge came to Princeton Seminary having been steeped in Presbyterianism's polity and confessional statements since his youth. His seminary years then were but an extension rather than a radical reorientation of his earliest religious training, and Alexander proved the pivotal figure in helping Hodge synthesize and then concretize systems of thought he had already long experienced in various church and school settings. In later years, Hodge often affirmed Alexander's importance in forming his thinking, proclaiming that he was "moulded more by the character and instructions of Dr. Archibald Alexander, than by all other external influences combined."[13]

Alexander's influence on Hodge is particularly evident in three areas: a benevolence that gave a distinct relational flavor to Hodge's theology, a pronounced biblicism, and a desire to make sense of theology as a coherent, interrelated system of thought. The profundity of Alexander's relational impact on Hodge has gone largely unnoticed by scholars. Alexander modeled a kind of theological elasticity when it came to dealing with men whom he admired or felt some degree of affection. The influence of such relational affinities colored Hodge's own theological propensities with a distinctly humane tinge. Often seen as the chief systematizer and enforcer of conservative Calvinism in America, Hodge had a distinctly softer side as seen how he tolerated the more liberal theological notions held by several of his later European friends.[14]

Alexander's intellectual influence on Hodge can be seen in the two major class notebooks—one on biblical criticism and the other on systematic theology—that survive from Hodge's student days at the Seminary. Hodge studied biblical criticism with Alexander during his first year, at a time when such criticism was undergoing a revolution in Europe. In Germany, J. G. Eichhorn and J. J. Greisbach had set in motion a new wave of biblical scholarship known as "Higher Criticism." Unlike "Lower Criticism," which focused entirely on the Bible as a pristine and uncorrupted text, forthright in its ability to be interpreted, Higher Criticism focused on historicizing the Bible by examining its transmission throughout the centuries. Such a historically sensitive view showed how defined cultural settings and distinct human personalities were critically important to biblical interpretation.[15]

When Alexander took charge of Princeton Seminary, American biblical scholarship was deeply entrenched in the Lower Criticism and had only begun to explore newer German scholarship. Alexander filled his lectures with references to ancient and Reformed scholars and did not once mention the more recent work being done in Europe.[16] Alexander was profoundly skeptical of the new German scholarship, and in the main he steered his students away from it.[17] His own views remained traditional. Unlike the Higher Criticism, which increasingly questioned the authorship and even content of books in both the Old and New Testaments, Alexander never questioned the Bible's reliability even considering its centuries-long history of translation and transmission.[18] In his mind, there simply were no good or compelling reasons to consider the biblical text as corrupt or that any of its books were authored by writers other than those whose names they bore.[19] Such traditionalism, however, did not mean that Alexander devalued rigorous intellectual engagement and argumentation. He frequently admonished his students: "Learn to think for yourselves. Depend rather on your own faculties than on those of other men."[20] Alexander steadfastly maintained that "faith which is weakened by discussion is mere prejudice, not true faith."[21]

The following year, Hodge followed his studies on biblical criticism with Alexander's course on systematic theology. In revealing fashion, Hodge copied the *Salutis Catena* (The Chain of Salvation) on the first page of his notebook. The *Salutis Catena* was a brief patristic Latin formula that linked together the activities of God, Christ, the Word, faith, witness, the sacraments and works.[22] The idea of a chain was a particularly apt metaphor. Rather than thinking of one aspect of Christian theology as isolated from other doctrines and lines of reasoning, systematic theologies focused on conceptualizing Christian doctrine as one harmonic, interrelated whole. Systematic theology studied the relationship between the natural and supernatural worlds, the revelation of God, and the propensities of the human heart.

Only two Americans had produced books that could properly be called systematic theologies prior to Alexander teaching the topic at the seminary: Samuel Willard's *Compleat Body of Divinity* (1687–1706) and Samuel Hopkins's *System of Doctrines* (1793).[23] Both Willard and Hopkins used their works to provide integrative overviews of Christian thinking that attempted to harmonize doctrine, polity, and human behavior. As the systematic theologies developed during the nineteenth century, their authors placed ever greater emphasis on explaining theological doctrine in relation to different fields of study such as science, history, and anthropology, but in the opening years of the century, theologians remained content with less encyclopedic endeavors.[24]

Hodge's notes from the systematic theology course filled nearly three hundred closely written notebook pages. The content and style of this course proved hugely influential in Hodge's own later theological lectures and the *Systematic Theology* he published in the 1870s. Hodge's notes reveal that he dutifully recorded Alexander's catechism-style lectures by writing over five hundred questions and their answers. Alexander began by establishing the reliability of the biblical text. He then moved to examining what he called the "Philosophy of the Mind," lectures addressing such thinkers as Hume, Berkeley, Locke, and Reid and how they each sought to understand the human capacity to distinguish truth from falsehood. Alexander's central concern in his early lectures focused on how one might apprehend the truth, a fact that comes across in the first question he posed to the class, namely: "What is Truth?"[25]

After exploring a range of options, Alexander quickly moved to argue for the primacy of Scottish Common Sense Realism in the search for truth. In true Common Sense fashion, Alexander taught that God revealed himself to the human senses (which were thoroughly reliable in their function) both through the Bible and through natural phenomena. He then further refined what humans might "sense" about God by constantly referencing the work of the Swiss Reformed theologian, Francis Turretin, who provided the single best explication of the lessons one learned about God from scripture and nature.[26] Turretin's massive, multivolume *Institutes of Elenctic Theology* stood as one of the most respected systematic theologies in the Reformed tradition, and Alexander revered it and soon inspired Hodge to do the same. Turretin's *Institutes* remained *the* primary textbook at Princeton Seminary until the early 1870s, when it was finally replaced with Hodge's own *Systematic Theology*.[27]

Aside from his strict Calvinist orthodoxy, perhaps the most important characteristic of the *Institutes* resided in Turretin's historical-mindedness when discussing central Christian doctrines. He carefully laid out the development of each doctrine and only then commented on the contemporary challenges facing that doctrine.[28] With such an approach, Turretin modeled for Hodge an ability to engage and historicize controversies. Consequently, Hodge learned to make historical arguments supporting or refuting certain doctrinal positions, while also being able to recognize that many of the controversies of his own day were but variations of problems that had confronted the Protestant Church since the time of Calvin.[29] For example, Turretin took great exception to the views of the Amyraldians who espoused an early brand of universalist thinking. For Hodge, the growing popularity of Unitarianism and Universalism in New England was but the latest manifestation of Amyraldian thought. Years later, when Hodge took over Alexander's role as Professor of Didactic Theology at the Seminary, he paid tribute to Turretin by writing that on the whole he stands as "the best systematic theological writer with whom we are acquainted" and his work "is remarkably adapted to the present state of theology in this country."[30]

Hodge's courses with Alexander reveal just how thoroughly he was trained in the Reformed scholastic tradition. While many other denominations were satisfied to send out ministers with minimal training, Princeton Seminary distinguished itself as a school firmly committed to pursuing a demanding study of Reformed theology, absolutely convinced that well-reasoned orthodox belief could not help but prevail. After all, according to Scottish Common Sense Realism, the truth was both self-evident and available to every properly cultivated individual.[31] Expose people to the truth, and they could not help but find it convincing. It was a view that the ensuing decades would sorely test.

12

"WHERE AM I TO GO?"

As his seminary graduation neared, Hodge grew increasingly worried about his future, frequently "asking the question—'Where am I to go?' or 'What am I to do?'"[1] Unlike two of his closest friends, William Nevins and Charles McIlvaine, who had decided to accept a call to become missionaries to South America (a call they would never fulfill because of the chaotic nature of the region), Hodge had no specific sense of what he might do after graduation. His one clear leaning was that he knew he wanted to preach, feeling that "preaching the gospel is a privilege superior to any other intrusted to men."[2] Another one of his classmates, Samuel Davis, planned to become a traveling missionary to the western and southern states and attempted to talk Hodge into accompanying him. Unbeknownst to Hodge, Davis even talked with Archibald Alexander to enlist his aid in convincing Hodge to join him in the mission field.

Davis's strategy of approaching Alexander is just one of many examples of how the Seminary's two professors often functioned as gatekeepers to the careers various seminarians pursued after their studies. In the winter of his final year, when Hodge joked with Alexander that he would soon need to get rid of him, Alexander responded with a smile and said: "Yes. Take care. I may shock you when I come to tell you what to do."[3] Shock him he did.

Hodge's final year was his busiest yet with a heavy course load and a full slate of evening meetings focused on everything from prayer to the weekly Friday-evening theological debates.[4] For Alexander, the year was equally challenging as the growing student body was beginning to take a serious toll on his health. He became ill three different times, forcing him to convalesce in bed and repeatedly miss or reschedule his classes. It was becoming abundantly clear as the Seminary's class sizes continued to grow that the General Assembly's original seminary plan of appointing three professors

Figure 12.1 *John Johns*: John Johns turned down the opportunity to teach at Princeton Theological Seminary in order to pursue Episcopalian ordination. He eventually served as an influential bishop in Virginia, president of William and Mary College, and president of Virginia Theological Seminary. [*Princeton University Library*]

needed to be enacted. A professor of languages was needed, particularly to teach Hebrew. Alexander, who never viewed languages as his forte anyway, was especially eager to free himself from all responsibilities in language instruction.

In choosing the Seminary's next professor, Alexander acted on his longtime desire to have the post filled by one of the school's graduates. What better testimony could there be to the efficacy of the school's training than the fact that it was producing men capable of training other men? Alexander originally asked Hodge's best friend and roommate, John Johns, to consider the teaching position. Johns had long distinguished himself as the brightest student in Hodge's class. Hodge noted that in all settings Johns was always the best-prepared student, able to recite the correct answer to any question upon demand without ever needing help or correction from the teacher. As Hodge succinctly put it: "Johns was always first—first everywhere, and first in everything."[5]

Johns, however, had grown up in Newcastle, Delaware, a town with two churches: one Episcopalian and the other Presbyterian. The ministers of the two congregations coordinated their preaching so that one preached in the morning and the other in the afternoon, so that the townspeople always had the option of attending both services if they wished. Such exposure to both Protestant traditions gave Johns a thorough familiarity with each, and during his final seminary year, he was forced to decide whether to become a Presbyterian pastor or an Episcopalian priest. Ultimately, Johns chose the latter, but in making this choice, he had also decided against Alexander's offer to teach at the Seminary.

When recounting these events years later, Hodge reflected that Johns's "decision although neither of us at the time knew anything about it, determined the whole course of my life."[6] When Johns made his intentions clear, Alexander turned to Hodge to fill the position. In many ways, Hodge was a natural next choice. He had proven himself an incredibly diligent student in his seminary studies, gaining a reputation for an astounding work ethic among his peers.[7] His natural linguistic ability made him a perfect choice to fill a post that was particularly focused on language work. In addition to his intellectual gifts, Hodge had a long history with Alexander, who clearly had a great affection for him.

Upon visiting Alexander one day at his home, Hodge's mentor suddenly changed the topic of his conversation and asked his protégé: "How would you like to be a professor in the Seminary?" Utterly surprised by the question, Hodge did not know how to answer. Most recently, he had musing over the possibility of serving as a missionary in the frontier states, and now Alexander was asking him about staying at Princeton to teach. Alexander quickly qualified his question noting that he did not have the power to determine such a thing. It lay in the hands of the General Assembly, but he wished Hodge to give it some thought. Alexander, however, tipped his hand and showed that he had given some thought to the possibility of retaining Hodge at Princeton by asking Hodge to spend the following "winter in Philadelphia learning to read the Hebrew language with points with some competent instructor."[8]

There was something of the youthful, adventuresome spirit that made Hodge question the wisdom of remaining in Princeton. He wondered if he might be missing something by not testing himself in a new setting. Measured against these thoughts in

Hodge's mind was Alexander's desire for Hodge to join him on the Seminary's faculty. Hodge was also acutely aware of what good he might accomplish teaching at the Seminary. He wrote his mother that "It is evident that the moral influence of Drs. Alexander and Miller on the character of the Church is almost inconceivable; for they in a measure impart their own spirit to each of their pupils, who bear it hence to spread it through the lesser spheres of which they may become centres. The very fact, therefore, of a man being pious in this situation makes him the means of incalculable good."[9]

In the end, Hodge was drawn by the fact that he might have a greater influence in a post at the Seminary than elsewhere. In addition, a Seminary post meant that he did not necessarily have to give up his dream of preaching since the Seminary faculty did almost as much preaching as those who held a traditional pastorate. He also realized that Alexander had only offered him the possibility of a temporary position. At its worst, he could make the most of the opportunity by refining his knowledge of the biblical languages before moving into the pastorate. Initially, Hodge had no plans to make the teaching position at the Seminary permanent. Little did he suspect just how permanent the move would prove to be.

Before he took up his new position, however, Hodge returned to Philadelphia to live with his mother after finishing his seminary studies in September 1819. Hodge's brother Hugh had graduated from medical school a year earlier and had almost immediately set sail as a ship's surgeon on a voyage to Calcutta.[10] Such voyages for young doctors were common at the time, providing them both experience and a chance to see the wider world before they settled into a more standard, less exotic practice. With Hugh's absence, Mary became all the more eager to have Hodge near her, and she was thrilled by Alexander's recommendation that her son return to Philadelphia to study Hebrew.

The strain of her boys growing into men, however, was taking a toll on Mary. They had been her whole life. She had relocated several times, taken in boarders and even done manual labor to see her sons educated, and now her boys were embarking on lives of their own. No place was this tension more keenly felt for Hodge than in the romance which had started to flower with Sarah Bache, the daughter of the woman with whom he had boarded during his first year in seminary.

The strength of his attachment to Sarah becomes clear as one traces their relationship through a series of what Hodge's son would later call "remarkable love-letter[s]."[11] Hodge's letters to Sarah were filled with theological musings and everyday advice, and they were also considerably longer than the letters he was writing home to his mother. Mary Hodge was clearly jealous of Sarah's ascendancy in her son's affections. The mother who had sacrificed so much to raise her sons now saw her youngest moving away not only in terms of his vocation, but his affections.[12] She did not hesitate to tell Hodge that he could do better than a match with Sarah, even though Sarah's mother was a longtime friend and had even lived with the Hodges for a time in Princeton. Eventually, Mary found herself forced to be less critical of Sarah. In a more conciliatory tone, she wrote Hodge that she would never do anything to stand in the way of his happiness, declaring that she would have certainly not mentioned her reservations if she had known how far their romantic attachment had gone.[13]

It is during these months leading up to his return to Princeton Seminary that Hodge kept one of the only two diaries of his life. This decision to keep a journal was probably the result of being in what he saw as a time of pivotal transition. He was now done with school, and a ministry career awaited him. The question became: what shape would his career take? Alexander had raised the option of teaching at Princeton, but the General Assembly still needed to approve it. Once in Philadelphia, the local presbytery licensed him to preach in the area. For Hodge, there was a romantic lure to preaching, and he felt that he could see over the next few months whether he did indeed have a gift for preaching. He even toyed with the idea of shortening his stay as a Seminary instructor, or skipping the opportunity altogether, if he performed well in the pulpit.

As he set upon preaching for the first time, Hodge began to keep a record of his pulpit experiences. Deeply impressed by the power one might exercise through sermons, his journal became a weekly reflection on how well he had preached and what he might improve. When it came to his dairy, no day aside from Sunday mattered. He was solely concerned with his weekly sermon and its delivery.

Hodge's reflections on preaching exhibited a kind of spiritual introspection that he had inherited from Alexander, who had carefully modeled rituals of devotional practice for his students through his own untiring commitment to personal prayer, fasting, and self-examination. He had drilled into his students that there was no more important duty than cultivating a "devotion of spirit," keeping always in mind that it is "in vain that preachers of the gospel might be multiplied "unless at the same time their piety and prudence are increased."[14] Gauging such piety and prudence was a difficult thing, for the human heart was capable of great deception, but keeping a careful watch on one's own emotions and behavior was a key step in cultivating true piety.

This pronounced emphasis on piety was a key component in Princeton Seminary's training, and it was profoundly linked to the Scottish Common Sense Realist stress on evidentiary proof.[15] Scottish Common Sense with its relentless demand for evidence fostered a piety closely tied to careful self-examination. To discover the state of one's relationship with God, it was necessary to search one's heart for spiritual clues. For the Common Sense Realists of Princeton, this emphasis on daily self-reflection in pursuit of sanctification superseded the importance of conversion itself, because a true conversion could only be determined if the converted's life exhibited the marks of a spiritually renewed heart. Such marks included visible manifestations of Christ's commands toward love, charity, and humility. The Princetonian stress on self-reflective sanctification played a key role in the coming years as religious revivalism spread across the nation. While hosts of revival and camp meeting preachers focused on the moment of conversion, Hodge and his Princeton brethren held fast to an emphasis on piety. Conversion—to be true conversion—had to bear certain types of fruit, and this type of harvest could only be judged over a period of time.

So, Hodge committed himself for several months to a written discipline of pietistic introspection, convinced that "the first requisite for preaching is fervent piety."[16] Hodge believed that to speak to others' hearts, his own heart must first be touched. His anxiety over his ability to preach seems to have been well founded. Although there is every indication that he was a competent preacher, both in these early years and later in life, he was by no means an exceptional one. After another lackluster pulpit performance, he "felt almost depressed under the apprehension that I shd never become even a moderately acceptable preacher."[17] In the following months, he began to despair that he had not yet seen any "visible fruit resulting from my labours."[18] During his seven months of supplying pulpits in and around Philadelphia, Hodge saw neither conversions nor many signs of deepening piety among his listeners. He began to ponder if he could preach at all.

In between these anxiety-producing Sundays, Hodge spent most of his time carrying out Alexander's wishes in studying Hebrew. Here, he enjoyed greater success. Alexander had recommended that Hodge study with Reverend Joseph Banks, a professor at a local seminary in Philadelphia, and one of the best Hebrew scholars in the country. Banks was a thoroughly enthusiastic teacher, who would "talk all day on any thing connected with Hebrew."[19] Banks was particularly excited about the language's finer linguistic intricacies, including its written system of accents and vowel points. The ancient language had fallen out of use in the centuries following the birth of Christ and to help determine how it was actually spoken, a system of accents and points had been developed and was in use by the fifth century.[20] This system was an attempt to recover how the Hebrew words had actually been pronounced. Hodge immersed himself in Hebrew and mastered both the system of accents and points, preparing himself for a potential call to Princeton to teach the language.

In the last entry of his diary, on May 21, 1820, Hodge commented that he "felt much interested in my Brethren & for the result of the important question soon to come before the assembly in which I am so much concerned."[21] Because of a broken carriage, Hodge had not been able to reach his appointed pulpit that Sabbath and instead attended services at his family's longstanding church home, Second Presbyterian Church. There, as the service proceeded, he sat preoccupied with thoughts of a teaching position at Princeton Seminary. Preaching had not gone well for him. Was this disappointment in some way a sign that God had other plans? The answer came just five days later when, a few blocks from Hodge's home, the General Assembly voted to authorize a position at Princeton Seminary for the teaching of "the original languages of Scripture."[22] The post paid $400 a year, and the Assembly offered the position to Hodge, who immediately accepted it. Preaching was not his gift; perhaps teaching was. One month later, Hodge was on his way back to Princeton. He was going home.

PART III

The 1820s

Young Professor

Figure 13.1 *Hodge Portrait by Rembrandt Peale, 1830:* The famous American portraitist Rembrandt Peale painted this picture of Hodge in 1830. It is the earliest-known visual representation of Hodge, and the only picture of him without his glasses. [*Presbyterian Historical Society, Presbyterian Church (U.S.A) (Philadelphia, PA)*]

13

"THE MOST ELIGIBLE SITUATION FOR IMPROVEMENT"

People stared as Hodge rode his horse through the small towns that dotted his path back to Princeton. Some even went so far as to stop their work and laugh. The day he chose for his return was "so excessively hot" that he had been forced to stop and purchase a piece of cardboard and fashion it into an awkward-looking wide-brimmed hat.[1] As ridiculous as he may have looked, he arrived in Princeton none the worse for wear, a fact that he eagerly attributed to his inventiveness along the way.

He immediately went to Alexander's home, where he planned to board for the next several months. As Hodge unpacked his few belongings, he found himself in the same room where the first seminary classes had met some eight years before. It was also the room where Alexander had originally broached the possibility of him joining the Seminary's faculty. Hodge was thrilled with his home. He was but a few short blocks from the Seminary building, and he was convinced that being in such close proximity to Alexander could not "fail of being very profitable."[2]

Not all was going well, however, as Hodge's health once again became an issue. This time the problem was a painful nerve condition in his right thigh that bore all the symptoms of an acute rheumatism. Frequently writing his family of his illness, he solicited his brother's medical advice on possible treatments. Nothing he had tried proved able to lessen his pain. His leg particularly hurt after strenuous exertion, but he felt it important to keep up some kind of exercise routine, so he rode daily. At the same time, he carefully watched how much he walked, knowing that excessive fatigue quickly resulted in noticeable pain. Hodge was experiencing the first symptoms of a debilitating leg condition that proved so crippling in the years to come that it would reduce him for a time to a bedridden state.

He also continued to worry about money. His salary proved barely enough to pay for his food, lodging, care for his horse, clothes, and books. Making matters worse was the fact that his salary payments were erratic. He frequently found himself forced to borrow money from his brother, mother, and other relatives to cobble together enough on which to live. His finances caused him endless anxiety partly because Hugh had yet to establish a thriving medical practice and Hodge knew borrowing from his family added to their own financial problems.[3]

Once the fall term began, Hodge divided his time between his duties at the Seminary and his responsibility for supplying three pulpits in the area: churches at New Brunswick, Georgetown, and Lambertville. The shortage of Presbyterian clergy was not only a national problem, it was a local issue as well. Both Alexander and Miller regularly supplied pulpits in the area. Hodge took his turn in helping out local congregations. By spring, he was preaching regularly at Lambertville, a town some twenty miles west of Princeton. Unlike his earlier forays into the pulpit, here he enjoyed considerable success, tending the small congregation until it found a full-time minister in the person of Peter Studdiford, one of Hodge's former classmates.

After Lambertville, the New Brunswick Presbytery assigned Hodge to Trenton First Church in the small town of Ewing. Up until this point, Hodge had simply been a licentiate under the care of his local Presbytery, but in the fall of 1821 he applied for ordination. In November, Samuel Miller presided over his ordination service. He was thrilled by how events were unfolding and wrote his mother: "Indeed, were I permitted to mould my own lot, I do not think I could devise a plan of life more suited to my desires, than the one Providence appears opening before me."[4]

Hodge's teaching responsibilities proved arduous.[5] Along with sermon preparation, Hodge lectured, heard recitations, and composed special addresses for various occasions around the Seminary.[6] The Seminary's enrollment had grown to some eighty students, and Hodge worked diligently to make them all proficient in Greek and Hebrew for their later biblical studies. Soon, additional duties were assigned to him. He began teaching on various Old and New Testament books including Isaiah, the minor prophets, Acts, Hebrews, and several of the Pauline epistles. He also began teaching a course entitled "History of Criticism," which covered such topics as biblical criticism, hermeneutics, the nature of language, and the history of biblical interpretation.[7] The more he was asked to do, the more inadequate he felt himself to be. He increasingly felt his want of more advanced theological training and began to think of ways he might obtain it.

One way he devised to better himself involved establishing informal study groups on various topics. Just months after his arrival, he formed "The Society for Improvement in Biblical Literature," a forum where he could work with others to translate difficult biblical passages and discuss weightier matters of biblical interpretation and criticism.[8] As the group's founder, he also served as its first president and its inaugural presenter. In December 1821, he offered the small gathering an essay titled: "A Dissertation on the Importance of Biblical Literature."[9] This "Dissertation" became vitally important six months later, as it played a pivotal role in Hodge obtaining a more permanent position at the Seminary.

Hodge had worked well with Alexander and Miller as their junior colleague, but by 1822 the temporary nature of his appointment began to wear on him. He yearned for a degree of job stability that might allow him to make longer range plans. He felt this need particularly in regard to his relationship with Sarah. They wished to get married but had agreed to wait until Hodge had gained a permanent position at the Seminary or elsewhere. So, Hodge began to seek clarification from his colleagues on the status of his Seminary post. If it did not promise to become permanent, he wished to begin looking for a pastoral position.[10]

Alexander and Miller both wanted Hodge to remain, but it was Miller who proved the more politically savvy of the two, as he helped orchestrate Hodge's retention. Miller knew that the General Assembly would ultimately determine Hodge's fate as a possible third professor at the Seminary.[11] Keeping this fact in mind, he proposed that Hodge publish a pamphlet to announce himself in wider Presbyterian circles.[12] Hodge readily concurred and quickly worked to publish and then circulate his recently composed "Dissertation."

The "Dissertation" was Hodge's first publication, and it proved to be a striking harbinger of the argumentative style and doctrinal views that later became trademarks of his thinking. In devastatingly clear prose, Hodge set forth two principals that remained constant throughout his entire career: first, the Bible was an utterly trustworthy document; and second, readers whose hearts are "most like those of the sacred writers" and enjoyed "the influences of the same all-teaching Spirit . . . will best understand" the sacred scriptures.[13] Simply put: the scriptures are reliable and one needs more than a keen mind, one needs a spiritually sensitive heart, to understand them. Even in the coming years as Hodge distinguished himself by his systematic, rational theological thinking, he never strayed far from a pronounced emphasis on the central role of heartfelt piety in the study of theology.

One other facet of Hodge's "Dissertation" is noteworthy. He lost no opportunity in its pages to rail against the "false doctrines" being propagated in Germany, doctrines built on a view that the scriptures were but "a mere human production."[14] Hodge took direct aim at the German thinking that Harvard Unitarians and similar thinkers were using to question the Bible's trustworthiness and such key Christian doctrines as the Trinity.[15] Hodge saw no end to the evils of German biblical criticism, lamenting that he was not "better acquainted with the history of opinion in Germany, and the nature of its institutions" so that he might more forcefully combat the criticism's poisonous

spread across the American theological landscape.[16] Ultimately, Hodge felt the dangers of the new European theological thinking so acutely that he spent two years in Germany equipping himself to battle the very theological notions that he increasingly saw battering the walls of Christian orthodoxy in America.

Hodge's first publication did its work. In May 1822, the General Assembly appointed him to the post of Seminary professor, and in so doing, effectively established a department of biblical and oriental languages at the school. With the new appointment came a commensurate increase in pay. His salary jumped from $400 to $1000 a year. Hodge was elated, viewing his new position as "the most eligible situation for improvement, for satisfaction, and for usefulness, which our church affords."[17]

His promotion cleared the path for him to finally marry Sarah Bache after a nearly-nine-year romance. Sarah, a great-granddaughter of Benjamin Franklin, had captured Hodge's heart soon after they first met in 1813 when she and her family began boarding with Mary Hodge in Princeton.[18] The young Sarah was strikingly beautiful with penetrating blue-grey eyes and dark auburn hair.[19] Hodge's brother, Hugh, described her as "handsome, full of imagination, and exceedingly enthusiastic, unconscious of self and absorbed in whatever claimed her attention; a most agreeable companion."[20] She had such a sharp intellect that Dr. Miller offered to tutor her in a diverse range of subjects including religion, history, philosophy, literature, astronomy, and chemistry.[21] Like Hodge, she had spent her early years in Philadelphia where her physician father died while she was young, leaving his family with a distinguished name but little money. Once Hodge heard of his faculty appointment, the two lost no time in getting married. They gave even their closest friends less than a week's notice of their wedding plans, and Dr. Miller could not adjust his schedule to be back in Princeton in time to attend their ceremony on June 17.[22]

Just thirteen months later, Sarah gave birth to their first child, christened Archibald Alexander Hodge. With the arrival of little Archie, Hodge decided to approach the Seminary's board of trustees for a land grant just a few hundred feet from the western side of the Seminary's main hall in order to build a house. The trustees agreed to the request, stipulating that the home not cost more than $5,000 and that the Seminary would have a say in any future sale of the home.[23]

Hodge turned to John Haviland to design his house.[24] Born and trained in England, Haviland immigrated to the United States in 1816, where he quickly established himself as one of Philadelphia's most respected and sought-after architects.[25] Haviland's stature in the city's architectural circles is testified to by the number of important buildings he designed, including additions to City Hall, the United States Mint, the Franklin Institute, and the Walnut Street Theatre. Later, he gained a national reputation as the country's foremost designer of penitentiaries. What had brought him to Hodge's attention was his work in designing some of Philadelphia's most beautiful

Figure 13.2 *Sarah Bache*: Sarah Bache Hodge was Hodge's much beloved first wife and the mother of their eight children. He was devastated upon her death, calling her: "Blesst saint; companion of my boyhood – my first and only love." [*Special Collections, Princeton Theological Seminary Libraries*]

early nineteenth-century churches, including First Presbyterian Church. This commission placed him firmly within the Philadelphia social and religious circles frequented by Hodge's family, and it credentialed him as an architect worthy of designing a structure to be placed on the campus of Presbyterianism's illustrious new seminary.

The house Haviland designed thoroughly fit Hodge's personality. Everything abut it was systematic, forthright, and functional. In the late 1810s, Haviland had written a popular pattern book on architecture that offered advice for designing a wide range of buildings. True to his own advice, Haviland designed Hodge's home with doorways across from each other to increase cross ventilation and hallways carefully positioned for the same purpose.[26] Haviland also designed the house so that Hodge's study might

Figure 13.3 *Hodge's House*: Designed by the famous Philadelphia architect John Haviland, Hodge's home became a center for Seminary life and learning after its completion in 1825. The door with small porch and stairs at the side of the house led directly into Hodge's study and stood but a few hundred feet from Alexander Hall. [*Special Collections, Princeton Theological Seminary Libraries*]

stand in the front corner nearest the Seminary's main hall. An exterior door was placed there, so that Hodge could leave through that door and travel no more than two hundred paces to the building that housed the majority of the Seminary's students and classrooms.

The house, however, was far more than a simple testament to the functional. It also reverberated with symbolism. Haviland had long shown a preference for Roman architecture, and Hodge's new home showed this enchantment. Haviland framed the three-story home's front door with twin columns, an unusual design for the Princeton area of the time, when front porches or plain storefront facades dominated. He also placed a Roman arch over the home's front entrance, crowned with a sunburst ornament. The house's classical flourishes and formidable size at once served as distant echoes of Hodge's once socially prominent Philadelphia roots, as well as timely reminders of the republican ideals of duty and virtue so highly prized in the ancient Roman Republic and so rigorously internalized by Hodge in his youth.

Hodge's home took nearly a year to design and build, and it was finally finished in 1825 amid unexpected cost overruns and troublesome delays.[27] Hodge financed the house by mortgaging the greater part of his new salary and selling land, which was all that remained of Sarah's inheritance from the Bache side of her family.[28] In building such a distinguished home, he clearly signaled an awareness of what his family name had once meant and what it might mean again. As the house neared completion, Sarah and Charles welcomed their second child into the world, a little girl they named after Hodge's mother Mary. Now numbering four, and employing household servants, Hodge found himself the master of a new family, a new house, and a new professorship all in the span of three short years.

NEW ENGLAND'S THEOLOGICAL LANDSCAPE

Before Hodge began teaching at the Seminary in November of 1820, he took a three-week trip to Boston with Benjamin Wisner, one of his seminary classmates. Wisner had been asked to be a candidate for the pastoral position at Boston's Old South Church and asked Hodge to accompany him. Hodge was thrilled by the opportunity to visit the birthplace of his mother and the seat of so much important theological activity. It proved a particularly important trip as it provided Hodge the opportunity to meet several of the nation's leading theological figures.

On the way to Boston, Hodge and Wisner stopped in New Haven to visit Nathaniel Taylor. The thirty-four-year-old Taylor had established himself as one of southern Connecticut's most influential preachers, and he welcomed the Princetonians, engaging them late into the night in "animated though temperate" theological conversation.[1] Two years later, Yale named Taylor as its newly formed theological department's first Dwight Professor of Didactic Theology. Taylor used this position to develop and teach a variation on traditional Reformed Calvinism that came to be called the "New Haven Theology." Taylor's "New Haven Theology" would play a critical role in one of the American Presbyterianism's most painful moments, its 1837 schism.[2] Hodge enjoyed his first meeting with Taylor thoroughly, reveling in the opportunity to spar with such a keen debater. He wrote that this visit was "one of the most improving incidents in our journey."[3]

After reaching Boston, Hodge eagerly sought out some of the most important men in city's academic and theological circles. He spent a "tantalizing hour" with Edward Everett, who had just taken a post at Harvard as a professor of literature. Everett had spent the previous four years studying in Europe, becoming the first American to receive a Ph.D. (a degree not yet available in the United States). While there, Everett had mastered seven languages and rigorously studied the German biblical criticism.

Figure 14.1 *Nathaniel Taylor*: Pictured here at the age of twenty-one, Nathaniel Taylor graduated from Yale where he had studied under Timothy Dwight. In 1822, after having served for a decade as the pastor of First Church of New Haven, he was appointed Yale Divinity School's first professor, a position he held for thirty-five years. [*Private Collection*]

An avowed and articulate Unitarian, Everett fascinated Hodge with tales of his experiences abroad. He yearned to spend more time with Everett, but poor weather and full schedules did not permit another visit.

Hodge was more fortunate in getting time with faculty members at Andover Seminary. He was particularly pleased to meet Moses Stuart, his senior by seventeen years but more important, his counterpart at the Seminary in ancient language instruction. Stuart, a linguistic genius, had taught himself Hebrew, Syriac, Chaldee, and Arabic. When he began teaching Hebrew at Andover, he purchased a set of Hebrew type along with other printing equipment so that he might produce a grammar for his students, a work he composed in his basement to become the first such grammar printed in the United States. Stuart also taught himself German to make himself better able to study German biblical criticism in order to refute the Unitarians who so heavily depended on its methods and insights.[4] During their conversations, Stuart encouraged Hodge to learn German for the same reason.

Hodge met with Stuart several times, and these meetings helped him set his own scholarly agenda for the next few years. He wrote his mother that Stuart "has done me great good, has marked out my road, and told me the right path, and enlarged my views as to the extent and importance of the study [of ancient languages], more than I could have conceived possible."[5] Far from seeing Hodge as a simple Greek and Hebrew tutor, Stuart waxed eloquent on how there was no higher calling than teaching students how to read the scriptures in their original languages. Correct scriptural interpretation depended on a knowledge of these languages. Without this linguistic knowledge, the Bible could quickly become nothing more than an ambiguous and ultimately unintelligible "enigma."[6]

For Stuart, the mind of God as manifest through human language made a correct understanding of the biblical tongues the single greatest weapon in the war against Unitarianism and other heterodox views. Stuart took the historical bent of German biblical criticism and turned it to his own conservative ends. The meanings of words found in the Bible must be interpreted through a sound knowledge of what those words meant in their original, historical usage. Stuart proclaimed that if a biblical scholar could accomplish such a feat, he could fight all manner of threats to traditional Reformed theological orthodoxy. In a less coherent form, Hodge already adhered to this line of reasoning, but Stuart clarified his thinking and gave him a champion of significant stature with which to stand. So convincing was Stuart on the topic of language that once he returned to Princeton, Hodge ordered one hundred of Stuart's Hebrew grammars for his students.[7] Over the ensuing decade, Stuart and Hodge continued to correspond about the study of Hebrew, and Stuart proved a key catalyst in Hodge's own European trip to pursue more advanced theological and language studies.[8]

Hodge's meetings with Taylor, Everett, and Stuart highlight not only the interconnected nature of the New England theological culture, but how this culture was becoming increasingly diverse and fractious. A theological revolution was afoot in

New England as the traditional Calvinism of such Puritan giants as Cotton Mather, John Owen, and Jonathan Edwards was confronted by the theological pressures of the German Higher Criticism, as well as unique aspects of the American context including massive immigration, widespread revivalism, an expanding frontier, and the country's ideological commitments to egalitarianism and democracy.[9] In the first three decades of the nineteenth century, American Calvinism entered a highly fluid state as charismatic leaders and important educational institutions worked to codify and then spread their own variations of the more traditional brands of Calvinism favored by their Puritan forefathers. The situation in the Boston area is particularly instructive in regard to the growing fissures in New England Protestant thought.

The rising liberal theological consensus at Edward Everett's Harvard became emblematic of just how radically American Protestantism was changing during this period. Although a movement toward a more liberal brand of Calvinism had long been afoot at Harvard, a pivotal moment for the school came in 1803 with the death of the theologically moderate and widely respected David Tappan, the school's Hollis Professor of Divinity.[10] Tappan's death spurred two years of debate and political maneuvering, which reached a crisis point when two Unitarians took key leadership roles at Harvard. Henry Ware replaced Tappan as the Hollis Professor of Divinity in 1805, while the following year the Harvard board named the equally liberal Samuel Webber as the school's president. With the ascendency of Ware and Webber, Unitarianism moved from the fringes of Harvard's intellectual community to its center. Such a transition may have thrilled Boston liberal intellectuals, but it horrified more conservative Christians across New England.

Many viewed the appointments of Ware and Webber as acts that placed Harvard beyond the pale of Calvinist orthodoxy. American Unitarianism developed slowly over the next fifteen years. Unitarians themselves remained a largely undefined and uncoordinated body of adherents until 1819, when the noted New England divine William Ellery Channing gave a more solid identity to the group when he delivered his famous "Unitarian Christianity" sermon at his Federal Street Church in Boston. For the first time, Channing clearly set forth the basic tenets of a theology that had taken firm root at Harvard.[11] He identified Unitarianism has having three key characteristics. First, Unitarians favored a type of biblical interpretation (heavily influenced by the rising school of German biblical criticism) that stressed philology and historicity. Second, Unitarians believed that a rigorous study of the ancient biblical texts revealed the Godhead to be a unitary entity composed only of God the Father—later Christian creeds, not the Bible itself had introduced the doctrine of the Trinity. Finally, Unitarians agreed with European Romantic and Enlightenment thinking that exalted a range of innate human abilities.[13]

Harvard's liberal theological revolution began a chain reaction which profoundly influenced the development of a number of New England seminaries over the next two decades. The most immediate response came from a group of Boston clergy led by Eliphalet Pearson, Jedidiah Morse, and Leonard Woods. By 1808, these men had mobilized New England's more conservative elements to found Andover Theological Seminary, whose explicit purpose was to "breast the gales that beat against Puritan orthodoxy."[14] While Harvard was embracing the influences of European scholarship, Andover stood firmly by the traditional Calvinist tenets found in the Westminster Confession. Morse, Pearson, and Woods demanded that every five years each Andover professor publically acknowledge his full agreement with the beliefs found in the Westminster Shorter Catechism and unequivocally renounce the teachings of "Atheists and infidels . . . Jews, Mahommetans, Arians, Pelagians, Antinomians, Arminians, Socinians, Unitarians, and Universalists."[15] No Ware or Webber would find a home at Andover.

In the coming years, Andover became known for a type of Hopkinsian Calvinism most powerfully articulated by Leonard Woods, Moses Stuart, and later Edwards Amasa Park.[16] Basing much of their theology on the thinking of Jonathan Edwards as later interpreted by Edwards's student Samuel Hopkins, Andover became a bastion for the "New Divinity" (also known as the "New England Theology"). Andover's brand of New Divinity fused Edwards's Calvinism with his revivalist sympathies. Woods and Stuart referred to themselves as "consistent Calvinists." Others, however, chose to call them "hyper-Calvinists" because of their extreme commitments to a belief in God's sovereignty and benevolence.[17] Their stress on God's benevolence was particularly important because it made Andover sympathetic to revivalist movements and their methods, seeing such endeavors as a chance to separate the elect wheat from the unelect chaff. Eventually, Andover espoused a theology which foregrounded a person's ability to fight sin using one's will. For many, including those at Princeton, such a belief was anything but "consistent Calvinism" because it so heavily weighted human agency in God's redemptive process.[18]

Yale with its New Haven Theology occupied a theological space somewhere between liberal Unitarian Harvard and conservative Hopkinsian Andover. Hodge's old acquaintance, Nathaniel Taylor, became the chief architect of the New Haven Theology as he blended American Congregationalism with nineteenth-century revivalism. The New Haven Theology mixed the Calvinism found in the standard Reformed confessions with European Enlightenment notions of innate human ability. A growing American democratic sensibility with its optimistic view of the individual power and importance of the common citizen also subtly influenced Taylor's belief in human moral ability and choice. Taylor emphasized the human role in pursuing God's salvation, thus downplaying the much-favored Calvinist doctrines of election and God's absolute sovereignty. He taught that human sin had its root in individual volition, stressing that men and women had freely chosen to sin (with the slight adjustment that their fallen natures gave them no other choice). According to Taylor, a person's desire to pursue a new life in Christ was "an act of the will or heart."[19] Such a view made Taylorism tremendously popular among revivalists, who often went to great lengths to get their listeners to "choose" for Christ.

Harvard, Andover, and Yale stood as three highly influential educational centers on New England's theological map. Together, they highlighted how the intellectual currents of European thinking, Reformed Confessionalism, and democratic ideology were swirling in ever-faster and more interconnected circuits throughout American Protestant theology. They also stood as theological markers against which Princeton Seminary both measured and defined itself in the opening decades of the nineteenth century. Hodge, along with Alexander and Miller, staked out theological territory that was in many ways more conservative in its ties to the traditional Reformed confessional statements than any of these schools.

If Harvard occupied the liberal left wing of the Calvinist theological spectrum, then Princeton set itself as the guardian of the beliefs that composed the conservative far right. Princeton positioned itself as the country's greatest champion of Confessional Calvinism. Ultimately, much of Hodge's reputation and most incisive theological thinking emerged as a result of the passionate, sophisticated, and sometimes vitriolic debates that raged between the theologies emanating from these four schools in the coming decades.

15

DEMOCRATIC CHRISTIANITY

More than a steadfast commitment to confessional Calvinism helped shape the identity and theology of Princeton Seminary. In many ways, the school also positioned itself in firm opposition to American's post-Revolutionary exaltation of individuality, autonomy, and self-empowerment. Such characteristics found rich soil in America's democratic ideology, which reveled in human achievement and egalitarian notions of personal opportunity and success. By the 1820s, a growing belief in advancement being tied not to lineage but to ability had taken root at every level of society as Americans increasingly embraced a more egalitarian ethic based on a belief that every one of the nation's citizens (at least its white male citizens) stood on an equal footing.

The presidential election of Andrew Jackson captured the spirit of the age. Standing against the more elite and property-minded Whig Party, Jackson positioned himself as the champion of the common man, seeking to enfranchise not just land owners, but all adult white males in the country's governance structures. For his presidential inauguration celebration, Jackson threw open the White House's doors to every American who wished to come. The White House took months to recover from the havoc wreaked upon it by partygoers who muddied its carpets, soaked its furnishings with wine, and destroyed thousands of dollars worth of china and glassware.[1] This new era of "Jacksonian Democracy" elevated the social position and identity of common Americans to unprecedented heights, and its unrelenting democratic spirit had far-reaching consequences for every aspect of American culture, including American Protestantism.

The historian Nathan Hatch has convincingly argued that democratic ideology totally revolutionized American Christianity in this period.[2] One result of this "democratization" centered on how grassroots religious movements, with their exaltation of every person's ability to interpret scripture and exercise spiritual leadership,

94

increasingly questioned time-honored forms of Protestant clerical authority and ecclesiastical tradition. Where once an educated, refined, and dignified class of ministers
was considered the cornerstone of the country's moral leadership, early nineteenth-
century American Protestantism—in the words of one disgruntled Episcopalian
priest—had come "under the supreme control of tinkers and tailors, weavers, shoe-
makers, and country mechanics of all kinds."[3]

So worrisome was this popular notion of Christian leadership that Timothy
Dwight passionately warned against the manifold dangers posed by improperly
trained ministers in his christening address at Andover Seminary's opening in 1808. He
bemoaned the fact that Americans insisted "that their property . . . be managed by
skilful agents, their judicial causes directed by learned advocates, and their children,
when sick, attended by able physicians," yet were "satisfied to place their Religion,
their souls, and their salvation, under the guidance of quackery."[4] The leveling notions
of democracy terrified Dwight when he considered the future of the American church.

Standing stalwartly against the dangers of democracy run amok was Princeton
Seminary with its rigorous standards of Presbyterian clerical training. David Rice, a
Princeton Seminary graduate and the first permanent Presbyterian minister in Kentucky, captures the tension of the age. In reporting to the General Assembly, Rice
stood amazed at how Christian services throughout his state were run by those who
consider "themselves called of God to preach the gospel . . . relying on their inward
call, neglecting almost every ministerial qualification required in the sacred Scriptures.
Some of them utter a strange mixture of sense and non-sense, truth and error, medicine and poison, with as much confidence as if all been [sic] inspired by infinite wisdom. No preachers less qualified, and none more confident."[5] Presbyterians looked
down on such poorly trained and misguided religious leadership and refused to coun-
tenance improperly prepared clergy within their ranks.

While Presbyterians remained fully committed to high standards of clergy qualification, denominations such as the Baptists and Methodists embraced a much broader
vision of lay and professional ministry. Their belief that even the most unlearned
reader of scripture might be able to interpret the Bible and establish a church sent
splintering shockwaves throughout American Protestantism, contributing to what
one historian called the country's "fragmenting evangelical ethos."[6] In the decades
leading up to the Civil War, American Congregationalists, Presbyterians, and Episcopalians with their highly education-centric traditions lost considerable ground, especially in the country's Western frontier regions as the Baptists, Methodists, and other
more democratically minded Protestants gained large followings among the laboring,
less educated and poorest classes.

At the time of the American Revolution, American Presbyterians were the country's second-largest denomination behind Congregationalism.[7] By 1850, the number of

Presbyterian congregants had fallen rapidly behind the tremendous growth of the Baptists, Methodists, and Catholics.[8] The Methodists in particular experienced great success on the frontier through their more flexible clergy ordination processes and their tolerance for strongly autonomous congregations. Large numbers of Methodist circuit riders penetrated into less settled areas of the country, bringing both the gospel and a conviction that less educated and refined individuals could serve as God's ministers. Methodists also embraced an Arminian-inflected theology that put the stress on individual choice for salvation rather than the more monarchal—read here "less democratic and thus less American"—views of God's sovereignty favored by most Presbyterians.

Democratizing trends in American Christianity had profound implications for Princeton Seminary, whose faculty were heavily marked by social prominence and elitism. Green, Alexander, Miller, and Hodge were all born into distinguished families who held to a high Federalist ideal, purporting that the most educated and most cultured individuals were the most capable of leading both the nation and the church. In this regard, Hodge and his compatriots were particularly influenced by the Scottish Presbyterian tradition, traceable back to Witherspoon, which revered all forms of church authority, whether that authority was divine, ecclesiastical, or clerical. For the Federalist-bent Princetonians, authority was to be obeyed, and thus the Seminary taught the greatest respect for ordination, church courts, and a centralized denominational governmental structure.[9]

For the Princeton faculty, such a high regard for authority found its deepest root in the belief that God was absolutely sovereign in all that he chose to do. His choices could not be influenced or thwarted by anything outside himself. There was no mob in heaven directing the actions of the Almighty. Princeton's theology was strikingly undemocratic for the time as the Seminary's faculty refused to bow to pressures that compromised its views on thorough clerical training and the proper obedience due to recognized sources of divine authority. Those at Princeton firmly believed that just as God was best able to manage the heavens and the earth, so were seminary-trained ministers best able to manage the affairs of God on earth. Such earthly management was serious business, and its proper execution required the best theological education. The Princeton faculty felt the weight of the mission entrusted to them; they were training young men to steward God's redemptive plan for America, and that training was rooted in the confessional statements of the Reformation, not the morass of new theological corruptions springing forth from more democratic notions of human ability and God's subservience to the preferences of his creation.

16

THE BIRTH OF THE *BIBLICAL REPERTORY*

While the Seminary adamantly opposed new democratically inflected theological ideas, it embraced many of the technologies nurtured by the country's reigning ideology. Hodge, in particular, turned to the democratic medium of print to convey Princeton's message of Reformed orthodoxy to the widest possible audience. Learning from how influential his own first publication had been in helping attain his faculty position at the Seminary, Hodge quickly became a master at using the persuasive medium of print to spread the Seminary's views.

Hodge became enamored with the power of print just as the country's publishing marketplace was undergoing radical change. The 1820s comprised a watershed moment for American publishing. Whereas a print run of two thousand copies of a book was the industry standard before 1820, after that date a number of factors coalesced that enabled publishers to print several hundred thousand copies of a title if they wished. Improvements in publishing technologies such as papermaking, power printing, and stereotyping all contributed to this change, as did key cultural shifts in American society, such as rising literacy rates, ideologies which emphasized reading, and better transportation networks to help disseminate printed material. These diverse factors worked together as the nineteenth century progressed to make the United States a society that was increasingly formed, framed, and fractured by the power of print.

Religious publishers were on the forefront of the country's print revolution. Once spreading God's word had primarily been the purview of preachers, but as printed material began to flood the nation, countless Protestants began to see publishing as a key means of turning the tide against countless American evils. So great did many believe the power of print to be that Horace Bushnell was led to comment that American

Christians had convinced themselves that "types of lead and sheets of paper may be the light of the World."[1] The opening decades of the nineteenth century saw Protestants join together in spirit of ecumenical optimism to form a "bond of union" which resulted in the formation of three incredibly influential, interdenominational societies: the American Bible Society (ABS) in 1816, the American Sunday School Union (ASSU) in 1824, and the American Tract Society (ATS) in 1825.[2] Using power presses, stereotyping, and sophisticated grassroots distribution networks, each of these societies became a master of using print to spread its message. By the early 1830s, these societies were annually dispersing millions of pages of printed material, dwarfing the efforts of even their largest secular publishing counterparts.

Presbyterians joined with these societies in recognizing the potential of the press in spreading the Gospel message. In 1822, the same year he retired as the president of Princeton College, Ashbel Green took over the *The Presbyterian*, the denomination's monthly newspaper.[3] He changed its name almost immediately to the less sectarian *Christian Advocate*, turning the newspaper into a widely read, conservative Presbyterian periodical. For over a decade, Green wrote without pause for his *Christian Advocate*. He also enlisted other like-minded conservative Presbyterians to contribute to his paper, including Princeton Seminary professors Alexander, Miller, and Hodge, who wrote essays on everything from literature and music to religious education and foreign missions.

By 1825, Hodge had decided to marshal the power of print on behalf of Princeton orthodoxy by publishing an academic quarterly journal. He was particularly interested in providing a scholarly counterbalance to Harvard's erudite efforts to undermine traditional Calvinist Trinitarian thinking. With this goal in mind, Hodge commenced the *Biblical Repertory*, subtitled *A Collection of Tracts in Biblical Literature*.[4] Hodge used the *Repertory* as a platform to collect, translate, and distribute articles on theological topics that buttressed the Seminary's views on scripture translation and interpretation. He did so with the firm Scottish Common Sense conviction that if he provided readers with good sound scholarship, their innate ability to recognize and respond to truth would bear bounteous orthodox fruit for both the Presbyterian Church and the nation more generally.

Hodge declared in his introduction to the journal's inaugural volume that the *Repertory's* central aim was making available the best and most current scholarship on biblical translation and right biblical interpretation.[5] It is telling that in the first two years of the journal's circulation, the *Repertory* contained twenty-seven articles, twelve of which dealt with German hermeneutic, translation, or church polity issues. That nearly half of the *Repertory's* content dealt with German theology and ecclesiology reveals much about Hodge's own mind during the time; by the mid-1820s, Hodge had become fixated with various developments in European—and particularly

German—theology. As he settled into his faculty position at the Seminary, he became ever-more convinced that the German Higher Criticism posed one of the greatest threats to Reformed orthodox thinking.

Hodge saw two primary threats in the German thinking. First, its emphasis on the historicity of the sacred text laid the sacred scriptures open to the charge that the Bible as it was currently studied was a hopelessly flawed text because it was not based on the best scholarly translations of the ancient manuscripts. Second, and equally damaging, was the German Criticism's belief that these corrupted renditions of the ancient scriptures had led to dangerously inaccurate interpretations of the sacred scriptures. Such inaccuracy inevitably insinuated that all current church doctrine and practice had been built on the flimsiest of foundations. Hodge intended his *Repertory* to serve as a beacon of light dispelling the darkness spread through the claims of the German Higher Criticism.

Hodge even turned to German scholarship not associated with the Higher Criticism to bolster his case for his traditional Calvinist views on scripture and its interpretation. He chose as the *Repertory's* inaugural article a 122-page translation of Beckii's 1803 *Monogrammata Hermeneutices*. In it, Christian Daniel Beck (1757–1832), a professor of ancient languages and history at Leipzig University, argued for the reliability of the sacred scriptures in their current state by providing an exhaustive and exhausting overview of biblical interpretation from the patristic fathers down through the turn of the eighteenth century. Equally important for Hodge was Beck's strong belief that the single most important interpretative aid to correct biblical interpretation lay in a heavy dependence on divine inspiration, an attribute Beck called "a candid and pious sense of feeling."[6] In choosing to focus on the *Monogrammata*, Hodge clearly set himself against the intellectualism and German interpretative practices of European Higher Criticism so favored by the Harvard faculty.[7] While those at Harvard were interested in using German thinking to create a new kind of American Protestantism in Unitarianism, Hodge was using German thinking to buttress Princeton's time-honored stands on Calvinism.

When it came to the articles in the *Repertory*, Hodge did much of the translation work himself. By the time of the journal's first issue, Hodge had studied seven languages (Hebrew, Greek, Syriac, Arabic, Latin, French, and German). He also turned to a number of friends and colleagues for help.[8] Pivotal in this regard was the Reverend Robert Bridges Patton, who became the journal's second most important proponent in its earliest years. Patton had joined the faculty of Princeton College as the Professor of Greek in November 1825 and immediately made a favorable impression both on his students and on Hodge, who shared his love of languages and his fervor for sound biblical exegesis.[9]

Aside from mutual interests and a growing friendship, Patton became important in Hodge's life because after he had graduated from Yale in 1817, he had traveled to

Göttingen, Germany, where he became the second American behind Edward Everett to earn a European Ph.D.[10] As the two spent time together, Hodge became ever more serious about Stuart's idea to spend extended time in Europe studying.[11] Patton fired his imagination about Europe's countless scholarly possibilities, all the while reinforcing Hodge's own suspicions that to truly grapple with the challenges posed by German biblical criticism, he would need to go to Germany itself.

German Higher Criticism's current influence on American theology coupled with Patton's own conviction that the best way to fight that influence was to study in its country of origin pushed Hodge to consider once again the possibility of a European study leave. In the late summer of 1826, he wrote his brother that he labored under the constant feeling of "the most painful sense of unfitness of my work."[12] In every regard, he felt that he could be better equipped to advocate skills and viewpoints essential to a right understanding of Reformed orthodoxy by further study, and Patton continued to press upon him his belief that the best places for such study were the great universities of Europe. Finally, in August 1826, Hodge approached the Seminary's board of directors for permission to embark on an extended educational leave in Europe.

17

THE TRIP TO EUROPE

Hodge faced numerous obstacles as he contemplated study abroad. The first involved finances. Although Robert Patton worked hard to convince him that one could actually live cheaper in Europe than in Princeton, Hodge found it hard to believe that he could afford such a trip. He worried both about the uncertainty of the actual costs and leaving his family adequately provided for in his absence. Finally, he thought that if the Seminary's board of directors could be convinced to continue paying his salary while he was gone, he might well be able to manage it. Part of Hodge's financial strategy was to offer to rent his new house "for a sum sufficient to employ an assistant to take my place in the Seminary," thus lessening the Seminary's financial burden.[1]

An even greater obstacle than money, however, was the effect such an extended trip would have on Sarah and their children. Hodge had been married just over four years and had two young children, Archie age three and Mary age one. He was so attached to his family that Dr. Alexander sincerely doubted whether he could "remain six months" without them.[2] His wife, Sarah, was supportive of the idea of a study leave in Europe, but she assumed the entire family would go. After long and heated discussions, Hodge decided against taking his family with him. He simply thought that it would prove too difficult to focus on both his family and his studies. Even days before his departure, Hodge wavered on his decision, assuring Sarah that he would send for them if it seemed at all practicable.[3] Such a summons never came.

Considering Hodge's unwavering affection for his family, it is a measure of both his professional ambition and insecurities that he decided to leave his young family for a two-year study abroad. In one sense, many nineteenth-century professions separated families for long periods of time. Today's relatively instant travel via automobiles and airplanes was completely unknown in the 1820s, where in an age even before railroads simple journeys could take days, if not weeks. In this way, the long absences demanded by various occupations of the period strain the credulity of our twenty-first-century sensibilities. Hodge's own shipping-magnate ancestors had forced captains and their crews to be away from home on voyages that could take months or years to complete. American whalers were also absent for long periods of time, as were those involved in beaver trapping, traveling sales, and mining. Yet, Hodge was no manual laborer or low-level clerk whose work demanded his absence. He had complete choice in opting to foist a two-year separation upon his family, a decision which offers some indication of just how profound was his "inordinate and morbid impression" that he had no "adequate qualification" to be instructing seminarians for the ministry.[4]

Hodge left his family in Philadelphia, under the care of his mother and brother. Sarah and the two children settled in with Mary Hodge, while Hodge entrusted his brother with Sarah's finances, knowing that his brother would make up for any short-falls caused by Hodge's sporadic salary payments.[5] Hugh was not a wealthy man at this point, but the financial care he exercised during these two years began a longstanding pattern of financial generosity toward his brother's family. Hodge wrote years later that when it came to financial matters his brother "without having to be asked, always helped me through. He seemed to regard me as himself, and my children as his own."[6]

Hodge also contended with Archibald Alexander's ambivalence toward studying overseas. Alexander, a man Hodge had come to refer to as his "dear father," had two hesitations about Hodge's European study excursion.[7] He did not endorse Hodge's long separation from his family, and he feared that Hodge would be corrupted by a prolonged exposure to the subtle and insidious influences of German rationalism. So prevalent had such rationalism become in the German theological circles of the day that it came to have its own name: "Neology" from the Greek for new (theo)-ology.[8] Before Hodge left, Alexander warned him: ". . . remember that you breathe a poisoned atmosphere. If you lose the lively and deep impression of divine truth, if you fall into skepticism or even into coldness you will lose more than you gain from the German professors and libraries."[9] In Alexander's mind, Neology was made dangerous because of how its rationalist tendencies robbed the Christian faith of its vitally important mys-tical and emotional aspects. In the end, Alexander succumbed to Hodge's heartfelt desire to further his education. In all likelihood, Alexander sensed that something in his young protégé needed this adventure to lay to rest lingering doubts about his intel-lectual training and ability.

So Drs. Alexander and Miller wrote to the Seminary's board of directors in support of Hodge's idea for an extended period of European study. They made special mention (with Harvard clearly in mind) of the training he would be able to attain there in "Bib-lical criticism" and "that many of the most enlightened and important institutions of our country have adopted a measure of this kind."[10] As an added inducement, they mentioned that Hodge might serve as the Seminary's agent in soliciting funds and procuring books for the school's library. In executing this duty, Hodge proved particularly successful. Aside from the books he attained during his trip, Hodge inaugurated what turned into a thirty-year practice of collecting books for the Seminary from various German booksellers.[11] Alexander and Miller made a convincing case on Hodge's behalf. In its September 1826 meeting, the Seminary's board of directors granted Hodge's request to pursue further studies in Europe while still paying his yearly salary.

Hodge left his house, the *Biblical Repertory*, and his teaching position in capable hands. The first two were taken over by Robert Patton, while the recent Seminary graduate John Williamson Nevin was tapped to teach his courses while he was away. Unfortunately, Patton was forced to leave Princeton before Hodge returned. In 1828, Princeton College once again found itself with too few students and too many expenses and decided to meet its financial shortfalls by reducing its faculty salaries. Patton was forced to resign as he could no longer support his family on such a meager income.[12]

Once the Seminary's board approved his trip, it took Hodge less than a month to find himself on the packet ship *Edward Quesnel*. Packet ships were postal vessels employed primarily for their speed, and Hodge joined a small number of other passengers along with all manner of correspondence and cargo in his journey to Europe. Twenty-five days after he left New York City, he arrived in the port city of Le Havre in Normandy, France. Because of inclement weather, the trip took somewhat longer than usual, and the volatile rain storms forced Hodge to spend much of the "boisterous" journey huddled in his cabin.[13]

According to a plan he had worked out with Patton, Hodge had determined to spend half of his European sojourn in Paris and the other half at the Georg-August University of Göttingen, Germany. Patton had studied in Göttingen, and the city's university had become a popular destination for American students ever since 1815 when Edward Everett had chosen to study there. Many of those who followed Everett became influential professors at Harvard, including the immensely literary George Ticknor, the great Unitarian sage Frederic Henry Hedge, the American historian George Bancroft, and the internationally famous poet Henry Wadsworth Longfellow.[14] Hodge was attracted to Göttingen's educational reputation, and initially he saw no reason to deviate from what was becoming a well-worn path for American students.

From Le Havre, Hodge traveled quickly through the countryside, stopping one night in Rouen before arriving in Paris. In Paris, he took up residence with the family of a librarian by the name of Oberlin who held an appointment in the city's world-renowned King's Library. Hodge soon learned that even though he had studied both French and German, his knowledge of these languages was woefully inadequate. He knew neither language well enough to engage in everyday conversation, much less

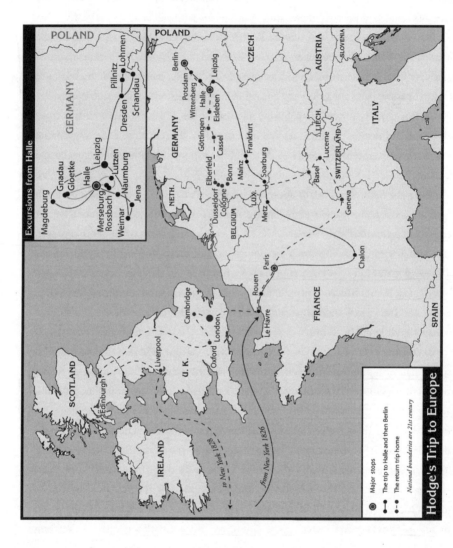

Figure 17.1 *Europe Travel Map*

advanced studies, and the Oberlin household spoke no English. At first, he had to resort to Latin to make any type of prolonged communication possible. Thus, his first order of business was improving his language skills. Just days after settling into his new home, he enlisted the aid of a French tutor who paid him daily visits.[15]

Hodge remained in Paris for three and a half months, dedicating himself to language study, both modern and ancient. Along with his French tutorials, he attended the lectures of Sylvestre de Sacy, the man who had attracted him to Paris.[16] De Sacy was the world's foremost Western authority on Middle Eastern languages, having gained his reputation by publishing several major works on Arabic texts and cofounding the city's Asiatic Society, which was doing pioneering work on Middle Eastern culture. De Sacy also enjoyed a reputation for taking pious students under his wing and nurturing their interest in the intersections between religion and the study of ancient languages.

Hodge enrolled himself at the University of Paris and began attending as many as six "lectures" a week taught by de Sacy, classes that consisted of seven or eight students working through various texts in order to master the languages. Hodge studied both Arabic and Syriac with de Sacy, and then sat in on other university classes to further refine his understandings of Arabic, Syriac, and Hebrew grammar. The University of Paris offered its courses as "public and gratuitous," so Hodge worked at a fevered pitch to cram in as many lectures as possible each week.[17] He wrote Dr. Alexander that he was simply amazed at the language studies available in Paris, commenting that "the advantages for the study of the Oriental languages here are very considerable," noting that the university offered "almost all the Eastern languages; Sanskrit, Chinese, Bengalee, Hindoostanee" along with various ancient, Arabic, and Persian dialects.[18]

Hodge pursued his studies with single-minded devotion. His typical day began with his French tutor arriving at eight A.M., followed by personal study before afternoon classes with de Sacy and another noted French orientalist at the University of Paris, Armand-Pierre Caussin de Perceval.[19] He then studied until midnight, only to rise early the next day to repeat the regimen. On most days, he relieved his studies only by taking meals, occasional midday walks, and observing the Sabbath. Hodge's prodigious work ethic enabled him to return to Princeton with several notebooks filled to overflowing with details of Hebrew and Arabic grammar.[20]

When Hodge did take an evening off from his studies, he spent the time with friends sharing a meal and discussing a wide range of theological topics. Notable among Hodge's Paris friends was the Swiss politician and philosopher Phillip Stapfer, who had settled in Paris. Hodge's friendship with Stapfer lasted long after his return to Princeton. Hodge translated and published an essay on the life of Kant by Stapfer in the *Biblical Repertory*, and in turn Stapfer proved to be a major force in getting Hodge's commentary translated and circulated in France. Stapfer also became the vice president of the Paris Protestant Society and corresponded with Hodge about what role Americans might play in evangelizing the heavily Catholic France.

Hodge also made time to see various Paris sights such as the garden of the Tuileries, the Louvre, and the celebration of mass in the king's chapel.[21] He even paid to see the king dine with the royal family.[22] He did not, however, visit any of Paris's great theaters. He so shunned the stage that his dramatic abstinence was commented upon by his Paris friends and even some of his fellow Americans. Princeton was conservative in its views of both dancing and acting, seeing them as seed beds for immorality. Hodge took his anti-drama views so far that throughout their youth he discouraged his children from staying at parties which introduced the parlor game of charades. Hodge's ability to hold his beliefs with adamantine firmness became an earmark not only of his time in Europe, but his life as a whole.

On several occasions, Hodge did find time to preach to a small English-speaking congregation in the city that had been founded by the pioneering English missionary, Mark Wilks.[23] Hodge's friendship with Wilks and his frequent preaching at his Paris chapel points out a crucial aspect of Hodge's time in Europe. Wilks had arrived in Paris in 1815. Over the ensuing decade, largely through his own writing and his efforts to see important works of Reformed theology translated into French, Wilks had become a key individual in France's Réveil, a Protestant revival that was slowly blossoming across the country. Both in Paris, and later in Germany, Hodge quickly formed critically important friendships with men who were intimately tied to what could be termed "evangelical" revival activity in those countries. Men like Wilks, who remained firmly committed to the importance of personal piety and the divinely inspired nature of the sacred scriptures, served as pivotal encouragers for Hodge as they insulated him from, and helped him interpret, less vital and more rationalist tendencies in European theology and religious life.

Hodge formed important friendships outside evangelical revival circles as well. During one of his sermons in Wilks's chapel, Marie-Joseph Paul Marquis de Lafayette and his family paid him a visit. Hodge had received an introduction to the famous French hero of the American Revolution from his friend Judge Samuel D. Southard, who was Secretary of the Navy.[24] While in Paris, Hodge had called on General Lafayette several times, only to be disappointed each time in finding the general to be out. He finally left his card. Lafayette sent him a kind note in return and then visited him along with "half a dozen of his daughters and grand-daughters" to hear him preach.[25] Later, Lafayette invited Hodge to his home where he was first introduced to the internationally famous explorer and scientist Alexander von Humboldt. During his international travels, Humboldt had visited Philadelphia and become friends with Caspar Wistar, Hugh Hodge's beloved medical mentor. Upon hearing of Hodge's plans to visit Germany, Humboldt graciously offered to write Hodge letters of introduction to prominent men in that country.[26]

As the winter months passed, Hodge needed to make a decision concerning his next step. He felt he had accomplished a great deal in Paris, but he was eager to begin his theological studies in Germany. While in Paris, Hodge had relinquished his plans of studying in Göttingen. Largely on the advice of Edward Robinson, a student of Moses Stuart, who was also studying theology in Germany, Hodge decided to instead to pursue his studies in Halle.[27] Robinson convinced Hodge that Göttingen's faculty were not only liberal in their theological views, but getting too old to be effective teachers. Johann Gottfried Eichhorn, the founder of modern Old Testament criticism, was in his seventies, and influential German theologian Gottlieb Jakob Planck was in exceedingly poor health due to epilepsy. In Robinson's mind, Göttingen was not the school it once had been, and it was particularly ill-suited for the study of any type of orthodox Reformed theology.

Halle, on the other hand, paid more attention to biblical studies than any other German university. It was a school that had been founded in the last decade of the seventeenth century under the guidance of two eminent Pietists, Philip Jakob Spener and August Hermann Francke, both of whom had stressed personal piety and intensive biblical study over the examination of forms and theories of biblical interpretation.[28] Two centuries later, Halle was harking back to these roots by having recently appointed the twenty-eight-year-old wunderkind August Tholuck, a man as famous for his heartfelt evangelical beliefs as his insightful scholarship and teaching.[29] By the late 1820s, Tholuck had already mastered fifteen languages, published an important essay on the ancient Persians, and completed a commentary on Romans that Stapfer hailed as the best work ever published on this critical New Testament book.[30] In addition to Tholuck, Halle had one further virtue of no small importance to Hodge: it was a cheaper place to live than Göttingen.[31]

18

HALLE

In mid-February 1827, Hodge began his thirteen-day stagecoach trip to Halle. Rather than take the most direct route, he decided to travel south in order to see more of France. He journeyed to Chalon and only then made his way north to Halle, passing through Metz, Saarbrücken, Mainz, Frankfurt, and Leipzig before finally arriving in Halle at two in the morning on February 28. It had proved to be a brutal trip, a fatiguing, start-and-stop stagecoach journey over snow-covered roads and treacherous rivers.

Hodge's first impressions of Halle were dour. He wrote Sarah that it was "beyond dispute the dirtiest, ugliest, gloomiest town of its size I have ever seen."[1] His initial bleakness was offset by the warm welcome he received from Edward Robinson, who had secured the room next to his in a boarding house owned (and also partly occupied) by Wilhelm Gesenius, one of the professors who had brought Hodge to Halle. Hodge considered Gesenius the "first Hebrew scholar probably in the world," and even though Gesenius was a devout rationalist, Hodge looked forward to learning from the great linguist.[2] The day after Hodge arrived in Halle, Robinson introduced him to the university's major theological and language scholars, including August Tholuck, a newly appointed theological professor who was just a year younger than Hodge.[3]

Sharing houses first in Halle and then later in Berlin helped Hodge and Robinson form a friendship that lasted for decades. Robinson remained longer in Germany than did Hodge and married the daughter of a philosophy professor at Halle, a union that forever linked him to important German theological circles. When Robinson returned home with his new bride, he took up a faculty position at Andover Seminary, where he became the country's first internationally recognized biblical scholar.[4] His travels in Palestine led him to formulate intricate and widely accepted theories on how the geography of the Holy Land served as an indispensable apologetic to prove the trust-worthiness of the Christian scriptures.

In Halle, Hodge again faced language difficulties, and within days of his arrival he hired a tutor to help him with his German, a language he found "exceedingly difficult" to master.[5] His tutor turned out to be a young Prussian by the name of George Müller. In his early student days at Halle, Müller had distinguished himself as a drunkard, gambler, liar, and thief, but when he arrived to help Hodge, he was a newly converted Christian. Hodge could not possibly have known that this "pious young man" would later become the driving force behind a number of internationally recognized benevolent enterprises, including a host of orphanages, which by the time of his death some seventy years later had touched the lives of one hundred thousand children.[6] As Hodge settled in, he met daily with Müller to work on his German.

Hodge broadened his academic interests in Halle. He took courses in ancient languages, but he attended other classes as well. Hodge attended the lectures of the famed German rationalist, Julius Wegscheider, in order to expose himself to more-liberal German thinking.[7] At one point Hodge records that Wegscheider satirically proclaimed that "Paul taught the doctrine of predestination just as the Calvinists hold it" and then urged this as "proof of the little dependence we can place upon this apostle."[8] For Hodge, such a statement bordered on blasphemy. He had come to Europe to confront German biblical criticism, and in Wegscheider's thinking Hodge vividly glimpsed what had so worried Archibald Alexander about German Neology.

It quickly became apparent as Hodge began his studies in Halle that there existed a rich complexity and diversity of theological thought in Germany.[9] Not all Germans favored the liberal Neological views that Alexander so feared and Harvard so eagerly embraced. While certain German scholars were hard at work developing highly rationalist approaches to biblical study, much of 1820s Germany and Prussia was in the midst of a revival experience known throughout the region as the "Awakening" (*Erweckungsbewegung*), a movement born of Lutheran Pietism and Romanticist mysticism.[10] Everywhere the "Awakening" produced "evidence that vital religion was very much increasing."[11]

Tholuck was both a product of this revivalist sentiment and eventually one of its greatest champions as he worked to combine orthodox doctrine, personal piety, rigorous biblicism and select insights from recent German theological scholarship.[12] Throughout his career, Tholuck read recent developments in German biblical criticism against personal and orthodox views of supernatural intervention. He pushed against any type of historical rationalism that robbed the Gospel message of its mystical and emotive power.[13] While Hodge would never agree with all of Tholuck's scholarly sympathies, including his deep admiration for Schleiermacher, he found in Tholuck a kindred spirit, a man who fused heartfelt personal devotion to an unwavering belief in the Bible's divine inspiration.[14]

Hodge's European journal is full of descriptions of discussions with Tholuck. They moved from topics ranging from the efficacy of enforcing God's moral law among those who did not believe in God to the likelihood of damnation for those who died never having heard the Gospel.[15] Tholuck stopped by Hodge's room at least three or four times a week, but sometimes as frequently as twice a day, to invite Hodge to join him to take a stroll and talk.[16] In the coming months, they came to dine daily in each other's company.[17] Through their walks, shared meals, and extended evening discussions, Tholuck became Hodge's most significant and enduring friend from his time in Europe, and served as yet one more example of Hodge's remarkable ability to make and sustain significant, long-lasting friendships. The two corresponded sporadically throughout the rest of their lives, and as late as 1877 Tholuck sent Hodge a picture of himself, which Hodge prominently displayed in his study until his death a year later.[18]

His fondness for Tholuck also points to an interesting theological flexibility on Hodge's part. Tholuck's contributions to theology were diverse, and yet a common thread found running through each of them was his conviction that communion with God was best accomplished though the sacramental and the mystical rather than the rational. Based on this line of reasoning, Tholuck showed himself open to an ecumenism that set him apart from much of the denominational squabbling of the day.[19] Tholuck inspired a wide range of American theologians, including John Williamson Nevin, who adopted much of the German's thinking as he developed his Mercersberg Theology. In the coming years, Hodge took exception to the Mercersberg Theology, all the while tolerating Tholuck. Hodge's strong sense of personal loyalty influenced his openness to Tholuck's views, but he also appreciated his friend's cultural context. Hodge had firsthand knowledge of a Germany beset by theological rationalism and thus took into account the stresses that influenced Tholuck's more mystical theology. In the end, Hodge saw Tholuck's Pietism as a beacon of light in a German sea of metaphysical speculation, whereas he saw the Mercersberg Theology as a needless and misguided variation on the vibrant Calvinism one could find in the United States.[20]

Amid his intensive studies at the University of Halle, Hodge intensely missed his wife and children. Although Hodge never had much patience for keeping a diary, while in Germany he kept the most complete journal of his life. He used an epistolary fiction to motivate himself to keep an almost daily record of his trip. He pretended each journal entry was part of "A long Letter to my *Dear Sarah*."[21] Once he returned to Princeton, he occasionally noted important events or personal thoughts in a daily memorandum book, but never again did he keep as thoughtful a diary as the one he kept while in Europe.

Cost seems to have once again been a consideration when he decided to undertake his "long letter" to Sarah. Not only was sending letters across the Atlantic a painfully slow process, but it was expensive as well. Sarah was also aware of both the cost and time involved in writing her husband. In her own letters, she frequently notes the time elapsed between hearing from him, knowing that it took a minimum of forty-eight days between the arrival of the particular packet ships that might bring a letter from Halle. She also was careful to keep her letters to a single piece of paper, noting how expensive even a single page was to send overseas.[22] Such economy resulted in incredibly cramped letters, full of news told in tiny handwriting, sometimes even written in the "crisscross" letter style where the writer would write a page and then turn that same page ninety degrees and proceed to write another full page on top of the lines just written.

In his journal entries, one is able to glimpse Hodge's theological development (or stasis) during this period. For the first time in his life, Hodge was placed in educational settings significantly outside his Presbyterian-centered background. One might expect that these new settings would have had a broadening effect on his theology, but such was decidedly not the case. Although he showed a limited tolerance for views that differed from his own if they came from friends such as Tholuck, Hodge's own theological views never wavered from those he had adopted as a youth. His time in Europe deepened his theological convictions rather than broadened them. Nothing he was exposed to in Europe moved Hodge's thinking on key Reformed doctrines such as imputation, atonement, and depravity, and he used his own views of these key doctrines to measure whatever new ideas he came across. Hodge remained untouched by strains of Lutheran Pietism, German Romanticism, and various forms of rationalism and the Higher Criticism throughout his time in Europe.

When Hodge encountered some new theological or philosophical idea, he quickly took the role of cataloguer and judge. New views were set against what he already believed and measured accordingly. It is as if he arrived in Europe ready to rebut, rather than engage, new theological ideas. When it came to the most central beliefs of Reformed orthodoxy, Hodge was as immoveable as the Rock of Gibraltar. He arrived in Europe with the conservative Calvinist views he had learned from Drs. Green, Alexander, and Miller, and in these views he never deviated. The principles he had learned in his youth remained the standards against which he measured every theological point of view he came across in Europe.

Hodge, however, was not completely untouched by what he experienced in Europe. While he was not open to shifting stances on any core beliefs of Christian doctrine, he did show a willingness to embrace change in other areas. He proved open to new ideas concerning various religious practices. For example, he appreciated the use of trumpets in worship services and was much taken with the notion of having a confirmation ceremony for those who had been baptized as infants.[23] While in Halle, he witnessed one such ceremony wherein some one hundred and fifty children stood before their congregation acknowledging their agreement with the Apostle's Creed. In response, the congregation recognized them forthwith as members of the church. Hodge wrote "that however little authority there may be for rebut, as of divine appointment, that some service of the kind might" show itself immensely useful in the American Presbyterian Church.[24] For the remainder of his life, Hodge believed that such a ceremony would do great service as a means of more formally bringing the young into the life of the church.[25] .

Hodge stayed in Halle just under eight months. To offset the long hours he spent studying, he took numerous excursions into the surrounding region. These explorations came to compose his own version of the European grand tour. Hodge was a keen observer and could not help but compare Europe with the United States. His letters home are filled with vivid descriptions of the countryside, farming, women at work, clothing, children, Catholic Church services, and what decorated the homes he visited. In general, he found the towns and people of Europe to have a rather worn, though healthy, look but generally lacking American characteristics of "comfort, independence and cultivation."[26]

Making short excursions from Halle, Hodge preferred to visit locations that held particular historical or cultural significance. He made it a point to visit the famous Napoleonic battlefields of Rossbach, Weimar, and Jena.[27] He rode one day to see the battlefield near Merseburg where Frederick the Great defeated the French and then visited the battlefield near Lutzen where the great Swedish warrior-king Gustavus Adolphus fell in battle in 1632.[28] He also spent time in the region's most important cities, including Magdeburg, Dresden, and Leipzig.

He traveled to Dresden to visit the city's art gallery, which was widely considered "to be the finest in modern Europe." Once he had seen it, however, he thought it suffered in comparison to the Louvre.[29] Disappointed by much of the art he saw there by such masters as Correggio and Rubens, he found himself absolutely mesmerized by Raphael's *Sistine Madonna*, in which he thought the infant captured "the expression of the eye [which] belongs to no human infant," and saw the Virgin as "the ideal of human purity and beauty."[30] Hodge did not have a sophisticated vocabulary for that which he found pleasing, but his journal entries on both art and music clearly show just how important the heart was in his judgments. As rational as his descriptions of various works might be, for any piece of art to make an "impression" upon him it needed to strike an unexplainable—almost mystical—chord within him, not unlike how he viewed the need for the special touch of the Holy Spirit to incite any real understanding of God.[31]

Hodge also had a chance to see the Elbe River in its mountainous setting as it flowed through a region commonly known as Saxon Switzerland. Traveling once again with Tholuck, Hodge stood awestruck before the rugged and romantic beauty of the region. Dining at small villages along their stage route, Hodge and Tholuck eventually arrived at the famous citadel at Königstein, a rock fortress built into the mountains and supposedly never successfully assaulted by an enemy force. In the same region, ever interested in scientific and medical matters, Hodge stopped in the small town of Schandau to visit a hospital and asylum for the insane.[32]

When Hodge and Tholuck returned to Halle, Hodge had to decide where to spend his remaining time in Europe. A new winter school term was approaching, and he needed to determine if Halle were the best place to pursue his studies during his final winter in Europe. Tholuck helped convince him that he should spend his last months studying in Berlin, Prussia's capital city and an important center of both intellectual and "Awakening" activity.[33]

Hodge opted for Berlin. As he made his way north in October 1827, he stopped in Wittenberg, a city Hodge viewed as the birthplace of Protestantism. While there, he carefully traced as much of Martin Luther's life and history as his short, two-day stay would allow. He visited Luther's church, home, grave, and the famous door upon which he had nailed his Ninety-Five Theses. He also spent time in the house once occupied by Luther's disciple Melanathon.[35] For someone like Hodge who was thoroughly steeped in the history and tradition of the Reformation, Wittenberg was as close to holy ground as any place on earth.

19

BERLIN AND THE RETURN HOME

Arriving in Berlin on October 12, Hodge reunited with Tholuck, who happened to be visiting the city and his good friend Ernst Wilhem Hengstenberg.[1] Just twenty-five years old, Hengstenberg was quickly distinguishing himself both as a scholar of Middle Eastern languages and as an important voice in the "Awakening" movement through his editorship of one of the most influential orthodox journals in Europe, *Evangelische Kirchenzeitung*. Hengstenberg's career bore a striking resemblance to Hodge's. His journal was similar to the *Repertory* in its strident advocacy of conservative evangelical views, his university teaching was marked by a pronounced orthodox and pious fervor, and he published a great deal during his lifetime.

Hengstenberg quickly became good friends with Hodge. Hengstenberg appreciated Hodge's "simplicity, modesty, and sincerity," and provides one more example of how Hodge's earnestness, quick mind and keen sense of humor gave him a low-key, yet powerfully magnetic, personality that drew others to him.[2] Tholuck, Hodge, and Hengstenberg made for a young and extremely intelligent trio as they spent countless evenings together in the company of various "Awakening" circles found throughout Berlin.[3] These *Erweckungsbewegung* groups introduced Hodge to several other German neo-Pietist luminaries including Otto von Gerlach, the founder of the Berlin Foreign Missionary Society and a man Tholuck fondly characterized as "the Wesley of Berlin."[4] Von Gerlach came from a prominent political family in Berlin. His father had been Lord Mayor of the city, and his older brother Ludwig was carving out his own remarkable political career. As fervent as Otto was in his Christian faith, Hodge became better friends with Ludwig, a man so passionate about fusing the mind of Christ into political affairs that Hodge was hard pressed to find another European who "excited more love and respect" in him.[5]

While in Berlin, Hodge also became friends with the brilliant church historian, Johann Neander. Born into a poor Jewish peddler's family, Neander possessed such an amazing intellect that he was able to rise above his humble origins and earn a student spot at the University of Halle. While there he fell under the spell of Friedrich Schleiermacher, who inspired Neander's lifelong meditative, almost mystical, approach to Christianity. Neander's personal motto was "the heart makes the theologian," and throughout his career he stressed the importance of personal holiness and the ecumenical fellowship of all believers.[6] So close did Hodge and Neander become in Berlin that when Hodge prepared to leave, both men broke down into tears, providing Hodge with a parting he said he could "never forget."[7]

By the time Neander entered the University of Halle, Schleiermacher had already established himself as one of Germany's most influential theologians as he sought to reconcile Protestant theology with Enlightenment rationalism. Schleiermacher argued that such reconciliation could be found in realizing that Christianity was at its core a way of life, not a set of doctrines. His stress on Christianity's emotional aspects and the unifying power of religious feeling made many view him as a pantheist, but he proved a pivotal influence on some of the most important young conservative Christian theologians of his age. He sparked spiritual awakenings in Neander and Tholuck, and both men believed that Schleiermacher's ability to turn people from hollow rationalism to meaningful spiritual introspection made him an extremely important, if not entirely orthodox, theologian.[8] Although Hodge met Schleiermacher and heard him preach on several occasions, he was never able to muster much admiration for the man, going so far as to write in his journal that he found his theology so "vague and indefinite" as to be useless.[9]

How Hodge spent his time in Berlin differed from how he had filled his days in Paris and Halle. He attended theological classes, including Old Testament lectures by Hengstenberg and New Testament lectures by Neander.[10] Then, no longer hampered by poor French and German, Hodge spent his evenings surrounded by friends in prayer meetings and lively theological discussions. On the weekends, he visited local churches and listened to the preaching of such eminent figures as Friedrich Gustave Lisco, Johannes Evangelista Gossner, and the "too violent" David Friedrich Strauss, the young German theologian who later became an international sensation when he published his historical *Life of Jesus*, which denied Jesus' divinity.[11]

Hodge also ventured into different parts of Berlin and the surrounding region. Not wishing to waste a single moment of his time in Europe, Hodge only undertook trips that promised to teach him something of German history and culture. He visited schools for reformed teenage criminals and for the blind, as well as the *Gewerbs Institut*, which trained artists and mechanics and reminded Hodge of Philadelphia's much smaller Franklin Institute.[12] He also spent a day visiting a prison near Berlin which among its four hundred prisoners housed some ninety women, most of whom were serving life sentences for having killed their own infants. Always fascinated with the practical expressions of human depravity, Hodge showed a particular interest in European crime rates (which were much higher than those found in the United States) and how prisoners were punished for their sins against society.[13]

Hodge traveled to Potsdam and was able to see such memorable sights as Napoleon's hat, captured at the Battle of Waterloo, and the grave of Frederick the Great.[14] He had one of his most disturbing European moments when he visited Voltaire's home, a house that had become a kind of shrine honoring rationalist anti-religious sentiment. As Hodge entered Voltaire's house, he felt himself becoming physically ill, later writing that he considered the anti-Christian Voltaire to be "of all men who ever lived" the one who "most excites my bad feelings."[15] Hodge's visceral response to Voltaire's lingering ghost made him happy to leave Potsdam.

Hodge considered his time in Berlin to be the highlight of his stay in Europe.[16] He had made a number of close friends in the city, reveled in the spiritually vibrant *Erweckungsbewegung* gatherings, and met some of the greatest European thinkers of the age. Perhaps most remarkable among men in this latter category stood Baron Alexander von Humboldt, the great Prussian naturalist, geographer, and explorer. Considered Europe's most famous man after Napoleon, Humboldt's reputation was equally grand in the United States, where Thomas Jefferson had once declared him to be the greatest scientific mind alive.[17] Humboldt had made his reputation through his ambitious scientific expeditions to South and Central America, producing scholarly works from these travels that placed him among the most admired naturalists of his time.

Between November 1827 and April 1828—a period of time almost exactly corresponding to Hodge's time in the city—Humboldt offered a series of "Physical Geography" lectures at Berlin University that covered an extraordinary breadth of topics ranging from geology to global climate to astronomy to botany to biology. So immense was Humboldt's iconic reputation that obtaining a ticket to these lectures was extremely difficult. Having met Humboldt months before in Paris, Hodge applied to Humboldt himself for a seat in the auditorium, which he readily received. In the months that followed, Hodge religiously attended these lectures and his journal becomes largely an extended meditation on Humboldt's teaching.[18] That he would fill his long letter "to his dear Sarah" with pages of scientific notes on ocean currents, planetary movement, and climate differences once again shows just how voracious was Hodge's scientific appetite.

Hodge was particularly interested in Humboldt's thoughts on the different races of humanity. Humboldt held an unbending egalitarian view of "the unity of the human race" and was utterly convinced that all races shared a common origin, with no one race being superior to another.[19] He believed that races had intermixed and that these mixtures emphasized certain racial features, but in no way changed the universally shared nature of the human race as a whole. His conviction concerning basic human equality lay at the root of the one issue that could transform Humboldt's legendary congenial demeanor into one of wrath: slavery.[20] While Hodge agreed with Humboldt's thinking on humanity's common origin and nature, he differed on matters of social and political theory. In the coming years, Hodge made it clear that he believed there to be room (buttressed by biblical warrants) for the institution of slavery as long as slaves were treated with the dignity God had bestowed upon every person.

Hodge was linked to Humboldt's thinking in yet another way, as the great naturalist spent the final years of his life pursuing a project that Hodge would echo in his own *Systematic Theology*. At the age of seventy-six, Humboldt began writing a grand compendium of his thinking that eventually emerged as his titanic, multivolume *Cosmos* (published between 1845–1858). In this mammoth work, Humboldt attempted to make sense of the entire world by linking small biological and geographic details to grander general theories of the earth's development. *Cosmos* stood as Humboldt's rationalist attempt to bring order out of chaos, to understand the interrelated particulars of all the natural world's diversity. Nearly twenty-five years after the appearance of *Cosmos*'s first volume, Hodge attempted a similar feat, although with a distinctly more theological bent, when he composed his massive three-volume *Systematic Theology*.

In their own ways, both men stood as products of the Enlightenment impulse to catalog countless details and then provide schemas that served to explain the relationships of these particulars to an overall whole. Humboldt dreamed of writing a single work in which he might explain the interconnectedness of the entire material universe. Hodge's *Systematic Theology* was similar in that it aimed at providing a comprehensive interpretation of God's relationship to his entire creation. While Humboldt was concerned with explaining the relationships that existed between all aspects of the material world, Hodge's primary concern was explaining the vast array of relationships that existed between the spiritual and material worlds. Today such grand comprehensive interpretive schemes may seem to be nothing short of delusional, but in the nineteenth century there clearly existed an optimism in human rationality that spurred on such scholarly ambitions.

By April 1828, Hodge was planning his return journey to the United States. Knowing that this might well be his last time in Europe, he carefully planned his return trip to include as many important European universities and historical Reformation points of interest as possible. He traveled to the universities in Göttingen and Bonn. He then stopped in Eisleben, the birthplace of Martin Luther, where he marveled at a room near the apartment of Luther's birth full of "relics of the Reformer; such as his table, desk, letters, &c."[21]

Leaving Germany, Hodge entered Calvin's Switzerland and passed through Basel, Lucern, and Geneva. He found himself totally overwhelmed by the magnificence of the Swiss Alps. Upon seeing these towering mountains for the first time, he wrote Sarah that it was the first moment in his life "in which I felt overwhelmed. Every thing I had ever previously seen seemed absolutely nothing."[22] Hodge proceeded to visit Mont Blanc, Jungfrau and the Eiger. Ultimately, he was far more impressed with the natural beauty of the country than he was with any of the cities associated with the Reformation.

The rapture he felt as a result of encountering the Alps' incredible and sublime beauty became a reigning metaphor for Hodge's devotional life. In the ensuing years when he entreated others to flee anything that hardened their hearts and deadened "the delicate sensibility of the soul to moral truth and beauty," he invoked the sense of heartfelt wonder he had experienced amid the Swiss Alps. Upon his return, he included in his comments to the Seminary's new students: "Let a man, when contemplating the grandeur of alpine scenery, begin to examine the structure of the mountains, and study their geological character; what becomes of his emotions of sublimity? Thus also religious truth, viewed in the general, produces devotion; metaphysically analyzing it destroys it."[23] Hodge was clearly responding to the metaphysical rationalism that he had found so stultifying to the cause of true religion in Germany.

In the years immediately following his time in Europe, Hodge became known as a professor who took every opportunity to encourage his students to approach God in a spirit of awe and wonder, not a spirit of metaphysical mastery and rationalist dissection. Reminiscent of his alpine awe, Hodge believed that the immensity of God's mercy should wash over the believer, not be approached so rationally as to diminish its infinite, all-encompassing grandeur. In one sense, Hodge's extended exposure to France's *Réveil* and Germany's *Erweckungsbewegung* had helped push the pendulum of his theological thinking in a decidedly Pietistic direction, laying stress on the importance of the heart in encountering God. Forty years later, with the memories and threats of German rationalism a distant memory, the pendulum swung in the other direction as Hodge composed much of his *Systematic Theology* as an apologetic for the pivotal role the mind played in the process of understanding and appreciating God and his redemptive work.

Upon leaving Switzerland, Hodge made his way back through France, stopping once again in Paris before embarking for England and Scotland. He stopped briefly in London, taking time there to indulge his political interests by visiting both houses of Parliament. He was impressed when he heard the Duke of Wellington rise to address the House of Lords, but on whole he thought he had "never heard so much poor speaking" in his life.[24] He could only hope that the American Congress acquitted itself better in this regard. He then moved to visit the great universities at Cambridge and Oxford, where he was impressed by these magnificent educational institutions.

While in Great Britain, Hodge could not pass up the opportunity to close out his grand Reformation tour by detouring north to see the great mecca of Presbyterianism,

John Knox's Edinburgh. Having visited the city and such sites as St. Andrews University and Knox's church, St. Giles Cathedral, Hodge could now say that he had left no major point on the Reformation's compass untouched. He had visited Luther's Wittenberg, Calvin's Geneva, and now Knox's Edinburgh. In the coming years, he often salted his musings on these giants of the Reformation when conversing with students with anecdotes of his visits to the cities where they once lived.

As Hodge journeyed home, he became increasingly thoughtful about the usefulness of his two years abroad. In the spring, he wrote Archibald Alexander directly addressing the question "what has been gained" though his time in Europe.[25] Alexander had believed that Hodge stood to gain little by visiting Europe, and Hodge now contritely confessed to Alexander that he had not expected to learn "*so* little."[26] He went on to comment, however, that the fruits of the trip had come in the confidence he had gained concerning his own training and abilities. Having "seen German professors and German universities, [and] observed the manner of instruction," Hodge had become "convinced that learning is not obtained by magic even in Germany."[27] Far from regretting his decision to go abroad, Hodge exulted in the fact that his European studies had not shaken his faith "in the doctrines of the church" but quite "the reverse."[28]

Hodge had traveled to Europe as a young man eager to study the most recent scholarly innovations in ancient-language study and biblical studies. He had sought this knowledge in order to be better equipped to grapple with the threats that such German scholarship posed to American theology. If his time in Europe had taught him anything, it had convinced him that he no longer need fear German theology. Familiarity had bred contempt. In the coming years, rather than cower before European scholasticism and its American champions, Hodge became one of conservative American Protestantism's most skillful crusaders against the German biblical criticism and its wayward American adherents.

20

A SENSE OF MISSION

Hodge returned to Princeton in September 1828 a changed man.[1] Gone were his doubts about his own training and his ability to train others. His travels had convinced him that although he had certainly learned things in Europe, particularly in regard to his work in ancient languages, American theological education was not nearly as inferior and defective as men like Edward Everett and Moses Stuart had been led to believe. His personal encounters with the great scholars of Europe had only served to bolster this view. He told Sarah that the same men who had seemed theological giants when "viewed from the other side of the Atlantic" shrank after he actually met them, becoming nothing more than mere mortals "made of very vulgar clay."[2]

The thirty-one-year-old Hodge returned from Europe finally able to leave his student status behind. He had discovered that he could discuss theology as a peer with the greatest theological minds of his era, an impression reinforced by the fact that so many of these great minds were roughly Hodge's age. Tholuck was twenty-eight, Otto von Gerlach was twenty-seven, Hengstenberg was twenty-six, and Neander was thirty-nine although Hodge believed him to be thirty-five.[3] In countless evening conversations, classes, and social settings, these and other noteworthy European theologians had become simply men to Hodge. Many of them had also become good friends. Far from being intimidated by such scholars, Hodge found himself their equal.

Hodge arrived back in Princeton ready to take on the mantle of a crusader, and it is this spirit of righteous energy that the renowned artist Rembrandt Peale captured in his 1830 portrait of Hodge (see figure 13.1). Peale had risen to prominence by painting the portraits of such renowned men as George Washington, Thomas Jefferson, and even Hodge's recent acquaintance, Alexander von Humboldt. Among all the representations that exist of Hodge, Peale's vision is unique. He gives the young Hodge a vibrant and slightly windblown look, so full of energy that he almost bursts forth from the canvas. He then accents this sense of vitality by offering the only known picture of Hodge without his glasses, transforming Hodge from a cloistered scholar into a determined man of action. Peale perfectly captures the self-assurance and determination that marked Hodge upon his return from Europe.

Once he was settled back into his routines of family life and teaching, Hodge focused his energies on two causes he felt to be of paramount importance: Christian missions and public- education reform. Far from being disparate endeavors, he viewed missions and education as inextricably tied. His time in Europe had convinced him that the United States was the single most important country for the future of humanity. He argued both privately and publicly that any careful observer could not escape the conclusion that "from its physical character, from its local advantages, from the character of its population, and the nature of its institutions," the United States would "have greater influence on the human family than any other nation that has ever existed."[4] Its expansive resources coupled with its pioneering emphasis on civil liberty uniquely positioned the young United States to be a fount of unprecedented goodness for the entire world.

Because the United States was founded on democratic principles, Hodge was just one of an entire strata of Americans who believed it absolutely essential to educate Americans as thoroughly as possible to ensure that the country was guided by thoughtful, cultured, and well-considered decisions. Central to such an educational vision were notions of virtue and morality. For Hodge, this meant that from the earliest age, the young needed to be taught sound religious principles. He took for his model the school system he had found in Prussia, where "religion is as regularly and systematically taught as any other subject."[5] He recounted that so universal and thorough was this religious education that he never met a Prussian boy "selling matches in the street (and I made several experiments of the kind) who could not answer any common question on the historical parts of the Old and New Testaments."[6] By the age of fifteen, every Prussian school boy and girl—whether they were Protestant, Catholic, or Jewish—had mastered the most fundamental principals of the Christian religion, a fund of knowledge Hodge noted as sorely lacking in the United States. Without religion serving as the bedrock foundation for commonly held ideals of public and private virtue, American democracy itself was at risk, and the freedoms Americans enjoyed could become the most malevolent of forces.[7] For the next thirty years, Hodge waged a tireless campaign to champion educational reforms that might head off just such a disaster.

Hodge's fervor for educational reform was also fueled by the fact that his own children were fast approaching school age.[8] As little Alexander and Mary grew older, one senses in Hodge a growing interest and urgency when it came to matters of educating the young. Hodge wrote his mother that "everything must be made secondary" to the vow he and Sarah had made "to educate [their children] for heaven."[9] Mary Hodge most surely appreciated her son's sentiments; she had been relentless in her own quest to make sure that Charles and Hugh had received the best, and most religiously sound, schooling possible.[10]

Hodge's educational campaigns took several forms, but they were all driven by the central idea that religion must be taught in the public school system, even if this meant simply reading the Bible in the classroom.[11] When he began to doubt whether religion would ever hold a prominent place in the public school curricula, Hodge turned his attention to the possibilities of founding more denominationally centered schools for the young. By the 1840s, Hodge had begun advocating the establishment of Presbyterian parochial schools as a means of teaching orthodox Protestant tenets (as defined by his own brand of conservative Presbyterianism) to the nation's children. The need for such conservatively bent denominational schools became all the more urgent as his own denomination struggled with internal divisions and the nation's Roman Catholic population continued to grow through the massive waves of Catholic immigration from Ireland, Germany, and Italy.[12]

Linked to his almost-prophetic sense of America's global destiny was Hodge's rekindled interest in international missions. Hodge's time in Europe had given him a much-broader view of Protestantism, and in turn he had become convinced of the importance of the United States in the efforts of world evangelization. Hodge formulated a theory that vital Christian belief underwent certain cycles. "During one age, there are many revivals of religion, and a general prevalence of evangelical spirit and exertion; to this succeeds a period of coldness and declension; and to this, either a period of revival or of open departure from the faith."[13] Hodge saw the massive and ubiquitous revivals happening in America as a sign that the United States was near the apex of the religious cycle, with an unrivaled ability to spread the message of God's grace. At the same time, even with the Protestant revival movements that dotted the French and German landscapes, he saw the state of religion on the European continent as being at a low ebb.

Hodge had been interested in world missions even before his trip to Europe. While a seminary student, he had participated in the Society of Inquiry on Missions and the General State of Religion, a club not unlike the Whigs, which had been first founded as a secret society in 1814 and eventually blossomed into an ever-more-inclusive organization promoting missions awareness among seminarians for nearly half a century.[14] Members of this society met on the first day of every month to pray for world missions and discuss various topics related to both domestic and foreign evangelization. The society not only maintained an extensive correspondence with other like-minded societies across the country and around the world, but it collected books on topics pertaining to missions and even maintained a cabinet of "false gods" that had been sent to the Seminary by various missionaries as material reminders of what people around the world were worshiping instead of Jesus Christ.

Groups such as Princeton's Society of Inquiry played a key role in fostering interest in missions among American Protestants at the turn of the nineteenth century. Beginning with what became known as the Haystack Prayer Meeting of 1806 when a violent thunderstorm forced a group of Williams College students to move their prayer meeting under a haystack, a new era of interest in Protestant missions was born in the United States. Amid flashes of lightning and peals of thunder, these students committed themselves to spreading the Gospel overseas, taking as their motto "We can do it if we will."[15] By 1810, a number of Protestants denominations had joined together to establish the American Board of Commissioners for Foreign Missions.

Missionary optimism permeated the day as advances in transportation technologies led many to believe that the Great Commission might be accomplished during their lifetimes. Hodge's old mentor Ashbel Green was swept up by the possibility of global evangelization. When Hodge departed for Europe, Green asked him to send any "missionary intelligence" he could gather to be printed in the *Christian Advocate*.[16] As a result, Hodge paid close attention to the state of Christianity in every country he visited, but he wrote to Green most extensively concerning the heavily Catholic France, a country many Protestants considered so long "under the curse of Romanism and infidelity, that it seems like a field that has been burned over by the fire, and in which every appearance of life has been consumed."[17]

When Hodge arrived in France in 1826, he estimated France's Protestant population to be somewhere between 1,500,000 and 2,000,000. Far from being dispirited by a number that represented but a small fraction of France's thirty-three million inhabitants, Hodge's early exposure to France's *Réveil* movement through the British missionary Mark Wilks heartened him. Wilks had arrived in Paris one year after Louis XVIII's 1814 restoration to the throne. Louis XVIII's Bourbon Restoration proved a great boon to French Protestantism, as the king's greater tolerance for non-Catholics inspired his government to set aside money to fund clergy salaries and the construction of Protestant churches.[18] Louis XVIII also permitted French Protestants to receive greater international aid. As a result, British and Swiss Protestants began to provide France with missionaries and resources such as Bibles and other printed material to aid the growth of country's Protestant Church.[19]

This openness to Protestantism also aligned with other cultural changes within France. After decades of wars and bloody internal revolutions, the French no longer unquestioningly revered the Enlightenment ideals of rationalism and human moral progress. Instead, the French increasingly turned to personal spirituality and organized religion to help them interpret their lives.[20] Belief in something greater than human ability became the watchword for the day, and French Protestants seized on this newfound spiritual openness to foster the *Réveil*.[21] Once in Paris, Hodge quickly began to move in the circles frequented by these revival-minded Protestants. His primary connection to these revivalists was the Monod family, led by the family's patriarch, Jean Monod. Hodge first exposure to the famous Monod family came when he met Frederic Monod, the oldest of Jean's sons, who was staying in Paris at the same time as Hodge.[22] Frederic was in the midst of the daunting task of translating Scott's biblical commentary, a multivolume conservative Calvinist gloss on the Bible. Frederic's theological bent quickly endeared him to Hodge, and in the ensuing months Hodge developed friendships with several Monod brothers.

The brother to whom Hodge grew closest was Guillaume "Billy" Monod, who lodged in the same Berlin boarding house as Hodge during the winter months of 1827 and 1828.[23] Billy was considered the firebrand of the Monod clan. So great was his evangelistic passion that in the early 1830s he was institutionalized for a time because of his outspoken and erratic behavior.[24] During their time together in Berlin, Hodge and Billy Monod led several worship services together and "the most wonderful and wildest stories" circulated about their evangelistic partnership.[25]

Hodge's friendship with the Monods continued long after he left Europe. One of the Monod brothers translated Hodge's commentary on Romans into French and Adolphe Monod, eventually the most celebrated revivalist of the family, wrote an introduction to the volume. This translation immensely pleased the Seminary's board because it promised to propagate Princeton Seminary's particular brand of Calvinism among the French. In gratitude, the board granted Adolphe an honorary doctorate degree.[26] For his part, Hodge published Adolphe's "The Religious Prospects of France" in the *Biblical Repertory*.

Through his friendship with the Monods, Hodge became the single most important figure in Princeton Seminary's longstanding "bond of mission" with France.[27] When the Bourbon government gave way in 1830 to the even-more-Protestant-tolerant July Monarchy of Louis-Philippe, American Protestants took advantage of the moment by forming the "French Committee," a mission society created to focus specifically on France. Princeton Seminary and its graduates proved critical players in this committee's work.[28] Hodge encouraged several of his students to join the Monods' revivalist cause in France, including John Proudfit (1831), Flavel Mines (1834), Robert Baird (1835), and Edward Kirk (1837). Hodge also made sure to connect two of Archibald Alexander's sons (James and Addison) to the Monods when they made their own study trips abroad to Europe.[29]

In these and other ways, Hodge helped make Princeton Seminary a driving force in the American Christian missionary movement. He even passed on his zeal for world missions to his children. In 1833, when Archie was but ten years old and Mary was eight, they composed a letter to one of their father's former students, James Read Eckard, who was serving as a missionary in Ceylon (known today as Sri Lanka). They wished Mr. Eckard to read their letter to the people to whom he ministered:

> Dear Heathen:
> The Lord Jesus Christ hath promised the earth shall be His Kingdom. And God is not a man that he should lie nor the son of man that He should repent. And if this was promised by a Being who cannot lie, why do you not help it to come sooner by reading the Bible, and attending to the words of our teachers, and loving God, and renouncing your idols, take Christianity into your temples? And soon there will be not a nation, no, not a space of ground as large as a footstep, that will want a missionary. My sister and myself have, by small self-denials, procured two dollars which are enclosed in this letter to buy tracts and Bibles to teach you.
>
> Archibald Alexander Hodge
> Mary Eliz. Hodge
> Friends of the Heathen[30]

So great was little Archie's interest in missions that after graduating from the Seminary fourteen years later, he decided to become a missionary in India.

In 1829, Hodge deepened his involvement in world missions by accepting an appointment to a five-member General Assembly committee charged to consider the possibility of establishing a school to train missionaries.[31] Perhaps not surprisingly, because Archibald Alexander and Samuel Miller also sat on this committee, the General Assembly voted to appoint Princeton Seminary the denomination's new home for missionary training, a decision that included giving the Seminary a fourth professor who would conduct such training. In 1836 the Seminary hired one of Hodge's old college and seminary classmates, John Breckinridge, to the position of Professor of Pastoral Theology and Missionary Instruction.

In creating Breckinridge's position, the Seminary had established the first professorship of missions in the world. In the first half of the nineteenth century, Princeton Seminary was the only seminary or university that offered a course on missions as a part of its official curriculum.[32] Breckinridge occupied this professorship for a mere two years before taking up the more general leadership of the Presbyterian Board of Foreign Missions. Upon leaving the Seminary, he was not replaced, but a course on missions continued to be taught at the Seminary into the 1850s. The creation of Breckinridge's professorship and the enduring curricular changes it brought clearly demonstrated how interested Hodge and his fellow professors were in furthering the missionary cause.

Figure 20.1 *John Breckinridge*: John Breckinridge was Hodge's college and seminary classmate and had deep ties to Princeton. He was related to Samuel Stanhope Smith, Samuel Miller (through marriage to Miller's daughter) and one of Hodge's faculty successors, Benjamin Breckinridge Warfield. [*Special Collections, Princeton Theological Seminary Libraries*]

Hodge himself remained devoted his entire life to the missionary cause. He served on both the Presbyterian Board of Foreign Missions and the Presbyterian Board of Domestic Missions from the mid-1840s until 1870. He even served for two years as the president of the Board of Foreign Missions (1868–1870).[33] In 1848, he preached a Sunday-evening sermon before the Board of Foreign Missions entitled "The Teaching Office of the Church." Hodge built his sermon around the basic question: how is the injunction found in the Book of Acts to "Go ye, therefore, and make disciples of all nations" to be performed?[34] His answer was both simple and profound. Disciples, in his mind, were both followers and learners. They must know Christ's commands and the doctrines of the church, and central to their discipleship was their baptism and their religious education. In addition, Hodge stressed the role of the Holy Spirit in missionary activity. Declaring that "the truth is powerless, without the demonstration of the Spirit," Hodge urged his listeners to never forget that while men and women might teach the truths of the Gospel, the Spirit was the only power that could "give that teaching effect."[35] The sermon was reprinted in a host of different venues both before and after his death, and it became the baseline characterization in Presbyterian circles of true Christian missionary activity.

21

THE *REPERTORY* REBORN

While Hodge rejoiced at the promise of global missions, he despaired at the state of Reformed orthodoxy in American Protestantism. He showed great tolerance for various shades of Protestant theology overseas as he saw the challenges there so great that any furthering of the Gospel was welcome, but at home he was far more particular about what he considered acceptable standards of Gospel orthodoxy.[1] Throughout the 1830s, Hodge struggled with how to best draw deeper and darker lines around the doctrines he thought essential to Reformed theology. This decade saw Hodge emerge as one of the most articulate and passionate advocates for Princeton's brand of conservative theological thinking. His advocacy led him to become one of his denomination's most influential figures, a power he exercised both in the classroom and in his masterful manipulation of the persuasive medium of print.

Hodge's newfound post-European confidence led him to change the nature (and name) of the *Biblical Repertory* when he once again began editing the journal in 1829. When he had founded the *Repertory* four years earlier, he had conceived of it primarily as a means to reprint and disseminate the most current scholarship—much of it European—on various aspects of biblical studies. Hodge now had a new vision. No longer content to simply reprint European scholarship, he wished to give American Presbyterians their own voice, and he intended to do this by filling his journal with contributions from his colleagues, friends, and a handful of other like-minded thinkers. Hodge signaled the changing nature of the journal in three ways. He renamed it *Biblical Repertory. A Journal of Biblical Literature and Theological Science, Conducted by an Association of Gentlemen.* (One year later he would simplify the title to *Biblical Repertory and Theological Review.*) He also renumbered the newly renamed *Repertory* starting with volume one and alerted readers on the title page that "A New Series" had begun.

Hodge's "New Series" had far more ambitious goals than the journal's prior incarnation. Rather than just targeting professional clergy and assorted students of theology, Hodge hoped that the new *Repertory* might appeal to "all intelligent Christians."[2] In the wake of the growing influence of the American Bible Society and other voluntary societies, which were flooding the nation with copies of the Bible, Hodge saw it of "the utmost importance to afford to the people, every possible facility for a right understanding of the divine oracles."[3] Hodge recognized the power of the press in not only getting Bibles into the hands of Americans, but also in providing materials that would help them interpret those Bibles. He heartily desired that the *Repertory* might become a key contributor in helping Americans understand the world's most important book, and so he purposefully aimed the "New Series" at a wider audience.

Although Hodge originally hoped that his new *Repertory* might reach less theologically educated readers, it remained a periodical primarily read in Presbyterian clerical circles. One reason for its failure to appeal to more common readers was its highly erudite, complexly argued articles.[4] The other reason was cost. The price of the journal remained largely constant under Hodge's entire editorship. In 1825, a yearly subscription cost four dollars, but beginning in 1828 the cost was lowered to an annual rate of three dollars and remained at this level until he retired as the journal's editor in 1871.[5] Of course, adjusted for inflation, the journal was cheaper and more affordable in 1871. In its early years, three dollars represented nearly a week's wages for the common New England laborer. With the same money, a laborer could buy some twenty pounds of sugar or two bushels of potatoes along with a bushel of corn.[6] The journal's high cost inevitably narrowed its audience. By 1836, the *Repertory* was being circulated to 650 subscribers, a considerable number for a theological journal but a paltry figure compared to the thousands of readers who subscribed to the more popular magazines and newspapers of the day. The *Repertory*'s high cost and intellectually rigorous content destined it to be a journal for the highly educated and the more affluent.

As Hodge embarked on his "New Series," it would be misleading to say that editing the journal was solely a one-man affair. Over the years, Hodge may have served as the first among equals when it came to guiding the *Repertory*, but he had substantial help in producing it, including several men who took on significant editorial responsibilities for varying lengths of time.[7] One such key figure was Archibald Alexander's third son, Joseph Addison (known to all simply as "Addison"), who Hodge engaged as his associate editor in 1829 at the tender age of twenty. Addison was a child prodigy and grew into a gifted linguist and scholar. By the age of seventeen, he had read the Koran in Arabic and made progress in learning Persian and Syriac. Eventually, he mastered some twenty ancient and modern languages, and made widely recognized theological contributions through his attempts to fuse European biblical scholarship with conservative views of American Calvinism. In the years to come, he became one

Figure 21.1 *Joseph Addison Alexander*: Joseph Addison Alexander (known to everyone simply as "Addison") was a linguistic genius and read the Bible daily in six languages. He was also a social recluse, never marrying but devoting his every energy to his scholarship and teaching. He was a great favorite among children, and when Caspar Wistar Hodge Sr. was a boy, he served as his private tutor. Hodge said that Addison was "incomparably the greatest man I ever knew, incomparably the greatest man our church has ever produced," an amazing statement considering the distinguished circles in which Hodge moved. [*Library of the Author*]

of the *Repertory*'s most prolific contributors, publishing ninety-five essays in its pages between 1829 and 1863 (the last of which appeared posthumously).[8]

Aside from Addison, Hodge quickly gathered around himself a loosely defined editorial board, which became known as the "Association of Gentlemen" mentioned in the New Series' title. Hodge led this editorial team, which included many of the journal's most regular and important contributors: Archibald Alexander and his son Addison, Samuel Miller, James W. Alexander, James Carnahan (the then president of Princeton College), John Maclean Jr. (a future Princeton College president), and

Albert Dod.[9] Hodge may have led this "Association," but this did not give him final say over the contents of the periodical. Votes were taken on contentious issues, and sometimes he found himself overruled.

This editorial board evolved over the years, but the periodical always had some governing body that met at regular intervals to discuss the journal's direction and content. Throughout the early and mid-1830s, this board clearly attempted to make the periodical appeal to both New and Old School Presbyterians, even seeking in print to disassociate the periodical from Princeton Seminary in an attempt to emphasize its orthodox content over against any impressions of Princeton Seminary–based partisanship. Once the New and Old School Presbyterians split in 1837, Hodge abandoned any such pretense, and he changed the name of the journal yet again. After the 1837 Presbyterian schism, the journal took the name it would retain through the rest of Hodge's life: the *Biblical Repertory and Princeton Review*, a title that unabashedly identified it with Princeton Seminary and the school's Old School theological views.

PART IV

The 1830s

Crusader

Figure 22.1 *Hodge in the 1830s*: Hodge is pictured here during the years of American Presbyterianism's great schism. [*Presbyterian Historical Society, Presbyterian Church (U.S.A) (Philadelphia, PA)*]

22

THE IMPUTATION CONTROVERSY

Proclaiming Princeton's views became an ever-more-urgent endeavor in the minds of the Seminary's faculty as the next few years proved to be turbulent ones for American Presbyterianism. Swept along by widespread religious revivals throughout the Northeast, Presbyterians struggled to find a balance between the theology they taught and the practical realities and consequences of large-scale conversions. Due largely to the pressure of these revivals, factions arose within Presbyterianism which came to be called "Old School" and "New School."[1] The Old School was characterized by a more strident commitment to the traditional Calvinism found in the Westminster Confession as taught by such seventeenth-century scholastics as Turretin. The New School, on the other hand, distinguished itself largely through its revivalist sympathies.

New School Presbyterians fused their pro-revivalism tendencies with theologies that stressed the power of human agency in conversion over traditional Calvinist notions of God's absolute sovereignty.[2] They were profoundly influenced by Nathaniel Taylor and his New Haven Theology. While traditional Calvinism taught that all sin found its root in Adam's first act of disobedience in Eden, Taylor subtly shifted the emphasis away from Adam's choice to eat the apple.[3] Instead, Taylor placed the responsibility for sin squarely on the shoulders of each individual. In perhaps his most famous formulation of his position on sin, Taylor proclaimed that sin was "man's own act, consisting in a free choice of some object rather than God, as his chief end and good."[4] Such an emphasis on personal agency and free choice appealed to Americans who, in the country's democratic milieu, were increasingly showing a penchant to believe that they controlled their own destiny both as individuals and as a nation.

The New Haven Theology provided a critical ideological underpinning for revivalist activity. This revivalism had its symbolic beginnings in an 1801 week-long camp meeting in Cane Ridge, Kentucky, when somewhere between ten and twenty-five thousand people gathered to hear the Gospel message. Such gatherings, which as a body came to be known as the Second Great Awakening, peaked in frequency and force in the 1820s and then again in the 1850s. Many revival leaders adopted, sometimes unknowingly, Taylor's notions of human agency. Eschewing notions that God alone determines who might be saved, revivalists of the period instead emphasized a person's ability to choose for salvation.

As the New Haven Theology began to take root among Presbyterians in the late 1820s, Hodge and his fellow Seminary professors became uneasy. They were careful, however, not to engage these issues in an aggressive, belligerent style, but approached them instead in a spirit of reasoned and rigorous debate. Choosing Hodge's new *Biblical Repertory* as a principle means of engaging New Schoolers on key issues, the Princeton faculty wrote a series of articles addressing their concerns with the denomination's increasing embrace of Taylor's thinking and Finney's methods. Dr. Alexander offered the first salvo in what would build into a Presbyterian war of words over the next several years when he published his 1830 *Repertory* article, "The Early History of Pelagianism." Alexander made it clear to astute American Presbyterians that Princeton had little patience with Taylor's theological views by drawing parallels between the fundamental errors of the fifth-century monk Pelagius and the New Haven Theology.

At the root of Pelagius's errors was his denial of humanity's innately sinful nature, teaching "that man was born without sin; and that he could be saved by his own exertions."[5] For Alexander, such a denial was unmitigated heresy, and he set out in painstakingly thorough fashion to show how Augustine and all the reformers with "one consent . . . held that the sin of Adam was imputed to his posterity."[6] Central to Alexander's argument against Pelagius's "monstrous errors" was his repeated references to the fifth chapter of Romans, the most important and oft-cited biblical proof-text in support of the belief that all of Adam's descendants were the heirs of his sinful nature.[7]

Those who leaned toward a more expansive view of the power of human volition felt the force of Alexander's attack on the New Haven Theology. At issue was what theologians commonly termed "imputation." Imputation dealt with the belief that the responsibility (and thus the punishment) for Adam's initial sin in Eden was *imputed* to all future generations. When it came to the doctrine of imputation, Hodge and his Princeton colleagues were stolid Augustinian Calvinists, Christians who believed like Augustine (a vehement foe of Pelagius) that Adam chose to sin and both he and his posterity were punishable for that choice. For Hodge and his compatriots, this view was of particular importance because it provided the key to understanding the importance of Jesus' crucifixion. According to the Princetonians, God held all humanity guilty for Adam's first sinful action—the Original Sin. God was also willing to forego the punishment for this initial sin and all the sin to which it gave birth through another single action: Jesus'—the new Adam—death on the cross.[8]

Pelagius offered a rival interpretation. He placed responsibility for sin on those who actually committed the sin, not on the far-distant and long-dead Adam. The power of human agency stood at the center of his thinking on sin. In critiquing Pelagius, Alexander was critiquing Nathaniel Taylor. Alexander's article, however, did not

Figure 22.2 *Moses Stuart*: Moses Stuart served as a professor at Andover Theological Seminary from 1810 to 1848. He strongly encouraged Hodge to further his theological and language studies by traveling to Europe. Both Stuart and Hodge wrote important commentaries on the book of Romans. These commentaries highlighted their different conceptions of humanity's moral sense; Stuart argued – in distinction from Hodge's strict Calvinism—that all people had an innate ability to choose between good and evil. [*Franklin Trask Library, Andover Newton Theological School*]

immediately rouse Taylor or any of his New School adherents to respond in print. Instead, a champion for Taylor arose from another quarter: the immensely respected Andover scholar, Moses Stuart.[9]

By the 1830s, Moses Stuart had become the leading conservative biblical exegetical scholar in the United States, and his theology mirrored Taylor's in many respects. Stuart was also a longtime friend of Taylor, the man who had taken over his much-beloved pulpit at New Haven's First Church when Stuart left to take his teaching position at Andover in 1820. In an article published in Yale's *The Quarterly Christian Spectator* entitled "Inquiries Respecting the Doctrine of Imputation," Stuart took exception to the parallels Alexander drew between Pelagianism and modern American thinking on imputation. The battle had been joined. Over the next four years no fewer than ten articles appeared in both the *Biblical Repertory* and *The Quarterly Christian Spectator* arguing Yale's and Princeton's competing views of imputation. Hodge wrote several of the articles articulating the Princeton position.[10]

Frustrated with the narrow scope of argumentation journal articles necessarily mandated, Stuart decided to write *A Commentary on the Epistle to the Romans* (1832), a book-length treatise that he intended to be the decisive word concerning the knotty issues surrounding God's sovereignty and human agency. Romans, more than any other biblical book, contained the key texts Christians used to discuss such pivotal doctrines as humanity's sinful nature, God's absolute sovereignty, predestination, and imputation. Stuart believed that there was no better way to explain and justify his (and Taylor's) theological stances than by showing how they were fully grounded in, and supported by, St. Paul's own master theological treatise.

Stuart's commentary did not go unnoticed by Princeton's seminary faculty. Hodge immediately gave it a long and ultimately damning review in the *Repertory*, calling it a work full of "very numerous and very serious faults."[11] Stuart, however, was a Congregationalist and therefore outside the Presbyterian fold. A much more serious threat to Princeton's theological positions came from Albert Barnes, an 1824 graduate of Princeton Seminary who had become the head pastor of Philadelphia's rich and influential First Presbyterian Church. Barnes used his pulpit to become one of New School Presbyterianism's most potent advocates. Even more dangerous than his preaching was his publishing. In the early 1830s, Barnes began writing a New Testament commentary series which would make him one of America's most read and quoted biblical exegetes of his generation. Americans purchased more than one million copies of Barnes's commentaries before the Civil War.[12]

The most famous of Barnes's early commentaries was his *Notes on Romans* (1834). In it, Barnes freely admitted to deviating from certain tenets of the Westminster Catechism as he interpreted Romans' fifth chapter in accordance to the human volitional emphasis favored by both Nathaniel Taylor and Moses Stuart. When Hodge read

Figure 22.3 *Albert Barnes*: Albert Barnes was one of the most influential and beloved leaders of New School Presbyterianism. Serving as the head pastor of Philadelphia's affluent First Presbyterian Church for thirty-seven years (1830–1867), Barnes became internationally famous for his immensely popular eleven-volume New Testament commentary series and his vocal opposition to slavery. [*Presbyterian Historical Society, Presbyterian Church (U.S.A) (Philadelphia, PA)*]

Barnes's *Notes on Romans*, he saw precious little difference between it and Stuart's commentary on the most important doctrinal portions of Paul's letter.[13]

Hodge savaged Barnes's commentary in a fifty-five-page *Repertory* review, lamenting that Barnes had little understanding of Paul's most complex letter. In Hodge's mind, Barnes constantly undercut his arguments by his almost total "neglect of analytic method" and his constant and ill-considered objections to the most standard and well-established doctrines of the Protestant Church.[14] So misguided were his conclusions that Hodge goes so far as to state that Barnes himself should "be surprised at the supercilious tone of his decisions."[15] As merciless as Hodge was in his review of Barnes's *Notes on Romans*, he could not escape the fact that Barnes was having a huge influence not only on the Presbyterian clergy, but on Presbyterian lay people as well. Between Stuart's and Barnes's work on Romans, he felt that the time had come for him to enter the ring with his own book-length treatment on the issues that were proving so divisive in his denomination. Hodge decided to meet Stuart and Barnes on their own ground with his own, more orthodox, commentary on Paul's epistle to the Romans.[16]

23

ROMANS

While still in Europe, Hodge wrote in his journal: "We preach as by Paul with his wisdom & faithfulness—& each truth in proportion to its importance—*regeneration & atonement above all*."[1] Hodge's absolute conviction that these two doctrines stood at the center of the Gospel drew him to his lifelong engagement with the book of Romans because it was in this Pauline epistle that one found the best means of understanding the doctrines of regeneration (the role of God's Holy Spirit in moving a person to pursue a new spiritual life in Christ) and the Atonement (how sin is forgiven in the action of Christ on the cross).[2] In Hodge's mind, every other doctrine stood as secondary to these two, and he felt that Taylor's theology, now being widely adopted by New Schoolers, dangerously threatened orthodox renderings of both doctrines.

Hodge's teaching responsibilities at the Seminary had prepared him well to produce a Romans commentary. Upon his return from Europe his teaching responsibilities included not only courses on Old Testament literature and the Hebrew language, but he also regularly taught New Testament literature and biblical Greek. His mornings were dedicated to teaching Hebrew and lessons on the Old Testament, while his afternoons were filled with teaching classes on the New Testament, biblical criticism, and sacred geography.

As early as 1823, just a year after becoming the Seminary's third professor, Hodge had begun to write lecture notes on the Book of Romans.[3] By the early 1830s, he had become the Seminary's principal instructor of the New Testament epistles, regularly offering the junior class exegetical lectures on these books. He became so proficient in this area and enjoyed it so much that he offered his New Testament lectures every year until he retired from teaching, a span just short of half a century.[4] As a consequence, Hodge already had composed extensive notes on Romans when he finally sat down in the late autumn months of 1834 to begin on his commentary. He completed the work in a matter of months, taking every free moment he had during Princeton's frigid winter to finish the manuscript. As he wrote, he solicited Dr. Alexander's comments on each chapter and revised the work according to his mentor's advice.[5]

As he wrote and revised, Hodge kept ever mindful of his desire to reach an audience beyond professional theologians. Taking his cue from Barnes, and quite frankly fearing the threat a readable yet deeply doctrinally flawed commentary posed, Hodge set out to make his work a serious piece of scholarship that might be useful to the laity as well.[6] Along with the standard analysis of the biblical text found in all the commentaries of the day, Hodge reached out to a wider readership by concluding each of his chapters with a section entitled "Remarks." In these chapter codas, Hodge offered insights to how the epistle's content might apply to the lives of his nineteenth-century readers. For example, when considering how Paul encouraged the Saints in Rome to help their sister Phebe at the beginning of the book's sixteenth chapter, Hodge reminded his reader that "It is the duty of Christians to receive kindly their brethren and to aid them in every way within their power."[7] By giving his commentary this practical edge, Hodge strove to match the utility and accessibility of Barnes's work.

Hodge wished for far more, however, than a broad audience for his commentary. He devoutly desired that his work stand as a thoughtful, thoroughly Reformed commentary on Paul's epistle that might also make available a concise and forthright articulation of Princeton's views on the key doctrines of the Presbyterian Church. Believing that there "can be no solid foundation for theological opinion, but the original text of Scripture fairly interpreted," Hodge's commentary set out to anchor the central doctrines of the church to their biblical foundations.[8] With these doctrinal justifications in mind, Hodge specifically included a section in each chapter called "Doctrines," where he matched specific verses with the Christian doctrines they supported.

Knowing the doctrinal stakes that were in play as the rival commentaries of Stuart and Barnes circulated among American readers, Hodge dedicated himself to the careful explication of passages that addressed the doctrines most under debate. In so doing, he followed Stuart's lead and paid the most attention—over 11 percent of his commentary's total content—to explicating the Book of Roman's fifth chapter.[9] In the doctrinal war being waged by competing Romans commentaries, the most contested ground was the book's fifth chapter, particularly its twelfth verse: "Wherefore, as by one man sin entered into the world, and death by sin; and so death passed upon all men, for that all have sinned" (King James Version).

As in so many theological controversies, this one centered on a matter of emphasis. Hodge stressed the phrase "by one man" in his interpretation of Romans 5, linking Adam to the guilt, suffering, and death that he passed down to every human through his choice to eat the apple Eve had offered him. Stuart and Barnes offered interpretations that shifted the weight of the passage to emphasize the last three words of the verse: "all have sinned." In opposition to Hodge and the more traditional Calvinists for whom he spoke, they stressed it was the moral choices made by each individual that make them liable to God's judgment for their disobedience.

The idea of moral choice proved pivotal for both Stuart and Barnes, who placed far greater importance on the moral sense posited by Scottish Common Sense Realism than did Hodge. Stuart, in particular, made it clear that his brand of Scottish Realism differed from that held by Hodge. While Hodge stressed the philosophy's evidentiary aspects, Stuart focused on its moral teachings, holding that humans were endowed with a moral sense that allowed them to tell intuitively the difference between moral and immoral actions.[10] Such a finely tuned moral sense thus made humans more capable of making moral choices and more culpable for the choices they did make. Hodge was not nearly as willing to give totally depraved humans such intuitive power. In his mind, only the Holy Spirit could enlighten the heart to help men and women choose what is good.

Hodge was concerned with more than Stuart's faith in humanity's moral intuition. He saw Stuart's thinking as not only flawed in its moral metaphysics with its overly optimistic view of humanity, but in the exegetical conclusions it drew from the biblical text. A closer examination of Stuart's and Hodge's commentaries and their different scholarly approaches reveals the two paths American antebellum biblical scholars were beginning to pursue as the science of biblical interpretation took its own distinct form in the United States. Taken together, these two commentaries provide a window into a watershed moment in American biblical criticism when the effects of European scholasticism in general, and German biblical criticism in particular, can be seen as fostering a new, more critical age in the American study of the Bible.[11]

Stuart used his commentary on Romans as a chance to display his profound appreciation for many aspects of European biblical criticism. His commentary bears all the marks of serious European philological scholarship, which put a premium on accurately translating the core text and then attempting to recover the meaning the text's words held in their original context. Stuart's work is full of linguistic and grammatical comments focused on helping to elucidate larger doctrinal points. Readers might have found themselves overmatched, or simply bored, by Stuart's intense interest in language and its historical context, but they were left in no doubt that they were in the presence of a mind who had studied the Bible and biblical scholarship for decades.

Hodge was also serious about his scholarship, and his philological training is evident throughout his work. It is significant that both scholars put a high premium on offering their readers the best translation possible of the most ancient (and therefore accurate) version of the text available. Although both men paid careful attention to matters of philology, Hodge did not make such language study the most important exegetical tool in the construction of his argument. Unlike Stuart, who constantly keyed his analytical insights, and thus his exegetical conclusions, to the translation of certain words and phrases, Hodge used church doctrines as defined in the confessional statements of the Reformation as the bedrock upon which he chose to interpret Paul's text.

Hodge's son and biographer, Archibald Alexander, readily admitted that his father favored the church confessional tradition over philology when it came to his explications of scripture.[12] Rather than explain a text by examining it at the level of original words and phrases, Hodge was at his best when he rose to a more panoramic view of a passage or book, concentrating on the larger contours and meaning of a biblical writer's argument. Benjamin Warfield, the Princeton theologian who came to dominate the Seminary's intellectual life after Hodge's death, wrote of his predecessor that "few men could equal" Hodge is capturing a passage's "general flow of thought," but he had little patience for "the technicalities of Exegesis" and was guided more often by "theological predilection" than an attempt to struggle with the finer philological points of a text.[13]

What Warfield characterized as "theological predilection" was Hodge's firm commitment to Reformed theology as interpreted in the Westminster Confession and through such established figures as Augustine and Calvin. Stuart on the other hand placed a higher premium on human reason and the advancements in biblical historical criticism and language. He hated simply accepting lines of reasoning that were grounded in centuries of tradition and were credentialed by such a pedigree. He wished to struggle with the passages themselves in order to recover their original meanings.

Because of his commitment to this method of philological investigation, Stuart was willing to change his view of a passage if his study led him to a new understanding of its meaning. Having published the first edition of his commentary on Romans in 1832, he published a revision of this commentary in 1835 largely in response to Hodge.[14] In this second edition, he expanded his treatment of the fifth chapter of the book in order to do specific battle with Hodge's views. Of particular interest here is how Stuart changed some of his theological positions between his first and second editions, having shifted his understanding of certain passages after further study.

The changes and corrections Stuart made in his second edition are probably less important than his willingness to change them at all. Stating in his second edition's introduction that "if there be any whose first impressions are always right and only right" they will probably find little reason to sympathize either with his method or its results, Stuart told his readers that he was far from satisfied with his first efforts of explicating Romans and had worked hard in his second edition to ascertain whether his first conclusions would "abide a thorough scrutiny" of a second look.[15] Some of his language work and conclusions had, in fact, not survived the scrutiny, and Stuart made what he considered to be the appropriate changes in his second edition. In so doing, Stuart modeled an evolutionary view of biblical exegesis where opinions might change on substantive issues as better source materials and methods of study became available to scholars.

Because Hodge put a higher premium on the interpretations of traditional, accepted authorities, he was far less flexible than Stuart on the meaning of various biblical texts. This approach also made Hodge's theological prejudices more immediately apparent than Stuart's. In explicating passages and defending doctrines such as imputation, Hodge was willing to cite a plethora of historical sources—but only those who agreed with his point of view. He did not introduce at length, nor argue, with materials that were not in line with his doctrinal stances. When their differing degrees of philological work were peeled away, it became clear through their argumentation that Stuart hated a priori understandings of a passage, while Hodge depended heavily upon them.

It is this difference between the two scholars that proved representative of the diverging paths of American biblical scholarship that lay ahead. Stuart represented an openness to new lines of theological thinking, even strands of German biblical criticism, while Hodge remained firmly ensconced in the traditional biblical views taught by leaders of the Reformation and their disciples. It is important to note, however, that both the commentaries of Hodge and Stuart show just how much European biblical scholarship was being taken seriously in America. German biblical criticism was pushing American biblical interpreters to new levels of historical and philological sophistication in their scholarship. Hodge and Stuart become representative touch points for how different biblical scholars responded these approaches. They both acknowledged the importance of language and history in their work, but in the end Hodge was far more tied to the confessional scholastic tradition than was Stuart. While Stuart attempted to mix European scholarly insights into his method of studying the scriptures, Hodge used his considerable training and keen analytical mind to make his commentary on Romans a model of American biblical scholarship in the confessional tradition.

With the release of his commentary on Romans, Hodge had turned a corner. As important and influential as his work with the *Biblical Repertory* was, it was his Romans commentary that established him as not only one of the leading American biblical exegetes of the period, but one of the most important voices within the Presbyterian Church. One year after its release, he furthered the work's reach by offering an abridged version intended to be even easier to use for lay readers. So popular were Hodge's commentary and its abridgement that they appeared in sixteen editions before the Civil

War. In 1866, Hodge returned to revise the commentary one last time, paying even greater attention to the book's fifth chapter and its relationship to the doctrines of imputation and Original Sin. The commentary also gave him an international reputation as the Monod brothers worked to see the volume translated into French in 1841.[16] Through his Romans commentary, Hodge had established himself as one of the key spokesman for conservative Calvinism both in the United States and Europe.

24

CRIPPLED IN BODY, BUT NOT IN MIND

Hodge's work on Romans marked the culmination of an intensely prolific period in his life. Before he published his commentary, his abridged version of that commentary, and his study guide on Romans for Sunday Schools, all of which appeared in 1835 and 1836, Hodge had also published nearly twenty sizeable articles for the *Repertory*. Oddly, even amid his formidable teaching responsibilities and his impressive publishing endeavors, Hodge could not escape the feeling that he had "as yet done little or nothing."[1] His characteristic optimism persisted, but nagging feelings of inadequacy increasingly plagued these years. Life was short. Was he making the most of the gifts and abilities God had given him?

Two events in the early 1830s combined to catalyze Hodge's more frequent periods of dour self-reflection. In the spring of 1832, his mother died suddenly. It happened so quickly that he was not even able to make the day-long trip to Philadelphia to be at her bedside before she expired. Ashbel Green, who now resided in Philadelphia, performed the funeral service. He had married Hodge's parents, and now he had buried them both.[2]

Hodge had grown apart from his mother in the last years of her life, complaining to his brother that he did not know how to "get near her" either emotionally or physically.[3] In part, the emotional distance between Hodge and his mother may have been a case of two similar people unable to find common ground. Their strong wills had clashed over such important issues as whom he should marry and whether he should go into the ministry, and upon his return from Europe, there seemed to be a greater than ever distance between them. She may have resented the way in which he had left his family behind for two years, or she may have felt abandoned herself by his excursion. It is also likely that their relationship grew more complicated as Dr. Alexander's influence over Hodge grew. His mother may have resented her diminishing role. In her later years, Mary Hodge leaned much more on Hugh, her responsible elder and certainly more proximate son. It is interesting to speculate that Hugh's late marriage was in part due to his close relationship to his mother. In any case, after his European tour, Mary showed a strong predilection to stay in Philadelphia near Hugh rather than make any extended trips to Princeton.

Hodge was further reminded of life's brevity when, in the same year his mother died, Asiatic cholera struck New England for the first time.[4] Arriving from Europe where the disease had killed nearly one hundred thousand people in France alone, this cholera strain initially appeared in Canada and then worked its way south to cities including New York and Philadelphia. Three thousand people died in New York before the disease eventually disappeared in the winter months of 1832. Several people in Princeton died of the disease, and both College and Seminary students were given leave to return home in the middle of the school term if they wished. Hodge quickly became active in tending the sick and did all in his power to research the best treatments for the disease. It was almost as if the Philadelphia yellow-fever epidemics, which had taken the life of his father, drove him to do all in his power to head off the terrible and deadly effects of a potentially devastating epidemic.

As he struggled with the disease's appearance in Princeton, Hodge wrote to his brother Hugh for information and advice.[5] Hodge and his brother had kept up a regular correspondence since Hodge's return from Europe, exchanging several letters each month, but the appearance of cholera significantly quickened the pace of their writing. During the worst of the epidemic, Hodge sometimes wrote Hugh as often as three times a week. The cholera epidemic played an important role in establishing Hugh as one of Philadelphia's leading physicians. Having served as a ship's surgeon on a voyage to Calcutta after finishing his medical training in 1818, Hugh gained a priceless first-hand knowledge of cholera in India. He brought his experience to bear with great effect when cholera broke out in Philadelphia in 1832.[6] Building on this success, a few years later Hugh was named Professor of Obstetrics and the Diseases of Women at the University of Pennsylvania's medical school. Hugh had arrived. With his medical practice and reputation firmly established, Hugh solidified his position in Philadelphia's more elite social circles by purchasing an impressive $28,000 residence on an affluent stretch of Philadelphia's Walnut Street.[7]

Hodge drew heavily upon his brother's expertise as he visited every victim of the disease he could find in Princeton. His voracious interest in the disease and its possible treatments showed that while Hodge had decided against a medical career, his interest in medicine continued unabated. The human body and its ills remained a lifelong fascination for him, and through his own extensive reading and boundless medical curiosity, he often proved more knowledgeable on various diseases and their treatments than Princeton's local physicians.

Figure 24.1 *Hugh L. Hodge*: Hugh Hodge was a pivotal figure in establishing the specialities of gynecology and obstetrics in the United States. His medical writings gained him an international reputation, and variations of his "Hodge Pessary," which he invented to treat various cervix conditions, are still in use today. [*Presbyterian Historical Society, Presbyterian Church (U.S.A) (Philadelphia, PA)*]

Hodge's interest in medicine was tested to its limits beginning in the spring of 1833 when, amid colds, fevers, and chest ailments, the leg condition that had irritated him since his teenage years became much more serious. By the summer, he had totally lost the use of the limb and was experiencing severe pain in his hip, groin, and knee. His failing health made him mindful once again of life's precarious nature and imbued his teaching and writing with a renewed sense of urgency and mission. He wished his life to count for something, so even amid his illnesses, Hodge worked at a feverish pace.

The inciting incident for his leg's collapse seems to have been a series of arduous fund-raising tours Hodge made in New York City during the winter and early spring months of 1833. He had spent hours walking great distances in the city as he solicited money to help build a new chapel for the Seminary.[8] The exertion proved too much for him, and the pain in his hip became so great that he soon found himself bedridden. In the coming weeks, he was transferred each morning with the aid of family and servants to the couch located in his study, where he would remain for the rest of the day. His bed was moved to a room next to his study, so that he need not climb his house's central stairs at any point during the day. For the next three years, Hodge hardly traveled ten steps from his house. He did, however, at times ride a horse or take trips in trains and carriages. As time passed, he grew strong enough to take longer excursions if they did not include much walking. He traveled upon occasion to Philadelphia to visit his brother and visited the Atlantic Ocean at places like Old Point Comfort, Virginia, and Cape May, New Jersey, with the hope that the salt water might somehow improve the condition of his debilitated limb.

Although we cannot be certain as to the exact nature of Hodge's leg condition, the evidence from his correspondence and diary entries indicates that he probably suffered from a congenital deformity in his right hip joint, which weakened his leg and created pain when it was overused. His extensive fund-raising tours in New York City probably aggravated his condition by creating the opportunity for a bacterial infection to nest in his deformed hip joint, resulting in his leg becoming first painful and then useless.

During his years as an invalid, Hodge held classes and wrote while sitting on a couch in his study with his leg up. He learned to write on a leather-covered board, which he held upon his breast with his left arm while he wrote with his right. In the winter months of 1834 and 1835, while in considerable pain, he completed his entire commentary on Romans by writing on this board while his leg lay in a steel splint.[9] Hodge so perfected this method of writing that he continued it long after he had recovered and only abandoned it twenty years later when his wife induced him to substitute a small table for his much-worn board.[10]

One catches a glimpse of Hodge's tendency toward the known, the established, and the functional in his hesitancy to give up his writing board in favor of a table. Not only in the area of doctrine, but in the area of behavior, Hodge demonstrated a lifelong penchant to be slow to abandon that which was familiar to him for something untested and new. In 1839, Hugh made a present of a chair to his brother.[11] At first, Hodge hesitated to move the chair into a prominent place in his study. Personifying his much-beloved couch upon which he had spent so many hours convalescing, he wrote his brother:

My old couch was still in its place where all my books & writing instruments were & the chair was obliged to stand on one side, until the couch had been regularly displaced from the office. As it had held its situation for six years without a rival, it manifested some reluctance to give place to the handsome stranger. At last I persuaded it to assume the post of honour & with new draping to pass itself off for a divan sofa with the promise that it should support all my distinguished visitors.[12]

This new chair soon became Hodge's favorite spot in his entire home. Until his death, he sat in it daily to write, tutor students, and receive visitors. For almost four decades, his visitors expected to find him sitting in his chair when they entered his study. When illness forced him to his bed just a few days before his death, Hodge sensed that he had sat in his chair for the last time and lamented the loss by telling his family: "this chair and I for forty year have been growing to each other very closely."[13]

His desire to stay with established patterns influenced not only his choice of furniture, but his choice of clothes. From his earliest days in Princeton until his death sixty years later and despite the encouragement of family, friends, and students, he continued to buy the same fashion of clothes at the same store. Although the store itself underwent numerous changes and several different owners, Hodge never failed to patronize it. In every aspect of his life, Hodge loved the familiar, commenting that he

Figure 24.2 *Hodge's Chair:* Over the course of four decades visitors to his study grew accustomed to seeing Hodge at work in his beloved chair with its accompanying ottoman. [*Special Collections, Princeton Theological Seminary Libraries*]

even surprised himself by how "fixed I get & disposed" to frequent only known "fixtures and localities."[14]

Throughout the 1830s, Hodge constantly conversed with his brother about his condition, soliciting his medical advice, as well as advice of family friends and other physicians. He tirelessly tried new treatments that varied in their character and intensity. At first, he rubbed his leg with iodine and salves. He then moved on to lancing procedures around the hip area. At one point, he even subjected himself to the "moxa," a procedure that burned his leg from his hip to his knee with actual fire.[15] Nothing worked.

As time passed, Hodge sought even more experimental treatments. So desperate did he become that he approached Joseph Henry, a science professor at Princeton College who later became the founding president of the Smithsonian Institution, with an idea. Henry had become internationally famous for his experiments with magnetism and electricity, so Hodge asked him to attach his leg to one of his mammoth electric batteries to see if the electric current might do something to revive his limb.[16] Henry acquiesced, but even this extreme treatment brought no change. Hodge's invitation to Henry, however, does offer a glimpse into his continued fascination with both medicine and science.[17]

Hodge eventually settled into an almost-motionless existence, but this did not deter him from continuing to search for a cure. His letters throughout the 1830s are full of comments about his engagement with new doctors, new drugs, and new treatments. He even made the trip to New York City to visit one of the city's most famous physicians, Alexander Stevens, a professor at New York's College of Physicians and a future president of the American Medical Association.[18] Stevens found Hodge's case to be fascinating, but told him not to expect to recover anytime soon. Later, Hodge embarked on a new set of treatments involving hot and cold bathing.[19] He toyed with the idea of returning to Europe to visit either the hot baths of London or the mineral springs of Baden, Germany, but eventually settled for constructing a large bathtub off the rear of his house, which he filled with heated water from a special boiler.[20] Still, his condition lingered.

One happy result of Hodge's confinement was how it created the opportunity for the formation of a small society of friends that gathered almost nightly in Hodge's study for after-dinner discussions on a wide range of topics from philosophy to politics to theology to science. If Hodge was not accessible to his colleagues in the usual and casual interactions which they enjoyed with each other throughout the day, such lost opportunities were more than compensated for by these evening gatherings. Faculty members from both the College and the Seminary became regular members of this informal and congenial group. Frequent attendees included Archibald Alexander, his son James Alexander, Samuel Miller, President James Carnahan of Princeton College, Albert Dod, John Maclean Jr., and Joseph Henry.[21]

Figure 24.3 *Joseph Henry:* Joseph Henry served for a time as a professor of natural philosophy at Princeton College, where A.A. Hodge became his favorite student and one-time lab assistant. In 1846, he was named the founding president of the Smithsonian Institution. Hodge's last public appearance was the prayer he offered at Henry's funeral in Washington D.C., an event that closed down the nation's government as the President, Congress and the Supreme Court adjourned in order to attend the ceremony. [*Presbyterian Historical Society, Presbyterian Church (U.S.A) (Philadelphia, PA)*]

Hodge's confinement to his study finally ended in 1836 when he once again found himself able to walk with the aid of a cane from his study to the classrooms in the Seminary's main hall. He was destined to use a cane the rest of his life, but he was able to make ever-longer excursions with its help. It was not until June 1843 that he was finally able to walk the half mile to the village of Princeton, a journey he noted in his daily memorandum book that he had not made "in ten years."[22]

While Hodge struggled in these years with the loss of his mother, a potential plague besetting Princeton, and his own debilitating lameness, he also enjoyed his first great phase of publishing productivity. Between the reputation he was gaining through his work on the *Biblical Repertory* and his commentary on Romans, Hodge had begun his steady ascent to prominence not only in his own denomination, but also in American Protestantism more generally. The late 1830s, however, would prove to be some of the most challenging years of his life as his growing national reputation and his position at the Seminary made him a key figure in the debates that threatened to tear American Presbyterianism asunder.

25

HOME LIFE

In November 1830, Hodge purchased six acres of land immediately west of the Seminary.[1] In the years to come, he would use this land to provide a home and grazing space for his horse, as well as to grow vegetables for his family. Hodge loved horses and farming. From his earliest days as a seminary instructor, he kept a horse and rode it regularly. He appreciated fine horses much like someone today might appreciate a fine automobile. He also read widely about livestock and farming and eagerly sought opportunities to converse with others who shared his interests. He liked nothing better than to take a special trip to inspect an animal that had acquired some degree of local renown and talk with its owner.

The six acres Hodge cultivated near his seminary home—and later the farm he bought a little over a mile away—provided him with blissful breaks from his heavily intellectual labors. In his usual systematic and carefully considered way, he oversaw the planting of his land and its daily care. He immersed himself in agricultural works that might be able to help refine his farming strategies and techniques. Every morning he recorded the temperature, the direction of the wind, and the weather in a ledger he kept so that he might better understand the connections between seasonal weather conditions and his crops.[2] He was proud of what he grew and was not above boasting that he produced more per square foot than any farm in the neighborhood. Those who knew him well commented that it is the only bragging they ever heard from his lips. He also built a greenhouse near his house, so that he might be able to grow plants less suited to Princeton's frigid winters such as lemon trees, as well as to cultivate certain flowers year-round like roses and camellias.[3]

As Hodge's land holdings expanded, so did his family. By 1840, he and Sarah had grown their family to include eight children. Between their six-acre farm and large family, the Hodges found themselves in great need of domestic help. At first, he and Sarah simply hired a string of domestic servants, but found it extremely difficult to find and retain dependable, affordable workers. Hodge's letters to Hugh abound with woeful tales of trying to find good help. In one particularly memorable case, the Hodges employed an Irish serving girl who turned out to be mentally unstable, a fact they discovered when she attempted to injure herself one night by jumping from their third-story garret window. Hodge said of the incident that it caused him the "most dreadful night I ever passed." The following day, he found a place for the girl in a home for the "deranged."[4]

Ultimately, in 1828 these labor struggles led the Hodges to purchase their first slave, Henrietta, at the cost of seventy-five dollars.[5] Another slave, Lena, would also come into their possession a few years later, most likely as part of his mother's estate upon her death.[6] In addition, the Hodges employed at least two other African American servants during the 1830s, John and Cato, although it is impossible to determine exactly whether they were slaves or simply wage laborers.[7]

In his decision to become a slave owner, Hodge showed himself to be a product of his upbringing, his associations, and the place where he lived. Along with his mother, many of those closest to Hodge owned slaves or came from slave-owning families. Archibald Alexander and Samuel Miller came from families who had owned slaves, and as late as 1830, Samuel Miller still owned a slave in Princeton.[8] Princeton was also a place which, although situated in the North, was particularly amenable to slavery. New Jersey had actually passed an emancipation law in 1804 that guaranteed freedom after a certain age to every person of African descent who was born after July 4, 1804. (Male slave children born after this date were freed at the age of twenty-five, and female slave children were freed at age twenty-one.) If you were born before this date, it was a master's choice whether or not to free a slave.[9] The effect of this law was that while slavery did not aggressively grow in New Jersey, it did remain a relatively stable institution long after its popularity had begun to recede in other Northern states.

If New Jersey was on a slow road to emancipation, Princeton was on a slower one. The 1830 federal census shows that Princeton had one of the highest concentrations of black residents in the state, and the social climate of the town reflected this figure. Both the College and the Seminary were highly tolerant of the institution, a fact probably closely linked to the College's longstanding ties to the South, a region whose economy and very culture had become inextricably tied to slavery in the wake of the wide adoption of the cotton gin after its invention in 1793.[10] Before the Civil War, Southern states provided about one-third of the College's student population and roughly one-tenth of the Seminary's.

It is easy to forget that as the United States entered the nineteenth century, three-quarters of the entire world's population was repressed in some form of physical slavery

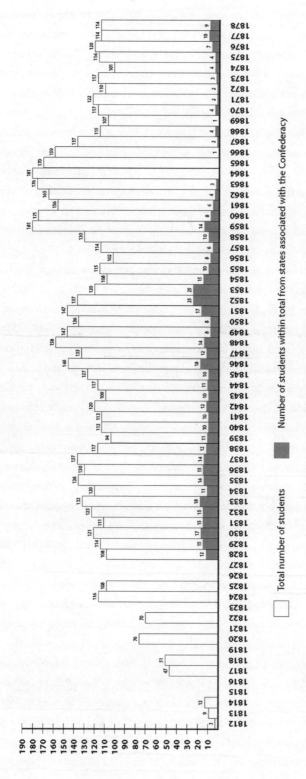

Princeton Theological Seminary Student Population

Number of students within total from states associated with the Confederacy

Total number of students

Figure 25.1   *Princeton Seminary Student Population*

or serfdom. At the height of the slave trade, close to eighty thousand Africans were transported annually to American shores.[11] As the historian Seymore Drescher has so aptly put it: "Freedom, not slavery, was the peculiar institution."[12] Such a slavery-soaked world began to change first in England and then in the United States around the turn of the nineteenth century, but in the early 1800s Princeton was still a place where slavery was a widely accepted and valued social institution. When he purchased slaves, Hodge was simply following his long-established pattern of embracing entrenched cultural traditions that he saw as not conflicting with scripture. As the issue of slavery became ever more contentious, Hodge would provide sophisticated biblical explanations of his slavery views, but when he made his first slave purchase in 1828, those around him saw the event as utterly unremarkable. In bringing a slave into his household, he was doing little more than establishing himself as one of Princeton's more prominent gentlemen who had the financial resources to not only own land, but a slave as well.

One needs to understand the premium Hodge put on the idea of personal improvement to understand accurately his relationship to his family, his household servants, and his slaves.[13] For Hodge, every aspect of life took on characteristics similar to those found in the Christian doctrine of sanctification, the gradual Spirit-led process of transforming a broken sinner into the image of Christ. With the end of divinely guided improvement in mind, Hodge made sure that both his slaves and hired servants had access to religious education and services. Later, when he employed Irish Catholic servant girls as cooks and nurses, he encouraged them to regularly attend mass.

Hodge's commitment to the linked ideas of sanctification and improvement can be seen in how he approached parenthood as well. He prayed daily with his family. Each morning at family devotions he had the entire family recite the Apostle's Creed and a creed of his own formulation. He then gathered them again each evening for prayer. Religion permeated the household in a way that was "always subconsciously felt," but it was not a topic of constant, overt conversation.[14] One of Hodge's grandsons described the atmosphere of the house as the most "sunny, genial, kindly and tolerant" he had ever experienced, with lively and "brilliant" talk of such things as books and music, farming and art.[15] Another grandson noted that the home was so full of "dignity and serenity, a hospitality and loving-kindness" that it stood as a haven where "friends and relatives and their children loved to congregate; where all found a boundless love and welcome."[16]

Hodge had the great gift as a parent of being able to set a tone of security, comfort, and assurance in his home. Believing less in corporal punishment than the power of influence, he once wrote Sarah that "[c]hildren's characters are formed more by the silent influence of example than by the best precept. . . . Let a child see the devout reverence of a Parent for God and divine things and he will feel that reverence too. Let us, my dear love, never forget that it is only by being good that we can hope to make our children good."[17] Hodge passionately believed that a good example was a child's best teacher.

Hodge also tied his notion of improvement to his children's educations. He constantly urged his children to be ever learning, no matter how gradual or small their intellectual or moral progress might be. Sarah, with her own impressive intellect, proved pivotal in the early education of the Hodges' five sons and three daughters. She had been well educated in her youth, and when Hodge was in Europe, she had visited chemistry lectures at the University of Pennsylvania and read widely concerning political events while she lived with Mary Hodge in Philadelphia.[18] She passed on her voracious intellectual curiosity to her children. When her children reached the age of four, she began teaching them Isaac Watt's infant catechism and hymns. She instructed each of her children at home during their grammar-school years, and she carefully prepared the boys with Hodge's help for the more advanced academies and colleges they would enter as they grew older.[19]

Hodge also used his extreme sociability as a means toward family improvement. He hosted countless "simple evening parties" where he invited guests to share their varied life experiences.[20] He made a habit of allowing his children free and constant access to him, even to the point that he added springs to his study doors while he was lame and couch-bound, so that the doors might swing closed behind the little feet that constantly entered and exited the room.[21] Because one of his study's doors led to the outside, his study became a kind of thoroughfare, but he never discouraged his children from using it as such.

Hodge was careful to make sure he treated all of his children as individuals and worked diligently to nurture their varying personalities. Archie, Hodge's eldest, loved animals and kept numerous rabbits as a youth. Hodge seemed to take as much interest in them as Archie did.[22] When his second son, Caspar Wistar, showed an inclination toward music, Hodge once again took up the flute he had played while a youth. He then bought a violin for Caspar, and became so intrigued by the instrument that he learned to play it himself.[23] And when Mary, his oldest daughter, showed a keen appetite for reading and a love of Latin, Hodge encouraged her by helping her acquire books and augmenting her language lessons.[24]

The values of family and improvement that so undergirded Hodge's outlook on life caused him tremendous pain in the 1830s as he saw his beloved Presbyterian Church torn apart by a series of internecine struggles. As he first tried to mediate these conflicts and then was ultimately forced to choose sides, he struggled with what it meant to be a family at a denominational level. He saw neither familial love nor sanctifying improvement in much of what tore American Presbyterianism apart in these years, and their absence rent his heart. In the midst of his denomination's struggles, however, he eventually established himself as one of the most powerful voices in bringing about a division he had sought so mightily to avoid, yet ultimately bowed to as inevitable.

26

THE COMING STORM

Hodge had hoped that his commentary on Romans might have done more to stop the growth of New School thought within the Presbyterian ranks, but he had not written the commentary as a declaration of war against New School men and what he saw as their dangerous Taylorite positions. It was a work emblematic of Princeton Seminary's commitment in the early 1830s to reasoned and civil engagement with theological issues that faced their denomination as a whole. The Seminary's faculty wished their school to serve the entire denomination, so although their own theological leanings may have been Old School, they worked hard not to alienate their New School brethren.[1] Hodge joined Drs. Alexander and Miller in a belief that little was to be gained by sowing seeds of theological division when many of the differences between the Old and New School were matters of degree and form rather than wholesale doctrinal disputes. The Princeton faculty went to great lengths to stress what they believed to be of theological importance without overtly taking sides on specific issues.

The Seminary faculty's middle-of-the-road approach made the Princeton faculty few friends in either camp. Archibald Alexander eldest son, James, commented on the vexed nature of the strategy in writing a friend: "There certainly is such a thing as righteous moderation, and those who have practiced it have, as far as I know, in every age stood between two fires, incurring the wrath of both sides."[2] The Old School faction was particularly upset with the Seminary. They knew of the faculty's theological predilections and wished for more-forceful support. A particular sore spot was the fact that Hodge and his compatriots refused to make the *Repertory* an overtly Old School organ in the midst of the growing controversies.

The Seminary's middle course became even more problematic when, in 1834, several Old School men under the leadership of Ashbel Green and Robert Jefferson

Breckinridge—a feisty Kentuckian whose older brother, John Breckinridge, would become Professor of Pastoral Theology at Princeton Seminary one year later—met in Philadelphia and drafted a public declaration to the churches known as the "Act and Testimony." The document set forth matters of faulty doctrine and misuses of denominational governing practice that the Old School thought threatened the very integrity of orthodox American Presbyterianism.

Thirty-seven ministers and almost as many elders originally signed the "Act and Testimony," and then circulated it among Presbyterian churches so that "all the friends of sound doctrine and of Presbyterian order" could add their names to the document.[3] Not only did those of the New School refuse to sign it, but many Old Schoolers declined as well, seeing it as an unauthorized test of orthodoxy. More-moderate Old School men worried that this manifesto might divide rather than unify Presbyterianism, and Ashbel Green soon reinforced these fears by openly declaring that the "Act and Testimony" had been designed to purify the Presbyterian Church. He did not hide the fact that such purification might well mean the secession of the more conservative elements from the denomination.[4]

Hodge rose as a vocal advocate for a more measured approach to addressing infirmities found in current American Presbyterian doctrine and governance when he wrote a two-part critique of the "Act and Testimony" for the *Repertory*. In the essay, he was careful to praise the Old School men who had written the document for their "tone of solemn earnestness, which carries to every heart the conviction of their sincerity, and their sense of the importance, as well as the truth, of the sentiments which they advance."[5] He then goes into painstaking detail on why many worthy men on either side of the controversy could not in good conscience sign the document. Hodge had two primary concerns. First, he argued that men of sound doctrine may find the "Act and Testimony" offensive because it stood as an "extra-constitutional method" to number the orthodox and cast out the heretical.[6] Second, he listed various changes to Presbyterian polity and policy advocated in the document that would be more properly pursued through the established channels of change found in the Presbyterian Constitution and General Assembly. In Hodge's mind, the document attempted to force change through improper means. Hodge could entertain that change might be necessary, but he was convinced that the "Act and Testimony" was not the best way of pursuing such change.

Hodge attempted to walk a middle ground as he used the *Repertory* to provide an extended critique of the "Act and Testimony." Many Old School critics had already written off Princeton Seminary as hopelessly lukewarm in its advocacy of true orthodoxy, and some had even begun to point to the new Presbyterian seminary in Pittsburgh as the new bastion of conservative Presbyterian thinking.[7] Hodge's own position was even more embattled when Robert Breckinridge announced that Hodge's criticism of the "Act and Testimony" astonished him since he claimed that he consulted with Hodge while composing the document.[8]

Hodge had been in Philadelphia before embarking on a therapeutic trip to the sea for his lame leg when Robert Breckinridge visited him to solicit his opinion on the document. Far from providing ideas for the "Act and Testimony," Hodge had raised serious reservations about drafting such a document.[9] Breckinridge's very public sense of betrayal excited so much Old School ill-feeling toward Hodge and the Seminary that two close friends of Hodge, Albert Dod and John Maclean Jr., felt it necessary to publish letters in Philadelphia's *The Presbyterian*, the most powerful Old School periodical, declaring that Hodge had only given the most general advice and had no hand in actually writing the document.[10]

The vitriolic tenor of this uproar, and the strong measures taken to counteract any impression that Hodge had a part in writing the "Act and Testimony," shows just how tense relations between the Seminary's faculty and many of the Old School's leaders had become.[11] As events proceeded, Hodge found himself more and more at odds with Green and his conservative cohort, who he had begun to call "Ultras" because of their extreme and unbending views on Presbyterian orthodoxy.[12] Hodge saw many of their actions as needlessly divisive, and he continued to reach out to the broadest possible spectrum of Presbyterian pastors and congregants to avert any type of denominational schism.

The "Act and Testimony" did not bring about the Old School's goal of a purer and more orthodox denomination, but it did clearly establish just how wide the fissures were growing between various Presbyterian factions. Tensions continued to flare around particular issues in the mid-1830s, one of the most pronounced being revivalism. The fact that different theologies circulated with regularity among Presbyterians found clear expression in 1835 when the great revivalist Charles Finney, who served as the head pastor for the large Second Presbyterian Church in New York City (Chantam Street Chapel), decided to withdraw his Presbyterian ordination and align himself instead with the more theologically accommodating Congregationalists.

A lawyer who had been raised in upstate New York, Finney had undergone a dramatic conversion experience when he was nearly thirty years old that led him to dedicate his life to the ministry. In 1824, he became an ordained Presbyterian minister and his preaching quickly sparked a number of revivals in upstate New York. His revival activity was so successful that he began to lecture and publish on his methods, which had come to be called "New Measures."

Finney had not cut his New Measures from whole cloth, but instead had made a close study of many Methodist practices. So impressed was Finney with the Methodists' evangelistic fervor that he exhorted everyone to follow their lead "or the devil will have the people, except what the Methodists can save."[13] Finney freely adopted and adapted

Figure 26.1 *Charles Finney*: Charles Finney began his ministry career as a Presbyterian. During his ordination process, he confessed that he had never even read the Westminster Confession of Faith. Such a cavalier attitude toward the confessional tradition and his high view of human ability forever put him outside the pale of what Hodge considered to be orthodox Protestant belief. Eventually Finney began to espouse a belief in human perfectionism, a view Hodge considered utterly ridiculous. [*Allen Memorial Art Museum, Oberlin College, Ohio; Gift of Lewis Tappan to Oberlin College, 1858.*]

many of their more controversial practices, including letting women pray in public, praying for people by name, entering towns without the permission of the local pastors, and using something called the "Anxious Bench" where people thought to be on the verge of conversion were seated and intensely preached at during revival meetings.[14]

Finney switched his denominational allegiances because of his recent appointment as Professor of Theology at the newly formed Oberlin College in Ohio. As a Congregational minister, Finney knew he would have far more latitude to pursue his pro-revivalist, pro-slavery activities without Presbyterianism's more restrictive forms of denominational oversight and accountability. In the same year he moved to Oberlin, he published his immensely popular *Lectures on Revivals in Religion*, a book that not only spelled out his own revivalist views but also served as a stinging condemnation of his former denomination. Finney's theology on revival exalted human agency far above the comfort level of many Old Schoolers. He preached that revivals were "not a miracle, or dependent on a miracle in any sense," but were "purely philosophical result[s] of the right use of the constituted means."[15] What Finney meant by "philosophical" here we might translate today as "scientific." He saw revivals as quasi-mechanical in nature. If one created the proper environment, revivals would arise. People, not God, thus became the initiator in God's redemptive plan. For many Presbyterians, Finney inappropriately exalted the power of both revivalist preachers and the sinners they were seeking to save.

Finney's teaching put him far outside the Princeton theological fold, and his views were radical enough to unsettle even many New School Presbyterians. As troubling as his theology might be, his opinions of Presbyterians caused even more rancor. He turned his considerable rhetorical gifts to denigrating the evangelistic efforts of the Presbyterians, who he considered far too timid and dispassionate when it came to the activity of saving souls. Presbyterians, he declared, lacked emotional fire and conviction in their preaching. He called for them to emulate the Methodists and Baptists who addressed the unconverted with sermons laced with persuasive emotion.[16] Finney was even more damning when it came to Presbyterian polity. He mused that Presbyterian leaders spent precious time arguing over trivial issues rather than saving souls. His view of the Presbyterian leadership was so low that he proclaimed that their "contentions and janglings are so ridiculous, so wicked, so outrageous, that no doubt there is a jubilee in hell every year, about the time of the meeting of the General Assembly."[17]

Finney's teachings gained wide currency among diverse Protestant constituencies, and they put considerable pressure on the Princeton Seminary faculty to answer his claims. Soon after Finney released his *Lectures*, Hodge turned to the *Repertory's* inner editorial circle and asked recent Seminary graduate Albert Dod to answer Finney's teachings on revival. Dod, a mathematical genius who had decided to take an appointment as Princeton College's Professor of Mathematics over a pastoral position elsewhere, offered just such an answer in an almost-one-hundred-page essay that ran in two consecutive issues of the *Repertory*. In a withering and unrelenting critique, Dod called Finney's *Lectures* "mainly, if not entirely, composed of exploded errors and condemned heresies."[18] Aside from countless instances of propounding wrong views on such key doctrines as regeneration and Original Sin, Dod was particularly upset with what he saw as Finney's unbelievable arrogance. For Dod, to read Finney was to encounter a man who thought he alone had not bent his knee to Baal. Finney wrote as if the "whole world is wrong, and he proposes to set them right."[19]

It would be a terrible mistake, however, to take Dod's essay as a signal that the Seminary's faculty had no interest or investment in the waves of revivalism that swept back and forth across the country prior to the Civil War. In fact, the Seminary faculty had a long established sympathy with revivals. Revivals had been instrumental in the conversions of Archibald Alexander and Hodge, and both men encouraged an openness to revivalism even if they had serious disagreements with Taylor's New Haven Theology or Finney's New Measures. As one might expect, their approach to revivals was more measured, intellectual, and subdued in comparison to the emotional fervor so favored by Finney and the Methodists.

Dr. Alexander was a much-sought-after speaker in various churches that felt they were primed for revival activity, and he regularly lectured Seminary students on the topic of revivals. His tempered approach to revival activity became a standard throughout much of the Presbyterian Church. Many New Schoolers appreciated Alexander's wisdom concerning revivals, although they often felt that he was not as aggressive as he might be in adopting some of the more popular means of bringing sinners to a realization of their fallen state. Alexander taught that more overt and aggressive conversion techniques could lead to a false confidence in the converted and often led to conversions of short duration. Instead, he argued a line of reasoning that Hodge wholeheartedly adopted, which held that true revivals exhorted "sinners to be found in the use of God's appointed means; that is, to be diligent in attendance on the word, and at the throne of grace. . . . While they are reading, or hearing, or meditating, or praying, God may, by his Holy Spirit, work faith in their hearts."[20] For Alexander as for Hodge, the work of conversion was God's work. The revivalist preacher and the exhorted sinner were absolutely dependent on God's initiative and guiding hand.

Although differences in theology lay at the root of many of Presbyterianism's conflicts, there were a number of other divisive topics that fueled the conflict between the Old and New school factions in the mid-1830s.[21] One notable issue in this regard was the difference in opinion over Presbyterianism's relationship with the nation's growing voluntary evangelical societies. By the 1830s, a number of societies had arisen in the United States to help spread the Christian Gospel. In the broadest sense, these societies came to be known as the "Evangelical united front."[22] Each society had a specific mandate. The American Bible Society (1816) focused on making the Bible accessible to everyone in the United States, while the American Tract Society (1825) produced thousands of religious tracts and books to be distributed both nationally and internationally. The American Sunday School Union (1817) focused on the religious education of both the old and young, and the American Home Mission Society (1826) concerned itself with evangelizing the sparsely churched western frontier. A host of other societies attacked other areas of American society with the goal of penetrating it with the message of Christ.

As these societies grew in power and influence, many Presbyterians began to question whether such societies were the best way to attempt cultural and religious change. The Old School was particularly concerned with this issue because it worried that the interdenominational nature of many of these ventures gutted any hope of a truly orthodox Gospel message reaching the masses. In their quest to link the efforts of various denominational bodies, these societies had to make theological compromises that were acceptable to Arminian Methodists as well as Calvinist Presbyterians, and many in the Old School found this type of lowest-common-denominator theological union repulsive.[23] They were particularly aggravated by the non-Calvinist views such societies held and promulgated. As they saw these societies trample on some of their most sacred theological tenets, conservative Presbyterians began to advocate a withdrawal from such societies. They argued that it was far better to pour the denomination's resources into its own churches and boards, which they could be confident would carry a properly Presbyterian concept of the Gospel to Americans.

Alongside the troubling theological elasticity of these societies, there was also the concern that they were not ecclesiastical bodies in the same sense that denominations were. It was on this issue that Hodge offered one of the most cogent and well-reasoned critiques of voluntary societies and the dangers they posed to the Presbyterian Church in particular and denominational churches more generally. In an article he wrote for the *Repertory*, Hodge responded to a proposal set before the 1836 General Assembly that Presbyterian boards should join together with societies that shared common areas of interest and activity.[24] Hodge focused his response mainly on the relationship of the American Home Missionary Society to the Assembly's own Board of Foreign Missions.[25]

Hodge carefully made the case that societies were certainly a viable way to engage the wider culture with the Gospel, but societies had certain limitations because they were not the Church proper. Specifically, they were well within their bounds and immensely useful in certain cases that did not involve the direct use of trained ministers. Particularly noteworthy in this regard were the Bible and tract societies and the ways in which they used lay people to spread divinely inspired literature.[26] In the end, however, although he did not oppose the existence of voluntary societies, Hodge thought it of the utmost importance that such societies should not be confused with the actual Protestant Church. Unlike denominations, voluntary societies had no authority to train and ordain clergy or discipline their membership. Keeping these distinctions in mind, Hodge argued that societies often posed a threat to the doctrinal and political integrity of denominational bodies because they touched the lives of denominational congregants without their denomination having any control over their activities.[27]

Hodge's complaints against societies centered on the Presbyterian point of view that it was the denominational, ordaining body that had the right to determine "the place or character" of a missionary's labor.[28] Such direction was primarily the purview of the presbytery that had trained and ordained the missionary. Ministers might be financed by a given society for a specific mission, but ultimately those ministers were responsible to their ordaining denominational body. Hodge argued that to place a society before his denomination's governing structure was "a practical subversion of the whole system of our church."[29]

Such a stance—which Old Schoolers readily embraced—would have particularly important consequences in the next few years for the New School, which was more open to the work of voluntary societies. Large numbers of Presbyterian ministers were supported by voluntary associations, particularly on the western frontier. The American Home Missionary Society alone supported almost half of the Presbyterian ministers located west of the Alleghenies.[30] As the Old School moved against voluntary societies by seeking to emphasize the Presbyterian denomination's own Boards of Education and Foreign Missions, many Presbyterian ministers in the West were forced to make decisions regarding their denominational allegiances. When the Old and New School Presbyterians finally split their denomination in 1837, many ministers funded by the American Home Missionary Society sided with the New School simply because of its more supportive attitude toward the voluntary societies of the "Evangelical united front," an ecumenical stance that the Old School in no way shared.[31]

Hodge's own advocacy of limiting the power of voluntary societies had two results. It moved him closer to the Old School, although in 1836 he was still carefully attempting to maintain a middle ground on key issues between the denomination's rival factions. It also set the course for a kind of Presbyterian insularity for which he and the Old School would become famous in the comings years. In seeking to protect orthodoxy and denominational autonomy, Hodge had embarked on a type of anti-ecumenicalism that would mark Princeton Seminary and limit the influence of the very orthodoxy he so dearly wanted embraced by every American.

27

THE SLAVERY QUESTION

While fissures were widening among Presbyterians on the issues of revivalism and voluntary societies, yet another divisive issue became every more urgent as the 1830s progressed: slavery. The issue came to the fore in the critical events of August 1831 when a Virginian slave by the name of Nat Turner led a slave insurrection that eventually led to the death of fifty-seven white men, women, and children. What quickly became known as "Turner's Rebellion" sent shockwaves of terror throughout the South. Hodge carefully followed news of Turner's exploits and their aftermath. At one point, he wrote his brother that "I heard today that fresh murders had been committed and that one planter had called up four of his slaves and caused them to be shot without the preface of a trail and that it was feared that a dreadful massacre of blacks might yet occur."[1] Turner's Rebellion proved to be a turning point for the South as whites throughout the region became increasingly wary of any voice critical of slavery, fearing that such sentiments might spur slaves toward similar killing sprees.[2]

In the same year as Turner's rampage, the abolitionist activist William Lloyd Garrison began publishing his influential and inflammatory antislavery newspaper, *The Liberator*. Once a man who had believed in gradual emancipation, Garrison had become an ardent "abolitionist," a term that came to signify someone committed to the immediate and complete emancipation of every American slave. In 1832, Garrison founded the New-England Anti-Slavery Society and the next year he co-founded the American Anti-Slavery Society.[3] Using these organizations and the rhetorical power of *The Liberator*, Garrison became the most visible crusader against slavery in the United States.[4]

American Presbyterians felt the effects of the Garrison's fervor. In 1837, a pro-slavery mob murdered Elijah P. Lovejoy, a Princeton Seminary graduate, in Alton, Illinois, because of his Garrisonian leanings and the antislavery newspaper he published.[5]

Hodge took Lovejoy's death particularly hard, writing Hugh: "The Alton riot is a dreadful affair. Poor Lovejoy was one of our students, whom we all knew very well. . . . A few more such incidents and we shall have a civil war."[6]

For Hodge and his fellow Presbyterians, the Alton riot was yet one more chapter in the denomination's long and vexed relationship with slavery. As early as 1787, the Presbyterian Synods of New York and Philadelphia (the precursor to the General Assembly) drew up and published a declaration stating they did "highly approve the general principles in favour of universal liberty that prevail in America, and the interest which many of the states have taken in promoting the abolition of slavery."[7] Thus, Presbyterians stated their interest in abolishing slavery, but offered no timetable for such abolition. Not a great deal resulted from this statement of general principals.

The Presbyterian leadership once again revisited the issue when the 1818 General Assembly universally recommended that every Presbyterian "use the most prudent measures, consistent with the interests and the state of civil society . . . to procure eventually the final abolition of slavery in America."[8] The 1818 pronouncement became Presbyterianism's most famous condemnation of slavery, but its very wording showed that it was a product of the denomination's long-conflicted feelings concerning the issue.[9] Since 1787, Presbyterians had declared slavery to be immoral and a hideous violation of the laws of God, but they also held that immediate emancipation would be a grievous wrong to both slave and master. In both the 1787 and 1818 documents, Presbyterians declared that slaves needed to be better educated in order to make proper use of their freedom. To free them without the proper preparation would likely lead former slaves to "destroy themselves and others."[10]

So, although the Presbyterian Church was theoretically behind abolition, it advocated a slow road toward that goal. This gradualist approach made the denomination's stance acceptable to slave owners and non–slave owners alike. Slave owners faced no timetable for freeing their slaves, and non–slave owners could convince themselves that something was indeed happening as the General Assembly encouraged its slave-owning members to do all in their power to educate their slaves to prepare them for a vaguely defined future moment of freedom.

The role of ex-slaves in the larger society was a primary concern for many Presbyterians who held to the period's accepted wisdom that whites and black could never peacefully and productively coexist. Archibald Alexander himself believed that it would take "a thousand years" before blacks and whites could live harmoniously in the same society.[11] Because he believed that an integrated society was doomed to failure, Alexander joined a number of Presbyterian leaders who became enthusiastic supporters of the American Colonization Society (ACS), a voluntary association founded in 1816 to relocate slaves either to some defined, segregated region within the United States or return them to Africa. Eventually, the ACS focused all its energies to relocating slaves to Liberia, a private colony on Africa's Ivory Coast that the society had founded with the explicit purpose of returning ex-slaves to their mother country.[12] The ACS thus made it possible for Presbyterians to entertain an idea of emancipation without the complication of actually being forced to live in the same society with ex-slaves.

The ACS leadership was not only full of Presbyterians, but the society had deep ties to Princeton as well. The ACS had held its first public meeting in Princeton's First Presbyterian Church in 1816, and Drs. Alexander and Miller took an early and heartfelt interest in the society that lasted their entire lives.[13] Both men served as auxiliary officers in the New Jersey chapter of the ACS as did Hodge later on.[14] So committed was Alexander to the society's vision that late in life he produced the first major history of the society entitled *Colonization on the Western Coast of Africa*.[15]

While colonization seemed like a viable solution when the ACS was first founded, it was a solution that soon proved untenable. It quickly became apparent that ex-slaves could not be transported to Africa at a rate that even matched the birthrate of new slaves in America, much less accommodate adult slaves who might be freed.[16] Added to the logistical challenges of deporting freed slaves was the simple fact that many ex-slaves had no desire to leave the United States. They did not wish to travel to a completely unknown country with nothing more than promises about what might await them there.

In the midst of these rising doubts about the efficacy of the ACS, certain Presbyterian leaders began to advocate emancipation strategies disentangled from efforts to establish colonies of ex-slaves in Africa. Some even saw the ACS as a stumbling block toward eventual emancipation by leading people to waste their energy on a scheme that could never resolve the country's slavery question.[17] Perhaps not surprisingly, New Schoolers with their more egalitarian ethics and greater confidence in human ability and the social agendas that accompanied such confidence stood in the vanguard of Presbyterians interested in bypassing strategies of distant colonization. Not as bound by traditional modes of thinking on theological and social issues, the New School proved more open to radical solutions to the slavery question.[18]

As the 1830s progressed, several prominent antislavery New School voices became ever louder and more insistent. Albert Barnes and Charles Finney preached and wrote extensively on the urgent need to abolish slavery. Finney went so far as to declare "that slavery is, pre-eminently, the *sin of the Church*," and that the spread of the Christian Gospel would go "no farther and faster than the church take right ground upon the subject."[19] Along with individual voices, more coordinated efforts arose at the level of the General Assembly as various New School constituencies repeatedly submitted petitions and resolutions on the slavery issue in an attempt to move the Assembly beyond its gradualist abolitionist positions of 1787 and 1818.

An early and powerful locus of fervent Presbyterian antislavery sentiment was located in the Chillocothe Presbytery of southern Ohio.[20] The Chillocothe Presbytery took such a strong stand on slavery that it forbade its slave-owing congregants to take communion and threatened them with expulsion from the Presbyterian Church if they did not repent. The land encompassed by this presbytery became one of the great thoroughfares for the underground railroad in the years leading up to the Civil War as an estimated fifty thousand fugitive slaves passed through its boundaries on their way farther north.[21]

The Chillocothe Presbytery made its views known at the national level by not only sending an unceasing stream of petitions and resolutions to the General Assembly, but to Congress as well. Congress grew so weary of the Chillocothe Presbyterians that it ordered a gag rule on any further correspondence from them, a move that the General Assembly imitated. In 1835, however, in a sign that the New School was gaining power, one set of Chillocothe resolutions made it to the floor of the General Assembly. The resolutions were read and Old School members quickly maneuvered to have the resolutions referred to a committee to be considered and reported on the following year. Samuel Miller had tried to block the resolutions from the floor of the Assembly, but failing that, he got himself named to the committee which would report back to the General Assembly the following year.

As Miller worked with his committee to prepare a report for the next General Assembly, Hodge sat down to help his colleague with what promised to be a fractious Assembly debate by writing an extended article on slavery for the *Biblical Repertory*. Hodge sensed that New Schoolers were coming to view the 1836 General Assembly as their opportunity to push forward a more aggressive denominational agenda for emancipation, and so Hodge believed that writing a *Repertory* article to clarify the theological issues at stake was "the best service" he could render his fellow Presbyterians.[22] His overriding concern was denominational unity.[23] Knowing full well just how little common ground existed between the Old and New Schools on the slavery issue, he wanted to do all within his power to keep the two sides from drifting further apart.

The coming Assembly discussions on slavery threatened the denomination's unity on a regional front as well. Hodge was aware that there was a growing fear among Southern Presbyterians concerning what their Northern counterparts might do when it came to the issue of slavery. Anything but a commitment to gradual emancipation was suspect to the majority of Southern Presbyterians. If the Chillocothe Resolutions gained wide acceptance in the Assembly, the denomination could split regionally overnight. As their fears grew, Southern Presbyterians moved in ever greater numbers to ally themselves with those in the Old School who remained firmly behind the Assembly's prior statements on the issue of slavery.[24]

Hodge was also not blind to the implications the slavery question might have when it came to denominational support of Princeton Seminary. By the mid-1830s, the

New School had all but given up on Princeton, which they saw as tacitly—if not yet vocally—aligned with Old School views and practices. The New School's frustrations with the too traditional, and thus too moderate, stances of Princeton manifested themselves most forcefully in 1836 when several influential New School leaders helped found Union Theological Seminary in New York City, a school created to embody more-pronounced New School theological leanings and to function outside the control of the General Assembly.[25] It was impossible for Hodge and his fellow faculty members to take the founding of Union as anything other than a vote of "no confidence" on Princeton. Union posed a double danger: it threatened to take students away from Princeton and it threatened to institutionalize the theological fissures which already existed between the Old and New Schools.

The resulting essay, a piece he simply entitled "Slavery," was Hodge's first attempt to convey his thoughts on the slavery issue, a task he found exceedingly time-consuming and challenging. He wrote Hugh, "I had no fixed opinions when I began to write and therefore had to think the matter out for my own satisfaction in the first place."[26] In it, he laid out a carefully crafted biblical argument on slavery meant to show that Princeton stood above the tempestuous seas of factionalism, giving its allegiance not to one party or the other, but to the Word of God. "Slavery" appeared in the *Repertory* just one month before the General Assembly in May. Almost overnight, it became one of Hodge's most read and quoted articles as many in both Old School and Southern Presbyterian circles came to treat it as the best single distillation of their own position on slavery prior to the Civil War.

Ostensibly a review of William Ellery Channing's 1835 book entitled *Slavery*, Hodge crafted his article as the consummate argument for the lack of any biblical warrant for aggressive abolitionism. Quite to the contrary, his essay was a biblical manifesto defending the institution of slavery in the United States. In later years, Hodge described the article as a giant, targeted salvo meant to utterly destroy any radical abolitionist argument against slavery bold enough to use the Bible as its rationale for immediate emancipation.[27] Hodge maintained the views he set forth in this essay with his usual unswerving consistency and conviction until the middle years of the Civil War. It was only twenty-five years later that he experienced what one historian has called his one "antislavery moment," an epiphany brought on by his growing realization that unbiblical conceptions of race tainted the institution of slavery in the United States.[28] After the war, however, Hodge denied that he had ever strayed from the Bibliocentric views he first had set down in his 1836 "Slavery" article.

From the article's outset, Hodge acknowledges the country's growing turmoil over the slavery issue and throws down a gauntlet, proclaiming that the time has come "for every man to clarify his own thinking on the subject. Men can no longer be neutral."[29] In attempting to push his readers to take a stand, Hodge proceeds to set forth in devastatingly clear prose his most central line of argumentation: if the Bible nowhere condemns slavery then how can we condemn it? Taking direct aim at radical abolitionists—who he principally blamed for the nation's growing unrest over the slavery issue—Hodge argues that the institution had existed in the time of Christ and nowhere does Jesus or a single biblical author condemn it. As an even more conclusive rebuttal to radical Garrisonian abolitionism, Hodge notes that slave masters are nowhere exhorted in the New Testament even to liberate their slaves.[30] Hodge writes: "If we are right in insisting that slaveholding is one of the greatest of all sins; that it should be immediately and universally abandoned as a condition of church communion, or admission into heaven, how comes it that Christ and his apostles did not pursue the same course?"[31] For Hodge, the ultimate arbiter of moral choice was the Bible, and if the Bible was at best silent on the issue of slavery, it went beyond the purview of the church to mandate a radical abolitionist course of action.

Hodge deepens his argument by layering it with his thoughts on social organization. He argues that slavery is but one of many viable institutions different societies have used throughout history to organize themselves.[32] He freely admits that certain types of societal organization are preferable to others, and although he personally did not consider slavery a "desirable institution," there was no historical or biblical precedent for categorically forbidding it.[33]

As with all intellectual and theological positions, Hodge's thoughts on slavery were not born in a vacuum. They rose, in part, from his personality with its profound predilection against change coupled with his own life experiences. Unlike Garrison, who was able to embrace the possibilities resulting from radical societal reorientation, Hodge was constitutionally unable to conceive of drastically altering a fundamental and ingrained social institution such as slavery. His own thinking was always guided by precedent, not utopian notions of what might be. He fused his natural, conservative predisposition to his own experiences with slavery and poverty.

The importance of Hodge's life experiences to his thinking about slavery vividly comes across in how he justified the institution by making a crucial distinction between slaveholding and slave laws.[34] Slaveholding was not condemned by scripture, but certain slave laws clearly went against certain biblical mandates concerning how God commands people treat one another. Hodge had no trouble denominating slaves as property. What concerned him was that different forms of property be dealt with according to their nature. If a society defined a class of humans as property, that society still must treat that property as human, obeying God's commands concerning how every human should be treated.[35] Slavery became a sin when the laws that governed it ran counter to the commands of God. If slave owners did such things as forbid slaves to marry, separated families, interfered with the authority parents exercised over their children, failed to provide them the staples of life like adequate food and clothing, or deliberately opposed their "intellectual, moral or religious improvement," then that slave owner was clearly guilty of sin and subject to God's judgment.[36]

Hodge's conceptual distinction between the institution of slavery and the actual practices of slaveholding was so finely wrought that he showed himself a victim of his own limited exposure to slavery and the insularity of his life in Princeton. The type of slaveholding he had personally practiced (and to which he had been exposed in Princeton) was a much milder form of the institution than was found in other parts of the country. Hodge tipped his hand to his idealized view of the institution when he answered a critique of American slavery by declaring that American slaves were "far less severely tasked . . . better fed, clothed and lodged, and all their physical wants better provided for," than manual laborers one might find in England.[37] In general, Hodge believed that Americans treated their slaves in a manner calculated to improve their moral, physical, and emotional well-being.

Here, Hodge was using his own experience as a slaveholder as his template. Of utmost importance for him in considering the institution of slavery was not the degree to which any society curtailed a person's freedoms (every society limited the freedoms of its members to some extent), but the degree to which a society promoted or retarded "the progress of human happiness and virtue."[38] For poor African Americans, undereducated and ill-suited to fend for themselves, Hodge saw slavery as a means of gradually equipping them to take their place as productive members of a free society. With this end in mind, Hodge himself had taken great care in making religious education available to his own slaves, Henrietta and Lena, thereby demonstrating how firmly he believed that a slave owner could use the institution for good. There was a profound problem, however, in the fact that the milder brand of New Jersey slavery practiced by Hodge and his fellow Princetonians bore little resemblance to slavery found in other parts of the country. On the cotton plantations of the Deep South, for example, masters viewed educating slaves as a dangerous practice that might lead to sedition, and the Southern culture was largely without moral imperatives that encouraged slave owners to prepare their slaves for eventual freedom.

Hodge's conception of the difference between slaveholding and slave laws also stemmed from his adamantine commitment to property rights. Because much of his youth had been spent in relative poverty compared to the socially elite circles in which he moved, Hodge had a profound appreciation for the importance and sacred nature of personal property. For someone who had known want and been taught to value property even when he did not own much of it, Hodge was not about to dismiss the importance of property claims. He considered it no small thing that certain abolitionist legal policies might have drastic effects on slaveholders whose property had long been protected and guaranteed under various laws. Thomas Jefferson's embargo acts during the War of 1812 had proved devastating to Hodge's family, plunging his mother into poverty as she attempted to care for her two sons. Hodge was slow to pursue radical policy changes that might leave countless slaveholders in a similar situation.

Hodge ended his essay, "Slavery," with a clear reminder that while slaves might be considered property under the law, they remained human beings. He enjoined his readers in the clearest possible manner to pursue vigorously "the gradual elevation of the slaves in intelligence, virtue and wealth," which would insure more than any other single goal "the peaceable and speedy extinction of slavery."[39] Hodge was convinced that slavery was not going to last forever, and improving the lot of the slave was the surest and quickest way to its eradication. Such improvement at the individual level would ultimately pay rich societal dividends. American society would inevitably enjoy greater prosperity if a greater number of its members were better educated and able to be self-sufficient.

Hodge's gradualist stance on emancipation at the end of his essay did not satisfy every reader. It proved particularly unpopular among Southerners, who had little desire to free their workforce and even less desire to live alongside that workforce if it was freed. The extent of Southern abhorrence to Hodge's gradual emancipation ethic is seen in how E. N. Elliott excised the final paragraphs of his essay, which most clearly stated his gradualist ideas, when nearly a quarter of a century later he republished (without permission) Hodge's article in his famous and widely circulated 1859 pro-slavery polemic, *Cotton is King*.[40] By the late 1850s, Elliott and many other Southerners had come to believe that American slavery was an institution that should exist in perpetuity. Even as early as 1836, Hodge abhorred such perpetual notions of slavery.

In the end, Hodge's article did little more than help establish ever-more-sophisticated theological and political distinctions between Presbyterianism's Old and New Schools. It promoted some dialogue on the topic of slavery, but it did not bring about the unity Hodge so desperately sought. When Samuel Miller and his committee reported back to the 1836 General Assembly on the Chillocothe Resolutions, they reported that such an aggressive stance toward abolition could not possibly be endorsed by the General Assembly on practical and biblical grounds. Motions to discuss and change the denomination's stance toward slavery were all "indefinitely postponed."[41] The New School saw such a postponement as not only inconsistent with scripture, but also yet one more indication of just how much they differed from the Old School brethren. Hodge's dream of denominational unity was badly shaken during the 1836 General Assembly, but slavery was not the issue that would ultimately destroy the denomination's unity. Theological differences rooted in rival interpretations of the Westminster Confession would do that.

28

THE SCHISM

While the Old School was winning the debate on how best to deal with the slavery issue on the floor of the General Assembly in 1836, the gathering had an even more fractious issue on its docket. A year earlier, the Philadelphia Presbytery had chosen to accuse Albert Barnes, the immensely popular New School pastor of the city's First Presbyterian Church, of heresy. At the center of Barnes's trial was the contention that he went against the most basic tenets of the Westminster Confession in his 1834 *Notes on Romans* on such key issues as Original Sin, justification by faith, and human depravity. For almost a year, Barnes had elected to sit silently in the front pew of his own church while he waited for his case to be appealed to the General Assembly, the denomination's highest court. Hodge had little patience with what he saw as theatrical silence on the part of Barnes. The General Assembly put no strictures on his preaching until his case was tried. Hodge thought the move a canny maneuver by Barnes to bring both sympathy to himself and attention to the doctrinal controversies brewing within the denomination.[1]

It was not the first time that the Old School had put Barnes on trial. In 1829, Barnes preached his most famous—or as his opponents would have it, his most infamous—sermon: "The Way of Salvation." In it, Barnes showed his sympathy toward a belief in innate human ability to choose against sin, a stance many believed slapped in the face the traditional Calvinist doctrine of total depravity. The sermon was controversial, but not enough to stop the wealthy and influential First Presbyterian Church of Philadelphia a year later from calling the oratorically gifted and charismatic Barnes to be its pastor. This call placed Barnes in the heart of Philadelphia's nationally powerful Old School presbytery, and his presence outraged the this presbytery's decidedly conservative leaders, men including Ashbel Green and William Engles.[2] The Philadelphia

Presbytery wasted little time in charging Barnes with heresy in order to block his appointment and presented as their principal piece of evidence the views he had set forth in "The Way of Salvation." Eventually, the 1831 General Assembly acquitted Barnes, stating that while he might have been incautious in his use of language, his views did not differ enough from the Westminster Confession to be considered heretical.

The Old School leaders were outraged, but not totally defeated. They knew Barnes would give them another opportunity to try his views. He did not disappoint. When he published his *Notes on Romans*, his enemies immediately accused the text of reiterating Barnes's earlier heretical deviations from confessional Calvinism. Pointing to Barnes's *Notes*, Ashbel Green and his compatriots successfully maneuvered the local synod into censuring Barnes and leaving him to appeal his status to the General Assembly. Since the Assembly met only annually, Barnes found himself in a position where he needed to wait nearly a year to have his case heard. When the General Assembly did meet in May 1836, it spent two contentious weeks debating the Barnes issue. Eventually, because the New School was in the majority, the Assembly acquitted Barnes and reinstated him to his pulpit.

For the Old School, Barnes stood as the embodiment of the New School's deviance from confessional orthodoxy and his second acquittal was evidence enough that the denomination was forsaking "the faith once delivered to the saints" through how clearly it had decided to give "aid and comfort to the enemies of the truth."[3] Old School gloom deepened as they feared that the New School had gained too much power within the governing bodies of Presbyterianism. With the exception of 1835, the New School had held the majority of seats at every General Assembly since 1831. In the eyes of the Old School, the New School majorities during both Barnes trials had allowed apostasy to go unchecked. After the 1836 General Assembly, radical Old Schoolers no longer showed any interest at working within such a corrupt system. Instead, they turned their considerable energies to figuring out how to sever their ties with the New School.

Old Schoolers traced much of the New School's corruptive power to the 1801 "Plan of Union" between Presbyterians and their Congregational brethren. The root stock of the American Presbyterian Church had come from Scottish and Scotch-Irish immigrants who had primarily settled in the middle colonies of New York, New Jersey, Pennsylvania, and Delaware. The Congregational churches in New England had come mainly from those in England who wished to purify the Anglican Church. In terms of creedal and doctrinal beliefs, early Presbyterians and Congregationalists agreed on many issues.[4] Their main differences in the eighteenth century came in how they viewed church polity and some minor church traditions. Because of their similarities, these two bodies had decided to work together to help provide churches and religious instruction for an ever-expanding young United States as settlers poured into western

New York and northern Ohio. This partnership was formalized in 1801 and called the "Plan of Union."

The Old School had determined by the mid-1830s that the "Plan of Union" had done more harm than good, and much of the evil had come from the Congregationalists' strong commitment to local, individual church governance. Congregational churches were largely autonomous, answering only to themselves or to loose confederations or "associations" of other Congregational churches. Congregationalists passed on this same independent spirit to the many voluntary organizations they were instrumental in founding such as the American Education and Home Mission Societies. Many in the Old School were as worried about Congregationalism's lack of a central authority structure as they were about the wildly divergent theological views found among Congregationalists.[5] In a democratic culture that tended to favor individualism over traditional forms of societal order and power, Congregationalism provided no adequate check on the "widespread and ever restless spirit of *radicalism*, manifest both in the church and the state" that was leveling "all order to the dust."[6] The Old School saw the lack of effective central authority as an invitation to "transmute . . . pure faith into destructive heresy, . . . scriptural order into confusion and misrule."[7]

Presbyterianism was much more formalized and hierarchical. Presbyterian churches were tied together in local presbyteries. These presbyteries were then joined together into regional synods. These synods in turn met annually as the General Assembly, which theoretically had the ability to enforce conformity on issues of Christian doctrine and practice. Presbyterian ministers were accountable in both thought and action to their larger governing bodies at every level. Standards of orthodox doctrine and behavior were thus easier to enforce because the whole Presbyterian system depended to a greater degree on interlinked layers of guidance and accountability.

A majority of Older Schoolers had come to believe that Congregationalism's renegade spirit had penetrated too far into the more elegant and hierarchical polity of Presbyterianism. Many of the Presbyterian churches located outside the middle states were under the control of ministers appointed and paid by loosely governed voluntary societies, or only answerable to ill-defined confederations of Congregational and Presbyterian churches. Those in the Old School saw as equally problematic the allowance the "Plan" made for the transfer of ordination between Presbyterian and Congregational churches, making it possible for a pastor with little or no knowledge of Presbyterianism to shepherd a Presbyterian flock. Finally, the Old Schoolers hated the fact that the "Plan of Union" gave Congregational churches—which were overwhelmingly New School in their sympathies—a voting voice at the General Assembly.

In addition to these numerous problems surrounding church governance, Old Schoolers were disturbed by what they saw as unbridled theological variation on traditional Calvinism among Congregationalists.[8] Throughout the 1820s, Andover's New

Divinity and Yale's New Haven Theology had increasingly gained ground in Congregationalist and New School Presbyterian circles. The popularity of these theological strains was particularly troubling to those in the Old School who so highly prized their confessional notions of doctrinal purity.

While the second Barnes trial lit the fuse, the actual bomb that ultimately blew apart the Presbyterian Church did not explode until the following year when the Old School found itself in the majority at the 1837 General Assembly. Playing a pivotal part in the Old School's ascendancy at the General Assembly was the large number of Southern Presbyterians who had recently thrown in their lot with the Old School. Just the previous year, Southerners had largely voted to acquit Barnes of heresy charges, handing the New School an important victory. In a single year, things had drastically changed. Due to the denomination's growing conflicts over slavery, by the time the 1837 Assembly arrived, dozens of Southerners had firmly planted themselves in the Old School camp because of its clear pro-slavery position.[9] Such a majority in the Assembly was not an opportunity to be missed. Once the Old School had established that it outnumbered their New School brethren, they pursued a series of motions calculated to expel New School from their midst.

The Old School was truly surprised by their majority in the 1837 Assembly, but even before the Assembly convened, they had determined to use the meeting as their moment to separate themselves from the New School. Old School leaders had gathered several days before the General Assembly to strategize over how best to accomplish the division.[10] This meeting had produced the stinging "Testimony and Memorial," a paper carefully documenting the heresies embraced by the New School.[11] The "Testimony and Memorial" was the foundation upon which the Old School built its case for the need to separate the doctrinally pure Old Schoolers from their wandering New School brethren.

The Old School saw their majority status at the General Assembly as God's hand at work. He had made their task of division infinitely easier by allowing them to gain voting control of the Assembly. They made the first order of official business the consideration of their "Memorial," which was quickly adopted with only slight alterations. They then moved to see if there might be some amicable way of separating the Old and New Schools. Not surprisingly, the New School had many ministers who did not wish to see their denomination divided. A sizeable portion of New Schoolers balked at the Old School's encouragement to go establish their own denomination. Once the New School rebuffed these more measured calls for separation, the Old School brought all their force to bear to expel those aligned with the New School from the denomination.

The Old School quickly moved to declare null and void the "Plan of Union" as an unconstitutional act of the General Assembly of 1801. This action, in itself, was well within the bounds of the Assembly, which could certainly vote at any time to overturn one of its previous decisions. The Old School, however, went beyond the limits of constitutionality when it further moved to rescind all recognition of Presbyterian churches that had been formed under this plan. In one fell swoop, the Old School erased over thirty-five years of church development and demanded that any Presbyterian church founded under the "Plan of Union" reapply for denominational membership. These motions of excommunication came to be called the "Abscinding Acts," a series of legislative actions that stripped official denominational recognition from various synods, presbyteries, and churches.

The Old School was most interested in expelling the Synod of Western Reserve, which was both a hotbed of New School theology and radical revivalism. It was also a place where only one in four churches was officially Presbyterian, yet many of the Presbyterian-Congregational (Presbygational) churches in the region had a right to represent themselves at the annual General Assembly.[12] These "mongrel congregations" had power to "organize without elders, to permit congregationalists to constitute our sessions and presbyteries, to give to men the privilege of governing us, who refused to be governed by us."[13] The Old School voted to remove the entire synod from the denomination.

The Old School did not satisfy itself with simply moving to excise the heavily Congregational Synod of Western Reserve. It was interested in clearing out as many vestiges of Congregationalism and New School theology as possible. With this goal in mind, Old Schoolers moved to cut off three additional, much more Presbyterian, synods in western New York (Utica, Geneva, and Genesee), which had sprung from the Synod of Western Reserve under the "Plan of Union." Because these synods were the offspring of the dissolute Western Reserve, Old Schoolers judged them as bearing the same dangerous taint of poor governance and uncontrolled theology as found in the Western Reserve. They also moved to cut ties with the American Home Missionary Society and American Board of Education. The New School leanings of these societies, coupled with the reality that they were not answerable to Presbyterian bodies of authority, made them dangers both in terms of doctrine and polity. Finally, the Old School moved to abolish Philadelphia's third presbytery, a presbytery which had been set up largely as a buffer to shield Albert Barnes from his Old School foes in Philadelphia.

No one could doubt that the Old School was using their majority in the 1837 General Assembly to clean house. By the time the dust had settled, the General Assembly had dismissed 28 presbyteries, 509 ministers, and 60,000 church members, or nearly one-fifth of the entire American Presbyterian Church. In the Assembly itself, the New School lost in an instant nearly half of its voting strength.[14] The blow was so massive and so unexpected that the New School fell into complete disarray. Only in the weeks following the Assembly did they begin to realize the true extent and implications of the Assembly's actions.

As forceful as the actions of the Old School were in its maneuvers at the General Assembly, it was not a monolithic entity. Hodge himself had deep reservations about how the Old School was going about its crusade of purification. Largely due to his lameness and his lack of seniority, Hodge did not play a major role in the General Assembly events of 1837. In fact, he did not even attend the Assembly. Dr. Alexander had gone to represent the Princeton faculty. Hodge did have strong opinions about the momentous events at the Assembly, opinions he was eager to put into print.[15]

When the Old School elements of the 1837 General Assembly were attempting to figure out the best way to cleanse the body of the New School, several different plans of action were proposed. One such plan was put forward by Dr. Cornelius Cuyler, the pastor of Hugh Hodge's Second Presbyterian Church in Philadelphia. He proposed a more moderate plan. Cuyler advocated that all Congregational or Presbygational churches that wanted to be part of the General Assembly reorganize themselves as Presbyterian churches, as well as having the denomination recognize the current Presbyterian churches in the threatened synods in Ohio and New York as full and rightful participants in the General Assembly. Cuyler saw that there was much to lose and little to gain in expelling whole synods en masse.

Hodge strongly favored Cuyler's middle course of denominational reorganization.[16] He considered it decidedly unfair to excise certain Presbyterian churches just because they were founded under the 1801 "Plan of Union." If they were Presbyterian churches in good standing, they should have the right to remain so. In Hodge's mind, the 1837 General Assembly could undo its recognition of the "Plan of Union," but it could not backtrack and cast off every church founded under that plan that claimed Presbyterian ties.[17]

For Hodge, the question was not whether the separation of the Old and New School was necessary. He believed it was. His quibbles were with how the Old School had pursued the separation. He later wrote that he and the other Princeton professors "were in entire sympathy with the Old-school party" as to matters of theology and aim, but the methods used to achieve the disunion were ill-considered and unconstitutional in his mind.[18] He was particularly at odds with the decision to excise the three New York synods. When it came to writing the article recapping the 1837 General Assembly, Hodge wanted it noted that he favored Cuyler's plan over the one adopted.[19] In a display of how Hodge could not simply put into the *Repertory* whatever he wished, he lost this particular battle in a series of meetings with the "Association of Gentlemen" who voted against him writing anything that could be possibly interpreted as Princeton's dissension against the Old School's actions and policies at the General Assembly.

Ultimately, he was forced to settle for noting his hesitancies about the Old School's course in a vague footnote attached to his article.

Hodge's dissension here, however, is worthy of note. His increasingly fractious relationship with Green and his "Ultras" found yet another expression in how they chose to go about dividing the Presbyterian Church. Hodge clearly was not in absolute agreement with his Old School brethren in every regard, and the freedom he felt to disagree appeared repeatedly in the coming years. He saw it as a dangerous precedent to so grossly bend, if not break altogether, the constitutional procedures of the General Assembly, and he was worried that much of what was accomplished during the 1837 General Assembly might come back to haunt the men who had so cavalierly set aside established forms to accomplish their goals. In many respects, the next two years would show just how well founded his fears were.

29

THE NEW SCHOOL FIGHTS BACK

Although he had his reservations about how the separation was accomplished, Hodge wrote his brother after the Assembly in an exultant mood, proclaiming that "the New School experienced a Waterloo defeat."[1] Hodge knew that the New School had suffered a devastating, perhaps a mortal, blow in the 1837 General Assembly. Accomplished with constitutional legality or not, the churches of four synods had been stripped of their denominational recognition, and now all their lands, buildings, and financial accounts were subject to reversion to the denomination that had just thrown them out. The New School, however, was not going to give up without a fight.

Two months after the 1837 General Assembly, nearly 170 ministers and lay delegates representing some 30 presbyteries gathered in Auburn, New York.[2] The time had come to figure out how to respond to the "Abscinding Acts." This "Auburn Convention" became the first step in the New School forming its own denominational polity. Those who attended determined to attack the "Abscinding Acts" head on, declaring them unconstitutional. Those in Auburn decided that their best course was to have churches retain their present organization, and they agreed that "the Presbyteries send their commissioners to the next General Assembly, as usual."[3] Thus, the stage was set for a cataclysmic confrontation at the 1838 General Assembly.

When the 1838 General Assembly gathered at the Seventh Presbyterian Church in Philadelphia on May 17, word had already spread that the New School men planned to take their seats at the Assembly. To frustrate these plans, members of the Old School arrived early at the church and quickly occupied all the seats nearest the moderator. At the same time, other Old Schoolers locked a set of strategic doors, so that the New School representatives were forced to sit behind the Old School men and fill the upper galleries. When the proceedings began, the New School continually attempted to gain recognition from the moderator who refused to even acknowledge their presence in the building. What began as palpable tension transformed into chaos as Assembly delegates of both parties began to stamp their feet, stand on the pews, and shout at one another. One observer was so astounded by the scene that they thought its actors "were rather a company broken loose from a lunatic asylum, or a state penitentiary, than an association of grave and dignified ministers of any church."[4]

Eventually, the New School men moved into the church's central isle and began their own proceedings. They went through the proper motions to form a legally constituted General Assembly of their own. As soon as the New Schoolers had established their own Assembly, complete with moderator, they moved to adjourn and reconvene at Barnes's First Presbyterian Church a few blocks away.[5]

For the next several days, Philadelphia served as the home to two opposing General Assemblies, both of which claimed the constitutional right of succession to lead the Presbyterian Church in America.[6] To the utter astonishment of the Old School, those who decided to join the rival Assembly were made up of much more than the four synods that had been excised the year before. The rival Assembly had gathered to its fold 85 presbyteries and 1,200 ministers. These presbyteries and their ministers represented roughly 100,000 church members. On an otherwise unremarkable spring day in 1838, it became clear that the Old School's attempt to purify the Presbyterian Church in America had come at great cost. Attaining purity had meant losing nearly one half of the total number of Presbyterians in America.

If such mass defection was not insult enough, the Old School found itself in an even more awkward place when the New School Assembly took the Old School to court on the issue of the constitutionality of their expulsion. The Presbyterian Church had incorporated under a charter in the state of Pennsylvania in 1799. The New School brought a case before the Pennsylvania bar seeking to declare themselves as the rightful trustees to the church under this charter of incorporation.[7] The New School Assembly was fighting for the right to legally establish itself as the preeminent General Assembly of the Presbyterian Church in America, and thus gain control of all the property, finances, and land owned by the denomination.

The Waterloo-like defeat of the New School Hodge had celebrated just months before was about to be reversed. After a protracted legal battle, a judge and special jury handed down a decision on March 4, 1839, which stunned the Old School. The court found in favor of the New School General Assembly, stating that their expulsion had indeed lacked constitutionality. On this basis, the court recognized the New School's claim as the denomination's rightful trustees. The Old School's hasty and questionable actions in pushing through the abrogation of the "Plan of Union" had backfired. Hodge characterized the court's decision to his brother as "a very great calamity, and as a very severe judgment of God."[8]

The blow could spell the end of the Princeton Seminary as he knew it. If the court decision were to stand, it would mean that the Seminary would come under the New School's control, and the New School already had named Union as its most important seat of theological instruction. At best, Princeton might be allowed to continue its mission, but it would occupy a second tier in the denomination's educational structure.[9] Such a reduced position would have serious consequences for the type of resources and students Princeton could hope to receive.

The Old School General Assembly appealed the decision, but the months before the Supreme Court of Pennsylvania took up the appeal were dark indeed. Hodge told his friend Henry Boardman that it was "one of the most trying periods in our whole history."[10] Hodge feared that if the State's Supreme Court decided in favor of the New School Assembly that the Old School would not hold together. He saw no hope of reconciliation with the New School and was unsure whether such a reconciliation would be a good thing. Without property, financial resources, or even legal standing, Hodge feared that the Old School would simply "break into little fragments and cease to have much power to do good."[11] Such fragmentation would mean an end not only to the confessionally centered Presbyterian Church in America, but most probably to Princeton Seminary as well.

Hodge's own anxieties about the future of the church and the Seminary were complicated by his own growing financial worries. Partly due to the civil war within the church, and partly due to a severe economic depression that had struck the country in 1837, the Seminary found itself under extreme financial pressures in the closing years of the 1830s. Its student population declined drastically in the midst of the schism, and its faculty failed to receive their salaries from the General Assembly on a regular basis. These financial problems remained with the Seminary through the early 1840s. Hodge was reduced to asking Hugh continually for money with such plaintive letters as: "Only think of seven mouths, seven pair of feet, seven empty heads, and worse than all seven pairs of knees and elbows."[12]

In the end, the Old School survived its own Waterloo when the Supreme Court of Pennsylvania handed down a decision in its favor.[13] Amid the chaos and debris caused by the General Assemblies of 1837 and 1838, Princeton Seminary found itself now free to follow a more pronounced Old School road. With the New School element largely gone, the Old School Assembly enjoyed a time of "almost unprecedented doctrinal homogeneity" all centered on "the Westminster Confession and Catechisms."[14] The homogeneity allowed Princeton to thrive in a new way. No longer burdened with needing to satisfy a wide and varied theological constituency that ranged from hyper-Calvinists to New School Taylorites, Princeton quickly established itself as an unfettered, consistent, and clear voice in articulating the conservative confessional nature of American Presbyterian Calvinism in the United States. In the ensuing years, no one commanded this voice more soundly and with greater authority than Charles Hodge.

30

WRITING HISTORY

Hodge remained almost entirely confined to his house as the Presbyterian crisis of 1837-1838 unfolded. Acutely crippled by the pain in his leg, he spent his days in his book-lined study, seated in his chair, either talking with his family and friends, teaching his students, or being busy writing on the wooden board that lay constantly propped against his chest. In many ways, the timing was perfect when a delegation of prominent Philadelphia ministers approached him in 1838 to see if he might be interested in writing a definitive history of the Presbyterian Church in the United States.

Institutional and denominational histories frequently appear in moments when their subjects are in crisis.[1] Writers of such histories often find themselves asked to compose chronicles that not only record past triumphs but also serve to justify current, and possible future, courses of action. An historian's attempt to look at the past in order to help make sense of an angst-ridden present can do a great deal to assuage contemporary anxieties. Thus, it is not surprising that the 1837 schism brought forth two significant works of Presbyterian history. Samuel Miller wrote the first history of Princeton Seminary in 1838, and Hodge produced a two-volume constitutional history of the Presbyterian Church in the United States (1839, 1840).[2]

Writing such a history proved to be exceedingly difficult for Hodge. It was an endeavor that fit neither his interests nor his expertise, leading his son Archie to call it "the least natural, and most laborious work he ever undertook."[3] Hodge knew that such a denominational history could be a great use, however, and his crippled state spurred him on to want to do something useful. Confined largely to his study, Hodge thought it an auspicious time to undertake a project that required a great deal of research and patience. He readily admitted that he might not be the best person for the job, but he was willing and available.

Even before he had agreed to write his denomination's history, Hodge had already begun to distinguish himself as a Presbyterian historian of sorts. In 1834, Ashbel Green had begun to include a series of articles on the proceedings of the annual General Assembly in his *Christian Advocate*.[4] Not surprisingly, Green's recapitulation of the General Assembly's work had a pronounced Old School bias in both the selection and interpretation of events. Wishing to offer his fellow clergy a more balanced account of the proceedings of the denomination's highest ruling body, Hodge took it upon himself the following year to begin what would become an annual installment in the summer issue of the *Repertory* reviewing the key discussion and actions of that year's General Assembly. To emphasize his own neutrality, Hodge told his readers that he wished to offer them "the most important questions debated" by presenting them "a general view of the arguments on both sides."[5] Unlike Green, Hodge aimed at "perfect impartiality," even though he acknowledged that such balance was impossible to attain.[6] After the denomination's split in 1838, Hodge found himself the historian of the Old School Assembly and no longer felt the need to tread so lightly on Presbyterian views that differed from a standard Old School line.

Through these yearly articles—written with absolute regularity from 1835 to 1867 with the single exception of 1841—Hodge became a kind of de facto historian of the denomination. He captured in print what he considered to be the key issues and developments in the denomination each year as they appeared and were discussed in Presbyterianism's supreme governing body, often paying special attention to the constitutionality of the issues discussed. So popular did these yearly summaries of the General Assembly become that other contributors to the *Repertory* lamented that "there is no inducement to prepare a good article for the July number, because every one turns at once to that on the General Assembly, which absorbs all the interest."[7]

It was perhaps his role as the denomination's unofficial historian that made Hodge a logical choice to write a history of the American Presbyterian Church. An idea for such a history had been floated in the past. An earlier attempt had been made to enlist Ashbel Green to chair a committee to undertake the project.[8] Green had even begun to gather the necessary materials, but he had never found time to begin the work in earnest. When Hodge agreed to the project, he asked Green for the materials he had already gathered. Green consented to give the materials to Hodge, but it is telling that their interaction took place through mediators.[9] By 1838, Hodge had become completely alienated from his former pastor and teacher. He felt that Green and his "Ultras" had done great damage to Presbyterianism in their ceaseless battle against the New School. Green's uncompromising views and combative tactics pushed Hodge beyond the limits of his usual benevolent tolerance and made it impossible for him to interact personally with Green in the years immediately following the schism.

Hodge soon cobbled together a multitude of sources and finished a two-volume, four-hundred-page history of Presbyterianism in United States. He found writing such an extensive history particularly difficult because his confinement made it impossible for him to do much in the way of gathering the source material himself. He told Hugh that his "lameness is more in my way now than it ever has been, as I have to depend on others to make search for old things in my behalf."[10] As he collected source material, he placed much of it in a rotating bookcase within arm's reach of his chair.[11] Working at a feverish pace that pushed him at times to write for seven hours a day, he completed the work in two years.[12]

To read Hodge's finished work is to come face-to-face with his views on the uses of history. Hodge was not a historian in the sense that many might use the term today. In writing history, he was not so much interested in making sense of people, events, and ideas as they changed over time. Instead, he saw history as a repository of key bits of evidence that could be used to frame various understandings of the contemporary world. In this sense, one might call Hodge a polemic historian. He used the past to teach lessons about the present. It is as if his aversion to change bled over into how he conceptualized history and its uses. Certainly people, places, and things did change over time, but such change was not Hodge's central concern as he recorded the events of a given General Assembly or some aspect of eighteenth-century Presbyterianism for his history.

Hodge decided to tackle his history project in parts. As he embarked on his research, he did not know how popular the work might be, so he had decided to write about Presbyterianism's early days in America and see if there were enough interest to continue the work.[13] In the end, he completed two volumes of his history. The first volume covered from 1705 to the split between the Old and New Sides in 1741, while the second volume narrated the denomination's development from 1741 to 1788. Once Hodge saw the success of the first two volumes, he began considering embarking on a third that would take the denomination into the mid-1820s, but other pressures kept him from ever starting this final volume in earnest.[14]

With Hodge's presentist orientation toward history, one is forced to wonder why he had no interest in taking his work up to the current moment. The momentous events of the 1830s certainly cried out to be memorialized, but Hodge wrote his friend Henry Boardman that he did not know whether he had the "courage to undertake the labor of bringing the History to the Present time. It may be too soon to write the history of the last ten years."[15] He was content to leave the recent struggles of the New and Old School to another historian.

Even with these sentiments, the careful reader of Hodge's history soon discovers that his chronicle of the denomination's first eighty years is, in fact, largely a thinly veiled polemical gloss on the "last ten years." At many points, his history reads as a barely disguised commentary on the momentous events that engulfed his denomination in the 1830s. That Hodge called his work a "Constitutional History" offers but the first clue to how deeply invested his historical account was in providing a justification for the Old School's constitutional machinations that had led to the schism of 1837. As Hodge recounted the eighteenth-century struggles of the Old and New Sides over issues of church government, as well as competing theologies of revivalism and vital religion, he composed a narrative that offered insight after insight on the Presbyterian struggles of the 1830s. In Hodge's hands, the struggle between the New and Old Sides provided an incredibly constructive lens through which one might be able to interpret the Old and New School battles of his own day.

Just how far recent events impinged on Hodge's historical account comes across clearly in the three central claims around which he builds the first volume of his history: first, the Presbyterian Church did not owe its existence to Congregationalists; second, the Presbyterian Church in the United States was a true Presbyterian church modeled on the Church of Scotland and has always been properly Presbyterian in its government and its doctrines; and third, the Westminister Confession of Faith had always been the condition for being ordained a minister in the Church.[16] Taking each of these claims in turn, it is easy to see how Hodge mapped his current historical moment onto the past and used his history to justify the Old School in the controversies of his day.

Hodge begins by making it clear in narrating the Puritan migration to the colonies that not all "the Puritans were . . . Congregationalists."[17] Some four thousand Presbyterians had arrived in New England before 1640, and many Puritans embraced the Presbyterian form of church government.[18] His conclusion was simple, yet strongly worded: "nothing but a sectional vanity little less than insane, could lead to the assertion that Congregationalism was the basis of Presbyterianism in this country."[19] The implication was clear. The arguments many had made in defending the 1801 "Plan of Union" by reasoning that Congregationalism had been the wellspring of the Presbyterian Church in America were unfounded. Hodge was careful to note that even in 1766 when the Presbyterian Church agreed to partner with certain Congregational churches in various activities that the Presbyterian churches would "subsist entire and independent" from their Congregationalist counterparts "notwithstanding this union."[20] For Hodge, there was absolutely no doubt that Presbyterianism had always existed as its own entity in America.

Hodge further documents that while many Congregationalists held to the same Reformed views of Calvinism as Presbyterians, they had never been committed to the presbytery notion of church polity. Hodge carefully argues that from its inception on American shores, the Presbyterian Church had exercised a church government which firmly rested "upon the Presbyteries; that is, the clerical and lay elders."[21] As early as

1716, presbyteries were joining together to form synods.[22] These synods later joined together to function in larger bodies, eventually leading to the formation of the General Assembly. Whether it be at the presbytery, synod, or General Assembly level, Hodge wished his readers to know that Presbyterians had governed themselves within a presbytery structure for well over a century. The more loosely confederated Congregationalists could lay no claim to being Presbyterians when Presbyterians had so clearly distinguished their own identity and so clearly "thought themselves Presbyterians."[23]

Hodge built upon his assertion that Presbyterians had long been present as a distinct denomination in the New World by forcefully arguing that from the outset all early Presbyterian "ministers were Calvinists," and the proof of their Calvinism could be found in the Adopting Act of 1729 when all Presbyterian Churches in the colonies agreed to "make the adoption of the Westminster Confession a condition of ministerial communion."[24] Positioning the Westminster Confession as the standard of orthodoxy—a view held so dearly by the Old School—had been Presbyterianism's undeniable practice for nearly a century. In rhetoric eerily reminiscent of Ashbel Green's Old School's Ultras, Hodge muses at one point that in adopting the Westminster Confession as their church's theological cornerstone, early Presbyterians established "the most pious, laborious, and useful churches. And the strictest age of any particular church has almost always been its best age."[25]

In his second volume, Hodge turns his attention to offering an extended discussion of "the great revival of religion" that took place between 1740 and 1745, which brought forth the New Side/Old Side schism of 1741.[26] Those of the New Side mainly distinguished themselves from their Old Side counterparts by their commitment to emotional, fiery preaching, their pronounced emphasis on the importance of vital, personal piety and their openness to moving beyond traditional notions of church government and inter-church relations. The Old Siders, on the other hand, viewed new evangelical methods, new approaches to running worship services, and new rules for itinerant preaching with considerable skepticism and suspicion.

Hodge's treatment of the schism of 1741 turned almost entirely into a critique of the more outwardly emotional forms of revivalism. He made the Pennsylvania pastor and evangelist, Gilbert Tennent, the focal point of his critique. Tennent had been one of the founding fathers of the New Side faction, a man Hodge characterized as "so completely the soul of the party to which he belonged, that without him it never would have existed."[27] What most concerned Hodge about Tennent was the way in which he so easily disregarded the larger ecclesiastical authority of the Presbyterian Church and so freely took it upon himself to condemn ministers he saw as lacking true religion.

For Hodge, Tennent was the quintessential threat to Presbyterian order, authority, and polity: a power that functioned autonomously without check or balance from other bodies within the denomination. Tennent's commitment to his own agenda and his disregard for Presbyterian government made him a danger to the denomination as a whole. Hodge vehemently decried how Tennent set himself up as judge over his fellow clerics, a role appropriate for only a presbytery or synod to take.[28] In paying close attention to Tennent's famous Nottingham sermon, where he exhorted congregants who found themselves under the teaching and direction of "pharisee-shepherds or unconverted teachers" to leave those unredeemed pastors, Hodge argued that Tennent served as "one of the principal causes of the schism" of 1741.[29]

As a result of his inability to follow any course but his own, Tennent helped lead the New Brunswick Presbytery to separate from the denomination's other presbyteries. Although Tennent and other New Siders never wavered from their commitment to the Westminster Confession and Catechisms (a fact, for Hodge, that made them decidedly different than their New School counterparts), they had no confidence that other presbyteries were as eager to encourage vital religion to the extent they were. Tennent also refused to grant clergymen outside his own presbytery the power to veto the ordination of a minister whom he endorsed. Tennent later recanted many of these stances, but in the early 1740s he proved a central figure in bringing about the first major rupture in the American Presbyterian Church.

In Hodge's mind, when considering the 1741 schism, ecclesiastical polity and order were the critical issues. Tennent and the his fellow New Siders were sound in their commitment to the Westminster Confession and Catechisms, but they proved unwilling to submit to any higher church authority when they believed they were in the right. Hodge's stress on proper order takes on an almost-obsessive quality when he recounted the various dynamics present in the revivals of the mid-eighteenth century. Repeatedly, he condemns every person and action bringing disorder and confusion, while he praises everything and everyone promoting a spirit of peace, orderliness, and unity.[30]

To reinforce his case about the need for order, Hodge pointed to two other disruptive characters worthy of his special censure: the traveling evangelists George Whitefield and James Davenport. Not only were Whitefield and Davenport friends of Tennent, but they shared his penchant for condemning ministers who they felt were dead to true religion. Early in their careers, both men made a habit of questioning the salvation of ministers who disagreed with them. Whitefield and Davenport also felt free to disregard the accepted rules of preaching in another minister's domain without the home minister's consent, convinced that the importance of preaching the Gospel message overrode all commonly accepted rules of clerical etiquette. Whitefield was fond of saying that if church doors were closed to his preaching, open fields always stood nearby.

Aside from their blatant disregard for ministerial decorum, Hodge looked askance at how Whitefield and Davenport credited vibrant, bodily manifestations of the Holy Spirit as signs of true conversion. He saw their preaching as too often bent on encouraging such outward signs when they had little or no correlation to true conversion. He found offensive Whitefield's comment that "he never saw a more glorious sight, than when the people were fainting all round him, and crying out in such a manner as to drown his own voice."[31] Violent shaking, shouting, hysterical convulsions, fainting, and wild laughter had little to do with Hodge's precious sense of order. He very much doubted whether the Holy Spirit could be the force behind such chaos.

Hodge went so far as to characterize such phenomena as belonging to a "whole class of nervous diseases."[32] As he prepared his second volume, he wrote his brother requesting information that might elucidate "the contagious nature of certain nervous disorders" he so readily associated with revival activity.[33] Hodge was convinced that such "nervous phenomena, & . . . their rapid progression thro' large assemblies of ours & the Methodists especially" could be traced to natural, not spiritual, causes.[34] In his usual careful, scriptural manner Hodge argued that "[t]he testimony of the Scriptures is not merely negative on" the bodily manifestations of religious enthusiasm found so often at revivals but "[t]heir authority is directly opposed to all such disorders."[35]

By dedicating the first two chapters of his second volume to close examinations of Tennent, Whitefield, and Davenport, Hodge carefully built an argument that their revival practices and blatant disregard for Presbyterian Church polity led to the schism of 1741. His attacks on these three figures are easily connected to the anger he felt against those of his own day who stood against traditional church order in favor of radical revivalism and so-called "vital religion." He even openly conflates his own period with eighteenth-century events when he likens Whitefield's and Davenport's activities to the "Western revivals" of his own time, helping his readers draw connections between these colonial revivalists and the work of Finney in his own day.[36] His critiques of emotional oratory, disregard for rules of pulpit exchange, and denunciations of fellow ministers all had the familiar ring of events lifted right off the pages of Presbyterian periodicals circulating throughout the 1830s.

There is a certain amount of irony in Hodge's strong condemnation of the New Side. After all, his own ancestors had been deeply and personally indebted to the work of George Whitefield and Gilbert Tennent. Hodge's own great-aunt, Hannah Hodge, had been converted under Whitefield's ministry, and his family had been founding members of Philadelphia's Second Presbyterian Church, which had called Tennent to be its first pastor.[37] Hodge's ancestors had been prominent members in Philadelphia's early New Side community. Hodge was also currently a member of the very New Brunswick Presbytery that Gilbert Tennent had split off from the larger denomination in 1741.

The irony deepens when one pauses to realize that Hodge's much-beloved Princeton College had grown out of the efforts of key New Side ministers. Jonathan Dickinson, Aaron Burr, Samuel Davies, and Samuel Finley were all early presidents of the College, and they had all been aligned with the New Side. In fact, after the two factions joined

Figure 30.1 *Camp Meetings:* Western, or frontier, revivals took many different forms during the nineteenth century, but among their most famous manifestations were "Camp Meetings." Such gatherings could attract thousands of participants and last for several days. Charles Finney was one of the greatest champions of these events, while Hodge favored a less emotional conversion process keyed to a lifelong pursuit of personal sanctification. [*The Library Company of Philadelphia*]

together once again in 1758, the influence of the New Side became the dominant strain in American Presbyterianism. During the schism, the number of Old Side churches had remained largely the same, while the New Side had seen radical growth. The Presbyterianism that had established itself by the time of the Revolutionary War was deeply inflected with New Side pietism and aggressive evangelism.

Archibald Alexander had also been the product of New Side revivalism, and perhaps the most serious disagreement he ever had with Hodge concerned what he considered to be Hodge's unfair treatment of the New Side in his history. In a long letter, Alexander tells how he felt Hodge had dealt rather too roughly with the New Side. Hodge told his friend Henry Boardman that Alexander believed "that the Old Side were a great deal worse and the New Side a great deal better than I had represented them."[38] So egregious did Alexander find some of Hodge's New Side interpretations that he began to produce his own essays and sermons on Gilbert Tennent and his family. He eventually collected and published these works in a slim volume entitled *Biographical Sketches of the Founder and Principal Alumni of the Log College* to which he gave the telling subtitle *Together with an Account of the Revivals of Religion Under Their Ministry.*[39]

Alexander's critique gave Hodge "a great deal of uneasiness."[40] In writing his history, Hodge was sure that "many of our good old people will think it dreadful," but he was equally convinced that he needed to be true to his interpretation of the documents before him.[41] Thus, he decided against publishing his history with the Presbyterian Board of Publication because of the various prejudices and editorial changes the board might require. Instead, he turned to the Philadelphia firm of Wm. S. Martien to publish the work. Since he had decided not to publish it with the Presbyterian Board, Hodge also took an active role in getting Martien to advertise the book to his Presbyterian brethren and other interested readers. He believed in the project, but he also knew that it would have to be "put in the way of people" in order for it to sell.[42] Thus, he encouraged Martien to advertise it widely and send it to book stores not only in New England, but also in such far-off places as Pittsburgh, Cincinnati, Louisville, and Lexington. Due partly to Hodge's efforts, the book did sell quite well. Eventually the Presbyterian Board of Publication acquired its copyright in 1851, but Hodge's early decision to step outside the expected channels of Presbyterian publishing to bring forth his history signaled the highly sensitive nature of the topics and interpretations his history offered. It was also a decision that showed that as much as he was a party man when it came to his denomination, he still exercised considerable freedom in his own intellectual convictions. He was not afraid to stand by his own interpretations and conclusions, a trait that would bring him to considerable grief in the coming decade as he set forth his highly contentious views on such issues as Roman Catholic baptism.

PART V

The 1840s

Professor of Theology

Figure 31.1 *1846 Portrait of Hodge by Daniel Huntington:* Daniel Huntington painted this portrait in 1846 when Hodge served as Moderator of the General Assembly. [*Special Collections, Princeton Theological Seminary Libraries*]

31

THE WAY OF LIFE

In May 1840, as Hodge presented his publisher with the final pages of the second volume of his history, he faced one of the most wrenching turning points of his life. His beloved mentor and father figure, Archibald Alexander, had decided it was time to step aside as Princeton Seminary's lead professor. Having made up his mind, Alexander moved to handpick his successor. Samuel Miller was not an option. He was three years older than Alexander and in bad health. The only logical choice was Hodge, who had distinguished himself during his nearly twenty years at the Seminary as a beloved teacher, an orthodox theologian, and someone totally devoted to the institution itself. It came as no surprise that Alexander considered Hodge the perfect person to replace him as the Seminary's guiding hand.

Alexander officially requested that Hodge become his successor at the 1840 meeting of the General Assembly. At the same time, he approached the Assembly to name Hodge as the Seminary's principle theology instructor, Alexander asked if he might be able to take a less onerous and more pastoral position at the Seminary, a new post tailored specifically for him that the faculty had agreed to call "Professor of Pastoral and Polemic Theology." In such a role, Alexander planned to spend his time counseling students, training them in the practical matters of being a minister, and helping them with their preaching. Not a single voice was raised in dissent against Alexander's requests; the Assembly quickly approved the new positions for both men.

Showing his characteristic aversion to change, Hodge had hoped that the Assembly might fail to endorse Alexander's wishes. He had little desire to move from his department in oriental and biblical literature. He wrote his brother that he "would give five thousand dollars, if I had them to be let off" from taking Alexander's post.[1] He bemoaned the fact that "The new arrangement knocks all my plans in the head; & will increase my official labours for years to come four fold."[2] As it turns out, many of Hodge's "plans" were intimately tied to various publishing dreams. By the early 1840s, Hodge had written two versions of his Romans commentary, a study guide on Romans, and two volumes of Presbyterian history. Having tasted success with all of these works, Hodge had begun to formulate plans for several more books. Not only was he thinking of a third history volume, but he also wished to use his lecture notes on the Pauline epistles as the basis for a new commentary on the book of Ephesians (a work, as it turns out, he would not find time to write for another sixteen years).

Hodge not only enjoyed writing, but in the past few years his book royalties had provided an important supplement to his annual seminary salary of $1,500.[3] His Romans commentary had brought him $1,100 in its first two years in print, and Martiens had printed a large edition of his history that promised to give him as much as $750 in profit. His ever-erratic salary payments from the Seminary along with the demands of his large household made the money he made from his books vitally important. He wrote Hugh that it was immensely comforting to find that publishers were willing to pay substantial sums "for my brains."[4] In the coming years, he chose his publishers partly on the basis of how much they might be able to offer him for his books, commenting to his friend Henry Boardman, "Having eight children, being no great economist, I feel it a duty to help myself & family by making something from my books when I can."[5]

As he was elevated to Alexander's old position, Hodge faced the stark reality that "I shall have no time to do anything but prepare for my class, my History, my commentary, or commentaries & other matters must stop—I regret the change exceedingly."[6] The "class" to which Hodge referred was the students' coursework in theology. He bemoaned the fact that he was now expected to teach a course of study he had "not studied at all systematically since I left the Seminary."[7] He rightly anticipated that preparing lectures for a theological curriculum would be a taxing endeavor. He found the work so "laborous," in fact, that he did not begin presenting his own lectures on the subject until 1845, and even then he team-taught the seminary's theological courses with Alexander for several years.[8] All the while, Hodge continued to offer the junior class lectures on the Pauline epistles as he struggled with the transition of taking on many of Alexander's administrative responsibilities.

Alexander's resignation not only symbolically signaled that the formative era of the Seminary was ending, but it also gave a glimpse into how the Seminary would replace its most revered leaders in the coming decades. Hodge's succession to Alexander's position inaugurated a pattern of dynastic replacement at the Seminary. Alexander did more than choose Hodge as his successor; he also facilitated the appointment of his son, J. Addison Alexander, to Hodge's former position as the Professor of Oriental and Biblical Literature.

Alexander's choice to replace Hodge with his son did not mean that nepotism had won out over competency. It turned out that Addison's immense intellectual gifts and solitary temperament made him uniquely well suited for a professorial career. His work with the Old Testament gained the Seminary an international reputation in the fields of Old Testament language studies and biblical exegesis as he became one of America's leading conservative scholars in critically engaging European biblical criticism. His own scholarship built upon and challenged the work generated by the German school, declaring that "the true course with respect to German labours and researches is not to look away from them or cover them with dust, but to seize upon their valuable products and convert them to our own use."[9] Addison's great contribution to American theological thinking was the middle ground he forged between the historical demands of the Higher Criticism and the attention to form and detail favored by the Lower Criticism.

Over the next fifty years, the Seminary's dynastic faculty decisions included a number of Alexanders and Hodges. Alexander's first son, James Waddel, served for a short time as the Seminary's Professor of Ecclesiastical History and Church Government after Samuel Miller retired from his duties in 1849. Hodge had two of his own sons join the Seminary's faculty: Caspar Wistar Hodge Sr. served as school's Professor of New Testament Literature and Greek Exegesis from 1860 until his death in 1891, and Archibald Alexander Hodge (called "Professor Arch" by his students when he was not around) replaced his father as Professor of Didactic and Exegetical Theology in 1878. The Hodge line continued well into the twentieth century as Hodge's grandson, Caspar Wistar Hodge Jr. became a professor at the Seminary in 1901, ensuring that a Hodge sat on the school's faculty with only one short hiatus from 1822 to 1937. That such a long line of Alexanders and Hodges came to populate the Seminary's faculty ranks had a dual effect: it facilitated a continuity of theology and tone at the school, but it also led to a kind of insularity in its thought, methods, and predilections.

Even though Hodge was reluctant to take over Alexander's position, he only voiced his reservations to his family. He repeatedly told his brother that he wished to remain in his current post, but he did not feel that he could go against either his beloved mentor's wishes or his duty to do "just what the church bid."[10] When the 1840 General Assembly voted to make him the new Professor of Exegetical and Didactic Theology, Hodge did not offer the slightest murmur of dissent. He quietly bowed to what he could only view as God's providential leading.

Years later, A. A. Hodge testified to just how providential this career choice proved to be for his father.[11] Believing that his father had possessed a unique blend of theological training and natural intellectual ability, he saw him as being far better suited to teach theology than biblical literature. Hodge's extensive work in the Bible's original languages, fused with his intimate knowledge of the new German Higher Criticism

Figure 31.2 *James Waddel Alexander*: James Waddel Alexander, the oldest son of Archibald Alexander, began his studies at the Seminary in 1822 and became one of Hodge's first students. A spell-binding preacher and teacher, his career was varied. He served as a pastor, editor of *The Presbyterian*, professor of rhetoric and belles lettres at Princeton College, as well as a professor at Princeton Theological Seminary. [*Library of the Author*]

and his unwavering commitment to the standards of the Westminster Confession made him a formidable conservative theological scholar. Furthermore, his encyclopedic and logical mind made him the perfect candidate to undertake the systematic teaching of theology. Hodge proved to be a committed textual scholar who knew the complexities and genealogies of church doctrine, as well as the multifaceted philological and historical challenges of contemporary biblical scholarship.

Figure 31.3 *Caspar Wister Hodge Sr.*: Caspar Wister Hodge, Sr. was perhaps the quietest and most retiring of Hodge's children. In his youth, he was tutored by the immensely learned Joseph Addison Alexander. After his college graduation, he worked for a time as an assistant to professor Joseph Henry. When Joseph Addison Alexander died, Caspar left his pastorate to take his former mentor's faculty position at the Seminary. [*Special Collections, Princeton Theological Seminary Libraries*]

While Hodge did not have time to embark on any long and scholarly monographs as he took up his new position, he did work feverishly to complete a small apologetics volume he had promised to the American Sunday School Union.[12] It was a book he believed he could complete with relative ease because he knew the material so well. Hodge had wished to name the slender volume *The Narrow Way* (a nod to his own conservative Calvinist views), but the American Sunday School Union thought the name too uninviting and instead urged Hodge to consider naming it *The Way of Life*.[13] Hodge thought the Union's name a bit vague and his family complained that it made the little book sound more like an allegorical tale of religious fiction in the mode of Bunyan's *Pilgrim's Progress* than a primer on Christian doctrine, but he eventually acquiesced to the society's choice of title.[14]

It was a book that met with immediate success as it appealed to a wide range of readers. Those in the Old and New School embraced it, as did a great many Congregationalists and Episcopalians. The London Religious Tract Society immediately reprinted it, and missionaries in India had it translated into Hindustani to aid their work.[15] Eventually, the book sold thirty-five thousand copies in America and became Hodge's single most popular work during his lifetime.[16] Hodge realized only $250 from the sale of the copyright of the book to the American Sunday School Union and another 50£ (the rough equivalent of another $250) from the London Religious Tract Society, but the book's popularity among seminary professors, pastors, educated laymen, and those as lowly as "a servant girl and a hand-loom weaver" was a source of immense satisfaction to him.[17]

More important than the profits he received from the book was the opportune timing of its composition. Hodge used *The Way of Life* as a means of synthesizing his own thinking on Christianity's most basic doctrines. It became a blueprint of the theology he would spend the rest of his life teaching seminarians as he built the book around three foundational questions: "Are the Scriptures really a revelation from God? If they are, what doctrines do they teach? And what influence should those doctrines exert on our heart and life?"[18] Through these three questions, Hodge wished his readers to become more self-reflective about their own relationship to the Bible and its teaching. Just as importantly, he wanted to show his readers that "theology" was simply a fancy word for bringing ordered meaning to the myriad lessons and stories which filled the Bible.

In *The Way of Life*, Hodge presented his own overall understanding of the Bible's incredibly diverse contents. Different denominations had long depended on specific and time-honored confessional and creedal statements to help interpret the Bible's teachings as a coherent whole. Questions concerning the nature of baptism, the character of conversion, the exact role of Jesus in God's redemptive plan, the efficacy of the Lord's Supper, and the ultimate end for which humans had been created were topics explained through a religious tradition's confessional statements. As a Presbyterian, Hodge turned to the Westminster Confession to help him bring coherence to the teachings he found in the Bible's sixty-six books. In addition, Hodge's thinking bore the clear impress of his mentor, Archibald Alexander, whose philosophical predilections and theological stances proved to be the single most important interpreter for Hodge of both the Bible and the Westminster Confession.

One of Alexander's clearest marks on *The Way of Life* dated all the way back to the systematic theology course Hodge had taken from him nearly a quarter of century earlier. In this course Alexander had announced his clear conviction that all theological thought was rooted in Scottish Common Sense philosophy. In the same way, Hodge began his *The Way of Life* asserting a strict Scottish Common Sense philosophical line that declared evidence of God's existence and work in the world was available to everyone if they only paid attention to what their senses told them. In this fashion, Hodge held that the Bible's truths were universally accessible. At this point, however, Hodge followed Alexander in deviating from certain implications of Scottish Common Sense Realism because he did not believe that truth alone compelled people to accept God's offer of salvation. Hodge had to take into account the doctrines of human depravity and imputation.[19]

When considering these two doctrines, Hodge argued in *The Way of Life* that it was God's initiative, not just an exposure to truth, that ultimately activated people's moral sense and drew them toward salvation.[20] For Hodge, two people could be exposed to the exact same evidence of God's presence, but it is ultimately the work of God's Holy Spirit that quickens one person's heart and not another's to accept and act on the evidence available to all.[21] In such a stance, Hodge made his allegiance to Calvin's vision of predestination clear: God saved who he wanted to save and individual agency had little to do with it.

One should note here, however, the inherent tensions between Scottish Common Sense Realism's notion of a moral sense and Calvinism's doctrine of the Holy Spirit that Hodge was carefully trying to navigate in *The Way of Life*. Scottish Realism put a tremendous emphasis on humanity's moral intuition and its ability to detect and be moved by truth. Calvinism, with its doctrine of total depravity, held a much lower view of human moral ability. In its eyes, humans had no hope of detecting truth unless first touched and regenerated by the work of the Holy Spirit. In his own writings, Hodge vacillated between these two positions depending on the setting and the purpose of his work.

In *The Way of Life*, Hodge sought to set before his readers the most basic and important tenets of Christian doctrine, and he did so by stressing a more Calvinist approach to the detection and appreciation of truth. In later works, such as the opening section of his massive *Systematic Theology*, Hodge swings toward emphasizing the importance of the Baconian method and a Scottish Realist dependence on the senses in apprehending what is true, and in doing so emphasized human ability in the pursuit of truth in a way his more devotional works did not.[22] In broad strokes, he relied more heavily on Scottish Realism in relation to truth later in his career.

Hodge's earlier career bears a more marked response to his time in Europe, where his prolonged exposure to the *Erweckungsbewegung* in Germany and France's *Réveil* incited him to take every opportunity to stress the role of the Holy Spirit over and against the power of human intellect and innate moral sensibilities German metaphysical thought so idolized. By the time he sat down forty years later to write his great *Systematic Theology*, Hodge was more interested in proving that science and religion were not at odds with one another, so his pietistic tone receded as he pushed forward a strong Baconian belief in the power of the human senses to detect and act on the truth. In the end, Hodge proved inconsistent in his alliances to Calvinist and Scottish Realist thought, depending on one line of reasoning to prove a certain point at a certain time and changing his allegiances later when that suited his purpose. For all his famed consistency, Hodge's writing reveals just how fickle he could be in explaining the role of the Holy Spirit versus what one might expect from human moral intuition.

At the same time Hodge foregrounded his Calvinism in *The Way of Life*, he also used the work to show just how thoroughly his thinking was tied to the writings of St. Paul. The lessons found in Paul's epistles, rather than the more narrative theology found in the Gospels and historical books, the didactic lessons of the Old Testament's wisdom literature, or the revelatory writings of the prophets and Revelation, serve as the most foundational element in Hodge's own theological thinking. His annual courses on the Pauline epistles (and his Romans commentary) laid a bedrock foundation upon which he raised the edifice of all his future theological thinking. His commitment to Pauline theology comes across in his frequent references to Paul's writings throughout *The Way of Life*. Along with countless undocumented biblical references, Hodge includes 317 footnotes in the book. Of these notes, nearly 40 percent reference Paul's writings.

The Way of Life also serves as an indication of Hodge's larger contribution to the course of the Seminary and the theology taught there. Nowhere is this influence more clearly seen than in how Hodge chose to end his book. Hodge cared deeply about linking an appreciation of God's truth to one's actions, and in this spirit he entitled *The Way of Life's* final chapter "Holy Living." Here, he explored the causes, characteristics, and outcomes of the sanctified life. More common words for such a life might be "pious" or "holy." Such a life was defined by a person's daily commitment to living a Christ-like life in both word and deed. Hodge spent his book's final pages making it unmistakably clear that true religion consisted "in love to God and man," the former manifest "in reverence, devotion and obedience," while the latter showed itself chiefly in "benevolence and justice."[23]

For Hodge, "the necessity of holiness [was] absolute."[24] He believed it to be the single greatest mark of a transformed heart. In this way, *The Way of Life* serves as Hodge's own meditative reflection on the type of life he himself sought to live. True to the high value he put on improvement over time, Hodge considered the pursuit of holiness to be a gradual affair. It was not being "religious only on certain occasions."[25]

Using his last chapter to once again decry the passing religious fervency found in revivalism, Hodge wrote that genuine sanctified piety was not found where believers "pass from convulsions to fainting, and from fainting to convulsions," but instead, true religion was "steady, active and progressive."[26]

His commitment to living a sanctified life through the pursuit of personal piety also explains much in terms of what some of his contemporaries might have called an anemic eschatology. Hodge did not spend a great deal of time thinking, or teaching, about heaven, Christ's Second Coming, or the Final Judgment. The early 1840s was a time when vast numbers of Americans were caught up in debates about when Jesus might return to the earth to inaugurate his kingdom and judge humankind.

Most visible among those obsessed with these questions were the Millerites, a Protestant sect named after the prophet and leader William Miller. Miller had prophesied that Jesus would return by March 21, 1844. At the height of his popularity, tens—if not hundreds—of thousands were swayed by Miller's teaching. Miller spread his prophecies largely through the medium of print. Over four million pieces of literature penetrated even the country's most rural areas with his predictions of Christ's imminent return.[27] As Miller's date approached, some families gave away all their earthly possessions, others abandoned their crops, while still others laid aside every aspect of their normal lives as they simply stood in fields straining their eyes skyward in an attempt to be the first to see Christ descend from the clouds. When Christ failed to appear, Miller readily admitted he had been wrong and industriously made various biblical recalculations, which pointed to the new date of October 22, 1844, for Christ's return. Christ yet again failed to appear, leading everyone to call Miller's second prediction "The Great Disappointment."[28]

Hodge had little patience for Miller and those like him who felt they could predict the timing of what Christian doctrine called Christ's "Second Advent." He absolutely refused to spend time guessing when Christ might return. The Bible clearly taught that no man knew the time, and that settled the matter for Hodge.[29] He also showed little concern with whether Christ's Second Coming would usher in or follow the Millennium (the Christian belief that Christ's return would inaugurate a thousand-year reign of peace upon the earth.) In this regard, Hodge followed the traditional Reformed amillenial position on Christ's Second Coming: there was going to be no Millennium. Holding such a position, Hodge tended to idealize the events of the book of Revelation and other end-time prophecies, concentrating on the spiritual truths they illuminated rather than puzzling out exact timelines.

For Hodge, heaven was both "a place & a state," and in his own life and teaching he clearly stressed the latter.[30] Believing it "vain to ask" any details about heaven as a place, Hodge taught that the Christian's primary concern—the way of life—was to seek to partake of the Kingdom of Heaven on earth.[31] For this to happen, Christians had to commit themselves to wholehearted personal piety, or as he had called it in *The Way of Life*, "Holy Living." For Hodge, obtaining a foretaste of heaven on earth was only possible if one lived in harmony with God's leading. It was this very commitment to personal holiness that distinctly marked how he approached his new position of Professor of Theology at the Seminary.

Aside from *The Way of Life*'s immense popularity, the book is important for how it showed Hodge's desire to reach a wider audience with the theology taught at Princeton. Famous for this sophisticated and erudite theological thinking, Hodge was a man who could make himself understood when he wished among the less learned. He displayed this ability in a variety of settings, which ranged from the religious education of his own children and household servants to his gentle way of bringing first-year Seminary students along in their theological studies. His prose also revealed his ability to set out even difficult concepts with clarity and poise. It was such clarity that Hodge would be called on to use again and again in the coming years as he took over Alexander's position as the Seminary's chief spokesman, a role he also increasingly played for the Old School more generally until his voice came to represent the standard of conservative confessional orthodoxy among American Presbyterians.

32

DIDACTIC THEOLOGY

Admitting that God alone could know the condition of a person's heart, Hodge used the closing pages of *The Way of Life* to lay out what he considered to be the two most important (visible) characteristics of a true believer: "Knowledge and Piety."[1] For Hodge, these two characteristics were inseparably bound, for he believed that "the truth is the best means of promoting holiness."[2] One needed to be exposed to the truth in order to act upon it. Thus, the possibility of conversion and then the process of sanctification were heavily keyed to men and women being properly educated. It was this quest for proper education which lay at the heart of Hodge's senior course on didactic theology, a term which basically referred to the most fundamental doctrines of faith taught in the Bible.

Hodge had begun to share the teaching of the senior course in theology with Dr. Alexander during the winter of 1845–1846. Over the next five years, Alexander's presence in the theology course gradually receded as he turned his attention to serving as the Seminary's librarian and teaching homiletics. In his final years, Alexander found some of his greatest joy in listening to, and critiquing, student sermons.[3]

By the early 1850s, Hodge had largely completed writing the theology lectures he would give until he began teaching using his own *Systematic Theology* in the early 1870s. For a quarter of a century, the content of Hodge's theology lectures remained largely unchanged. His teaching manuscripts as well as class notes taken by his students reveal a striking consistency in the content of his lectures from the mid-1840s to the early 1870s. Only when Hodge began to compose his grand *Systematic* did the emphasis and content of his lectures change to any significant degree. In his *Systematic*, Hodge substantially revised his lecture material to emphasize the power of Baconian rationalism in the study of theology. In this way, Hodge's later theological teaching shifted to embrace the rational promise of the human mind over the less rationally explicable activities of the Holy Spirit.

Underlying Hodge's entire course in theology was his belief that the Protestant's "Rule of Faith" was nothing more nor less than an absolute reliance on the teachings of the Bible. Hodge most succinctly captures the core belief that oriented his entire theology in the opening lines of his "The Rule of Faith" lecture: "The word of God, which is contained in the Sacred Scriptures of the Old and New Testaments is [the] only infallible rule of faith & practice."[4] All Christian belief and action was *ruled* unequivocally by biblical teaching. As a consequence, a right understanding of the Bible was essential, and the best interpretative gloss on the teachings found in the Bible lay in the doctrines enunciated in the Westminster Confession.

As foundational as Hodge's views on the Bible were, he did not begin his theology course with his "Rule of Faith" first lecture. Like Alexander, Hodge began with a more panoramic disquisition on the "Nature and Sources of Theology." He then made a slightly more surprising move. His next lecture again forestalled his treatment of the "Rule of Faith" in favor of addressing the topic of "Enthusiasm." Before directly addressing the importance of the Bible, Hodge wished his students to understand the crucial role of the Holy Spirit in the study of theology. Hodge's "Enthusiasm" lecture clearly show the pietistic strains in his thought as he sought to convince his listeners that theology was not simply a rational exercise of putting all the pieces into their proper place. It was dependent on an inner light given by the Spirit of Christ. One could cultivate this light and then receive more wisdom through its illumination, but one could not hope to understand any important aspect of theology without the light shed by the Holy Spirit.

Hodge wished his students to appreciate the central role of the Holy Spirit in all aspects of scriptural study and moral reasoning. For Hodge, the Holy Spirit was "the immediate & Supreme authority."[5] All true Christians "must obey him."[6] In contrast to the Quakers who waited to be told by the Holy Spirit in their meetings what God might be saying, Hodge made it clear that "the present office and work of the Spirit on the minds of men is not the revelation of new truths, but the spiritual apprehension of those truths which are already objectively revealed & authenticated in the [Sacred Scriptures]."[7] The Quakers and those who held a more radical stance on the inner light of the Holy Spirit worked too independently of scripture for Hodge's taste, and it was these looser views of the centrality of scripture that led Christians into hopeless confusion in both doctrine and practice.

Hodge foregrounded his thoughts on the Holy Spirit's work not just to highlight his differences with the Quakers, but to also lay the groundwork for his distrust of the emotionalism so often found in revival activity. Among revivalists, the work of the Holy Spirit was often cited as the source for the shaking, the falling, the feinting, and the prophecies that sprang forth at camp meetings and prayer services. Hodge made it clear that the Holy Spirit had little to do with such behavioral and revelatory excesses; the Spirit's principal role was to confirm and guide revelation already given through God's Word. The Spirit did not send forth new prophets with new divine utterances to usher in new eras of the church, but instead worked closely with the biblical writings to lead individuals and communities toward redemption and sanctification.

If the Quakers erred on the side of trusting too much to the inner light outside the constraints of scripture, the Catholics erred in a different direction. In yet another early theology lecture entitled "Romish Doctrine as to the Rule of Faith," he argued that while the Catholics taught that the Bible was an important part of God's revelation, they also believed that it was hard to tell which books "are of divine authority, & therefore entitled to a place in the canon or rule of faith."[8] To compound this problem, Catholics taught that the common man or woman was "not competent to decide on the meaning of Scripture."[9] Instead, Catholics invested power in sources of divine authority other than scripture such as their traditions and their priesthood. The Quakers looked to the inner light as dependable revelation. The Catholics looked to the Holy Catholic Church and the Pope for revelation. Hodge covered all these points in order to outline Protestantism's distinctive nature and underline its most central theological belief, namely that scripture alone stood as the Rule of Faith.

The great body of Hodge's theology lectures, however, expounded on the teachings found in the Westminster Confession. His lectures provide a sophisticated analysis of the most central tenets of the Confession, and Hodge pursued this analysis by primarily following the Confession's own order of presentation. For those who had been catechized in their youth using the Confession, Hodge's lectures might have appeared as a highly advanced and detailed exposition of the same questions and propositions they had memorized as children. Beginning with the inspiration of holy scriptures and the central role of those scriptures in all theological study, Hodge moved on to discuss such key topics as the three members of the Godhead, the creation, and the central doctrines associated with God's redemptive plan: Original Sin, election, imputation, regeneration, sanctification, the Atonement, and justification.

At points, Hodge decided to explore in greater detail some of the implications of the doctrines found in the Westminster Confession. Particularly noteworthy is his frequent use of Roman Catholic and Lutheran doctrines as foils to standard Calvinist orthodoxy. The Catholics and Lutherans offered instructive lessons on where certain Christian traditions had strayed from a strict adherence to the Bible as the Rule of Faith. Hodge stressed notable touch points of Catholic and Lutheran error by dedicating the final nine of his course's sixty-eight lectures to extended discussions of the two Protestant sacraments: communion and baptism.

Beginning his discussion of the sacraments with the admission that "extreme difficulty has been encountered in fixing on any satisfactory definition of a sacrament," Hodge began his final lectures by tracing the various usages of the term. Not surprising, he concludes this terminological overview by telling his students that it is only by looking at the sacred scriptures and their teachings on baptism and the Lord's Supper that one might arrive at the true meaning of the word "sacrament."[10] Hodge distills the nature of the sacraments down to three characteristics: (1) they are ordinances instituted by God and executed by Christians; (2) they must involve sensible signs; (3) they must "be appointed to signify, seal & apply Christ & the benefits of the new covenant."[11]

To draw out the full implications of these three characteristics, Hodge carefully lays out how this particular view of the sacraments differs from those held by the Catholic and Lutheran traditions. On the one hand, Catholics invested the sacraments with inherent virtue and power, enabling them to be efficacious independent of the spiritual state of the recipient.[12] As a consequence, people could enjoy the benefits of God's grace if they simply partook of the sacraments whether they had faith or not. For Catholics, the power of the sacrament resided in the sacrament itself and its priestly administration, not in the recipient's faith. Here, Hodge saw the role of the priest as particularly important because the priest's faith helped invest the sacrament with the necessary power to bring grace even to those who lack faith.[13] The Lutherans, on the other hand, may not have gone as far as the Catholics in bestowing innate power in their sacraments, but they nevertheless believed the sacraments to have a degree of efficacy independent of the recipient's faith. Lutherans reasoned that sacraments wielded some power "not in the virtue of any thing in them, but by reason of the word of God, or promise of remission of sins, which by divine appointment is connected with them."[14]

In illustrating this point for his students, Hodge cited one of Luther's favorite sacramental illustrations: the story in Mark's Gospel where a woman with a flow of blood is cured by touching the hem of Christ's garment. Luther cited this story as an illustration that while the woman's faith brought about the healing, it was the "real virtue in Christ" which made her faith work.[15] The woman did not need any larger understanding of who Jesus truly was. She did not need to be a participant in any kind of Christian faith community. She simply needed some faith that was then completed by the power inherent in the person of Jesus. In a similar way, taught Luther, the sacraments have power in and of themselves, but to access that power a certain element of faith on the part of the recipient also needs to be present. It was this element of faith on the part of the recipient, not on the part of any priest, that set the Lutherans apart from the Catholics.

Hodge was not comfortable in going as far as Luther in granting the sacraments some form of innate power. For Hodge, sacraments were signs and seals of God's grace, but they contained absolutely no inherent, quasi-magical powers. He repeatedly stated that the efficacy of the sacraments was "not due either to them, or to him that doth administer them, but solely to the blessing of [Christ] & the working of his Spirit" in the recipient.[16]

In this way, Hodge differed even from Calvin on the subject of sacraments (and from American Reformed traditions such as the Mercersburg Theology that held more closely to Calvin's sacramental views). Calvin had held that there was a mysterious power in the sacraments beyond human understanding that touched those who received them with God's grace. For Calvin, not everything connected to the administration and reception of the sacraments was rational and easily explained. Throughout his lectures, Hodge took a harder line against any notions that the sacraments had a mysterious, inexplicable power.[17] Without reservation, he stressed that the efficacy of the sacraments was solely tied to the faith of the recipient. The sacrament was neither a sign nor a seal of God's grace without faith on the part of those who partook of it.

One problem with Hodge's sacramental views—and the views of the Reformed tradition more generally—was found in the sacrament of baptism, where Presbyterians baptized infants who were not able to make choices based on their own faith in God. Because the faith of the recipient played no part in an infant's baptism, Hodge dedicated three lectures to explaining the sacrament of baptism as a whole. He began these lectures by declaring that the mode of baptism (sprinkling or immersion) was not nearly as important as the intent behind the sacrament. Placing too much stress on the baptismal mode was "contrary to the whole spirit of the gospel."[18] Baptism's central importance lay in how it signaled purification, and through this signification helped convey "the benefits of the New Covenant" by showing the baptized person's commitment to living a life of faith in the context of a community of believers.[19] In adults, the sacrament needed to meet with faith in the recipient to be effectual, but in the case of infants who were too young to exercise their own faith, the sacrament could be administered as a promise of future state of grace if the one being baptized had at least one Christian parent.

This particular view of baptism depended on the expansive Reformed conception of the "church as visible & invisible—the latter as embracing only true believers, the former including those who have only an external connection with true believers—either by professing the same faith, or by some other bonds."[20] Simply put, the visible church will always be a mixture of believers and nonbelievers, and it is not the duty of the church to discern every person's heart, but to err on the side of inclusion. If a person demonstrated enough outward signs of faith, they could be included in the faith community. Only God could ultimately judge who was a true member of his church and who was not.

Following this line of reasoning, Hodge believed infants to be members of the visible church because of their bond to at least one believing parent. As members of the visible church, children were baptized as a signification that the promises of Christ would come to pass due, in part, to the parent's faith (because, as Hodge reminded his students, scripture "everywhere" teaches "the promises made to the father have come to us").[21] The historical precedent for this line of argumentation most vividly showed up in the rite of circumcision for the ancient Jews who distinguished their children as partakers in God's promises by physically marking them with a sign of God's covenant with the entire Jewish nation. Similarly, those in the Reformed tradition held that until a child of a believing parent was old enough to have his or her own individual faith, that child could partake of the grace of Christian community and the seal of God's love through the sacrament of baptism.

Throughout his discussions on the sacraments, Hodge stressed that following the teachings of scriptures, not simply taking the sacraments, led to salvation. The sacraments held no "magical influence" in obtaining the favor of Christ.[22] Hodge taught that it was only through the Bible's teachings and faith in those teachings—his own rendition of *Sola Scriptura, Sola Fide*—that any person might take advantage of the grace offered by God. In this way, Hodge's theology exalted the Bible above all else, as the power and authority of the sacraments, those in ecclesiastical positions of power, and even church tradition needed to bow before its teachings.

33

TEACHING AND PREACHING

When Hodge became the Seminary's Professor of Theology, he stood at the zenith of his powers in the classroom.[1] By the mid-1840s, the Seminary was enrolling around 140 students a year. By the time Hodge had finished his fifty-six-year teaching career, he had trained over three thousand students. His longevity in the classroom and the unrivaled consistency of his thought rendered him a peerless advocate for the tenets of conservative Calvinist Christianity in America. No single American professor trained more graduate students in any field than did Hodge during the nineteenth century. Among his students one finds such theological luminaries as John Williamson Nevin, Albert Barnes, the famed Irish professor of theology Robert Watts, the founder of the Southern Baptist's first great seminary, James Petigru Boyce, and his eventual successor at Princeton, the internationally renowned conservative Calvinist theologian Benjamin Breckinridge Warfield. The influence of his students, however, reached far beyond the field of theology, as literally thousands of them entered the pastoral and missionary fields.

While Hodge might have become most famous for his theology lectures, the course that he taught for the longest period of time was his junior class seminar on the Pauline Epistles. By the time Hodge began his theology lectures in the mid-1840s, he had already regularly taught the Pauline epistles for nearly two decades. Once Hodge took the position of Professor of Theology, his lectures on didactic theology and the writings of Paul became the backbone of his teaching load at the Seminary.

Hodge held both these classes twice each week in the afternoons. He met for one hour with the juniors to discuss Paul on Tuesdays and Thursday, and then turned his attention to his senior class course on theology for one hour on Wednesday and Friday. There was both rigor and rhythm in this schedule. Hodge lectured on the first

meeting day of the week and then assigned students to write answers to between twenty-five and forty questions by the second class day of the following week. Hodge used these second class periods to engage his students in a Socratic manner that pushed them to defend and elaborate on their written answers. By all accounts, Hodge's logical mind and encyclopedic knowledge made his Socratic method a wonder to behold, as he reduced students to seeing fallacious positions they held or encouraged them to follow their lines of reasoning to even more forceful conclusions. Through these written and oral question-and-answer exercises, each student carried away from his seminary experience between two and six quarto-sized volumes. In an age before formal textbooks existed, Hodge made each of his students compose his own textbooks for future reference.[2]

At various times, Hodge was questioned about what he considered essential to good pedagogy. Often these questions came from former students who were embarking on their own teaching careers. Lyman Atwater, who eventually became a faculty member both at Princeton College and Princeton Seminary, recalled that when he asked what made for a good teacher, Hodge had replied: "Knowledge, Ability, Fidelity and Tact," and then smiling he went on to add "many who have the first three, fail for the want of the last."[3] Even in this aphoristic reply, one sees the kind of gentle humor that was an earmark of his classroom presence.

William Swan Plumer, who had become a professor at Western Theological Seminary in Pennsylvania and would later teach at Columbia Theological Seminary in Georgia, also asked his former mentor for specifics on good classroom practice. In a thoughtful and lengthy reply, Hodge argued that four key components needed to be present for a good learning experience.[4] First, students needed a foundational book or books to which they could refer as they began the study of a particular topic. Second, students needed an able teacher who could guide them through their initial explorations of the topic under discussion. Third, a teacher must push his students to write a great deal on the topic themselves. Hodge saw writing as a way to compel students to be thorough, logical, and clear in their formulations and expositions of theological positions.[5] Finally, it was necessary to drill each student through oral question-and-answer examinations both to clarify their thinking and enable them to advocate various points of view. It is evident from surviving student notes that every class Hodge taught bore the impress of these four elements.

Until he began to use his own *Systematic Theology* in the final years of his life, Hodge assigned Turretin's *Institutes for Elenctic Theology* as his core textbook in his theology course. Hodge built his course around these *Institutes*, having his students read twenty to forty pages of Turretin in Latin to prepare for class.[6] He often commented that he believed Turretin's *Institutes* to be "incomparably the best book as a whole on systematic theology."[7]

Such an opinion did not keep him from using a wide range of other books when he addressed specific doctrines such as the Trinity, sin, total depravity and grace. Hodge prepared his classes by reading everything he "could command on the subject in hand, making notes of each author."[8] He regularly assigned the published lectures of prominent theologians such as the Scotsmen George Hill and John Dick and the German Georg Christian Knapp, all of whom were distinctly conservative and Reformed in their thinking.[9] Systematically reading through these writers and others, Hodge carefully synthesized everything he had read to make it accessible to his students. His presentations were so clear, logical, and sequential that it was a commonplace among his students that "his thoughts move in rows."[10]

Hodge's students, when reflecting on their classroom experience with him, repeatedly described his teaching as marked with extreme erudition, commanding logic, and a spirit of gentle holiness. It is as if Hodge encapsulated Aristotle's ideal of the effective communicator: a speaker who commanded the perfect balance of *pathos* (the compassion to seek to understand one's audience), *logos* (a clear understanding of the knowledge one wishes to convey), and *ethos* (a trustworthy character). Aside from everyone's immense respect for Hodge's mastery of his material and his ability to teach it, his *ethos*, or pious character, perhaps left the deepest impression on his students. James Boyce, a student of Hodge's who later became the founding president of Southern Baptist Theological Seminary in Kentucky, spoke for the multitude when he characterized Hodge as "one of the most excellent of men . . . so modest and yet so wise, so kind and fatherly in his manner, and yet of so giant an intellect" that he deserved "a world of praise."[11]

As Hodge repeated his lectures year after year, many wished to see him publish them for a wider audience. Hodge himself was in favor of such a plan. Published lectures were a common way to make available and popularize certain strains of current theological thought. Examples of such published lectures not only included the work of some of Hodge's favorite theologians such as Dick, Hill, and Knapp, but also of some of his antagonists such as Charles Finney.

Hodge also thought of publishing his lectures because as he repeated the course annually, students and even professional copyists began to transcribe them for wider dissemination. If written copies of his lectures were to circulate, Hodge wished for greater control over their content and perhaps some royalty income for his work. Hodge's own son, Archie, who had entered the Seminary in 1843 (and was often kidded by his classmates that the combination of names "Archibald Alexander" and "Hodge" placed great expectations upon him) joined the first formal group to attempt to transcribe his father's theological lectures verbatim.[12] What Archie and his friends had undertaken as a sign of respect for his father came to be a source of constant irritation for Hodge as the years passed. He disliked the presence of these copied notes because he found that students who had them either failed to attend his lectures or came to his classroom with a lackadaisical attitude since they need not toil to make their own notes.

Ultimately, Hodge postponed writing down the content of his lectures largely due to the constant pleas of the Seminary's board of directors. The board repeatedly implored him not to publish his lectures because they thought it would hurt the Seminary's enrollment.[13] Many students came to Princeton Seminary specifically to study with Hodge. If they could acquire his thinking through a book, they may not come at all.

As Hodge neared the end of his teaching career, the Seminary's board relented and even encouraged him to write down his theological thinking for future generations. As a result, Hodge reworked his lecture material into his grand *Systematic Theology*. Ultimately, the completion of the *Systematic* improved Hodge's teaching, as he replaced Turretin with his own work to acquaint his student with the fundamentals and intricacies of Christian doctrine and theology. Assigning sections from his *Systematic*, Hodge no longer lectured in his classes but gave over the entire time to engaging his students in a Socratic dialogue over what they had read for the week. He considered these final years of teaching among his best.[14]

It would be a terrible mistake to think that all of Hodge's teaching happened in the narrow confines of the Seminary's classrooms. He regularly took the opportunity to supply pulpits in New Jersey and Philadelphia.[15] He also frequently preached at the College Chapel. Hodge, however, was never known as anything but a solid, if not overly inspiring, preacher.[16] He could be powerful in his occasional sermons, particularly those he preached at the funerals of close friends.[17] The eulogies he offered for Dr. Miller's son, Edward, Dr. Alexander's son, Addison, and his dear friend Albert Dod ranked among his most moving and eloquent offerings. In the main, however, Hodge never gained the preaching reputation enjoyed by his senior colleagues. Miller had long been known for his witty, learned manner in the pulpit and was a great favorite among more cultured and urbane listeners.[18] Alexander had learned his trade in the revival and country church pulpits of Virginia, and he was well known for his ability to move his audience with vivid illustrations and dynamic rhetoric.[19]

Hodge was less comfortable in the pulpit than either of his senior colleagues, perhaps because he did not have their same experience in the traditional pastorate. He was also a man able to develop deep and lasting friendships, but seemed far less able to make particularly good first impressions. When people first encountered him, he often came across as reserved and aloof. James W. Alexander once described a first acquaintance with Hodge as not "generally very assuring or attractive to strangers."[20] Such aloofness in an initial encounter could not have served Hodge well when he supplied pulpits where he more often came across as a learned man rather than a passionate preacher. He was at his best in both preaching and teaching when his audience knew him more personally. His character and life added weight to his words, so visiting new settings to preach often left him offering valuable insights but without the added heft of his listeners being able to weigh his words against a more intimate knowledge of his life. Such a knowledge was one of Hodge's greatest assets when it came to driving home a message. In a certain sense, the consistency and piety of Hodge's own life was his single most powerful sermon illustration.

There was a teaching setting, however, outside the classroom where he did truly excel. It was a place where the intimacy of the setting and his familiarity with his audience allowed his character to compliment the messages he offered. All who knew Hodge in the final third of his life agreed that he was at his absolute best when he offered his heartfelt scripture meditations at the Seminary's weekly "Sabbath afternoon Conferences."[21]

What students knew as the Sabbath afternoon Conference had begun in the earliest days of the Seminary and were held in the largest meeting room of the Seminary's main building, the Oratory. These early meetings began with students offering their own reflections on a topic or biblical passage and then one of the Seminary's professors would add his own thoughts. Appropriately enough, Hodge had actually been the very first student to give a public address in the Oratory soon after Alexander Hall had opened its doors in 1817. Over time, students took a less active role in presenting material at these meetings, and the Seminary's professors took turns in each conference to drive home practical points of Christian devotion to accent the more intellectual pursuits that characterized the students' classroom training.[22]

While Alexander and Miller played a constant and important role in the Sabbath afternoon Conferences, it was Hodge who turned these meetings into the perfect blend of devotional exhortation and practical religious knowledge. In recounting his father's contributions in this setting, Archie commented that for students "who were diligent in taking notes," these sessions provided them a huge "mass of coherent thought for permanent use."[23] Hodge took each of these sessions as seriously as he did his time in the classroom. Among the papers discovered after his death were reams of preparatory notes for these conferences.

Even though the Seminary's students cycled through every three years, there is no indication that Hodge ever delivered the same conference meditation twice. He created a new conference paper for each and every Sabbath afternoon he led, sometimes carefully reworking the same theme or passage over a series of decades.[24] For example, over a twelve-year period he offered three meditations entitled "Backsliding," a topic of great interest to him because of the burden he felt to equip every student to move daily toward Christ in obedience and faith.[25]

Like his conference papers on backsliding, the vast majority of Hodge's Sabbath afternoon talks were topical. He addressed a diverse array of issues, using such titles as

"Fasting," "Assurance," "Ambition," and "Satan." Hodge based slightly less than half his meditations on a scriptural passage. Instead, he favored picking a topic and ranging widely from doctrine to scripture to human experience as he addressed the issue. When he did base his talks in scripture, he overwhelmingly favored the New Testament epistles with an even more pronounced favoritism for the letters of Paul. One out of four of his scripturally based conference meditations came from Paul's writings. Only 24 of his still extant 379 conference talks were solely rooted in passages from the Old Testament.[26]

The meditations themselves followed a basic pattern. Hodge began each meditation with a simple statement that pertained to the topic at hand. Titling the meditation he gave on Christmas Day, 1853, "The Advent," Hodge began his meditation with that statement: "The observance of Christmas is not commanded."[27] Then, in usual logical and crystal-clear manner, he moved point by point to explore the holiday's history, relations to scripture, and finally the benefits of its observance. As with so many of his meditations, he ended with an injunction to practical action. In so doing, he continued a tradition he had begun in his Romans commentary by capping his expository thoughts with practical inferences rooted in his exposition. Using this strategy of exposition and application, Hodge drove home his conviction that all of scripture's lessons should lead to life-changing, personal action. He argued, in this case, that the Advent should move the human heart to gratitude, joy, obedience, and devotion.[28]

In all of Hodge's teaching, whether it took the form of his published writings or his time before students or church congregations, there was a pronounced emphasis on piety born of knowledge. He modeled much of his own method on the apostle Paul, who was fond of logical argumentation to expound Gospel truths and then make those truths applicable to real-life situations. In settings such as the Sabbath afternoon Conferences, Hodge showed just how convinced he was that teaching, in whatever form it took, was a matter of both head and heart. He wished to make his every listener someone who came away from his lessons not only with a better understanding of what the Bible said on a given topic, but with some idea of the practical, life-changing consequences of taking those Bible lessons seriously. As he had driven home in his *The Way of Life*, the Christian needed to attain knowledge, but only if that knowledge led to a life marked by charitable action and greater holiness.

34

THE PUBLIC FACE OF THE SEMINARY

In 1846, Hodge decided to sit for another portrait. Hugh had suggested that his brother once again give the commission to Rembrandt Peale, but Hodge turned instead to Daniel Huntington, perhaps the nation's most-sought-after portrait artist of the day. Huntington was so highly regarded that he served an unprecedented twenty-one years as the president of the National Academy of the Arts. His reputation rested not only on his substantial artistic ability, but on his strong Protestant beliefs, which showed up in the frequent appearance of lofty, if slightly sentimental, religious symbols and characters in his work. His reputation, talent, and piety made him a natural choice to paint a second portrait of Hodge.

The difference between Huntington's vision of Hodge and Peale's reveals much. By the mid-1840s, Hodge had transformed from the Seminary's vibrant junior professor to its established leader. Huntington paints a mature Hodge, a man with a confident, straightforward gaze and the two defining marks of his clerical vocation: a white necktie and an open Bible (see figure 31.1). Far from Peale's electric vision of Hodge as a windblown, youthful crusader, Huntington paints Hodge as a man exuding the thoughtful steadiness of an accomplished scholar and denominational statesman.

Hodge not only stood center stage on Huntington's canvas, but he increasingly took the most prominent place in the affairs of the Seminary. One indication of this fact is the way in which he became a key person in receiving and entertaining important visitors to the school. From Adolphe Monod of France to the great German Lutheran historian and theologian Isaak Dorner, Hodge stood as a pivotal figure of hospitality and intellectual exchange as the Seminary hosted some of his era's most prominent Protestants.[1] Memorable among such visitors—and someone who exercised a profound influence on Hodge's thinking about denominational financial governance—was William Cunningham, the famous Scottish churchman and reformer. Cunningham had come to America in 1843 as an ambassador from the newly established Free Presbyterian Church in Scotland. The Free Church had just broken from Scotland's Established Church over the issue of who held the right to appoint church ministers: the congregants themselves or higher powers who manipulated appointments through elaborate networks of patronage. The Free Church wished their ministers to be elected solely "by the people and for the people."[2] Cunningham visited Princeton (and stayed in Hodge's home) twice during his five-month American tour. The Seminary's faculty and board were so impressed with him that they awarded him an honorary doctorate degree.

In deciding to break from Scotland's Established Church, the newly formed Free Church had been thrown entirely upon its own financial resources. No longer could they count on state aid for their activities. As a result, the Scottish Free Church pioneered the idea of a common "sustenation" fund to sustain its clergy, a fund born out of dire necessity as the congregations that had seceded pooled their resources for their very survival. Hodge was immensely impressed by how the fund both embodied St. Paul's exhortations about partnership in the Gospel and sought to distribute equitably the church's resources between congregations that had more and those that had less. Inspired in large measure by the Free Church's "sustenation" fund, Hodge campaigned in the coming years for a similar resource to help pay American Presbyterian ministers.

Cunningham, along with Thomas Chalmers, was one of the most important leaders of Scotland's Free Church movement. In 1842 the newly established Free Church appointed him one of the first professors at New College, the Free Church's first seminary.[3] Firmly convinced that training evangelical and competent ministers was one of the most important challenges facing the Free Church, Cunningham took the position but wished to visit America to see firsthand how the American seminaries educated their clergy. He also hoped that an American trip would help him gain much-needed financial support for the fledgling Free Church. Cunningham's American mission led him to tour most of the country's major cities including New York, Philadelphia, Boston, Richmond, and Baltimore.[4]

Standing six feet tall with a head covered with massive and dense curly locks, Cunningham was an imposing figure.[5] James W. Alexander found him to be "the most satisfactory foreigner" he had ever seen, although he did quibble with Cunningham's pronounced attachment to snuff.[6] Cunningham was erudite and impressive in the breadth of his reading and conversed easily on an endless array of topics. He was such a gifted orator that both friends and foes remarked that few rivaled his powers of persuasion. Hodge took an instant liking to the Scottish crusader. He later commented that he did "not recollect of ever having met anyone to whom I was so much drawn, and for whom I entertained so high a respect and so warm a regard as I did for him, on such short acquaintance."[7] Hodge considered the Scotsman's visits to Princeton as "sunny spots which, whenever I look back on my life, my eyes rest with delight."[8]

James Alexander described Hodge's friendship with Cunningham as "friendship at first sight," a remarkable occurrence in his opinion because of Hodge's noted tendency to make less-than-inviting first impressions.[9] Cunningham drew Hodge to him through his own ardent evangelical, thoroughly Reformed faith. Both men shared a love of Turretin and an unwavering commitment to the basic tenets of the Westminster Confession.[10] They also agreed on a high view of scripture, a conviction that kept both men from denouncing the institution of slavery.[11]

In Scotland, the Presbyterian battle lines demarcated two basic camps, one denominated "Evangelical" and the other "Moderate." The Moderates, as the name implied, took a more broad-minded, less-strident view of the tenets set forth in the Westminster Confession.[12] By the time of "the Great Disruption," the moment when the Free Church split from Scotland's Established Church, Moderates had gained the reputation of resembling the American Unitarians.[13] In the main, the Scottish Moderates held a high view of what humans could accomplish and often openly disdained Calvinism. While the Great Disruption found its breaking point in issues of patronage and church government, the split between the Scottish Moderates and Evangelicals played no less a role in the Free Church separating from the Established Church. As one Scottish minister put it: "The Disruption was the separation of two religions," the liberal-leaning Moderates and the orthodox Calvinist Evangelicals.[14]

Cunningham hated how the Moderates denigrated God's initiative and grace, and he became one of their most implacable foes. Hodge saw Cunningham as a man standing for the central orthodoxies of the Christian religion in a Scottish climate that was growing ever more cold to the plain truths of the Gospel. The confirmed theological conservatism of both men bound them together as brothers. In later years, when a student approached Cunningham to see if a course he wished to take overseas with Hodge might count toward his degree in Scotland, Cunningham took a pinch of snuff and told the student that the only question he needed to ask himself about any course taken with Hodge was whether it should count for two courses rather than just one.[15]

35

MODERATOR OF THE GENERAL ASSEMBLY

As the septuagenarian Alexander's star dimmed, Hodge's shone all the brighter. As he increasingly shouldered the burdens of the Seminary's lead professor, his visibility grew on the national Presbyterian stage as well. In 1842, he attended the Presbyterian General Assembly for the first time as an official representative from his local presbytery, a role that Drs. Alexander or Miller had played in the past. Hodge was now the one called upon to represent the Seminary's needs and accomplishments to his Presbyterian brethren. In the years that followed, Hodge regularly took his turn as a delegate to the Assembly where he came to serve on a number of national committees and boards. The exact measure of Hodge's growing stature within the denomination became clear in 1846 when his fellow Presbyterians elected him the Assembly's moderator.

The General Assembly over which Hodge presided was uneventful by the standards of the Assemblies convened a decade earlier, convocations which had weathered the storms of the revival controversies, the Barnes trial, and ultimately the schism. The 1846 session, however, did revisit with slightly less volcanic variations some of the issues that had troubled the denomination over the past decade. Hodge had to use his considerable diplomatic skills as moderator to help guide two potentially divisive issues through his year's session: slavery and Presbyterian parochial schools.

The 1846 Assembly once again grappled with the lingering specter of slavery when several petitions and memorials from a range of sources—including the Presbyterian Churches of Canada and Ireland—reached its floor. Ultimately, the Assembly answered these petitions in the same way it had for decades, declaring that while the practice of slavery was regrettable and should eventually be abolished, it was an institution in no way prohibited by scripture.[1] Assembly delegates reasoned that more aggressive denunciations of slavery denigrated scripture's teaching and risked over-stepping the church's authority by interfering in civil matters.

Hodge himself had revisited the issue of slavery just two years before when he reviewed for the *Repertory* four recently published works that debated the institution's biblical justification. In his article, he addressed the growing tensions between those who advocated "that slave holders should not be admitted to the communion of the church, and that slavery should immediately, under all circumstances and regardless of all consequences, be abolished" (the abolitionist stance) and those who saw the institution as evil but advocated a course of gradual eradication.[2] Throughout his review, Hodge did not deviate from the position he had first made public in 1836, namely that although slavery was often a detestable institution in practice, there was nothing in scripture to forbid it.[3]

Hodge's 1844 piece is telling, however, in how it shows Hodge's growing distaste for abolitionists. Just as Hodge had no patience with the radical enthusiasts who advocated more emotional measures in revivalism, he showed little tolerance for those who took an emotional, rather than scriptural, position against slavery. He denounced abolitionists as possessing "an evil spirit; a spirit of railing, of bitterness, of exaggeration; a spirit which leads to the perversion of facts, and to assertions which often shock the common sense and moral feelings of the community."[4] Abolitionists, in his mind, were blinded by their own misguided ambitions, totally untrustworthy in their methods, and sadly unaware of the utterly ruinous consequences of their agenda.

Hodge bolstered his attack on abolitionists by detailing how they troubled the nation to a degree far out of proportion to their actual numbers. The fallacious nature of their views could be seen in how they had "failed to command the assent of the great body of the intelligent and pious men of the country."[5] Even the casual observer could see that the vast majority of American Christians, the "Congregationalists of New England, the Episcopalians, the Presbyterians, the Baptists, the Methodists, have one and all refused to sanction the unscriptural doctrine on which the whole structure of moral abolitionism rests."[6] To Hodge's way of thinking, how could so many Christians be wrong? His commitment to Scottish Common Sense Realist philosophy testified that the shared sentiment of so many moral men and women was a convincing indicator of what was truly morally just. Hodge was also too much of a Federalist at heart to allow society's precious order and harmony to be upset by the misguided actions of a handful of radicals who seemed bent on ruining rather than building up his beloved country.

In his retrospective essay on the 1846 General Assembly, Hodge continued to advocate a more moderate, less confrontational approach to slavery than that favored by William Garrison and those of his ilk. Although matters would radically shift just a few years later, in 1846 Hodge could write that he knew not "a single presbyterian minister, either south or north, who has ever ventured to teach that slavery is a desirable institution which ought to be rendered permanent."[7] The answer, therefore, remained one of gradual reform, not abrupt change. He knew that if the abolitionists had their way, Southern Presbyterians would see no option but to separate from their Northern brethren, a division that horrified him. In the midst of his gradualist rhetoric, however, Hodge found himself moving ever more firmly to a position that held slavery to be an institution marked by such a propensity toward human degradation and evil that the country was better off without it.[8] By the mid-1840s, Hodge held a profoundly paradoxical stance on slavery. He had hardened in his distaste for abolitionism, but he had also come to a firmer conviction that slavery in the United States must be abolished. It was a tension that would grow both for him, and his nation, over the next fifteen years.

One other issue which demanded much of the Assembly's time, and was dear to Hodge's own heart, centered on the possibility of establishing Presbyterian parochial schools across the nation. Hodge had entertained such an idea ever since his return from Europe nearly twenty years before. Now he joined many of his Presbyterian brethren in declaring that the country's "common school system is rapidly assuming not a mere negative, but a positively anti-Christian character."[9] In an attempt to pursue one of the Church's most important functions, namely educating every Presbyterian child in orthodox Christian doctrine, Hodge allied himself with those who wished to see Presbyterian parochial schools developed alongside every Presbyterian church in the country.[10]

Ultimately, plans to develop a Presbyterian parochial school system lacked the broad-based support necessary to make them a reality, but Hodge never wavered in his desire to see proper doctrine catechized into every child of believing parents. Sunday Schools could not hope to adequately teach children the fundamentals of the Christian faith when they only had an hour a week to do so, and the country's common schools were moving so far from religion that even regularly reading the Bible in schools was fast becoming a practice of the past.[11] Not surprisingly for someone who had given his life to education, Hodge saw the development of Presbyterian parochial schools as a key element in strengthening both the church and the country. It was a dream he never completely abandoned, but he also never saw fulfilled.

The following year when the General Assembly met in Richmond, Virginia, Hodge offered its opening sermon, an honor granted every outgoing moderator.[12] He took as his text 1 Corinthians 9:14: "Even so hath the Lord ordained, that they which preach the gospel should live the gospel." Hodge used this most important of Presbyterian stages to argue one of his long-held convictions that had recently been reignited by the time he had spent with William Cunningham, namely that ministers should be paid enough to execute their office without having to worry about their personal finances. Hodge argued that Paul had been unequivocal in his views on supporting those in the ministry. Paul taught "that those who devoted themselves to the preaching of the gospel are entitled to live by the gospel. A competent support for themselves & for their families . . . it is not a gratuity, it is not a favour, but a matter of justice and divine right."[13] In a sermon that ran some forty handwritten pages, Hodge strove to show through scriptural warrant and historical precedent that it had always been the "common obligation" of the church to support its ministers, and that this duty is currently so neglected by Presbyterians that their negligence was an affront to the cause of Christ.[14]

Hodge argued that the very nature of Presbyterian Church polity implied that congregations should bind together in mutual support. He advocated that larger, even national funds, be collected and then dispersed to support equitably Presbyterian churches across the country. Thus, rich urban churches would help support poor frontier congregations.[15] Hodge angled for a larger, more coherent vision of the American Presbyterian Church. He saw the issue of "sustenation" as a place where the Presbyterian Church could gain a more vibrant sense of its national and international mission through the congregational partnerships such a fund would facilitate. Hodge's impassioned pleas on the subject proved to make no "sensible impression" upon the Assembly, and no plans were pursued to better accommodate the support of ministers.[16]

Even with this particular failure, the topic of ministerial "sustenation" remained on Hodge's mind, and he visited the topic again and again in the coming years in both public and private settings. Just one month after the close of the Civil War, the General Assembly entertained a number of overtures from different presbyteries for establishing a general denominational fund to financially support clergy. Although the General Assembly made no formal decisions, Hodge was thrilled that his denomination now seemed "awake to the importance of the subject."[17] Taking advantage of the moment, Hodge dusted off his nearly-two-decade-old sermon to rouse support for the idea at Princeton. The sermon once again catalyzed Hodge's passion on the issue, and he wrote a forceful plea on behalf of the idea for the next issue of the *Repertory*.[18] So strongly did Hodge feel about "sustenation" that he approached a local printer to publish the essay independently in pamphlet form so that it might be widely distributed among his Presbyterian brethren.[19]

Although Hodge would not live to see the formation and implementation of a national "sustenation" fund, he never lost an opportunity to advocate the idea during his lifetime. In part, he was driven not only by Paul's clear teaching on the subject, but by his own his conception of the church universal. The ideas of equity and partnership that were so highly prized values throughout the New Testament church completely resonated for him with the idea of a "sustenation" fund. Such a fund would signal to all the grand coherence of vision and resources that should mark Christ's visible church on earth. In this way, the "sustenation" fund was both about providing for the denomination's ministers, but also it was a way of signaling the world at large that the American Presbyterian Church was indeed serious about more accurately mirroring scripture's aspiration of a universal church.

36

"THE NONSENSICAL DIALECT OF TRANSCENDENTALISM"

The idea of a universal church may have seemed little more than a pipe dream as the nineteenth century progressed and American Christianity splintered into ever-more-numerous denominations, sects, and innovative religious traditions. Even new manifestations of Christianity in the United States such as the New England Unitarians began to fragment. One of the most prominent Unitarian factions to arise by the late 1830s was Transcendentalism. Ill-defined at first, and composed of marked diversity of thinking within its own ranks, great debates arose as to what it exactly meant to be a Transcendentalist. As the movement coalesced through the 1840s, certain broad generalizations came to distinguish it: most major figures of the movement had significant ties to Unitarianism, many were connected to Harvard, and all eschewed the British and Scottish empiricism championed by thinkers such as Locke and Reid in favor of the more Romantic German Idealism of Immanuel Kant, Johann Fichte, Frederick Schelling and G. W. F. Hegel.[1] The growing presence and power of Transcendentalist thought troubled professors not only at the Seminary, but also at Princeton College where James Alexander saw "an increasing number in our ambitious students every year who babble the nonsensical dialect of transcendentalism."[2]

Transcendentalism had been forged out of Unitarianism's engagement with the German Higher Criticism. Beginning in the 1810s, an ever-growing number of intellectually gifted New Englanders traveled to Europe to study theology. Several of these scholars became influential members of Harvard's faculty including Edward Everett, Charles Ticknor, George Bancroft and Frederic Hedge. While studying in Europe, each of these men imbibed the latest trends in German philosophy and biblical criticism. Others such as Ralph Waldo Emerson had the opportunity to travel in Europe, if not study there, and still others brought Europe to America like the Boston Unitarian ministers George Ripley and Theodore Parker, who voraciously read both German and French philosophers and theologians connected with the Higher Criticism.

German Higher Criticism was characterized by a commitment to understanding the Bible's language as thoroughly dependent on its historical setting rather than on a belief that the words themselves had unchangeable natures and thus universal, immutable meanings. German Higher Critics taught that to understand the Bible, one must situate its words in their original context. It was a type of history-centric scholarship that inspired a generation of gifted textual scholars including such notable European intellectuals as J. G. Eichhorn, J. J. Griesbach, and Karl Lachmann to dedicate themselves to determining what ancient biblical manuscripts were the oldest and thus most reliable versions of the sacred scriptures. Their work held out the promise of more accurate primary biblical texts for scholars who wished to understand the Bible's works in relation to their original historical settings.

Debates about how best to understand biblical language led several more radical Unitarians to conclude that the true meaning of the Bible's words was beyond the reach of the rational faculties alone. Instead of stressing the intellectual, scientific work of translation, this group believed that biblical language had a poetic element that was best understood not by the mind, but by the heart. For them, the key to arriving at the true intent of a biblical passage came in understanding it in a figurative rather than literal sense. Such Romantic thinking became one of the great distinguishing marks of the Transcendentalist movement.

For these more Romantic Unitarians, the writings of Samuel Coleridge became particularly important. The first American edition of Coleridge's immensely influential treatise on language entitled *Aids to Reflection* appeared in 1829 and quickly gained a wide readership among New England intellectuals.[3] Coleridge held that language was too pregnant with meaning and nuance to be easily comprehended. Language, he argued, needed to be understood not only by the intellect, but by one's emotional intuition as well. His emphasis on an intuitive aspect of textual interpretation gave more adventurous Unitarians a way out of the potentially fractious debates fostered by the German Higher Criticism. While German Higher Criticism threatened to destabilize the Bible's influence by implying that its truest text might never be fully recovered, Coleridge's poetic view of language made understanding the scripture a more elastic, emotive endeavor. Crucial terms in the Bible no longer needed to be understood strictly in terms dictated by dictionary-driven preconceptions and one's intellectual training. Instead, "the inward and subjective nature" of words could be revealed by a transcendent, divinely attuned perceptive ability found in every person.[4]

There was an added benefit in Coleridge's Romantic approaches to language. It promised to revitalize religion by once again engaging the heart. In the rigorous scholastic circles of Harvard, where immensely learned men spent their lives pursuing the proper understanding of Hebrew vowel points or ferreting out tiny corruptions in ancient biblical manuscripts, many younger Unitarian ministers felt that the heart had been ripped out of their religion. Such men yearned to find a more experiential, emotionally vibrant type of spirituality. A poetic view of language perfectly matched this desire. For Coleridge and his followers, all one needed to do to connect with the Divine was turn to the religiously sensitive intuition of one's heart.

Those Unitarians who felt a special burden to once again stress religion's emotional component found one of their greatest inspirations in the German theologian Friedrich Schleiermacher, a towering European figure who Hodge had heard preach and teach on several occasions during his time in Germany.[5] Schleiermacher was both a widely respected preacher and influential university professor in Berlin who attempted to bridge the gap between the intellectual rationality that characterized the Higher Criticism and the more common, emotional aspects of leading a Christ-like life. Similar to Coleridge, Schleiermacher stressed that true religion was primarily rooted in one's heart, not one's head.

The emotionalism advocated by Schleiermacher in particular, and found in German Idealism more generally, offered many Unitarians a far more attractive path than the intense rationalism of British empiricism. Unlike Locke and his later Scottish followers who based the acquisition of all knowledge on external sensory experience, the German Idealism of Kant and his adherents maintained that every person had an innate ability that allowed them to make sense of exterior phenomena. For the German Idealists, the senses may retrieve data, but without processing that data through a person's intuitive faculty, such data was doomed to remain jumbled and meaningless.[6] Locke's blank slate, his *Tabula Rasa,* made no sense to Idealists who held that certain ideas needed to be generated by the intuition prior to categorizing, synthesizing and ultimately understanding any sensory data.

Central to German Idealism was the belief that humans had an innate intuitive faculty that allowed them to make sense of their world. Those who came to call themselves "Transcendentalists" viewed this faculty as both divinely inspired and present in all sentient beings. It was a *transcendental* quality. Unlike traditional Calvinists who believed that every person had such a corrupted nature that their only hope of glimpsing God was to look outside themselves, Transcendentalists believed that every person contained a portion of the Divine. As a consequence, they held that encountering God began not from the penetrating touch of the Holy Spirit but from within oneself. In attempting to characterize the movement a half century after its first stirring, George Ripley wrote that Transcendentalism was "the assertion of the high powers, dignity, and integrity of the soul; its absolute independence and right to interpret the meaning of life, untrammeled by tradition and conventions."[7] Every person had the ability to tap into the Divine themselves if they could only learn to rely on their own divinely attuned intuitive sense.

As both those inside and outside Unitarian ranks began to study and critique the emergence of Transcendentalist thought, Transcendentalists came to think of their movement in divinely mandated, providential terms. The early Transcendentalist Orestes Brownson captured the movement's sense of destiny when he proclaimed that the history of human religion was but a tale of stages where belief systems were constantly replaced by better, more comprehensive, and thus truer alternatives.[8] As a consequence, Transcendentalism could be seen as a type of religious evolution: Protestantism had supplanted Catholicism; Protestantism had in turn given way to Unitarianism; Transcendentalism was but a refinement of Unitarianism. Each stage built upon the last, and each stage brought humanity one step closer to comprehending the Divine in its truest sense.

Those at Princeton saw Transcendentalism as evolutionary in a much more negative sense. It was but a horrifying extension of the worst elements of Unitarianism's liberal heresies, and several prominent Princeton thinkers moved quickly to attack Unitarianism's newest variation. Hodge joined with his fellow Princetonians Albert Dod and James W. Alexander to write one of the earliest, and most thoughtful, critiques of Transcendentalism to appear before the Civil War. Together, the three men composed two *Repertory* articles that were intended to serve as a double shotgun blast bent on demolishing the philosophical underpinnings of Transcendentalism.

Dod and Alexander wrote the first article. The essay offered a systematic examination of the philosophical roots of Transcendentalism by reviewing the work of Victor Cousin, Immanuel Kant, J. G. Ficte, Friedrich Schelling and Georg Hegel. The piece is marked by a distinct lack of patience with any of the basic tenets held by these German Idealists. Dod and Alexander wryly comment on the Transcendentalist's German penchant to so twist language that words become meaningless. They gleefully marveled when the Transcendentalists in their eagerness to follow in the footsteps of Hegel failed to see the patent absurdity in his "discovery—certainly the most wonderful in the history of human research—that *Something and Nothing are the same!*"[9]

For Dod and Alexander, worse than these misguided linguistic gymnastics was the Transcendentalist belief that "[t]he infinite chasm between heaven and earth is no more. Human action is the action of the infinite. Man can know the infinite by immediate insight, because he is himself infinite."[10] For the Princeton Calvinists, such a view of humanity was the worst type of blasphemous hubris, and there was no more unsettling advocate for this view of humankind's divine grandeur than Ralph Waldo Emerson.

Emerson earned Princeton Seminary's undying antipathy in 1838 when he delivered the graduation sermon to the senior class of Harvard's Divinity School, a sermon that eventually became known simply as the "Divinity School Address." In it, Emerson lambasted historical Christianity's "noxious exaggeration about the *person* of Jesus."[11] For Emerson, Jesus was the truest expression of all that any man or woman might be, but he could claim no divine attribute not also available to every human. This line of argument led Emerson to intimate that people properly in touch with their own sacred self might claim exactly the same status as Jesus, and thus be able to say with him: "I am divine, Through me, God acts; through me, speaks. Would you see God, see me."[12]

Emerson was so outspoken in his denigration of Jesus's divine status and his exultation of humanity that those at Princeton were not alone in their outrage. Emerson's remarks caused such uneasiness among Harvard's faculty and students that there arose a serious debate on whether his remarks should even be accorded the customary practice of being published for the wider public. Eventually a handful of students raised funds to publish privately Emerson's address in pamphlet form, and it was this slender volume of thirty-one pages that Dod and Alexander scrutinized in their *Repertory* essay.

Dod and Alexander argued that Emerson's address reached such heretical heights that they declared a "want of words with which to express our sense of the nonsense and impiety which pervade it."[13] They saw Emerson as a deluded practitioner of the German Idealist thought advocated by Cousin and others, and he was all the more dangerous because he encouraged young ministers to propagate views that Satan himself might find cause to celebrate. In noting that "not a single truth or sentiment" in Emerson's entire address "is borrowed from the Scriptures," Dod and Alexander excoriated Emerson's view of the "*infinitude of man*."[14] His encouragement to have young ministers look "into their own souls for the truth," made him—and his followers—a menace to all that orthodox Christianity held dear.[15] In the end, they declared Emerson to be nothing but "an infidel and an atheist," and they could only thank him for showing just how dangerous Unitarianism had become in its latest and most virulent Transcendental form.[16]

Emerson's "Divinity School Address" had long-lasting repercussions in Unitarian circles as well. It so disturbed a number of Unitarian stalwarts that distinguished Harvard faculty members including Henry Ware Jr. and Andrews Norton felt obliged to respond to Emerson.[17] One year after Emerson's "Divinity School Address," Norton offered his own Unitarian manifesto before the inaugural meeting of the "Association of the Alumni of the Cambridge Theological School" (a body composed of many of the more conservative Unitarians Emerson had so boldly challenged the previous year). Norton aptly named his proclamation on Unitarianism's true nature and the dangers to be found in its bastard offspring, Transcendentalism, *A Discourse on the Latest Form of Infidelity*.

Emerson had been a student of Norton's at Harvard, but precious little of Norton had rubbed off on Emerson during their time together. The two men could not have been more different. A slight, reclusive man who secluded himself for long hours in his study behind closed shutters, Norton was known as a gifted—if cantankerous—scholar. He had none of Emerson's mystical charisma or profound love of public speaking (it was said that his voice could hardly carry in even the smallest room), but his reputation among the liberal theological elements of Cambridge and Boston was so great that he had acquired the sobriquet: "The Unitarian Pope."[18] It was from this position of unparalleled respect that Norton attacked Emerson before the Harvard alumni in the summer of 1839.

Norton's complaints against Emerson were many, but at their root lay his conviction that true Christianity was a revelation given by a personal God, not some impersonal transcendent Over Soul. God had commissioned Jesus' earthly mission and attested to this commission through miracles. Miracles, as defined by traditional Christianity, not by Emerson and those of his ilk who saw them in the smallest drop of rain or the wings of a butterfly, were central to Norton's notion of true Christianity. God attested to the truth of Christ's message through the supernatural miracles that surrounded the Savior's life. Norton considered denying the miracles found in the Gospels as tantamount to denying "the existence of God."[19] Norton also had little patience for the feeling-oriented emphasis of the more radical Unitarians and their love of Schleiermacher.[20] He advocated an intellectually rigorous religion based on sound biblical scholarship.[21]

It was in response to Norton's *A Discourse on the Latest Form of Infidelity* and a prominent defense of Emerson offered by George Ripley (Emerson's cousin) that Hodge offered his own critique of Transcendentalism. While Dod and Alexander had laid out the philosophical underpinnings of the new Unitarian school of thought, Hodge's critique was more focused. Stating that the *Repertory* had already "exhibited, at considerable length, the nature of the prevalent system of German theology and philosophy," Hodge bent his energies to showing how closely American Transcendentalism resembled German Hegelianism, while also offering his own definition of true Christianity.[22]

Perhaps no man came better prepared to engage the strains of thought pulling Unitarianism apart than Hodge. He had studied both the Higher Criticism and German Idealism in Germany, he had actually met and listened to sermons delivered by Schleiermacher, and he was thoroughly acquainted with German studies in biblical manuscript collation that had most recently showed itself in the work of Karl Lachmann.[23] So when Hodge sat down to review Norton's condemnation of Transcendentalism and Ripley's response to Norton's venomous denunciations, he took to task both ends of the spectrum of Unitarian thought by speaking from firsthand experience with the scholarship and philosophy that undergirded the arguments each side was making.

Hodge forcefully disagreed with both Unitarianism proper and its wayward child, Transcendentalism. He dissented from Norton's view that miracles provided the only adequate proof of divine revelation and the Transcendentalists' belief that a common, divinely attuned innate intuition was the best divining rod of Christian truth. Hodge believed that the Bible itself as a divinely inspired document and nature's concurrence everywhere with the teachings of scripture were two critical testimonies to God's work in the world.[24] Hodge went on to argue that Emerson's reasoning was Hegelian to the core, and the similarities were particularly vivid when one looked at David Strauss's recently published *Life of Jesus* (1837). A disciple of Hegel, Strauss used his *Life of Jesus* to argue against Christ's divinity, sharing Emerson's view that Jesus was simply the best example of a man who understood and cultivated the divinity that lies within every person.

To do battle with Transcendentalism and its Hegelian roots, Hodge turned to the writings of two of his German friends: Ernst Hengstenberg and August Tholuck. Hodge shows that he had kept current with a wide array of contemporary German theological and philosophical debates concerning Hegel, Schleiermacher, and Strauss by reading a number of German writers and regularly delving into Hengstenberg's *Evangelische Kirchenzeitung*, the hyper-orthodox German journal that served as a theological counterbalance to a wide range of German philosophical thought. Hodge constantly cites the writings of both these friends as he denounces American Transcendentalism as but a dim reflection of the school of Hegelianism found in Germany.[25]

While Norton's enemies took much joy in the fact that Norton did not seem to be anything approaching a competent scholar on the current German philosophical discussions of the day, no such accusation could be laid against Hodge. At one point in his pamphlet, Ripley accuses Norton of making no fewer than fourteen errors when translating a mere twenty-one lines from the writings of Wilhelm De Wette, one of Schleiermacher's theological colleagues at the University of Berlin.[26] Hodge, on the other hand, made it absolutely clear that he had a well-earned competency in matters of contemporary German theology and philosophy. He works tirelessly in his essay to show that his comments on Transcendentalism were based not only on his extensive study of the subject, but a knowledge of parallel discussions taking place in Germany on similar topics.

It was a sign of just how angry Norton was at the Transcendentalists that he decided to reprint the two *Repertory* essays on Transcendentalism for wide distribution among his Unitarian brethren in a pamphlet entitled: *Transcendentalism of the Germans and of Cousin and its Influence on Opinion in the Country*.[27] Norton saw Emerson's brand of thinking as so dangerous that he was willing to make common cause with the Calvinists of Princeton. Like many a Princeton seminarian, Norton turned to the Princeton faculty's rigorous engagement with the "portentous and disastrous character of the speculations of the infidel metaphysicians and theosophists of Germany" to combat a philosophy that offered little more than "an universal solvent, reducing all forms of opinion into vague formulas, into which every man may insinuate what sense he pleases."[28] Although Norton disagreed with Hodge on a great many things— he once characterized Hodge's views as "very foreign from Christianity"—in republishing Hodge's critique of Transcendentalism, the Unitarian Pope had become a Princetonian.[29]

37

ROMAN CATHOLIC BAPTISM

While Norton had done the once unthinkable in making common cause with Princeton, many Presbyterians began to wonder about Hodge's own theological loyalties when, in 1845, he refused to join the General Assembly in denouncing the efficacy of Roman Catholic baptism. Questions concerning Hodge's Catholic sympathies arose just when anti-Catholic sentiment was reaching an all-time high in the United States. His thoughtful and carefully circumscribed defense of Catholicism's sacrament of baptism subjected him to some of the most pointed and aggressive criticism of his career.[1]

The depth of anti-Catholic sentiment among Presbyterians can be seen in how by the mid-1840s the denomination had added a special time during its General Assemblies for the preaching of a sermon against Catholicism. By 1845, anti-Catholic sympathies were running so strong that a group of Ohio ministers introduced a motion in the General Assembly to declare Catholic baptism invalid, arguing that it was "the unanimous opinion of all the Reformed churches that the whole papal body, though a branch of the visible church, has long since become unutterably corrupt and hopeless apostate."[2] The motion passed with a tidal wave of support. One hundred and sixty-nine delegates voted in favor, while only eight stood in opposition and six more abstained. Hodge viewed everything about this motion and the resulting vote in its support as a tragic mistake.

Presbyterian animosity toward Catholicism was but a reflection of American culture at large. Much of the nation's distaste for Catholicism lay in the fact that since the 1830s, immigrants had been flooding into the United States from all over Europe, but particularly from Germany and Ireland, where there were significant Catholic populations.[3] Between 1845 and 1855, nearly three million immigrants arrived in the United

States, comprising a sizeable 14.5 percent of the general population.[4] The demographic shifts caused by such a massive population influx played a critical role in the development of antebellum American society. New York City stood as a particularly poignant example of population shifts rooted in immigration as roughly 50 percent of the city's residents were foreign born by 1855.[5]

American Protestants saw the massive influx of Catholics among these immigrants as a threat to both American religious and political values. Protestants railed against the Catholic belief that only priests—not common believers—were capable of interpreting the Bible. They saw this dependence on the guidance of an all-powerful priesthood as decidedly dangerous and undemocratic. It was this perceived undemocratic spirit that bled over into American politics. "Native" Americans played on the fear that the Pope himself wished to subvert American democracy by establishing priests as a new kind of aristocracy in a country where every man was supposed to think (and vote) for himself.[6]

Tensions between American Protestants and Catholics often took violent and deadly forms. Cities such as New York, Baltimore, Boston, and Philadelphia all experienced significant unrest in the decades leading up to the Civil War as Americans repeatedly turned against Catholics by attacking their convents, churches, and schools. One of the most cataclysmic confrontations took place in the streets of Philadelphia in the summer of 1844 when hundreds of Protestants vented their rage against the Catholic bishop Francis Patrick Kenrick's request to the city's board of controllers that Catholic children be allowed to use their own version of the Bible and have their own religious instruction in the city's schools. Protestants interpreted such a request as a deadly knife thrust to the very heart of their beliefs. Violence erupted just a few miles from the home of Hodge's brother, Hugh, as roaming groups of Philadelphians destroyed whole blocks of Catholic housing, and then turned their attention to burning and pillaging three Catholic churches, a convent, and a Catholic seminary.[7]

In the General Assembly that followed, the Philadelphia riots became the place where Presbyterians chose to make their own statement against the rising Catholic menace. That this General Assembly met in Cincinnati, Ohio, only helped fan the flames of anti-Catholic sentiment as it had become a much-publicized fact that the Vatican had targeted the city as the chief recipient of papal funds to settle Catholic immigrants once they moved away from the Atlantic seaboard.[8] Because of the Vatican's interest in Cincinnati, many Ohio Presbyterians felt that the city was especially vulnerable to the country's growing Catholic menace. So, it came as no surprise that a group of Ohio delegates initiated the motion to invalidate Catholic baptism, an act that declared all Catholics outside the pale of Christ's earthly church.[9]

Hodge, who did not make the long trip to Cincinnati to attend the Assembly, found himself "overwhelmed by such a vote."[10] He was astonished that the Assembly could have declared "Calvin, Luther, and all the men of that generation, as well as thousands who with no other than Romish baptism" who had long "been received into the Protestant churches, to have lived and died unbaptized."[11] He felt sure that the majority of the nation's Presbyterians would join him in balking at the Assembly's decision because it stood "in opposition to all previous practice, and to the principles of every other Protestant church."[12] That year Hodge spent roughly two-thirds of his annual *Repertory* review article on the General Assembly questioning the wisdom of invalidating Catholic baptism. It was his first, but certainly not his last, extended statement in support of Catholic baptism, a support that it turned out precious few of his Presbyterian brethren were willing to embrace.

Hodge's defense of Catholic baptism stands as a vivid example of just how important historical precedent was to his theological reasoning. Although inevitably influenced by the culture in which he lived and moved, Hodge never acknowledged that anything other than biblical teaching and established church traditions flavored his doctrinal reasoning. When it came to the issue of Catholic baptism, he argued almost solely from historical precedent. Hodge was willing to oppose his brethren on this issue not because he loved Catholicism, but because he aligned himself with every orthodox Christian dating back to the patristic fathers in affirming that Catholic baptism was a valid sacramental form.

Revealing clues behind Hodge's handling of the issue of Catholic baptism are evident as early as 1838 when he reviewed John Henry Newman and the Oxford Movement's *The Tracts for the Times* for the *Repertory*. While Hodge made it unmistakably clear that he had grave reservations about certain aspects of the Oxford Movement, particularly its Catholic drift toward investing the sacraments with inherent power, he was not prepared to denounce them as heretics.[13] He wrote: "We prefer our own form, but we do not denounce theirs. We shrink from the idea of renouncing communion with the holy Catholic church, the congregation of Christian people dispersed throughout the whole world."[14] Hodge reasoned from this same general spirit of tolerance when he defended Catholic baptism to his Presbyterian brethren.

Hodge's argument concerning Catholic baptism was complex, but it came down to a basic belief that although the Catholic Church was certainly "corrupted and overlaid by false and soul-destroying abuses and errors," it was still a body of believers that professed the essential elements of true Christianity.[15] For Hodge, these essentials were all important, because it would be both without biblical warrant and hugely impractical for the Presbyterian Church to stand as judge over every doctrinal error found throughout the Christian world. No tradition was without error; one simply needed to decide whether those errors were heretical enough to expel a given religious body from the Christian ranks. Hodge saw no reason to expunge either those in the Oxford Movement or Roman Catholics from the larger universal church because of their baptismal doctrine and practice. If narrow definitions of baptism were put in force as the General Assembly wished, Hodge saw that Presbyterians would have no choice but to "unchurch almost the whole Christian world; and Presbyterians, instead of being the most catholic of churches, and admitting the being of a church, wherever we see the fruits of the Spirit, would become one of the narrowest and most bigoted of sects."[16]

Hodge defended Catholic baptism on three grounds: "the matter, form, and intention" of the sacrament.[17] He summarized his views by stating: "The matter, is the washing with water; the form, washing in the name of the Trinity; the intention, not the popish notion of the secret purpose of the priest, but the professed, ostensible design of the act."[18] Catholic baptism was valid because it followed the biblical injunction to wash with water, and because it was executed in the name of the Trinity (and Hodge was convinced that there was "not a church on earth which teaches the doctrine of the Trinity more accurately, thoroughly or minutely, according to the orthodoxy of the Lutheran and Reformed churches, than the church of Rome").[19] No matter how the Catholics had perverted the practice of baptism, they still executed it with the clear "intention of complying with the command of Christ, and of doing what he requires to be done, by those who accept the covenant of grace."[20]

It is telling that Hodge in his extended defense of Catholic baptism went to great lengths to point out the absolute necessity of baptizing a person "in the name of the Father, of the Son, and of the Holy Spirit."[21] The Trinity was all important to Hodge's notion of orthodoxy, and just as he was working hard to include Roman Catholics as members of the visible church because of their adherence to Trinitarian doctrine, he was working equally hard to exclude the Unitarians, who had abdicated all rights to Christian communion by holding the pernicious doctrine that the Trinity was a heretical concept rooted in corrupted renderings of the biblical text.

Hodge's stance on Catholic baptism was tremendously unpopular with his fellow Presbyterians, but it did show his ability to stand by his convictions. So much criticism was leveled at him that Hodge revisited the topic in yet another extended essay in the *Repertory* the following year.[22] He began his second article with a wry understatement: "It is very plain that our remarks, in our number for July last, in favour of the validity of Romish baptism, have not met the approbation of a large portion of our brethren."[23] In fact, his remarks had pleased practically no one, yet Hodge boldly declared that he remained absolutely convinced of "the correctness of our position."[24] When convinced of a position, Hodge was not easily swayed. The stubbornness his mother had lamented when Hodge was a boy manifested itself in a tenacity of belief that not even those closest to him could alter. As he had shown in writing his *Constitutional History of the Presbyterian Church in America*, not even his much beloved mentor, Archibald

Alexander, could move him from a position once he had become convinced of its biblical and historical soundness.

In his second essay, Hodge defended Catholic baptism mainly on the ground of defending Catholics as members of the visible church. Ranging far from the simple topic of baptism, Hodge used this article to delineate who he considered members of the larger universal community of Christians around the world. In Hodge's view, Catholics were certainly members of the visible church and were thus fully entitled to baptize their members.

In so arguing, Hodge showed a definite ecumenical tint in his thinking. He was willing to accept Catholicism within the fold of the universal Christian church because of its long and vitally important history. So much of Christian doctrine was rooted first in the Catholic Church and its early creedal councils that Hodge was loathe to expel the body that stood as the rootstock of the Christian Reformation. He certainly did not view the Catholic Church as anywhere near as pure and correct in their understandings of Christian doctrine as their Reformed successors, but it was a tradition that had certainly retained "truth enough to save the soul."[25] Hodge argued in a way that was reminiscent of his reasoning on the issue of slavery.[26] He viewed the institution of the Catholic Church very differently than he viewed Roman Catholics themselves, just as the institution of slavery was different from individual slaveholders. For Hodge, it was one thing to "denounce the Romish system, and another to say that Romanists are no part of the church catholic."[27] The Catholic Church may indeed be corrupt, but not so corrupt that it stood outside the communion of saints who Christ had promised would inherit heaven and earth.

38

THE INFECTION OF GERMAN IDEALISM

While Hodge extended grace toward Roman Catholicism, he showed far less tolerance for those in the Reformed tradition who deviated from the orthodoxy taught at Princeton. Hodge emerged as the guardian of Reformed orthodoxy in the wake of the 1837 schism as he battled with the New School over the nature of true Presbyterian belief in the United States. The Taylorite New School was not the only subject of Hodge's wrath. As the 1840s progressed, he turned his attention to a number of other supposedly Reformed theologies. His targets were many, but principal among them were John Williamson Nevin, Charles Finney, and Horace Bushnell. In Hodge's mind, each of these men had turned traitor as they elevated their own attachments to European philosophy above the well-established truths espoused by Augustine, Calvin, and the Westminster divines.[1]

Among these three men, perhaps no one tried Hodge's patience more than his former student, John Williamson Nevin. Nevin had both studied under Hodge at Princeton, and then served as his replacement at the Seminary when Hodge traveled to Europe. Nevin had remained Hodge's friend and Old School ally through the dark days of the 1830s, but during these years he began to immerse himself in the writings of Hodge's old European friend, Johann Neander. As a result, Nevin's thinking began to run in channels cut away by German Idealist thought.

In 1840, Nevin accepted a position at the small German Reformed Church Seminary in the isolated village of Mercersburg, Pennsylvania. It was while teaching there that he began to develop what would come to be called the "Mercersburg Theology." Crucial to the development of this new strain of Reformed theology was the towering intellectual figure of Philip Schaff, who joined Nevin at the seminary in 1844. Oddly enough, Schaff had his own connections to Hodge. Swiss by birth, Schaff had been

Figure 38.1 *John Williamson Nevin:* John Williamson Nevin, a former student of Hodge, was one of the principal architects of the Mercersburg Theology, a system of belief that emphasized Christ's incarnation and the continuance of Christ's life through his earthly Church. Although they had their differences, Nevin shared Hodge's skepticism about the more radical elements of revivalism. [*Courtesy of Archives and Special Collections, Franklin and Marshall College, Lancaster, PA*]

educated in Europe and then served as the personal secretary for none other than Hodge's dear friend, August Tholuck. Tholuck eventually recommended Schaff for a teaching position at University of Berlin, where Schaff came to idolize the historical work of Neander and immersed himself in the philosophical thought of the German Idealists.[2] Upon arriving in Pennsylvania, Schaff deepened Nevin's already-emergent German intellectual commitments. Together they developed a theology that, while it never gained widespread popularity in America, did attract a significant following in Europe. Popular in America or not, Hodge saw dangers to orthodoxy in the Mercersburg Theology that lead him to spend years calling down fire upon it.

In Hodge's mind, the Mercersburg Theology combined the worst elements of Transcendentalism and Roman Catholicism. It taught a notion of a unifying historical consciousness that bore a haunting resemblance to Emerson's Over Soul, and it deified the sacraments, giving them inherent power that denigrated the role of reason and preaching. These disturbing characteristics led Hodge to attack Nevin's theology on three fronts: its conception of the church, the priority it gave to the Incarnation over the Atonement, and its view of the sacraments.

At the very heart of the Mercersburg Theology lay what Nevin called the "Church Question."[3] Nevin had originally begun to formulate his theology as a response to the problem of factionalism in American Christianity. He had been deeply scarred by the Old/New School division within Presbyterianism, and he was particularly leery of the divisive nature of the revivalism spearheaded by Finney. As revivalism began to touch German Reformed congregations near Mercersburg, Nevin responded by publishing *The Anxious Bench* (1843), a stout warning against the dangers of emotionalism and church division inherent in revivals. Ultimately, Nevin's dismay at the splintered state of the American Church proved pivotal in leading him to develop an entire theology around a vision of a unified Christian church.

In a line of reasoning that resonated with Roman Catholic belief, Nevin argued that the church itself, not the Bible, was the most important means to accessing God's grace. A Christian could not be a Christian unless they stood within the communion of the church for the simple reason that the church was "the continuation of the earthly life of the Redeemer in the world."[4] Nevin proclaimed that "Out of the Church, then, or as separated from the general life of Christ in his people, there can be no true Christian character and no Christian salvation. Christianity and the Church are identical."[5] According to Nevin, Christ's spirit lived on in the visible form of the church. To be in relationship with Jesus was to be a member of his church.

Nevin and Schaff argued that the church was a dynamic entity. Similar to a human being, the church embodied a consciousness and evolved and matured over time.[6] They believed that the end of the church's life would be marked by the total, unified communion of all Christians. With such a harmonic end in mind, they taught that it was the obligation of every Christian to work toward this eventual unity. Hodge found such a dynamic view of the church unsettling. He was willing to admit that a knowledge of Christianity might grow over time, but its fundamental doctrines did not evolve. The notion that the church matured in form and doctrinal substance opposed every belief he held about the changeless nature of Christian orthodoxy.

Nevin and Schaff's view of the church also meant that there was no distinction between the visible and invisible church, running completely counter to Hodge's own thinking. Hodge held to the standard Calvinist belief that all Christians when taken as a whole were bound together and shared fellowship in an invisible, spiritual church.[7] In the eyes of the Mercersburg Theology, the invisible church was nothing but a worthless abstraction. Nevin made this sentiment absolutely clear when he declared: "the invisible Church, as it is called, can have no being whatever apart from the visible."[8]

The Mercersburg view of the visible church led to a tremendous emphasis on Christ's incarnation. Because the church was but the life of Christ continued, the most important moment in human redemptive history was the visible, earthly appearance of Christ. First and foremost, redemption hinged not on Christ's saving work on the cross, but in the fact that he had appeared on earth as a reconciling mediator between God and humankind.[9] Hodge's Augustinian view of the importance of the Atonement left him utterly speechless when it came the primacy Nevin and Schaff placed on the incarnation. For Hodge, the cross, not a stable in Bethlehem, marked the most pivotal point in human history.

Hodge first wrote about the Mercersburg Theology when he reviewed Schaff's *Principle of Protestantism as Related to the Present State of the Church* (1845) for the *Repertory*. He found Schaff's work "thoroughly German," characterized by language and thought "seldom very intelligible."[10] Even with this complaint, Hodge found much in the work to praise, although he did worry that Schaff both failed to put enough emphasis on the "the doctrine of justification by faith alone" and failed to recognize the true union of all believers as an invisible, spiritual phenomenon.[11] In the end, however, Hodge found Schaff's view of Protestantism to be "thoroughly evangelical."[12]

Hodge broke more decidedly with the Mercersburg Theology when he reviewed Nevin's *The Mystical Presence* (1846), using his essay to answer the pivotal question: "What was the real doctrine of the Reformed church on the Lord's Supper?"[13] In the course of fifty pages, Hodge took Nevin to task for his "loud, frequent, often apparently at least, contemptuous . . . reproaches of his brethren for their apostasy from the doctrines of the Reformation."[14] Nevin unabashedly believed that his view of the sacrament was closer to Calvin's than the majority of his Reformed brethren, charging that American Reformed divines like Hodge had so exalted the role of reason in their theological thinking that they had forgotten that not everything about God could be comprehended by the human mind.[15]

Nevin argued that a "mystical union" took place when the communion sacrament was administered, believing there to be a spiritual "force of the sacrament in the sacrament itself."[16] Disagreeing with Hodge's view that communion primarily functioned as a sign of God's work in the world, Nevin believed that the sacrament exercised an inherent redemptive power. Nevin's "mystical union" was a bit too vague and metaphysical for Hodge, who saw in Nevin's thinking nothing but an unsettling Reformed version of Emerson's Over Soul. Hodge thought Nevin's theology so collapsed the categories of the divine and the human that Christ became little more than a consciousness that pervaded every aspect of human existence.[17]

Hodge saw Nevin's drift toward seeing Christ as a pervasive, universally accessible consciousness as indicative of his not seeming "to know what to do with the Spirit."[18] For Hodge, the Holy Spirit quickened hearts and changed lives. It was a real and vitally important spiritual force, not some vague idealist notion. Hodge was convinced that Nevin's thinking on Christ and the Holy Spirit was little more than German Idealism mixed with Christian doctrine. It was a way of thinking that both eviscerated Christ's work on the cross and gave the sacraments magical powers that denigrated the Reformation's Rule of Faith: the Bible itself and the preaching of it.

In Hodge's view, Nevin and Schaff were not the only ones straying from the Reformation's clear and time-honored teachings. At the same time he attacked the Mercersburg Theology, Hodge was also finding dangerous deviations from Reformation orthodoxy in Charles Finney's Oberlin Theology. Once Finney had accepted the position of Professor of Theology at the newly formed Oberlin Collegiate Institute (later known as Oberlin College) in 1835, he began to lecture on, and write down, his revival-centered theology. Out of this process emerged his immensely influential *Lectures on Systematic Theology* (1846). Hodge reviewed these *Lectures* the following year, quickly concluding that the Oberlin Theology was as insidious as anything expounded by Nevin and Schaff.

Finney's pragmatic, results-oriented revivalist theological views had long troubled Hodge. His *Lectures* simply confirmed that Finney believed every person to be a moral agent capable of exercising complete freedom of the will. In his *Lectures*, Finney had adopted and adapted certain strains of European philosophy, particularly those concerned with human moral choice, as a means of cohering his teachings on the role of human agency in the midst of God's own role in redeeming humanity. Central to Finney's theology was his stress on the moral intuition found in every person. For Finney, the key to Christian conversion was found in activating a non-believer's moral intuition, or "intelligence" as he often referred to it, so that person might choose to embrace God's grace.[19] Finney held that human nature was not itself sinful, but tended toward evil until it was taught otherwise, and so the task of every believer was to activate the moral intuition of the unconverted and then focus that intuition on Jesus.[20]

Hodge considered Finney's theology as terribly "reckless."[21] In ways that echoed the stress upon human intuition favored among Transcendentalists, Hodge accused Finney of making the Scriptures—and even God himself—subordinate to a person's innate sense of morality. Finney's stress on human moral agency led him to embrace a moral rather than penal view of Christ's death on the cross. Following in the footsteps of the eleventh-century theologian Abelard, Finney turned away from the Reformed notion of penal atonement that saw Jesus's death on the cross as paying the penalty for all human sin. Instead, Finney held that Christ's work on the cross was primarily an act bent on evoking a moral response in the human heart that would enable men and women to respond to God's love.[22] Finney squarely put the responsibility for leading a godly life in the hands of the believer who could use, or ignore, their moral "intelligence" to respond to God. In the end, Hodge saw Finney in almost complete accord with "the modern German school, which makes God but a name for the moral law or order of the universe."[23]

For Hodge, Finney's great heresy was the way in which he de-emphasized God in favor of human moral reasoning. In fact, Finney's stress on the moral aspect of God's redemptive plan was so pronounced, Hodge declared that Finney should have called his book *Lectures on Moral Law and Philosophy*.[24] Hodge's complaints boiled down to a fundamental difference in approaches. He held that the true "Christian method is to begin with doctrines, and let them determine our philosophy, and not to begin with philosophy and allow it to give law to the doctrines."[25] Counter to sound, Reformed orthodox practice, Finney too often assumed "as axioms contested points of doctrine," building his sophisticated, yet flawed, reasoning upon principles that were undeniably "at variance with scripture, experience and the common consciousness of men."[26] In the end, Hodge stood amazed at how Finney so unequivocally championed the human moral ability to choose holiness when the Bible "in a multitude of places asserts just the reverse."[27]

Finney was not the only one who adopted German philosophical thinking to undergird his theology as the 1840s progressed. Hodge found a similarly disturbing infection of German Idealist thought in the theology of Horace Bushnell. Bushnell had studied theology at Yale under Nathaniel Taylor and after his ordination in 1833 became pastor of North Congregational Church in Hartfield, Connecticut, where he stayed for the next quarter century. Bushnell became widely known for his effectiveness in the pulpit, but his more extensive fame came through his published works.

Like Hodge, Bushnell disliked New England's growing spirit of revivalism and the theologies it cultivated. Partially spurred on by his own antipathy to revivals, Bushnell published his first book, *Discourses on Christian Nurture* (1847). In it, he argued that the family was the single most important means toward developing holiness in the individual believer. He laid particular stress on the role parents played in raising up

Figure 38.2 _Horace Bushnell_: A vigorous orator, Horace Bushnell made a name for himself first in the pulpit and then in print. His greater fame came after his death as his thinking proved foundational for the Social Gospel Movement's passionate commitment to the practice of heartfelt religion in a wide range of community settings. [_Library of the Author_]

godly children. Bushnell believed that true conversion resulted from the influence of a godly family over an extended period of time, not in the emotionally charged, instantaneous decisions so prized in tent meetings.

Although Bushnell's stress on the importance of the family was so widely accepted among New England Protestants that many complained his book was nothing but an exercise in the obvious, others found fault in how he de-emphasized the need for some process that actually ended in a defined moment of conversion and in how his theory of "Christian nurture" seemingly bypassed the need for the Holy Spirit to catalyze a person's journey toward salvation. The book's original publisher, The Massachusetts Sunday School Society, stopped printing the book amid these controversies, and another publisher had to be found to continue the book's publication. When Hodge reviewed the book for the *Repertory*, he found it "very much of an 'Old-School' cast" and considered Bushnell's ideas "in a high degree attractive and hopeful."[28] Hodge was well aware of the disputes that had begun to swirl around the slender volume, but he anticipated "immeasurably more good than evil from it publication."[29] In a way that did not exclude the "sovereignty of God," Hodge felt that Bushnell's great contribution was the way in which *Discourses* reinforced the important "connexion between faithful parental training and the salvation of children."[30] It was to be the most generous and positive review of a work by Bushnell that Hodge ever wrote.

Just two years later, Hodge's sympathy with Bushnell came to an abrupt end when he reviewed Bushnell's second book, *God in Christ* (1849). *God in Christ* was a compilation of three sermons Bushnell had delivered at New Haven, Cambridge, and Andover along with an extended essay he called "A Preliminary Dissertation on Language." It was an ambitious book, for in it Bushnell attempted to reach across the New England Orthodox/Unitarian divide and underline the commonalities of the traditions by proposing a more elastic notion of biblical language and by stressing an innate sense of human intuition over a cold, dogmatic rationalism. It was a treatise seeking common ground.

Drinking from the same philosophical well as the New England Transcendentalists, in *God in Christ* Bushnell turned to the English poet and philosopher Samuel Taylor Coleridge as a key source of inspiration. Following Coleridge's Romantic views of language, he argued that language portrayed conceptions of the things it signified, rather than the actual things themselves. This difference between idea and item inevitably led to gaps between what a speaker or writer intended to communicate and what their audience might actually understand their meaning to be.[31] To overcome the interpretative problems inherent in such gaps, Bushnell argued that the intuitive faculty provided the best means to arrive at the true spirit of language's meaning. Thus, when it came to understanding language, intuition not reason became the best arbiter of meaning.

Bushnell encapsulated what was at stake in his thinking when he declared early in "A Preliminary Dissertation on Language" that in considering language's poetic nature, he no longer saw "how anyone who rightly conceives its nature, can hope any longer to produce in it a real and proper system of dogmatic truth."[32] Building upon his notion of language gaps, he argued that the best way to make sense of competing "creeds of theory, or systematic dogma" was to consider them together, "letting them qualify, assist, and mitigate each other."[33] Seemingly competing creedal statements were but manifestations of the inexactness of language, but this inexactness could be overcome if one took large portions of creedal belief as a whole and looked for the spirit manifested in them as a group rather than trying to parse them out in the particular.

Bushnell was interested in looking at creeds and doctrine in their totality, trying to make sense of them as a whole rather than placing them in opposition to one another. Bushnell's reasoning throughout *God in Christ* tended toward a vision of organic wholeness that extended all the way to the unity of all believers, a godly community bound together by central truths arrived at through the heart, not the head. In this way, *God in Christ* was but a natural extension of *Discourses on Christian Nurture*, but focused this time on the entire family of believers rather than the biological family found in the domestic household.

For Hodge, Bushnell's *God in Christ* was "a failure" on almost every level, a hopeless montage of contradictions and absurdities.[34] He believed that even a casual perusal of the book soon showed that Bushnell's heart-centered approach to theology made him thoroughly incapable of being able to argue a cogent position. For Hodge, the study of theology involved approaching the Bible's teachings in a rational, systematic way. Bushnell proved himself utterly incapable of the rigors of such logical thinking. Bushnell had never held an academic post, and his writing demonstrated none of the intellectual rigor that was the coin of the realm in Hodge's academic circles. To Hodge's way of thinking, Bushnell was swimming in intellectual waters far too deep for him, and every page of *God in Christ* bore testimony to this fact.

Hodge was even more disturbed by the way in which Bushnell conceived of the form and function of language. Admitting that language could indeed have different meanings in given settings, Hodge found Bushnell taking this rather mundane insight to "the most absurd conclusions."[35] For Hodge, God had chosen to communicate himself through the scriptures, which could best be understood by the rational faculty, not some "esthetic principles of our nature."[36] That God had decided to speak to his people chiefly through the scriptures was evidence that they were a reliable medium of communication and that rational engagement with them brought out forthright meanings. The scriptures were not intended as a set of obscure, gap-filled language codes understandable only through the use of some innate, subjective intuition. Every rational person had the ability to understand them. Hodge argued that "[a]ll the operations of the Spirit are in connexion with the word, and the effects of his influence are always rational—i.e., they involve an intellectual apprehension of the truth, revealed in scriptures. The whole inward life, thus induced, is dependent on the written word and conformed to it."[37] Bushnell's elastic notion of language was reminiscent of German metaphysical thought that reveled more in paradox than clarity. Hodge thought Bushnell's belief that "language can convey no specific, definite truth to the understanding" was but the smallest step away from completely destroying "the authority of the Bible."[38]

Hodge believed that Bushnell's faulty logic, dependence on intuition over reasoning, and his elastic notion of language made *God in Christ* an incomprehensible theological muddle. The most vibrant testimony to Bushnell's inconsistent thinking came in how he vacillated on the positions he set forth concerning key doctrines of the Christian faith, most noticeably on the character and meaning of the Trinity and the Atonement. Hodge painstakingly revealed how Bushnell had a habit of holding contradictory stances on these two issues in particular. At points Bushnell seemed to hold a non-Trinitarian view of the Godhead and a moral theory of the Atonement, but as his discussions progressed he set forth more orthodox, time-honored conceptions of the Trinity and a more traditionally Reformed penal notion of Christ's death on the cross. By the end of *God in Christ*, Hodge declared that any reader would be hopelessly confused about Bushnell's actual stances on these key doctrinal issues. He noted that it was not easy to tell if Bushnell wished to "emancipate himself more completely from the teachings of the nursery, the Bible and the Spirit," or "save something from the wreck of his former faith."[39]

In the coming years, Bushnell attempted to clarify his thinking on the very issues Hodge found so obscurely treated in his *God in Christ*. Almost two decades after completing *God in Christ*, Bushnell released perhaps his most sophisticated book-length attempt to define his position on the key issue of the Atonement. He titled the book *The Vicarious Sacrifice* (1866), and in it he argued that Christ's death on the cross was a type of moral rather than penal atonement. Bushnell held that Christ's death on the cross did not satisfy God's sense of justice by serving as a propitiation for humankind's sin. It did nothing to change God's attitude toward humanity. Instead, it wrought a change in believers' hearts that allowed them to respond to God's love. It was a variation on the very atonement view held by Finney and despised by Hodge.

Hodge was so disgusted with *The Vicarious Sacrifice* that he deemed the book "a waste of time."[40] Hodge found the volume did not even have the virtue of the "poetic fire" and passion that characterized Bushnell's earlier works.[41] He remained thoroughly unimpressed with Bushnell's ability to mount an argument and took particular exception to the way in which Bushnell dismissed centuries of accepted orthodox Christian doctrine concerning God's justice and how that justice was appeased for all humanity through Christ's death on the cross. For Hodge, the Atonement was the "cardinal doctrine of the gospel," central to any understanding of how a sinner might "gain access to God" and "secure the pardon" for sins.[42] Building his argument from both the Bible and a long tradition of doctrinal interpretations rooted in the Bible, Hodge felt it "an insult to the common sense of men, to attempt to show that the sacrifices" practiced throughout history by God's people "were not expiatory, but reformatory; not intended to expiate the guilt of the offender, but to cleanse him from moral pollution."[43]

The cross stood as the historical moment when God's wrath was turned away by Christ's sacrifice, not a moment when human hearts came alive to the love of God. Bushnell's great error in Hodge's mind was how he took the focus and responsibility for salvation away from God and placed it instead squarely on humanity's shoulders. In one fell swoop, Bushnell had pushed "the guilty and trembling soul clear off the immoveable rock of Christ's righteousness" and "bid him rest all his hopes on what he himself is."[44]

Perhaps most disturbing for Hodge as he engaged the thinking of Nevin, Finney, and Bushnell was the fact that each of these men unsettled Reformed Christian orthodoxy from within. These men were not Unitarians, fractious Transcendentalists, or even Roman Catholics. Nevin and Finney had been Presbyterians and Bushnell considered himself a good Congregationalist. They had been nurtured in the midst of communities with close ties to his own Reformed theology, and yet German Idealism had completely ruined their thinking. Hodge had come to realize that the German idealist threats to Christian orthodoxy were increasingly coming from figures who had been nurtured in his own Reformed tradition. Such a realization led him in the coming years to spend a great deal of time defining the true church and its members as he attempted to sift theological wheat from chaff, not only in reference to Roman Catholicism and Unitarianism but among others who claimed an allegiance to the Reformed tradition as well.

39

"WHEN THE WILL OF THE WIFE IS THE OTHER WAY"

In October 1846, Archibald Alexander Hodge graduated from Princeton Seminary, inaugurating a period of intense and lasting change for the Hodge household. Within the year, Archie was licensed to preach, ordained, and married to Elizabeth Holliday of Winchester, Virginia. Long drawn to international missions work, no one was surprised when he and his new bride applied to the Presbyterian Board of Foreign Missions soon after their wedding. The Board quickly approved their application and before the year was out, they were on their way to Allahabad in Northern India. Archie's departure signaled the end of an epoch in Hodge's life. Until then, Hodge and Sarah had kept their eight children gathered in Princeton. The entire family was never again fully reunited, as Sarah would die before Archie and Elizabeth returned from India.

Hodge closely followed news of his son's trip to India and his subsequent three-year ministry there. The initial voyage was particularly difficult for Elizabeth, who "suffered dreadfully" in her cabin throughout much of the journey.[1] She was already pregnant with the couple's first child and at times became so ill that Archie sought the aid of physicians from other passing ships. Her illness was but a harbinger of things to come. Although she safely delivered a daughter and then another daughter almost exactly a year later, Elizabeth's time in India almost broke her health. Archie's health also began to deteriorate, forcing them to return to the United States in 1851.

Just three months after Archie and Elizabeth's wedding, Hodge's eldest daughter, Mary, also wed. Mary had met her future husband, William M. Scott, while he had been a student at Princeton Seminary. As their romance blossomed and an engagement was formalized, there grew to be some debate on when the marriage should take place. Mary and William discussed getting married soon after William's seminary graduation in the Fall of 1846, but Hodge and Sarah were adamant that the two not wed until William had found a paying position somewhere.[2] Waiting for such a position is exactly what Hodge and Sarah had done, and they felt strongly that it would be irresponsible to marry until a firm source of income was in hand. Both Hodge's and Sarah's childhood poverty played an important role here as they both sought to help their daughter avoid the same economic trials that had been so much a part of their early lives.

As strong as Hodge and Sarah's views were on certain aspects of their children's marriages, they never interfered with their choice of spouses.[3] Again, Hodge's own history with Sarah doubtless played a role here. He had been scarred by his own mother's initial displeasure at his choice to marry Sarah and so remained silent concerning his children's marriage choices. He had reasons to protest against both Elizabeth Holliday and William Scott.[4] Elizabeth came from an obscure family of little means, while William Scott's politics made him a fierce and unrepentant Democrat in the Jacksonian mold.[5] In an age when parents still exercised substantial control over their children's marriage choices, Hodge consistently let the preferences of his children, not his own, dictate who they married.

This support did not mean losing Mary to marriage was easy for Hodge. He keenly felt the impending loss of his favorite daughter, and the separation was not made easier by the fact that William wanted to become a seminary teacher rather than a pastor, a desire that decreased his chances of obtaining a position close to Princeton. While countless pastorates stood open throughout New England, William was forced to accept a faculty position as Professor of Ancient Languages at Centre College in Danville, Kentucky, in order to pursue a teaching career. Moving to Danville put Mary some seven hundred miles away from Princeton. For all practical purposes it may as well have been as far away as India.

As Mary's wedding passed, Hodge wrote his brother that Mary's departure had been "peculiarly painful," far more difficult than losing Archie had been just three months earlier.[6] Hodge found that Mary's love for William had forced upon him "a complete sacrifice of self," as he struggled to put Mary's good ahead of his own.[7] His sadness, however, did not stop him from officiating at her wedding, a ritual he would perform for each of his daughters and a number of his sons.[8] Hodge found comfort in officiating at his children's weddings, as the ceremonies served to remind him that his children were not his own but were ultimately wed to Christ. A few weeks later, Mary and William left for their new Kentucky home.

As events unfolded over the next few years, one is able to see some truth in the aphorism that sons tend to marry women like their mothers. In many ways, this was the case for Hodge. Sarah had much of the keen intellect and unbending spirit that had so marked Hodge's mother, Mary. Sarah was also a woman with a strong sense of right and wrong, an untiring work ethic, and laser-like focus on a goal once she had set her sights on it. Nowhere was her fixedness of purpose more evident than in her commitment to her children, yet another characteristic she shared in common with Hodge's mother. Sarah exhibited every ounce of her motherly love in summer of 1849 when her daughter Mary was due to deliver her first child.

Mary's pregnancy had proved to be both a physically grueling and a socially isolating time. She and William lived in a boarding house in Danville without the help of even one domestic servant. Mary had long lamented this fact to her parents, telling them it had proved impossible to hire help in a slave state. Sarah was particularly concerned about this lack of aid as the birth of the child neared because Mary and William were also without close friends and family in the area. Upon reflecting on Mary's situation, Sarah made up her mind that it was her first duty to help see that Mary delivered the child safely, something that could never be taken for granted in the nineteenth century, particularly in more rural settings.

Initially, Hodge was not supportive of Sarah's plans. He saw nothing but "certain danger" in the journey for his wife.[9] There was a cholera epidemic raging through much of the Midwest, and Hodge feared for Sarah's health as she traveled. She was already prone to headaches and fatigue; coming down with cholera in a strange town could quite possibly be a death sentence. He also worried about their other children, six of whom still lived in Hodge's house. He needed Sarah to care for them and feared being without her for any extended period of time.

Hodge's concerns were compounded by his own poor health. Since the previous summer, he had suffered from a strange nervous condition. It had begun as he prepared to take a preaching trip to New York in July 1848. While visiting with friends one afternoon, he had aspirated some tea while laughing. He began to cough violently, eventually passing out and striking his head against a nearby sofa. He was so unsteady after the incident that he needed to cancel his trip to New York.[10] What at first appeared to be but an unfortunate moment of swallowing incorrectly marked the beginning of a six-year period of constant dizziness and fatigue for Hodge. His own unsteadiness and lack of energy, a condition he came to refer to as his "feeble *inervation*," made him all the more eager to keep Sarah near him.[11]

Sarah, however, would not be dissuaded. She embarked on the arduous trip to Kentucky taking her third son, Charles Jr., who was on his summer break from his first year at Princeton College, as her traveling companion. Together they made the journey by taking a series of trains, stage coaches, canal boats, and river steamers.[12] They avoided towns and settlements that had been touched by cholera and arrived in late July just in time to help Mary deliver her first child, a red-headed boy who was christened "Charles Hodge Scott."

Mary's life did not become easier after the birth of her son. She developed a high puerperal fever and then an abscess on one of her breasts. The fever threatened Mary's life, and as the cholera epidemic crept closer to Danville, Sarah once again showed her indomitable will in overriding William's protests in insisting that Mary and her new grandchild be first moved to the home of friends in Lexington, Kentucky, and eventually all the way back to Princeton.[13] Later, Hodge commented that he was thankful that Sarah had followed her "'instinctive judgment,' the gift of your sex, rather than the advice that the wisdom of men dictate."[14] Forcing William to endure a lengthy separation from his wife, Mary remained with her newborn in Princeton for several months until her health was fully restored. Only then did she rejoin her husband in Kentucky.

Sarah's journey south highlights a great deal about the very real tensions between theory and reality when it came to the role of women both in his life and in larger society.[15] Hodge's views on a woman's place were primarily rooted in two sources: his male mentors and his own multi-decade immersion in the writings of Paul. Ashbel Green, Samuel Miller, and Archibald Alexander all taught and published on the role of women in church and society. Their writings consistently showed their thoroughly traditional, Pauline views on the subject.[16] Without exception, they believed women were best suited for training children, influencing other women, and encouraging the men in their lives toward greater godliness. All three stressed that women were not to take positions of public leadership over men, citing Paul's injunction that women should remain silent in church, and by extension, in public as well.[17] In his own teaching and writing, Hodge showed little variation with the thinking of these three men.

Hodge believed that God had set up natural hierarchies in his creation, placing himself at the top. Within this Divine system of order, men always occupied positions of leadership above women. If God's hierarchy were to become unsettled by women coming "forth in the liberty of men, to be our agents, our public lecturers, our committeemen, our rulers ... all order and all virtue would speedily be banished."[18] For Hodge, male superiority was a fact laid down in the scriptures and underscored by nature itself. Men were "larger, stronger, bolder" and had "more of those mental and moral qualities which are required in a leader. This is just as plain from history as that iron is heavier than water."[19]

Women were to follow the lead of men. Such submission did not mean that women could not pursue their own education or betterment. Sarah had attended chemistry lectures when Hodge was away in Europe, and Hodge had tutored Mary in Latin. Hodge even allowed that women might be superior to men in certain areas, but for him overall superiority rested with the male. To be true to biblical teaching, women needed to acknowledge male superiority and leadership. Hodge used these views, which he firmly rooted in Paul's teachings, to encourage seminarians in their own leadership roles, and he took comfort in them as he reflected on the fact that his daughter Mary had married "a faithful minister of the gospel, who will be her guide to heaven."[20]

In the cases of both his wife Sarah and his daughter Mary, certain realities trumped Hodge's finely wrought theories on biblical hierarchies and gendered leadership. In theory, the man led the household, but certain realities occasioned by the birth of Charles Hodge Scott brought into vivid relief just how much leadership could be exercised by women in Hodge's life. Hodge himself had experienced this firsthand from the youngest age with the willfulness and steadiness of purpose demonstrated by his mother. Hodge knew that women could be intelligent and forceful, and while he forever held that men were to take the primary leadership role in all settings, he harbored no illusions that men got their way in every setting in which they supposedly led. When his son Caspar Wistar did not wish his son to take his name, he lost the argument to his wife who insisted that their child be named Caspar Wistar Jr. With a wry comment to his brother, and in a manner that hinted at a wisdom borne of long experience, Hodge noted that Caspar never had a chance "when the will of the wife is the other way."[21]

40

"COVERED IN GLOOM"

While the 1840s brought the joy that accompanies weddings and grandchildren, Hodge faced times of profound grief during these years as well. In 1845, Albert Dod, one of Hodge's closest friends, died suddenly of pneumonia at the age of forty-one. Hodge took Dod's death exceedingly hard and carried his sorrow for years to come. A decade after Dod's passing, Hodge commented that he had "not yet ceased to mourn his departure as a personal loss" and later made a special effort to defend Dod in a *Repertory* article reviewing a recently reprinted volume of Victor Cousin's work with a new introduction by Caleb S. Henry.[1] Henry had impugned an earlier critique of Cousin by Dod, an outrage that Hodge took so personally that he accused Henry as being a "calumniator of the dead," noting that his "incompetent" remarks imposed "a solemn obligation on the surviving friends of [Dod], to vindicate his memory."[2] Hodge's gesture was but one more testimony of just how deeply his attachments to friends could run.

Dod had come to Princeton for his undergraduate studies at Princeton College. He eventually became a tutor at the school before he began to pursue theological studies at Princeton Seminary. Upon his graduation from the Seminary he was licensed to preach, but so pronounced were his mathematical abilities that he took a position in 1830 as the Professor of Mathematics at the College and soon became a frequent attendee of Hodge's evening faculty gatherings.

Like Hodge, Dod was a tremendously popular teacher. Hodge said of him: "There was nothing that he could not make plain," and his students readily agreed.[3] Hodge attempted to harness some of Dod's intellectual energy by assigning him key articles to write for the *Repertory* and by consulting him on an a wide range of issues both personal and professional. The bond between the two solidified further when Dod married Hodge's cousin, Caroline S. Bayard.

Figure 40.1 *Albert Dod*: Albert Dod attended Princeton Theological Seminary, but had such a genius for mathematics that he chose to become a mathematics professor at Princeton College rather than enter the ministry. He became an immensely popular teacher and one of Hodge's closest friends. [*Princeton University Library*]

Hodge served as Dod's constant bedside companion during his final days. As he slipped in and out of consciousness, he wanted Hodge to make sure that his students knew of his religious convictions even at the end and entreated him to tell them that "Jesus Christ is the God whom I worship."[4] Hodge used these words as the basis for a dramatically emotional eulogy he offered at Dod's funeral.[5] Hodge remained convinced in later years that had God prolonged Dod's life, he would have been "one of the most eminent and useful" men ever to grace the American Presbyterian Church.[6]

Dod's was but the first of a series of six deaths that personally touched Hodge's life within the span of just six years. In May 1848, at the age of eighty-six, Ashbel Green died. Appropriately enough, he was found dead in the posture of prayer.[7] Hodge had grown distant from Green since the outset of the New and Old School controversy over a decade earlier, but his passing brought into vivid relief that the era dominated by Princeton Seminary's founding triumvirate of Green, Alexander, and Miller was coming to an end.

The next death that visited Hodge was infinitely dearer to him. On Christmas Day 1849, just four months after her return to Princeton with her daughter and grandchild, Sarah "softly & sweetly fell asleep in Jesus."[8] She most probably fell victim to uterine cancer.[9] Sarah's health had begun to deteriorate soon after her return, and by December her condition was such that Hodge had lost all hope of her recovery.[10] In her final weeks, he personally nursed Sarah, spending countless hours simply lying next to her. During these times, he held her hand, and conversed with her when she had the strength.[11] The depth of their love remained so intense that Hodge later commented that "to the last she was like a girl in love."[12] During her final week, Sarah asked Hodge to tell her in detail "how much you love me," and they spent time recounting the high points of their life together.[13] Hodge's last hours with his wife were particularly poignant. As her life ebbed away, Sarah looked at her children gathered around her bed and quietly murmured "I give them to God."[14] Hodge then asked her if she had thought him a devoted husband to which she replied as "she sweetly passed her hand over" his face: "There never was such another."[15]

Soul mates to the end, Hodge was devastated by Sarah's death. So close had the two been that John Johns once commented that it was impossible to think of either of them "without seeing both."[16] Hodge had been unusually fortunate for a man living in the nineteenth century to have experienced so little death in his immediate family. Aside from his mother's death, once grown he had not suffered the loss of a wife, sibling, or child. Such good fortune made his Sarah's death all the more difficult. So great was the blow that in the ensuing weeks, Hodge doubted whether he would ever again be good for anything. Attempting to find a way to lift his brother out of his prolonged bouts of crying and melancholy, Hugh encouraged his brother to consider taking up his full duties again. Hugh saw work as perhaps the only antidote to his brother's grief, and so he wrote in the month after Sarah's death: "You must return fully & thoroughly to your *work*. This is your duty, & will be *now* your chief happiness."[17] Hugh coaxed Hodge along with reminders of how much both his family and his school still needed him.

More sadness came. Less than two weeks after losing Sarah, Samuel Miller died at the age of eighty. Miller's death was not as sudden or shocking as either Dod's or Sarah's.

His health had been declining for some months, and all those around him noticed that his body and mind were failing.[18] His passing reverberated throughout the Seminary. In the school's thirty-eight-year history, it had never before buried a professor. Dr. Alexander offered the eulogy, closing his remarks with the words "I am reminded that I must soon follow my departed brother and friend to the grave. There are many in this great assembly who will never hear my voice again," and with these words, he asked them for their prayers as he too would soon be bidding them good-bye.[19] Hodge sat among the listeners, buffeted by griefs past and thoughts of griefs to come.

Just eleven months after Miller's funeral, death came again as one of Hodge's nephews suddenly fell ill late one evening with a chill only to expire five dates later.[20] Now it became Hodge's turn to comfort Hugh who was overwhelmed by the lightning-strike loss of his son. Hodge attempted to console his brother by relating his own recent lessons in grief. He encouraged Hugh to pursue a "[p]ious sorrow, that is, sorrow mingled with pious feeling, with resignation, confidence in God, hope in his mercy and love" and not give into melancholy that he called "irreligious" and a "a cancer to true peace and spiritual health."[21] For a man who had experienced so little death for so many years, Hodge now found himself surrounded by it.

And yet, more grief was to come. Just ten months later, Dr. Alexander, the man Hodge had long considered his surrogate father, passed away. Nearing his eightieth year, Alexander's health had started its final downward spiral in the autumn of 1851. Having taken to bed a few days earlier, he died on October 22 in a state of "no ecstacy—but clear faith."[22] He found himself at peace believing that "after eighty he had never known a man to be useful, and he did not think it desirable for him to live and drag on a few years more a burden to himself and others."[23] He was absolutely confident in his salvation, and felt he had accomplished his every desire in his forty years as a professor at the Seminary.[24] His only remaining wish was that others in his family might have the same peace when it came their time to die.

In Alexander's final month, he repeatedly called Hodge to his bedside as he passed off to him various administrative details of the Seminary. He wished to leave all his affairs, including the affairs of the Seminary, in good order. During one of their evening meetings, their time together touched a much more personal note as Alexander presented Hodge with a white bone walking-stick, decorated with elaborate carvings, a gift he had been given by a chief in the Hawaiian Islands (see figure 58.1). In what became a particularly poignant and tearful exchange, Alexander solemnly commanded Hodge: "You must hand this to your successor in office, that it may be handed down as a kind of symbol of orthodoxy."[25] In so doing, Alexander passed his mantle to Hodge, his own chosen successor to guide the Seminary.

Alexander did not linger long. A few days before his death, he called Hodge one last time to his bedside. Upon entering his sickroom, Alexander reached out to his former student and longtime junior colleague and for the first time addressed him as his "dear son."[26] He then bid Hodge to keep silent while he said a few things. Most importantly, he wished Hodge to know that he considered it "one of my greatest blessings that I have been able to bring you forward."[27] He then bid him farewell. With Alexander's death, Hodge felt his world once again "covered in gloom."[28] He had not only lost a treasured mentor and a faithful colleague, but the man who, over the past forty years, had become his father. To show the depth of his attachment to Alexander, Hodge purposely walked in the same group as his sons during the funeral procession. In their four decades together, no single man had exercised a more profound influence on Hodge's life and thinking.

The deaths of Miller and Alexander marked the end of one of the greatest partnership Princeton Theological Seminary would ever know. Hodge later characterized their combined leadership and heartfelt mutual respect as having formed a "halo" of holiness over the Seminary.[29] Alexander said of Miller that he had "*never known a man more entirely free from vain glory, envy and jealousy,*" while Miller said of Alexander that he was forever thankful "that I ever saw the face of my venerated senior colleague. He has been, for thirty-six years, to me, a counselor, a guide, a prop, and a stay under God, to a degree, which it would not be easy for me to estimate or acknowledge."[30] When Alexander had bought forth Hodge as the Seminary's third professor, the three harmoniously guided the Seminary under "a uniform desire to promote, by all the means in their power, the best interests of the Seminary, as a nursery of ardent piety, and of sound biblical and theological knowledge."[31]

Hodge knew that Alexander's passing closed a chapter in the Seminary's history. He now stood as the school's most senior professor without the benefit of the wisdom of either of the men who had done so much to mold the school's character and curriculum. The passing of his senior colleagues also meant that two of the Seminary's most important leaders with extended pastoral experience were gone. Under Hodge's leadership, the academic nature of the Seminary's curriculum became ever more pronounced, and its professors increasingly came straight from academic backgrounds or with but a few years in pastoral positions. The Seminary's formative years were now clearly behind it. By the 1850s, it had become one of the most established schools for professional theological training in the country. Hodge spent the remainder of his life as the Seminary's principal guide both academically and spiritually.

PART VI

The 1850s

Inspired Churchman

Figure 41.1 *Charles Hodge in the 1850s [Presbyterian Historical Society, Presbyterian Church (U.S.A) (Philadelphia, PA)]*

41

COLLEGE TRUSTEE

The emotional and physical toll surrounding so many deaths of loved ones slowed Hodge's pace of life. As he continued to be plagued by uncontrollable bursts of weeping and incessant bouts of dizziness and fatigue, Hodge sought relief in various forms of mild recreation. He took long walks, rode, and visited Sarah's grave at least twice a week.[1] He also took more time to play games with friends and family. Although he continued to forbid his children to play cards and attend dances, he began to play backgammon along with his much-beloved chess during the evenings.[2] In the summer, he set up a croquet field on his front lawn outside his study's windows and enjoyed watching others play when he was not outside himself taking a turn. He also began to read novels for the first time in his life.[3] He chose them carefully and did not pursue the more salacious forms of fiction (he waited to read Henry Fielding's *Tom Jones* until the end of his life).[4] For the first time in his life, he began to read widely in genres that fell outside his usual interests in theology, politics or science.

Upon Samuel Miller's death, President Carnahan of Princeton College approached Hodge to take Miller's vacant place on the school's board of trustees. Carnahan was a longtime friend of Hodge. He frequented Hodge's evening gatherings, and the two men had worked closely together in a number of settings since 1826 when Carnahan had joined the Seminary's board of trustees. Their friendship had grown even closer when Carnahan became that board's president in 1843. Carnahan saw Hodge as a natural and valuable addition to the College's board. Being an ordained Presbyterian minister himself, he valued Hodge's religious commitments, as well as the fact that in every way Hodge had shown himself a devoted alumnus of his alma mater.

By the time Hodge took his seat on the College's board in 1850, the fifty-two-year-old Hodge had established himself as one of the most important and respected members of the Princeton community. He was well known among the College's faculty, and the trustees soon granted him the status of one of their elder statesman, giving great weight to his administrative common sense, diplomatic skills, and intellectual commitments. Hodge played a particularly important role in 1854 when he was called upon to help shepherd the College through the transition from one president to another.

When Carnahan announced his intention to relinquish his post, many supposed that Dr. John Maclean Jr., who had served the College in various capacities from tutor

Figure 41.2 *John Maclean Jr.:* John "Johnny" Maclean, Jr. was the son of Princeton College's first chemistry professor. Maclean became the College's professor of mathematics at the age of twenty-three, eventually rising to become the school's tenth president. [*Princeton University Library*]

all the way to vice president for thirty-five years, would become the next president. It came as a surprise then that a number of trustees found Maclean a bit too ordinary for such an august position, and wished to fill the presidential post with someone who would bring greater prestige to the College. The lay members among the trustees were particularly eager to have Joseph Henry return to the College after his 1846 departure to become the founding secretary of the newly founded Smithsonian Institution.[5] The clerical members of the trustees were solidly behind Maclean. Hodge, who had known Maclean since their undergraduate days together in Princeton, became a pivotal force in moving the board to appoint Maclean the College's tenth president.[6]

Maclean's administration turned out to be steady, but not innovative. Maclean continued Carnahan's firm commitment to keep the College from dividing into disparate schools. Both Carnahan and Maclean believed that each undergraduate should participate in a common, broad-based curriculum aimed at developing mental discipline and religious character. To this end, Maclean filled the College with gifted scholars who were also all orthodox Presbyterians of the Old School.[7] Hodge became a perfect partner in the execution of this agenda.

Not surprisingly, Hodge's single greatest contribution to the College as one of its trustees was his unwavering emphasis on the "the religious character of the College," which he believed should forever be "the first great aim of its administration."[8] He was particularly interested in the College's faculty appointments. He never faltered in making sure that every faculty candidate had two key characteristics: piety and intellectual expertise. He wished the College to be the home of some of the country's greatest minds, but because he was so convinced that teachers influenced as much through their moral example as through their intellect, he wished every one of them to be thoroughly Christian in their principles and practices. During his time as a trustee, such pious intellectual luminaries as the classicist Charles Augustus Aiken (future president of Union College), the great Swiss geologist Arnold Guyot, and the towering Scottish Common Sense philosopher and logician James McCosh joined the College's faculty.

Hodge also proved a key support for Maclean as the College weathered two of its most trying times. In 1854, Nassau Hall burned to the ground as a cinder fell through a ventilation grate in the northeast corner of the building. Before the general alarm was sounded and the fire brigade arrived, the fire had progressed too far to be extinguished. It took two years to rebuild Nassau Hall. Hodge and the other trustees worked tirelessly alongside Maclean to raise funds to see the centerpiece of the campus restored. Later came the countless trials associated with the Civil War, which included the College losing a large number of its southern students as well as the numerous decisions brought on by the deprivations accompanying the war.

Hodge served on the board until his death, attending his last trustees' meeting just weeks before he took to his bed for his final illness. In his last years, Hodge worked with James McCosh, the man who replaced Maclean as president, to once again preserve the school's traditional curriculum. Serving as a key member of various curricular review committees, Hodge coupled his longstanding desire for faculty piety and intellectual excellence with a passionate determination to see that the classical languages and the humanities did not suffer at the hands of the physical sciences. Hodge was in full agreement with McCosh's belief that the College must prevent at all costs "a narrowness and a one-sidedness of mind and training by requiring all to have a competent knowledge of certain fundamental branches of a liberal education."[9] Both Hodge and McCosh believed that a successful education avoided an all-too-common "exclusiveness and angularity" of mind that was cultivated by the teaching of "science without literature, or literature without science."[10] Hodge proved to be one of McCosh's most valuable lieutenants as McCosh made sure that every undergraduate took classes in traditional subjects such as Latin, Greek, and mathematics.

In Hodge's mind, work in the classics was a foundational building block for the study of theology, and he wished the College to remain a launching pad for ministerial careers. College was also about mental rigor and discipline, and there was no discipline better for teaching these skills than mathematics. So, Hodge did all in his power to see that the study of modern languages and work in the physical sciences did not displace classical studies and a firm grounding in mathematics.[11]

Hodge experienced great satisfaction through his work as a trustee, largely due to how closely his own educational sympathies matched those of both Maclean and McCosh. A broad-based, traditional curriculum that also included pronounced religious instruction marked Hodge's twenty-seven-year tenure as a College trustee. Up until the time of his death in 1878, the College's freshmen were still required to take Latin and Greek, as well as study the New Testament's parables and the poetical books of the Old Testament. Sophomores continued their work in the ancient languages and studied portions of the New Testament in Greek. Juniors worked their way through the prophetic books and Acts, while seniors studied Christian doctrine and went through the Book of Romans with President McCosh.[12] Hodge was gratified to see the dividends of such educational commitments when the school's 1877 graduating class, the last class he lived to see graduate, chose the ministry as their third most popular vocation, trailing only slightly behind law and medicine.[13] Although Hodge had given his life to religious education through the Seminary, he spent almost three decades serving as a critical force in making sure that his alma mater also remained a key source of pious instruction.

42

LANGUAGE AND FEELING

In the same year he became a College trustee, Hodge also embarked on one of the most titanic theological battles of his career. His opponent was Edwards Amasa Park, a man Hodge once characterized as having a "peculiar talent for making Old-school doctrines appear ridiculous and odious."[1] Park was the Abbot Professor of Christian Theology at Andover Seminary, a post he had taken over in 1847 from the legendary conservative Leonard Woods.

Park was Hodge's counterpart at Andover. He had arrived at the Andover in 1836, remaining there until his retirement from teaching in 1881. For nearly four decades, Park edited Andover's theological journal, *Bibliotheca Sacra*, the chief periodical trumpeting Andover's brand of New England Theology that stressed a traditional Calvinism mixed with some sympathy for revivalism and human agency. Like giant men-of-war raking each other with massive broadsides, over a two-year period Hodge and Park used their respective journals to pummel each other with tightly argued theological salvos on the nature of biblical language and the role of reason in biblical interpretation.[2]

One is as struck by the similarities of the two men as their differences. Like Hodge, Park was a devoted Calvinist who held reason in high regard. Both men venerated the Bible and considered it to be the ultimate arbiter of truth. They had also both studied with August Tholuck in Germany and had come away with an appreciation for the rigors of European theological scholarship, yet were troubled by certain aspects of German Idealist thought as it surfaced in New England. In this regard, they found Horace Bushnell's thoughts on biblical language particularly distressing. They took exception to Bushnell's poetic view of language and the way it destabilized traditional, Calvinist interpretations of the Bible. Park, however, differed from Hodge in the solution he offered to the threats posed by German Idealism and Bushnell.

Figure 42.1 *Edwards Amasa Park*: Edwards Amasa Park was named in honor of Jonathan Edwards and actually married one of Edwards's great granddaughters. He became one of Edwards last great nineteenth-century disciples and expositors. He spent his forty-five year career at Andover Seminary developing a theology that sought to harmonize certain key Calvinist beliefs concerning God's absolute sovereignty with the more liberal notions of human agency often tied to aggressive revivalism. [*Franklin Trask Library, Andover Newton Theological School*]

Park rooted his solution in a Calvinism different from Hodge's. In his attempt to harmonize revivalist fervor with Calvinist views of God's sovereignty, Park had developed a theology he called "Consistent Calvinism," a group of tenets he believed to be more in line with Calvin's own thinking than the teachings that had come to be taught under his name in the long centuries after his death.[3] One key attribute to Park's

"Consistent Calvinism" was its stress on the emotions. Park held a high view of the reasoning faculty, but he considered it absolutely essential to determine what place the emotions played in the religious life as well. He spent much of his career attempting to articulate the relationship between the heart and the mind. This quest lay at the root of his debate with Hodge.

In May 1850, Park delivered what many considered his most important, and certainly his most controversial, sermon at the Convention of Congregational Ministers of Massachusetts entitled, "The Theology of the Intellect and that of Feelings." In it, Park sympathized with Horace Bushnell's stress on the intuitive faculty in understanding the Bible and key points of Christian doctrine. Park's sympathy with Bushnell was by no measure total agreement. Bushnell asserted that a logical approach to the Bible "showed it the absurdist book in the world," a sentiment Park found repugnant.[4] Park, however, agreed with Bushnell's view that a heart-centered view of language promised peace for some of the more contentious theological debates plaguing New England.

The key insight Park offered in his "The Theology of the Intellect and that of Feelings" was that biblical, and by extension theological, language was best interpreted by using different modes of understanding. The intellect or "logical consciousness" was the best means of understanding matters expressed in the language of propositional and literal truths. The logical consciousness gravitated toward understanding theology as a science based on "plain, instructive, defensible" claims that helped explain the general, comprehensive nature of God's work in the world.[5] The heart or the "intuitive consciousness," on the other hand, was the best means of understanding God's truth as it was communicated in emotion-evoking images through figurative language.[6] Such figurative language was designed to appeal to one's affections. It aimed "to be impressive, whether it be or not minutely accurate," and thus followed Bushnell in claiming that "instead of being comprehensive, figurative language was elastic" in its meanings.[7]

For Park, humans comprehended God's truth in one of these two modes depending on how that truth was presented to them. He stressed, however, that no matter the mode of apprehension, God's truth was absolutely immutable. Park's theology of feeling and intellect attempted to slice through the rancorous theological debates of his day by encouraging theologians to realize that many of their points of argument were, in reality, the same position but arrived at through different means.

Disturbed by Park's musings about interpretative elasticity and different modes of apprehending truth, Hodge argued that the scriptures taught only "one definite form of faith."[8] It was a form that was fully comprehensible through the use of reason. Hodge had no use for Park's innovative view that not every passage in the Bible was "intended for logical proof; they may have been designed for passionate appeals and figure into the shape of argument, not to convince the reason but to carry the heart by a strong assault."[9] Hodge disagreed with Park's quasi-Bushnellian views on language, arguing that Park had gone too far in his accommodation of emotion. He was particularly aggrieved by Park's belief that theology derived from reason alone often found itself antiquated by scientific advances, whereas theology interpreted through the heart need not "always accommodate itself to scientific changes, but may often use its old statements, even if, when literally understood, they be incorrect, and it thus abides as permanent as are the main impressions of truth."[10] Hodge found such denigrations of scriptural truth fantastically dangerous. For him, any truth revealed in scripture always held up amid scientific scrutiny because scientific truth always agreed with God's revealed truth.

In the end, Hodge believed that Park's distinction between figurative and literal language was hopelessly confused and confusing. Much of the language Park called figurative was as literal as the literal language he claimed to be figurative. He was particularly troubled by how quickly Park denoted language as figurative that addressed doctrines with which he disagreed. Hodge maintained that language that led to standard beliefs such as "Christ bore our punishment; that he satisfied the law; that Adam's sin is imputed to us, and our sins to Christ" was not figurative in the least as Park believed.[11] Considering such language, Hodge declared that it was "impossible to pick out of the whole range of theological statements, any which are less impassioned, or which are more purely addressed to the intellect."[12] Hodge saw Park establishing himself as the sole arbiter of what was to be considered figurative or literal language, and he saw in Park's choices little more than a thinly disguised way of justifying personal theological predilections.[13] Hodge considered Park's theology of feeling as nothing but his "convenient way of getting rid of certain doctrines" he found "unpalatable."[14]

A prime example of the doctrinal danger of Park's method came in the issue of personal responsibility for sin. Along with Finney and other revivalists, Park favored a notion that a person could play an important role in initiating their own salvation. Hodge directly attacked such a view by stating that the "Bible plainly, not in impassioned language, but in the most direct terms, asserts the inability of men to certain acts necessary to their salvation. . . . This doctrine, however, is in conflict, not with other assertions of Scripture, for they are no counter statements, but with a peculiar theory of responsibility, which the author adopts."[15] Simply put, Hodge accused Park of shying away from the doctrine of total depravity, consigning it to the category of being present in scripture but running counter to the truer theology illuminated not by reason, but by intuitive feeling.

Hodge saw the consequence of Park's desire to make pronounced distinctions between words and the realities they represented as creating a great gulf between matter and form, the natural extension of which was that "the facts and doctrines of the Bible" became "mere forms of the spirit of Christianity."[16] In so emphasizing the spirit, Hodge saw Park arguing that it did not matter what forms the "spirit of Christianity" took as long as the spirit was true. In Park's way of thinking, doctrines that had stood for centuries could be wiped away if their "spirit" was deemed out of sync with the human heart. The test of orthodoxy for Park was no longer confined strictly to rational and systematic thought, but to how a tenet might appeal to "the wants of the well-trained heart."[17]

In the following two years, Hodge and Park exchanged articles that did little more than further define and distill their differences. For Hodge, Park had set out to attain the quixotic goal of reconciling the warring "Augustinian and Anti-Augustinian systems of theology," an aim he saw as a hopeless tilting at windmills.[18] He noted that from the earliest history of the Christian church, "there have been two great systems of doctrine in perpetual conflict. The one begins with God, the other with man."[19] Hodge believed that the middle ground that Park so desperately sought was but a figment of his imagination brought on by "a head made light by too much theorizing."[20] To stay true to either system, one was forced to deny the fundamental principles of its opposite. Park's dream of expanding the circle of acceptable orthodox belief by reaching out to Christians who adhered to other "allowable creeds" was at best misguided and at worst terribly dangerous.[21] True Christian belief meant only one thing for Hodge: Calvinist doctrine inflected by Augustinian thought. To compromise on these tenets was to endanger the entire Gospel message. Park's theology of feeling simply allowed him to foreground his own anti-Augustinian views against all systems of "doctrine embodied in the creeds of the Lutheran and Reformed Churches."[22]

The rancorous debate between Hodge and Park served a much more important role, however, than simply recapping long-held divisions of Protestant thought on human agency and the sovereignty of God. Their argument represented a fork in the road of New England Calvinist thought. Even though Park remained staunchly conservative in much of his theology until his death, his openness to the elasticity of language, and by extension a more elastic view of church doctrine, was a harbinger of Andover Seminary's eventual slide toward the liberal theology that came to characterize the school's teaching by the end of the century.[23] Hodge's Princeton took a different path. By remaining solidly rooted in a strong Common Sense view of language and a pronounced Augustinian Calvinism, Princeton eschewed every turn toward liberalism and became a key institution in the development of American Fundamentalism.[24]

On another level, the debate between Hodge and Park takes on special significance as an early hint of the coming separation of scientific and religious discourses in the nineteenth century. Up until the 1850s, American Protestants saw theology as a scientific discipline. Built upon the solid foundation of Scottish Common Sense philosophy and its reliance on factual evidence and human reason, theological studies were considered completely compatible with science in both method and content.[25] By mid-century, confidence in this compatibility was beginning to erode. Many began to question the ability of theology to explain the presence and purpose of various natural phenomena. New geological theories on the age of the earth wreaked havoc with traditional Protestant notions that the world had emerged only six thousand years ago in the Garden of Eden, and Darwin's theory of evolution proved equally unsettling as scientists began to question whether some more primitive form of primate, not Adam and Eve, stood as the rootstock of all humanity.[26] Theology stumbled as it continued to claim scientific certainty but then had difficulty coming to terms with new scientific theories.

For Park, the elasticity of figurative language became a way to reconcile science with scripture. Various theologians began to argue that the Bible was figurative when it spoke of "days" and "years," so that the earth could age exponentially and yet still square with key biblical passages.[27] Bushnell went farther than most when he proposed to separate entirely science and theology, arguing that the purview of the natural sciences was the study of the physical world while theology's only concern should be the spiritual universe of ideas.[28] Hodge was completely unwilling to condone such a separation, convinced that the two were utterly compatible.[29] He saw Park and Bushnell's stress on the figurative language and its attack on the rational faculty as a path toward total theological devastation. Such a line of reasoning threatened to destroy centuries of careful thinking on Christian doctrine and ultimately to concede that humans could have no precise and definite knowledge about God. Hodge believed that God wanted all men and women to have a definite knowledge of himself, and such knowledge came most clearly through the written revelation he had offered humanity in the clear and rationally accessible language of the Bible.

43

THE INSPIRATION OF SCRIPTURE

Park's arguments undermining the role of reason in the interpretation of the Bible moved Hodge to become one of American Protestantism's most vocal and articulate defenders of the reliability of both the Bible and the rational faculty. Combining his considerable intellect with his commitment to Scottish Realism, Hodge developed a highly sophisticated, if somewhat insular, view of how language worked, spurred on by his conviction that Park's views threatened "'common sense' the standard of all truth."[1] Following tenets dating back to Witherspoon, Hodge answered Park, Bushnell, and others by arguing that God had endowed every human with a commonly shared set of sensory and rational faculties which, when properly nurtured and employed, produced a reliable set of beliefs by which to live. Because all humanity had always shared these common faculties, cultural and chronological differences were no impediment for one set of people to understand another.

In true Common Sense fashion, Hodge believed that people of his day were fully capable of understanding people of bygone ages because of humanity's commonalities anchored by a universal moral sense. By extension, humanity's common nature allowed people throughout the ages to build shared, permanent systems of reliable knowledge. What was of paramount importance was that people employ their rationality to understand the truths found in both human and physical nature, so that they might shape their own thinking and behavior according to these truths. For Protestants, the best source of truth, both philosophical and physical, was found in the words of the Bible.

The German idealism of Park, Bushnell, and the Transcendentalists cut across the beliefs taught by Scottish Common Sense by unsettling the conviction that the mind was the court of first and last resort in understanding both language and the physical world. For such thinkers, the heart was a necessary, and often superior means, of understanding the world. Hodge saw himself as correcting this drift away from rationality. He was not entirely opposed to, or bereft of, emotions; he saw emotions as playing an essential role in the Christian's life as exhibited in how he constantly exhorted his family and his students toward a heartfelt piety.[2] He even taught that as important as it was to assent to truths such as "there is a God, that the soul is immortal, that there is a heaven," the emotions allowed a believer to "feel the power" of such truths.[3] Hodge contended not that emotions were irrelevant to truth, but that God's truths were "true to the intelligence in the precise sense in which they are true to the feelings."[4] He did not treat the activities of the heart and mind as independent modes of determining truth. If it was true, it was as true to a person's rational faculty as it was to that person's intuitive faculty.

In considering the role of emotions in the religious life, Hodge taught that emotions arose in response to the rational sensory apprehension of exterior stimuli. He wrote: "Intellectual apprehension produces feeling, and not feeling intellectual apprehension."[5] He believed this to be "specially true of the religious affections."[6] Pious feelings were inspired by the rational apprehension of God's truth.

Because the mind always needed to first apprehend external stimuli before emotion could be created, Hodge had little patience for those who taught that the Bible contained contradictory language whose meaning was unattainable through the mind alone. Hodge responded to such thinking with a sophisticated Common Sense view of the nature of biblical language and inspiration. He built his case for the importance of reason in the Christian life by first turning his attention to the Bible. Hodge realized that he must first prove that the Bible itself was a reliable document because Common Sense argued that the ability to determine and respond to truth was only as good as the source material with which it worked. Faulty material inevitably produced faulty reasoning and ultimately false conclusions. Good material led to good reasoning and true conclusions.[7]

Thus, Hodge began his counterattack on German Idealism's influence on biblical interpretation with an extended articulation of the absolute correctness and dependability of the Bible in an 1857 *Repertory* article entitled "The Inspiration of Holy Scripture." Here, Hodge declared that the Bible's message was infallible in a "plenary" or complete sense. Opposing all notions of partial biblical inspiration, Hodge held the Bible to be totally correct and reliable.[8] Hodge's notion of plenary inspiration reached well beyond the assertion that the Bible's content was conceptually sound. He held that the Bible's content was reliable down to the very "words employed."[9] If the Bible was indeed an inspired "record of truth," Hodge argued that it had to be absolutely correct in every one of its details, and these details extended down to the level of word choice.[10] Hodge declared that to deny "the control of the Spirit over the words of the sacred writer, is to deny inspiration altogether."[11]

Following his Scottish Realist convictions, Hodge believed that all words had fixed meanings comprehensible to humanity's common rational faculty. The Bible's conceptual content—its "spirit" in Park's thinking—could never be separated from its words. Just as "no man can have a wordless thought," form and substance were one and the same when it came to biblical language.[12] God had used words to convey himself to humanity, and he had chosen the *exact* words he wanted to accomplish this revelation. Although Hodge allowed for a biblical writer's own personality and culture to flavor his writings, the words themselves came straight from God and the meanings of those particular words were immutable.[13]

It is important to note that while Hodge held the words of scripture to be infallible, he never personally advocated that they were without error in their original manuscripts. (Later Princetonians like his son Archie and B. B. Warfield rose as the great champions of this "inerrant" view of the scriptures, a line of reasoning that Hodge had implied but never formally taught.[14]) Hodge conceded that minor errors in transcription had occurred over the centuries, but taken as a whole, Christians of his day could have complete confidence in the scriptural record.[15] Unlike the German Higher Criticism that stressed the need to understand the historical setting of biblical books and the implications of how various corruptions of the text had important theological ramifications, Hodge believed that such chronological matters and textual disruptions mattered little. For him, the Bible forever remained an entirely reliable document. The words it contained held common, universal meanings understandable to any person using their "common sense" and employing their rational faculty.

Biblical language was thus sacrosanct and fixed in a way that broached no compromise to considerations of time and place. One did not need to take into account the points of view of various biblical writers, their settings, or their motivations for writing a given passage or book. Their words were what was important, timeless words that were immutable in their meanings. The religious historian George Marsden characterized Hodge's view toward the scriptures as "analogous to the relationship between Ptolemaic and Copernican accounts of the universe."[16] The Ptolemic view held that the earth was a fixed point around which all other stars revolved. The Copernican view taught that all heavenly bodies were in motion, including the earth. Hodge's view was Ptolemaic in two respects: he believed words to be fixed in their meanings, and he believed truth itself to be a fixed point around which everything else revolved. German Idealism, and its more modern philosophical descendants, tended to view both words and truth as something to be gauged relative to variations in chronological time and the points of view of both author and audience. Hodge was convinced that God's words and the truths they conveyed were the same yesterday, today, and forever.

For Hodge, the proper activity of the interpreter was not to discover interpretation-laden gaps in figurative language or recover the historical moment in which a biblical author wrote. Instead, a good biblical interpreter carefully orders and then enumerates the truths found in the scriptures themselves. Like physical nature, the scriptures provide a repository of facts that simply needed to be studied and properly set in relation one to another in order to obtain a clear sense of the truths they revealed. In this line of reasoning, Hodge showed just how deeply he had come to be influenced by the renowned philosopher and empiricist Francis Bacon. Bacon's teaching encouraged Hodge to approach the words of scripture using a rigorous inductive method of examining the Bible's words and then grouping concepts together to make overall conclusions about the text's meaning. Hodge became one of the greatest practitioners of this scientific, systematic method of biblical observation and categorization.[17] He unabashedly taught that the job of any biblical interpreter rested not in proposing theories based on possibilities, but in simply uncovering the truths found through a careful examination of the very words of scripture.

Hodge's emphasis on humanity's common rationality and the universal meanings of words promised that the vast majority of people were capable of understanding the Bible. Adhering closely to the thinking of his much beloved Turretin, Hodge believed the Bible to be a book that God had intended to "be understood by the people, in the use of ordinary means."[18] Turretin had written that the scriptures were accessible to every person without "recourse to any tradition independent" of the Bible, whether such traditions be oral or written.[19] If recourse was to be sought, Hodge believed the best single distillation of scriptural interpretation was to be found in the Westminster Catechism, but the doctrines contained therein were nothing more than the summary of truths culled from the careful and thorough study of the entire scriptures.

Hodge's Common Sense view of biblical language, undergirded by his faith in the Baconian inductive method of observation and categorization, became increasingly less serviceable as the nineteenth century wore on. An influx of immigration and the heightened awareness of cultural differences that accompanied such immigration gave the lie to Common Sense notions of the universality of language and the unity of all humankind.[20] Hodge, however, did not live to see Scottish Common Sense Realism pushed to the country's philosophical margins as the Anglo-Saxon Protestant moral and religious consensus increasingly fractured at the turn of the twentieth century.[21] Hodge maintained throughout his life that there existed a commonality among all people from near and distant ages, as well as disparate societies and cultures, which affirmed certain unchanging, core truths found in the scriptures.

44

"GRACES OF THE SPIRIT"

Hodge's ascent from the depths of grief in the wake of his beloved Sarah's death was a slow, painful process. It became common practice for Hodge to recount milestones of Sarah's final months. He was especially sensitive to various types of anniversaries: the day she had returned from Kentucky, the last time she stayed with his brother Hugh, her final attendance at a public worship service, and the list goes on.[1] Beginning just the week after her death, he began to mark all time relative to her passing by denoting every Sabbath in his daily memorandum book as the "first Sunday after" and "second Sunday after" and so forth.[2] Even a year after her passing she so dominated his thoughts that he wrote his brother that it had been "sixty seven weeks (469 days)" since he had bid Sarah farewell.[3] As late as September 16, 1857, Hodge noted the day as the eighth anniversary of the last time Sarah heard him preach.[4]

In the weeks following Sarah's death, Hodge's family heard him frequently weeping in his study, and he made an almost-daily pilgrimage to her grave.[5] He spent grief-filled hours collecting and pouring over letters that he and Sarah exchanged over the years. Hodge commented to his brother in the midst of his grief that afflictions have a "sanctifying influence," and it was a man's "great duty & highest interest to endeavor to desire spiritual benefit from our bereavements & sorrows" because they are "designed principally to wean us from the world and to call into exercise the graces of the Spirit."[6] Hodge had great opportunity to pursue such "graces of the Spirit" as he struggled daily to find God's hand in what seemed so often to him an impossibly difficult loss.

Hodge did work hard in his attempts to normalize his family's life in the wake of his wife's death. He still had his three youngest children at home with him: Catherine (Kitty), Francis (Frank), and Sarah, who ranged in ages from ten to fourteen years old. He hired a family friend, Miss Craig, to serve as a type of house manager and nanny.[7]

He toyed with the idea of leaving Princeton because Sarah was "so associated with everything" about it, but he gradually reestablished a rhythm that revolved around his family and Seminary responsibilities.[8] Amidst his grief, he did find it terribly difficult to concentrate and struggled with a feeling of being "inefficient," telling his brother that he had "more than one book half finished—but when they will be done I cannot venture to conjecture."[9] Nothing seemed to come as easy for him as it once had.

Not every aspect of Hodge's life was desolate in the wake of his wife's death. His daughter Mary and her newborn son had been in Princeton when Sarah had died, and she served as a ray of hope in his most dismal days of grief. Mary stayed until the following summer when, with great reluctance, she returned to Kentucky to be with her husband. Mary missed William, but she found Kentucky a difficult place to live. She had been unable to make any meaningful friendships there, disliked the violence that marked so much Southern honor-based culture, and desperately missed the more refined society of the East Coast.[10] Mary's domestic life in Kentucky was further complicated by the fact that she and her husband did not have their own house, but lived in a boarding house for women, a situation she described as a thoroughly "unpleasant arrangement."[11] So unhappy did Mary become upon her return that William contemplated leaving his position and returning East.[12] Hodge strongly urged him to take no such step without a firm job in hand, and they remained for a time in Danville until they were able to relocate to Chicago, where William took a position as Professor of Biblical Literature and Exegesis at the Theological Seminary at Chicago.[13]

Another source of happiness for Hodge amid his grief was the return of Archie and his family from India in May of 1850.[14] Although he settled his family in Philadelphia, Archie proved himself a source of great consolation and companionship for Hodge. After supplying pulpits for six months and considering a post as a missionary to the Chickasaw Indians beyond the Appalachian mountains in Kentucky and Tennessee, in 1851 Archie finally accepted a pastorate in Lower West Nottingham, Maryland.[15] He served a double role there as both minister and farmer, since a small farm was given to him as part of his compensation for his pastoral duties. Unlike his father, Archie did not take naturally to farming, and this particularly rural position proved intellectually isolating for him.[16] Like his sister, he longed for the more refined society in which he had been raised. After four years in this post, Archie moved his family to a new pastoral position in Fredericksburg, Virginia.[17] His whole family found this larger, less rural community much more to their liking.

The way in which Hodges's emotional and relational world contracted with the death of Sarah was echoed in how he decided a year after her death to sell the eight acres of farmland adjacent to his home, land that he had assiduously cultivated for over twenty years. Richard Stockton, the current resident of Princeton's magnificent Morven estate, offered him $5,000 for the land, and Hodge agreed to sell.[18] Although the loss of his little farm saddened him, Hodge found that he no longer had the energy to pay it the necessary attention. He also desperately wished to be able to help both Mary and Archie live more comfortably with their new families, and he made generous gifts to them both with the money he realized from the sale of his farm.

Figure 44.1 *Mary Hunter Stockton Hodge*: Mary Hunter Stockton Hodge was widowed at the age of twenty-nine after the death of her husband, Samuel Witham Stockton, a Lieutenant in the United States Navy. Through her marriage to Samuel, she became connected to Princeton's famous Stockton family. Three years after Sarah's death, Hodge married Mary and embarked on a long and happy second marriage. [*Special Collections, Princeton Theological Seminary Libraries*]

A greater change was yet to come. On July 8, 1852, Hodge married for a second time. His bride, Mary Hunter Stockton, was the daughter of Andrew Hunter, a Presbyterian minister and a one-time professor of astronomy and mathematics at the College, and her brother would gain fame as a Civil War general.[19] Mary had married into Princeton's illustrious Stockton family by becoming the wife of Samuel Witham Stockton, a lieutenant in the United States Navy. She had become a young widow when Samuel had died in 1836, leaving her with two small children. By the time Hodge proposed, Mary was forty-five years old and her children had grown.

It gives but a taste of Princeton's tight social circles to note that while Mary married Hodge, her two children would wed two of Hodge's children. Her son, Samuel, married Hodge's youngest daughter, Sarah, and her daughter (also named Mary Hunter Stockton) married Hodge's second son, Caspar.[20] Caspar's marriage was tragically short-lived. His Mary died of consumption less then two years later, leaving him to remarry five years later, only to lose his second wife to consumption less than a year after their wedding.[21] Finally, in October 1869, Caspar married a woman with whom he would have two children and a long, happy marriage.

Mary had actually been an intimate of the Hodge family for years. Hodge had known her since she had been fifteen years old, and in the six or seven years before Sarah's death, Mary had become like "a sister" to his wife.[22] Long before their marriage, Mary had become a regular presence in the Hodge household, and no doubt her familiarity and great popularity with his family helped Hodge propose. Hodge's girls were particularly pleased with their new stepmother, and Hodge described his new bride as filling his long-saddened home with gleaming rays of "devout, cheerful sunlight."[23]

Hodge was as well suited to his second wife as he had been to his first. He was fortunate to have married well twice in his life. Mary proved to be a vivacious, social, and religious woman who immediately took charge of Hodge's household. She renovated rooms throughout the house, converted the attic into another bedroom for the girls, and began to once again provide Hodge's children with a sound and systematic education at home. Their twenty-six-year marriage was marked by happiness and mutual respect. Mary outlived Hodge by two years, dying in 1880. Archie, the child who had been closest to Sarah, commented after his stepmother's death that she had been a wonderful support to his father and to the entire family. He noted that she had always enjoyed the profound "affection and gratitude of all her children."[24]

45

THE BATTLE AGAINST "CHURCHIANITY"

As Hodge began to enjoy his new marriage, he finally found himself once again able to settle back into a regular writing schedule. In the coming years, there was one topic in particular to which he returned again and again: the nature of the Christian church. Throughout the 1850s, he published eleven lengthy articles in the *Repertory* on what Nevins had succinctly called the "Church Question."[1] So important did Hodge deem the topic that he considered writing a fourth volume to his *Systematic Theology* specifically devoted to the topic of the church.[2]

Hodge was not writing his thoughts about the church in a vacuum. The "Church Question" was a topic of vibrant discussion at the time not only in the United States, but around the world. Many of Hodge's European friends were leading figures in these interchanges. In Germany, August Neander set forth a conception of a constantly evolving, more organic church, while Ernst Hengstenberg and Ludwig Von Gerlach argued for conservative, hierarchical conceptions of the church in relation to both politics and society. William Cunningham continued his running battle with the Established Church of Scotland over issues of ecclesiastical authority.[3]

In the United States, there was no single genesis to the "Church Question," but by the 1840s, denominations were spending ever greater amounts of time articulating their views on what constituted the true Christian church. As frontier revivalism, European Catholic immigration, the appearance of quasi-Christian groups such as the Mormons, and primitivist movements like the Disciples of Christ all pushed against established denominations such as the Episcopalians, Presbyterians and Congregationalists, members of every party attempted to legitimate their own doctrinal stances, forms of church government, and denominational traditions. Hodge was acutely aware that his Presbyterians were losing ground to the Methodists, Baptists, and Catholics.

While one in three American Protestants were Methodists by 1840, fewer than one in ten were Presbyterians. For Presbyterians, this was a decline of almost 50 percent from the time of the American Revolution.[4] Competition among Protestants only intensified as the nineteenth century wore on, and the friction created by so many competing viewpoints catalyzed a plethora of exchanges on the character and membership of Christ's earthly bride, the church.[5]

Hodge became a major contributor to these discussions for two reasons. First, as Samuel Miller had aged and gradually retired from his position of teaching church history, Hodge had stepped in to begin offering lectures on topics related to the church.[6] His preparation for these lectures sparked in him a growing interest in matters of ecclesiology, and he used many of these lectures as the foundation for his later *Repertory* essays on the church.

Second, a broader range of intellectual crusades and denominational responsibilities pushed Hodge toward clarifying his own thinking on the nature of the church. As Hodge took a seat on his denomination's Board of Missions in the mid-1840s, attempted to defend Roman Catholic baptism without condoning the Catholic Church's every action, argued against various forms of Unitarianism, decried the activities of theologically unsound revivalism, and took many of his fellow Protestants to task for being unfaithful to the most basic tenets of the Reformation, he found it increasingly necessary to provide his own definition of the church. Unlike Bushnell, who he once accused of proposing ideas that overturned, but did "not erect," Hodge wished not only to argue against what he considered a heterodox view of the church, but also he desired to provide a scripturally based, soundly reasoned position on what defined Christ's true church.[7]

While many factors pushed Hodge to engage the church topic, it soon became clear that the attacks he had suffered for his defense of Roman Catholic baptism a few years earlier served as the single-most-important guiding force behind what he wrote. Stung by the persistent criticism that "Princeton has fairly turned out to be an apologist for Rome," Hodge composed many of his essays to highlight his belief that while Catholics were not outside the pale of Christian community, Protestantism offered an infinitely superior way to Christ.[8] No one could read far into Hodge's church writings and have any doubt about his absolute allegiance to Protestantism.

Hodge's first *Repertory* article on the "Church Question" appeared in 1846 and was entitled "The Unity of the Church." He had written this article during the height of the Presbyterian controversy over whether Roman Catholic baptism should be recognized by the Presbyterian Church in America as a viable sacrament. He had composed his "Unity" article to disarm all arguments against excommunicating every Catholic who had been baptized before the Reformation. He argued that if the Presbyterian Church took such a stance, Martin Luther himself could not claim to have been baptized.

Hodge wished to make it clear in his "Unity" article that while Catholics may have their doctrinal idiosyncrasies, these mistakes did not automatically make their sacrament of baptism meaningless.

By the early 1850s, Hodge showed himself to be much more battered by the criticism of his peers on the topic of Catholicism. In his church articles from this decade, he is infinitely more interested in demonstrating Protestantism's superiority over Catholicism. In 1853, he published his theoretical centerpiece on the nature of the church, a mammoth two-part *Repertory* essay entitled: "The Idea of the Church." In it, Hodge addressed what he considered the most crucial aspect of the "Church Question:" "whether we are to conceive of the Church, in its essential character, as an external society, or as the communion of saints."[9] His answer to this question showed just how far he had moved away from stressing Catholicism's inclusion in a more universal conception of the church.

"The Idea" offered three basic doctrinal paradigms that had come to distinguish various forms of the church through the ages: rationalistic, ritualistic, and evangelical.[10] The rationalistic form favored reason above all else and saw nothing supernatural in either Christ or Christianity. Certain Gnostic heresies, as well as the more liberal Unitarians of Hodge's own day, served as examples of this form.[11] Hodge spent little time in his church essays exploring the rationalist form of the church; he was far more interested in setting the ritualistic and evangelical forms against each other. Roman Catholicism (and the High Anglicanism of the Oxford Movement) most vibrantly captured the ritualistic form, an orientation that stressed the external form of the church and its divinely ordained power structure. The ritualistic form held that the institution and leaders of the church controlled "the exclusive channels of grace and salvation."[12]

Far superior to this ritualistic orientation was the "evangelical" form.[13] This form was found in the primitive church and was reborn in the Protestant Church of the Reformation. It placed the responsibility for salvation squarely on the shoulders of each individual, not on the clerical hierarchies or institutional apparatuses so favored by Catholics. The evangelical form rested "on the scriptures as its objective ground; and its inward or subjective ground is an enlightened conviction of sin."[14] Accordingly, members of the church were distinguished as those in whom Christ "dwells by his Spirit."[15] Although men and women could never know the hearts of others, the best single indicator as to whether a person might have this indwelling of the Holy Spirit was the manifestation of the fruits of the Spirit in his or her life. Such manifestations Hodge commonly called "works by love" and were the central distinguishing marks of a holy life.[16]

Throughout his church essays, Hodge used the formulation of the church found in the Apostles' Creed as the foundation for his own thinking; the church was best described as being "the communion of saints," and it was not "a visible society organized under one definite form."[17] In this respect, the Catholics were absolutely wrong in their assertion that there was only one true form of the church presided over by a pope. In contradistinction, Hodge maintained that the scriptures had little to say about the actual form of the church. He noted that "the Church can exist without a pope, without prelates, yea, without presbyters, if in its essential nature it is the communion of Saints."[18] The scriptures, however, were unequivocal in showing that the true church was composed of everyone whose heart had been enlightened by the Holy Spirit and as a result believed certain fundamental truths of the Gospel. For Hodge, the "vital bond between Christ and his body [was] the Holy Spirit."[19]

Hodge's emphasis on the church being defined by its believing membership made it a global, universal entity. Just as importantly, it was an invisible entity, defined by believing hearts, not by ordained clergy or physical institutions.[20] Hodge had no qualms about agreeing that believers throughout history had needed smaller bodies to help them live out their faith, but the church universal was the communion of all believers who had hearts transformed by the work of the Holy Spirit.[21] In this way, the Protestant's invisible church could claim to be the most catholic of all conceptions of the church even though its members were broken into smaller denominations and myriad local congregations.[22]

It was the stress on the invisible, universal church that made Hodge stand so adamantly against theologies that emphasized the visible church like the Catholics, the Oxford Movement and those at Mercersburg with their "Romanizing" tendencies.[23] These theologies partook too much of the ritualistic form and ultimately stood for a kind of "Churchianity, in distinction from Christianity."[24] Hodge sharply distinguished between "professing" and "true" Christians, the former not being Christians at all but only those who called themselves such.[25] The ritualistic form so stressed the externals that anyone who claimed membership in their ranks could also claim salvation.[26] Church membership, the blessing of priests, even the partaking of the sacraments was no sure sign of salvation or memberships within the communion of the saints for Hodge.[27] In the end, the only "distinguishing characteristic of the members of Christ's body, is the indwelling of the Holy Ghost."[28] The church did not make true believers as much as true believers made up the church.[29]

Hodge pounded away at the differences between the Protestant and Catholic conceptions of the church by writing article after article refuting key attributes the Catholics claimed to be defining marks of Christ's church. When Catholics said the church was visible as a single entity on the earth, Hodge countered by saying the church was visible "not as an organization, not as an external society, but as the living body of Christ; as a set of men distinguished from others as true Christians."[30] When Catholics declared that the church needed to be distinguished by a sense of perpetuity—an entity that followed a consistent set of doctrines and was guided by a leader who could trace his succession all the way back to Peter—Hodge agreed that "the Church is perpetual," but argued that "perpetual" meant nothing more than "the continued existence on earth of sincere believers who profess the true religion."[31] When Catholics were tempted to ask "Where was your Church before Luther?" Hodge replied with "the homely retort, where was your face this morning before it was washed?"[32] At every turn, Hodge used Roman Catholicism as his primary foil to explain his Protestant view of the church.

Hodge's stress on personal belief, so treasured in the evangelical paradigm, did raise a slightly different issue when it came to the salvation of those who were not able to repent and believe for themselves, most notably infants and young children. Of particular importance for Hodge here was the issue of infant damnation. Did God condemn to hell all those too young to understand and act on the basic tenets of the Gospel message? Hodge took on this particular question in 1858 when he reviewed R. B. Mayes' *The Tecnobaptist* for the *Repertory*, a book he told his readers that was profoundly interested in "the idea of the Church, and on the conditions of church membership."[33]

In a rare departure from his usual church essay, Hodge turned his attention away from Roman Catholicism as the negative counterpoint to bolster his arguments and instead used the Baptists as the misguided exponent of deluded doctrine. Hodge argued that Baptists were sadly mistaken in their views of the church's membership.[34] Hodge was relentless in asserting that the church's membership, by necessity and by long tradition, had always included the infants and young children of true believers. Citing an Irish Episcopal minister, Hodge exclaimed that "there are but two places into the whole universe of God from which infants are excluded. The one is hell; the other is the Baptist Church."[35] Arguing a line that included everyone in the evangelical church aside from the Baptists, as well as many in the ritual form, Hodge set before his readers a detailed argument drawn both from scripture and the Reformed creedal tradition that children were members of the church by virtue of their parents' membership. "In all covenants which God has ever formed with men," the children of true believers "have always been included."[36] Hodge held that an infant would not be damned upon its death if it had at least one of Christian parent.[37]

Hodge completely adhered with longstanding Reformed doctrine in stating that believing parents represent their children in the covenant of God's grace. Thus, children of true believers enjoyed the same grace as their parents until they come of age to make their own faith decision.[38] (Hodge agreed with many others of his day that the age of religious accountability was twelve.) In opposition to the Catholics, Episcopalians, Lutherans, and those at Mercersburg, Hodge argued that baptism did not mystically renew the infant's spirit and make him or her members of the church. Infants were members of the church solely by virtue of their parent's belief.

Aside from the contentious issue of the church's membership, Hodge also wrote extensively on the scripture's view of the church's government. The church might be invisible and universal, but the fact that its saints actually met together demanded that the scriptural view of such gatherings be addressed. In what might seem an uncharacteristically system-free gesture, Hodge wrote that no "one mode of organization is essential to being the church, nor that the details of any system of church polity are laid down in Scripture as universally obligatory."[39] He thought it "inconceivable that any one outward form of the church can be suited for" every age, every race, and every part of the globe.[40] As long as congregations held to the value of teaching God's Word and emphasizing the Holy Spirit's role in spiritual renewal, Hodge showed incredible flexibility in conceiving what forms different congregations might take.

Even with such elastic sentiments, Hodge did believe that the New Testament offered certain general principals that congregations should follow, and he sincerely believed that these principles found their truest expression in the Presbyterian form of church governance. There were three core principles set forth in the scriptures when it came to church organization: church members had a right to take part in matters of governance; a small section of the church's members must be appointed to permanent clerical positions to teach God's Word, administer the sacraments, and enforce church discipline; and the unity of the church depended on the subjection of smaller congregations to larger governing bodies.[41] In the end, Hodge proved himself a thorough Presbyterian, and in 1855 he published a small but popular book entitled *What is Presbyterianism?* This booklet came to serve as his most succinct articulation of the nature of God's church as manifested in Presbyterian polity.[42]

Hodge solidified his public ties to his beloved denomination by writing numerous essays on the distinctive characteristics of Presbyterianism and serving on a special committee called by the 1857 General Assembly to revise the denomination's *Book of Discipline*. Hodge may have believed that scripture advocated no exact form for the church, but he was equally convinced that it could not exist without some form of organization when it took a visible form. The *Book of Discipline* functioned as a manual of Presbyterian practice that set down general directions, admonitions, and exhortations to aid church leaders, and instructions on how to handle cases where church law has been violated.[43] The *Book of Discipline* was a cornerstone document in the governing practices of the church. Although it took no theological position declaring that there was but one form the church could take, for Presbyterianism it provided the fundamental source of acceptable denominational practices, without which Presbyterianism was in danger of falling into ineffectual disorganization and ultimately ecclesiastical chaos.

Beyond the uniformity signaled by his support of the denomination's *Book of Discipline*, Hodge paid attention to issues that brought a sense of shared identity among

Presbyterians when it came to worship practices. In this regard, he was particularly interested in the issue of liturgies: were liturgies acceptable in worship and how should they be used? Hodge maintained throughout his life that while the use of liturgies was certainly not compulsory, all Presbyterians would be well served if they had a book of liturgies compiled from the writings of "Calvin, Knox, and of the Reformed Churches" to which they could turn when planning and executing various religious services and sacraments.[44]

Even as he showed his bias for liturgies, Hodge again battled the specter of being called a Roman Catholic sympathizer. He felt it necessary once again to make it painfully clear that his own theological views were entirely grounded on the evangelical rather than ritualistic form of the church. He was careful to point out that while liturgies were a defining characteristic of "prelatical churches" such as Catholicism, the Presbyterian Church had a long liturgical tradition that in no way should be confused with its Romish counterpart.[45] Hodge wished all to know that "the use of liturgies was introduced into all the Protestant churches at the time of the Reformation, and that in the greater number of them, they continue in use to the present day."[46] There were liturgies that had been long used among Presbyterians, and their use had always done much to enliven the spiritual life of the church, particularly when it came to the issue of prayer. Even in his discussions of liturgies, Hodge wished to prove himself to be a product of the Protestant Reformation, a man who saw liturgies not as magical incantations but as useful tools to better bind together his brethren in both ecclesiastical form and doctrinal substance.

THORNWELL AND "THUS SAITH THE LORD"

Hodge's flexibility toward church form, even with his clear preference for Presbyterianism, did not please everyone within his denomination. Significant differences existed even between Old School Presbyterians when it came to definitions of the church. Nowhere was this more apparent than in Hodge's many arguments with Southern Presbyterianism's most intellectually gifted and vocal leader, James Henley Thornwell, a man who took exception to Hodge's notion that the scriptures had laid down no exact blueprint when it came to the governance of the church. Thornwell firmly believed the opposite. God had indeed set down the form of the church, and scripture made it clear that form was Presbyterianism.

Thornwell's arguments against Hodge's notions on church form manifested themselves most vividly in his crusade against the use of extra-biblical bodies such as voluntary societies and boards of governance within the Presbyterian Church. Hodge saw such voluntary societies and boards as good and necessary for American Presbyterianism, while Thornwell saw them as having no biblical warrant and posing a great threat to Presbyterian purity and autonomy. Their differing opinions led to one of the greatest confrontations to occur in the General Assembly since the denominational split of 1837. Over the period of eight days on the floor of the 1860 General Assembly, Hodge and Thornwell served as the lead debaters defending different positions on the nature of the Presbyterian Church.

One might little suspect the depth of animosity that existed between the two men given that they were both such prominent Old School leaders. They had much in common, even though Thornwell was Hodge's junior by fourteen years. Both had been left fatherless at young ages, and had grown up to be devoted husbands and fathers to large families. Both had also distinguished themselves through their prodigious

Figure 46.1 *James Henley Thornwell*: James Henley Thornwell was once described by the great American historian George Bancroft as "the most learned of the learned." He dominated antebellum Southern Presbyterianism first as a oratorically gifted minister and then as a faculty member and eventual president of South Carolina College. Thornwell taught that the Church was a spiritual body that should abstain from joining itself to secular institutions or causes. Hodge believed that Thornwell took the invisible nature of the Church too far and saw his position as undercutting the Church's ability to oppose social ills. [*Library of the Author*]

intellectual abilities and astounding work ethics. Thornwell showed himself to be so precociously intelligent as a young boy that leading men in his community rose up to sponsor his education. He then went on to study at South Carolina College in Columbia, Andover Seminary, and finally Harvard Divinity School. The North did not agree with him, however, as he found its climate too cold and its theologies too liberal. After his Northern studies he returned to South Carolina, where he served first as a minister and then took various positions at his alma mater including faculty member, chaplain, and ultimately president.

Thornwell appreciated much of Hodge's more theological treatises and made special mention of his Romans commentary as being particularly good. He felt, however, that Hodge's lack of pastoral experience was an insurmountable handicap when it came to understanding the church's form and the nature of its government.[1] As early as 1843, clear differences could be seen in the two men's thinking. Their first major battle centered on "the warrant, nature, and duties of the office of ruling elder in the Presbyterian Church," an issue that was debated in both the 1842 and 1843 General Assemblies.[2] At issue was the power and rank held by the ruling elder in the church's governing structure.

The 1843 General Assembly ultimately decided that ruling elders were different in both position and responsibility from ordained teaching elders (more commonly called ministers). They also affirmed the long-held tradition that ministers occupied a post ranking above other elders and were not members of their individual congregations. Instead, ministers were members of a larger presbytery that served a number of congregations in a defined geographical area.[3] One result of their special status was that under normal circumstances, ministers could only be ordained by a group of already ordained ministers, thus further widening the gap between ruling and teaching elders. Hodge fully endorsed the Assembly's views on the primacy of ministers and joined the majority in voting to adopt a sharp distinction between teaching and ruling elders by a 138–9 margin.[4]

Thornwell vehemently opposed the decision, believing that the distinction between ruling elders and ministers had no basis in scripture.[5] He believed the General Assembly's position both denigrated the role of the ruling elder and exalted too highly the role of the clergy.[6] He saw the decision as touching upon "a principle which lies at the very foundation of our system," namely the treasured participation of laymen in church governance.[7] By making such strong distinctions between ruling and teaching elders, Thornwell saw a way open up for "High Churchism and Popery," a tendency to so exalt ministers that all meaningful power was wrested from a church's congregation.[8] Presbyterianism was built upon the belief that all (male) members could contribute to church governance. Making the church's elected eldership so clearly inferior to the positions of ordained clergy put at risk the broad-based congregational participation that was a key distinctive of Presbyterianism.

A scant two years later, Hodge and Thornwell once again found themselves locked in combat when Thornwell became a major voice in the 1845 General Assembly vote that invalidated all Roman Catholic baptisms. Thornwell wrote his wife from the Cincinnati Assembly that "I made a speech to-day, *two hours long*, which was listened to with breathless attention, and, from what I can gather, is likely to settle the question."[9] His words did prove pivotal in the landslide vote against Catholic baptism. The national reputation Thornwell gained through this controversy helped him get elected as Hodge's replacement as General Assembly moderator in 1847, making him at age thirty-five the youngest man to ever hold the post.

As Thornwell stepped into the national spotlight, he wasted no time in showing just how disillusioned he had become with many of the views of his predecessor. As Hodge continued to defend the Catholic sacrament of baptism, Thornwell decided that the *Repertory*'s time had passed. In its place, he helped start *The Southern Presbyterian Review*, a rival theological journal intended to stand against all errant views, and he showed himself particularly keen to correct the mistakes he saw pouring forth from Princeton.[10] Over the next three decades, Thornwell's *Review* became the major platform for the articulation of Southern Presbyterian thought.

Thornwell based his every argument against Hodge, and his every position more generally, on a simple credo: "the Bible is our only rule, and that where it is silent we have no right to speak."[11] For Thornwell, historical precedent and the constitution of the Presbyterian Church in America weighed as nothing against the preeminence of scripture in determining any important church matter. Holding firmly to this principle, he distinguished himself as one of American Presbyterianism's strictest biblical constructionists. Thornwell's literalist approach showed up in every stance he took on religious practice and was well exemplified in his stand against the adoption of the organ in church services because he saw no place in scripture authorizing the use of instrumental music in worship.[12]

While Hodge may today enjoy a reputation as one of American Protestantism's most literal expositors of scripture, it is a reputation he earned only in part. His views on such issues as slavery do indeed show how committed he was to a literal approach to the Bible's teaching, but his approach to many ecclesiastical matters evince a pronounced interpretative flexibility. Hodge pales in comparison as a conservative biblical constructionist when set against Thornwell, a man so tied to what appeared—or did not appear—in the Bible that even Hodge considered his biblical hermeneutic to be untenable "superlative high churchism."[13] Next to Thornwell, Hodge comes across as a biblically pragmatist who believed that it was simply impossible to decide every issue by Thornwell's "Thus Saith the Lord" principle of adjudication.[14] A million different practical and cultural considerations led Hodge to assert that "Christ has, in his infinite wisdom, left his church free to modify her government, in accordance" with certain general scriptural principles.[15] Hodge argued that churches must be governed by general scriptural principles rather than hard and fast rules that apply equally to all congregations in every situation.

By the time of Hodge and Thornwell met for their last great face-to-face confrontation on the floor of the 1860 General Assembly, the two men had been sparring in print and in person for nearly two decades. Standing fast upon his stance that the "Bible is our only rule," Thornwell spent hours arguing against the existence of voluntary societies and denominational boards.[16] He reasoned that such structures had no place in scripture, and thus no place in the church; "God had laid down in the Scripture a form of church government, for which we are not at liberty to depart . . . we can no more create a new office, or a new organ for the church, than we can create a new article of faith."[17]

Hodge took the opposite view, positing lines of reasoning he had articulated as early as 1837.[18] In a role he commonly took against Thornwell, Hodge argued from what he saw as the spirit of scriptural intention when he defended certain church institutions against Thornwell's extreme biblical literalism. Rather than focus on the narrow details surrounding the existence of scriptural warrants for given voluntary societies and church boards, Hodge argued that the larger scriptural principle of preaching the gospel message to every creature took precedent. Furthermore, Hodge believed that scripture's vagueness on the issue of church form was intentional in that it gave church leaders "discretionary power as to matters of detail and modes of operation" that allowed for maximum flexibility and effectiveness in reaching humanity with the Gospel.[19]

Thornwell saw this as biblical pragmatism of the most dangerous kind, and his greatest fears about the crumbling nature of the American Presbyterian Church were realized when, much to his dismay, the 1860 General Assembly decisively defeated his position against extra-denominational societies and boards with a vote of 234–56.[20] It was a vote that did much to unsettle Thornwell's confidence in his fellow Presbyterians, and Hodge's reputation among Southern Presbyterians also suffered, for they saw in him a man even less committed to biblical warrants than they had hitherto believed. His stance on Roman baptism had troubled many of them; his unbiblical stance on voluntary societies further eroded their confidence in him.

For Thornwell, the Assembly's 1860 vote brought into vivid relief just how little his Northern brethren cared about the purity of the church and the supremacy of scripture. Partly due to his shaken faith in the American Presbyterian Church, Thornwell moved away from his Northern Presbyterian brethren in the coming months to become a founding member of the Presbyterian Church of the Confederate States of America.[21] He hoped to attain in this new church body his dream of a more "spiritual" church, a goal he no longer saw as possible in a unified American Presbyterian Church.

47

THE PAULINE COMMENTARIES

Hodge's new marriage brought him renewed energy for personal and professional projects. He returned to his love of agriculture in 1856 by buying a farm on the Millstone River about three miles from his house. He placed the farm under the care of his fourth son, John, who had never shown much interest in school or more scholarly endeavors. John wished to try his hand at farming, but worked his father's land for only three years before moving thirty miles northeast to take a post at a railroad office in South Amboy, New Jersey.[1] Even after John's departure, Hodge kept the farm and rented out the land. He took great joy later in life regularly visiting his farm and returning home with its vegetables, eggs, and chickens.

In the same year that he acquired the Millstone farm, Hodge approached Addison Alexander with the idea of working together to produce a commentary series on the entire New Testament. Hodge had been both impressed and chagrined by the immense popularity of Albert Barnes's New Testament commentaries. Barnes had set to work with the primary goal of providing a resource that would be equally useful to educated clergy and laymen alike. He eventually wrote eleven commentaries that sold tens of thousands of copies during the nineteenth century. Hodge wanted to produce a similar series, but one executed with an eye to Old School orthodoxy. Hodge proposed that he write on the doctrinal and epistolary books, while Addison devote himself to the historical and prophetic sections of the New Testament. Hodge proposed that the two men work in a parallel fashion, each attempting to complete a different book on roughly the same schedule. Addison was so thrilled by the idea that he found himself unable to imagine a "way in which we could both exert more influence" for the good of the church.[2]

Hodge could not have chosen a better partner for a commentary series he hoped would give thousands a sound, thoroughly Calvinist interpretation of the New Testament,

Not only had the two men been friends since their undergraduate days at Princeton College, but Addison was an internationally famous biblical linguist who had already, written two highly respected Old Testament commentaries. His closely reasoned and massively researched study of Isaiah (1847) turned out to be his masterpiece, an impressive display of how Princeton Old School theology attempted to confront and inculcate various strains of modern European biblical criticism without losing sight of Reformed orthodoxy. Addison had also published a mammoth, well-received three-volume set on the Psalms (1850).

While Barnes had shown himself wonderfully adept at being able to calibrate the content of his commentaries to a lay audience, both Hodge and Addison proved themselves far less nimble in this regard. Addison's first commentary for the series addressed the Book of Acts (1857), and it ended up being a dense, two-volume affair. He then moved on to complete treatments of the Gospels of Mark (1858) and Matthew (1860). Hodge turned his attention to the book of Ephesians (1856) and then to First and Second Corinthians (1857 and 1859). As Hodge and Addison proceeded with their work, they struggled to strike a balance between discussing the scholarly and practical angles of the texts they explored. In the end, while they got better at making their commentaries accessible to lay readers as their series progressed, they were never able to achieve the reader-friendly tone and content that Barnes had so ably mastered. Their commentaries on Acts and Ephesians, in particular, bore all the marks of intense Princeton erudition.

One does not need to read far into Hodge's volume on Ephesians to get a sense for how his ideal audience differed significantly from Barnes's. Hodge's analysis of Ephesians bore a much closer resemblance to his scholarly commentary on Romans than it did to anything written by Barnes. On the last page of his introduction to the book of Ephesians, Hodge gives his readers an overview of the best current scholarship on the text, citing a number of German critics. Thus, he signals early his desire to place his book in an international, scholarly conversation. As the commentary proceeds, Hodge constantly addresses critical concerns about the book's history, content, and relationship to various schools of theological thought both inside and outside Reformed circles. Whereas Barnes seldom deals with New Testament Greek in his commentaries, Hodge frequently cites passages in their original language and then offers extended footnotes in untranslated Latin and German. To further the scholarly aura of his commentary, Hodge deviated from the practice that made his Romans commentary so successful by failing to include practical sections at the end of each chapter highlighting how the teachings of the apostle might be applied to one's everyday life. Far from an accessible commentary similar to Barnes's work, Hodge's Ephesians commentary evinces a desire not so much to reach lay readers as to set the theology taught at Princeton before a highly educated audience.

Hodge's work on Ephesians also bears the marks of his most recent thinking on the church. His Ephesians commentary served as kind a coda on much of his ecclesiastical thinking of the previous decade. Hodge dedicated long portions of his commentary to explaining the invisible nature of the church, the communion of the saints, the sacraments (including infant baptism), and who might rightly be considered members of the church.[3] He also carefully noted how key passages in Ephesians severely undercut various teachings held dear by followers of Schleiermacher, Transcendentalists, Roman Catholics, and even Lutherans.[4]

Hodge also showed his continuing interest in the issue of slavery in his work on Ephesians. As various motions on slavery repeatedly made their way throughout the 1850s to the floor of the General Assembly, Hodge used his commentary to argue (in a line of reasoning that differed little from the one he had first offered in 1836) that nowhere in the Bible can one find "the doctrine that slave-holding is in itself sinful."[5] He spent considerable time directly addressing the much-discussed Ephesians passage on slavery from the book's sixth chapter:

> Servants [often translated as 'slaves'], be obedient to them that are your masters
> according to the flesh, with fear and trembling, in singleness of your heart, as
> unto Christ. Not with eyeservice, as menpleasers; but as the servants of Christ,
> doing the will of God from the heart. (Ephesians 6:5–6, KJV)

In his exegesis of this passage, Hodge once again declared his belief that too many people confounded "slave-laws with slavery."[6] He continued to believe that societies throughout history had always been based on various types of social hierarchies, and slavery had long held a place in such hierarchical structures. Hodge argued that Paul is neither "denouncing or commending slavery" to his Ephesian audience; he is simply acknowledging the institution's existence and setting forth the biblical injunctions that should govern its practice.[7]

Hodge did make it clear that while slavery was not prohibited by scripture, it was a practice that should be avoided if possible. As he had done before, he noted that "scriptural doctrine is opposed to the opinion that slavery is in itself a desirable institution, and as such to be cherished and perpetuated."[8] He was not yet ready to accept the radical reforms of abolitionism, but he was concerned that slavery not become an acceptable, perpetual institution in American society—the very position many Southern Presbyterians had already started to lean toward in the years leading up to the Civil War.

Hodge believed that as a Christian ethos increasingly enveloped the United States, slavery could not help but decline because it was so opposed to a host of scriptural mandates on human equality and compassion, values that preoccupied Paul in his letter to the Ephesians.[9] In Hodge's mind, Paul taught that as Christians sought their own sanctification, they could not but conclude that slavery was absolutely incompatible with the highest ideals of Christ. This realization may come gradually to Americans, but it was a view that Hodge believed would ultimately prevail. In the meantime, Hodge pointed slaveholders to Paul's teachings in Ephesians as the moral baseline for how they should treat their slaves.[10]

Throughout his treatment of slavery in Ephesians, Hodge once again shows just how little he appreciated the effects of slavery's more brutal aspects as it was practiced throughout much of the Union. As he sought to make clear how Paul sought to maintain the freedom of a slave's soul by giving a master authority over only a slave's external world, the degradation and cruelty of the institution is lost in the careful semantics of Hodge's prose.[11] For Hodge, the entire institution tended to remain on a highly conceptual plane. In the ideal scenario laid out by Paul, Christian masters worked for the religious uplift of their slaves, and Christian slaves could find "the highest mental elevation and spiritual freedom" by obeying their masters with a sanctified attitude of submission.[12] Hodge's notion of sanctification through obedience took no notice of the harsh realities of the broken families, back-breaking labor and pitiful living conditions that characterized slavery in America.

Hodge's biblical defense of the institution made his commentary, if not always himself, immensely popular among Southern Presbyterians who could not stomach the work of more rampant antislavery Presbyterians such as Albert Barnes.[13] Rather than doing close and literal exegetical work in a vein similar to Hodge, Barnes had published extensively against slavery, arguing that slavery was "against all laws which God has written on the human soul" and that all biblical exegesis defending the institution was "among the most remarkable instances of mistaken interpretation and unfounded reasoning furnished by the perversities of the human mind."[14] In Barnes's mind, Hodge's Ephesians commentary was perverse in the extreme, while Southern Presbyterians used it as a scriptural bulwark for their pro-slavery views.[15]

Upon completing his work on Ephesians, Hodge began collecting his lecture notes and preparing to write commentaries on First and Second Corinthians. He saw these two epistles as natural extensions of his work on Ephesians, as all three epistles were extended Pauline treatments on the nature of the church. Hodge's commentaries on First and Second Corinthians differed significantly, however, from his work on Ephesians. In his Corinthian commentaries, Hodge made a distinct move toward making his exegetical work more accessible to lay readers. Mimicking Barnes's style, Hodge spent less time keying on original language work, and he moved away from extended treatments of scholarly debates on doctrine and hermeneutics. Instead, he focused his energy on giving his readers lucid expositions of the books' central points.

Even the physical natures of Hodge's Corinthian commentaries reflected Hodge's change of tone and desire to reach a broader audience. His commentary on Ephesians had been an imposing quarto-sized volume, the same format the publisher had used to produce his Romans commentary. Reminiscent of the format that had been used to publish his immensely popular devotional *The Way of Life*, the Corinthian volumes reached their readers as considerably smaller octavo books, the size also long favored by Barnes for his commentaries. The octavo size was easier to carry and cheaper to purchase.[16] Hodge had made a choice to reach beyond his usual scholarly audience with these slender volumes, and as a result they became quite popular among more conservative Protestant lay readers as well as members of the clergy.

To read Hodge on the Corinthian epistles is peruse two books devoted to practical governance issues and membership requirements for Christ's earthly church. Hodge may have believed that the church need not take one exact form, but this flexibility did not preclude him from using Paul's letters to the Corinthians as case studies in practices that might unify the church amidst its "fondness for speculation" and debilitating "party spirit."[17] Hodge saw in Paul's Corinthian concerns many of the same battles he had waged against the speculative practices inherent in German Idealism and the factionalism brought on by competing denominational notions of the church. By addressing issues such as inappropriate administration of the sacraments and competition between church leaders, as well as foregrounding the proper use of church discipline and congregational financial support of the clergy, Hodge used these commentaries to show how the church might first sanctify itself and then the larger society that surrounded it.[18] Hodge saw in Paul's Corinthian teachings the best single example of his long-treasured gradualist ethic of personal and cultural transformation through the pursuit of personal and then communal holiness.[19]

As Addison and Hodge worked on their commentary series, Dr. Robert Breckinridge, one of Southern Old School Presbyterian's most revered patriarchs, offered a resolution before the 1858 General Assembly that the Presbyterian Board of Publication nominate men under the direction of the entire Assembly to write on each biblical book. Hodge opposed the idea from its inception, not because he feared competition to his own commentary series, but because he felt that it was a mistake for the General Assembly to put its imprimatur on a commentary series when there was such a wide range of opinion even among Old School Presbyterians on various biblical passages and the doctrinal points they were employed to defend.

Instead, Hodge aggressively argued that the Confession of Faith (the "Westminster confession and Catechisms [that] were declared to be parts of the Constitution of the Church") was the only common doctrinal ground needed by the General Assembly.[20] He wrote an extended essay in the *Repertory* entitled "Adoption of the Confession of Faith" that championed strict adherence to the confession. Its adoption had to be taken serious by all Presbyterian ministers, and they needed to adopt it with the historical sense of the document's meanings in mind. He was particularly careful to note that all who adopted the confession needed to do so in full accordance with its words "taken in their plain, historical sense," a distinction aimed against the New School, which he believed had given certain essential articles in Presbyterianism's key doctrinal statements markedly different meanings than had been intended by their original writers.[21] He strongly felt that it was well beyond the bounds of practicality and wisdom to require the adoption of a more elaborate uniformity among Old School clergy that an officially sanctioned commentary series implied. Hodge felt that it was enough to adopt the Confession of Faith, a document and a system for determining doctrinal allegiance that had served the American Presbyterian Church well since it was instituted in the Adopting Act of 1729.[22]

Sadly, Hodge's partnership with Addison on their New Testament commentary set came to a premature end in 1860 when Addison died after suffering for a year from poor health. Always a rotund man, Addison had never taken good care of himself. Hodge once wrote that "it would be hard to find an educated man more profoundly ignorant of the structure of the human body or the functions of its organs. Hence he was constantly violating the laws of health. He was a whole year seriously ill without knowing it; and only two or three days before his death, he said to me, 'Don't look so sad, I'm as well as you are.'"[23] Many believed that Addison's health began to fail when he heard of the death of his brother, James Waddel. James had died of dysentery after a prolonged illness the previous year.[24] As he mourned his brother's passing, Addison continued to teach and work on his Matthew commentary, but his frame grew thin and his step unsteady. Eventually, he was forced to give up both his classroom duties and his writing, although he did fill many of his bedridden hours with reading.

As the winter months set in, Addison developed a terrible cold. He was plagued by an intermittent fever and began coughing up blood. After nearly a year of illness, he died in his sleep on January 28, 1860. The last note in his daily journal was an appropriate: "Reading as usual."[25] With the single exception of his wife Sarah's death, Hodge noted that the loss of Addison "was the greatest sorrow of his life."[26] With Addison's passing, Hodge abandoned his plans for the New Testament commentary series. He revised his commentary on Romans in 1864, but that would be his last entry into what had been planned as a sweeping addition to conservative biblical criticism in the United States. With Addison's death, Hodge no longer had the heart to finish alone a work he had shared with such a dear and treasured friend.

48

POLITICS AND CONSCIENCE

While Hodge struggled throughout much of the 1850s to stabilize his life in the wake of the deaths of family members and friends, turbulence on a national scale beset him on all sides. The country's politics were seemingly spinning out of control, and politics interested Hodge almost as much as theology. When Hodge finally sat down to write a few autobiographical remarks near the end of his life, he wished his children and grandchildren to know "that their ancestors and kindred were Presbyterians and Patriots."[1] In those few words, Hodge showed how closely intertwined he viewed the practices of politics and religion. He exhibited a lifelong, avid interest in governmental matters, devoting himself to reconciling the activities of God's kingdom with more earthly civil authorities. Three central tenets framed his engagement with political issues: a deep assurance of God's providence, a belief that civil and religious activity must sometimes overlap for the good of those governed, and an awareness that much of governmental rule revolved around the ownership, taxation, and distribution of property.

A strong Calvinist belief in God's providence cast the longest shadow over Hodge's political thinking. No matter what the issue, he never wavered in his view that God's hand guided human destiny. Every ruler and every government were "ordained of God in such a sense that the possession of [their] power" was under his merciful control.[2] While God's short-term plans might be obscure, Hodge was absolutely confident that all events worked together to bring about his redemptive promises.

Hodge was also passionately committed to a notion of political involvement. Here, he significantly differed from his two principal mentors at the Seminary. Archibald Alexander had little or no use for politics. He never voted and made it a point to avoid taking political stands in either the classroom or the pulpit. Samuel Miller had briefly flirted with political matters during his New York pastorate. He had been an early and ardent supporter of Thomas Jefferson's presidency, but became so disillusioned with Jefferson's administration that he forsook political involvement in his later years.

Hodge, on the other hand, believed politics "when connected with morals and the character and interests of the country, is a subject second only to religion in importance."[3] Unlike his older colleagues, Hodge never believed in completely separating the realms of politics and religion. He freely advocated various courses of political action he felt were sanctioned by the Bible's teachings. Because the nation was predominantly populated by Christians, Hodge held that the U.S. government had an obligation to follow "the will of God as revealed in his word."[4] He had no patience with the view that civil government should remain neutral in religious matters. Thus, Hodge stood as the only member of the Seminary's first three professors to involve himself in political discussions and causes, and he often did so with considerable passion.

Hodge's interest in politics took many forms. He voted regularly in local and national elections, and voraciously read the political papers Hugh sent him from Philadelphia. He wrote numerous political articles for the *Repertory*, beginning with an essay in 1831 that addressed the nation's need for Sabbath laws.[5] Hodge was also related to various politically prominent figures including his cousins Samuel Bayard, who clerked for the Supreme Court, and James Ashton Bayard, who represented Delaware in both houses of Congress. So pronounced was Hodge's interest in politics that one of his friends asked him in the turbulent years leading up to the Civil War whether he might "consent to be a candidate for the Presidency?"[6] It was by no means an outlandish notion considering Hodge's national reputation and prominence in conservative Protestant circles, although there is no evidence that he ever took the possibility seriously.

While scholars have paid some attention to Hodge's politics as they intersected with his views on providence and civic engagement, the critical role that property played in his political thinking has been almost totally ignored. Hodge's own family history did much to cement the connection between his conceptions of property and his interest in politics. The Hodges' precipitous fall from the heights of Philadelphia economic affluence to the poverty that marked his youth left an indelible mark on Hodge. Even though he was raised with extremely limited financial resources, Hodge maintained throughout his life a political framework that favored social prominence, wealth, and education. It was a framework that his affluent and politically active Philadelphia ancestors had helped forge, and it went by the name of "Federalism."

Hodge's grandfather, Andrew, and like-minded Federalists of his day had advocated that the country's most educated, genteel, and propertied men should take the important roles of political leadership. Hodge thoroughly embraced this view and once proudly proclaimed that "[e]very drop of blood in our veins is of the old federal stock.... We never had a blood relation in the world, so far as we know, who was not a federalist in the old sense of the word."[7] Federalists believed that office holders should have a financial stake in the fortunes of the country. Hodge once wrote Hugh that "[i]f we could have a Republic with the right of suffrage restricted to householders ... we could get along grandly."[8] The pivotal issue for Hodge here was property. He believed, in what to many might seem a rather idealist way, that men of property made the best leaders because they were more likely to act intelligently and from an ethic of civic mindedness rather than personal aggrandizement. In his thinking, they were already wealthy, so they need not use political offices to line their pockets. Because of the affluence of its members, the Federalist Party was sincerely devoted to the protection of private property, an ideal it saw as critical to the nation's growth and prosperity.

Federalists found their primary competitors at turn of the nineteenth century to be Thomas Jefferson's Republican Party.[9] Jefferson had a more expansive concept of who might participate in leading the nation and set forth his famous notion of America's yeoman farmer, a common man who tilled his land and added his voice to governing both community and nation.[10] Hodge made no secret of his dislike for Jefferson, whose Embargo Act of 1807 had financially ruined his mother. In an attempt to punish Britain for its aggressive and intrusive policies concerning American shipping, Jefferson had legislated a European embargo that strangled American commerce, thereby silencing the Philadelphia wharf, dockside store, and warehouse that provided almost all of Mary Hodge's income. Because of his anti-trade policies, Hodge blamed Jefferson for his family's poverty.

Hodge's distaste for Jeffersonian Republicanism led him to embrace the Whig Party that emerged in the 1820s from the ruins of various Federalist-minded coalitions. The Whigs provided the major political alternative to the common-man ethic first set forth by Jefferson and taken to unprecedented egalitarian extremes by Andrew Jackson.[11] The Whig Party built much of its identity on Federalist elite notions of governance. Whigs continued to trumpet the importance of property and education, and they used these values to emphasize the key characteristics of "discipline, improvement, and moral responsibility," which they wished to mark all aspects of both individual and community behavior.[12] In Hodge's mind, the Whigs stood for stability, duty, and moral improvement as opposed to Jeffersonian and then Jacksonian Democrats and their constant preoccupation with land acquisition, material progress, and equality for all men.[13]

As Andrew Jackson rose to political prominence, Hodge moved every deeper into the Whig camp. He despised many of Jackson's policies, and was particularly upset about how Jackson cultivated a spoils system of political appointments. Hodge saw Jackson and his followers as opportunistic politicians who were quick to award public posts not to the most qualified, but to those who had the best political connections.[14]

Hodge believed that such an approach to government would deter "'men of worth' from public service and ensure that the Jacksonian administration would be 'held together by no principle, but desire of office & power.'"[15]

He also disliked the cavalier and authoritarian manner with which Jackson wielded his power. Particularly disturbing was the way Jackson had ignored the rule of law in his quest to remove various eastern Native American tribes to new lands farther west.[16] Jackson overrode the Supreme Court itself to remove the Cherokees from their ancestral lands. Hodge found Jackson's disregard for previous treaties and established laws so troubling that he felt he "could join a rebellion" against Jackson "with a clear conscience, as I am sure I could with full heart."[17] For Hodge, a key attribute of established authority was its trustworthiness. Could it be counted on to act honestly and with determination to enforce the commitments it had made? Jackson's treatment of Native Americans left Hodge ashamed of his government and its unwillingness to keep its promises.

As the Whig Party continued to develop through the 1830s and 1840s, Hodge aligned himself with the Cotton Whigs, one of the party's more conservative factions. Cotton Whigs distinguished themselves by their strong commitment to national unity and their acceptance of slavery. Because of these stances, they were particularly numerous in the South. Cotton Whigs stood as the antithesis to Garrisonian abolitionists, who Hodge so despised for their volatile rhetoric and inflammatory actions. Cotton Whigs prized steadiness and incremental change, and they pursued policies that avoided anything that might drastically disrupt the nation's unity or economy.[18] Cotton Whigs provided a political home for Southern men of property and more conservative Northern men who may not have liked slavery, but were not willing to divide a nation over the issue.

Not even the conciliatory actions and compromise-filled strategies of the Cotton Whigs were enough to save the Whig Party by the mid-1850s. As the presidential election of 1856 approached, the Whigs found themselves unable to agree any longer on a broad range of issues and as a result the party simply disintegrated. Most central to the Whig Party's demise was the issue of the expansion of slavery into new territories. Antislavery Whigs proved successful in 1852 in preventing the nomination of their incumbent Whig president Millard Fillmore from running again on their ticket because they felt that he was too willing to appease the South with various pro-slavery policies. Instead, the Whig Party nominated the successful Mexican War general Winfield Scott as its candidate. His success on the battlefield, however, did not transfer to the political arena, and he was soundly defeated by the Democratic Party's Franklin Pierce. The political infighting that led to Scott's nomination was the beginning of the end for the Whig Party. As Whigs lost confidence in their party, they either fled politics altogether or attached themselves to rivals such as the strongly nativist Know-Nothings or the recently established Republicans.

Even before Scott's loss of the presidency, terrible fissures had begun to destabilize the Whig Party. It was a party that simply did not know how to deal with the Compromise of 1850, a series of Congressional bills that irretrievably fractured Whigs along pro-slavery and antislavery lines. Perhaps the most notorious and divisive aspect of the Compromise was its Fugitive Slave Law that required all American citizens to assist in the return of runaway slaves regardless of the state in which they were discovered. The law mandated that Northern states return fugitive slaves even if those states forbade the practice of slavery within their boundaries.

The Fugitive Slave Law brought home to many Northerners the injustices inherent in slavery and the seemingly voracious political appetites of the Southern states. In 1851, Hodge responded to the Fugitive Slave Law with the first of what would become a series of influential *Repertory* articles examining religion's relationship to sectional-driven politics as he reviewed Moses Stuart's book, *Conscience and the Constitution*. Stuart's book was an extended treatise supporting Daniel Webster's famous "The Constitution and the Union" speech. By declaring that he wanted to be seen "not as a Massachusetts man, nor as a Northern man but as an American," Webster used the speech to convince thousands to support the national unity made possible by the Compromise of 1850.[19]

Although Stuart was well known for his antislavery leanings, in his desire to join Webster in seeing the Union maintained, he made a compromise of his own and set forth a moderate slavery position in his *Conscience and the Constitution*. In fact, the view of slavery he laid before his readers in *Conscience and the Constitution* almost entirely matched Hodge's biblically literal stance on the issue. Stuart told his readers that his more than forty years "spent on the study of the Bible" had led him to the conclusion that the scriptures neither stood for nor against slavery.[20]

Channeling Hodge's views, Stuart argued that the Bible did not condemn slavery, so it could not be called a sin, and thus Northern abolitionists had no right to use the Bible to stand against the Fugitive Slave Law.[21] Stuart carefully dismantled many of the biblical arguments used by antislavery enthusiasts by painstakingly working through the passages found in Exodus and Deuteronomy so favored by abolitionists. Stuart's concluded: "If Abolitionists are right in their position, then Moses is greatly in the wrong."[22] Stuart also focused on the parallels between the Hebrews' legal code and the U.S. Constitution. He argued that both sets of laws had been established under the auspices of God and therefore demanded every citizen's obedience. Stuart claimed that all Americans were legally and honor bound to obey the various measures of the Compromise of 1850 until those measures were changed by working through the proper legislative channels of redress and correction.

Hodge applauded Stuart's views on a citizen's duty, agreeing "that the great body of people in every part of the Union" should join in supporting the Compromise of 1850.[23] If they disliked the Compromise, they should adhere strictly to a constitutional process of legal redress.[24] Only if the government could not be modified through peaceful means, even when a majority of its citizens sought change, was it appropriate to pursue the absolute last recourse of revolution. In Hodge's mind, this is what the patriots of the American Revolution had done in rebelling against England. It is also why he so admired European revolutionaries such as Lajos Kossuth, a man he told his brother was "beyond question one of the great men of the age" because of his tireless efforts to replace a hopelessly corrupt Hungarian government with a more democratic and just alternative.[25]

Hodge not only shared many of Stuart's thoughts on slavery and the proper way to address unsavory laws, but when it came to politics he shifted away from his often-conflicted and hesitant stance on humanity's innate moral sense to agree with Stuart on the power and importance of the moral reasoning that emanated from that shared moral sense. Hodge agreed with Stuart in foregrounding a moral sense capable of binding humanity with common conceptions of, and motivations toward, what was good and right. Hodge proclaimed that "[t]he allegiance of conscience is to God," and such a conscience (or moral sense) was crucial in guiding the country as a whole toward godliness.[26] The moral sense was particularly important when it came to how individuals determined their own relationship to larger communities and their laws. Hodge noted that whenever "a command is issued by one in authority over us, we immediately and almost unconsciously determine for ourselves, first whether he had the right to give the order; and secondly, whether it can be in good conscience obeyed."[27] Such is how the humanity's common moral sense worked. It provided every individual with an "instinctive sense" of the "self-evidence power" of what God had set forth as good.[28] If every person heeded his or her conscience, the world would inevitably move closer to the goodness and justice most perfectly evinced in God's character.

A decade before the onset of the Civil War, Hodge showed a clear belief in a shared moral conscience, one that would bind the nation together as its citizens pursued a common good. It was a belief that the Civil War sorely tested for Hodge, and one that did not survive entirely intact as Northerners and Southerners bloodied each other driven by consciences that seemed unable to agree on a common understanding of what was good for both individuals and for the nation. But, in the early 1850s, Hodge held that men and women were bound by similar consciences tuned to God's sovereign goodness. This philosophical stance allowed him to hope that a type of universal unity driven by a shared desire to partake of such goodness was achievable. Hodge put a pronounced emphasis on individual conscience, making it clear that people could judge governmental decrees for themselves, a doctrine he believed "essential to all religious liberty and to the religious sanction of civil government."[29]

By following the dictates of one's conscience, Hodge believed that citizens could discern what governmental laws were to be obeyed, and which could be ignored. Hodge retained a measure of optimism in the early 1850s about the national course of events largely because he believed that the country's sectional divisions were ultimately no match for the universally shared conscience of Americans that would help everyone distinguish and act on moral differences. After all, everyone could agree that activities such as theft and murder were evil. The heart knew right from wrong, and communities needed only find ways of cultivating this common moral sense in order to build cohesive and happy societies. Americans' shared moral conscience would thus lead them toward the good and bind the nation together.

There was a weakness, however, in Hodge's Common Sense–based political theory, and it was the same problem that faced Common Sense Realism more generally. Common Sense Realism touted that truth was objective and accessible, and yet there was a wide variance of belief on the exact nature and manifestations of truth.[30] The most rational and upright people might never agree on important points of what was seemingly true, and this was particularly dangerous when it came to politics. Hodge believed that humanity's common moral sense would provide the foundation for great commonalities of righteous belief and action. God's truth would eventually reign supreme and through its accessibility draw all humanity together. It was a highly optimistic, and ultimately incorrect, set of assumptions.

Just as there existed so many different schools of thought on various interpretations of the Bible, there also existed a multitude of opinions on American government and its relationship to its citizens. Common Sense Realism promised consensus and unified action through a shared moral sense, but such an optimistic view of the inevitability of moral unity proved to be naive indeed. The fiery divisions brought forth by the Fugitive Slave Law gave the lie to such optimism. A shared conscience that grew from a common moral sense did little to stop the growing fissures between the North and South.

These fissures were responsible for the collapse of the Whig Party in 1856. The party had already lost its luster by this point for Hodge. As various Whigs moved to nominate Winfield Scott for the presidency, Hodge threw his support behind John C. Fremont, the Republican candidate for president. Hodge's change of political allegiance shows just how disillusioned he had become with the Whig Party, which he saw as having no clear plan to stop the expansion of slavery and thereby check the South's unruly political ambitions. He was also unhappy with how the Whigs had so openly betrayed their Federalist roots by nominating as Fillmore's vice presidential running mate Andrew Jackson Donelson, the nephew of the grand architect of so many of the country's problems, the demonically democratic Andrew Jackson.[31]

For a man who hated change, Hodge's move to support Fremont is indicative of just how troubled he was by national events. For Hodge, Fremont offered the best solution to the growing tension between the North and the South. By the middle of the 1850s, a controlling political issue in Hodge's mind was the sovereignty crisis over the issue of slavery in the Kansas-Nebraska territories. In 1854, these territories had been created by the Kansas-Nebraska Act, but in their creation the Missouri Compromise of 1820 was repealed. The Missouri Compromise had guaranteed that there would be no slave territories established north of the 36°30' parallel except within the boundaries of Missouri. Due to the pro-slavery and Southern states' rights advocates in Congress, the Kansas-Nebraska Act enacted a policy of popular sovereignty in which each territory could vote for itself whether it would become a slave or free state.

As a result, pro- and antislavery factions from the North and South flooded the territories with their supporters in the hope of turning the issue one way or the other. The chaotic consequence was brutal violence not only in these territories but on the floor of the U.S. Senate as well. Charles Sumner, a senator from Massachusetts, was one of the principle opponents to the Kansas-Nebraska Act. In 1856, he was brutally beaten with a cane by the Southern Carolina representative Preston Brooks. It was an assault that left him incapacitated for years, but it also made him a mythic symbol for Northerners of slavery's evils. Hodge was outraged at Sumner's beating, and he was stunned that such a brutal act could occur in the nation's Senate chamber.

Hodge had decided to support Fremont "not for the man, but for the platform," as he became increasingly disturbed by how the South wished to exercise a control over the national government completely out of all proportion to the size of its population and economic importance.[32] He refused to grant that "300,000 slave-holders" were equivalent to "20,000,000 of the freemen" when it came to guiding the country.[33] This sense of inequity drove much of Hodge's political thinking in the years preceding the Civil War. He saw the principal political danger facing the nation's leaders to be the "divisions and concessions of the North" to the South.[34] The Union could not survive under such constant concessions, and Hodge saw the Republican Party as the only viable political force willing to stand against the expansion of slavery and other Southern political aggressions.

By 1860, Hodge had firmly aligned himself with the Republican Party as he voted for Abraham Lincoln for president. Lincoln had run as the Republican candidate with a straightforward platform against the expansion of slavery, protecting the rights of immigrants, and a firm commitment to preserving the Union. In a four-way race, Lincoln became the first Republican candidate elected to the presidency, and he won by capturing only 40 percent of the nation's popular vote.[35] Adding to his failure to attract a majority of the country's voters was the fact that his support came almost entirely from the North. He was not even listed on the ballot in nine Southern states.

Lincoln's election proved to be a watershed moment for the Union. Just weeks after his election, South Carolina made good on its threat to withdraw from the Union if Lincoln was elected. South Carolina was quickly followed by seven other Deep South, cotton-growing states. Together, these states formed the nucleus of the Confederate States of America. Four other states soon followed. The stage was set for the bloodiest war ever to be fought on American soil.

PART VII

The 1860s

Conflicted Unionist

Figure 49.1 *Charles Hodge in the 1860s*: Hodge around the time of the Civil War [*Presbyterian Historical Society, Presbyterian Church (U.S.A) (Philadelphia, PA)*]

49

THE STATE OF THE COUNTRY AND THE CHURCH

In November 1860, the same month as the country's presidential election, Hodge decided to add his voice to the political cacophony that was engulfing the nation by writing one of his most famous articles: "The State of the Country." He hoped to offer the general public a level-headed and biblically based case against secession. Hodge believed that both the North and the South were being driven by passions which, if left unchecked, would lead the country down a path of blood-soaked destruction. He felt the topic to be so important and urgent that he contemplated publishing it in advance of the January volume of the *Repertory*, so that it might appear before "the union may be dissolved."[1]

In the end, Hodge could not finish the article before January. While visiting Hugh in Philadelphia, Hodge read aloud a draft of the essay to his brother, whose eyesight had begun to fail in 1858. (In just a few years, Hugh would be forced to give up his medical practice due to blindness.)[2] Hugh made a number of suggestions that took Hodge time to incorporate into the essay's final version.[3] Hodge made the changes and presented the essay as the lead article in the 1861 *Repertory*.

Even before the essay appeared, however, controversy swirled around it. Henry Boardman, Hodge's close friend and partner in getting the *Repertory* published each quarter, was so disturbed by the piece that he asked the printer to halt work on the volume until he could implore Hodge to either withdraw the essay or modify its contents. Boardman told Hodge that he had composed a dangerous "fire-brand" that would do "a world of evil."[4] He believed that in Hodge's attempt to strike a middle ground, the article would please neither Northern nor Southern Presbyterians whose differing regional views were quickly hardening in the wake of Lincoln's election. Hodge refused to make any further changes to his essay, believing the piece to be a model of moderate reasoning. In Hodge's mind, if anyone was acting like a fire-brand it was Boardman himself whose sermons did much more to fan the flames of regional animosities than anything he had written in "The State of the Country."[5]

Hodge opened his article declaring that religion was essential to governing the country. He proclaimed that "there are periods in the history of every nation when its destiny for ages may be determined by the events of an hour. . . . On such occasions the distinction between secular and religious" voices are obliterated.[6] Hodge saw it as the "privilege and duty of all who have access in any way to the public ear, to endeavor to allay unholy feeling, and to bring truth to bear on the minds of their fellow-citizens."[7] In the nearly forty pages that followed, Hodge did all in his power to stop the country's headlong flight toward disunion. He was not only worried about the state of the Union, but he saw its fragmentation as a blow to the global cause of Christ.[8] The United States was a Christian beacon to the world. Its implosion would only mean that its redemptive light to the nations would be dimmed, possibly even extinguished.

In writing such an overtly political piece for the *Repertory*, Hodge showed just how little patience he had with fellow Presbyterians who believed that the church should play no role in political discussions. James Thornwell was one such Presbyterian who stood as a strong advocate for separating the realms of politics and religion.[9] Thornwell lived to see only a few months of the Civil War, as he died of consumption and overwork in 1862, but in his final years he spearheaded a Presbyterian entrenchment against allowing the church to mingle too closely with political matters. He argued that "to *unsecularize* the Church should be the great aim of all who are anxious that the ways of Zion should flourish."[10] He viewed Christ's church on earth as primarily a "*spiritual* body" whose principle aim was "the gathering and perfecting of saints, to the end of the world."[11]

Thornwell's separation of religion and politics became particularly important when it came to the issue of slavery. Like Hodge, Thornwell firmly believed that there was not a single passage of scripture that condemned the practice of slavery outright. Thornwell differed from Hodge, however, when he argued that slavery was "purely a civil relation, with which the Church, as such, has no right to interfere."[12] Hodge was anything but a radical reformer, but he severely disliked Thornwell's position because it too tightly circumscribed the church's ability to stand against any social evil or take any kind of political stand. Thornwell's thinking proved immensely influential, particularly in the South. His constant stress on the church's spiritual nature provided the theological framework for Southern Presbyterians to absent themselves from involvement in political and social issues before, during, and after the Civil War.[13]

Early in "The State of the Country" Hodge admitted that the South had "some just grounds of complaint, and that the existing animosity towards the North is neither unnatural nor unaccountable."[14] He largely blamed the divisive rhetoric and inflammatory actions of Garrisonian abolitionists for these problems, but he also made it clear that it was terribly misleading to judge the North by looking only at this "small band of fanatics."[15] While Hodge was disturbed by abolitionists' anarchic tendencies, he was equally aware of just how mighty a monarch old King Cotton was in the South. Whereas the total American export of cotton at the end of the eighteenth century had been roughly two hundred thousand pounds a year, the invention of the cotton gin and the growing use of slave labor in the South had moved this annual figure to an astounding 2.3 billion pounds. Three-quarters of the world's cotton was produced in the United States, and almost all of it was grown in the South. Cotton stood as the country's major export, often equaling—sometimes doubling—the value of all other American exports combined.[16] The great engine of the Cotton Kingdom was slavery, and Hodge knew it. He struck at the heart of the South when he used "The State of the Country" to argue that the South's main motive for secession was its desire *"to reopen the African slave trade."*[17]

Unlike Garrison's abolitionists, Hodge wished to position himself as a reasonable man. He did not push the South to abandon slavery altogether. Instead, he used two lines of reasoning to argue against national division. First, he advocated, along with Lincoln, that the best solution to the country's current turmoil could be found in reinstating the territorial agreements of the Missouri Compromise that had been thoughtlessly thrown aside in the Kansas-Nebraska Act.[18] Slavery could exist in states south of the parallel 36°30' and in the state of Missouri. Yet in the weeks after Lincoln's election, it became painfully clear that the time of the forty-year-old Missouri Compromise had passed.[19] Not only did the South have no interest in limiting slavery within certain defined geographical boundaries, but it now wished to argue that the Constitution had always intended that slavery should be permissible in every state.[20] Hodge later commented that the cause of the War had been built upon the Northern sentiment that "you may hold slaves, if you please, but you shall not make slaveholders of us."[21]

Second, Hodge decried the Southern claim that the federal government had never adequately supported the Fugitive Slave Law. Hodge believed that the federal government had done all in its power to enforce the Fugitive Slave Law.[22] He went so far as to add his own personal "condemnation of all resistance to the restoration of fugitive slaves" because it was the law of the land to do so.[23] If one could not obey the law, one had to accept the penalty for any noncompliance.[24] That was the way Christians should respond to the governing authorities that God had, in his provident wisdom, placed over them. In Hodge's mind, that the South was thinking of secession because it disagreed with governmental policy. Its unwillingness to work through the proper channels to address their complaints was a complete "breach of faith."[25]

Upon its release, Hodge's "State of the Country" instantly created a sensation. American Christians from a multitude of denominational backgrounds eagerly read what one of the nation's most prominent Presbyterians had to say about the state of their nation. Hodge himself commented that "no article every printed" in the *Repertory* "from the pen of its editor, ever excited greater attention" as it was reprinted at length in several prominent religious papers of the day and was circulated in the thousands as a stand-alone pamphlet.[26] In the end, however, it did nothing to accomplish Hodge's heartfelt goal of preserving the Union. The essay pleased no one. It outraged Northerners who felt that Hodge was too conciliatory toward treasonous states. Southerners saw the article as just one more example of how little the North appreciated the South's rights as sovereign states.

Perhaps somewhat surprisingly, it was James Thornwell, a man who had worked so hard to draw firm distinctions between religious and political activity, who became a major religious voice in the politics of the South's secession movement.[27] Thornwell wasted no time in publishing a forceful rebuttal to Hodge in the form of his own "State of the Country" essay, which he published in the winter volume of *The Southern Presbyterian Review*.[28] Thornwell offered the country the South's principal rationale for secession when he declared that "[t]he universal sentiment of all that the Constitution of the United States has been virtually repealed" with the election of Lincoln.[29] Thornwell argued that the Constitution by its very nature was supportive of slavery throughout the United States and that the federal government had systematically moved away from acknowledging and enforcing this fact. Thornwell argued that Southern secession had nothing to do with reopening the slave trade and everything to do with the rights of states to stand as sovereign entities when their government so clearly worked against their interests.

If Thornwell's essay did not make it crystal clear to Hodge that the dissolution of the Union was inevitable, the political events during the winter and spring of 1861 did. By June, eleven southern states had joined together to form the Confederate States of America. As state after Southern state slipped into the Confederacy, Hodge changed his tack from trying to save the Union to attempting to save the unity of the American Presbyterian Church.

American Old School Presbyterians had a proud history of unity in the years leading up to the Civil War. While the issue of slavery had fractured the Methodists along regional lines in 1844 and had done the same to the Baptists in 1845, the Old School Presbyterians had remained a coherent national entity since their theological split with the New School brethren in 1837. Hodge considered the value of this unity as being beyond measure. It testified to the power of right theology and the power of the bond of love shared by all those in Christ.

Hodge reponded to Thornwell's "State of the Country" article in the very next issue of the *Repertory* in an essay entitled "The Church and the Country." This piece was also widely distributed in pamphlet form and argued for maintaining the truly precious unity shared by both Southern and Northern Old School Presbyterians. To read the essay now, one marvels at just how little Hodge appreciated the deep resentments that had been long festering in the South and its Presbyterian churches. Hodge's basic argument was simple: "Neither state nor federal authorities have any control over the courts of the church. . . . We remain substantially one people despite of the disruption of the Union."[30] Hodge believed that all "antecedent reasons for our ecclesiastical union remain in full force," and a divided Presbyterian Church would "be a great calamity to the country and the world."[31] He held out to his fellow Presbyterians an even brighter hope, however, for he firmly believed that a single, unified Presbyterian Church could provide the nation with a profound model of unity and thus play a pivotal role in restoring "our political union."[32]

Hodge knew that if he was to convince Southern Presbyterians of the need for unity, he had to address directly Thornwell's "State of the Country" essay. Thornwell's immense stature among Southern Presbyterians could not be ignored, and no hope of Presbyterian unity remained if Thornwell's justifications for Southern secession were left unanswered. Thornwell's reasons for secession found some of their deepest roots in his conviction that slavery was based in natural law. Thornwell wrote that "if there be any property that can be called natural, in the sense that it spontaneously springs in the history of the species, it is the property of slaves."[33] Building upon this natural-law premise, Thornwell argued that the Constitution itself acknowledged it as "THE UNIVERSAL CUSTOM OF MANKIND," and to call it only a local or municipal law was "of 'all absurdities the motliest.'"[34] Because of slavery's universal nature, it had the right to go into "every territory from which it is not excluded by positive statute."[35] The natural state was one that allowed slavery to be practiced everywhere, a fact Thornwell believed was attested to throughout all history. Congress had no right to place Northern customs of non-slaveholding "upon the common soil of the Union."[36] Thornwell joined his countrymen in believing that the federal government was following an inevitable trajectory of Southern strangulation when it came to the national practice of slavery, making it obvious "that nothing more nor less is at stake in this controversy than the very life of the South."[37]

Although Hodge saw no biblical mandate against slavery, he had no interest in seeing the institution spread. His position had long been one of gradual emancipation, due to his believing that slavery was nothing more than a transitional institution in the United States that could be used as a means of uplifting the mental and moral qualities of African Americans so that they might be equipped to take their place in a more highly civilized Western society. Once slavery had done its work, African Americans and whites could more easily stand on an equal footing.

In looking at Thornwell and other aggressive pro-slavery Southern ministers, Hodge saw a distinctly troubling move toward slavery becoming "a good and desirable institution, which should be cherished, perpetuated, and extended."[38] Such a view found one of its most vocal proponents in Thornwell's protégé, Benjamin Morgan Palmer, a Presbyterian pastor so distinguished for his oratorical gifts that the General Assembly had offered him the chair of Pastoral Theology and Sacred Rhetoric at Princeton Theological Seminary in 1860.[39] Palmer turned down the position only to become Thornwell's successor at Columbia Seminary a few years later.

Palmer became a hero throughout the South when, in late November 1860, he preached what quickly became known as his "Thanksgiving Sermon," an eloquent diatribe that elaborated upon Thornwell's natural-law argument for slavery by boldly proclaiming that the "providential trust" of the Southern people was "to conserve and to perpetuate the institution of domestic slavery as now existing."[40] Palmer's "Thanksgiving Sermon" was immediately issued in pamphlet form, and soon, over thirty thousand copies were in circulation throughout the South. Newspapers also reprinted the sermon in its entirety, and the governor of Mississippi asked Palmer to visit his state, declaring that he was worth more than a thousand troops.[41]

Hodge found Palmer's sermon repugnant. He could not fathom why God might have ordained the South to "preserve and transmit our system of domestic servitude" in perpetuity.[42] It was a view totally antithetical to the teachings of scripture, and therefore he believed the Presbyterian Church could never sanction it. In the coming months, Hodge became such an implacable and vocal foe of Palmer's stance that he offhandedly commented to his brother that it "was a great mistake that the Southern Christians had not prayed for my death."[43] While alive, he would do all in his power to fight against any move to make slavery in the United States a permanent institution.

Hodge sought to dismantle Palmer's providential pro-slavery argument by directly attacking Thornwell's natural-law argument for slavery. Hodge made this attack by showing how the Constitution had never considered slavery as a manifestation of natural law. Citing a view accepted even by Alexander H. Stephens, the future vice president of the Confederacy, Hodge showed that the Founding Fathers had viewed slavery "in violation of the laws of nature; that it was wrong in principle, socially, morally, and politically."[44] The Founders had hoped that the institution of slavery "would be evanescent and pass away."[45] In this manner, and against the view purported by Thornwell and popularized by Palmer, slavery had no constitutional mandate. Slavery was a local issue, governed by local laws. There was nothing universal or natural about it.

Because Hodge was convinced that the Founders had never favored the institution of slavery when writing the Constitution, he reached back in "The Church and the Country" to decry the evil done by the 1857 Supreme Court decision in the Dred Scott case. In Hodge's mind, the Supreme Court had ignored the will of the Constitution's original framers when it decided that Scott, a slave who had lived for an extended period in free states and territories and therefore wished to be considered a freeman, had no legal right to be heard in the nation's federal court system when he sued for his freedom. What was at stake in the Dred Scott case was clear to all. If the Supreme Court decided in Scott's favor, Southerners placed their ownership of slaves at risk each time their slaves entered a Northern state. Hodge's anger against the Supreme Court's decision burned for two reasons. He hated the fact that slaves might never be accorded the same standing before the law enjoyed by other Americans, and he saw the decision as an invitation to open "all the territories now possessed, or hereafter to be acquired, to the introduction of slavery."[46]

Ultimately, Hodge was to be disappointed in his attempts to convince his Presbyterian brethren to hold fast to the "divinely appointed terms" of Christian and ministerial communion.[47] Just one month after publishing "The Church and the Country," Old School Presbyterians from both the North and the South gathered in Philadelphia for the annual General Assembly. Sectional tensions were present, but muted, until Dr. Gardiner Spring, a minister from New York, put forth a resolution obligating all Presbyterians "to promote and perpetuate, so far as in us lies, the integrity of the United States, and to strengthen and uphold the Federal government in the exercises of all its functions."[48] It was a blatantly Northern and divisive resolution, which everyone knew would be unpalatable to the Southerners in the Assembly. Hoping to preserve his precious notion of denominational unity, Hodge led a group in protest of the resolution. He argued that the General Assembly had no right to require its members to hold certain political allegiances. Hodge's protest went unheeded, however, and when Gardiner's resolution reached the floor of the Assembly, it was adopted 156 to 64, effectively killing any hope of keeping Old School Presbyterian unity intact.[49] Within the year, Thornwell and other leading Southern Presbyterians split from their northern brethren as they established the Presbyterian Church of the Confederate States of America. The war that was tearing apart the nation had now rent asunder American Presbyterianism as well.

50

HODGE'S FAMILY AT WAR

The magnitude of the Civil War touches us even today when we contemplate the conflict's horrific devastation. Over 623,000 soldiers died in the conflict, and there is no accurate estimation of the civilian dead. Other American wars pale in comparison. The combined American casualties of the Revolution, the War of 1812, the Mexican War, the Spanish-American War, both World Wars, and the Korean War roughly equal the number of men killed during the Civil War. If the rate of death is considered in terms of general population, a similar conflict today would produce six million fatalities.[1] Approximately one out of every eleven men of service age died in the war, leaving it difficult—if not impossible—to find an American family untouched by its rapaciously deadly grip.[2]

Hodge was certainly touched by the war, although he was fortunate enough not to lose any of his immediate family in its fighting. His fourth son, John, enlisted as a volunteer officer in the Union Army soon after hostilities began in 1861. John trained in Washington, D.C., but contracted typhoid fever there. He was sent home to Princeton to convalesce, but he was so weakened by the disease that he never returned to active service. He was eventually honorably discharged as an invalid in 1863.[3] Although John was severely disappointed about his discharge, it was no small mercy that he survived his bout with typhoid. During the war, twice as many soldiers died of disease as they did from being wounded in battle.[4]

Hodge was also linked to the war through his new wife's brother, David Hunter. Unlike John Hodge's almost-total anonymity as a Union soldier, David Hunter became a figure who generated great interest and even greater controversy. Having graduated from West Point in 1822, Hunter was a colonel when the war began. His views were strongly antislavery, and even before Lincoln's election, he began corresponding with

Figure 50.1 *General David Hunter*: General David Hunter distinguished himself during the Civil War by his hatred of slavery and his ruthlessness on the battlefield. His tactics were so brutal that one of Robert E. Lee's relatives wrote that Hunter's actions would bring upon his head the "curses of thousands" and "the scorn of the manly and upright and the hatred of the true and honorable." After the war, he served in the honor guard at Lincoln's funeral. President Andrew Johnson appointed him the president of the nine-man military tribunal that tried the conspirators in Lincoln's assassination. [*Library of the Author*]

Figure 50.2 *Hugh Lenox Scott*: Hugh Lenox Scott graduated from West Point in 1876. Hodge gave his nephew a Bible as graduation present with the following inscription:

Dear Lennie,

–Never pass a day without reading the Bible and calling upon God in prayer.

–Learn to pray always. The Lord Jesus is ever near you. It does not take long to say: "Lord preserve me: Lord help me; Lord keep me from sin." We need to say this a hundred times a day.

–Never gamble.

–Never drink intoxicating liquor.

–Never use profane language.

–Let no corrupt communication proceed out of your mouth.

–Never incur debt.

–Live peaceable with all men.

–Never be afraid to confess Christ.

–Let your last words every night be: "I take Jesus Christ to be my God and Saviour."

–May the blessing of God be upon you always and everywhere.

Your Loving Grandfather, Charles Hodge, Princeton, Sept. 15, 1876

[*Special Collections, Princeton Theological Seminary Libraries*] the future president about the need to free the slaves. Lincoln was so impressed with Hunter that he invited the colonel to ride in the train with him from Springfield, Illinois, to Washington, D.C., after his election. The budding friendship between the two men helped Hunter get quickly promoted to the rank of general.

After his marriage to Mary, Hodge occasionally made trips to Washington, D.C., to visit the Hunters. Through these visits and constant correspondence between the two families, Hodge received a steady stream of information concerning the Union's political and military affairs.[5] So close did the two families become that Hodge and his wife spent every May after the war until his death with the Hunters in Washington, D.C.[6]

Hunter was a vocal advocate of immediate emancipation. So unswerving was he in his convictions that soon after his appointment as commander of the Department of the South in 1862, he took it upon himself to free the slaves of Georgia, South Carolina, and Florida. Lincoln immediately rescinded the order, but Hunter continued his crusade against slavery by organizing one of the Union Army's first black regiments. In 1864, he led an army into the Shenandoah Valley that followed a scorched-earth policy, much like General Sherman's March to the Sea. Hunter's Shenandoah campaign of terror earned him the undying hatred of Southerners as his army freely looted every town it passed through and burned to the ground such revered Southern institutions as the Virginia Military Institute. Because of his extreme tactics, Southerners began to call him "Black Dave Hunter," both because of his antislavery views and what they considered to be the color of his merciless character.

Hodge's eldest son, Archie, was another of family member whose life was profoundly changed by the war. Archie and his family had lived in Virginia near Fredericksburg for five years when Southern states began seceding from the Union. Although he had become a preacher of considerable renown and made many good friends in the region, he became increasingly uneasy about what he eventually came to see as an inevitable clash between the North and the South. After the Confederacy began the war by attacking Fort Sumter in April 1861, Archie quickly decided there was not a moment to lose in moving his entire family to the North. He fled Virginia virtually overnight.

Archie traveled through West Virginia, Maryland, and Pennsylvania until he and his much-careworn family reached Hodge's house in Princeton.[7] When he arrived on his father's doorstep, he needed both a place to live and a means of supporting his family. He was fortunate that he was not long at his father's home before the congregation of the Presbyterian Church of Wilkes-Barré, Pennsylvania, called him to be its pastor. Wilkes-Barré was a thriving coal mining town roughly one hundred miles south of Princeton, and Archie was thrilled to take the position. He spent most of the war happily serving in this post until 1864, when he was called to a faculty position at Western Theology Seminary in Allegheny, Pennsylvania.

Figure 50.3 *William Berryman Scott*: William Berryman Scott, shown here during his undergraduate days at Princeton College, became a renowned scholar of geology and vertebrate paleontology at his *alma mater*. While an undergraduate, he proofread Hodge's manuscript for *What is Darwinism?* At the time he agreed with Hodge's view that Darwinism was but another name for atheism. After Hodge's death, Scott revised this view and gradually came to reconcile Darwin's theology of evolution with religion. Until his death, Scott venerated his grandfather. He named his first son after him. [*Princeton University Library*]

At the same time that Archie was moving back to Princeton, Hodge's second child, Mary, also found herself returning with her family to her father's home. For months her husband, William Scott, had been ill with consumption. His health had deteriorated to such a degree that he was forced to resign his professorship at Northwest Theological Seminary in Chicago and remove his family to Princeton in the autumn months of 1861.[8] The Scott family arrived just as Archie was moving to Wilkes-Barré. Only a few weeks after settling into her childhood home, Mary found herself burying her husband, leaving her and her two sons to become long-term members of Hodge's household.[9] Mary remained in her father's house until his death some seventeen years later.

Both of Mary's sons grew up to hold positions of importance. The older one had been named after Hodge's brother, Hugh. Hugh Lenox Scott, known to the family as "Lennie," graduated from West Point and joined the Seventh Calvary. He eventually served as the superintendent of West Point before being named chief of staff of the United States Army at the outset of the First World War. William "Willie" Scott eventually became a world-renowned professor of geology at Princeton College with a special interest in vertebrate paleontology.

Willie was destined to hold a special place in Hodge's heart. He was barely three years old when he arrived in Princeton, and within months of his arrival, the young boy found himself without a father. Hodge's own fatherless youth perhaps inspired the special bond that soon formed between the two. In the elderly Hodge, Willie found a dedicated, patient, and loving father figure. It was a common sight for Princetonians to see the abundant affection Hodge bestowed on the small boy as they strolled hand-in-hand through Princeton or shared a buggy ride to Hodge's much-beloved Millstone Farm. Willie later pointed to the years he spent growing up in Hodge's household as some of the happiest of his life, and Hodge considered Willie one of the greatest blessings of his final years.

51

THE UNITIES OF MANKIND

As his children and their families came and went from his home, Hodge kept a close eye on events both national and international. He sat in shocked disbelief as Confederate forces carved up one Union army after another in the opening months of the war. He became despondent over the early Union defeats at the First and Second Battles of Bull Run, grew anxious over a serious combat wound sustained by his brother-in-law, General Hunter, and hoped fervently for a major Union victory as what was supposed to be a short war promised to become a long one.[1] He bemoaned the fact that the "North somehow is not half so alert to raising troops as the South," outnumbering "us everywhere—tho' in all other respects they are worse off."[2] As the war continued, and hopes of a speedy Union victory fell away, Hodge became ever more depressed, losing both sleep and weight because of his country's troubles.[3]

The war sorely tried Hodge's usually sanguine temperament. He characterized the Union's terrible defeat at Fredericksburg as a "deplorable affair" and "an inexcusable & criminal sacrifice of life," and he bemoaned the carnage and lack of sound leadership at Antietam.[4] Overall, Hodge laid much of the blame for the disastrous early course of the war at the feet of Henry Halleck, the man who had replaced George McClellan (a man Hodge much admired) as general-in-chief of the Union's armies. Hodge came to share Lincoln's view that Halleck excelled at preparation for war, but proved utterly incompetent in actually winning battles.[5] By the end of 1862, Hodge's despair reached new depths as he noted that "thousands of lives have been sacrificed, millions of money have been squandered," and foreign nations have been "emboldened in their hostility" toward the United States.[6]

It was his concern over foreign affairs that made Hodge once again pick up his pen to write an unprecedentedly scathing *Repertory* article: "England and America." Hodge used the essay to entreat England not to enter the war on the side of evil, which in his mind the Confederacy so clearly represented. He took a hardline non-interventionist stance, a view inspired by Kossuth and shared by Lincoln, that foreign governments should not interfere with the internal problems of lawfully elected governments.[7] Aiming his prose at an English audience that he believed did not appreciate the magnitude of the South's sin in seceding from the Union, Hodge painstakingly described the reasons for the war and his regret at how "Constitutional, anti-slavery England throws the whole weight of her sympathy in favour of this unrighteous pro-slavery rebellion."[8]

Hodge was astonished that the British could even entertain the idea of supporting the rebellious South. He considered England one of the "great Protestant powers of the world," forming a partnership with the United States that did "more than all other nations combined, for what we both regard as the best interests of man and the advancement of the Redeemer's kingdom."[9] He wished those in England to know that it was not the goal of the North to subjugate the South, but simply to stay true to nation's founding democratic principles. The South wished its three hundred and fifty thousand slave-owners to have as much, if not more say, than the North's "thirty millions of our people."[10] Nothing less was at stake than democracy itself as the North sought freedom from the long powerful "tyrannical minority" of the South.[11]

Aside from the urgency of its content, what strikes one about Hodge's "England and America" essay is its charged, emotional tone. Hodge's two earlier political essays on the war, and his *Repertory* articles more generally, tended toward rational, evenhanded argumentation. Passion frequently marked his prose, but it did not overwhelm. Such even-handedness changed in "England and America" as Hodge described "the character of this rebellion" as "unprovoked" and "made simply in the interests of slavery" by "unprincipled men" who committed "acts of the grossest fraud, treachery, and spoliation."[12] Hodge had clearly shifted to a more aggressive rhetorical register than he had ever before used. For Hodge, the time for placation, mediation, and mild argumentation was over. His anger toward the South was palpable as he attempted to convince England to stay out of the war.

One cannot help but wonder if the reason for Hodge's change in tone was partly due to subtle shifts in his thinking about slavery as the war dragged on. As he became absolutely convinced that the South was waging the war "simply in the interests of slavery," Hodge reconsidered whether the rule of law and differing conceptions of property were truly the most central issues behind the South's commitment to America's peculiar institution.[13] By 1862, Hodge saw how central the issue of race was in the pro-slavery mindset of the South. The same year that "England and America" appeared, Hodge composed an article that directly addressed the issues of race and human equality. In his "Examination of some Reasonings against the Unity of Mankind,"

Hodge laid out his own thinking on the issue of race, namely his belief that all humans were indeed of the same species and thus equal.

As the war approached, Southerners increasingly denounced any notion of gradual emancipation, touting the view that African American slaves were a different human species, never capable of equality with whites. To give their views credibility, Southerners turned to new scientific work on species categorization that argued that different variations of humanity had appeared at different times in different parts of the world with defined, immutable core character and physical traits. It was a school of thought that came to be known as "polygenism," named after the many points of origin it favored.

Polygenism rose up in direct contrast to the biblical view of monogenism, a belief that all humans had descended from a single parental pair (most often, Adam and Eve) and then spread across the globe. Monogenists most commonly believed that the world's vastly differing environments had caused humans to change over time, but all humans remained descendants of a single pair of parents. Such a view of mutation ran counter to the immutable and innate species characteristics championed by polygenists. Monogenists believed that humans were capable of great change, and because of their common parentage, every human was a member of the same species and thus ultimately capable of attaining the same levels of intellectual, moral, and cultural achievement.

Hodge fully supported the monogenist view because it fit both with Genesis's creation account and his theological conviction that change was possible in the soul of any man or woman. If something as important as the soul could change, it was a small matter to have climates and cultures cause variations in skin color and intelligence. Discussions at Princeton on monogenism dated all the way back to Samuel Stanhope Smith, who had held the biblical position that all humans were descended from the same set of parents and then had moved throughout the earth only to change and adapt to various environmental and climatic influences.[14] This view remained the standard Princeton line throughout the nineteenth century, and Hodge never deviated from it.

Hodge's voracious scientific appetite, however, did lead him to read widely in the work of polygenists. He was particularly intrigued by the work of Hugh's anatomy colleague at the Pennsylvania Medical College: Samuel George Morton. In the 1830s, Morton began to espouse a set of scientific theories that would lead to polygenism, although he shied away from using the term himself because of his own mixed allegiances to the Christian creation story. Hodge's first foray into question of race and polygenism, however, was not addressed to the foundational work of Samuel Morton, but to the monogenist work of Dr. James Laurence Cabell, a professor of anatomy and surgery at the University of Virginia.

In 1858, Cabell published *The Testimony of Modern Science to the Unity of Mankind*, and Hodge took the opportunity in a lengthy *Repertory* review to launch a full-fledged attack on polygenism and its rather dubious scientific claims. In his usual crystalline prose, Hodge testified to the trustworthiness of Cabell's work and juxtaposed it to the shoddy intellectualism of polygenists with their penchant to separate their scientific theories from all regard for "[m]oral and religious truths" and ignore all facts that did not fall specifically "within their own department."[15] Hodge clearly believed polygenists incapable of lifting "their eyes above the dissecting table" and believing "that there is more in man than the knife can reveal," making them blind to the larger network of connections in which all scientific facts are embedded.[16] Such scientific myopia made polygenists act irresponsibly as scholars as they adopted theories "on the mere balance of probabilities, which supposes the Bible to be false, sin and redemption to be fictions, despite of all the evidence which sustains the authority of the Scriptures and the truth of its teachings."[17]

Hodge was most astounded by the fact that polygenists could not even agree on the meaning of their most central term: "species." Without a commonly accepted definition of this basic term, all their logical argumentation fell apart. Hodge marveled that anyone would "expect Christians to give up faith in the Bible, or renounce important doctrines of their religion" with theories based on so little certainty and such great confusion.[18]

Hodge criticized a number of specific polygenists—including Louis Agassiz of Harvard, a man he much admired—for claiming that humans did not share a common point of origin. Hodge maintained that far from human difference pointing to a variety of human species, human variation testified to humanity's "highest perfection," an ability to adapt to any number of cultural and physical settings.[19] He believed that the polygenist view that species were immutable was nonsense. One needed only look at the horse or the dog to see variety of type within the same species. A Labrador retriever (the breed of dog Hodge owned) and the bloodhound may look different, perform different tasks, and live in different climates, but they remained dogs by sharing both a common physiological and psychological nature. All humans, in a similar way, shared a common nature even if they differed in other respects. Most importantly, humans were bound together more tightly than any other species by virtue of the fact that each individual had a highly developed rational faculty and an "immortal soul."[20] Hodge's reference to the soul signaled his most basic objection to polygenism, namely that it was a theory "opposed to the authority of the Bible, and to the facts of our mental, moral and spiritual nature."[21]

As the war wore on, Hodge became ever more convinced that the "new doctrines" of polygenism lay "at the bottom of our present civil commotions" and were used to justify holding "black people in perpetual slavery to the whites."[22] In 1862, three years after his first massive defense of monogenism and a few months before Lincoln's Emancipation Proclamation, Hodge once again wrote against polygenism. This time he specifically focused on the problematic work of Samuel Morton. Morton had posited that the earth was populated with five distinct races of humans: Caucasian, Mongolian, Malay, American, and Negro, which could be further divided into twenty-five familial groups.[23] Although Morton never used the word "species" to describe these races or their subfamilies, he did believe that each race was characterized by a set of immutable characteristics. These characteristics arose from innate biological influences, and each group had remained the same since their first primordial appearance.

Morton offered these conclusions based on extensive work he had completed on the largest collection of human skulls extant in the United States, a collection partly owned by the Pennsylvania Medical College and partly by himself. He had performed a set of sophisticated craniometric measurements on the skulls using white pepper seed, which allowed him to determine the exact size and capacity of each skull.[24] Morton published his findings in his book *Crania Americana* (1839), and five years later followed up with *Crania Ægyptiaca* (1844), a study of Egyptians skulls he had received from a consular friend stationed in Egypt. Morton argued that his measurements provided conclusive evidence that different races had different cranial capacities (white Europeans had the largest while Ethiopians had the smallest), and such cranial capacities corresponded to substantially different intellectual and moral abilities.

One is struck by Hodge's timing and his focus on Morton's work. Hodge had made his first strike against polygenism by reviewing Cabell's book only months after its publication, but by denouncing Morton's research, which served as the basis for so much later polygenic theorization, Hodge was choosing to attack work that was some twenty years old. Morton became Hodge's target precisely because he served as the great scientific fountainhead of polygenism in the United States, and his disciples included such important polygenic spokesmen as Louis Agassiz, George Robin Gliddon and Josiah Nott. Morton's work had also come to serve as a touchstone for countless American phrenologists, including George Combe, who taught that the shape and size of a person's head was directly related to that person's mental ability and moral character.[25] Hodge sought to debunk Morton's work because he saw it as the rootstock of American polygenic science. To discredit Morton's work was to strike a blow against all who built upon it.[26]

Hodge undercut Morton's theories by arguing that his sample of skulls was far too small to bear the weight of his vast generalizations.[27] He was particularly interested in discrediting Mortonite theories that denigrated the humanity of African Americans. Hodge argued against African Americans being considered an inferior race incapable of substantial improvement, the possibility that African Americans serve as some sort of intermediary link between human and ape, and the claim that intermarriage

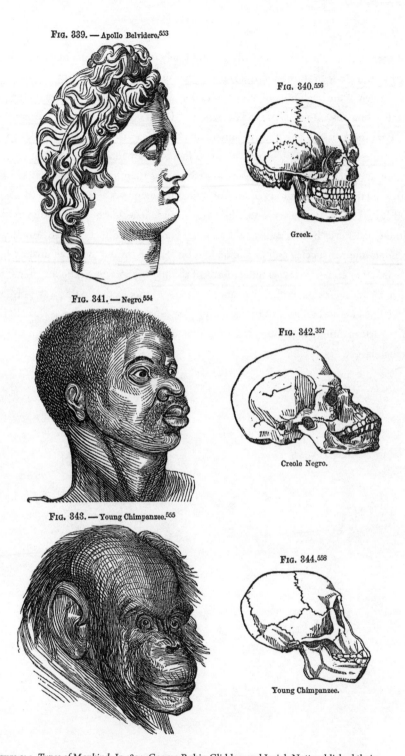

Figure 51.1 *Types of Mankind*: In 1854, George Robin Gliddon and Josiah Nott published their collaborative work in a book entitled: *Types of Mankind*. In this illustration from their text, one sees their belief that the African-American was nothing more than a quasi-human intermediary link between the idealized western, white man (as seen in the bust of Apollo) and the chimpanzee. [Courtesy Lilly Library, Indiana University, Bloomington, IN]

between African Americans and whites could only produce hybrid, infertile progeny. In the end, Hodge returned to the Bible as the "most probable account that has ever been given of the beginning of things," and the surest source of knowledge on the primacy of humans among all of God's creation and their equality one with another.[28]

For Hodge, it was one thing to adhere to a biblical argument in favor of slavery; it was quite another thing to begin to argue that African Americans did not share a common origin and as a result were something less than human. Such a view both affronted the Bible's creation account, as well as its unequivocal teaching on the availability of God's grace to everyone, whether male or female, Jew or Greek, bond or free. Hodge had never been a radical abolitionist, but the claim that African Americans were an inferior species and as such could be forever treated as slaves pushed him toward an openness to less gradual means of abolition.[29] So, when Lincoln offered his Emancipation Proclamation in January 1863, Hodge embraced it. In this way, polygenism helped nudge Hodge toward the abolitionist camp. In his mind, it was far better to offer African American slaves premature freedom rather than consign them to perpetual slavery.

52

THE DISUNITIES OF MANKIND

Although Hodge embraced Lincoln's Emancipation Proclamation, he did not let it pass without comment. He saw in it the potential to change the aim of the war from preserving the Union to abolishing slavery, something he wished to avoid at all costs. The proclamation itself consisted of two executive orders. Lincoln issued the first of these on September 22, 1862, and in it declared all slaves free in any state within the Confederate States of America if that state did not return to the Union by January 1, 1863. Lincoln issued the second order some one hundred days later on January 1, 1863, and in it he specifically listed the ten states in which now all slaves were free. Lincoln issued these orders by the authority invested in him as commander-in-chief as a tactical act necessary for a Northern victory. Lincoln had no power to free slaves in states loyal to the Union, but to the disloyal, he could attack their institution of slavery as a means of crippling their ability to fight.[1] The niceties of executive power were lost on many abolitionists, however, who roundly criticized Lincoln for taking such a weak step toward total emancipation.

Even as he offered the Emancipation Proclamation, Lincoln maintained that his principal goal in the war had not changed. He wrote Horace Greeley, the famous New York City newspaper mogul and outspoken abolitionist: "My paramount object in this struggle is to save the Union and is not either to save or destroy slavery. If I could save the Union without freeing any slave I would do it, and if I could save it by freeing all the slaves I would do it."[2] Hodge stood in total agreement with Lincoln, believing that to change the purpose of the war would be absolutely "fatal to our success."[3] Hodge saw the proclamation not as an act bent on abolition for its own sake, but as a key strategy in undermining the South's economy and much of its labor force. If the North could destabilize the institution of slavery in the South, the South would fall.

In the wake of Lincoln's Emancipation Proclamation, Hodge published an extended essay offering what he saw as "the bearing of the moral law" on the great questions facing the country.[4] In a *Repertory* article simply entitled "The War," Hodge argued that the justness of the war lay in its adherence to the Constitution, which clearly laid out the country's legal code and the systems of redress when that code was questioned. At the bottom of Hodge's thinking lay the all-important Calvinist doctrines of God's providence and sovereignty.[5] God's purposes behind the war were known only to him in his "mysterious wisdom."[6] The war may be a punishment for the nation's sins, or it might be a disciplining action of mercy, but there was no excuse to take any action that was not rooted in the Bible's teachings.[7] With this view in mind, it was of singular importance that citizens follow the biblical injunction to follow the laws of their sovereignly ordained rulers. The South had forsaken this sacred duty in flouting their country's Constitution, and thereby must face the penalty for their action.

Hodge went on to argue that the North could not simply use the war as an excuse to ignore the very rule of law it was seeking so desperately, and at such a high human cost, to protect and preserve. Hodge believed that Lincoln had acted well within his rights as commander-in-chief in pursuing a strategic policy bent on bringing an end to the war. In considering the Emancipation Proclamation, or any other tactic used to win the war, Hodge saw expediency as the great evil to be avoided. He pointed to Lincoln as a man who saw that a proper end should never be pursued by improper means. Hodge held that the Bible unequivocally taught that "those who teach that we may do evil that good may come" faced a just "damnation."[8] Slavery might be "hateful to the men of this generation, and therefore they are prone to make its extirpation the great end of the war," but every American was enjoined by scripture to heed their government and its Constitution.[9] Only by acting with the firm conviction that God was sovereign over the workings of duly elected governmental officials could the North hope to become "the abode of liberty and constitutional order."[10]

Hodge's firm belief in God's providence met one of its most severe tests when a Southern actor by the name of John Wilkes Booth stole into Lincoln's box at Ford's Theater on the evening of April 14, 1865, and fired a single bullet into the back of the president's head. After suffering through the night, Lincoln died the next morning in a house across the street from the theater, just days after General Robert E. Lee surrendered the Army of Northern Virginia to Union forces at Appomattox Court House. Hodge was devastated by Lincoln's death.

The first inkling of the tragedy actually came from his grandson, Willie, who told him that something bad had happened to the president. Hodge then sought out news from Seminary students, who told him that the president had been shot. Hodge cried "O, it cannot be, it cannot be," and burst into tears, wandering back to his study as one "bewildered by a sudden stroke."[11] He told his brother that he considered the day of

Lincoln's death "the saddest day in the whole history of our nation.... The death of no one man in all the world could have sent such a wave of sorrow over this nation as that of Mr. Lincoln."[12] On the day of Lincoln's funeral, as students and faculty gathered together to lament the president's death, Hodge offered up a prayer so filled with grief that his own sobbing almost drowned out his petitions. It was a sincerely affecting experience, and many present recalled for years afterward the depth of Hodge's sorrow at the event.[13]

Hodge retreated to his writing to help make sense of Lincoln's passing and produced a heartfelt *Repertory* lament to his fallen leader entitled: "President Lincoln." Hodge opened the essay by stating that "No Christian can look upon the events of the last four years without being deeply impressed with the conviction that they have been ordered by God to produce great and lasting changes in the state of the country, and probably the world."[14] Such momentous events were clearly all part of a divine plan. "Nothing happens by necessity or by chance. God governs all his creatures and all their actions."[15] God had guided every aspect of the war, and Americans must trust that his hand also controlled Lincoln's tragic death for some greater purpose.[16]

Aside from an extended excursus on God's providence, Hodge used the essay to align himself closely with the views Lincoln had so long championed. He repeated that the war had always been focused on the preservation of the Union. It never "became an anti-slavery war."[17] He rejoiced that Southern slavery was at an end because he believed the institution as practiced in the South had been "a great moral evil," but he also goes on to soften his stance by excusing many good Southern men who had acquiesced to the institution because they had "been born and educated under that system."[18] After all, even the great John Newton, who had written some of the church's great hymns—including "Amazing Grace"—continued to be a slave trader even after his conversion. Hodge pointed to Newton's example as evidence that not every man "who aided the rebellion was in heart a reprobate."[19]

Hodge's defense of his own pro-Lincoln position and the compassion he bestowed upon Southern Christians shows a profound shift in his thinking about the ethical dimensions of Scottish Common Sense philosophy. Gone was Hodge's faith in the power of a common moral sentiment being able to lead all people toward a unity of moral conviction and action. Instead of focusing on the ability to appeal to a common conscience that told everyone the difference between right and wrong, Hodge had come to believe that the views of men and women were not entirely determined by an inner moral sense, but by environmental factors as well. By the end of the war, he declared that the ways in which people determined the difference between right and wrong were largely due "to the controlling influence of public opinion, and of the life of the community to which they belong."[20] The notion of an über-human conscience capable of binding people together had faded away in the midst of the divisions he had witnessed between sincere Northern and Southern Christians during the Civil War.

The war had forced him to reconsider the efficacy of a common moral sentiment and the morally upright world that it might build.

In his essay on Lincoln, Hodge may have rejoiced that slavery's passing from the American scene was one of the "most momentous events in the history of the world," but the fact remained that many considered Hodge's long-held biblical positions on slavery to be morally indefensible.[21] Even his treasured friend, John Johns, reportedly told Hodge at their first meeting after the war: "Charley, you have been a bad boy, but I'll forgive you."[22] Others, however, had a hard time forgetting or forgiving the biblically based pro-slavery stance Hodge had advocated since 1836.

Hodge met the criticism of his less forgiving foes in the fall of 1865, when he published his last *Repertory* article on the war: "The Princeton Review on the State of the Country and of the Church." Responding to how he had been "widely and severely censured" for his political views over the past few years, Hodge wrote this article to exonerate himself by making it clear to all that his first allegiance was not to a political system or position, but to the Bible.[23] The article was an extended and aggressive defense of the positions he had taken throughout the war. He proudly declared at the article's outset that as he surveyed his political writings of the past five years, he could "find in them nothing which we wish to retract."[24] Nevertheless, Hodge was deeply wounded by the criticism. In a rare display of self-pity, Hodge told his critics that he could easily walk away from the *Repertory*, which he had carried as a prisoner carries "a ball-and-chain for forty years," receiving no "other compensation than the high privilege and honour of making it an organ for upholding sound Presbyterianism, the cause of the country, and the honour of our common Redeemer."[25]

In finding fault with Hodge, his critics chastised him for being too lukewarm in his Northern loyalties and too willing to provide biblical ammunition to support the South's slavery position. Hodge fired back that he never had "the slightest sympathy with the South in this great national conflict" and that his position on slavery "both as in its moral and political aspect" was the same as it had always been: the Bible never condemned the institution, so neither could he.[26] Hodge had made virtually the same claim a year earlier when he wrote that he wished it "distinctly understood, that we have not changed our ground on the subject of slavery. We hold now precisely what we held in 1836, when the subject was first argued in these pages."[27] His position on slavery had remained rock solid: "We have always held that gradual emancipation would be the best for all concerned."[28] And yet when it became clear that to preserve the life of the nation, slavery must be extinguished, he had agreed with the stance of the General Assembly that had unanimously declared that the time had "come when slavery should be at once and for ever abolished in the State and Territories of this Union."[29]

While many considered his stance on slavery to have changed during the war, Hodge believed until his death that he had only ever held one position on the slavery with question. To understand his slavery position is to understand his unwavering commitment to the Bible's teachings on the unity of humankind and the primacy of God's Word in all human counsels. It was a stance, however, full of it own problems and contradictions. In the course of the war, Hodge found himself increasingly unable to separate notions of slavery from the practices of slaveholding in the Southern states, where he had become convinced that slaves were held in the greatest degradation. Still, he never abandoned his conceptual separation between slavery and slaveholding when pushed on his slavery position.

His position of gradual emancipation led him into a conflicted stance on slavery even after the war. Hodge was hesitant to support the Fourteenth Amendment when it came to its final vote in 1868. He struggled with the amendment, as it ran counter to his old Federalist notions that the best and brightest should be privileged when it came to governmental decisions and positions. He did not yet believe former slaves were qualified to hold every right granted American citizens.[30] Although he believed that former slaves were fully human, he did not think them yet ready to be trusted with the rights of suffrage and political leadership. As he staunchly proclaimed the unity of all humankind, Hodge found himself unable to disassociate himself from the influences of his own genteel, Northern upbringing. In this way, a nagging sense of disunity dogged his own notions of black and white relations. In the end, Hodge never moved much beyond his own stance of gradual emancipation before his death. In keeping with this gradualist slavery stance, he was able to take a terribly long view of just how much time might be required for former American slaves to gain equality in every aspect of the American society.

53

REUNITING THE OLD AND NEW SCHOOLS

As the war concluded, it quickly became apparent that reunifying Old School Presbyterians from the North and South was not going to be easy. As the North's General Assembly met just one month after Lee's surrender, many present demanded that their Southern brethren publically repent and confess their mistake in seceding from the Union before they be readmitted to Presbyterian fellowship. Hodge strenuously argued against such a position, proclaiming that secession was not an ecclesiastical sin. Demanding Southern repentance for secession was not only theologically unsupportable, but it was unfairly singling out Southerners when thousands of Northerners had agreed with the South throughout the conflict.

Many Old School Southern Presbyterians felt both the animosity of their Northern peers and the loss of the war so keenly that they no longer desired fellowship with their Northern brethren. Although the Presbyterian Church in the Confederate States of America fell with the Confederacy, a sizeable contingent of Southern Old School Presbyterians refused reunion with their former colleagues and in 1866 established the Presbyterian Church in the United States. The continued separation grieved Hodge as he was slow to give up his dream of seeing all Old School Presbyterians once again reunited after the war.

While the war had served to estrange Northern and Southern Presbyterians, the conflict seemed to have catalyzed a broad-based interest in unity across the American religious spectrum. Spurred on by the devastating sense of division and chaos arising from the seemingly endless brutality of the Civil War, a number of New York City ministers worked together to develop "a Federal Union of all Evangelical Denominations."[1] Their hope was that each member of the Union might be able to retain its own distinctive character and spiritual institutions, but in a United Nations–type fashion members would also submit all questions arising from conflicting interests to a supreme panel representing the Union as a whole. It was a model based on a similar plan of Federated Nations proposed in Europe, but which had failed when faced with the practicalities involved in getting nation states to agree on terms of mutual submission.

This Federated Union of Evangelicals was but one manifestation of a much larger American interest in finding unifying elements to bind together different denominations and even different religions. One of the boldest examples of this quest for unity came in the form of the Free Religious Association, which was founded in 1867 "to remove all dividing lines and to unite all religious men in bonds of pure spirituality."[2] One of the Association's leaders, the Transcendentalist minister and author, Thomas Wentworth Higginson—perhaps best remembered now for his sponsorship of the reclusive Massachusetts's poet Emily Dickinson—helped spearhead a larger religious-unity movement in the United States by producing a widely circulated and much-imitated address entitled *The Sympathy of Religions* (1870).

Higginson proclaimed that ultimately all religions showed "the same aim, the same symbols, the same forms, the same weaknesses, the same aspirations."[3] His desire to prove that a sympathy did, in fact, exist between all spiritual traditions moved him to argue that any close study of the world's major religions revealed that Zoroaster, Christ, Buddha, and Mohammed were interchangeable figures and had all advocated the same basic teachings.[4] Higginson proved to be just one American among many who dedicated their intellectual energies to seeking common ground among the world's religions, a quest that became so pronounced that it ultimately helped produce the Parliament of the World's Religions held during the 1893 World Columbian Exposition in Chicago. This event was the first formal gathering of representatives of Eastern and Western spiritual traditions and began important interreligious dialogues between a number of these traditions.

The Presbyterians were not immune to the promise of power and peace to be found in unification, but their interests in this regard centered on their own denomination, not on bonding with other religious traditions. Such a Presbyterian-centric focus issued forth for the first time when during the 1862 Old School General Assembly in Columbus, Ohio, several delegates broached the possibility of seeking reconciliation with their New School brethren.[5] After a brief discussion, the Old School General Assembly put off the potentially emotional and contentious issue until a later date, but many of its members were intrigued enough by the idea that the Assembly appointed delegates to serve as official visitors to the next New School General Assembly.

The following year saw a number of Old School delegates visit the New School General Assembly, including a former chaplain to the United States Senate by the name of Rev. Dr. Septimus Tustin. The Old School Tustin took up the issue of reunification with a passion, declaring in an address to his New School colleagues that "the strife is at an end. The fierce war-cry that grated so long upon the heart of piety, has died away into an echo so indistinct as scarcely distinguishable. Our ecclesiastical war-steeds, if we may so speak, are reclining amidst the olive groves of peace."[6] Tustin and his fellow delegates took every opportunity to extol the bliss that awaited a reunited Presbyterian body. In this spirit, the following years saw the exchange of numerous delegates between the Old and New School General Assemblies.

Discussions of reunion soon became regular fixtures at both gatherings. The issue gained even greater momentum in November 1867 when the Synod of the Reformed Presbyterian Church sponsored "The National Presbyterian Union Convention," a convocation that gathered 313 representatives from each of the nation's six Presbyterian bodies.[7] For three days, speakers and delegates representing both the Old and New Schools joined with smaller bodies such as the Cumberland and Reformed Presbyterians in Philadelphia to celebrate and promote the Presbyterian heritage in America.

Hodge attended the gathering, but he had arrived under the misapprehension that the meeting would focus on prayer and Presbyterian fellowship. By the end of the first day of the three-day gathering, he felt he had been lured to Philadelphia under false pretenses. He soon determined that the National Presbyterian Union Convention was not a meeting principally intended to promote general fellowship among American Presbyterians; it was a calculated effort to catalyze measures that might bring all Presbyterians under one "general organic union" as a single unified denomination.[8] Hodge sat in silence through the first two days of meetings, and it was only at the end of the last day that he sought to temper the enthusiasm of his fellow Presbyterians on the topic of pursuing a wider, and to him an all-too-ill-defined, unity. Hodge rose during the afternoon of the last day and offered an exposition on the importance of adhering to the "Standards" set forth in the Westminster Confession and the Bible.[9] His position was simple: all who were to share true communion with the Old School Presbyterians needed to accept the positions taught in the Westminster Confession "without note or comment."[10] Hodge was not opposed to enjoying the fellowship of other Presbyterians, but he was leery of pursuing any course that might compromise the doctrinal integrity of the Old School. To have true unity, Presbyterians had to acknowledge the importance of a common vision when it came to central issues of doctrine.

The reservations Hodge voiced at the convention were but an echo of his views on reunification that he had first laid out two years earlier in an extended *Repertory* article entitled "Principles of Church Union, and the Reunion of the Old and New-School Presbyterians."[11] In this essay, Hodge was quick to acknowledge the widespread interest in reuniting the Old and New School wings of American Presbyterianism, and he thought that given enough time, such a reunion might well occur. Ever the gradualist, Hodge favored a slow and measured road to reunification. He believed that the best chance for success lay not in how Presbyterians shared a common concept of church government, but in establishing a clear, shared understanding of key points of doctrine. Coming to such an understanding would take time, and Hodge had no desire to rush the process. The denomination's long-term stability depended on all parties agreeing on the theology that would bind them together.

Others, however, wished to ride the tide of brotherly love and forge ahead with what they saw as the inevitability of reunion. Principal among those leading the reunion charge was Henry Boynton Smith of Union Theological Seminary. Smith had been one of the earliest New School advocates of the idea of reunification, raising the possibility at the 1863 New School General Assembly when he sat as that body's annual moderator. Over the next six years, Smith became the chief architect of, and advocate for, Presbyterian reunion.[12]

Smith was perfectly suited to handle the delicate politics and forceful personalities involved in the reunification cause. A leading faculty member at Union Theological Seminary, the New School's flagship training school, he had risen by the mid-1860s to be one of the New School's most influential and respected leaders. His theological approach was thoroughly Christocentric. Whereas the high Calvinists of Princeton tended to begin with a Sovereign God to guide their theological thinking and the New Haven–inflected New Schoolers emphasized human agency, Smith rooted his own theological approach in the figure of Christ and his role as a mediator between God and humanity. As an extension of his heavily Christocentric views, Smith saw his own role in denominational politics as a mediator dedicated to reconciling the warring sides of Old and New School Presbyterianism.[13]

Smith was able to woo large sections of the Old School because his own theological thinking was so conservative. He vigorously argued that the majority of New Schoolers were characterized by strong, traditional Calvinist beliefs. He repeatedly declared that the New School was not as radical as it had once been, and that New Haven (or Taylorite) New School Presbyterians were the exception rather than the rule.[14] He saw a thorough alignment between New and Old School views on key doctrinal points, and because of this harmonious agreement he argued that no substantial obstacles stood in the way of the two bodies reuniting.

Hodge appreciated Smith's work in seeking a common ground between the Old and New Schools, but he did not share Smith's belief that the New School's position on moral agency was either in line with the Westminster Confession or the Old School. He felt that the New School had a long history of ordaining Taylorite ministers and allowing Taylorite teaching in its seminaries and publications. For Hodge, it did not matter if only one in one hundred New School ministers favored the New Haven theology. (He even admitted that this indeed might be the case.)[15] The issue was not how many Taylorites were numbered in the New School, but what the New School

Figure 53.1 *Henry Boynton Smith*: Henry Boynton Smith was one of the foremost leaders of New School Presbyterianism. After training for the ministry at Andover and Bangor Seminaries, Smith spent three years in Germany studying theology under August Tholuck, Johann Neander and Ernst Hengstenberg. After returning to the United States, he dedicated much of his life to formulating a middle position between the theologies of New Haven and Princeton. He played a pivotal role in reuniting Old and New School Presbyterianism. He taught at Union Theological Seminary from 1850 until his health failed in 1874. [*Presbyterian Historical Society, Presbyterian Church (U.S.A) (Philadelphia, PA)*]

tolerated as acceptable doctrinal positions.[16] In Hodge's mind, the New School countenanced doctrinal stances that true Augustinian Calvinists could never find acceptable.[17] The sticking point for Hodge was not what individual New School ministers might believe, but that the New School as a whole admitted a dangerous and unbiblical "latitude in matters of doctrine and order, which the Old-school have conscientiously resisted."[18]

Hodge believed that to reunite the Old and New Schools while different theological leniencies were in force was simply to invite the same kind of conflict and confusion that rent the denomination asunder thirty years before.[19] Hodge was not opposed to working toward a common theological understanding that would once again reunite his denomination, but he felt that no such understanding was in place when both the Old and New School General Assemblies met in 1869 to render a final decision on whether or not to reunite the country's two main bodies of Presbyterians. Hodge was so opposed to what he saw as a precipitous step toward reunion that he rode nine miles while ill to attend the autumn meeting of his local presbytery to cast his vote against reunion.[20]

Ultimately, his efforts and his final vote proved futile. The following month, the New and Old School General Assemblies reported the presbyteries' votes: the New School's 113 presbyteries were unanimous in their support of reunion, while the Old School reported that 126 of its 144 presbyteries had voted for reunion (with 15 presbyteries not reporting and only 3 standing in opposition).[21] Hodge stood as a minority dissenting voice amid the overwhelming fervor for reunion.

Hodge's resistance to the reunion provides some interesting insights into his life-long aversion to change and his views on sharing fellowship with those who differed from him theologically. Thirty years earlier, Hodge had been one of the strongest advocates for exploring ways to keep the Presbyterian Church from dividing institutionally into New and Old School sides. Few had worked harder to try to limit the influence of Ashbel Green's theologically inflexible Ultra faction in an attempt to keep the denomination together. Three decades later, Smith had taken Hodge's former role as the moderating voice of reconciliation, while Hodge came to resemble Green or one of his Ultras from the 1830s. He could not support a return to a common Presbyterian body because like so many changes in his life he saw this one as utterly unnecessary. Each body had established itself as a respected and ably functioning entity. There was no need to disturb this equilibrium, particularly when he saw that it would mean compromising one another's theological views.

Hodge's opposition to the reunion also demonstrated his own principles when it came to communing with various Christian denominations that differed in theology. He was certainly not opposed to ecumenism. In the midst of the National Presbyterian Union Convention, he served as the Convention's goodwill ambassador to a major Episcopalian gathering that was meeting in Philadelphia at the same time. As he addressed that Episcopalian assembly, he pointed to his lifelong friends and Princeton classmates, Bishop McIlvaine and Bishop Johns, as exemplars of how members of the different denominations could work side-by-side in the cause of Christ.[22] Such men proved the truth that Presbyterians and Episcopalians stood together "one in faith, one in baptism, one in life, and one in our allegiance to your Lord and to our Lord."[23] Tears ran down the faces of many of the ministers at the gathering who listened to Hodge extol this interdenominational partnership in the Gospel.

As capacious as Hodge could be in embracing any person "who professes to be a worshipper of Christ," he showed far less tolerance when it came to the beliefs and actions of his fellow Presbyterians.[24] Throughout his life, Hodge held Presbyterians to a higher theological standard. Presbyterians were to adhere to the historical meanings of the tenets outlined in the Westminster Confession. Deviation from these tenets was nothing short of heresy. One might picture the tolerances of Hodge's theological opinions as a set of concentric rings, with Presbyterians occupying the center-most circle because their doctrines stood as the truest explanations of the teachings found in the sacred scriptures. Other Christian bodies occupied different rings that radiated outward from this Presbyterian center. Hodge had few qualms embracing Christians who inhabited the outer rings, as long as they professed acceptably orthodox theological views. Hodge also had no illusions that Presbyterians were the only Christians in the world. But, if one claimed to be a Presbyterian, Hodge held that person accountable to the most rigorous standards of Augustinian Calvinism because he or she was claiming a place in the most central circle of Christian orthodoxy.

Because Hodge saw himself as defending this most central circle, he dedicated himself to showing the folly of any premature move to Presbyterian reunification. He once again put pen to paper and wrote what would become the primary "Protest" against the reunion, declaring that a time for reunion might well come but as long as there was no clear agreement on key points of theological difference, that time had not yet arrived.[25] Few seemed interested in Hodge's article with its long historical explanations of the 1837 schism and dire predictions of future theological tension. Only a handful of like-minded conservatives joined Hodge in his protest. His voice, which for years had been a signal trumpet for the Old School, fell on deaf ears as hundreds of New and Old School Presbyterians embraced the idea of denominational reunion.

In a sense, history had passed Hodge by. It is worthy of note that the same Hodge who had clamored for union at the outset of the Civil War for the Old School in particular and for the nation as a whole, now found himself as one of the sole hold-outs against the kind of moderation and acceptance that could bring the New School back into the Old School fold. Hodge simply proved too adverse to change, too vivid in his remembrances of the 1837 schism, and too committed to Old School notions of Augustinian Calvinism to embrace any move toward the new brand of more ecumenical Presbyterianism favored by the vast majority of his ministerial brethren.

Hodge also failed to appreciate just how powerful the shared political commitment of both Old and New Schoolers to preserving the Union during the Civil War could be in reuniting the denomination. Although it had been theology that had driven the denomination apart in the 1830s, it was the cultural and political affinities of countless pro-Union Presbyterians that played a key role in helping forge the common ground that reunited the denomination.[26] Hodge was only able to see the Old and New Schools through the lens of theology. For countless Presbyterians, the war had shown the dangers of division and given them a renewed sense that what they held in common was more important than what separated them. Theological differences receded, as Presbyterians embraced each other with the hope of being more effective in combining their efforts to evangelize the American frontier, send missionaries abroad, and minister in their more traditional strongholds on the East Coast.

Hodge may not have rejoiced in his denomination's reunion, but once it was done, he did all in his power to see the newly reunited denomination flourish. Emblematic of his support, Hodge added his voice to those of his fellow Princeton College trustees as they approved a proposal to build a new hall on campus in honor of the Presbyterian reunion. In 1869, the trustees voted to construct "Reunion Hall," and a year later the moderator of the newly combined General Assembly of the Old and New Schools laid the building's cornerstone.[27] Hodge may have considered the reunion hurried and ill-advised, but once the presbyteries had voted, Hodge was too good a Presbyterian not to bow to the collective wisdom of God's people. In his heart, he desired to see his beloved denomination as solid and beautiful a structure as the newly erected Reunion Hall.

PART VIII

The 1870s
Systematic Theologian and Scientist

Figure 54.1 *Hodge, near the time of his 50th teaching anniversary in 1872:* [*Special Collections, Princeton Theological Seminary Libraries*]

54

THE *SYSTEMATIC THEOLOGY*

Robert Clinton, a scholar who has spent much of his career studying contemporary evangelical leaders, uses the term "afterglow" to describe the last stage of a Christian leader's life.[1] He has noted that a handful of prominent Christian leaders experience an "Afterglow or Celebration" phase near the end of their lives where the "fruit of a lifetime of ministry and growth culminates in an era of recognition and indirect influence at broad levels."[2] Such leaders serve as models of behavior and living storehouses of knowledge and experience. They glow with the wisdom and piety born of their lifelong journeys of faith, and those around them bask in their radiant aura.

By the 1870s, Hodge could be counted as one of the select few who had entered the "afterglow" stage of life. He had nothing left to prove. After protesting against the Presbyterian reunion of 1869, he showed little interest—with the one exception of his writing on Darwinism—in taking part in the pressing controversies of his day. He left theological and denominational struggles for other, younger men to handle.[3] He had even gradually handed off the editorial work of the *Repertory*. In 1869, Lyman Atwater became the journal's co-editor. The Professor of Mental and Moral Philosophy at Princeton College, Atwater had already contributed sixty-six articles to the *Repertory* before agreeing to help take the editorial reins of the journal.[4] Three years later, Hodge retired completely from his editorial duties, and Atwater was joined by Henry Boyton Smith as the journal embraced the New School faction at Union Theological Seminary and was renamed *Presbyterian Quarterly and Princeton Review*.

Even before his full retirement from the *Repertory*, Hodge had turned his attention to collecting, systematizing, and recording his five decades of theological thinking. Long discouraged by his colleagues from undertaking such a work for fear that it might discourage students from actually coming to the Seminary to study with him, in his

Figure 54.2 *Lyman Atwater*: Lyman Atwater enjoyed a long career at Princeton College, serving on its faculty from 1854 until his death in 1883. Although his students fondly lampooned his pear-like shape, they considered him an outstanding teacher in his courses on logic and moral philosophy. He co-edited the *Repertory* in its various forms from 1869 to 1878 and contributed more than 110 articles to its pages, making him one of the most prolific defenders of Old School Calvinism in the nineteenth century. [*Princeton University Library*]

final years Hodge wished to write a compendium of his theological thinking.[5] By 1867, Hodge was spending almost all of his free time writing what would become his magnum opus: his multifaceted, three-volume *Systematic Theology*.

Systematic theology is a study built on the principle of integration. As it was most commonly practiced in the nineteenth century, it was a branch of theological study focused on harmonizing the Bible's varied and diverse teachings, thereby exhibiting biblical doctrines "in their unity & mutual relations."[6] Hodge was fond of calling it "the brightest form of theology—as isolated truths assume a higher form when seen in their harmonious dependence."[7] He likened interlinked biblical truths to "the columns of a Grecian temple each symmetrical & beautiful" as they stand alone, but "something more & something higher, when seen as parts of a beautiful whole."[8] Systematic theology's emphasis on integration, however, came to function on a more ambitious level in Hodge's hands than it did for many of his contemporaries. Hodge did not simply seek to harmonize the Bible various teachings, but he sought to reveal the myriad linkages to be found between God and his creation. As a consequence, no topic stood beyond his purview as he sought to reveal the Bible's relationship to such diverse fields as medicine, psychology, law, geology, astronomy, political science, and philosophy.

As the nineteenth century wore on, a number of more conservative Protestant seminaries formalized their commitment to the integrative impulse in theological studies by establishing faculty positions in systematic theology. Along with Hodge, some of the century's most gifted Protestant professors held these posts, including: Leonard Woods (Andover), Charles Finney (Oberlin), Henry Boynton Smith and William G. T. Shedd (Union Theological Seminary in New York), Robert Lewis Dabney (Union Theological Seminary in Virginia), James Henley Thornwell and Benjamin Morgan Palmer (Columbia Seminary in Georgia), James P. Boyce (Southern Baptist Theological Seminary), and Miner Raymond (Garrett Biblical Institute).

Once he began his *Systematic* in earnest, Hodge worked steadily over a five-year period to produce the largest published systematic theology ever to come from an American. His work eventually comprised three massive volumes: Theology (the study of God), Anthropology (the nature of humankind), and finally Soteriology and Eschatology (God's plan for salvation and the culmination of His redemptive work). There are numerous clues that he toyed with writing a fourth volume on ecclesiology (the nature of the church), but in the end, he let his three volumes stand alone. For whatever reason, he felt that his comments on the church found throughout his first three volumes were sufficient.[9]

His son, Archie, noted that each word contained in the volumes was written using the same temperamental gold fountain pen whose use eluded everyone except his father.[10] Although Hodge had already published or taught on every issue he discussed in his *Systematic*, the extant manuscripts of the work reveal that he was not content with simply patching together previous writings and lectures to create his all-encompassing Reformed theological treatise. While one frequently finds a sentence or two from his lectures, commentaries, or sermons embedded in his larger work, one also quickly realizes that Hodge sat down and composed his *Systematic* anew, creating a work that flowed as a single, organic whole. The manuscript later recovered from his printer shows just how sure a hand Hodge exercised in recording a lifetime of theological thought. For a work that eventually reached 3,311 manuscript pages, there is amazingly little marginalia or interlinear correction defacing the work.[11] There are moments where Hodge crossed out pages or pasted in new paragraphs, but on the whole, Hodge's text is startlingly pristine. His ripened thoughts seemed to pour forth almost uninterrupted from his old, faithful pen.

Hodge's *Systematic* proved to be the brightest jewel in the crown of his distinguished publishing career. The same aversion to change that had marked his entire life found its way into its pages. It was a work of synthesis and distillation, not innovation. It was theology beyond the reach of cultural whims and contemporary moods, and Hodge's critics rightly pointed out that there was a wonderful naïveté in the work as it assumed "somewhere a line of succession in the Church, which in every age has taught just what he teaches," an idealized church that held the same doctrine in "every age of history."[12] Hodge wrote his *Systematic* with the unshakeable conviction that the true church and its teachings were utterly incapable of change. More importantly, he believed that these immutable teachings served as the core of Princeton Seminary's curriculum, and that his *Systematic* was simply the compendium of a line of theological thinking that had characterized the Seminary since its founding.

As in many areas of theological study, the Germans led in the composition of large systematic theological works in the nineteenth century. Notable in this regard are Friedrich Schleiermacher's two-volume *The Christian Faith* (1821–1822) and his student Richard Rothe's five-volume *Theologische Ethik* (1845–1848).[13] Both men wrote imposing, ambitious, and intellectually challenging works that boldly set forth complex theological systems. Their attempts to meld Christian biblical teaching with more current European philosophy made their scholarship immensely influential on both sides of the Atlantic.

Americans followed this European lead and began publishing notable systematic theological works as early as the 1840s. Hodge added the crowning touch to this publishing trend in the 1870s with his own *Systematic*, and any comparison of the work to other American systematics of the period testifies to Hodge's staggering achievement. Before Hodge, American systematic theologies consisted almost entirely of collections of published lecture notes on a range of related theological topics. Particularly popular works in this tradition include Charles Finney's *Lectures on Systematic Theology* (1846) and the published lectures of Henry B. Smith and Robert Dabney in the last half of the nineteenth century.[14] A few theologians such as Robert Breckinridge published more polished systematic theological works, but the appearance of Hodge's *Systematic* marked a pivotal change in how Americans pursued the genre.[15] Hodge did

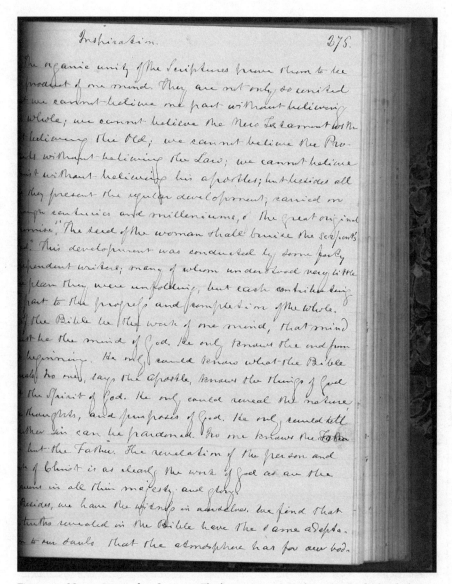

Figure 54.3 *Manuscript page from Systematic Theology manuscript.* Hodge wrote in a fluid and often flawless manner. The largely pristine nature of his original manuscript's pages reveal just how little he needed to change once he put pen to paper. [*Special Collections, Princeton Theological Seminary Libraries*]

not simply produce a longer and more complex work than his contemporaries, he offered a synthetic treatise of unprecedented intellectual range and encyclopedic scope.

It was only after the appearance of Hodge's landmark *Systematic* that other Americans turned their energies to projects of similar scope and ambition. The multi-volume works of the Methodist Miner Raymond (1877–1879), the Baptist Augustus Hopkins Strong (1886) and the Presbyterian William G. T. Shedd (1888–1894) stand as particularly noteworthy.[16] Raymond's own three-volume *Systematic Theology* attempted to stand as an Arminian counterpoint to Hodge's own Calvinist work, while the works of Strong and Shedd followed, with variations, in Hodge's Calvinist footsteps. With his *Systematic*, Hodge had inaugurated a new era of synthetic theological study in America.

While Hodge's *Systematic* was a product of a half century of theological study, it was also a work forged in the fires of the times in which he lived. The Civil War had gone a significant distance in replacing antebellum American post-millennial optimism with the fracturing questions that came from theodicy, the struggle to understand why God allowed suffering in the world. Post-millennialism posited that the world was on an upward, ever-improving trajectory that would ultimately culminate with the return of Christ. In this view, the Millennium (the thousand year reign of Christ) was not imposed from without, but was, in fact, already present in the advance of Christian civilization throughout the world.[17] The horrifying nature of the Civil War challenged such an optimistic view of the world. Any belief in a coherent plan, instituted by a merciful, sovereign God, came face to face with the terrible realities of not only the war itself, but the conflict's haunting aftermath, as thousands of soldiers returned home either physically or psychologically maimed, and myriad American families grappled with the grief caused by the loved ones who failed to return at all.[18] In partial response to the waves of profound grief and religious doubt that washed over the country in the war's wake, Hodge positioned his *Systematic* as a grand apologia for the omnipotence, benevolence, and constant presence of a merciful God.

Every page of Hodge's work was marked by his indomitable optimism. Self-characterized as an incurable optimist, Hodge lived his entire life as someone willing to believe the best about his God, his neighbors, his colleagues, his students, and the world at large. Even the depression that so marked his Civil War years quickly faded in the conflict's aftermath. After completing his *Systematic*, Hodge declared to his old and dear friend, John Johns, that "I really believe that the world, on the whole, is getting better, and that the cause of Christ is on the advance," and near his death he wrote in one of his last Conference Papers that he "believed that the vast majority of the human race were to share the beatitudes and glories of his Lord's redemption."[19] At its core, Hodge's *Systematic* reflected his unceasing optimism as it testified to the ability of the human mind to comprehend God's work, while also teaching that every facet of God's word and world attested to his sovereign and benevolent nature. Perhaps one of Hodge's greatest contributions to American Reformed Theology was this optimistic outlook, tempering the dour contours of earlier Puritan variations of Calvinism that had in some cases held such a high view of God that people were encouraged toward a willingness to be damned for his greater Glory.[20]

Hodge did more than use his *Systematic* to argue against the existential meaninglessness fostered in the minds of so many on account of the war. He used it as a powerful weapon to combat the rising influence of more liberal Protestant theology gaining ground across the country. Building on tendencies first evident among certain strains of German Romanticist theology in the vein of Schleiermacher and the early Transcendentalists, more progressive Protestant thinkers such as Henry Ward Beecher, Theodore Munger, Frederick W. Robertson, and Washington Gladden began to turn away from an unwavering belief in the power of the intellect to understand the Divine as they confronted a seemingly incomprehensible modern world characterized by the tremendous societal strains engendered by industrialization, urbanization, and an unprecedented technological savagery in warfare.

This new breed of American theologian eschewed Enlightenment-bound notions of seeing propositional truths as the surest means of understanding the Divine and instead turned to the heart.[21] Beecher encapsulated this new intuitive theological movement when he stated that true Christianity was found not in cold doctrine but in "a heart that breathes kindness and love."[22] For these more liberal American Protestants, the best path toward spiritual truth lay not through the mind, but through the emotions. Experience, not dull scriptural facts, was the key to true spiritual understanding. With this emphasis on the heart came a more "modern" view of scripture, which favored non-literalist interpretations of the Bible. Such readings of the Holy Writ emphasized the importance of understanding the broad intentions of the Bible's message rather than viewing the Bible's words as coming unmediated from God himself.[23]

Hodge stood aghast at such thinking and composed his *Systematic* to be a forceful response to those who no longer had confidence that the mind might be the best means of apprehending the Divine. It is his absolute confidence in the mind as an agent of spiritual understanding that drives much of the *Systematic's* early discussion on the methods behind theological study. Holding fast to his Scottish Common Sense philosophical roots, Hodge trumpeted the intellectual nature of theological study by arguing that theology was, in fact, a science. In his aptly named first chapter, "Theology as a Science," Hodge carefully and relentlessly made the case for the rational nature of theological study, a type of study that was the most fruitful when it was marked by the same rigorous methods of investigation, factual collation, and postulate formulation found in the best science of his day.[24]

His *Systematic Theology* was not the first time Hodge had posited that theology was a scientific endeavor. Such thinking can be traced all the way back to his study with Tholuck in Germany. Tholuck had held theology to be the "queen of the sciences" and had also underscored Hodge's already-budding commitment to the systematic nature of theology.[25] Through his exposure to Tholuck, his unwavering commitment to Common Sense Realism, and his skepticism of German higher biblical criticism, Hodge had spent his life stressing the importance of bringing one's intellect to bear on the Bible's content in order to formulate theological positions.

Even with Hodge's long history of seeing the scientific aspects of theological inquiry, one does detect a notable shift in emphasis when it comes to how Hodge chose to begin his *Systematic*. Never before in either his lectures or his writings had Hodge so foregrounded the intellect in understanding the divine. To answer the skepticism shown by those who no longer thought the mind adequate to understand God's will and character, Hodge turned to Bacon and his scientific method to buttress his own long-held inductive theological predilections. Nowhere is this change in emphasis more evident than when one considers Hodge's lectures in theology, which he began to offer in the 1840s. In his lecture notes, and the surviving notes of students who attended his classes, there is a stunning absence of any mention of Bacon and his scientific, inductive method. Instead, Hodge warned his students away from approaching theology as "the study of a system of truth . . . with the same spirit" in which one might open "a book of science, history or philosophy."[26] Ultimately, God revealed truth through "his Spirit, who searches all things even the deep things of God."[27]

By the late 1860s, however, Hodge had changed his point of emphasis in his teachings on theological method and had become a thorough Baconian. Although he still revered the Holy Spirit as the source of all divine knowledge, to rebut the rising tide of American liberal, heart-centered theology, Hodge placed Bacon's method front and center in the opening pages of his *Systematic*. His discussions on method in the *Systematic* reveal a clear shift toward the intellect when he states that "the true method of theology is" first and foremost found in "the inductive which assumes that the Bible contains all the facts or truths which form the contents of theology."[28]

Hodge had been drawn to the work of the seventeenth-century scientist and philosopher Francis Bacon because Bacon's method entailed an absolute commitment to empiricism that coincided with the Scottish Common Sense belief that one's senses could indeed be trusted to comprehend the world.[29] One's senses could be used to gather a wide range of reliable facts, which could then be synthesized to form general theories. Bacon's thinking buttressed a belief in Common Sense empiricism by stressing a systematic framework of investigation. The first job of any investigator involved a careful ordering of all the evidence at hand, avoiding all factually unsupported wanderings of reason or imagination. Evidence studied in such a systematic, rational way revealed patterns that led to generalizations. Evidence generated propositions; propositions could never be allowed to guide the interpretation of evidence.[30] In this way, Bacon led an entire generation of nineteenth-century Scottish Common Sense Realists to glory in the reliability of objective knowledge and treat facts with an almost-holy reverence.

In his *Systematic*, Hodge enlisted Bacon's method to attack those who favored an intuitive approach to religion. Far from needing to retreat from the use of the mind, Baconian science showed just how essential the intellect was in understanding God.

Hodge went to great lengths to dismiss heart-centered—what he often termed "mystical"—approaches to theological study in favor of the more intellectually rigorous pursuit of theology through the scientific application of one's mind. In his theology lectures, he had attacked such emotional approaches as "enthusiasm," but he now redoubled his efforts against emotive-based religion by declaring theology built on intuitive suppositions was the "great evil in the Church."[31] Truth was not primarily found in the heart; it was found in the careful study of facts, both natural (those found in nature) and supernatural (those found in the divinely inspired scriptures).[32] Collecting, collating, and synthesizing such facts was the surest method of illuminating the Divine.

While every human had access to natural facts, only believing Christians took full advantage of supernatural revelation and the important facts it contained. Hodge, thus, dedicated the majority of his *Systematic* to the study and explanation of the facts found in God's supernatural revelation to humanity, the Bible. Whether people recognized it or not, the Bible stood as one of the world's richest repository of indisputable facts. Hodge argued that Baconian systematic induction brought to bear on the Bible was the surest way to arrive at a right understanding of God. To prove this point, he chose to begin his *Systematic Theology* with what has become the work's most famous passage:

> The Bible is to the theologian what nature is to the man of science. It is his store-house of facts; and his method of ascertaining what the Bible teaches, is the same as that which the natural philosopher adopts to ascertain what nature teaches. . . . the duty of the Christian theologian is to ascertain, collect, and combine all the facts which God has revealed concerning himself and our relation to Him. These facts are all in the Bible. . . . It is in this sense that "The Bible, and the Bible alone, is the religion of the Protestants."[33]

Hodge makes it clear that the Bible, as a "store-house of facts," is the foundational source of knowledge about God. Principles about the character of humanity, the nature of the physical world, and the triune personality of God needed first and foremost to be derived from biblical facts. "The properties of matter, the laws of motion, of magnetism, of light, etc., are not framed by the mind. They are not laws of thought. They are deductions from facts."[34]

As Hodge and other systematic theologians of his era devoted themselves to the construction of interpretative frameworks bent on harmonizing the Bible's teachings both one to another and then to the greater world of natural phenomena, one discovers that overarching themes guided their harmonizing impulses. Such themes inevitably led systematic theologians to favor particular doctrinal schools of thought. In

Hodge's case, the systematic study of the Bible proved at every turn that the Westminster Confession provided the best single synopsis of the whole scope of God's creation and the doctrines taught in the Bible. With this truth in mind, Hodge thought it only natural to use the Confession itself as the basic organizational principle for his *Systematic*. It was the organizational principle he had used to structure his theological lectures of the last thirty years, and it had been the same principle that his mentor Archibald Alexander had used in formulating and sequencing his own theological lectures. Thus, Hodge's *Systematic* was utterly consistent with the basic theological form of doctrine and teaching that had always been taught at Princeton Seminary.

Because Hodge held closely to the Westminster Confession in basic outline and doctrinal content, his *Systematic* holds few surprises. At every point, he stressed his unwavering belief in the truth of conservative Augustinian Calvinist doctrinal positions. Following a trend he had first established in his commentary on Romans published thirty-five years earlier, Hodge used his *Systematic* to offer extended explanatory discussions on central Reformed lynchpin topics such as sin, the power of the human will, and God's sovereignty. A traditional Calvinist view of imputation played prominently in the work as a bulwark against the thinking of more modern, progressive Protestant theologians who continued the long American revival-born tradition of arguing for the power of human agency in the pursuit of salvation. Hodge dedicates almost a quarter of his second volume to the topic of imputation, while his *Systematic*'s largest single chapter, "The Means of Grace," is a nearly 250-page discussion of God as the sole arbiter in matters of salvation through a carefully argued discussion of the sacraments as vehicles of saving grace, not guarantors of it. Hodge's position throughout his *Systematic* is utterly Reformed in nature: God alone decides who is saved and who is not; there is no way to force his hand when it comes to matters of mercy and justice.

In every section of his *Systematic*, Hodge goes into far greater depth on the topics he chose to discuss than he had in his theological lectures. He was fully aware that while his *Systematic* might not be the last word in theological studies, it was his last word. So, he wrote with a comprehensive passion, pouring forth a lifetime of theological thought. He also wanted to make his thinking relevant to the current moment by putting it in the context of the day's contemporary theological discussions. Thus, his *Systematic* is full of passages citing a great range of current theological writing. For example, in his discussion of the sacrament of Communion, Hodge engaged the views of the German Lutheran Isaak Dorner and cited Dorner's immensely influential *Geschichte der protestantischen Theologie* (1867).[35] Since his time in Europe, Hodge had continued to read widely in German theology in its original language.

Two other characteristics of Hodge's *Systematic* are noteworthy. The first one concerns his long excursus on the nineteenth article of the Westminster Confession: "Of the Law of God." Hodge dedicates over two hundred pages of his *Systematic* to a detailed and culturally relevant exposition of the Ten Commandments. Hodge used the Decalogue as an opportunity to address topics of contemporary importance, including swearing oaths, observing the Sabbath, the responsibilities of parenting, political involvement, suicide, capital punishment, dueling, military service, celibacy, divorce, property law, socialism, and communism. In the midst of these wide-ranging discussions on theology's practical applications, there is a noticeable absence of any mention of slavery. Hodge incorporated much of his previous thinking found in forty years of *Repertory* articles into his *Systematic*, but on the issue of slavery he remained totally silent. After his final justification of his position soon after the Civil War, Hodge never again revisited the topic in print. Scripture may have made allowance for the institution of slavery, but American society no longer did. Obeying the sentiments of that particular shift, Hodge chose to remain silent on the institution he had done so much to defend biblically over the past forty years.

Second, one is struck by how Hodge's *Systematic* is often characterized by a softer tone than he exhibited in his *Repertory* essays. The main reason for this shift can likely be attributed to the fact that the *Systematic* was, in a way, a retrospective of his theology. He was not engaging theological issues in the heated moments of their debate as he had in the *Repertory* when he used the journal to combat various contemporary heresies. Instead, Hodge used his *Systematic* to present a panoramic view of Calvinism in the American context. A tendency toward conciliation comes across at several points in the text as exemplified when he declares that though "no sane man would deny" the truths of the Bible's Parthenon-like grandeur, there might be "a speck of sandstone" on its magnificent walls.[36] Or, when he turned his attention to Friedrich Schleiermacher, a theologian whose quasi-pantheistic ideas he had spent a lifetime attacking, and granted that this eminent German philosopher had ever been a pious and devout follower of Christ. Although Schleiermacher's teachings may have been full of error, Hodge went so far as to declare his confidence that God would overlook Schleiermacher's theological mistakes and allow him through the gates of heaven.[37]

The first two volumes of the *Systematic* were widely reviewed upon their release in 1872, and the significance of the work can be at least partially glimpsed in the fact that Baptists, Congregationalists, Methodists, Lutherans, Presbyterians, and even those at Mercersburg Seminary commented on the grandeur of the achievement. Over twenty reviews appeared by 1874, and it was clear that a wide spectrum of American Protestantism deemed the work worthy of serious consideration.[38] While each reviewer critiqued Hodge's Calvinism with differing degrees of sympathy, they universally praised the author. Hodge's long teaching career and his substantial contributions to American theological debate had earned him a place atop the theological pantheon of his day. With one voice, they agreed that the work stood as a towering "monument to the ability and untiring industry of one of the great theological instructors of this country."[39]

Hodge dotted the last "i" and crossed his last "t" on his manuscript in early October 1872, roughly a year after the appearance of the first two volumes. His final volume sped through the typesetting and printing processes, and just two months after he had submitted his final manuscript to his publisher, the Presbyterian Scribner family of New York, he held the last of three volumes in his hands.[40] The volumes sold for three dollars apiece, and Hodge received a 10 percent royalty on each volume. The *Systematic* sold at a pace that surprised both Hodge and his publisher. By the winter of 1873, readers had purchased over two thousand copies of the first two volumes, and Hodge was gratified to receive checks for some $2,600 in advances and royalties.[41] Such a sum was considerable in the publishing circles of the day. Although it was clear that the work stood more as a theological encyclopedia than a classroom textbook, sales were brisk enough that a publisher in Scotland printed two thousand copies as well.[42] So strong was the interest in the book that Hodge undertook with help of Caspar René Gregory, a recent Seminary graduate who also served as his part-time secretary, to produce an index for the three volumes. When the index appeared in 1873, it was widely lauded as the crowning touch to an already-momentous achievement.[43]

With the appearance of his *Systematic*'s third volume and an index to the entire work, Hodge stood at peace. His theology was now available not just within the hallowed halls of Princeton Seminary. God had given him enough time and energy to distill a lifetime of theological thinking and make it available for the entire English-speaking world.

55

"THE APEX OF MY LIFE"

While the *Systematic Theology* may have been the highpoint of his publishing career, the moment Hodge called the "apex of my life" took place on April 24, 1872, when over five hundred friends and family members gathered to celebrate his semi-centennial as a Seminary faculty member.[1] Such celebrations to honor long-serving and particularly eminent professors was a treasured tradition in Europe, but Hodge's jubilee was the first of its kind in an American institution of higher learning. The prime mover behind the event was Hodge's colleague and former pupil, William Henry Green, who suggested the idea to the Seminary's board of directors in the spring of 1871. The board immediately endorsed the plan with great enthusiasm and even encouraged Green to solicit funds for an endowed chair in Hodge's honor.

Green moved quickly. Within weeks he had enlisted seventy individuals from all over the country to help plan the event and solicit funds. In less than a year, Green's committee of seventy had collected over $45,000 to endow a teaching position in Hodge's honor. In addition, they had received numerous personal financial gifts for Hodge. On the day of the celebration, the committee proudly presented Hodge a check for $15,350 to do with as he saw fit.[2] Hodge was left speechless by an act of such great generosity.

As impressive as these financial gifts were, the actual event was even more striking. On the brisk April morning, over four hundred former students gathered at the Seminary and then marched in procession accompanied by other attendees to Princeton's First Presbyterian Church, where a long platform stood waiting in the chapel filled with chairs to seat an impressive number of dignitaries. As those in attendance filed in, Henry Boardman seated himself at one side of the stage while Hodge occupied the seat at the other. In between them sat delegates from various other seminaries and

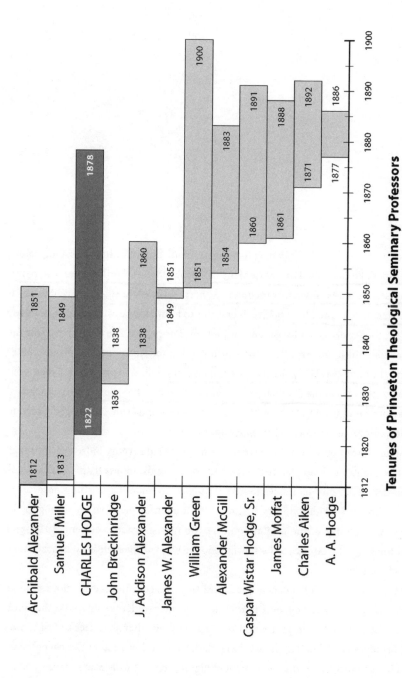

Tenures of Princeton Theological Seminary Professors

Figure 55.1 Graph of Princeton Seminary Faculty Tenures in the Nineteenth Century

colleges, as well as faculty, directors, and trustees of Princeton College and Princeton Seminary.

These dignitaries represented but a fraction of those who had been invited. Dozens who could not attend sent congratulatory letters offering their "warmest sympathies" for a man "who has so long stood among the very foremost of the defenders and expounders of revealed truth."[3] Samuel Hopkins of Auburn Theological Seminary best captured the hagiographic tone of the correspondence when he wrote that it was Hodge's "intellectual superiority commanding respect with broad good sense, cheerfulness, kindness, unaffected and unpretentious piety" that has "made him dear to so many hundreds of pupils and to so large a circle of friends."[4] Countless others sent telegrams congratulating Hodge on his accomplishments and apologizing for their absence.[5]

So great was the number in attendance that Hodge's jubilee dwarfed the Seminary's own semi-centennial celebration, which had taken place ten years earlier, an event diminished by being held in the midst of the Civil War. No such national calamity halted the splendor of Hodge's jubilee. Former students had traveled from as far away as California and Texas to attend the celebration, and missionaries on leave from India, Africa, and Ireland made the gathering global in nature. As the final members of the procession made their way into First Presbyterian Church's chapel, they found even standing room difficult to find.

After a time of prayer and singing, the gathering settled in for a morning of addresses. Appropriately, one of Hodge's former students offered the mornings opening and keynote address. The Rev. Dr. Joseph T. Duryea, class of 1859 and currently a pastor in Brooklyn, took as his inspiration the first two volumes of Hodge's recently published *Systematic Theology*. As the day progressed it became clear that Hodge's *Systematic* served as the event's intellectual centerpiece as speaker after speaker praised and commented upon the work. Many echoed the refrain that "[w]here you have taught scores, you will now teach hundreds; and where you have taught hundreds, you will now teach thousands."[6] Those assembled rejoiced at how his *Systematic* allowed Princeton's Reformed theology to be "dispersed over the four quarters of the globe."[7]

Rev. Duryea offered a largely extemporaneously oration, "The Title of Theology to Rank as a Science," an address in which he pointed to Hodge's principle contribution both in print and in the classroom as one of teaching "theology as a science."[8] Decrying the fact that the current age had sought to separate science and religion, thinking science to be concerned with knowledge and religion with faith, Duryea praised Hodge and his lifelong commitment to intimately tying the two together. Hodge's *Systematic* provided the most eloquent evidence that far from theology and science being separate endeavors, theology *was* a science. Echoing completely the sentiments Hodge had set forth in his *Systematic*, Duryea proclaimed that all truth came from the carefully executed, scientific study of natural and supernatural revelation using reason to rightly

Figure 55.2   Princeton Seminary Faculty, 1872: From left to right: James Clement Moffat, Alexander Taggart McGill, Caspar Wistar Hodge, Charles Augustus Aiken, Charles Hodge, William Henry Green. [*Special Collections, Princeton Theological Seminary Libraries*]

order and then understand the facts gathered by the senses.[9] It was a dry, erudite speech, which lasted barely forty-five minutes, but it was an able distillation of the guiding intellectual principles behind Hodge's *Systematic*.

The rest of the day was filled with more personal messages of admiration for Hodge's character, not necessarily his intellect. Directly following Duryea, Hodge's longtime friend, Henry Boardman, took the stage and represented the directors, trustees, and alumni of Princeton Seminary as he congratulated Hodge on the occasion. Boardman took time to thank Hodge for being such an "unselfish and sympathizing friend," and summed up his message by declaring that "while we honor him for the great head which God has given him, we *love* him for his still greater heart."[10]

It then came Hodge's turn to stand before those assembled, and as he left his chair to speak, every person in the chapel spontaneously rose with him. After thanking all those who came, Hodge attempted to deflect glory from himself and instead focused on the Seminary and its long tradition of orthodox teaching and its pious students. It was in the brief remarks that he offered that day that he uttered the defining, oracular statement of his life when he declared "a new idea never originated in this Seminary."[11] Reflecting on the long and distinguished history of orthodoxy inaugurated at the Seminary by Drs. Alexander and Miller, Hodge waxed eloquent on the immutable theological tradition that had forever stood as the bedrock of the school's teaching. With utter simplicity and conviction, Hodge stated that the Seminary had adhered to a single guiding principle, namely that "[t]he Bible is the word of God . . . what the Bible says, God says. That ends the matter."[12]

Critics of Hodge have long painted his comments about the Bible and the lack of originality at Princeton Seminary in the darkest hues possible, claiming that Princeton was hopelessly mired in its commitment to Reformed orthodoxy and biblical literalism. Hodge may have been a systematic thinker, but he certainly was not an innovative one. While the merits of such conclusions can be debated, such characterizations tend to devalue Hodge's greatest gift: his utter consistency of conviction. He was a man who had the rare ability to adhere to a set of doctrinal positions for an entire lifetime. For some, such consistency might show an inability to change and grow. To others, it signals a passionate ability to remain true to one's convictions. Taken in its original context, Hodge's comment does capture the very essence of the man. He was not interested in theological innovation because he believed it impossible to improve on orthodox belief. The only things that were new in orthodox theology were various heresies, and Hodge had no interest in distinguishing himself as a heretic. His role, and the role of the Seminary, had always been to be guardians of orthodoxy, not creators of new strains of Christian doctrine.

After lunch, distinguished men from all over New England continued to offer Hodge further congratulatory addresses. Among others, the impressive list of figures included James McCosh, the president of Princeton College; Henry B. Smith of Union Theological Seminary; Theodore Woolsey, the former president of Yale College; and Egbert Smyth of Andover Seminary. By the late afternoon, however, Hodge had tired, and he chose to spend the remainder of the day reclining on a sofa placed behind the speaking platform. Later, when Henry Boardman asked him how he had endured so much praise, Hodge smiled and replied that he pretended that the speakers had been talking about someone else.[13] Boardman pressed the issue by saying that Hodge should be happy indeed considering "what you have accomplished, and the universal feeling towards you."[14] Hodge stopped him at that point with a wave of his hand saying, "All that can be said is, that God has been pleased to take up a *poor little stick* and do something with it. What I have done is as nothing compared with what is done by a man who goes to Africa, and labors among a heathen tribe, and reduces their language to writing. I am not worthy to stoop down and *unloose the shoes* of such man."[15]

When evening came, Hodge retired to his home, where he continued to receive guests until late into the night. It was a particularly memorable evening because it was the last time so many of his own children would be gathered together with his brother and his family. Nine months later, Hugh returned home after visiting patients one particularly cold February night only to faint and be placed in his bed with labored breathing. As he lingered for another twenty-six hours, his family gathered around his bedside.[16] Hodge was notified of his brother's condition by telegram, but he was too sick himself with a severe fever to make the trip to Philadelphia. On February 26, 1873, Hugh Hodge died at the age of seventy-six, an unexpected and devastating blow for Hodge. Aside from his blindness, Hugh enjoyed unusually vigorous health, and there had been no hints that he might fail so quickly. Hodge soon lapsed into a deep depression complicated by a severe chest infection that lasted well over a month and nearly killed him. As he lay sick in his bed, Hodge took solace in writing his last remaining lifelong friend, John Johns, asking for his prayers and telling him that the two of them were now "left like two old trees standing almost alone."[17] Three years later, John Johns would die, leaving Hodge as the last tree standing.

56

SCIENCE AND DARWINISM

After deciding to forgo adding a fourth volume to his *Systematic* on the subject of the church, there is no indication that Hodge planned to write another book. Instead, he busied himself with enjoying his teaching and his family. Although he remained a trustee of Princeton College, he spent less and less time on administrative duties at both the College and the Seminary. He did continue to offer his Sunday afternoon conference talks in the Seminary's oratory, and occasionally he accepted invitations to preach at local churches and at important events. One such event took place in October 1873, when Hodge traveled to New York City to offer a keynote address at the Sixth General Conference of the Evangelical Alliance.

The Evangelical Alliance was an organization that had been founded in 1847 to link North American Protestants with their counterparts in Europe and Britain.[1] When the Evangelical Alliance gathered in New York in the fall of 1873, it boasted an impressive number of delegates from all over the world. The importance of the event is attested to by the fact that numerous papers, including the *New York Times*, covered it extensively in their pages, and after the conference closed, a number of attendees traveled en masse to Washington, D.C., where they met President Grant at the White House. (On their way to the nation's capital, the delegation stopped in Princeton to visit Hodge and the Seminary.)

The speech Hodge offered, "The Unity of the Church Based on Personal Union with Christ," was well received as many thought it eloquently captured the guiding spirit behind not only the New York gathering, but the ecumenical mission of the Evangelical Alliance as a whole.[2] Not everyone, however, was pleased with it, as more conservative elements among the Presbyterians, Congregationalists, Episcopalians, and Baptists felt Hodge had gone too far in his ecumenism, underplaying the importance of denominational distinctiveness.[3] Having spoken, Hodge spent the next day attending various other sessions at the event. After a talk offered by his friend James McCosh, the current president of Princeton College, entitled "Religious Aspects of the Doctrine of Development," Hodge rose and addressed an overflowing room by questioning the term "development," a word widely in use to describe various schools of thought on evolution and Darwinism. Hodge explained his query by stating

> The great question which divides theists from atheists—Christians from unbelievers—is this: Is development an intellectual process guided by God, or is it a blind process of unintelligible, unconscious force, which knows no end and adopts no means? In other words, is God the author of all we see, the creator of all the beauty and grandeur of this world, or is unintelligible force, gravity, electricity, and such like.[4]

Unknown to him at the time, this line of reasoning would become the intellectual backbone of his book, *What is Darwinism?*

The matter may have well ended with his question after McCosh's talk if the Princeton Club, a local association of Princeton's most prominent men, had not asked Hodge to spend an evening with them just three months later to speak on the question: What is Darwinism?[5] Hodge's time in New York had confirmed for him something that he had come to suspect, namely that Darwin's thinking on evolution was quickly becoming Christianity's greatest intellectual challenger. He took the opportunity of speaking to the Princeton Club to refine his own rebuttal to Darwinism. Princeton Club members received Hodge's thoughts on Darwinism so enthusiastically that he decided to spend the ensuing winter months expanding his notes on the subject into a full-length book manuscript. By the summer of 1874, Scribner, Armstrong and Company released Hodge's final book: *What is Darwinism?*

Neither Hodge's question at the Evangelical Alliance gathering, nor his talk at the Princeton Club represented his first intellectual grappling with Darwin. He had actually offered an extended critique of Darwin in his *Systematic*, where he called Darwin's theory of human development "a mere hypothesis" hopelessly weakened by the reality that it could not take into account countless facts that opposed it.[6] On the most fundamental level, Hodge dismissed Darwin's theories because they could not possibly be proved, an unforgivable sin in Hodge's mind when it came to scientific claims. Hodge held that there was a "vast difference between facts and theories," championing his old friend Joseph Henry's cardinal requirement of scientific investigation at the Smithsonian Institution, namely "that 'all unverified speculations' must be rejected."[7]

Hodge used his book on Darwinism as his final utterance on the importance of seeking a crucial harmony between science and religion in the pursuit of knowledge.

Building upon a lifelong love of science that dated all the way back to his early desire to follow his father into the field of medicine, Hodge had consistently argued throughout his life that the fields of science and theology were absolutely complementary in nature. Hodge summed up his unequivocal belief that the pursuits of science and theology were inextricably tied when he wrote: "Nature is as truly a revelation of God as the Bible, and we only interpret the Word of God by the Word of God when we interpret the Bible by science.... If the Bible cannot contradict science, neither can science contradict the Bible."[8]

Hodge's bedrock conviction that good science and sound theology were utterly compatible underlies his forty-year editorship at the *Repertory*, where nearly 20 percent of the journal's articles focused on matters of science.[9] At one point, Hodge even experimented with including a section in the *Repertory* dedicated to recent scientific advances under the title: "Quarterly Scientific Intelligence."[10] Hodge declared his desire to see the pursuit of science work hand-in-hand with theology when he wrote that "[n]o class of men stands deservedly higher in public estimation than men of science, who, while remaining faithful to their higher nature, have enlarged our knowledge of the wonderful works of God."[11]

One can see Hodge's willingness to incorporate current scientific thinking into his own theological positions throughout his *Systematic*. Particularly noticeable are the ways in which he used recent scientific work in the areas of geology and astronomy to help interpret the Bible. By the 1840s, a large number of scientists (most of whom were also devout Christians) had come to advocate the view that the world was the product of a long creation process, which made the earth much older than the commonly accepted age of some six thousand years.[12] The issue had then become: how does one reconcile Genesis's six-day creation account to the much longer creation process testified to by contemporary science? Although the strategies to reconcile the biblical and scientific accounts varied, one of the most common harmonizing methods came to be called "day-age" theories of creation, where the separate days recounted in Genesis were equated to various extended periods of geological time.[13]

Arnold Guyot, a Swiss geographer who joined the Princeton College faculty in 1854 as a professor of geology and physical geography, and a man who Hodge admired for his immense piety along with his towering intellect, made an important contribution to "day-age" scholarship by incorporating the nebular hypothesis of the French astronomer Pierre-Simon Laplace into theories of how the earth might have formed and developed. Laplace had posited a theory that our solar system had been born of a gaseous nebulae that had cooled and contracted over millions of years. Guyot taught that the different days of creation corresponded to various astronomical epochs. For example, on the first day, God formed the earth out of gaseous matter that produced light. On the second day, the nebulae had broken up into different planetary systems, while on the third day the earth had condensed into a solid globe, and so forth.[14] Hodge endorsed this "day-age" theory of Guynot's in his *Systematic Theology* and reveled in the immense benefits that came from considering God's natural and revealed revelations in tandem.[15]

The problem, as Hodge saw it, was that scientists were increasingly uninterested in weighing the truths found in scripture against what they saw as the truths of the natural world. He particularly disliked the ways in which scientists had grown to dismiss the scientific thinking of theologians and even admonished them to stay away from the sophisticated and specialized fields of scientific endeavor. Hodge passionately believed it inappropriate for scientists to "warn the theologian" away from science "as a trespasser."[16] By the time Hodge wrote *What is Darwinism?* he saw religion in a "fight for its life against a large class of scientific men" who no longer wished to pay attention to the scientific truths found in the Bible.[17]

Hodge saw the growing division between religious and scientific inquiry as "not only lamentable but revolting."[18] Infinite harm could be done when scientists recklessly formed "their theories without any regard to moral and religious truths."[19] Far worse, Hodge was disturbed by the way in which science was increasingly used as a means to denigrate and discredit Christian belief.[20] In writing *What is Darwinism?*, Hodge was doing more than engaging Darwin's thinking; he was arguing for the essential role theologians played in addressing the pressing scientific inquiries of the day.[21]

Hodge approached his critique of Darwinism in the same way he had approached countless controversial issues throughout his career. Before he set forth his argument, he clearly defined the terms involved in the issue under debate. *What is Darwinism?* was, at its core, Hodge's attempt to define exactly what one meant when one invoked Darwin's thinking, stating that "great confusion and diversity of opinion prevail as to the real views of the man whose writings have agitated the whole world, scientific and religious."[22] Hodge's book stood as an extended meditation on the essence of Darwin's thought and the implications of that thought for Reformed Christian orthodox belief.

The nub of Hodge's argument is revealed in his now famous retort to the question posed in the book's title, *What is Darwinism?* Hodge answered: "It is Atheism."[23] Darwinism was atheism not because it advocated a particular view of evolution or even that humans might be descended from apes (although he intensely disagreed with this point of view), but because "by far the most important and only distinctive element of his theory" was the idea that natural selection was "without design, being conducted by unintelligent physical causes."[24] Darwin provided a "theory of the universe" that excluded God as the agent who designed, created and sustained the world, and it was such exclusion that Hodge saw as absolutely antithetical to Christian belief.[25]

Hodge's critique of Darwin hinged on the issue of divine design, and to fully appreciate his argument, one must understand just how indebted Hodge was to William

Paley's views on natural religion. Hodge had first studied Paley as an undergraduate at Princeton College when Ashbel Green had forcefully reintroduced the work of the British philosopher into the College's curriculum. A string of major faculty figures (including Samuel Stanhope Smith, Archibald Alexander, and Samuel Miller) at both Princeton College and Seminary helped Hodge forge his concept of how theology related to the natural world. In true Paleyian fashion, Hodge saw the chief problem with Darwin's thinking to be how it argued against the critical notion of divine design.

Paley had explained nature's divine attributes through the analogy of a watch and its maker. Paley argued that if one found a watch lying by the side of a road and then proceeded to study that watch, one could not but be struck by the fact that all its parts fit together in a precise way to perform a precise function. Everything about the watch declared an intelligence behind its creation and purpose. In like manner, any prolonged investigation of the natural world could not but lead a thoughtful person to conclude that there existed a Grand Designer who had created the world with a specific purpose in mind.[26] Paley proclaimed this line of reasoning in his *Natural Theology's* subtitle: *Evidences of the Existence and Attributes of the Deity, Collected from the Appearances of Nature.*

In considering Darwin's work, it was this issue of design that most troubled Hodge. Darwin had not created the idea of evolution. (The idea could be traced back to the Greeks.) Darwin's great contribution came in a particular process of evolution he called "natural selection." Darwin had been moved forward in his thinking about evolution by puzzling over the troubling question of why there were so many different species so similar in form and function as to be practically indistinguishable. Why had a Creator chosen to create so many species that differed ever so slightly and basically fulfilled the same function? Why the needless repetition of purpose? Had a Divine Agent created a multitude of species specifically exhibiting only the slightest variations or were these species the result of "gradual accumulations of unintentional variations?"[27]

In seeking to answer this question, Darwin argued against the age-old accepted Christian wisdom that plants, animals, and humans had remained unchanged since the moment of their divine creation. Darwin argued against this eternal immutability and declared that the numerous variants found throughout nature were the result of "natural selection," a theory that posited change could be attributed to species adapting over time to different settings in order to survive. To insure survival, a species would maintain its most helpful attributes over time while those attributes that did nothing to help insure longevity fell away. Thus, for example, the reason behind such a wide variety of pigeons lay in the fact that various types of pigeons had adapted to different natural settings over time in order to survive.[28]

Hodge used *What is Darwinism?* as a full frontal assault on Darwin's notion of natural selection, arguing that Darwin substituted "the blind operation of natural causes" for God's sovereignty.[29] Darwin posited a theory of natural development that was "without design, being conducted by unintelligent physical causes."[30] The implications of Darwin's theory were profound, because his theory rejected all notions of divine teleology (the presence of design and purpose). Hodge saw no room in Darwin's thinking to account for changes in plants and animals as contingent upon "the continued cooperation and control of the divine mind, nor the original purpose of God in the constitution of the universe."[31] Instead of a Divine Being guiding nature, Darwin posed a theory whereby nature itself—through a set of random processes tied to the pursuit of survival—guided the world.

Fortunately, Hodge believed, "[t]his banishing God from the world is simply intolerable, and, blessed be his name, impossible."[32] To prove his case, Hodge called upon the longstanding tradition of the "two books" by which God could be known: the holy scriptures and the book of nature.[33] Citing the Westminster Catechism's distillation of the truths found throughout scripture, Hodge declared God to be "infinite, eternal, and unchangeable in his being, wisdom, power, holiness, goodness and truth."[34] The Bible was unequivocal in its teaching that God was everywhere powerful, present, and purposeful in his creation. Hodge then turned to nature and found nowhere evidence enough to support Darwin's ateleological claims. Quite to the contrary, nature through its endless complexities—from organs as complicated as the eye to the sophisticated processes of flower pollination—made it "absolutely impossible to believe that it is not a work of design."[35]

Essential to note here is that while Hodge was always willing to entertain science as a means to interpreting scripture, he varied in his openness to adjusting scriptural interpretations based on current scientific evidence. He showed himself receptive to the largely speculative claims being put forth in geology and astronomy in part because these theories were being widely accepted by a great number of religious men he respected. A veritable Who's Who of eminent Christian scientists, including Princeton's Arnold Guyot, Amherst's Edward Hitchcock, Scotland's Thomas Chalmers, the Smithsonian's Joseph Henry, McGill's John Dawson and Yale's Benjamin Silliman, all joined in testifying to the truth of the epoch theory when it came to reconciling the age of the earth with the creation account found in Genesis.[36] Hodge was willing to trust the Christian character and the scientific conclusions of these men, and allowed this trust to help him adjust his own views of scripture in light of recent scientific work in the physical sciences.

In contrast, Hodge proved far less open to considering changing his biblical interpretations in light of new scholarship in biology. Although Christian scholars, including his own friend James McCosh and the famed Harvard Botanist, Asa Gray, were sympathetic to strains of Darwin's thinking, Hodge sidestepped these endorsements and any biological evidence for "natural selection" because Darwin's theory so directly attacked his high Calvinist notion of the absolute sovereignty of God.[37] A career full of sustained and rigorous debate on the nature of human agency in revival, the salvific efficacy found in the sacraments, and the precise nature of Christ's atonement had hardened Hodge against any theory that questioned God's omnipotent involvement in every aspect of his creation. In the end, Hodge was suspect of advances in the biological sciences such as Darwin's because they argued against "any intention, purpose, or cooperation of God."[38] Such "advances" reduced humans (God's most magnificent creation) to accidental morally superior beings who, to use Darwin's own words, were "descended from a hairy quadruped, furnished with a tail and pointed ears, probably arboreal in its habits."[39] On the most fundamental level, Hodge could not reconcile Darwin's views "with the declarations of the Scriptures" concerning God's character, the teleological nature of his creation, and the fact that humans had been created in the image of God.[40] While science could certainly influence Hodge on certain scriptural interpretations, when it came to theories that threatened the core of his Confessional beliefs, Hodge was absolutely immoveable.

Hodge did make a distinction between being a Darwinist and being an evolutionist. Although he could not reconcile himself to evolution, he granted that many Christians of repute had. Hodge allowed for the possibility that Christians could be an evolutionist if they believed that it was God who introduced and then guided the processes of evolution to accomplish his purposes.[41] Not only did James McCosh and Asa Gray hold this position, but ultimately Hodge's son Archie, as well as his nephew Willie, would adopt this view.[42] Hodge respected Darwin's commitment to science, as seen in how during the final weeks of his life he reread Darwin's *Voyage of a Naturalist* and commented that he found the book "remarkable and delightful," but he never made peace with what he saw as Darwin's ateleological theory of natural selection.[43] He did, however, in making a distinction between Darwinism and evolution, help open the door to the adoption of the increasingly popular view of theistic evolution, namely that God had used evolution as means in accomplishing his greater goals in his creation. It was a door that many who came after Hodge at the Seminary walked through.

57

"O DEATH, WHERE IS THY STING?"

As Hodge was putting the finishing touches on *What is Darwinism?* the Seminary's trustees began to discuss who might replace him when he retired. They quickly came to the conclusion that the best choice was Hodge's own son, Archibald Alexander, who currently served as the Professor of Systematic Theology at Western Theological Seminary in western Pennsylvania. Hodge, however, thought such a move premature, so the matter dropped. Four years later when his health began to fail, he was willing to entertain the idea. Hodge had once commented to a friend that he wished to see his eightieth year, but had little desire to see his eighty-first (an echo of Archibald Alexander's own sentiment that men were of little use after eighty).[1] So, in 1877 after Hodge had reached his eightieth year, the trustees invited the younger Hodge to become his father's assistant and eventual successor. Archie accepted the invitation, and over the next year he taught alongside his father in the four classes Hodge continued to teach each week.[2]

With Archie as successor, the board of trustees ensured Hodge's theological legacy, at least for a time. Archie adhered to his father's confessional beliefs, with some minor variations, and through his own *Outlines of Theology*, *The Atonement*, and *Popular Lectures on Theological Themes*, he popularized the most central aspects of Hodge's teaching.[3] Archie proved to be an excellent teacher. When students were baffled by some particularly difficult theological concept, "he swept the universe for illustrations, and poured them out so copiously, and with such manifest spontaneity, that they overwhelmed him with their applause."[4] Sadly, he also had a tragically short career at Princeton, dying suddenly just nine years after taking up the post.

Hodge not only continued to teach, but he frequently contributed to the student Sunday afternoon conferences in the Seminary's oratory. His final conference talks

Figure 57.1 *Archibald Alexander Hodge*: Archibald Alexander Hodge graduated from Princeton Seminary in 1847. That same year he got married and left to become a missionary in India. Because of health problems, he returned to the United States after three years abroad. He then served in various pastoral and teaching positions until succeeding his father as Professor of Didactic and Exegetical Theology at Princeton Theological Seminary. [*Special Collections, Princeton Theological Seminary Libraries*]

became ever more focused on the eternal nature of God's Kingdom, and beginning in 1875, one notes that he increasingly took as his topic obtaining a place in heaven. One of his most striking offerings focused on 1 Corinthians 15:55: "O Death, Where is they Sting?" Here, while Hodge passionately declared that "Death is the King of Terrors, the event of all others the most to be dreaded," he just as earnestly exhorted his listeners to lead faithful lives in Christ in order to defeat death.[5] His final years saw him offer his students numerous heartfelt reflections on finishing the race of faith with titles such as: "Death," "Follow me," "No man having put his hand to the plow and looking back," "Loyalty to Christ," "Dying unto Sin," "Love Not the World," and (his final talk in the summer of 1877) "What Must I Do to Be Saved?"[6]

On May 16, 1878, Hodge traveled to Washington, D.C., to perform what turned out to be his last public duty. He journeyed to the nation's capital to offer a prayer at the funeral of his old friend, Joseph Henry. Henry's funeral was an affair of national pomp and circumstance. So famous had Henry become through his role as founding president of the Smithsonian Institution that the White House, Congress, and the Supreme Court all closed down to attend the funeral ceremony. Thus, after singing an anthem by Mendelssohn, Hodge stood and prayed before President Rutherford B. Hayes, Vice President William A. Wheeler, Supreme Court Justices, Congressmen and the countless other dignitaries packed into the New York Avenue Presbyterian Church to mourn the loss of one of the country's most renowned scientific minds.[7] Overcome by his own grief, Hodge found it difficult at first even to stand for his prayer, but he quickly rallied and delivered such an energetic and heartfelt prayer that the moment seemed to transform the frail and elderly Hodge into a much younger man.

Henry had once said that Hodge "had made the best use of his talents his life through of any man he ever knew."[8] Hodge now offered similar kind words regarding Henry. In his prayer, Hodge rejoiced that "Almighty God" had endowed Henry with "such rare gifts—intellectual, moral and spiritual," and had spared him to a "good old age . . . to accomplish so much for the increase of human knowledge and for the good of his fellow men."[9] It was a moving prayer, and unknown to anyone there, including Hodge himself, it would be the last time he would ever set foot inside a church.

Hodge's health rapidly declined after the ceremony. He was so weak as he made his way back to Princeton that Wolcot Jackson, a family friend and the general superintendent of the New Jersey division of the Pennsylvania Railroad Company, ordered an express train to make a special stop at Princeton Junction railway station to deliver Hodge home from Baltimore.[10] By early June, Hodge could no longer negotiate the stairs up to his bedroom, so a bed was made up for him in his house's back parlor, a room adjacent to his study. With help, Hodge shuffled to his beloved chair in his office for a portion of each day to read or write letters. On the Monday before his death, he showed a particular reticence to get up from his chair, rightly suspecting that he would never sit in it again.

Hodge took time in his final days to set his affairs in order. He asked two of his seminary colleagues, Charles Aiken and William Green, to come to his study to witness the signing of his last will and testament. It was a strikingly simple document. He made few special bequests, leaving two-thirds of his property to his wife and the rest to his children, who he enjoined to "share and share alike."[11] Then, on June 19, at six in the evening, Hodge quietly passed from life into death, his bedside surrounded by his wife, children, and older grandchildren. Near the end, he murmured to his wife, "My mind is at rest, but I am too weak to talk about it," but upon seeing the sadness in his daughter Mary's face, he said: "to be absent from the body is to be present with the Lord."[12] His death came in the middle of Princeton College's annual commencement celebrations, and it sent waves of grief through the multitude who had gathered for the week's events.

As news of his death spread, memorials and messages of condolence flooded in from around the world. One writer captured the sentiment of the moment by lamenting that with Hodge's passing, Princeton had "lost its greatest ornament, the Presbyterian Church its most precious gem, the American Church her greatest earth-born luminary."[13] Those who paid him honor agreed with a single voice that his influence on American and European Christian thought "was greater than that of any man in the Presbyterian Church," and that "no Protestant divine in our day has done more than he in the elucidation and defence of the doctrines set forth in our Confession and Catechism."[14] Even those who disagreed with his theological views were quick to admit that his "mind and beautifully adorned life [represented] the greatest result of our Christian intellectual development."[15] Many a memorial writer affirmed that Hodge had been "the ablest and most distinguished representative of theological scholarship which America has produced."[16]

As laudatory as the remarks upon his contributions to the church and theology were, one is struck by an even stronger note of praise running through these testimonials. Hodge may have had an incredible mind, but he touched lives in a more profound way through his pious and benevolent character. Those who knew him well were quick to recall a man "luminous with the spirit of the indwelling Christ," and remembered him for his "[d]evout, reverent, sincere, fearless, intensely earnest and honest" character.[17] Many agreed that his "genuine kindliness of heart and largeness of soul" challenged the Calvinist stereotypes of sternness and severity.[18] Others recalled him as "the sweetest, gentlest and most lovable of men. His face itself was a benediction."[19] Hodge's colleague William Green reminded those who had known Hodge of his "cheerful affability, rising at times into hilarity."[20] Hodge had loved to laugh, and he liked nothing better than a good joke or a humorous story. The editor of one journal wrote that he had "seldom seen a man more genial and attractive than this representative of the American Presbyterians" and that his "parlour-study [was] one of the cheeriest glimpses" he had ever had of the inside of an American home.[21] In summing up Hodge, Lyman Atwater noted that there were precious "few men who had so many elements of greatness, with so little that one could wish otherwise."[22] Posterity might remember Hodge for his magnificent mind, but for those who knew him best, what set him apart was his even-more-magnificent heart.

Hodge was buried in Princeton's central cemetery, located less than a half a mile from Nassau Hall. As his sons lowered their father's body into the grave, Hodge came to rest just yards away from a host of American Protestant luminaries, including his treasured mentors and colleagues, Archibald Alexander and Samuel Miller, as well as Jonathan Edwards and John Witherspoon. Buried in such sacred ground, Hodge—a man who one mourner described as "not only *par excellence* the Calvinist theologian of America, but the Nestor of all American theology"—joined God's invisible communion of the saints in death as he had in life.[23]

EPILOGUE

HODGE'S LEGACY

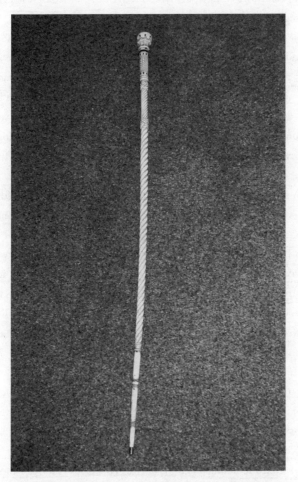

Figure 58.1 *The Cane of Orthodoxy*: While on his deathbed, Ar-chibald Alexander presented this ornately-carved bone walking stick, a gift he had received from an Hawaiian king, to Hodge. He then told Hodge: "You must leave this to your successor in office, that it may be handed down as a kind of symbol of orthodoxy." [*Special Collections, Princeton Theological Seminary Libraries*]

Even allowing for the hyperbole that so often fills funeral orations and obituary notices, it was clear that Hodge's contemporaries considered him to be the leading conservative theologian of his day, calling him "one of the ripest scholars and most comprehensive thinkers that America" had ever produced.[1] Yet today, Hodge has drifted to the outer margins of the American religious history, a largely forgotten and forgettable figure. Given this disparity between Hodge's time and our own, one wonders whether Hodge is as totally absent from the American Protestant landscape as might first appear. More simply put: Does Hodge have a theological legacy, and if he does, what might it be?

The answer to such a query is by necessity complex, and perhaps the best place to begin is in looking at the reunion of the Old and New Schools in 1869. Hodge had stood solidly against the reunion because he felt that while the two factions shared certain common cultural and political affinities, they did not agree on key points of doctrine. Hodge feared that nothing but vitriolic and hurtful discord would eventually result from a reunion that lacked any mutually-agreed-upon theological foundation. In many ways, his dour forecasts of a Presbyterian unified future proved prophetic.

On the heels of the reunion, both the Old and New Schools enacted various ventures intended to bind the two groups together. Emblematic of such endeavors was the renaming and reconceptualizing of the *Princeton Review*. A. A. Hodge joined with Charles Briggs of Union Theological Seminary to inaugurate a new, more inclusive journal called *The Presbyterian Review* in 1880. The journal was intended as a place where the Old and New Schools might come together to discuss the key theological and ecclesiastical issues facing the denomination as Hodge solicited articles from the conservative Old School perspective and Briggs did the same for the New School.

Even with these harmonious intentions, *The Presbyterian Review's* essays became ever-more-rancorous, as did the discussions they catalyzed. Its articles captured many of the longstanding tensions between the two schools. Conservative Old Schoolers positioned themselves as the guardians and preservers of historic Reformed orthodoxy. New Schoolers saw themselves as more modern in their impulses and more ready to strike mediating positions between historic orthodoxy and new cultural settings and scientific discoveries.[2] These two basic impulses, conservative and modernizing, could not hold together in the coming years, and Princeton Seminary in the opening decades of the twentieth century became one of the great battlegrounds between these two factions.

The Old School patriarch Archibald Alexander had symbolized the fixed nature of historic orthodoxy on his deathbed by giving Hodge an ornately carved bone cane, entreating his younger colleague to leave it to his successor in like manner as

Figure 58.2 *Benjamin Breckinridge Warfield*: Benjamin Breckinridge Warfield studied under Hodge at Princeton Theological Seminary and then continued his studies in Europe. He succeeded A. A. Hodge as Professor of Didactic and Polemic Theology in 1887 and taught at the Seminary until his death in 1921. [*Special Collections, Princeton Theological Seminary Libraries*]

"kind of symbol of orthodoxy."[3] Hodge treasured the cane and Alexander's theologically conservative vision for the Seminary throughout his long career. While Hodge did not literally pass off the walking stick at his death, he along with the Seminary's trustees metaphorically gave the symbolic cane to Archie when they appointed him his father's successor in 1878. In this way, Archie came to embody Hodge's theological legacy.

Upon Archie's death, the cane once again symbolically passed from one conservative hand to another, this time to Benjamin Breckinridge Warfield, a former student of Hodge's and the most prolific and brilliant of those who would take up Hodge's theological mantle at Princeton. Warfield taught at the Seminary for thirty-four years. While there, he instructed 2,700 students and published dozens of monographs, essays, and short reflections, as well as editing *The Presbyterian and Reformed Review* (later renamed *The Princeton Theological Review*) for over twenty years. Although Warfield did not agree with Hodge on every issue (as seen in his great respect for Darwin), he became one of the most vigorous and thoughtful defenders of Princeton's conservative brand of Reformed theology. His views were aptly and succinctly captured when he wrote: "Calvinism is just religion in its purity. We have only, therefore, to conceive of religion in its purity, and that is Calvinism."[4]

When Warfield died in 1921, the cane of orthodoxy metaphorically passed once again, this time into the hands of one of Warfield's students, J. Gresham Machen, who had joined the Seminary faculty in 1906 and became its Assistant Professor of the New Testament in 1914. In the coming years, Machen became the Seminary's foremost defender of its long-held conservative notions of historic Reformed orthodoxy and published influential books championing the tradition such as *The Origin of Paul's Religion* (1921) and *Christianity and Liberalism* (1923).

Machen became convinced that the modern and conservative elements of Christianity would be best served if separated, and Princeton Seminary became a microcosm of these larger tensions in American Presbyterianism more specifically and American Protestantism more generally. As the Seminary increasingly welcomed into its faculty ranks more progressive Christian thinkers, Machen felt that the school had betrayed its theological heritage. In 1929, he helped lead a group of disgruntled conservative Princeton professors to leave the Seminary and found Westminster Seminary in Philadelphia. Eventually expelled from the American Presbyterian Church for his conservative views and the relentless conviction with which he pursued them, Machen proved pivotal in the founding of the Orthodox Presbyterian Church in the United States. Machen and his compatriots built much of their rebellion against Princeton and the organization of a rival conservative seminary on an unwavering

Figure 58.3 *J. Gresham Machen*: J. Gresham Machen studied under B. B. Warfield at Princeton Theological Seminary. He took a teaching post at the Seminary in 1906. He became one of the nation's leading New Testament scholars and spent much of his career denouncing the insidious influence of modernism on historic Presbyterian orthodoxy. In 1929, his convictions led him to withdraw from Princeton Theological Seminary with a number of other professors to found the more conservative Westminster Theological Seminary in Philadelphia. [*Special Collections, Princeton Theological Seminary Libraries*]

commitment to the conservative, Old School theological tradition championed by Charles Hodge.[5]

In one sense then, Hodge's legacy moved from Princeton to the more conservative confines of Westminster Seminary, and from the American Presbyterian Church more generally to the Orthodox Presbyterian Church. Through their teaching and writing, Warfield and Machen also made Hodge a much-cited and respected figure in the growing Protestant Fundamentalist movement of the early twentieth century. Named for the twelve-volume paperback series called *The Fundamentals* (1910–1915), American Protestant Fundamentalism showed itself to be preoccupied in the opening decades of the twentieth century with matters of doctrine, a primary concern for Hodge and his successors. Even though many Fundamentalists did not agree with many of the age-old Princeton beliefs because of their dispensational pre-millennial propensities, they did appreciate Hodge's longstanding commitments to God's sovereignty, humanity's total depravity, the reality of miracles, and his view of the sacraments as signs not guarantees of God's salvation.

Perhaps most importantly, Fundamentalists adhered closely to the writings of both the younger and older Hodges, as well as B. B. Warfield, on the inspiration and inerrancy of scripture. Warfield was particularly important in this regard. Beginning with a landmark essay entitled "Inspiration" he coauthored with A. A. Hodge, Warfield spent his career carefully crafting a position on the inerrant nature of the scriptures in their original manuscripts.[6] It was a line of thinking Charles Hodge had hinted at, but had not codified with Warfield's vigor.[7] Warfield went so far as to declare in later writings that the weight of evidence was on others to disprove his theory on inerrancy by somehow discovering the original manuscripts to show him that they did indeed contain errors.[8] As late as the 1970s, Warfield was still serving as a pivotal authority on the inerrant nature of scripture for Fundamentalists as they found themselves engaged in a "Battle for the Bible" with various wings of American Protestantism, a fight inspired by Harold Lindsell's book of the same name.[9] Thus, Hodge's thoughts on biblical inspiration as popularized through Warfield's writings helped establish Hodge as a type of patron saint of inerrancy for countless twentieth-century Fundamentalist Bible colleges and seminaries.[10]

While Hodge's thinking has been long revered in these more conservative circles, his theological legacy has by no means been confined there. The views Hodge developed, refined, and propagated helped shape many pivotal strains of Calvinism that run throughout a broader spectrum of twentieth- and twentieth-first-century American Christian evangelicalism.[11] In this larger context, perhaps Hodge's most enduring influence came in his life's dual intellectual focus: a strict adherence to a brand of Calvinism interpreted through the Westminster Confession and the Enlightenment philosophical school known as Scottish Common Sense Realism.

Calvinism provided the backbone of all of Hodge's theology. Memorizing its central tenets as a boy through his study of the Westminster Catechism, Hodge remained solidly committed throughout his life to the confessional faith he learned as a youth. His theological thinking became the Calvinist plumb line not only for such important Presbyterian figures as Machen and Warfield, but for legions of conservative thinkers in a wide array of denominations from early Baptists such as James Boyce, the founding president of Southern Baptist Theological Seminary in Kentucky, to more recent conservative evangelical thinkers such as R. C. Sproul, John F. MacArthur, and John Piper.[12]

Hodge had also been exposed early to Scottish Common Sense Realism and became an immensely influential disseminator of this philosophical school of thought among American Protestants. Scottish Realism provided Hodge with an unshakeable belief in the human ability to arrive at a right conception of the truth by using one's mind to sift through the evidence the world presented to one's senses. Hodge's twin convictions that sensory input was reliable and that God had provided clear clues to his presence in the world became cornerstone beliefs for much of twentieth-century American evangelical theology. The apologetics movement of the later twentieth century, where theologians like E. J. Carnell and popularizers like Josh McDowell held forth that the world carefully studied and rightly interpreted provided ample "evidence that demands a verdict" concerning the truth of Christ's teachings, is but one of the most vibrant continuations of a type of thinking Hodge was pivotal in weaving into the warp and woof of American Protestantism.[13]

Hodge's Common Sense exaltation of the role and ability of reason in biblical interpretation helped establish a kind of extreme evidential, systematic biblicism in the decades following his life. Hodge considered the Bible to be humanity's primary storehouse of "truth which the theologian" must "collect, authenticate, arrange, and exhibit in their internal relation to each other."[14] His work in systematizing and harmonizing various biblical texts had two long-lasting consequences. First, it laid the groundwork for countless evangelical theologians who followed him. Just one example can be found in the work of Lewis Sperry Chafer, the founding president of Dallas Theological Seminary, a bastion of American Dispensational theology, an evangelical theological tradition that owes much to Hodge's commitment to Common Sense Realism.[15] Chafer seemingly channeled Hodge when he composed his eight-volume *Systematic Theology* (1947), where he defined theology as the "collecting, scientifically arranging, comparing, exhibiting, and defending of all facts from" the Bible and other manifestations of God's work.[16]

Second, the centrality Hodge placed on the Bible and the confidence he put in the human mind's ability to understand it helped establish a pronounced *sola scriptura* ethos among twenty and twenty-first-century American evangelicals.[17] For them, there existed no higher praise than to be known like their Reformation and Puritan forefathers as a People of the Book, or, more commonly: "Bible-believing Christians."[18] In a way that even Hodge would have tempered, large sections of American Protestants over the past century have emphasized the Bible—not religious traditions, creeds, or cultural variations—as the taproot of theology and the only right source of guidance on issues both religious and secular.

Hodge also relentlessly championed the view that all people could understand the Bible. In true Scottish Realist fashion, he argued that the language and meaning of the scriptures was "self-evident." Although the Bible could be difficult to understand at points, in it God had not given us a puzzle too obscure to understand. Hodge never turned from his belief that the Bible could be understood by all people simply by the "use of ordinary means."[19] Everyone could be comforted by the fact that the Bible said what it meant and meant what it said.[20] Hodge's debates with Horace Bushnell and Edwards Amasa Park provided a defensive bulwark utilized by a host of later conservative biblical commentators who argued against the need for advanced theological degrees and fancy philosophical training in order to understand the plain truths of the Bible. They agreed with Hodge that interpreting the Bible was a simple and straightforward process, accessible to any pious and fair-minded man or woman.

Finally, Hodge's work on the definition of the church and its role in politics still has admirers today. Hodge spent much of the last third of his life struggling with just how one might define the church and what responsibility the church and its members had in larger societal settings. The Civil War forced him to confront issues of civic involvement that reached far beyond traditional notions of the separate spheres of church and state. Hodge engaged in discussions that focused on what it meant to be both a Christian and an American citizen, offering a sophisticated—and sometimes contradictory—understanding of how the church was not in the business of legislating morality, yet there were moments when moral action was demanded of the church, tasking Christians with a sacred duty to "bring truth to bear on the minds of their fellow-citizens."[21]

The figure of Hodge may have largely disappeared from the historical landscape of American religion, but his thinking has remained a vibrant part of a wide range of American Protestant theology up to the current day. Hodge was no theological innovator, and he reveled in the fact that he was not. He was, however, an articulate defender of a certain Reformed Calvinist theological tradition rooted in the interpretative prowess of such figures as Francis Turretin. More liberal American Protestantism may have little use for such traditional Augustinian Calvinism, but in many conservative theological circles Hodge's influence is still felt and his work is still appreciated. Countless American Christians still carry some portion of Princeton Seminary's cane of orthodoxy, many of whom having no idea that it was Charles Hodge who passed it on to them.

NOTES

Abbreviations Used in Notes

ACR *American Church Review*

AGP Ashbel Green Papers, 1744–1958, Collection #C0257, Firestone Library, Department of Rare Books and Special Collections, Princeton University.

APR *American Presbyterian Review*

AQ *American Quarterly*

BDA *Boston Daily Advertiser*

BOQR *Boston Quarterly Review*

BQ *Baptist Quarterly*

BQR *Baptist Quarterly Review*

BR *Biblical Repertory: A Collection of Tracts in Biblical Literature*

BRPR *Biblical Repertory and Princeton Review*

BRQR *British Quarterly Review*

BRTR *Biblical Repertory and Theological Review*

BS *Bibliotheca Sacra*

CA *Christian Advocate*

CH *Church History*

CHM Charles Hodge Manuscript Collection, Princeton Theological Seminary, Library Special Collections.

CHP Charles Hodge Papers, 1773–1930, Collection #C0261, Firestone Library, Department of Rare Books and Special Collections, Princeton University.

CHPC Charles Hodge, *The Constitutional History of the Presbyterian Church*, 2 vols. (Philadelphia, Pa.: William S. Martien, 1839–1840).

CHR John W. Stewart and James H. Moorhead, eds., *Charles Hodge Revisited: A Critical Appraisal of His Life and Work* (Grand Rapids, Mich.: William B. Eerdmans Publishing, 2002).

CONH Charles Hodge, *The Constitutional History of the Presbyterian Church in the United States of America*, 2 vols. (Philadelphia, Pa.: Presbyterian Board of Publication, 1851).

CQ *Congregational Quarterly*

CR *Christian Review*

CU *Christian Union*

FL Firestone Library, Department of Rare Books and Special Collections, Princeton University.

FYFL John Hall, ed., *Forty Year's Familiar Letters of James W. Alexander*, 2 vols. (New York: Charles Scribner, 1860).

HSP Historical Society of Pennsylvania

JAH	*Journal of American History*
JEH	*Journal of Ecclesiastical History*
JET	Hodge's Journal of European Travels, Charles Hodge Manuscript Collection, Box 16, Folder 4, Princeton Theological Seminary, Library Special Collections.
JHI	*Journal of the History of Ideas*
JPH	*Journal of Presbyterian History*
LAA	James W. Alexander, *The Life of Archibald Alexander* (New York: Charles Scribner, 1854).
LCH	Archibald Alexander Hodge, *The Life of Charles Hodge* (New York: Charles Scribner's Sons, 1880).
LSM	Samuel Miller Jr., *The Life of Samuel Miller*, 2 vols. (Philadelphia, Pa.: Claxton, Remsen and Haffelfinger, 1869).
MFH	Hugh L. Hodge, *Memoranda of Family History Dictated by Hugh L. Hodge* (n.p., 1903).
MIN	*Minutes of the General Assembly of the Presbyterian Church in the United States of America* (Philadelphia, Pa.: Stated Clerk of the General Assembly, 1789–1869).
MQR	*Methodist Quarterly Review*
MR	*Mercersburg Review*
MUDD	Seeley G. Mudd Manuscript Library, Princeton University Archives, Department of Rare Books and Special Collections, Princeton University Library.
NA	*North American*
NAT	*The Nation*
NE	*New Englander*
NEQ	*New England Quarterly*
NYO	*New York Observer*
NYT	*New York Times*
PG	*Pennsylvania Gazette*
PH	*Princeton History*
PMHB	*Pennsylvania Magazine of History and Biography*
PQPR	*Presbyterian Quarterly and Princeton Review*
PR	*Presbyterian Review*
PRE	*Presbyterian*
PRR	*The Presbyterian and Reformed Review*
PSB	*Princeton Seminary Bulletin*
PTS	Princeton Theological Seminary, Library Special Collections
PULC	*The Princeton University Library Chronicle*
QCS	*Quarterly Christian Spectator*
QR	*Quarterly Review of the Evangelical Lutheran Church*
RO	Charles Hodge, *A Commentary on the Epistle to the Romans* (Philadelphia, Pa.: Grigg & Elliot, 1835).
SPR	*Southern Presbyterian Review*
ST	Charles Hodge, *Systematic Theology*, 3 vols. (New York: Charles Scribner's Sons, 1872–1873).

TAPS   *Transactions of the American Philosophical Society*
WID   Charles Hodge, *What is Darwinism?* (New York: Scribner, Armstrong, and
        Company, 1874).
WMQ   *William and Mary Quarterly*
WTJ   *Westminster Theological Journal*
WOL   Charles Hodge, *The Way of Life* (Philadelphia, Pa.: American Sunday-
        School Union, 1841).

Notes

Large portions of the Special Collections of the Firestone Library at Princeton University, the Princeton University Archives located in the Seely G. Mudd Manuscript Library at Princeton University, and the Special Collections of Princeton Theological Seminary Libraries have been used in the course of this biography by the kind permission of each of these institutions.

Prologue

1. Weather recorded in Charles Hodge Memorandum Book, Vol. 6, p. 115, CHM, Box 30, Folder 3.
2. Letter from Columbia faculty, Apr. 8, 1872, CHM, Box 32, Folder 5.
3. LCH, 257.
4. Ralph J. Danhof, *Charles Hodge as Dogmatician* (Goes, the Netherlands: Osterbaan and le Cointre, 1929), 171. D. James Kennedy and Jerry Newcombe, *How Would Jesus Vote?* (Colorado Springs, Colo.: Waterbrook Press, 2008), 56.
5. In the spring of 1989, a group of Princeton Theological Seminary students removed Hodge's portrait from its place in Hodge Hall and replaced it with a signed petition protesting the school's "commemoration of a man who advocated the enslavement, oppression, and disenfranchisement of African Americans and women." Hodge's portrait was eventually rehung, but not before a flurry of documents were circulated on the appropriateness of publicly remembering him as a key figure in the school's history. PTS, William Harris's personal loose file on Charles Hodge.
6. Danhof, *Charles Hodge*, 172. See also Sydney E. Ahlstrom, "Theology in America: A Historical Survey," in *The Shaping of American Religion*, ed. James Ward Smith and A. Leland Jamison (Princeton, N.J.: Princeton University Press, 1961), 262–263.
7. John W. Stewart, "Introducing Charles Hodge to Postmoderns," CHR, 36–39.

Chapter 1: Andrew Hodge, Family Patriarch

1. It is estimated that as many as one-quarter of a million Scotch-Irish came to settle in the colonies in the eighteenth century, about one in ten Americans at the time. Ron Chepesiuk, *The Scotch-Irish: From the North of Ireland to the Making of America* (Jefferson, N.C.: McFarland, 2000), 137. See also Wayland Fuller Dunaway, *The Scotch-Irish of Colonial Pennsylvania* (Chapel Hill: University of North Carolina Press, 1944), 34–35; Russell F. Weigley et al., *Philadelphia: A 300-Year History* (New York: W. W. Norton, 1982), 45. An excellent treatment of the role of the Scotch-Irish in the founding of early New England culture can be found in Patrick Griffin, *The People with No Name: Ireland's Ulster Scots, America's Scots Irish, and the Creation of a British Atlantic World, 1689–1764* (Princeton, N.J.: Princeton University Press, 2001).

2. For information on the shipping schedules and destinations of the Hodges' ships, see PG, Apr. 3, 1740; July 17, 1740; Dec. 4, 1740; Oct. 1, 1741. The Hodges had added another ship, *The Dolphin*, to their fleet by 1751. PG, June 6, 1751.

3. Frank Willing Leach, "The Philadelphia of our Ancestors," NA (Sunday, June 14, 1908): 1.

4. PG, June 7, 1764.

5. Weigley, *Philadelphia*, 208.

6. Harrold E. Gillingham, "Some Colonial Ships Built in Philadelphia," PMHB 56:2 (1932): 181. Whitfield J. Bell Jr., "Addenda to Watson's Annals of Philadelphia," PMHB 98:2 (Apr. 1974): 139.

7. One mark of Andrew Hodge's business success can be seen in how he was able to join an influential Philadelphia business consortium in 1767 which bought large tracts of land in Nova Scotia to sell to potential settlers. The venture had mixed results, but it was a clear indication of Andrew Hodge's wealth and importance in Philadelphia's business community. William Otis Sawtelle, "Acadia: The Pre-Loyalist Migration and the Philadelphia Plantation," PMHB 51 (1927): 278–284. PG, Jan. 23, 1767 and Apr. 7, 1768.

8. MFH, 21.

9. Bell, "Addenda to Watson's Annals," 140.

10. For the importance of carriages in early Philadelphian society, see Robert F. Oaks, "Big Wheels in Philadelphia: Du Simitiere's List of Carriage Owners," PMHB 95:3 (July 1971): 351–362. Andrew Hodge's equipage is noted on page 360.

11. Ruth Y. Johnston, "American Privateers in French Ports, 1776-1778" PMHB 53:4 (1929): 368.

12. Leach, "Philadelphia of our Ancestors," 1.

13. PG, July 5, 1780.

14. Andrew Hodge's oldest daughter, Margaret, married John Bubenheim Bayard, a respected and well-to-do merchant in Philadelphia, who was elected to the Continental Congress in 1785, and became close friends with Alexander Hamilton and Elias Boudinot. Andrew and Jane's second daughter, Agnes, married James Ashton Bayard, a medical doctor who lived in Wilmington, Delaware. Providing yet more evidence of the profound interconnectedness of the families, James received his medical training alongside Charles Hodge's father, Hugh Hodge, under Dr. Cadwalder, with whom they both held medical apprenticeships. A good overview of the Bayard family and their influence in America can be found in James Grant Wilson, *Colonel John Bayard and the Bayard Family of America* (New York: Trow's Printing & Bookbinding, 1885).

Chapter 2: Presbyterian Heritage

1. Wayland Fuller Dunaway, *The Scotch-Irish of Colonial Pennsylvania* (Chapel Hill: University of North Carolina Press), 33.

2. Harry S. Stout, *The Divine Dramatist: George Whitefield and the Rise of Modern Evangelicalism* (Grand Rapids, Mich.: William B. Eerdmans, 1991), 85.

3. Stout, *Divine Dramatist*, 33.

4. Russell F. Weigley et al., *Philadelphia: A 300-Year History* (New York: W. W. Norton, 1982), 49.

5. J. Thomas Scharf and Thompson Westcott, *History of Philadelphia* (Philadelphia: L. H. Everts, 1884), 2:1264.

6. As quoted in Weigley, *Philadelphia*, 49. In the 1740s, Franklin became the first American publisher of Whitefield's sermons and later served as the Pennsylvania agent for collecting funds for Whitefield's Georgia orphanage. Stout, *Divine Dramatist*, 220.

7. E. R. Beadle, *The Old and the New, 1743–1876* (n.p., 1876), 25.

8. These distinctions between New and Old Sides are, of course, simplified. The differences that motivated each party were complex, driven both by doctrinal differences and the various personalities involved. A concise statement of the differences between the two parties can be found in L. H. Butterfield, *John Witherspoon Comes to America: A Documentary Account Based Largely on New Material* (Princeton, N.J.: Princeton University Library, 1953), 1–2.

9. Beadle, *Old and the New*, 21–22.

10. Beadle, *Old and the New*, 22.

11. LCH, 4.

12. Beadle, *Old and the New*, 26–27.

13. Beadle, *Old and the New*, 26.

14. Milton J. Coalter, *Gilbert Tennent, A Son of Thunder: A Case Study of Continental Pietism's Impact on the First Great Awakening in the Middle Colonies* (Westport, Conn.: Greenwood Press, 1986), 44–45; 73.

15. Coalter, *Gilbert Tennent*, 75; 185.

16. Samuel Finley, *The Successful Minister of Christ Distinguished in Glory* (Philadelphia, Pa.: William Bradford, 1764), 20.

17. Finley, *Successful Minister*, vi.

18. Russell T. Hitt, ed., *Heroic Colonial Christians* (Philadelphia: J. B. Lippincott Company, 1966), 114.

19. "Historic Philadelphia from the Founding until the Early Nineteenth Century," TAPS, n.s., 43:1 (1953): 221.

20. Stout, *Divine Dramatist*, 92–93.

21. A brief sketch of Rev. James Sproat's life can be found at the end of Ashbel Green's funeral sermon for Rev. Sproat. Ashbel Green, "A Sermon Occasioned by the Death of the Rev. James Sproat, D.D." (Philadelphia, Pa.: William Young, 1794), 20–25.

22. Green, "A Sermon Occasioned by the Death," 21.

23. Mark A. Noll, *America's God: From Jonathan Edwards to Abraham Lincoln* (New York: Oxford University Press, 2002), 26; 29.

24. CHPC, 2:71–73.

Chapter 3: Hodge's Parents

1. MFH, 17.

2. PG, Oct. 13, 1773.

3. For a brief biography of Thomas Cadwalader, see J. Thomas Scharf and Thompson Westcott, *History of Philadelphia* (Philadelphia: L. H. Everts, 1884), 2:1581–1582.

4. MFH, 17. J. M. Toner, *The Medical Men of the Revolution* (Philadelphia, Pa.: Collins, 1876), 96.

5. MFH, 20–21.

6. For a good overview of various theories concerning the cause of disease in the eighteenth and nineteenth centuries, see Lester S. King, *Transformations in American Medicine: From Benjamin Rush to William Osler* (Baltimore, Md.: Johns Hopkins University Press, 1991), 142–181. For an overview of fevers and their treatments in the eighteenth century, see Lester S. King, *The Medical World of the Eighteenth Century* (Chicago: University of Chicago Press, 1958).

7. MFH, 22.

8. John Powell, *Bring Out Your Dead: the Great Plague of Yellow Fever in Philadelphia in 1793* (New York: Time, 1965), 80–81.

9. Harriot W. Warner, *The Autobiography of Charles Caldwell, M.D.* (Philadelphia, Pa.: Lippincott, Grambo & Co., 1855), 184. Richard A. Harrison, *Princetonians, 1769–1775* (Princeton, N.J.: Princeton University Press, 1980), 295–297.

10. Warner, *Autobiography of Charles Caldwell*, 184.

11. L. H. Butterfield, *Letters of Benjamin Rush* (Princeton, N.J.: Princeton University Press, 1951), 2:718. Powell, *Bring Out Your Dead*, 287.

12. LCH, 9.

13. MFH, 20.

14. LCH, 10. William Berryman Scott, *Some Memories of a Palaeontologist* (Princeton, N.J.: Princeton University Press, 1939), 3.

15. MFH, 19.

16. LCH, 8. MFH, 20.

17. James Grant Wilson, *Colonel John Bayard and the Bayard Family of America* (New York: Trow's Printing and Bookbinding, 1885), 14.

18. MFH, 23. E. R. Beadle, *The Old and the New, 1743–1876* (n.p., 1876), 38.

19. MFH, 24, 25.

20. One of her earliest boarders was the Reverend Jacob Janeway, who had been hired at the Second Presbyterian Church to help Ashbel Green with his duties. MFH, 24.

21. MFH, 25.

22. MFH, 25–26.

23. MFH, 25.

Chapter 4: The Beginnings of Self

1. Lawrence Cremin, *American Education: The Colonial Experience 1607–1783* (New York: Harper & Row, 1970), 402. "Historic Philadelphia from the Founding until the Early Nineteenth Century," TAPS, n.s., 43:1 (1953): 179–180. By 1805, there were over fifty teachers listed in the Philadelphia directories, the vast majority serving as the heads of their own schools. James Robinson, *The Philadelphia Directory for 1805* (n.p.: Printed for the Publisher, 1805).

2. LCH, 12.

3. Lefferts A. Loetscher, *The Broadening Church: A Study of Theological Issues in the Presbyterian Church since 1869* (Philadelphia: University of Pennsylvania Press, 1954), 40.

4. A more detailed discussion of Hodge's theological commitments can be found in David F. Wells, "Charles Hodge," in *Reformed Theology in America: A History of Its Modern Development*, ed. David F. Wells (Grand Rapids, Mich.: Baker Books, 1997), 39–62.

5. LCH, 13.

6. MFH, 27.

7. Grace Clark, Jessie Havens, and Stewart Hoagland, *Somerset County, 1688–1938: A Chronology with Tales from the Past* (Somerville, N.J.: Somerset Press, 1976), 70.

8. Abraham Messler, *First Things in Old Somerset, A Collection of Articles Relating to Somerset County, N.J.* (Somerville, N.J.: Somerville Publishing Company, 1899), 102–104.

9. Messler, *First Things in Old Somerset*, 38.

10. Abraham Messler, *Centennial History of Somerset County* (Somerville, N.J.: C. M. Jameson Publisher, 1878), 174.

11. Mary Hodge to Hugh and Charles Hodge, May 13, 1810, CHP, Box 7, Folder 4.

12. LCH, 14–15.

13. The most comprehensive biography of Theodore Frelinghuysen is Robert J. Ells, *Forgotten Saint: The Life of Theodore Frelinghuysen; A Case Study of Christian Leadership* (Lanham, Md.: University Press of America, 1987).

14. Mary Hodge to Hugh and Charles Hodge, Jan. 13, 1810, CHP, Box 7, Folder 4.

15. Mary Hodge to Hugh and Charles Hodge, Jan. 13, 1810, CHP, Box 7, Folder 4. See also Mary Hodge to Hugh and Charles Hodge, Jan. 20, 1811, CHP, Box 7, Folder 4; Mary Hodge to Hugh and Charles Hodge, Feb. 10, 1811, CHP, Box 7, Folder 4.

16. Mary Hodge to Hugh and Charles Hodge, Dec. 9, 1810, CHP, Box 7, Folder 4. Mary Hodge to Charles Hodge, Jan. 6, 1811, CHP, Box 7, Folder 4. Mary Hodge to Charles Hodge, Nov. 18, 1811, CHP, Box 7, Folder 4.

17. Mary Hodge to Hugh and Charles Hodge, Mar. 13, 1810, CHP, Box 7, Folder 4.

18. Mary Hodge to Hugh and Charles Hodge, May 20, 1810, CHP, Box 7, Folder 4.

19. Mary Hodge to Hugh Hodge, Feb. 8, 1812, CHP, Box 7, Folder 4.

20. Mary Hodge to Charles Hodge, Mar. 11, 1811, CHP, Box 7, Folder 4. Mary Hodge to Hugh and Charles Hodge, Nov. 25, 1811, CHP, Box 7, Folder 4.

21. Mary Hodge to Hugh and Charles Hodge, Feb. 3, 1811, CHP, Box 7, Folder 4. Mary Hodge to Charles Hodge, Dec. 16, 1811, CHP, Box 7, Folder 4. Mary Hodge to Hugh and Charles Hodge, Jan. 27, 1811, CHP, Box 7, Folder 4. Mary Hodge to Charles Hodge, Jan. 26, 1812, C0261, Box 7, Folder 4. Mary Hodge to Hugh Hodge, Dec. 11, 1811, CHP, Box 7, Folder 4. Mary Hodge to Charles Hodge, Jan. 15, 1812, CHP, Box 7, Folder 4.

22. Mary Hodge to Hugh and Charles Hodge, Feb. 3, 1811, CHP, Box 7, Folder 4.

23. Mary Hodge to Charles Hodge, Oct. 29, 1810, CHP, Box 7, Folder 4.

24. Mary Hodge to Hugh Hodge, Jan. 6, 1811, CHP, Box 7, Folder 4. Mary Hodge to Hugh Hodge, Feb. 23, 1812, CHP, Box 7, Folder 4.

25. Mary Hodge to Hugh and Charles Hodge, May 20, 1810, CHP, Box 7, Folder 4.

26. Mary Hodge to Hugh and Charles Hodge, Jan. 27, 1811, CHP, Box 7, Folder 4.

27. Daniel Walker Howe, *Making the American Self: Jonathan Edwards to Abraham Lincoln* (New York: Oxford University Press, 1997), 3. Howe offers an excellent discussion of early American conceptions of self-identity and self-development.

28. Howe, *Making the American Self*, 11.

29. Charles Hodge to Hugh Hodge, Dec. 29, 1847, CHP, Box 11, Folder 6.

30. Mary Hodge to Charles Hodge, Feb. 8, 1812, CHP, Box 7, Folder 4.

31. MFH, 31–32.

32. LCH, 11. MFH, 32.

33. Mary Hodge to Charles Hodge, Mar. 24, 1811, CHP, Box 7, Folder 4.

Chapter 5: Prince's Town

1. John F. Hageman, *The History of Princeton and Its Institutions*, 2nd ed. (Philadelphia, Pa.: J. B. Lippincott, 1879), 2:43.

2. Hageman, *History of Princeton*, 1:229.

3. Hageman, *History of Princeton*, 1:245.

4. Thomas Jefferson Wertenbaker, *Princeton, 1746–1896* (Princeton, N.J.: Princeton University Press, 1946), 15.

5. Wertenbaker, *Princeton*, 17.

6. Wertenbaker, *Princeton*, 18.

7. Wertenbaker, *Princeton*, 19. For a complete discussion of the political travails of getting the state governor to approve the College's charter, see John Maclean, *History of the College of New Jersey, From Its Origin in 1746 to the Commencement of 1854* (Philadelphia, Pa.: J. B. Lippincott, 1877), 1:36–49.

8. Wertenbaker, *Princeton*, 38. Courtney Anderson et al., *Heroic Colonial Christians* (Philadelphia, Pa.: J. B. Lippincott, 1966), 219.

9. Andrew Hodge helped sell lottery tickets in Philadelphia (printed by Benjamin Franklin) to help fund the College, and Tennent took a two-year leave from his Philadelphia pastorate to travel across the British Isles to secure funds for the College. Don Oberdorfer, *Princeton University: The First 250 Years* (Princeton, N.J.: Princeton University Press, 1995), 13. Wertenbaker, *Princeton*, 31.

10. Wertenbaker, *Princeton*, 39.

11. MFH, 27.

12. MFH, 32.

13. MFH, 31. Hageman, *History of Princeton*, 1:186.

14. MFH, 33.

Chapter 6: Witherspoon's Common Sense

1. L. H. Butterfield, *John Witherspoon Comes to America: A Documentary Account Based Largely on New Material* (Princeton, N.J.: Princeton University Library, 1953), xii.

2. Ashbel Green, *The Life of the Revd. John Witherspoon* (Princeton, N.J.: Princeton University Press, 1973), 130.

3. Varnum Lansing Collins, *President Witherspoon, A Biography* (Princeton, N.J.: Princeton University Press, 1925), 1:102–103. Green, *Life of the Revd. John Witherspoon*, 120.

4. Mark Noll, *Princeton and the Republic, 1768–1822* (Princeton, N.J.: Princeton University Press, 1989), 18.

5. Thomas Jefferson Wertenbaker, *Princeton, 1746–1896* (Princeton, N.J.: Princeton University Press), 76.

6. Noll, *Princeton and the Republic*, 53.

7. Green, *Life of the Revd. John Witherspoon*, 273.

8. Wertenbaker, *Princeton*, 108–109.

9. Noll, *Princeton and the Republic*, 36–37.

10. E. Brooks Holifield, *Theology in America: Christian Thought from the Age of the Puritans to the Civil War* (New Haven, Conn.: Yale University Press, 2003), 175.

11. Mark Noll, Introduction to *The Way of Life*, by Charles Hodge (New York: Paulist Press, 1987), 25.

12. A good overview of the basic components of Scottish Common Sense Realism in America is Mark Noll, "Common Sense Traditions and American Evangelical Thought," AQ 37:2 (1985): 220–225.

13. Darrell Guder, "The History of Belles Lettres at Princeton" (Ph.D. diss., University of Hamburg, 1964), 154–155.

14. Mark Noll, *America's God: From Jonathan Edwards to Abraham Lincoln* (New York: Oxford University Press, 2002), 100.

15. Jonathan Dickinson, *The True Scripture-Doctrine Concerning Some Important Points of Christian Faith* (Boston, Mass.: D. Fowle, 1741), 217.

16. Noll, *America's God*, 98.

17. An insightful discussion of the acceptance of Scottish Common Sense moral reasoning in the colonies can be found in Noll, *America's God*, 93–103.

18. Norman Fiering, *Moral Philosophy at Seventeenth-Century Harvard: A Discipline in Transition* (Chapel Hill: University of North Carolina Press, 1981), 300.

19. Wertenbaker, *Princeton*, 132.

20. Noll, *Princeton and the Republic*, 9.

21. Noll, *Princeton and the Republic*, 163.

22. A good account of this riot and the way the students draped themselves in revolutionary rhetoric is found in Mark Noll, "Before the Storm: Life at Princeton College 1806–1807," PULC 42 (1981): 145–164.

23. John Maclean, *History of the College of New Jersey, From Its Origin in 1746 to the Commencement of 1854* (Philadelphia, Pa.: J. B. Lippincott, 1877), 2:78.

24. Steven J. Novak, *The Rights of Youth: American Colleges and Student Revolt, 1798–1815* (Cambridge, Mass.: Harvard University Press, 1977), 32.

25. Noll, *Princeton and the Republic*, 172.

26. In fairness to Smith, it should be noted that Princeton College was not alone in its experience of student revolt. In speaking of student unrest, Yale's president Timothy Dwight wrote of Princeton: "the cause in which the governors of the College of New Jersey are engaged is the common cause of all colleges." As early as 1799, the University of North Carolina experienced a significant student uprising, which included students beating the college's president and stoning two other faculty members. Riotous activity, however, seemed to reach a peak in the years 1807–1809. Students at Harvard (1807), Williams (1808), William and Mary (1808), Dartmouth (1809), and a number of other schools rose in rebellion in these years. So many students were expelled in this decade that college presidents began circulating lists of students who had been banned from their campuses and reached an agreement that no expelled student would gain admittance to a second institution of higher learning. As a mark of the tenor of the times, the incoming students at the University of North Carolina were required to swear upon their honor that they had never been expelled from another college. Novak, *Rights of Youth*, 31; 19; 24.

27. Wertenbaker, *Princeton*, 144.

28. Maclean, *History of the College of New Jersey*, 2:72.

29. Ashbel Green kept a diary throughout his life. Evidence for his reluctance to take Princeton College's presidency can be found in entries throughout August and September 1812. AGP, Box 11.

Chapter 7: "Classick Learning"

1. Darell Guder, "The History of Belles Lettres at Princeton" (Ph.D. diss., University of Hamburg, 1964), 233.

2. David B. Calhoun, *Princeton Seminary* (Carlisle, Pa.: The Banner of Truth Trust, 1994), 1:37.

3. Ashbel Green, *The Life of the Revd. John Witherspoon* (Princeton, N.J.: Princeton University Press, 1973), 273.

4. Mark Noll, *Princeton and the Republic, 1768–1822* (Princeton, N.J.: Princeton University Press, 1989), 158. Steven J. Novak, *The Rights of Youth: American Colleges and Student Revolt, 1798–1815* (Cambridge, Mass.: Harvard University Press, 1977), 21.

5. Ashbel Green, *An Address to the Students of the College of New-Jersey: Delivered May 6th 1802* (Trenton, N.J.: Sherman & Mershon, 1802), 4.

6. Guder, "History of Belles Lettres at Princeton,"231.

7. Ashbel Green, *The Life of Ashbel Green, V.D.M. Begun to be Written by Himself in his Eighty–Second Year and Continued to his Eighty-Fourth* (New York: Robert Carter & Brothers, 1849), 345.

8. Noll, *Princeton and the Republic*, 274. Ashbel Green, "Report to the Trustees, Apr. 1813," AGP, Box 8, Folder 7, pp. 4–5, 13, 64, 68.

9. Noll, *Princeton and the Republic*, 275. *Laws of the College of New Jersey; Revised, Amended, and Adopted by the Board of Trustees, Sept. 30, 1813* (Trenton, N.J.: n.p., 1813).

10. Noll, *Princeton and the Republic*, 275. Guder, "History of Belles Lettres at Princeton," 227. The most comprehensive treatment of the use of Paley's works in American colleges is Wilson Smith, "William Paley's Theological Utilitarianism in America," WMQ 11:2 (Apr. 1954): 402–424.

11. Guder, "History of Belles Lettres at Princeton," 234.

12. John Maclean, *History of the College of New Jersey, From Its Origin in 1746 to the Commencement of 1854* (Philadelphia, Pa.: J. B. Lippincott, 1877), 2:198.

13. Maclean, *History of the College of New Jersey*, 2:198.

14. Green, *Life of Ashbel Green*, 343.

15. George P. Schmidt, *Princeton and Rutgers* (Princeton, N.J.: D. Van Nostrand Company, 1964), 42.

16. Maclean, *History of the College of New Jersey*, 2:150–151.

17. Schmidt, *Princeton and Rutgers*, 42–43. Don Oberdorfer, *Princeton University: The First 250 Years* (Princeton, N.J.: Princeton University Press, 1995), 26–27.

18. For a good overview of Princeton College's early curriculum, see Francis L. Broderick, "Pulpit, Physics, and Politics: The Curriculum of the College of New Jersey, 1746–1794," WMQ 6:1 (Jan. 1949): 42–68. See also Guder, "History of Belles Lettres at Princeton," 107–134.

19. Guder, "History of Belles Lettres at Princeton," 245–247.

20. The standard histories of these societies are: *Addresses and Proceedings at the Celebration of the One Hundredth Anniversary of the Founding of the American Whig Society of the College of New Jersey* (Princeton, N.J.: Stelle & Smith Publishers, 1871) and Charles Richard Williams, *The Cliosophic Society, Princeton University* (Princeton, N.J.: Princeton University Press, 1916).

21. Guder, "History of Belles Lettres at Princeton," 121.

22. *Catalogue of the Honorary and Graduate Members of the American Whig Society, Instituted in the College of New Jersey, in 1769* (Princeton, N.J.: John Bogart, 1837), 3. See also *Addresses and Proceedings*, 6–7.

23. *Catalogue of the Honorary and Graduate Members*, 3–10.

24. Henry Lyttleton Savage, *Nassau Hall, 1756–1956* (Princeton, N.J.: Princeton University Press, 1956), 115.

25. Guder, "History of Belles Lettres at Princeton," 261.

26. American Whig Collection, MUDD, Box 192.

27. "Whig Final Minutes," American Whig Collection, MUDD, Box 4, entries for June 6, 1814; July 26, 1814; Feb. 21, 1815.

28. "Whig Final Minutes," American Whig Collection, MUDD, Box 4, entries for Jan. 5, 1812; Mar. 2, 1813; Feb. 14, 1814; Mar. 7, 1814; May 30, 1814.

29. "1820 Whig Constitution and By-Laws", American Whig Collection, MUDD, Box 169, Article 4.

30. Annual History of 1815, American Whig Collection, MUDD, Box 153, Folder 1.

31. Typescript diary, AGP, Box 11, entries for Mar. 28, 1815; June 9, 1815; July 25, 1815; Aug. 15, 1815.
32. "Faculty Minutes Book, 1812–1820," MUDD (Feb. 12, 1813), 31–32.
33. "Faculty Minutes Book, 1812–1820," MUDD (Jan. 8 & 9, 1814), 84–85.
34. "Faculty Minutes Book, 1812–1820," MUDD (Jan. 8 & 9, 1814), 84–85. Green, *Life of Ashbel Green*, 361.
35. Green, *Life of Ashbel Green*, 361.

Chapter 8: Enlisting under the Banner of King Jesus

1. MFH, 28.
2. LCH, 28.
3. Ashbel Green, *A Report to the Trustees of the College of New Jersey Relative to a Revival of Religion Among the Students of Said College* (Philadelphia, Pa.: William Fry, 1815), 6.
4. Green, *Report to the Trustees*, 12.
5. Green, *Report to the Trustees*, 21–25.
6. Green, *Report to the Trustees*, 14. Charles Hodge to Hugh L. Hodge, Princeton, Feb. 1815, CHP, Box 9, Folder 1.
7. Green, *Report to the Trustees*, 8.
8. Green, *Report to the Trustees*, 8–11.
9. LCH, 35.
10. LCH, 13. Mary Hodge also commented on Hodge's early religious nature by describing him as someone whose "attention to religious duties . . . [had] long been a leading feature" of his life. Mary Hodge to Hugh Hodge, Jan. 23, 1815, CHP, Box 9, Folder 1.
11. LCH, 13.
12. LCH, 13.
13. LCH, 30.
14. "Faculty Minutes Book, 1812-1820," MUDD, Apr. 3, 1815; Aug. 7–16, 1815.
15. James Waddel Alexander, *Princeton—Old and New: Recollections of Undergraduate Life* (New York: Charles Scribner's Sons, 1898), 48; 74. George P. Schmidt, *Princeton and Rutgers* (Princeton, N.J.: D. Van Nostrand Company, 1964), 57–58.
16. LCH, 32. Mary Hodge to Hugh Hodge, Jan. 23, 1815, CHP, Box 9, Folder 1.

Chapter 9: Happy Jaunts and the "Man of Men"

1. Rhamanthus M. Stocker, *Centennial History of Susquehanna County, Pennsylvania* (Philadelphia: R. T. Peck & Co. 1887), 500.
2. Charles Hodge to Mary Hodge, Silver Lake, July 11, 1816, CHP, Box 7, Folder 3.
3. Charles Hodge to Mary Hodge, Silver Lake, July 27, 1816, CHP, Box 7, Folder 3.
4. Charles Hodge to Mary Hodge, Silver Lake, July 27, 1816, CHP, Box 7, Folder 3.
5. LCH, 18.
6. LCH, 18.
7. LAA, 114; 276.
8. LAA, 44.
9. LAA, 45.
10. LAA, 114.
11. LCH. 45.

12. LCH, 44.

13. LCH, 45.

14. LCH, 45.

15. LCH, 45.

Chapter 10: "Give Us Ministers!"

1. Mark Noll, *Princeton and the Republic, 1768–1822* (Princeton, N.J.: Princeton University Press, 1989), 171–172.

2. Mark Noll, "The Founding of Princeton Seminary," WTJ 42 (Fall 1979): 76.

3. Noll, "Founding of Princeton Seminary," 87.

4. Noll, "Founding of Princeton Seminary," 87. William K. Selden, *Princeton Theological Seminary: A Narrative History, 1812–1992* (Princeton, N.J.: Princeton University Press, 1992), 14.

5. Noll, *Princeton and the Republic*, 172.

6. Mark Noll, "The Response of Elias Boudinot to the Student Rebellion of 1807: Visions of Honor, Order, and Morality," PULC 43 (Aug. 1981): 20.

7. Mark Noll, *America's God: From Jonathan Edwards to Abraham Lincoln* (New York: Oxford University Press, 2002), 259–262.

8. Archibald Alexander, *A Sermon Delivered at the Opening of the General Assembly of the Presbyterian Church in the United States, May, 1808* (Philadelphia, Pa.: Hopkins & Earle, 1808), 30–37.

9. "Trustee's Minutes," MUDD, Sept. 25, 1806.

10. Noll, "Founding of Princeton Seminary," 98.

11. Noll, "Founding of Princeton Seminary," 78–79.

12. LSM, 1:14.

13. LSM, 1:393.

14. Belden C. Lane, "Miller and the Eldership: A Knickerbocker Goes to Nassau," PSB 6:3 (1985): 213.

15. LSM, 1:326.

16. LSM, 1:359.

17. For a good, concise overview of Miller's career, see Lane, "Miller and the Eldership," 211–224.

18. "Minutes of the Proceedings of the Board of Directors," PTS (Sept. 30, 1813): 71. For the most complete account of the construction of Alexander Hall, see Robert S. Beaman, "Alexander Hall at the Princeton Theological Seminary: Construction of a Building and the Establishment of an Institution," PH 2 (1977): 43–58.

Chapter 11: Student Years at the Seminary

1. LCH, 47.

2. William K. Selden, *Princeton Theological Seminary: A Narrative History, 1812–1992* (Princeton, N.J.: Princeton University Press, 1992), 48.

3. Charles Hodge to Mary Hodge, Princeton, Nov. 10, 1817, CHP, Box 7, Folder 3.

4. LCH, 56.

5. A good overview of William Graham's career can be found in Henry Alexander White, *Southern Presbyterian Leaders* (New York: Neale Publishing, 1911), 124–139.

6. On the educational training of Dr. Alexander, see Lefferts A. Loetscher, *Facing the Enlightenment and Pietism: Archibald Alexander and the Founding of Princeton Theological Seminary*

(Westport, Conn.: Greenwood Press, 1983), 27–40; James M. Garretson, *Princeton and Preaching: Archibald Alexander and the Christian Ministry* (Carlisle, Pa.: Banner of Truth Trust, 2005), 6–10; LAA, 105–110.

7. Loetscher, *Facing the Enlightenment and Pietism*, 17–26.

8. E. Brooks Holifield, *Theology in America: Christian Thought from the Age of the Puritans to the Civil War* (New Haven, Conn.: Yale University Press, 2003), 11.

9. Mark A. Noll, ed., *The Princeton Theology, 1812–1921* (Grand Rapids, Mich.: Baker Book House, 1983), 13; 27–33.

10. Loetscher, *Facing the Enlightenment and Pietism*, 76.

11. George M. Marsden, *The Evangelical Mind and the New School Presbyterian Experience* (Eugene, Oreg.: Wipf & Stock Publishers, 1970), 14.

12. Robert Baird, *Religion in the United States of America* (Glasgow and Edinburgh, Scotland: Blackie & Son, 1844), 368–369.

13. LCH, 47.

14. John Oliver Nelson, "The Rise of the Princeton Theology: A Genetic Study of American Presbyterianism until 1850" (Ph.D. diss., Religion, Yale University, 1935), 352.

15. Henry S. Nash, *The History of the Higher Criticism of the New Testament* (New York: Macmillan Company, 1900), 89–99.

16. Loetscher, *Facing the Enlightenment and Pietism*, 217.

17. Samuel Miller to Benjamin B. Wisner, Apr. 15, 1822, FL, Samuel Miller Papers, Collection #C0277, Firestone Library, Department of Rare Books and Special Collections, Princeton University, Box 3, Folder 111.

18. Charles Hodge, "Critica Sacra or Biblical Criticism," Princeton, Dec. 31, 1817, CHM, Box 12, Folder 2, pp. 93–95.

19. To prove his position, Alexander cited the work of Benjamin Kennicott, who had compared nearly seven hundred manuscripts over a twenty year period in the latter half of the eighteenth century, to propose which parts of the Bible were most reliable and why. Not surprisingly, the German critics found fault with much of Kennicott's work and methodology, but Alexander used Kennicott's work to undergird his views on the absolute trustworthiness of the Bible. Charles Hodge, "Critica Sacra or Biblical Criticism," Princeton, Dec. 31, 1817, CHM, Box 12, Folder 2, pp. 39–41.

20. Archibald Alexander, "Introductory Lecture," Nov. 1815, Archibald Alexander Manuscript Collection, PTS, Box 7, No. 3.

21. Archibald Alexander, *The Canon of the Old and New Testaments Ascertained* (New York: A.D. Borrenstein for G. & C. Carvill, 1826), 13.

22. Charles Hodge, Lecture Notes on Theology, Princeton, Jan. 1818, CHM, Box 12, Folder 3, p. 1.

23. Holifield, *Theology in America*, 65.

24. Holifield, *Theology in America*, 173.

25. Charles Hodge, Lecture Notes on Theology, Princeton, Jan. 1818, CHM, Box 12, Folder 3, p. 2.

26. A good, brief biographical treatment of Turretin and his descendants can be found in James W. Alexander, *"Institutio Theologiae Elencticae"* BRPR 20:3 (July 1848): 452–463.

27. Noll, *Princeton Theology*, 28–29. Turretin's writings were available in their original Latin to Hodge during his seminary days, and Dr. Alexander made large sections of his *Institutes* required student reading. Hodge's extensive and intensive study of Turretin made the Swiss theologian one of the greatest influences on his own thinking. So profound and enduring was his respect for Turretin that in the middle of his career at Princeton Theological Seminary,

Hodge requested that George Musgrave Giger, a classics professor at Princeton College, undertake the massive project of translating Turretin's *Institutes* into English. Begun in 1848, Giger eventually produced over eight thousand pages of handwritten translation text. As he worked on the manuscript, Giger made his notes available (again at Hodge's request) to the Seminary's students, so as they studied Hodge's lectures on theology they would also have ready access to Turretin's thinking. Francis Turretin, *Institutes of Elenctic Theology*, trans. George Musgrave Giger, ed. James T. Dennison Jr. (Phillipsburg, N.J.: P&R Publishing, 1997), 1:xxvii.

28. Nelson, "Rise of the Princeton Theology," 36.
29. Alexander, *"Institutio Theologiae Elencticae,"* 453.
30. Charles Hodge, "Short Notices" BRPR 17:1 (Jan. 1845): 190.
31. Holifield, *Theology in America*, 195. Loetscher, *Facing the Enlightenment and Pietism*, 219.

Chapter 12: "Where Am I To Go?"

1. Charles Hodge to Mary Hodge, Princeton, Feb. 1, 1819, CHP, Box 7, Folder 3.
2. Charles Hodge to Mary Hodge, Princeton, May 13, 1819, CHP, Box 7, Folder 3.
3. Charles Hodge to Mary Hodge, Princeton, Feb. 10, 1819, CHP, Box 7, Folder 3.
4. Charles Hodge to Mary Hodge, Princeton, Apr. 21, 1819, CHP, Box 7, Folder 3.
5. LCH, 64–65.
6. LCH, 64.
7. Charles Hodge to Mary Hodge, Princeton, Apr. 21, 1819, CHP, Box 7, Folder 3.
8. LCH, 65.
9. LCH, 66.
10. MFH, 42.
11. LCH, 58.
12. Charles Hodge to Mary Hodge, Princeton, June 22, 1820, CHP, Box 7, Folder 1.
13. Mary Hodge to Charles Hodge, Philadelphia, June 30, 1820, CHP, Box 7, Folder 1.
14. "Introductory Lecture, June 30, 1820," "Introductory Lecture, July 2, 1819," Archibald Alexander Manuscript Collection, PTS, Box 7, Folders 5 and 6.
15. Charles D. Cashdollar, "The Pursuit of Piety: Charles Hodge's Diary, 1819–1820," JPH 55 (1977): 267. Elwyn Allen Smith, *The Presbyterian Ministry in American Culture: A Study in Changing Concepts, 1700–1900* (Philadelphia, Pa.: Westminster Press, 1962), 143–150.
16. Hodge Diary, Jan. 30, 1820, CHP, Box 1, Folder 3.
17. Hodge Diary, Dec. 26, 1819, CHP, Box 1, Folder 3.
18. Hodge Diary, Mar. 12, 1820, CHP, Box 1, Folder 3.
19. Charles Hodge to Archibald Alexander, Philadelphia, Dec. 16, 1819, CHP, Box 13, Folder 17.
20. Charles Hodge, "Critica Sacra or Biblical Criticism," Princeton, Dec. 31, 1817, CHM, Box 12, Folder 2, p. 85.
21. Hodge Diary, May 21, 1820, CHP, Box 1, Folder 3.
22. *Minutes of the General Assembly of the Presbyterian Church in the United States* (Philadelphia, Pa.: Presbyterian Board of Publication, 1847), 720.

Chapter 13: "The Most Eligible Situation for Improvement"

1. Charles Hodge to Mary Hodge, Princeton, June 22, 1820, CHP, Box 7, Folder 1.
2. Charles Hodge to Hugh Hodge, Princeton, July 10, 1820, CHP, Box 9, Folder 1.
3. Charles Hodge to Hugh Hodge, Aug. 28, 1820; Apr. 21, 1821; Nov. 23, 1821, CHP, Box 9, Folder 1.

4. Charles Hodge to Mary Hodge, Princeton, Dec. 19, 1821, CHP, Box 7, Folder 1.

5. LCH, 84.

6. Charles Hodge to Hugh Hodge, Princeton, Nov. 11, 1822, CHP, Box 9, Folder 1.

7. Notes for Hodge's early lectures at the Seminary can be found in CHM, Boxes 13–15.

8. Charles Hodge to Mary Hodge, Princeton, Dec. 19, 1821, CHP, Box 7, Folder 1. Charles Hodge, *A Dissertation on the Importance of Biblical Literature* (Trenton, N.J.: George Sherman, 1822), 4. David B. Calhoun, *Princeton Seminary* (Carlisle, Pa.: Banner of Truth Trust, 1994), 1:112. LCH, 87.

9. Charles Hodge to Hugh Hodge, Princeton, Jan. 1, 1822, CHP, Box 9, Folder 1.

10. Charles Hodge to Hugh Hodge, Princeton, May 2, 1822, CHP, Box 9, Folder 1.

11. Charles Hodge to Mary Hodge, Princeton, Dec. 19, 1821, CHP, Box 7, Folder 1.

12. Charles Hodge to Mary Hodge, Princeton, Jan. 19, 1822, CHP, Box 7, Folder 1.

13. Hodge, *Dissertation*, 49.

14. Hodge, *Dissertation*, 43; 48.

15. Hodge, *Dissertation*, 32; 41.

16. Hodge, *Dissertation*, 43.

17. LCH, 91.

18. Leonard W. Labaree, ed., *The Papers of Benjamin Franklin* (New Haven, Conn.: Yale University Press, 1959), 1:lxiv.

19. LCH, 95.

20. LCH, 29.

21. Calhoun, *Princeton Seminary*, 1:113.

22. Samuel Miller to Charles Hodge, Princeton, June 15, 1822, CHP, Box 17, Folder 63.

23. Charles Hodge to the Board of Directors, Princeton, May 17, 1824, in the Treasurer's Office, Miscellaneous Papers, Packet 1824–1898, PTS, Box 200.

24. John Dehaviland to Charles Hodge, July 1, 1824, CHP, Box 16, Folder 37. Dehaviland charged Hodge $85.00 for two sets of drawings and a trip out to Princeton to survey the site for the house.

25. Roger W. Moss, *Historical Sacred Places of Philadelphia* (Philadelphia: University of Pennsylvania Press, 2005), 120. For Haviland's role in the design of American prisons, see Michael Meranze, *Laboratories of Virtue: Punishment, Revolution, and Authority in Philadelphia, 1760–1835* (Chapel Hill, N.C.: Institute of Early American History and Culture, 1996), 247–251.

26. John Haviland, *The Builder's Assistant, Containing Five Orders of Architecture* (Philadelphia, Pa.: John Bioren, 1818), 1:31.

27. Sarah Hodge to Charles Hodge, Philadelphia, June 11, 1824, CHP, Box 8, Folder 1.

28. Robert Smith to Charles Hodge, Philadelphia, July 22, 1822, CHP, Box 17, Folder 80. Some thirty years after his house was built, Hodge requested that the Seminary pay off his mortgage since the homes of other Seminary professors were included in their salary contracts. In this request, Hodge noted that it was Sarah's money that largely helped pay for the initial construction of the house. The board agreed to pay off the mortgage. Minutes of the Board of Trustees, Princeton Theological Seminary, PTS, Vol. 1, May 13, 1857.

Chapter 14: New England's Theological Landscape

1. Charles Hodge to Mary Hodge, Boston, Oct. 9, 1820, CHP, Box 7, Folder 3.

2. Douglas A. Sweeney, *Nathaniel Taylor, New Haven Theology, and the Legacy of Jonathan Edwards* (New York: Oxford University Press, 2003), 3; 149–150. George M. Marsden, *The*

Evangelical Mind and the New School Presbyterian Experience (New Haven, Conn.: Yale University Press, 1970), 46–52; 65.

3. Charles Hodge to Mary Hodge, Boston, Oct. 9, 1820, CHP, Box 7, Folder 3.

4. Moses Stuart, "On the Study of the German Language," CR 6 (1841): 448.

5. Charles Hodge to Mary Hodge, Boston, Oct. 25, 1820, CHP, Box 7, Folder 3.

6. Moses Stuart to Charles Hodge, Andover, Feb. 4, 1822, CHP, Box 18, Folder 96.

7. Moses Stuart to Charles Hodge, Andover, Mar. 20, 1821, CHP, Box 18, Folder 96.

8. Moses Stuart to Charles Hodge, Andover, Apr. 28, 1829; June 23, 1826, CHP, Box 18, Folder 96. Richard Gardiner, "Princeton and Paris: An Early Nineteenth Century Bond of Mission" (Senior Thesis, History Dept., Princeton Theological Seminary, 1994), 35.

9. Mark Noll, *America's God: From Jonathan Edwards to Abraham Lincoln* (New York: Oxford University Press, 2002), 262–268.

10. Perry Miller, "Jonathan Edwards to Emerson," NEQ 13:4 (1940): 612.

11. Noll, *America's God*, 285.

12. Paul C. Gutjahr, *An American Bible: A History of the Good Book in the United States, 1777–1880* (Stanford, Calif.: Stanford University Press, 1999), 95–99.

13. The best comprehensive treatment of Unitarianism's philosophical underpinnings is Daniel Walker Howe, *The Unitarian Conscience: Harvard Moral Philosophy, 1805–1861* (Middletown, Conn.: Wesleyan University Press, 1988), 27–148.

14. Henry K. Rowe, *History of Andover Theological Seminary* (Newton, Mass.: Thomas Todd, 1933), 1.

15. Rowe, *History of Andover Theological Seminary*, 14.

16. A good overview of Hopkinsian thought can be found in E. Brooks Holifield, *Theology in America* (New Haven, Conn.: Yale University Press, 2003), 139–148.

17. Rowe, *History of Andover Theological Seminary*, 8.

18. Rowe, *History of Andover Theological Seminary*, 8; 17.

19. Nathaniel W. Taylor, "Spring on the Means of Regeneration," QCS 1 (1829): 19.

Chapter 15: Democratic Christianity

1. Sean Wilentz, *The Rise of American Democracy: Jefferson to Lincoln* (New York: W. W. Norton, 2005), 313.

2. The best single treatment of the influence of democratic ideology on early American religion remains Nathan Hatch, *The Democratization of American Christianity* (New Haven, Conn.: Yale University Press, 1989).

3. Devereux Jarratt, *The Life of the Reverend Devereux Jarratt* (Baltimore, Md.: n.p. 1806), 14–15; 181.

4. Timothy Dwight, *A Sermon Preached at the Opening of the Theological Institution in Andover* (Boston, Ma.: n.p. 1808), 7–8.

5. David Rice wrote two different reports to the Presbyterian General Assembly: *An Epistle to the Citizens of Kentucky Professing Christianity, Especially Those that Are, or Have Been, Denominated Presbyterians* (Lexington, Ky.: 1805) and *A Second Epistle to the Citizens of Kentucky, Professing the Christian Religion, Especially those Who are, or Have Been Denominated Presbyterians* (Lexington, Ky.: 1808). The excerpt quoted here can be found in a reprint of Rice letters in Robert H. Bishop, *An Outline of the History of the Church in the State of Kentucky, During a*

Period of Forty Years: Containing the Memoirs of Rev. David Rice (Lexington, Ky.: T. T. Skillman, 1824), 353.

6. George A. Rawlyk, *Ravished By the Spirit: Religious Revivals, Baptists, and Henry Alline* (Kingston, Ont.: McGill-Queen's University Press, 1984), 145.

7. Roger Finke and Rodney Stark, *The Churching of America 1776–1990* (New Brunswick, N.J.: Rutgers University Press, 1992), 25.

8. Finke and Stark, *Churching of America*, 55.

9. H. Shelton Smith et al., *American Christianity: An Historical Interpretation with Representative Documents* (New York: Charles Scribner's Sons, 1963), 2:89.

Chapter 16: The Birth of the Biblical Repertory

1. Quoted in Joan Brumberg, *Mission for Life: The Judson Family and American Evangelical Culture* (New York: New York University Press, 1984), 67.

2. The best overview of religious printing in this period can be found in David P. Nord, *Faith In Reading: Religious Publishing and the Birth of Mass Media in America, 1790–1860* (New York: Oxford University Press, 2004). See also Stephen Elmer Slocum Jr., "The American Tract Society: 1825–1975: An Evangelical Effort to Influence the Religious and Moral Life of the United States" (Ph.D. diss., New York University, 1975).

3. Ashbel Green, *The Life of Ashbel Green* (New York: Robert Carter & Brothers, 1849), 439–447.

4. There are two good comprehensive histories of this journal: "The Princeton Review Series and The Contribution of Princeton Theological Seminary to Presbyterian Quarterly Magazines," Princeton, N.J., 1943, PTS, typescript copy; and Mark Noll, "The Princeton Theological Review: 1825–1929," WTJ 50 (Fall 1988): 283–304.

5. "Introduction," BR 1:1 (1825): first page.

6. "Translation of Beckii Monogrammata Hermeneutices N.T.," BR 1:1 (1825): 59.

7. It should be noted that even at Harvard, there was a division among the faculty concerning the utility and accuracy of recent developments in German theology. Andrews Norton, the Dexter Professor of Sacred Literature at Harvard during this period, was so opposed to certain German theological developments that he forbade his son to study the German language, thinking that it might lead to a corruption of his Unitarianism. This is particularly interesting considering that Norton spoke and read the language himself. Henry A. Pochmann, *German Culture in America: Philosophical and Literary Influences: 1600–1900* (Madison: University of Wisconsin Press, 1957), 561.

8. LCH, 98–99.

9. For Patton's popularity as a teacher, see Thomas Jefferson Wertenbaker, *Princeton, 1746–1896* (Princeton, N.J.: Princeton University Press, 1946), 160–161.

10. Pochmann, *German Culture in America*, 533.

11. Jacob N. Beam, "Charles Hodge's Student Years in Germany," PULC 8:3 (Apr. 1947): 105.

12. Charles Hodge to Hugh Hodge, Princeton, Aug. 29, 1826, CHP, Box 9, Folder 2.

Chapter 17: The Trip to Europe

1. Charles Hodge to Hugh Hodge, Princeton, Aug. 26, 1826, CHP, Box 9, Folder 2.

2. Charles Hodge to Hugh Hodge, Princeton, Aug. 29, 1826, CHP, Box 9, Folder 2.

3. Charles Hodge to Sarah Hodge, Philadelphia, Sept. 1, 1826, CHP, Box 8, Folder 3.

4. These are Samuel Miller's words regarding Hodge's inability to appreciate his importance to the Seminary. LCH, 160.

5. Charles Hodge to Sarah Hodge, New York, Sept. 30, 1826, CHP, Box 8, Folder 3.

6. LCH, 11.

7. Charles Hodge to Archibald Alexander, Paris, Nov. 2, 1826, CHP, Box 13, Folder 17.

8. Jurgen Herbst, *The German Historical School in American Scholarship* (Ithaca, N.Y.: Cornell University Press, 1965), 77. For a concise overview of "Neology" as it was seen in the 1830s, see "Neology," QCS 6:3 (Sept. 1834): 509–512.

9. Archibald Alexander to Charles Hodge, Princeton, Mar. 24, 1827, CHP, Box 13, Folder 17.

10. LCH, 102.

11. While in Halle, Hodge bought books through Waisenhaus Buchhandlung and would continue to use this book agent as a source for German books on theology and philosophy long after he returned to Princeton. Jacob N. Beam, "Charles Hodge's Student Years in Germany," PULC 8:3 (Apr. 1947): 105.

12. Thomas Jefferson Wertenbaker, *Princeton, 1746–1896* (Princeton, N.J.: Princeton University Press, 1946), 179; John Maclean, *History of the College of New Jersey, From Its Origin in 1746 to the Commencement of 1854* (Philadelphia, Pa.: J. B. Lippincott, 1877), 2:276–277.

13. Charles Hodge to Archibald Alexander, Paris, Nov. 2, 1826, CHP, Box 13, Folder 17.

14. The most complete list of nineteenth-century Americans who studied in Gottingen is found in Daniel B. Shumway, "The American Students of the University of Gottingen," *German American Annals* 8:5–6 (Sept.–Dec. 1910): 171–254. Shumway points to the patronage the university enjoyed from the British House of Hanover as one of the reasons both British and American students made it one of their favorite schools in Germany.

15. Charles Hodge to Sarah Hodge, Paris, Dec. 28, 1826, CHP, Box 8, Folder 3.

16. Charles Hodge, "The State of Religion in France," CA (Oct. 1827): 501. James Lynn Osen, "The Revival of the French Reformed Church, 1830–1852" (Ph.D. diss., University of Wisconsin, 1966), 34.

17. Charles Hodge to Archibald Alexander, Paris, Jan. 29, 1827, CHP, Box 13, Folder 17. See also Hodge, "State of Religion in France," 499.

18. Charles Hodge to Archibald Alexander, Paris, Jan. 29, 1827, CHP, Box 13, Folder 17.

19. Charles Hodge to Archibald Alexander, Paris, Jan. 29, 1827, CHP, Box 13, Folder 17.

20. These notebooks are located in CHP, Box 2, Folders 1, 2, 9.

21. Charles Hodge to Archibald Alexander, Paris, Nov. 2, 1826, CHP, Box 13, Folder 17.

22. Charles Hodge to Sarah Hodge, Paris, Nov. 20, 1826, CHP, Box 8, Folder 3.

23. For information on Mark Wilks, see Kenneth J. Stewart, *Restoring the Reformation: British Evangelicalism and the Francophone 'Réveil' 1816–1849* (Waynesboro, Ga.: Paternoster, 2006), 120; 124–125; 128; 158–159; and Richard Gardiner, "Princeton and Paris: An Early Nineteenth Century Bond of Mission" (Senior Thesis, History Dept., Princeton Theological Seminary, 1994), 15; 45; 47.

24. Charles Hodge to Sarah Hodge, New York, Sept. 30, 1826, CHP, Box 8, Folder 3.

25. Charles Hodge to Sarah Hodge, Paris, Feb. 12, 1827, CHP, Box 8, Folder 3.

26. Beam, "Charles Hodge's Student Years in Germany," 109. Douglas Botting, *Humboldt and the Cosmos* (New York: Harper & Row, 1973), 168.

27. James Hall, ed., *Forty Years' Familiar Letters of James W. Alexander, D.D.* (New York: Charles Scribner, 1860), 1:105.

28. A brief description of the theological history of the university at Halle can be found in Leonard Woods Jr.'s translation of George Christian Knapp, *Lectures on Christian Theology* (New York: N. Tibbals, 1872), 9–22.

29. For a good biographical sketch of Tholuck, see Edwards Amasa Park, *Sketch of the Life and Character of Prof. Tholuck* (Edinburgh: Thomas Clark, 1840). See also Karl Barth, *Protestant Theology in the Nineteenth Century: Its Background and History* (London: SCM Press, 1972), 508–518.

30. Charles Hodge to Sarah Hodge, Halle, Mar. 11, 1827, CHP, Box 8, Folder 3. Charles Hodge to Archibald Alexander, Paris, Jan. 29, 1827, CHP, Box 13, Folder 17.

31. Charles Hodge to Sarah Hodge, Paris, December 21, 1826, CHP, Box 8, Folder 3.

Chapter 18: Halle

1. Charles Hodge to Sarah Hodge, Halle, Feb. 28, 1827, CHP, Box 8, Folder 3.
2. Charles Hodge to Mary Hodge, Halle, Mar. 1, 1827, CHP, Box 7, Folder 2.
3. JET (Mar. 3, 1827), 2.
4. An informative, short biography of Edward Robinson is Henry Boynton Smith and Roswell D. Hitchcock's *The Life, Writings and Character of Edward Robinson* (New York: A. D. F. Randolph, 1863). A treatment of Robinson's importance to American biblical scholarship can be found in Jerry Wayne Brown, *The Rise of Biblical Criticism in America, 1800–1870* (Middletown, Conn.: Wesleyan University Press, 1969), 111–124.
5. Charles Hodge to Sarah Hodge, Halle, Feb. 28, 1827, CHP, Box 8, Folder 3.
6. JET (Mar. 13, 1827), 10.
7. JET (Mar. 7, 1827), 6–7.
8. JET (Mar. 22, 1827), 18.
9. B. A. Gerrish, "Charles Hodge and the Europeans," CHR, 144.
10. A good overview of the "Awakening" in Germany and Prussia during this period can be found in Walter H. Conser Jr., *Church and Confession: Conservative Theologians in Germany, England, and America, 1815–1866* (Macon, Ga.: Mercer University Press, 1984), 27–38. See also Helmut Walser Smith, ed., *Protestants, Catholics and Jews in Germany, 1800–1914* (New York: Berg, 2001), 71–74.
11. LCH, 120.
12. Karl Barth, *Protestant Theology in the Nineteenth Century: Its Background and History* (London: SCM Press, 1972), 508–509.
13. Barth, *Protestant Theology in the Nineteenth Century*, 513–516.
14. LCH, 120.
15. JET (Mar. 22 & 24, 1827), 17–19.
16. Charles Hodge to Sarah Hodge, Halle, Mar. 11, 1827, CHP, Box 8, Folder 3. JET (Mar. 8, 1827), 8.
17. JET (May 12, 1827), 48.
18. LCH, 117.
19. LCH, 150–151.
20. For a good overview of Hodge's objections to the Mercersburg Theology, see E. Brooks Holifield, "Mercersburg, Princeton, and the South: The Sacramental Controversy in the Nineteenth Century," JPH 54 (1976): 238–257.
21. JET, unpaginated second page.
22. Sarah Hodge to Charles Hodge, Philadelphia, Nov. 10, 1826, CHP, Box 8, Folder 1.
23. JET (Apr. 8, 1827), 25.
24. JET (Apr. 8, 1827), 26–27.
25. LCH, 126.
26. Charles Hodge to Archibald Alexander, Paris, Nov. 2, 1826, CHP, Box 13, Folder 17.

27. JET (Sept. 10, 1827), 72.

28. JET (Apr. 11, 1827), 29.

29. JET (Aug. 27, 1827), 60.

30. JET (Aug. 27, 1827), 61.

31. JET (Aug. 27, 1827), 62.

32. JET (Sept. 1, 1827), 68.

33. JET (Mar. 24; May 12, 1827), 18; 48. Conser, *Church and Confession*, 35.

34. JET (Oct. 10, 1827), 78–80.

Chapter 19: Berlin and the Return Home

1. JET (Oct. 12, 1827), 81.

2. As quoted in LCH, 154 (from I. Bachman, *The Life of Hengstenberg* [1879], 2:30).

3. Walter H. Conser Jr. *Church and Confession: Conservative Theologians in Germany, England, and America, 1815–1866* (Macon, Ga.: Mercer University Press, 1984), 35.

4. JET (Oct. 12, 1827), 81.

5. JET (Dec. 27, 1827), 95.

6. Robert Clemmer, "Historical Transcendentalism in Pennsylvania," JHI 30:4 (Oct.–Dec. 1969): 585.

7. LCH, 188.

8. JET (Jan. 18, 1828), 117.

9. JET (Oct. 14, 1827), 82.

10. CHP, Box 2, Folders 3–5; *Das Apostolische Zeitalter von Neander*, CHM, Box 16, Folder 3. See also JET (Oct. 14, 1827), 82; and JET (Dec. 30, 1827), 102.

11. JET (Mar. 23, 1828), 144; JET (Mar. 30, 1828), 155; JET (Dec. 30, 1827), 99.

12. JET (Apr. 15, 1828), 175.

13. JET (Apr. 15, 1828), 174.

14. LCH, 186.

15. LCH, 186.

16. LCH, 188.

17. Douglas Botting, *Humboldt and the Cosmos* (New York: Harper & Row, 1973), 172. See also Aaron Sachs, *The Humboldt Current: Nineteenth-Century Exploration and the Roots of American Environmentalism* (New York: Viking, 2006), 2.

18. Examples of notes on Humboldt's lectures can be found in JET (various dates), 97–98; 105–107; 110; 115–116; 119–124; 126; 128–130; 133–143; 148–153; 159–162; 166–171;173; 176–181.

19. "Lecture on the Races of Men, CHP, Box 2, Folder 6.

20. Botting, *Humboldt and the Cosmos*, 79.

21. LCH, 190.

22. LCH, 190.

23. Charles Hodge, "Lecture Addressed to the Students of the Theological Seminary," BRTR 1:1 (Jan. 1829): 96.

24. LCH, 200.

25. Charles Hodge to Archibald Alexander, Apr. 4, 1828, CHP, Box 13, Folder 17.

26. Charles Hodge to Archibald Alexander, Apr. 4, 1828, CHP, Box 13, Folder 17.

27. Charles Hodge to Archibald Alexander, Apr. 4, 1828, CHP, Box 13, Folder 17.

28. Charles Hodge to Archibald Alexander, Apr. 4, 1828, CHP, Box 13, Folder 17.

Chapter 20: A Sense of Mission

1. LCH, 207.
2. Charles Hodge to Sarah Hodge, Halle, Mar. 1, 1827, CHP, Box 8, Folder 1.
3. JET (Sept. 4, 1827), 69.
4. Charles Hodge, "Anniversary Address: American Home Missionary Society," *The Home Missionary* 2:2 (June 1, 1829): 18. Copy found in CHM, Box 28, Folder 67.
5. Charles Hodge, "Lecture Addressed to the Students of the Theological Seminary," BR 1:1 (Jan. 1829): 85.
6. Hodge, "Lecture Addressed to the Students of the Theological Seminary," 87–88.
7. Hodge, "Lecture Addressed to the Students of the Theological Seminary," 87.
8. Charles Hodge, "Review of Sprague's *Lectures to Young People*," BRTR, 3:3 (July 1831): 300–301.
9. Charles Hodge to Mary Hodge, Princeton, December 25, 1825, CHP, Box 7, Folder 2.
10. For an example of Mary Hodge's strong views on the importance of early education, see Mary Hodge to Charles Hodge, Philadelphia, Apr. 19, 1828, CHP, Box 7, Folder 1.
11. Charles Hodge, "Lecture Addressed to the Students of the Theological Seminary," 86. David Neil Murchie, "Morality and Social Ethics in the Thought of Charles Hodge" (Ph.D. diss., Drew University, 1980), 274–275.
12. The most complete treatment of Hodge's views on public education reform is found in Andrew D. Witmer, "'To Educate For Heaven': Charles Hodge and Religious Instruction in American Common Schools, 1825–1850" (M.A. thesis, History, University of Virginia, May 2002). Concerning the emergence of Presbyterian schools for the young, see Lewis Joseph Sherrill, *Presbyterian Parochial Schools, 1846–1870* (New Haven, Conn.: Yale University Press, 1932).
13. Hodge, "Lecture Addressed to the Students of the Theological Seminary," 93.
14. The Society for Inquiry was one of three educational secret societies in which Hodge participated at Princeton. The first was the Whigs, and the last was the earliest incarnation of the Chi Phi fraternity, which was founded at Princeton College by Robert Baird (then a tutor at the College) on December 24, 1824. Hodges was twice an officer for the Society of Inquiry. See PTS, Minutes of the Society of Inquiry, Box 14, Folder 1 (1812–1842). The most comprehensive study of Princeton Theological Seminary's commitment to missions during the early nineteenth century is David Calhoun, "The Last Command: Princeton Theological Seminary and Missions (1812–1862)" (Ph.D. diss., Princeton Theological Seminary, 1983).
15. Interest in missions predated the "Haystack Prayer Meeting," but this event served a largely symbolic purpose in commemorating the beginning of a major American Protestant interest in global evangelization. Calhoun, "Last Command," 58–59.
16. Charles Hodge to Archibald Alexander, Paris, Jan. 19, 1827, CHP, Box 13, Folder 17. So great was Green's interest in missions that he published a book on the subject: *A Historical Sketch or Compendious View of Domestic and Foreign Missions in the Presbyterian Church of the United States of America* (Philadelphia: William S. Martien, 1838).
17. Robert Baird, *Boston Recorder*, June 2, 1836.
18. James Lynn Osen, "The Revival of the French Reformed Church, 1830–1852 (Ph.D. diss., History, University of Wisconsin, 1966), 27–28.
19. Osen, "Revival of the French Reformed Church," 28–29; 77–81.
20. Osen, "Revival of the French Reformed Church," 28.

21. Osen, "Revival of the French Reformed Church," 29–30.

22. LCH, 110.

23. LCH, 154.

24. Frederic Monod to Charles Hodge, Paris, December 23, 1833, CHP, Box 17, Folder 68. For perceptions of Billy's "fanatick" behavior, see "Billy" Monod to Charles Hodge, St. Quentin France, CHP, Box 17, Folder 67.

25. As reprinted in an excerpt in LCH, 154 (from I. Bachman, *The Life of Hengstenberg* [1879], 2:30).

26. Richard Gardiner, "Princeton and Paris: An Early Nineteenth Century Bond of Mission" (Senior Thesis, History Dept., Princeton Theological Seminary, 1994), 70. Hodge tells his friend Henry Boardman that "It was not Adolphe Monod, but a younger brother, who translated the commentary on Romans. There are four Monods in the ministry. Adolphe wrote the Preface." Charles Hodge to Henry A. Boardman, Princeton, June 29, 1848, CHP, Box 14, Folder 23.

27. "Billy" Monod to Charles Hodge, St. Quentin France, Aug. 17, 1831, CHP, Box 17, Folder 67. See also Gardiner, "Princeton and Paris," 21.

28. The various incarnations of the "French Committee" were: "French Association" (1833); "Foreign Evangelical Association," (1836); Foreign Evangelical Society" (1839); and finally, the "Evangelical Alliance" (1846). Gardiner, "Princeton and Paris," 28.

29. Gardiner, "Princeton and Paris," 77.

30. Letter printed in the *Banner*, church paper published by the Doylestown Presbyterian Church, n.d., as cited in Calhoun, "Last Command," 425–426.

31. MIN (1830), 18. See also Calhoun, "Last Command," 197–198.

32. Calhoun, "Last Command," 208.

33. LCH, 384.

34. Charles Hodge, "The Teaching Office of the Church," *The Foreign Missionary Chronicle* 16:6 (June 1848): 161.

35. Hodge, "Teaching Office of the Church," 169.

Chapter 21: The Repertory Reborn

1. Charles Hodge, "The Inspiration of Holy Scripture," BRPR 29:4 (Oct. 1857): 695.

2. BR 1:1 (1829): Advertisement.

3. Paul C. Gutjahr, *An American Bible: A History of the Good Book in the United States, 1777–1880* (Stanford, Calif.: Stanford University Press, 1999), 29–33. BR 1:1 (1829): Advertisement.

4. John Backus to Charles Hodge, Philadelphia, Jan. 4, 1836, CHP, Box 14, Folder 1.

5. Kenneth S. Gapp, "The Princeton Review Series and the Contribution of Princeton Theological Seminary to Presbyterian Quarterly Magazines," (Princeton, N.J.: 1943, PTS, typescript), 13. Mark A. Noll. "The Princeton Theological Review: 1825–1929," WTJ 50 (Fall 1988): 286. Some subscribers received the *Repertory* for less than the $3.00 annual fee. Matthew Hope, who helped manage the periodical in the 1840s, reported that at least twenty subscribers received the periodical for $2.25 per year. He believed the circulation would go up if the price was lowered. Matthew Hope to Charles Hodge, Philadelphia, December 14, 1841, CHP, Box 16, Folder 49.

6. Cathy N. Davidson, *Revolution and the Word: The Rise of the Novel in America* (New York: Oxford University Press, 1986), 25.

7. Others who served as editor or co-editor of the *Biblical Repertory* included Robert Patton, James W. Alexander, Joseph A. Alexander, Albert Dod, and Lyman Atwater. Another important person for the *Repertory* was Matthew Boyd Hope, a Princeton Theological Seminary graduate who would later teach at Princeton College. From 1840 to 1848, he served as the publisher of the journal and handled its financial affairs.

8. For a good overview of the life and writings of Joseph Addison Alexander, see "Alexander, Joseph Addison," BRPR, *Index 1825–1868* (Philadelphia, Pa.: Peter Walker, 1871): 82–91.

9. Gapp, "Princeton Review Series," 21.

Chapter 22: The Imputation Controversy

1. The terms "Old School" and "New School" had been circulating since the late 1820s, but it was Ashbel Green who popularized them when he used them as key reference labels in a series of ten articles entitled "The Present State of the Presbyterian Church," which appeared in his *Christian Advocate* in 1831 and 1832. The Old and New School factions had some similarities to the Old and New Side factions of the previous century, but there were no direct lines of descent between the Old Side and Old School and New Side and New School. One important distinction lay in the fact that the eighteenth-century Old and New Sides remained committed to Calvinism although they differed on certain issues surrounding revival activity. A good summary of these issues can be found in Theodore Dwight Bozeman, *Protestants in an Age of Science: The Baconian Ideal and Antebellum American Religious Thought* (Chapel Hill: University of North Carolina Press, 1977), 32–38.

2. Key theological differences between the Old and New School are neatly encapsulated in Isaac Van Arsdale Brown, *A Historical Vindication of the Abrogation of the Plan of Union* (Philadelphia, Pa.: Wm. S. & Alfred Martien, 1855), 288–308.

3. For a thorough treatment of the New Haven Theology and its influence in early nineteenth-century Presbyterianism, see Earl A. Pope, "The Rise of the New Haven Theology," JPH 44:1 (1966): 24–44; and Earl A. Pope, "The Rise of the New Haven Theology II," JPH 44:2 (1966): 106–121.

4. Nathaniel Taylor, *Concio ad Clerum: A Sermon Delivered in the Chapel of Yale College, Sept. 1828* (New Haven, Conn.: Maltby and Homan Hallock, 1842), 8.

5. Archibald Alexander, "The Early History of Pelagianism," BRTR 2:1 (Jan. 1830): 89.

6. Alexander, "Early History of Pelagianism," 92.

7. Alexander, "Early History of Pelagianism," 78.

8. Alexander outlines the traditional view of imputation held by both Augustine and the Princeton faculty in his article on Pelagius. For a concise treatment of the definition of imputation, see Alexander, "Early History of Pelagianism," 90.

9. For a good treatment of Stuart's view of imputation and Original Sin, see John H. Giltner, *Moses Stuart: The Father of Biblical Science in America* (Atlanta, Ga.: Scholars Press, 1988), 111–116.

10. From the Princeton side, these articles included Charles Hodge, "Review of an Article in the June number of the Christian Spectator, entitled, 'Inquiries respecting the Doctrine of Imputation," BRTR 2:3 (July 1830): 425–472; Archibald Alexander, "The Doctrine of Original Sin as held by the Church, Both Before and After the Reformation," BRTR 2:4 (Oct. 1830): 481–503; Archibald Alexander, "An Inquiry into that Inability under which the Sinner Labours, and Whether It Furnishes Any Excuse for His Neglect of Duty," BRTR 3:3 (July

1831): 360–383; Charles Hodge, "The Christian Spectator on the Doctrine of Imputation," BRTR 3:3 (July 1831): 407–443; Charles Hodge, "The New Divinity Tried," BRTR 4:2 (Apr. 1832): 278–304. From the Yale side, the articles included Moses Stuart, "Remarks of a Protestant on the Biblical Repertory," QCS 3:1 (Mar. 1831): 156–168; "Case of the Rev. Mr. Barnes," QCS 3:2 (June 1831): 292–336; Moses Stuart, "The *Biblical Repertory* on the Doctrine of Imputation," QCS 3:3 (Sept. 1831): 497–512; "What is the Real difference between the New-Haven Divines and those who oppose them?" QCS 5:4 (December 1833): 657–672; "The Scriptural View of Divine Influence as opposed to Pelagian and other Views," QCS 7:4 (Dec. 1835): 591–597.

11. Charles Hodge, "Stuart on Romans," BRTR 5:3 (July 1833): 382.

12. Earl A. Pope, "Albert Barnes, The Way of Salvation, and Theological Controversy," JPH 57:1 (Jan. 1979): 21.

13. Charles Hodge, "Barnes on the Epistle of the Romans," BRTR 7:2 (Apr. 1835): 303.

14. Charles Hodge, "Notes, Explanatory and Practical, on the Epistle to the Romans, designed for Bible-Classes and Sunday Schools," BRTR 5:3 (Apr. 1835): 288; 286.

15. Hodge, "Notes, Explanatory and Practical," 286.

16. It is likely that Hodge initially conceived of his Romans commentary as a rebuttal to Stuart's 1832 work. He wrote his brother that he was over half finished with his commentary before he first heard of Barnes's *Notes on Romans*. Once Barnes's commentary appeared, Hodge felt an even greater need to publish a corrective to Stuart's, and then Barnes's, faulty biblical interpretations. Charles Hodge to Hugh Hodge, Princeton, Apr. 6, 1835, CHP, Box 9, Folder 5.

Chapter 23: Romans

1. JET (Jan. 7, 1828), 106. Hodge would later repeat the importance he placed on these doctrines in the lecture he gave at the opening of the 1829 seminary school year: "Wherever you find vital piety, that is, penitence, and a devotional spirit, there you find, the doctrines of the fall, of depravity, of regeneration, of atonement, and the Deity of Jesus Christ." Charles Hodge, "Lecture Addressed to the Students of the Theological Seminary," BRTR 1:1 (Jan. 1829): 94–95.

2. Scott Robert Wright, "Regeneration and Redemptive History" (Ph.D. diss., Westminster Theological Seminary, 1999), 95.

3. Epistle to the Romans, 1823, CHP, Box 5, Folder 3. Hodge recorded his first notes to the all-important fifth chapter of Romans in Jan. 1824. Over time, he wrote three separate collections of notes on Romans 5:12–21. Even in his earliest notes from 1824, he paid an inordinate amount of attention to these nine verses.

4. LCH, 205

5. LCH, 273–277.

6. Hodge's desire to reach an audience beyond the professional clergy can be seen in how upon completing his commentary he immediately proceeded to write another 175-page book containing questions and materials on Romans designed to be used in Bible and Sunday school classes: *Questions on the Epistle to the Romans: Designed for Bible Classes and Sunday Schools* (Philadelphia: Grigg & Elliot, 1835).

7. Hodge, RO, 586.

8. Charles Hodge, "Stuart on Romans," BRTR 5:3 (July 1833): 382.

9. Mark Noll, "Charles Hodge," in *Reading Romans through the Centuries*, ed. Jeffrey P. Greenman and Timothy Larsen (Grand Rapids, Mich.: Brazos Press, 2005), 182.

10. Moses Stuart, *A Commentary on the Epistle to the Romans*, 2nd. ed. (Andover, Mass.: Gould & Newman, 1835), 610; 614; 616. Mark Noll, *America's God: From Jonathan Edwards to Abraham Lincoln* (New York: Oxford University Press, 2002), 306.

11. The best single treatment of the differences between these two commentaries and changes in American biblical scholarship that these differences signal is Stephen J. Stein, "Stuart and Hodge on Romans 5:12–21: An Exegetical Controversy About Original Sin," JPH 47:4 (Dec. 1969): 340–358.

12. LCH, 271–272.

13. LCH, 590–591.

14. Stuart, *Commentary on the Epistle to the Romans*, 2nd ed., 1835.

15. Moses Stuart, *A Commentary on the Epistle to the Romans*, 4nd ed. (Glasgow, Scotland: Thomas Tegg and Son, 1838), vii.

16. "Dr. Hodge's Commentary on Romans in French." PRE 11 (Mar. 27, 1841): 50. For Stapfer's role in the French translation, see LCH, 277.

Chapter 24: Crippled in Body, But Not in Mind

1. Charles Hodge to Hugh Hodge, Princeton, June 4, 1832, CHP, Box 9, Folder 3.

2. MFH, 79.

3. Charles Hodge to Hugh Hodge, Princeton, July 21, 1829, CHP, Box 9, Folder 3.

4. For the most comprehensive treatment of this epidemic, see Charles E. Rosenberg, *The Cholera Years: The United States in 1832, 1849 and 1866* (Chicago: University of Chicago Press, 1987).

5. For a sampling of Hodge's activity and interest in this wave of cholera, see Charles Hodge to Hugh Hodge, Princeton, July 10, 1832; July 24, 1832; Aug. 4, 1832; Aug. 7, 1832; CHP, Box 9, Folder 3; and Hugh Hodge to Charles Hodge, Philadelphia, Aug. 25, 1832, CHP, Box 28, Folder 5.

6. Hugh Hodge enhanced his reputation by later publishing a much-read medical journal article on how best to treat cholera. Hugh L. Hodge, "Lecture on Cholera Morbus; on the Pathology and Therapeutics of Cholera Maligna," *American Journal of the Medical Sciences* 12 (1833): 293–306; 386–432.

7. Charles Hodge to Hugh Hodge, Princeton, Apr. 23, 1836, CHP, Box 10, Folder 2.

8. LCH, 234–235.

9. LCH, 271.

10. LCH, 239.

11. Charles Hodge to Hugh Hodge, Princeton, Nov. 9, 1839 and Nov. 24, 1839, CHP, Box 10, Folder 4.

12. Charles Hodge to Hugh Hodge, Princeton, Dec. 5, 1839, CHP, Box 10, Folder 4.

13. LCH, 236.

14. Charles Hodge to Hugh Hodge, Nov. 24, 1839, CHP, Box 10, Folder 4.

15. LCH, 237.

16. The best biography of Joseph Henry is Albert E. Moyer, *Joseph Henry: The Rise of an American Scientist* (Washington, D.C.: Smithsonian Institution Press, 1997). Henry considered Archibald Alexander Hodge his favorite student. Henry's relationship with A. A. Hodge is chronicled in David B. Calhoun, *Princeton Seminary* (Carlisle, Pa.: Banner of Truth Trust, 1994), 1:268.

17. It is interesting to note that Hugh Hodge encouraged Charles to give up his attempts to find a cure through the use of electric current. Charles Hodge to Hugh Hodge, Princeton, Oct. 22, 1834, CHP, Box 9, Folder 5.

18. Charles Hodge to Hugh Hodge, Princeton, June 23, 1836, Box 10, Folder 2.

19. On the subject of water treatments, Hodge read and was much influenced by John Bell's *On Baths and Mineral Waters* (Philadelphia, Pa.: Henry H. Porter, 1831). Charles Hodge to Hugh Hodge, Princeton, June 5, 1838, CHP, Box 10, Folder 3.

20. Charles Hodge to Hugh Hodge, Princeton, Jan. 16, 1838; May 19, 1838; May 20, 1838, CHP, Box 10, Folder 3.

21. LCH, 239.

22. LCH, 238.

Chapter 25: Home Life

1. Charles Hodge to Hugh Hodge, Princeton, Nov. 20, 1830, CHP, Box 9, Folder 3. Hodge bought the land for $1560. He paid $60 down and mortgaged the remainder.

2. LCH, 236.

3. Charles Hodge to Hugh Hodge, Princeton, Jan. 5, 1835, CHP, Box 10, Folder 1.

4. Charles Hodge to Hugh Hodge, Princeton, Aug. 22, 1836 and Aug. 27, 1836, CHP, Box 10, Folder 2.

5. Charles Hodge to Hugh Hodge, Princeton, Dec. 12, 1828, CHP, Box 9, Folder 3.

6. David Torbett, *Theology and Slavery: Charles Hodge and Horace Bushnell* (Macon, Ga.: Mercer University Press, 2006), 70–71.

7. Cato was probably married to Henrietta. Charles Hodge to Hugh Hodge, Princeton, Jan. 16, 1832, CHP, Box 9, Folder 3.

8. LAA, 280–282. LSM, 1:90; 2:300. Allen C. Guelzo, "Charles Hodge's Antislavery Moment," CHR, 304.

9. Arthur Zilversmit, *The First Emancipation of Slavery in the North* (Chicago: University of Chicago Press, 1967), 193. Graham Russell Hodges, *Slavery and Freedom in the Rural North: African Americans in Monmouth County, New Jersey, 1665–1865* (Madison, Wisc.: Madison House, 1997), 147–152.

10. Guelzo, "Charles Hodge's Antislavery Moment," 303. Ernest Trice Thompson, *Presbyterians in the South* (Richmond, Va.: John Knox Press, 1963), 1:334–335.

11. Adam Hochschild, *Bury the Chains: Prophets and Rebels in the Fight to Free an Empire's Slaves* (New York: Houghton Mifflin, 2005), 2.

12. Seymour Drescher, *Capitalism and Antislavery: British Mobilization in Comparative Perspective* (New York: Oxford University Press, 1987), x.

13. This emphasis on improvement is similar to a line of reasoning elaborated in Torbett, *Theology and Slavery*, 69.

14. William Berryman Scott, *Some Memories of a Palaeontologist* (Princeton, N.J.: Princeton University Press, 1939), 7.

15. Scott, *Some Memories of a Palaeontologist*, 8.

16. Hugh Lenox Scott, *Some Memories of a Soldier* (New York: The Century Co., 1928), 3.

17. Charles Hodge to Sarah Hodge, Apr. 9, 1827, CHP, Box 8, Folder 3.

18. Charles Hodge to Sarah Hodge, Jan. 20, 1827, CHP, Box 8, Folder 3.

19. Louise L. Stevenson, "Charles Hodge, Womanly Women, and Manly Ministers," CHR, 171–172.

20. Scott, *Some Memories of a Palaeontologist*, 8.

21. LCH, 227

22. Charles Hodge to Hugh Hodge, Princeton, Aug. 15, 1835, CHP, Box 10, Folder 1.

23. LCH, 227–228. Charles Hodge to Hugh Hodge, Princeton, June 3, 1840, CHP, Box 10, Folder 4.
24. Charles Hodge to Hugh Hodge, Princeton, Sept. 24, 1838, CHP, Box 10, Folder 3.

Chapter 26: The Coming Storm

1. David B. Calhoun, *Princeton Seminary: Faith and Learning 1812–1868* (Carlisle, Pa.: Banner of Truth Trust, 1994), 1:242.
2. FYFL, 1:170.
3. BRPR, Index Volume from 1825–1868 (1871): 20. Green published a copy of the "Act and Testimony" in his CA (June 1834): 269–272.
4. BRPR, Index Volume, 22.
5. Charles Hodge, "The Act and Testimony" BRTR (Oct. 1834): 505.
6. Hodge, "Act and Testimony," 508.
7. Charles Hodge to Hugh Hodge, Princeton, Nov. 21, 1834, CHP, Box 10, Folder 1.
8. Robert Breckinridge, "A Plain Statement," PRE 5:16 (Apr. 16, 1835): 1.
9. LCH, 313–314.
10. Letters (both dated Apr. 17, 1835) from John MacLean and Albert Dod appeared in *The Presbyterian* one week after Breckinridge's article. See PRE 5:17 (Apr. 23, 1835): 66. Earl A. Pope, "Albert Barnes, The Way of Salvation," JPH 57:1 (Jan. 1979): 29.
11. Charles Hodge to Hugh Hodge, Princeton, Nov. 7, 1834, CHP, Box 10, Folder 1.
12. Charles Hodge to Hugh Hodge, Princeton, Nov. 21, 1834, CHP, Box 10, Folder 1. Hugh T. Kerr, ed., *Sons of the Prophets: Leaders in Protestantism from Princeton Seminary* (Princeton, N.J.: Princeton University Press, 1963), 34. Green embraced the term. In speaking of his compatriots in his own *Christian Advocate*, he characterized the conservative side with the words: "Ultraism—high church notions." Ashbel Green, "A Solemn Warning to the Presbyterian Church," CA (Feb. 1834): 64.
13. Charles Grandison Finney, *Lectures on Revivals of Religion* (New York: Leavitt, Lord & Company, 1835), 253.
14. Richard Carwardine, "The Second Great Awakening in the Urban Centers: An Examination of Methodism and the 'New Measures,'" JAH 59:2 (Sept. 1972): 327–340. John H. Wigger, *Taking Heaven by Storm: Methodism and the Rise of Popular Christianity in America* (Urbana: University of Illinois Press, 1998), 79; 96–97; 106; 118; 151–161. Nathan O. Hatch, *The Democratization of American Christianity* (New Haven, Conn.: Yale University Press, 1989), 49–56; 79; 197–201.
15. Charles Finney, *Lectures on Revivals of Religion* (New York: Leavitt, Lord, 1835), 12.
16. Finney, *Lectures on Revivals of Religion*, 253. For a more complete discussion of Finney's thoughts on preaching, see Keith J. Hardman, *Charles Grandison Finney, 1792–1875* (Grand Rapids, Mich.: Baker Book House, 1987), 282–283.
17. Finney, *Lectures on Revivals of Religion*, 269.
18. Albert B. Dod, "Lectures on Revivals of Religion," BRTR 7:3 (July 1835): 482.
19. Dod, "Lectures on Revivals of Religion," 484.
20. Archibald Alexander, "An Inquiry into that Inability under which the Sinner Labours, and Whether It Furnishes any Excuse of his Neglect of Duty," BRTR 3:3 (July, 1831): 381–382.
21. For the most cogent and concise analysis of the Presbyterian schism and the centrality of theology to the split, see George M. Marsden, *The Evangelical Mind and the New School Presbyterian Experience* (Eugene, Oreg.: Wipf & Stock, 2003), 66–67.
22. Marsden, *Evangelical Mind*, 71. Calhoun, *Princeton Seminary*, 1:239–240.
23. LCH, 327.

24. Sydney E. Ahlstrom, *A Religious History of the American People*. (New Haven, Conn.: Yale University Press, 1972), 467.

25. For details of the arguments surrounding the General Assembly, its Foreign Missionary Board, and voluntary societies, see Charles Hodge, "The General Assembly of 1836," BRTR 8:3 (July 1836): 416–440.

26. Charles Hodge, "Voluntary Societies and Ecclesiastical Organizations" BRPR 9:1 (Jan. 1837): 103. Hodge, "General Assembly of 1836," 429.

27. Hodge, "Voluntary Societies," 106.

28. Hodge, "Voluntary Societies," 114.

29. Hodge, "Voluntary Societies," 114.

30. Marsden, *Evangelical Mind*, 74. See also Earl R. MacCormac, "Missions and the Presbyterian Schism of 1837," CH 32:1 (Mar. 1963): 32–45.

31. Robert Baird, *Religion in the United States* (Glasgow and Edinburgh, Scotland: Blackie & Son, 1844), 552.

Chapter 27: The Slavery Question

1. Charles Hodge to Hugh Hodge, Princeton, Oct. 1, 1831, CHP, Box 9, Folder 3.

2. Daniel Walker Howe, *What Hath God Wrought: The Transformation of America, 1815–1848* (New York: Oxford University Press, 2007), 323–327. Kenneth M. Stampp, *The Peculiar Institution: Slavery in the Ante-Bellum South* (New York: Vintage Books, 1989), 132–134.

3. Howe, *What Hath God Wrought*, 425–426.

4. Matthew Mason, *Slavery and Politics in the Early American Republic* (New York: Oxford University Press, 2006), 228–229.

5. Andrew E. Murray, *Presbyterians and the Negro—A History* (Philadelphia, Pa.: Presbyterian Historical Society, 1966), 99.

6. Charles Hodge to Hugh Hodge, Princeton, Nov. 27, 1837, CHP, Box 10, Folder 3.

7. *A Digest Compiled from the Records of the General Assembly of the Presbyterian Church in the United States* (Philadelphia, Pa.: R. P. M'Colloh, 1820), 338.

8. *Digest*, 338–339.

9. Just how much compromise was involved in the 1818 declaration is discussed in Murray, *Presbyterians and the Negro*, 20–28.

10. *Digest*, 344.

11. Archibald Alexander, *A History of Colonization of the Western Coast of Africa* (Philadelphia, Pa.: William S. Martien, 1846), 17. See also James Oliver Horton and Lois E. Horton, *Slavery and the Making of America* (New York: Oxford University Press, 2005), 87.

12. Eric Burin, *Slavery and the Peculiar Solution: A History of the American Colonization Society* (Gainesville: University Press of Florida, 2005), 15.

13. Alexander, *History of Colonization*, 80; P. J. Staudenraus, *The African Colonization Movement 1816–1865* (New York: Columbia University Press, 1961), 19; LAA, 450.

14. *The Twelfth Annual Report of the American Society for Colonizing Free People of Colour of the United States* (Georgetown D.C.: James C. Dunn, 1829), 72; Staudenraus, *African Colonization Movement*, 85.

15. More recent histories of the African Colonization Society include Staudenraus, *African Colonization Movement*; Amos Beyan, *The American Colonization Society and the Creation of the*

Liberian State (Lanham, Md.: University Press of America, 1991); and Burin, *Slavery and the Peculiar Solution.*

16. Drew Gilpin Faust, *The Ideology of Slavery: Proslavery Thought in the Antebellum South, 1830–1860* (Baton Rouge: Louisiana State University Press, 1981), 49–50; Murray, *Presbyterians and the Negro,* 84.

17. Murray, *Presbyterians and the Negro,* 83.

18. George M. Marsden, *The Evangelical Mind and the New School Presbyterian Experience* (Eugene, Oreg.: Wipf & Stock, 2003), 100.

19. Charles Finney, *Lectures on Revivals of Religion* (New York: Leavitt, Lord, 1835), 278.

20. Murray, *Presbyterians and the Negro,* 92.

21. Murray, *Presbyterians and the Negro,* 93.

22. Charles Hodge, "Slavery," BRTR 8:2 (Apr. 1836): 274.

23. Hodge wrote that wrong thinking on the issue of slavery "does much to retard the progress of freedom; it embitters and divides the members of the community, and distracts the Christian Church." Hodge, "Slavery," 298.

24. Marsden, *Evangelical Mind,* 97–100.

25. Robert T. Handy, *A History of Union Theological Seminary in New York* (New York: Columbia University Press, 1987), 5. Ezra Hall Gillet, *History of the Presbyterian Church in the United States of America* (Philadelphia, Pa.: Presbyterian Publication Committee, 1964), 2:501.

26. Charles Hodge to Hugh Hodge, Princeton, May 15, 1836, CHP, Box 10, Folder 2.

27. Charles Hodge, "Conscience and the Constitution," BRPR 23:1 (Jan. 1851): 128.

28. Allen Guelzo coined the phrase "antislavery moment." Although I agree with Guelzo that Hodge changed his position on slavery for a time during the Civil War, my own interpretation of what brought on this "moment" differs from Guelzo. I place greater emphasis on the issue of race in Hodge's reconsideration of slavery. Allen C. Guelzo, "Charles Hodge's Antislavery Moment," CHR, 299–325.

29. Hodge, "Slavery," 273.

30. Hodge, "Slavery," 276.

31. Hodge, "Slavery," 277.

32. Hodge, "Slavery," 292.

33. Hodge, "Slavery," 302.

34. Hodge, "Slavery," 278. See also David Neil Murchie, "Morality and Social Ethics in the Thought of Charles Hodge" (Ph.D. diss., Drew University, 1980), 294–308.

35. Hodge, "Slavery," 293.

36. Hodge, "Slavery," 303. Hodge attempted to make good on his strong conviction that slave families should be kept together by exploring the possibility of purchasing the son of his slave, Lena, from a family a few hours ride from Princeton. The complicated nature of slavery and ethics, however, becomes clear when Hodge decided against the purchase upon discovering that the boy was consumptive. Hodge feared bringing the disease into his household. Charles Hodge to Hugh Hodge, Princeton, Jan. 9, 1836, CHP, Box 10, Folder 2.

37. Hodge, "A Narrative of the Visit to the American Churches," BRTR 7:4 (Oct. 1835): 624.

38. Hodge, "Slavery," 289–291.

39. Hodge, "Slavery," 304.

40. Guelzo, "Charles Hodge's Antislavery Moment," 324.

41. Charles Hodge, "The General Assembly of 1836," BRTR 8:3 (July 1836): 441.

Chapter 28: The Schism

1. Charles Hodge to Hugh Hodge, Princeton, Nov. 9, 1835, CHP, Box 10, Folder 1.
2. Albert Barnes, "The Way of Salvation" (Morris-Town, N.J.: Jacob Mann, 1830), 6; 10; 13. For a good analysis of "The Way of Salvation" as a source of controversy, see Earl A. Pope, "Albert Barnes, The Way of Salvation," JPH 57:1 (Jan. 1979): 20–34. See also E. Brooks Holifield, *Theology in America* (New Haven, Conn.: Yale University Press, 2003), 375.
3. Lewis Cheeseman, *Differences between Old and New School Presbyterians* (Rochester, N.Y.: Erastus Darrow, 1848), 8. Pope, "Albert Barnes, The Way of Salvation," 21.
4. James H. Moorhead, "The 'Restless Spirit of Radicalism': Old School Fears and the Schism of 1837," JPH 78:1 (Spring 2000): 19–20.
5. Moorhead, "Restless Spirit of Radicalism," 25–32.
6. MIN (1837), 507.
7. MIN (1837), 507.
8. Moorhead, "Restless Spirit of Radicalism," 23–25.
9. George M. Marsden, *The Evangelical Mind and the New School Presbyterian Experience* (Eugene, Oreg.: Wipf & Stock, 2003), 97.
10. Ezra Hall Gillet, *History of the Presbyterian Church in the United States of America* (Philadelphia, Pa.: Presbyterian Publication Committee, 1964), 2:495–496.
11. For a copy of the "Testimony and Memorial," see Isaac Van Arsdale Brown, *A Historical Vindication of the Abrogation of the Plan of Union* (Philadelphia, Pa.: Wm. S. & Alfred Martien, 1855), 216–226.
12. LCH, 301.
13. Charles Hodge, "General Assembly of 1837," BRPR 9:3 (July 1837): 424–425.
14. Marsden, *Evangelical Mind*, 63.
15. LCH, 285.
16. LCH, 305.
17. LCH, 303.
18. Charles Hodge, "Retrospect of the History of the Princeton Review," BRPR, Index Volume (1871): 19.
19. Charles Hodge to Hugh Hodge, Princeton, July 26, 1837, CHP, Box 10, Folder 3.

Chapter 29: The New School Fights Back

1. Charles Hodge to Hugh Hodge, Princeton, June 11, 1837, CHP, Box 10, Folder 3.
2. Ezra Hall Gillet, *History of the Presbyterian Church in the United States of America* (Philadelphia, Pa.: Presbyterian Publication Committee, 1964), 2:532.
3. Samuel Baird, *A History of the New School* (Lansing: University of Michigan Library, 2006), 541.
4. Isaac Van Arsdale Brown, *A Historical Vindication of the Abrogation of the Plan of Union* (Philadelphia, Pa.: Wm. S. & Alfred Martien, 1855), 260.
5. For accounts of the events of the 1838 Old School General Assembly, see "General Assembly," PRE 8:20 (May 19, 1838): 78; "The Schism," PRE 8:21 (May 26, 1838): 82; Baird, *History of the New School*, 545–553; Brown, *Historical Vindication*, 258–260; George M. Marsden, *Evangelical Mind and the New School Presbyterian Experience* (Eugene, Oreg.: Wipf & Stock, 2003), 64–66.
6. Marsden, *Evangelical Mind*, 65.
7. LCH, 315.

8. Charles Hodge to Hugh Hodge, Princeton, Mar. 27, 1839, CHP, Box 10, Folder 4.

9. Charles Hodge to Hugh Hodge, Princeton, Mar. 27, 1839, CHP, Box 10, Folder 4.

10. Charles Hodge to Henry A. Boardman, Princeton, Apr. 13, 1839, CHP, Box 14, Folder 23.

11. Charles Hodge to Henry A. Boardman, Princeton, Mar. 28, 1839, CHP, Box 14, Folder 23.

12. Charles Hodge to Hugh Hodge, Princeton, Apr. 28, 1840, CHP, Box 10, Folder 4.

13. For a copy of key moments of the Supreme Court's proceedings, see Brown, *A Historical Vindication*, 262–287. Henry A. Boardman kept Hodge informed of the March trial in minute detail through writing him of the daily proceedings in a series of letters. The letters are located in CHP, Box 14, Folder 23.

14. *Presbyterian Re-Union Memorial Volume* (New York: De-Witt C. Lent, 1870), 11.

Chapter 30: Writing History

1. Peter J. Wosh, *Spreading the Word: The Bible Business in Nineteenth-Century America* (Ithaca, N.Y.: Cornell University Press, 1994), 115.

2. Samuel Miller, *A Brief History of the Theological Seminary of the Presbyterian Church at Princeton New Jersey* (Princeton, N.J.: Printed by John Bogart, 1838).

3. LCH, 279.

4. Ashbel Green, "Extracts from the Minutes of the General Assembly of 1834," CA (July 1834): 322–329; "Proceedings of the General Assembly of the Presbyterian Church in May and June, 1834," CA (Aug. 1834): 362–369; "Proceedings of the General Assembly of the Presbyterian Church in May and June, 1834," CA (Sept. 1834): 410–418; "Proceedings of the General Assembly of the Presbyterian Church in May and June, 1834," CA (Oct. 1834): 459–467; "Proceedings of the General Assembly of the Presbyterian Church in May and June, 1834," CA (Nov. 1834): 503–512; "Proceedings of the General Assembly of the Presbyterian Church in May and June, 1834," CA (Dec. 1834): 556–561.

5. Charles Hodge, "The General Assembly of 1835," BRTR (July 1835): 440.

6. Hodge, "General Assembly of 1835," 440.

7. "Charles Hodge," BRPR, Index Volume (1871): 206.

8. CONH, 1:vi.

9. Hugh T. Kerr, ed., *Sons of the Prophets: Leaders in Protestantism from Princeton Seminary* (Princeton, N.J.: Princeton University Press, 1963), 36.

10. Charles Hodge to Hugh Hodge, Princeton, Oct. 12, 1838, CHP, Box 10, Folder 3.

11. LCH, 239.

12. Charles Hodge to Hugh Hodge, Princeton, Jan. 28, 1839, CHP, Box 10, Folder 4.

13. Charles Hodge to Hugh Hodge, Princeton, Jan. 28, 1838, CHP, Box 10, Folder 3.

14. Charles Hodge to Hugh Hodge, Princeton, July 16, 1840, CHP, Box 10, Folder 4.

15. Charles Hodge to Henry Boardman, Princeton, Jan. 21, 1840, CHP, Box 14, Folder 23.

16. CONH, 1:214–215. LCH, 281.

17. CONH, 1:34; 59.

18. CONH, 1:34; 52.

19. CONH, 1:60.

20. CONH, 2:369.

21. CONH, 1:91.

22. CONH, 1:108.

23. CONH, 1:90–91.

24. CONH, 1:86–87.

25. CONH, 1:133.

26. CONH, 2:11.

27. CONH, 2:133.

28. CONH, 2:140.

29. CONH, 2:126.

30. Representative examples of Hodge's preoccupation with the terms "order" and "disorder" can be found in CONH, 2:176–182.

31. CONH, 2:71.

32. CONH, 2:73.

33. Charles Hodge to Hugh Hodge, Princeton, July 25, 1839, CHP, Box 10, Folder 4.

34. Charles Hodge to Hugh Hodge, Princeton, July 25, 1839, CHP, Box 10, Folder 4.

35. CONH, 2:80.

36. CONH, 2:78.

37. Hodge even uses the memoirs of Hannah Hodge as source material for his history. CONH, 2:29.

38. Charles Hodge to Henry A. Boardman, Princeton, Jan. 21, 1840, CHP, Box 14, Folder 23.

39. Archibald Alexander, *Biographical Sketches of the Founder and Principal Alumni of the Log College* (Philadelphia, Pa.: Presbyterian Board of Publication, 1851).

40. Charles Hodge to Henry A. Boardman, Princeton, Jan. 21, 1840, CHP, Box 14, Folder 23.

41. Charles Hodge to Henry A. Boardman, Princeton, Jan. 21, 1840, CHP, Box 14, Folder 23.

42. Charles Hodge to William Martien, Princeton, June 18, 1839, CHP, Box 28, Folder 62.

Chapter 31: The Way of Life

1. Charles Hodge to Hugh Hodge, Princeton, May 11, 1840, CHP, Box 10, Folder 4.

2. Charles Hodge to Hugh Hodge, Princeton, May 11, 1840, CHP, Box 10, Folder 4.

3. Hodge's salary was raised by the Seminary's board of directors on May 19, 1828 to $1500.00. William O. Harris, ed., *A Digest of the Minutes of the Board of Directors, 1812–1929* (1992), 20. Special Collections, Princeton Theological Seminary Library.

4. Charles Hodge to Hugh Hodge, Princeton, Apr. 1, 1836, CHP, Box 10, Folder 2.

5. Charles Hodge to Henry Boardman, Princeton, Apr. 7, 1841, CHP, Box 11, Folder 1. (This letter is misfiled and can be found in the correspondence between Hodge and his brother Hugh.)

6. Charles Hodge to Hugh Hodge, Princeton, July 17, 1840; May 18, 1837, CHP, Box 10, Folder 3.

7. Charles Hodge to Frederick Packard, December 15, 1840. Samuel Perkins Collections, HSP, Phi 494 Am. 112, vol. 2, G–M.

8. Charles Hodge to Frederick Packard, Apr. 25, 1841. Samuel Perkins Collections, HSP, Phi 494 Am. 112, vol. 2, G–M. LCH, 323.

9. Joseph Addison Alexander, "A Cyclopedia of Biblical Literature," BRPR 18:4 (Oct. 1846): 561–562.

10. Charles Hodge to Hugh Hodge, Princeton, May 11, 1840, CHP, Box 10, Folder 4.

11. LCH, 322–323.

12. Charles Hodge to Frederick Packard, Jan. 9, 1840, Samuel Perkins Collections, HSP, Phi 494 Am. 112, vol. 2, G–M.

13. Hodge considered a number of titles at the urging of friends and the American Sunday School Union, including *The Path of Peace* and *Scripture Truth Illustrated by Christian Experience.* Mark Noll, Introduction to *The Way of Life* (Mahwah, N.J.: Paulist Press, 1987), 47.

Charles Hodge to Frederick Packard, Sept. 20, 1841. Samuel Perkins Collections, HSP, Phi 494 Am. 112, vol. 2, G–M.

14. Charles Hodge to Frederick Packard, Nov. 24, 1841. Samuel Perkins Collections, HSP, Phi 494 Am. 112, vol. 2, G–M.

15. LCH, 325.

16. LCH, 325.

17. The amount of the American copyright is noted in a letter from Charles Hodge to Frederick Packard, Nov. 11, 1841, Samuel Perkins Collections, HSP, Phi 494 Am. 112, vol. 2, G–M. The British copyright sum is found in Noll, Introduction to *The Way of Life*, 48. Dr. James McCosh in *Proceedings connected with the Semi-Centennial Commemoration of the Professorship of Rev. Charles Hodge* (New York: Anson D. F. Randolph & Co., 1872), 64. See also FYFL, 1:389.

18. WOL, 3.

19. WOL, 72–73.

20. WOL, 26–27.

21. WOL, 23–24.

22. A good discussion of this tension between Calvinism and Scottish Common Sense Realism in Hodge's thought can be found in Mark Noll, *America's God: From Jonathan Edwards to Abraham Lincoln* (New York: Oxford University Press, 2002), 316–319.

23. WOL, 314.

24. WOL, 315.

25. WOL, 294.

26. WOL, 294.

27. Nathan O. Hatch, "Elias Smith and the Rise of Religious Journalism," in William L. Joyce et al, *Printing and Society in Early America* (Worcester, MA: American Antiquarian Society, 1983), 251.

28. David Morgan, *Protestants and Pictures: Religion, Visual Culture, and the Age of American Mass Production* (New York: Oxford University Press, 1999), 162.

29. Charles Hodge, "Second Advent," Dec. 1, 1846, CHM, Box 2, Folder 22, p. 4.

30. Charles Hodge, "Final Judgement," Nov. 8, 1846, CHM, Box 2, Folder 23, p. 6.

31. Charles Hodge, "Final Judgement," Nov. 8, 1846, CHM, Box 2, Folder 23, p. 7.

Chapter 32: Didactic Theology

1. WOL, 283.

2. WOL, 3.

3. John Broadus, *A Gentleman and a Scholar: Memoir of James P. Boyce* (New York: A.C. Armstrong & Son, 1893), 67–69.

4. Charles Hodge, "Protestant Doctrine as to the Rule of Faith," n.d, CHM, Box 1, Folder 3, p. 1. No exact dates exist on these manuscripts, but evidence points to these notes being used in lectures beginning in the late 1840s.

5. Charles Hodge "Enthusiasm," n.d., CHM, Box 1, Folder 2, p. 1.

6. Charles Hodge, "Enthusiasm," n.d., CHM, Box 1, Folder 2, p. 1.

7. Charles Hodge, "Enthusiasm,"n.d., CHM, Box 1, Folder 2, p. 2.

8. Charles Hodge, "Romish Doctrine as to the Rule of Faith," n.d., CHM, Box 1, Folder 4, p. 1.

9. Charles Hodge, "Romish Doctrine as to the Rule of Faith," n.d., CHM, Box 1, Folder 4, p. 1.

10. Charles Hodge, "Sacraments," n.d., CHM, Box 2, Folder 24, p. 1.

11. Charles Hodge, "Sacraments," n.d., CHM, Box 2, Folder 24, p. 3.

12. Charles Hodge, "Lutheran Doctrine of the Efficacy of the Sacraments," n.d., CHM, Box 2, Folder 25, p. 2.

13. Charles Hodge, "Sacraments," n.d., CHM, Box 2, Folder 24, p. 7.

14. Charles Hodge, "Lutheran Doctrine of the Efficacy of the Sacraments," n.d.,CHM, Box 2, Folder 25, p. 2.

15. Charles Hodge, "Sacraments," n.d., CHM, Box 2, Folder 24, p. 8.

16. Charles Hodge, "Sacraments," n.d., CHM, Box 2, Folder 24, p. 10.

17. D. G. Hart, *John Williamson Nevin: High Church Calvinist* (Phillipsburg, N.J.: P&R Publishing, 2005), 126–127.

18. Charles Hodge, "Baptism," n.d., CHM, Box 2, Folder 26, p. 2.

19. Charles Hodge, "Baptism," n.d., CHM, Box 2, Folder 26, p. 8.

20. Charles Hodge, "Subjects of Baptism," n.d., CHM, Box 2, Folder 27, p. 9.

21. Charles Hodge, "Baptism," n.d., CHM, Box 2, Folder 26, p. 10.

22. Charles Hodge, "Baptism," n.d., CHM, Box 2, Folder 26, p. 9.

Chapter 33: Teaching and Preaching

1. LCH, 323.

2. CHM, Boxes 35, 36; 39–42. These boxes contain volumes on Hodge's lectures on Didactic Theology, compiled by the following students: Henry V. Rankin (1845–1846); Thomas R. Markham (1850–1851); Caspar Wistar Hodge, Sr. (1852–1853); Henry A. Harlow (1856–1857); and Edward B. Hodge (1863).

3. Lyman H. Atwater, *A Discourse Commemorative of the Late Dr. Charles Hodge* (Princeton, N.J.: Charles S. Robinson, 1878), 10.

4. LCH, 389.

5. Charles Hodge, *Conference Papers* (New York: Charles Scribner's Sons, 1879), vii.

6. David Calhoun, *Princeton Seminary* (Carlisle, Pa.: Banner of Truth Trust, 1994), 1:262.

7. Charles Hodge to William S. Plumer, Princeton, July 25, 1854, CHP, Box 18, Folder 30.

8. Charles Hodge to William S. Plumer, Princeton, July 25, 1854, CHP, Box 18, Folder 30.

9. Calhoun, *Princeton Seminary*, 1:262. George Hill, *Lectures on Divinity* (Philadelphia, Pa.: Herman Hooker, 1844); John Dick, *Lectures on Theology*, 2 vols. (Philadelphia, Pa.: F.W. Greenough, 1838); George Christian Knapp, *Lectures on Christian Theology* (New York: M.W. Dodd, 1850).

10. John Broadus, *A Gentleman and a Scholar: Memoir of James P. Boyce* (New York: A.C. Armstrong and Son, 1893), 73.

11. Broadus, *Gentleman and a Scholar*, 78. A good recent biography of Boyce is Thomas J. Nettles, *James Petigru Boyce: A Southern Baptist Statesman* (Phillipsburg, N.J.: P&R Publishing, 2009).

12. Calhoun, *Princeton Seminary*, 1:268.

13. LCH, 388.

14. LCH, 388.

15. FYFL, 1:150.

16. LCH, 205.

17. Atwater, *Discourse*, 22.

18. Calhoun, *Princeton Seminary*, 1:66–67.

19. LAA, 118–119; 122.

20. Robert Rainy and James Mackenzie, *Life of William Cunningham, D.D.* (London: T. Nelson & Sons, 1871), 206.
21. Hodge, *Conference Papers*, vi.
22. Hodge, *Conference Papers*, iii.
23. Hodge, *Conference Papers*, vii.
24. Hodge, *Conference Papers*, vii.
25. Charles Hodge, Sermons, CHM, Box 23, Folder 21; Box 24, Folder 57; Box 25, Folder 80.
26. Hodge's Conference Talks are found in the CHM, Boxes 23–27.
27. Hodge, *Conference Papers*, 26.
28. Hodge, *Conference Papers*, 26–27.

Chapter 34: The Public Face of the Seminary

1. LCH, 588.
2. Robert Rainy and James Mackenzie, *Life of William Cunningham, D.D.* (London: T. Nelson & Sons, 1871), 61.
3. FYFL, 1:387.
4. Rainy and Mackenzie, *Life of William Cunningham*, 204.
5. Rainy and Mackenzie, *Life of William Cunningham*, 65; 205. FYFL, 1:386.
6. FYFL, 1:386.
7. Rainy and Mackenzie, *Life of William Cunningham*, 206.
8. Rainy and Mackenzie, *Life of William Cunningham*, 206.
9. Rainy and Mackenzie, *Life of William Cunningham*, 206.
10. John Macleod, *Scottish Theology in Relation to Church History since the Reformation* (Carlisle, Pa.: Banner of Truth Trust, 1974), 269.
11. Charles Hodge, "General Assembly, 1846," BRPR 18:3 (July 1846): 424. William Cunningham to Charles Hodge, Edinburgh, July 15, 1844, CHP, Box 15, Folder 16. Although they agreed on much in terms of slavery, Cunningham did have qualms with some of Hodge's views. Cunningham thought no man could be made to give up his natural right "to control his time and labor" except through his own consent. He also believed that it was the right of every slave to attempt escape. William Cunningham to Charles Hodge, Edinburgh, Apr. 26, 1845, Charles Hodge Collection, CHP, Box 15, Folder 16.
12. Macleod, *Scottish Theology*, 198–206.
13. Rainy and Mackenzie, *Life of William Cunningham*, 190–201; 63.
14. Rainy and Mackenzie, *Life of William Cunningham*, 191.
15. Macleod, *Scottish Theology*, 271.

Chapter 35: Moderator of the General Assembly

1. Charles Hodge, "General Assembly, 1846," BRPR 18:3 (July 1846): 422.
2. Charles Hodge, "The Integrity of our National Union vs. Abolitionism," BRPR 16:3 (Oct. 1844): 546.
3. Hodge, "Integrity of our National Union," 568; 573; 580.
4. Hodge, "Integrity of our National Union," 549.
5. Hodge, "Integrity of our National Union," 551.
6. Hodge, "Integrity of our National Union," 553.

7. Hodge, "General Assembly, 1846," 425.

8. Hodge, "General Assembly, 1846," 426

9. Hodge, "General Assembly, 1846," 439.

10. Hodge, "General Assembly, 1846," 435.

11. Hodge, "General Assembly, 1846," 438.

12. MIN (May 20, 1847), 372.

13. Charles Hodge, "They Which Preach the Gospel," Feb. 21, 1847, CHM, Box 21, Folder 2, p. 4. Hodge had first delivered this sermon three months earlier for a chapel service at the Seminary. Although there would be inevitable changes to accommodate the new setting of the General Assembly, there is little reason to doubt that the core of the sermon remained the same between when he first delivered it in February and then repeated it in May.

14. Hodge, "They Which Preach the Gospel," Feb. 21, 1847, CHM, Box 21, Folder 2, p. 37.

15. Hodge, "They Which Preach the Gospel," Feb. 21, 1847, CHM, Box 21, Folder 2, p. 17.

16. Charles Hodge, "Sustentation Fund," BRPR 38:1 (Jan. 1866): 2.

17. Hodge, "Sustentation Fund," 2.

18. He delivered the sermon once again on October 22, 1865, as noted in his sermon notes, CHM, Box 21, Folder 2. Hodge, "Sustentation Fund," 1–24.

19. Charles Hodge, Adequate Support of the Ministry: Sustentation Fund (Princeton, N.J.: Blanchard, 1866). Hodge, "Sustentation Fund," 9.

Chapter 36: "The Nonsensical Dialect of Transcendentalism"

1. Philip F. Gura, American Transcendentalism: A History (New York: Hill & Wang, 2007), 5–6. Gura's volume provides the best general treatment of American Transcendentalism. Much of my own discussion of Transcendentalism here is indebted to this fine synthetic work. Another insightful, if slightly more focused, treatment of Transcendentalism can be found in Dean Grodzins, American Heretic: Theodore Parker and Transcendentalism (Chapel Hill: University of North Carolina Press, 2002), 175–247.

2. FYFL, 1:363.

3. Gura, American Transcendentalism, 50.

4. James Marsh, "Stuart's Commentary on the Epistle to the Hebrews," QCS 1 (1829): 147.

5. Gura, American Transcendentalism, 81.

6. Albert B. Dod and James W. Alexander, "Elements of Psychology," BRPR 11:1 (Jan. 1839): 46.

7. George Ripley and George P. Bradford, "Philosophic Thought in Boston," in The Memorial History of Boston, ed. Justin Winsor, 4 vols. (Boston, Mass.: J.R. Osgood 1881), 4:305.

8. Gura, American Transcendentalism, 76–77.

9. Dod and Alexander, "Elements of Psychology," 61.

10. Dod and Alexander, "Elements of Psychology," 55.

11. Ralph Waldo Emerson, "Divinity School Address," in Transcendentalism: A Reader, ed. Joel Myerson (New York: Oxford University Press, 2000), 236.

12. Emerson, "Divinity School Address," 235.

13. Dod and Alexander, "Elements of Psychology," 95.

14. Dod and Alexander, "Elements of Psychology," 97; 96.

15. Dod and Alexander, "Elements of Psychology," 97.

16. Dod and Alexander, "Elements of Psychology," 97–98.

17. Two months after Emerson addressed Harvard's senior class of divinity students, Ware delivered a rousing sermon against Emerson's views in his "The Personality of the Deity. A Sermon

Preached in the Chapel of Harvard University, Sept. 23, 1838 (Boston, Mass.: n.p., 1838). Andrews Norton, *A Discourse on the Latest Form of Infidelity* (Cambridge, Mass.: John Owen, 1839).

18. William Sprague, *Annals of the American Pulpit* (New York: Robert Carter & Brothers, 1857), 8:432. Orestes Brownson, "Review of *Two Articles from the Princeton Review*," BOQR 3 (July 1840): 269. Samuel Eliot Morison, *Three Centuries of Harvard* (Cambridge, Mass.: Harvard University Press, 1936), 242.

19. Norton, *Discourse on the Latest Form of Infidelity*, 11.

20. Andres Norton, "The New School in Literature and Religion," BDA (Aug. 27, 1838): 2. Along with his condemnation of Schleiermacher, Norton also took this opportunity to denounce the French Idealists and their influence on various Unitarians.

21. A. P. Peabody wrote that Norton had the "most skeptical mind that I was every acquainted with. He held in utter distrust all appeals to the emotional nature." In this regard, he bore a close resemblance to many of Hodge's own views. Sprague, *Annals of the American Pulpit*, 8:435.

22. Charles Hodge, "A Discourse on the Latest Form of Infidelity," BRPR 12:1 (Jan. 1840): 46.

23. In 1834, Hodge had written a twelve-page review of Lachmann's textual work on the New Testament in the *Biblical Repertory*, in which he offers a glimpse of his extensive knowledge of the history of biblical manuscript collation. Charles Hodge, "Lachmann's New Testament," BRPR 6:2 (Apr. 1834): 269–281.

24. Hodge, "Discourse on the Latest Form of Infidelity," 33.

25. Hodge, "Discourse on the Latest Form of Infidelity," 46, 47,48, 51, 53, 54, 62, 68.

26. George Ripley, *Defence of "The Latest From of Infidelity" Examined: A Second Letter to Mr. Andrews Norton* (Boston, Mass.: J. Munroe, 1839), 150.

27. Norton approached Hodge with the idea of reprinting his article soon after he first read it. He clearly thought that their similarities outweighed their differences when it came to the German Idealists. Andrews Norton to Charles Hodge, Cambridge, Mass., Feb. 21, 1840, CHP, Box 18, Folder 9. See also Andrews Norton to Charles Hodge, Cambridge, Mass., Mar. 4, 1840, CHP, Box 18, Folder 9.

28. Andrews Norton to Charles Hodge, Cambridge, Mass., Feb. 21, 1840, CHP, Box 18, Folder 9. Hodge, "Discourse on the Latest Form of Infidelity," 38.

29. Andrews Norton to Charles Hodge, Cambridge, Mass., Feb. 21, 1840, CHP, Box 18, Folder 9. Hodge's respect for Norton is evident in two letters he wrote in regard to Norton's desire to reprint "A Discourse on the Latest Form of Infidelity." Charles Hodge to Andrews Norton, Princeton, Feb. 27, 1840; Mar. 12, 1840, Andrews Norton Papers, Houghton Library Special Collections, Harvard University.

Chapter 37: Roman Catholic Baptism

1. For the longevity and force of the sentiment against Hodge's stance on Catholic baptism, see Matthew Hope to Charles Hodge, Philadelphia, Feb. 4, 1846, CHP, Box 16, Folder 49.

2. MIN (1845), 406.

3. Tyler Anbinder, *Nativism and Slavery: The Northern Know Nothings and the Politics of the 1850s* (New York: Oxford University Press, 1992), 4–5.

4. Anbinder, *Nativism and Slavery*, 3.

5. Edward K. Spann, *The New Metropolis: New York City, 1840–1857* (New York: Columbia University Press, 1981), 24.

6. Lyman Beecher, *A Plea for the West* (Cincinnati, Truman & Smith; New York, Leavitt, Lord, 1835), 59–61.

7. Ray Allen Billington, *The Protestant Crusade, 1800–1860* (New York: The Macmillan Company, 1938), 225–229.

8. Paul C. Gutjahr, "'Hundreds of Souls in the Balance': An Eastern Congregational Minister Ponders Moving West to Iowa," *Palimpsest* 74:2 (Summer 1993): 56.

9. Charles Hodge, "The General Assembly of 1845," BRPR 17:3 (July 1845): 444.

10. Hodge, "General Assembly of 1845," 444.

11. Hodge, "General Assembly of 1845," 444.

12. Hodge, "General Assembly of 1845," 444.

13. Charles Hodge, "The Tracts of the Times," BRPR 10:1 (Jan. 1838): 90.

14. Hodge, "Tracts of the Times," 97.

15. LCH, 340.

16. Hodge, "General Assembly of 1845," 452.

17. Hodge, "General Assembly of 1845," 448.

18. Hodge, "General Assembly of 1845," 448.

19. Hodge, "General Assembly of 1845," 450.

20. Hodge, "General Assembly of 1845," 450; 448.

21. Hodge, "General Assembly of 1845," 458.

22. Charles Hodge, "Essays in the Presbyterian by Theophilus on the Question: Is Baptism in the Church of Rome Valid," BRPR 18:2 (Apr. 1846): 320–344.

23. Hodge, "Essays in the Presbyterian by Theophilus," 320.

24. Hodge, "Essays in the Presbyterian by Theophilus," 320.

25. Hodge, "General Assembly of 1845," 465.

26. Hodge himself draws this parallel in his second treatment of Catholic baptism in *The Repertory*. Hodge, "Essays in the Presbyterian by Theophilus," 321–322.

27. Hodge, "General Assembly of 1845," 471.

Chapter 38: The Infection of German Idealism

1. Charles Hodge, "Finney's Lectures on Theology," BRPR 19:2 (Apr. 1847): 240.

2. James Hastings Nichols, ed., *The Mercersburg Theology* (New York: Oxford University Press, 1966), 6.

3. J. W. Nevin, "The Church," in Nichols, *Mercersburg Theology*, 73.

4. Philip Schaff, *The Principle of Protestantism* (Philadelphia, Pa.: United Church Press, 1964), 220.

5. Nevin, "Church," in Nichols, *Mercersburg Theology*, 60.

6. Charles Hodge, "The Mystical Presence," BRPR 20:2 (Apr. 1848): 228; John W. Nevin, *The Mystical Presence and Other Writings on the Eucharist* (Philadelphia, Pa.: United Church Press, 1966), 261–262.

7. Hodge, "Mystical Presence," 228; Nevin, *Mystical Presence*, 273.

8. Nevin, "Church," in Nichols, *Mercersburg Theology*, 68.

9. Nevin, "Church," in Nichols, *Mercersburg Theology*, 79.

10. Charles Hodge, "Principle of Protestantism as Related to the Present State of the Church," BRPR 7:4 (Oct. 1845): 626.

11. Hodge, "Principle of Protestantism," 628; 631.

12. Hodge, "Principle of Protestantism," 628.

13. Hodge, "Mystical Presence," 227.

14. Hodge, "Mystical Presence," 264.

15. D. G. Hart, *John Williamson Nevin* (Phillipsburg, N.J.: P&R Publishing, 2005), 127–137.

16. Hodge, "Mystical Presence," 228; Nevin, *Mystical Presence*, 183.

17. Hodge, "Mystical Presence," 228; Nevin, *Mystical Presence*, 260–262.

18. Hodge, "Mystical Presence," 228; Nevin, *Mystical Presence*, 277.

19. Charles G. Finney, *Lectures on Systematic Theology* (Oberlin, Ohio: James M. Fitch, 1846), 237–238.

20. Finney, *Lectures on Systematic Theology*, 488.

21. Charles Hodge, "Finney's Lectures on Systematic Theology," BRPR 19:2 (Apr. 1847): 237.

22. Keith J. Hardman, *Charles Grandison Finney, 1792-1875: Revivalist and Reformer* (Grand Rapids, Mich.: Baker Book House, 1987), 385.

23. Hodge, "Finney's Lectures on Systematic Theology," 239.

24. Hodge, "Finney's Lectures on Systematic Theology," 240.

25. Hodge, "Finney's Lectures on Systematic Theology," 240.

26. Hodge, "Finney's Lectures on Systematic Theology," 249.

27. Hodge, "Finney's Lectures on Systematic Theology," 244.

28. Charles Hodge, "Discourses on Christian Nurture," BRPR 19:4 (Oct. 1847): 502.

29. Hodge, "Discourses on Christian Nurture," 504.

30. Hodge, "Discourses on Christian Nurture," 507.

31. A good treatment of Bushnell's view of language is found in Philip F. Gura, *The Wisdom of Words: Language, Theology and Literature in the New England Renaissance* (Middletown, Conn.: Wesleyan University Press, 1981), 56–68.

32. Horace Bushnell, *God in Christ* (New York: Charles Scribner's Sons, 1876), 21.

33. Bushnell, *God in Christ*, 83.

34. Charles Hodge, "God in Christ," BRPR 21:2 (Apr. 1849): 260. See also Robert Bruce Mullin, *The Puritan as Yankee: A Life of Horace Bushnell* (Grand Rapids, Mich.: William B. Eerdmans Publishing, 2002), 157–160.

35. Hodge, "God in Christ," 266.

36. Hodge, "God in Christ," 268.

37. Hodge, "God in Christ," 273–274.

38. Hodge, "God in Christ," 267.

39. Hodge, "God in Christ," 262.

40. Charles Hodge, "The Vicarious Sacrifice," BRPR 38:2 (Apr. 1866): 161.

41. Hodge, "Vicarious Sacrifice," 162.

42. Charles Hodge, "Christ, the Only Sacrifice," BRPR 17:1 (Jan. 1845): 84; 85.

43. Hodge, "Vicarious Sacrifice," 169.

44. Hodge, "Vicarious Sacrifice," 173.

Chapter 39: "When the Will of the Wife is the Other Way"

1. Charles Hodge to Hugh Hodge, Princeton, Mar. 30, 1848, CHP, Box 11, Folder 6.

2. Charles Hodge to William M. Scott, Princeton, Oct. 24, 1846, CHM, Box 28, Folder 58.

3. An extended discussion of Hodge's views on marrying off his children is found in Charles Hodge to Hugh Hodge, Princeton, Oct. 29, 1850, CHP, Box 12, Folder 1.

4. Louise L. Stevenson, "Charles Hodge, Womanly Women, and Manly Ministers," CHR, 174–175.

5. Charles Hodge to Hugh Hodge, Princeton, Jan. 10, 1851, CHP, Box 12, Folder 1.

6. Charles Hodge to Hugh Hodge, Princeton, Sept. 14, 1847, CHP, Box 11, Folder 5.

7. Charles Hodge to Hugh Hodge, Princeton, Sept. 14, 1847, CHP, Box 11, Folder 5.

8. For a text of Hodge's wedding ceremony, see CHM, Box 18, Folder 13.

9. Charles Hodge to Hugh Hodge, Princeton, June 27, 1849, CHP, Box 11, Folder 6.

10. Charles Hodge to Hugh Hodge, Princeton, July 14, 1848, CHP, Box 11, Folder 6.

11. Charles Hodge to Hugh Hodge, Princeton, July 19, 1848, CHP, Box 11, Folder 6.

12. Charles Hodge to Hugh Hodge, Princeton, July 13, 1849, CHP, Box 11, Folder 6.

13. Charles Hodge to Hugh Hodge, Princeton, Sept. 6, 1849, CHP, Box 11, Folder 6.

14. Charles Hodge to Hugh Hodge, Princeton, Sept. 6, 1849, CHP, Box 11, Folder 6.

15. Little attention has been paid to Hodge's view on the role of women both in church and in society more generally. Two notable exceptions to this lack of scholarship include Stevenson, "Charles Hodge, Womanly Women, and Manly Ministers," 159–179, and Ronald Hogeland, "Charles Hodge, The Association of Gentlemen and Ornamental Womanhood: 1825–1855," JPH 53 (1975): 239–255.

16. Ashbel Green, "The Christian Duty of Christian Women," (Princeton, N.J.: Princeton Press, 1825); Samuel Miller, *The Appropriate Duty and Ornament of the Female Sex," A Sermon, Preached March 13, 1808* (New York: Hopkins and Seymour, 1808); Archibald Alexander, "Hints for Young Men in the Choice of a Wife," (n.p.: n.d.), copy found in PTS. See also Hogeland, "Charles Hodge, The Association of Gentlemen," 244–245.

17. Hodge clearly stated his agreement with these sentiments in his First Corinthians Commentary. (See the exposition of 1 Corinthians 14:34). Charles Hodge, *An Exposition of the First Epistle to the Corinthians* (New York: Robert Carter & Brothers, 1857), 304.

18. Charles Hodge, "An Account of the Present State of the Island of Puerto Rico," BRPR 10:4 (Oct. 1838): 604.

19. Charles Hodge, *A Commentary on the Epistle to the Ephesians* (New York: Robert Carter & Brothers, 1858), 312.

20. John Johns to Charles Hodge, Richmond, Va., Apr. 17, 1848, CHP, Box 16, Folder 66.

21. Charles Hodge to Hugh Hodge, Princeton, Nov. 28, 1870, CHP, Box 12, Folder 3.

Chapter 40: "Covered in Gloom"

1. LCH, 364.

2. Charles Hodge, "The Elements of Psychology," BRPR 28:2 (Apr. 1856): 387; 337.

3. LCH, 365. John Frelinghuysen Hageman, *History of Princeton and Its Institutions* (Philadelphia, Pa.: J. B. Lippincott), 1:278.

4. LCH, 596.

5. LCH, 596

6. LCH, 366.

7. Alfred Nevin, *Encyclopedia of the Presbyterian Church in the United States* (Philadelphia, Pa.: Presbyterian Publishing, 1884), 275.

8. Charles Hodge Memorandum Book, Dec. 17, 1849, CHM, Box 29, Folder 5.

9. Hodge records that his brother Hugh diagnosed Sarah as having a "uterine tumor." Charles Hodge Memorandum Book, Dec. 17, 1849, CHM, Box 29, Folder 5.

10. "The Late Mrs. Hodge," PRE 20 (Jan. 12, 1850): 6.

11. Charles Hodge to Hugh Hodge, Princeton, Jan. 26, 1850, CHP, Box 12, Folder 1.

12. Charles Hodge to Hugh Hodge, Princeton, Jan. 26, 1850, CHP, Box 12, Folder 1.

13. Charles Hodge to Hugh Hodge, Princeton, Jan. 26, 1850, CHP, Box 12, Folder 1.
14. Charles Hodge Memorandum Book, Dec. 17, 1849, CHM, Box 29, Folder 5.
15. Charles Hodge Memorandum Book, Dec. 17, 1849, CHM, Box 29, Folder 5.
16. John Johns to Charles Hodge, Williamsburgh, Va., Mar. 19, 1850, CHP, Box 16, Folder 66.
17. Hugh Hodge to Charles Hodge, Philadelphia, Jan. 19, 1850, CHP, Box 12, Folder 1.
18. LSM, 2:540–541.
19. LSM, 2:544.
20. Hugh L. Hodge, *Memoranda of Family History Dictated by Hugh L. Hodge M.D. LL.D.* (n.p., 1903), 93.
21. Charles Hodge to Hugh Hodge, Princeton, Dec. 16, 1850, CHP, Box 12, Folder 1.
22. LAA, 613.
23. Charles Hodge to Hugh Hodge, Princeton, Oct. 15, 1851, CHP, Box 12, Folder 1.
24. LAA, 613.
25. LCH, 382.
26. Charles Hodge to Hugh Hodge, Princeton, Oct. 15, 1851, CHP, Box 12, Folder 1.
27. Charles Hodge to Hugh Hodge, Princeton, Oct. 15, 1851, CHP, Box 12, Folder 1.
28. Charles Hodge to Hugh Hodge, Princeton, Oct. 15, 1851, CHP, Box 12, Folder 1.
29. Charles Hodge, "The Life of Archibald Alexander," BRPR 27:1 (Jan. 1855): 158.
30. LSM, 2:544; 513.
31. LSM, 2:503.

Chapter 41: College Trustee

1. Charles Hodge to Hugh Hodge, Princeton, June 6, 1851, CHP, Box 12, Folder 1.
2. Charles Hodge to William Cameron, Princeton, Apr. 1, 1853, CHP, Box 14, Folder 52.
3. LCH, 377.
4. William Berryman Scott, *Some Memories of a Palaeontologist* (Princeton, N.J.: Princeton University Press, 1939), 75.
5. John Maclean, *History of the College of New Jersey, From Its Origin in 1746 to the Commencement of 1854* (Philadelphia, Pa.: J. B. Lippincott, 1877), 2:336.
6. Thomas Jefferson Wertenbaker, *Princeton, 1746–1896* (Princeton, N.J.: Princeton University Press, 1946), 256–257.
7. Wertenbaker, *Princeton*, 259.
8. LCH, 386.
9. Trustee Bound Volumes (1868–1878), MUDD, 5:649.
10. Trustee Bound Volumes (1868–1878), MUDD, 5:649–650.
11. LCH, 387.
12. Trustee Bound Volumes (1868–1878), MUDD, 5:589–581.
13. Trustee Bound Volumes (1868–1878), MUDD, 5:581.

Chapter 42: Language and Feeling

1. Charles Hodge, "Presbyterian Reunion," BRPR 40:1 (Jan. 1868): 61.
2. The warring articles were published in the following order: Edwards Amasa Park, "The Theology of the Intellect and That of Feelings," BS 7:26 (1850): 533–569; reprinted as *The Theology of Intellect of the Feelings* (Andover: Warren F. Draper, 1850); Charles Hodge, "The

Theology of the Intellect and that of the Feelings," BRPR 22:4 (Oct. 1850): 642–674; Edwards Amasa Park, "Remarks on the Princeton Review," BS 8:29 (1851): 135–180; Charles Hodge, "Prof. Park's Remarks on the Princeton Review," BRPR 23:2 (Apr. 1851): 306–347; Edwards Amasa Park, "Unity and Diversities of Belief even on Imputed and Involuntary Sin; with Comments on a Second Article in the Princeton Review," BS 8:31 (1851): 594–667; Charles Hodge, "Unity and Diversities of Belief even on Imputed and Involuntary Sin," BRPR 23:4 (Oct. 1851): 674–695; Edwards Amasa Park, "New England Theology," BS 9:33 (1852): 170–220.

3. D. G. Hart, "Divided between Heart and Mind: The Critical Period for Protestant Thought in America," JEH 38 (Apr. 1987): 263.

4. Horace Bushnell, *God in Christ* (New York: Charles Scribner's Sons, 1876), 69.

5. Hodge, "Theology of the Intellect and that of Feelings," 646. Park, *Theology of the Intellect and of the Feelings*, 4.

6. Hodge, "Theology of the Intellect and that of Feelings," 646.

7. Park, *Theology of the Intellect and of the Feelings*, 6.

8. Hodge, "Theology of the Intellect and that of Feelings," 659.

9. Park, *Theology of the Intellect and of the Feelings*, 9.

10. Park, *Theology of the Intellect and of the Feelings*, 10.

11. Hodge, "Theology of the Intellect and that of Feelings," 648.

12. Hodge, "Theology of the Intellect and that of Feelings," 648.

13. Hodge, "Theology of the Intellect and that of Feelings," 652.

14. Hodge, "Theology of the Intellect and that of Feelings," 646.

15. Hodge, "Theology of the Intellect and that of Feelings," 656.

16. Hodge, "Theology of the Intellect and that of Feelings," 642–643.

17. Hodge, "Theology of the Intellect and that of Feelings," 649.

18. Hodge, "Unity and Diversities of Belief," 675.

19. Hodge, "Remarks on the Princeton Review," 308.

20. Hodge, "Theology of the Intellect and that of Feelings," 656.

21. Hodge, "Remarks on the Princeton Review," 322.

22. Hodge, "Remarks on the Princeton Review," 307. By saying that the heart could better understand certain biblical passages, Park had opened up a space that allowed a "Calvinist" to say there was some power in human agency instead of strictly stressing the supremacy and sovereignty of God. Hodge stood aghast that anyone who called himself a "Calvinist" could so lean against an ultimate view of God's sovereignty. To make his case, he once again returned to one of his favorite battlegrounds, the doctrine of imputation, to prove just how far Park had strayed from proper Calvinist doctrine. In responding to Park, Hodge turned to the Augsburg Confession, the Council of Dort and a number of established Reformed seventeenth-century apologists including the Dutch theologians Simon Episcopius and Philipp van Limborch to establish that the Bible plainly taught the doctrine of imputation as accepted by churches grounded in the Reformed tradition. Hodge, "Remarks on the Princeton Review," 309–317.

23. D. G. Hart, "Poems, Propositions, and Dogma: The Controversy over Religious Language in American Learning," CH 57 (Sept. 1988): 311.

24. George M. Marsden, *Fundamentalism and American Culture: The Shaping of Twentieth-Century Evangelicalism, 1870–1925* (New York: Oxford University Press, 1980), 109–118.

25. George M. Marsden, "Everyone One's Own Interpreter? The Bible, Science, and Authority in Mid-Nineteenth-Century America," in *The Bible in America: Essays in Cultural History*, ed.

Nathan O. Hatch and Mark A. Noll (New York: Oxford University Press, 1982), 82–84; Hart, "Poems, Propositions, and Dogma," 312.

26. James Turner, *Without God, Without Creed: The Origins of Unbelief in America* (Baltimore, Md.: Johns Hopkins University Press, 1985), 96–104.

27. Marsden, "Everyone One's Own Interpreter?" 87; 93.

28. Hart, "Poems, Propositions, and Dogma," 313.

29. Hodge, "The Inspiration of Holy Scripture," 683.

Chapter 43: The Inspiration of Scripture

1. Charles Hodge, "The Theology of the Intellect and that of Feelings," BRPR 22:4 (Oct. 1850): 642.

2. For an extended treatment of Hodge's piety, see Andrew Hoffecker, "Beauty and the Princeton Piety," in *Soli Deo Gloria: Essays in Reformed Theology*, ed. R.C. Sproul (Nutley, N.J.: Presbyterian and Reformed Publishing, 1976), 118–133.

3. Sermon, "Jesus is the Son of God," I John 5:5, Apr. 16, 1843, CHM, Box 20, Folder 19.

4. Hodge, "Theology of the Intellect and that of Feelings," 652.

5. Charles Hodge, "The Inspiration of Holy Scripture," BRPR 29:4 (Oct. 1857): 692.

6. Hodge, "Inspiration of Holy Scripture," 692.

7. Terence Martin, *The Instructed Vision: Scottish Common Sense Philosophy and the Origins of American Fiction*, Indiana University Humanities Series Number 48 (Bloomington: Indiana University Press, 1961), 85–103.

8. Hodge, "Inspiration of Holy Scripture," 664.

9. Hodge, "Inspiration of Holy Scripture," 675.

10. Hodge, "Inspiration of Holy Scripture," 675. Hodge did allow that there were indeed certain contradictory passages in the Bible, but these contradictions were of such small consequence, they were not worthy of notice. Hodge, "Inspiration of Holy Scripture," 686. See also ST, 1:169–170.

11. Hodge, "Inspiration of Holy Scripture," 675.

12. Hodge, "Inspiration of Holy Scripture," 677.

13. Hodge, "Inspiration of Holy Scripture," 681.

14. Ernest R. Sandeen, "The Princeton Theology: One Source of Biblical Literalism in American Protestantism," CH 31 (Sept. 1962): 315.

15. Hodge, "Inspiration of Holy Scripture," 687.

16. George Marsden, *Fundamentalism and American Culture: The Shaping of Twentieth-Century Evangelicalism, 1870–1925* (New York: Oxford University Press, 1980): 114.

17. The clearest articulation of Hodge's respect for a Baconian system of biblical interpretation is found in ST, 1:1–3; 9–17. The best discussion of Old School Presbyterianism's ties to Baconian thought is Theodore Dwight Bozeman, *Protestants in an Age of Science: The Baconian Ideal and Antebellum American Religious Thought* (Chapel Hill: University of North Carolina Press, 1977), 138–159.

18. ST, 1:152.

19. Francis Turretin, *Institutes of Elenctic Theology*, trans. Georege Musgrave Giger, ed. James T. Dennison Jr. (Phillipsburg, N.J.: P&R Publishing), 1:136.

20. Marsden, *Fundamentalism and American Culture*, 114.

21. Scottish Common Sense Realism's marginalization did not mean that Hodge's views on inspiration had no power after the nineteenth century. They became a pivotal influence

among more conservative evangelicals like Benjamin Warfield and J. Gresham Machen. The best single article on the longevity of the Princeton Theology's impact on views of American biblical literalism remains Sandeen, "Princeton Theology," 307–321.

Chapter 44: "Graces of the Spirit"

1. Charles Hodge to Hugh Hodge, Princeton, Sept. 16, 1850; July 2, 1851, CHP, Box 12, Folder 1.
2. Charles Hodge Memorandum Book, CHM, Box 29, Folder 5, entries beginning Dec. 30, 1849.
3. Charles Hodge to Hugh Hodge, Princeton, Jan. 26, 1850; Feb. 20, 1850; Apr. 5, 1851, CHP, Box 12, Folder 1.
4. Andrew Hoffecker, "Beauty and the Princeton Piety," in *Soli Deo Gloria: Essays in Reformed Theology*, ed. R. C. Sproul (Nutley, N.J.: Presbyterian and Reformed Publishing, 1976), 122.
5. Charles Hodge to Hugh Hodge, Princeton, Jan. 10, 1851, CHP, Box 12, Folder 1.
6. Charles Hodge to Hugh Hodge, Princeton, Dec. 10, 1851, CHP, Box 12, Folder 1.
7. Charles Hodge to Hugh Hodge, Princeton, Jan. 26, 1850, CHP, Box 12, Folder 1.
8. Charles Hodge to Hugh Hodge, Princeton, June 18, 1850, CHP, Box 12, Folder 1.
9. Charles Hodge to Hugh Hodge, Princeton, July 8, 1850, CHP, Box 12, Folder 1.
10. Charles Hodge to Hugh Hodge, Princeton, May 4, 1852, CHP, Box 12, Folder 2.
11. Charles Hodge to Hugh Hodge, Princeton, Apr. 16, 1851, CHP, Box 12, Folder 1.
12. Charles Hodge to Hugh Hodge, Princeton, Mar. 10, 1851, CHP, Box 12, Folder 2.
13. LCH, 367.
14. Charles Hodge to Hugh Hodge, Princeton, May 18, 1850, CHP, Box 12, Folder 1.
15. Charles Hodge to Hugh Hodge, Princeton, Jan. 4, 1850, CHP, Box 12, Folder 1.
16. Charles Hodge to Hugh Hodge, Princeton, Apr. 14, 1852, CHP, Box 12, Folder 2.
17. MFH, 112.
18. Charles Hodge to Hugh Hodge, Princeton, Dec. 5, 1850; Dec. 6, 1850, CHP, Box 12, Folder 2.
19. David B. Calhoun, *Princeton Seminary* (Carlisle, Pa.: Banner of Truth Trust, 1994), 1:366.
20. MFH, 118.
21. MFH, 115.
22. Charles Hodge to John Johns, Princeton, Aug. 27, 1852, CHP, Box 16, Folder 66.
23. Charles Hodge to Hugh Hodge, Princeton, July 29, 1852, CHP, Box 12, Folder 2.
24. LCH, 392.

Chapter 45: The Battle against "Churchianity"

1. J. W. Nevin, "The Church," in *The Mercersburg Theology*, ed. James Hastings Nichols (New York: Oxford University Press, 1966), 73. Hodge's extensive writings on the topic of the church were gathered after his death by one of his former students, William Durant, and published as Charles Hodge, *Discussions in Church Polity* (New York: Charles Scribner's Sons, 1878).
2. Hodge, *Discussions in Church Polity*, iii.
3. On the international nature of the "Church question," see E. Brooks Holifield, *Theology in America* (New Haven, Conn.: Yale University Press, 2003), 472.
4. Roger Finke and Rodney Stark, *The Churching of America 1776–1990* (New Brunswick, N.J.: Rutgers University Press, 1992), 55.
5. Lefferts A. Loetscher, "The Problem of Christian Unity in Early Nineteenth-Century America," CH 32:1 (Mar. 1963): 7.

6. LCH, 420.

7. Charles Hodge, "God in Christ," BRPR 21:2 (Apr. 1849): 260.

8. Benjamin Morgan Palmer, *The Life and Letters of James Henley Thornwell* (Richmond, Va.: Whittet & Shepperson, 1875), 288.

9. Charles Hodge, "Idea of the Church, Part I," BRPR 25:2 (Apr. 1853): 268; 264.

10. Charles Hodge, "Idea of the Church, Part II," BRPR 25:3 (July 1853): 539–342. Charles Hodge, "The Unity of the Church," BRPR 18:1 (Apr. 1846): 138.

11. Hodge, "Unity of the Church," 138

12. Hodge, "Idea of the Church, Part II," 341.

13. Hodge, "Idea of the Church, Part II," 342.

14. Hodge, "Unity of the Church," 140.

15. Hodge, "Unity of the Church," 140–141.

16. Hodge, "Unity of the Church," 140–141.

17. Hodge, "Idea of the Church, Part I," 249.

18. Hodge, "Idea of the Church, Part I," 278.

19. Hodge, "Unity of the Church," 143.

20. Hodge, "Idea of the Church, Part I," 264.

21. Hodge, "Unity of the Church," 143.

22. Hodge, "Unity of the Church," 145.

23. Hodge, "Idea of the Church, Part I," 269. Charles Hodge, "History of the Apostolic Church," BRPR 26:1 (Jan. 1854): 149. In the midst of Hodge's numerous articles on the church, he wrote an extended review of Philip Schaff's *History of the Apostolic Church* in which he critiqued Schaff's sympathies with several Roman Catholic doctrines.

24. Hodge, "Unity of the Church," 148.

25. Hodge, "Idea of the Church, Part I," 261.

26. Hodge, "Idea of the Church, Part I," 266.

27. Hodge, "Unity of the Church," 148. Hodge, "Idea of the Church, Part II," 357.

28. Hodge, "Idea of the Church, Part I," 262.

29. Hodge, "Idea of the Church, Part II," 345.

30. Charles Hodge, "The Visibility of the Church," BRPR 25:4 (Apr. 1853): 672.

31. Hodge, "The Church—Its Perpetuity," BRPR 28:4 (Oct. 1856): 689; 696.

32. Hodge, "Visibility of the Church," 682.

33. Hodge, "The Tecnobaptist," BRPR 30:2 (Apr. 1858): 348. "Tecnobaptist" comes from the Greek words denoting the baptism of children ($\tau\epsilon\chi\nu\omega\nu\ \beta\alpha\pi\tau\iota\sigma\mu\alpha$).

34. Hodge, "Tecnobaptist," 349.

35. Hodge, "Tecnobaptist," 355.

36. Hodge, "Tecnobaptist," 355.

37. Hodge, "Tecnobaptist," 373–376.

38. Hodge, "Tecnobaptist," 373; 389.

39. Charles Hodge, "American Board of Commissioners," BRPR 21:1 (Jan. 1849): 6.

40. Hodge, "American Board of Commissioners," 7.

41. LCH, 419. See also Charles Hodge, *What is Presbyterianism?* (Philadelphia, Pa.: Presbyterian Board of Publication, 1855), 6–7.

42. *What is Presbyterianism?* came from an address Hodge gave before an anniversary meeting of the Presbyterian Historical Society in Philadelphia on May 1, 1855.

43. Charles Hodge, "The Revised Book of Discipline," BRPR 30:4 (Oct. 1858): 694–695.

44. Charles Hodge, "Eutaxia; or, the Presbyterian Liturgies," BRPR 27:3 (July 1855): 460.
45. Hodge, "Eutaxia," 445.
46. Hodge, "Eutaxia," 446.

Chapter 46: Thornwell and "Thus Saith the Lord"

1. James H. Thornwell, *Collected Writings* (Richmond, Va.: Presbyterian Board of Publication, 1873), 4:243–244. So heartily did Thornwell disapprove of Hodge's views on the issues of voluntary societies, boards of governance outside the denomination, and the role of ruling elders that he wrote Hodge had "never touched the questions connected with the nature and organization of the Church without being singularly unhappy." Thornwell, *Collected Writings*, 4:244.
2. This phrase is taken from the title of a book on the subject by Samuel Miller. Samuel Miller, *An Essay on the Warrant, Nature and Duties of the Office of The Ruling Elder in the Presbyterian Church* (Philadelphia, Pa.: Presbyterian Board of Publication, 1832).
3. Charles Hodge, "The General Assembly of 1843," BRPR 15:3 (July 1843): 422.
4. Charles Hodge, "Presbyterianism," BRPR 32:3 (July 1860): 561. Hodge agreed with his former colleague Samuel Miller on the role and position of ruling elders. Miller, *Essay on the Warrant, Nature and Duties*. Hodge, "General Assembly of 1843," 433.
5. A thorough discussion of Thornwell's views on the position of elder can be found in James H. Thornwell, "The Elder Question," *Southern Presbyterian Review* 2:1 (June 1848): 1–67.
6. James Oscar Farmer Jr., *The Metaphysical Confederacy: James Henley Thornwell and the Synthesis of Southern Values* (Macon, Ga.: Mercer University Press, 1986), 186. Additional material on Thornwell's position on elders can be found in James H. Thornwell, "Dr. Thornwell on Ruling Elders," *Southern Presbyterian Review* 18:1 (July 1867): 30–46.
7. Benjamin Morgan Palmer, *The Life and Letters of James Henley Thornwell* (Richmond, Va.: Whittet & Shepperson, 1875), 253.
8. Palmer, *Life and Letters*, 255.
9. Palmer, *Life and Letters*, 286.
10. Palmer, *Life and Letters*, 289–90; 296.
11. Palmer, *Life and Letters*, 225.
12. Farmer, *Metaphysical Confederacy*, 186–187.
13. Hodge, "Presbyterianism," 564.
14. Hodge, "Presbyterianism," 553; 564. LCH, 402.
15. Charles Hodge, "Rights of Ruling Elders," BRPR 15:2 (Apr. 1843): 320.
16. The most complete account of the 1860 General Assembly debate can be found in Thornwell, *Collected Writings*, 4:173–241. See also Hodge, "Presbyterianism," 546–567.
17. Charles Hodge, "General Assembly of 1860," BRPR 32:3 (July 1860): 515–516.
18. Charles Hodge, "A Plea for Voluntary Societies," BRPR 9:1 (Jan. 1837): 128–137.
19. Charles Hodge, "General Assembly of 1860," 518.
20. Charles Hodge, "General Assembly of 1860," 513.
21. Palmer, *Life and Letters*, 499–512.

Chapter 47: The Pauline Commentaries

1. MFH, 116.
2. Henry C. Alexander, *The Life of Joseph Addison Alexander* (New York: Charles Scribner, 1870), 2:780.

3. Charles Hodge, *A Commentary on the Epistle to the Ephesians* (New York: Robert Carter & Brothers, 1858), 171–175; 194–195; 312–354; 340–346; 318–328.

4. Hodge, *Commentary on the Epistle to the Ephesians*, 342–344.

5. Hodge, *Commentary on the Epistle to the Ephesians*, 362.

6. Hodge, *Commentary on the Epistle to the Ephesians*, 363.

7. Hodge, *Commentary on the Epistle to the Ephesians*, 363.

8. Hodge, *Commentary on the Epistle to the Ephesians*, 362.

9. Hodge, *Commentary on the Epistle to the Ephesians*, 362.

10. Hodge, *Commentary on the Epistle to the Ephesians*, 364–370.

11. Hodge, *Commentary on the Epistle to the Ephesians*, 363.

12. Hodge, *Commentary on the Epistle to the Ephesians*, 364.

13. Albert Barnes, *An Inquiry into the Scriptural Views of Slavery* (Philadelphia, Pa.: Perkins & Purves, 1846), 258. For a longer discussion of the hermeneutics involved in the slavery debate, see E. Brooks Holifield, *Theology in America* (New Haven, Conn.: Yale University Press, 2003), 497–504.

14. Barnes, *Inquiry into the Scriptural Views of Slavery*, 381.

15. Charles Hodge to Dr. John C. Backus, New York, Dec. 28, 1860, CHP, Box 14, Folder 1.

16. Hodge's Romans and Ephesians commentaries probably sold for $3.00 apiece. The price of each Corinthian volume was $1.75. As late as 1866, the Corinthian commentaries were still being printed, and Hodge was receiving nice royalties from the publisher. "Note regarding I & II Corinthians," CHM, Box 46, Folder 27.

17. Charles Hodge, *An Exposition of the First Epistle to the Corinthians* (New York: Robert Carter & Brothers, 1857), viii.

18. Hodge, *Exposition of the First Epistle to the Corinthians*, 170–196; 46–56; 80–88. Charles Hodge, *An Exposition of the Second Epistle to the Corinthians* (New York: Robert Carter & Brothers, 1860), 191–197; 213–222.

19. Hodge, *Exposition of the First Epistle to the Corinthians*, xi.

20. Charles Hodge, "Adoption of the Confession of Faith," BRPR 30:4 (Oct. 1858): 677.

21. Hodge, "Adoption of the Confession of Faith," 671.

22. Hodge, "Adoption of the Confession of Faith," 675.

23. Charles Hodge, *A Discourse Delivered at the Re-Opening of the Chapel, Sept. 27, 1874* (Princeton: Chas. S. Robinson, 1874), 26.

24. "The Late Dr. Alexander," NYT, Aug. 5, 1859.

25. Alexander, *Life of J. A. Alexander*, 2:882.

26. LCH, 437.

Chapter 48: Politics and Conscience

1. LCH, 5. Hodge's concern with politics had deep roots dating back to the American Revolution. As a young girl, Hodge's mother had sat on the lap of Major-General Joseph Warren, who eventually died at Bunker Hill, and listened to him tell stories of the great conflict with England. LCH, 8. Hodge's own grandfather's home had been burned to ground for his support of the American cause. Frank Willing Leach, "The Philadelphia of our Ancestors," NA, Sunday, June 14, 1908, 1.

2. Charles Hodge, "Conscience and the Constitution," BRPR 23:1 (Jan. 1851): 134.

3. Charles Hodge to Hugh Hodge, Princeton, Mar. 8, 1825, CHP, Box 9, Folder 2.

4. Charles Hodge, "Sunday Laws," BRPR 31:4 (Oct. 1859): 742; Hodge, "The *American Quarterly Review* on Sunday Mails," BRTR 3:1 (Jan. 1831): 127–129. See also Richard J. Carwardine, "The Politics of Charles Hodge," CHR, 252.

5. Hodge, "*American Quarterly Review* on Sunday Mails," 86–134.

6. Cortland Van Rensselaer to Charles Hodge, Dec. 29, 1851, CHP, Box 19, Folder 24.

7. Charles Hodge, "The Church and the Country," BRPR 33:2 (Jan. 1861): 333.

8. Charles Hodge to Hugh Hodge, Princeton, Oct. 10, 1839, CHP, Box 10, Folder 4.

9. Stanley Elkins and Eric McKitrick, *The Age of Federalism* (New York: Oxford University Press, 1993), 555.

10. Elkins and McKitrick, *Age of Federalism*, 195–208.

11. Daniel Walker Howe, *What Hath God Wrought: The Transformation of America, 1815–1848* (New York: Oxford University Press, 2007), 210.

12. Carwardine, "Politics of Charles Hodge," 266.

13. Daniel Walker Howe, *The Political Culture of the American Whigs* (Chicago: University of Chicago Press, 1979), 21.

14. William W. Freehling, *The Road to Disunion: Secessionists at Bay* (New York: Oxford University Press, 1990), 450.

15. Charles Hodge to Hugh Hodge, Princeton, Dec. 15, 1829; Dec. 5, 1833, CHP, Box 9, Folders 3 and 4.

16. Howe, *What Hath God Wrought*, 342–357.

17. Charles Hodge to Hugh Hodge, Princeton, Oct. 1, 1831, CHP, Box 9, Folder 3.

18. Thomas H. O'Connor, *Lords of the Loom: The Cotton Whigs and the Coming of the Civil War* (New York: Scribner, 1968), 58–68.

19. *Webster's Speeches* (Boston, Mass.: Ginn & Co., 1897), 103.

20. Moses Stuart, *Conscience and the Constitution* (Boston, Mass.: Crocker & Brewster, 1850), 5.

21. John H. Giltner, *Moses Stuart: The Father of Biblical Science in America* (Atlanta, Ga.: Scholars Press, 1988), 124.

22. Stuart, *Conscience and the Constitution*, 31–32; 35.

23. Hodge, "Conscience and the Constitution," 125.

24. Hodge, "Conscience and the Constitution," 153.

25. Charles Hodge to Hugh Hodge, Princeton, Feb. 16, 1852, CHP, Box 12, Folder 2. See also Charles Hodge to Hugh Hodge, Princeton, Dec. 29, 1851, CHP, Box 12, Folder 2. A Good overview of the Hungarian revolution of the late 1840s and the role Kossuth played in it can be found in Mike Rapport, *1814: Year of Revolution* (New York: Basic Books, 2008), 301–380.

26. Hodge, "Conscience and the Constitution," 147.

27. Hodge, "Conscience and the Constitution," 146.

28. Hodge, "Conscience and the Constitution," 146.

29. Hodge, "Conscience and the Constitution," 149.

30. George M. Marsden, *Fundamentalism and American Culture: The Shaping of Twentieth-Century Evangelicalism 1870–1925* (New York: Oxford University Press, 1980), 114.

31. Michael F. Holt, *The Rise and Fall of the American Whig Party: Jacksonian Politics and the Onset of the Civil War* (New York: Oxford University Press, 1999), 969.

32. Charles Hodge to Hugh Hodge, Princeton, July 8, 1856, CHP, Box 12, Folder 2.

33. Charles Hodge to Hugh Hodge, Princeton, July 8, 1856, CHP, Box 12, Folder 2.

34. Charles Hodge to Hugh Hodge, Princeton, July 8, 1856, CHP, Box 12, Folder 2.

35. Sean Wilentz, *The Rise of American Democracy: Jefferson to Lincoln* (New York: W.W. Norton, 2005), 765.

Chapter 49: The State of the Country and the Church

1. Charles Hodge to Hugh Hodge, Princeton, Nov. 22, 1860, CHP, Box 12, Folder 2.
2. MFH, 103.
3. Charles Hodge to Hugh Hodge, Princeton, Dec. 13, 1860, CHP, Box 12, Folder 2.
4. Charles Hodge to Hugh Hodge, Princeton, Dec. 13, 1860, CHP, Box 12, Folder 2.
5. Charles Hodge to Hugh Hodge, Princeton, Dec. 13, 1860, CHP, Box 12, Folder 2.
6. Charles Hodge, "The State of the Country," BRPR 33:1 (Jan. 1861): 1.
7. Hodge, "State of the Country," 1. Hodge would repeat this sentiment in a later article on the war, as well as devote an entire essay to the topic of the proper relations between religious activity and politics. Of interest in the latter article is how Hodge shows that he does believe that religion and politics should, as a rule, be confined to separate spheres. The boundaries between the two are most often by necessity permeable. Charles Hodge, "The War," BRPR 35:1 (Jan. 1863): 140. Charles Hodge, "Relation of the Church and State," BRPR 35:4 (Oct. 1863): 679–693.
8. Hodge, "State of the Country," 1.
9. Shelton Smith, "The Church and the Social Order in the Old South as Interpreted by James H. Thornwell," CH 7:2 (June 1938): 116–118.
10. Benjamin Morgan Palmer, *The Life and Letters of James Henley Thornwell* (Richmond, Va.: Whittet & Shepperson, 1875), 291.
11. Palmer, *Life and Letters*, 303.
12. Palmer, *Life and Letters*, 286.
13. Palmer, *Life and Letters*, 303. James Oscar Farmer Jr., *The Metaphysical Confederacy: James Henley Thornwell and the Synthesis of Southern Values* (Macon, Ga.: Mercer University Press, 1986), 189.
14. Hodge, "State of the Country," 6.
15. Hodge, "State of the Country," 15.
16. Irving Stoddard Kull, "Presbyterian Attitudes Toward Slavery," CH 7:2 (June 1938): 104.
17. Hodge, "State of the Country," 6.
18. Hodge, "State of the Country," 12.
19. Hodge, "State of the Country," 36.
20. Charles Hodge to Hugh Hodge, Princeton, Apr. 28, 1861, CHP, Box 12, Folder 2.
21. Charles Hodge, "England and America," BRPR 34:1 (Jan. 1862): 165.
22. Hodge, "State of the Country," 22; 27.
23. Hodge, "State of the Country," 20.
24. Hodge, "State of the Country," 20.
25. Hodge, "State of the Country," 29.
26. Hodge, "The Princeton Review on the State of the Country and of the Church," BRPR 37:4 (Oct. 1865): 629.
27. Smith, "The Church and the Social Order in the Old South," 124. Elizabeth Fox-Genovese and Eugene D. Genovese, *The Mind of the Master Class: History and Faith in the Southern Slaveholders' Worldview,* (New York: Cambridge University Press, 2005): 615.
28. James H. Thornwell, "The State of the Country," SPR 13:4 (Jan. 1861): 860–889. Farmer, *Metaphysical Confederacy,* 266.
29. Thornwell, "State of the Country," 863; 883.
30. Hodge, "Church and the Country," 323.

31. Hodge, "Church and the Country," 323; 324
32. Hodge "Church and the Country," 326.
33. Thornwell, "State of the Country," 870–871.
34. Thornwell, "State of the Country," 871.
35. Thornwell, "State of the Country," 871.
36. Thornwell, "State of the Country," 871.
37. Thornwell, "State of the Country," 883.
38. Hodge, "Church and the Country," 346.
39. Thomas Cary Johnson, *The Life and Letters of Benjamin Morgan Palmer* (Carlisle, Pa.: Banner of Truth Trust, 1906), 235.
40. Johnson, *Life and Letters of Benjamin Morgan Palmer*, 211.
41. Fox-Genovese, *Mind of the Master Class*, 616–618.
42. Johnson, *Life and Letters of Benjamin Morgan Palmer*, 213. Hodge, "Church and the Country," 347.
43. Charles Hodge to Hugh Hodge, Princeton, Sept. 6, 1861, CHP, Box 12, Folder 2.
44. Hodge, "Church and the Country," 359.
45. Hodge, "Church and the Country," 359.
46. Hodge, "Church and the Country," 373.
47. Hodge, "Church and the Country," 375.
48. Charles Hodge, "The General Assembly of 1861," BRPR 33:3 (July 1861): 546.
49. Hodge, "General Assembly," 551.

Chapter 50: Hodge's Family at War

1. Drew Gilpin Faust, *This Republic of Suffering: Death and the American Civil War* (New York: Alfred A. Knopf, 2008), xi.
2. Ronald C. White Jr., *Lincoln's Greatest Speech: The Second Inaugural* (New York: Simon & Schuster, 2002), 23–24.
3. Charles Hodge to Hugh Hodge, Princeton, Nov. 1, 1862; Nov. 19, 1862; Dec. 7, 1862; Jan. 31, 1963, CHP, Box 12, Folders 2 and 3.
4. Faust, *This Republic of Suffering*, 4.
5. Charles Hodge to Hugh Hodge, Washington, D.C., July 24, 1861, CHP, Box 12, Folder 2.
6. LCH, 450.
7. MFH, 112.
8. Charles Hodge to Hugh Hodge, Princeton, Oct. 31, 1861, CHP, Box 12, Folder 2.
9. MFH, 113.

Chapter 51: The Unities of Mankind

1. Charles Hodge to Hugh Hodge, Princeton, July 24, 1861, CHP, Box 12, Folder 2.
2. Charles to Hugh Hodge, Princeton, Aug. 9, 1861, CHP, Box 12, Folder 2.
3. Charles to Hugh Hodge, Princeton, Jan. 9, 1861, CHP, Box 12, Folder 2.
4. Undated letter fragment, CHP, Box 12, Folder 2. Charles Hodge to Hugh Hodge, Princeton, Dec. 24, 1862, CHP, Box 12, Folder 2.
5. Charles Hodge to Hugh Hodge, Princeton, Dec. 24, 1862, CHP, Box 12, Folder 2.
6. Charles Hodge to Hugh Hodge, Princeton, Dec. 24, 1862, CHP, Box 12, Folder 2.

7. Charles to Hugh Hodge, Princeton, Dec. 29, 1851, CHP, Box 12, Folder 1. Abraham Lincoln, "Resolutions in Behalf of Hungarian Freedom," in *The Language of Liberty*, ed. Joseph R. Fornieri (Washington, D.C.: Regnery Publishing, 2009), 127.

8. Charles Hodge, "England and America," BRPR 34:1 (Jan. 1862): 149.

9. Hodge, "England and America," 147.

10. Hodge, "England and America," 170.

11. Hodge, "England and America," 175.

12. Hodge, "England and America," 149.

13. Hodge, "England and America," 149.

14. John P. Jackson Jr. and Nadine M. Weidman, *Race, Racism and Science: Social Impact and Interaction* (Santa Barbara, Calif.: ABC-CLIO, 2004), 38–39.

15. Charles Hodge, "The Testimony of Modern Science to the Unity of Mankind," BRPR 31:1 (Jan. 1859): 105.

16. Hodge, "Testimony of Modern Science," 149.

17. Hodge, "Testimony of Modern Science," 105.

18. Hodge, "Testimony of Modern Science," 114.

19. Hodge, "Testimony of Modern Science," 119.

20. Hodge, "Testimony of Modern Science," 132.

21. Hodge, "Testimony of Modern Science," 148.

22. Hodge, "Examination of some Reasonings against the Unity of Mankind" BRPR 34:3 (July 1862): 437.

23. Hodge, "Examination of some Reasonings," 437.

24. Jackson, *Race, Racism and Science*, 47.

25. Hodge, "Examination of some Reasonings," 441. George Combe (1788–1858) was a popular writer and lecturer on phrenology. One of his essays was sometimes included in later printed editions of Morton's *Crania Americana*. Morton was never an advocate of phrenology although phrenologists eagerly adapted his work to substantiate their own scientific views.

26. Hodge, "Examination of some Reasonings," 436–437.

27. Hodge, "Examination of some Reasonings," 444–446.

28. Hodge, "Examination of some Reasonings," 464.

29. Irving Stoddard Kull, "Presbyterian Attitudes Toward Slavery," CH 7:2 (June 1938): 109; 113.

Chapter 52: The Disunities of Mankind

1. James M. McPherson, *Battle Cry of Freedom: The Civil War Era* (New York: Oxford University Press, 1988), 502–504.

2. McPherson, *Battle Cry of Freedom*, 510.

3. Charles Hodge, "The War," BRPR 35:1 (Jan. 1863): 153–154.

4. Hodge, "War," 159.

5. A longer discussion of Hodge's views on divine providence during the Civil War can be found in Mark A. Noll, *The Civil War as a Theological Crisis* (Chapel Hill: University of North Carolina Press, 2006), 82–84.

6. Hodge, "War," 147.

7. Hodge, "War," 141–147.

8. Hodge, "War," 156.

9. Hodge, "War," 153.

10. Hodge, "War," 169.

11. LCH, 482.

12. Charles Hodge to Hugh Hodge, Princeton, Apr. 15, 1865, CHP, Box 12, Folder 3.

13. LCH, 483.

14. Charles Hodge, "President Lincoln," BRPR 37:3 (July 1865): 436.

15. Hodge, "President Lincoln," 435.

16. Hodge, "President Lincoln," 444.

17. Hodge, "President Lincoln," 449.

18. Hodge, "President Lincoln," 450–451.

19. Hodge, "President Lincoln," 453.

20. Hodge, "The General Assembly of 1865," BRPR 37:3 (July 1865): 506.

21. Hodge, "President Lincoln," 439.

22. LCH, 565.

23. Charles Hodge, "The Princeton Review on the State of the Country and of the Church," BRPR 37:4 (Oct. 1865): 656.

24. Hodge, "Princeton Review," 628.

25. Hodge, "Princeton Review," 657.

26. Hodge, "Princeton Review," 633; 637.

27. Hodge, "General Assembly of 1865," 548.

28. Hodge, "Princeton Review," 639.

29. Hodge, "Princeton Review," 640–641.

30. Charles Hodge to Hugh Hodge, Princeton, Oct. 3, 1866, CHP, Box 12, Folder 3. See also Richard J. Carwardine, "The Politics of Charles Hodge," CHR, 282–283.

Chapter 53:   Reuniting the Old and New Schools

1. Charles Hodge, "Principles of Church Union, and the Reunion of the Old and New-school Presbyterians," BRPR 37:2 (Apr. 1865): 271.

2. Octavius Brooks Frothingham, *Recollections and Impressions, 1822–1890* (New York: G. P. Putnam's Sons, 1891), 120.

3. Thomas Wentworth Higginson, *The Sympathy of Religions* (Boston, Mass.: Reprinted from the Radical, 1871), 2. A more complete discussion of Higginson and the Free Religious Association can be found in Leigh Eric Schmidt, *Restless Souls: The Making of American Spirituality from Emerson to Oprah* (San Francisco: HarperCollins, 2005), 111–138.

4. Higginson, *Sympathy of Religions*, 4.

5. Charles Hodge, "The General Assembly of 1862," BRPR 34:3 (July 1862): 497.

6. Charles Hodge, "The General Assembly of 1863," BRPR 35:3 (July 1863): 445.

7. LCH, 505; "Meeting of the Presbyterian National Union Convention," NYT, Nov. 8, 1867, 5. *The American Annual Cyclopædia and Register of Important Events of the Year 1867* (New York: D. Appleton, 1869), 7:630–631.

8. LCH, 505.

9. LCH, 505.

10. Charles Hodge, "Presbyterian Reunion," BRPR 40:1 (Jan. 1868): 79–80.

11. Hodge, "Principles of Church Union," 271–313.

12. Lefferts A. Loetscher, *The Broadening Church: A Study of Theological Issues in the Presbyterian Church since 1869* (Philadelphia: University of Pennsylvania Press, 1954), 26.

13. Robert T. Handy, *A History of Union Theological Seminary in New York* (New York: Columbia University Press, 1987), 36.

14. Hodge, "Presbyterian Reunion," 79–80.

15. Hodge, "Presbyterian Reunion," 60.

16. Charles Hodge, "Protest and Answer," BRPR 40:3 (July 1868): 475.

17. Hodge, "Presbyterian Reunion," 58–59.

18. Hodge, "Presbyterian Reunion," 57.

19. Hodge, "Protest and Answer," 460.

20. LCH, 504.

21. Handy, *History of Union Theological Seminary*, 44.

22. LCH, 506.

23. LCH, 507.

24. Charles Hodge, "The Visibility of the Church," BRPR 25:4 (Oct. 1853), 680.

25. LCH, 504; Hodge, "Protest and Answer," 456–477.

26. Loetscher, *Broadening Church*, 7.

27. Trustee Minutes, Bound Volume 5 (1868–1878), MUDD, June 29, 1869, 77. Charles Hodge Memorandum Book, May 28, 1870, CHM, Box 30, Folder 3.

Chapter 54: The Systematic Theology

1. Robert J. Clinton, *The Making of a Leader* (Colorado Springs, Colo.: Navpress, 1988), 44.

2. Clinton, *Making of a Leader*, 47.

3. LCH, 531–532.

4. Mark A. Noll, "The Princeton Review," WTJ 50 (Fall 1988): 291. BRPR, Index Volume (1871): 94–96. Mark A. Noll, ed., *The Princeton Theology, 1812–1921* (Grand Rapids, Mich.: Baker Book House, 1983), 24.

5. LCH, 388.

6. Charles Hodge, Lecture, "The Study of Theology," delivered Aug. 27, 1847, CHM, Box 11, Folder 5, p. 18.

7. Charles Hodge, Lecture, "The Study of Theology," delivered Aug. 27, 1847, CHM, Box 11, Folder 5, p. 18.

8. Charles Hodge, Lecture, "The Study of Theology," delivered Aug. 27, 1847, CHM, Box 11, Folder 5, p. 18.

9. Charles Hodge, *Discussions in Church Polity* (New York: Charles Scribner's Sons, 1878), iii. ST, 1:32.

10. LCH, 451.

11. The original written manuscript for the *Systematic* was recovered from the printer and bound in eight volumes at the request of Princeton Theological Seminary's faculty and placed in the seminary's library. CHM, Boxes 5–9.

12. "*Systematic Theology*," MR 19 (Apr. 1872): 318.

13. Friedrich Schleiermacher, *The Christian Faith*, 2 vols. (New York: Harper Torch Books, 1963); Richard Rothe, *Theologische Ethik*, 5 vols. (Wittenberg,Germany: Zimmermannsche Buchhandlung, 1867).

14. Charles Finney, *Lectures on Systematic Theology* (1846); Henry B. Smith, *System of Christian Theology* (1884); Robert L. Dabney, *Lectures in Systematic Theology* (1878). Dabney's lectures have been reprinted by Banner of Truth Trust under the title *Systematic Theology* (1985).

15. Robert J. Breckinridge, *The Knowledge of God Objectively Considered* (New York: Robert Carter and Brothers, 1858); Robert J. Breckinridge, *The Knowledge of God Subjectively Considered* (New York: Robert Carter and Brothers, 1859).

16. Miner Raymond, *Systematic Theology*, 3 vols. (New York: Phillips & Hunt, 1877–1879); Augustus H. Strong, *Systematic Theology*, 3 vols. (Philadelphia, Pa.: Griffith & Rowland Press, 1907); William G.T. Shedd, *Dogmatic Theology*, 3 vols. (New York: Charles Scribner's Sons, 1889–1894).

17. Theodore Dwight Bozeman, *Protestants in an Age of Science* (Chapel Hill: University of North Carolina Press, 1977), 119–120. Perry Miller, *The Life of the Mind in America from the Revolution to the Civil War* (New York: Harcourt Brace Jovanovich, 1965), 79–80. Ernest Lee Tuveson, *Redeemer Nation: The Idea of America's Millennial Role* (Chicago: University of Chicago Press, 1968), 52–90. Timothy L. Smith, *Revivalism and Social Reform in the Mid–Nineteenth-Century America* (New York: Abingdon Press, 1957), 225–237.

18. James Turner, *Without God, Without Creed: The Origins of Unbelief in America* (Baltimore, Md.: Johns Hopkins University Press, 1985), 204.

19. Charles Hodge to John Johns, Princeton, Nov. 13, 1874, CHP, Box 16, Folder 66. LCH, 532.

20. Williston Walker, *Ten New England Leaders* (New York: Silver, Burdett, 1901), 346. Samuel Hopkins, *Works of Samuel Hopkins, D.D.* (Boston, Mass.: Doctrinal Tract and Book Society, 1854), 2:756.

21. Gary Dorrien, *The Making of American Liberal Theology: Imagining Progressive Religion, 1805–1900* (Louisville, Ky.: Westminster John Knox Press, 2001), 265.

22. Henry Ward Beecher, "The True Religion," in *Sermons, Preached in Plymouth Church, Brooklyn, New York* (London: Richard D. Dickinson, 1871), 207. Turner, *Without God, Without Creed*, 112; 196–197.

23. A good overview of the rise of this type of modern, liberal Protestant theology can be found in Dorrien, *Making of American Liberal Theology*, 261–392.

24. ST, 1:1.

25. Walter H. Conser Jr., *God and the Natural World: Religion and Science in Antebellum America* (Columbia: University of South Carolina Press, 1993), 69.

26. Hodge, "Study of Theology" (delivered Aug. 27, 1847), 6.

27. Hodge, "Study of Theology" (delivered Aug. 27, 1847), 5.

28. ST, 1:16–17.

29. Bozeman, *Protestants in an Age of Science*, 21.

30. Bozeman, *Protestants in an Age of Science*, 17.

31. ST, 1:7; 9; 5–6.

32. Charles Hodge, "Scripture and Science," NYO, Mar. 26, 1863, 98–99.

33. ST, 1:10, 11.

34. ST, 1:13.

35. ST, 3:676.

36. ST, 1:170.

37. ST, 2:440.

38. Reviews include: "Hodge's *Systematic Theology* (vol. II)," NE 31 (Apr. 1872): 371–372; "Hodge's Theology," APR 3 (Oct. 1871): 651; "Literary Review" [of *Systematic Theology*, vol. 1], CQ 13 (Oct. 1871): 604–605; "Literary Review" [of *Systematic Theology*, vol. 2], CQ 14 (Apr. 1872): 333–335; "Systematic Theology, vols. 1 and 2, by Charles Hodge," MQR 54 (Apr. 1872): 337–338; "*Systematic Theology* and *Index to Systematic Theology*, by Charles Hodge,"

MQR 55 (July 1873): 500–503; "*Systematic Theology. . .* by Charles Hodge," ACR 25 (Apr. 1873): 293–296; "*Systematic Theology* by Charles Hodge," BQ 36 (Jan. 1872): 115–116; "*Systematic Theology* by Charles Hodge," BQ 36 (Jan. 1872): 115–116; "*Systematic Theology* by Charles Hodge," BQ 37 (Apr. 1872): 248–249; "*Systematic Theology* by Charles Hodge," BQ 38 (Jan. 1873): 124–125; "*Systematic Theology* by Charles Hodge," BRQR 55 (Jan. 1872): 164; "*Systematic Theology* by Charles Hodge," BRQR 55 (Apr. 1872): 309–310; "*Systematic Theology* by Charles Hodge," BRQR 57 (Jan. 1874): 293; "*Systematic Theology* by Charles Hodge," MR 19 (Apr. 1872): 318–321; "*Systematic Theology* by Charles Hodge," MR 20 (Jan. 1873): 177–179; "*Systematic Theology*, vol. 2, by Charles Hodge," NAT 446 (Jan. 15, 1874): 44–46; "*Systematic Theology* by Charles Hodge," NE 30 (1871): 744–745; "*Systematic Theology* . . . by Charles Hodge," NYT, Oct. 23, 1871, 2; "*Systematic Theology* . . . by Charles Hodge," PQPR 2 (Jan. 1873): 174; "*Systematic Theology* by Charles Hodge," QR 3 (Jan. 1873): 156–157.

39. "*Systematic Theology* by Charles Hodge," MR 20 (Jan. 1873): 179.

40. Charles Hodge Memorandum Book, Vol. 6 (Mar. 1, 1866–Mar. 1, 1878), Oct. 8, 1872, p. 124; Dec. 7, 1872, p. 128, CHM, Box 30, Folder 3. Charles Hodge to Caspar René Gregory, Princeton, July 10, 1871, CHM, Box 28, Folder 44. Charles Scribner to Charles Hodge, New York, Apr. 10, 1872, CHP, Box 18, Folder 63. Charles Hodge to Hugh Hodge, Princeton, Jan. 7, 1872; Feb. 17, 1873, CHP, Box 12, Folder 3.

41. Charles Scribner to Charles Hodge, New York, Oct. 1, 1871; Apr. 10, 1872; Apr. 18, 1872, CHP, Box 18, Folder 63. Charles Hodge to Hugh Hodge, Princeton, Feb. 17, 1873, CHP, Box 12, Folder 3.

42. "*Systematic Theology* by Charles Hodge," BQ 36 (Jan. 1872): 116. Charles Hodge to Hugh Hodge, Princeton, Feb. 17, 1873, CHP, Box 12, Folder 3.

43. Manuscript for the *Index to Systematic Theology*, CHM, Box 9, Folders 2–4. "*Index to Systematic Theology* by Charles Hodge," BS 31 (Apr. 1874): 197.

Chapter 55: "The Apex of My Life"

1. Charles Hodge Memorandum Book, Vol. 6 (Mar. 1, 1866–Mar. 1, 1878), Apr. 24, 1872, CHM, Box 30, Folder 3, p. 115.

2. LCH, 512.

3. Letter from faculty of Glesina College; Letter from Williams College, CHM, Box 32, Folder 8, Letters 47 and 49. Some fifty congratulatory letters for this event are found in CHM, Box 32.

4. Samuel M. Hopkins to Semi-Centennial Committee, Apr. 9, 1872, CHM, Box 32, Folder 5, Letter 4.

5. *Proceedings Connected with the Semi-Centennial Commemoration of the Professorship of Rev. Charles Hodge* (New York: Anson D. F. Randolph, 1872), 45.

6. *Proceedings Connected with the Semi-Centennial Commemoration*, 45.

7. *Proceedings Connected with the Semi-Centennial Commemoration*, 45.

8. *Proceedings Connected with the Semi-Centennial Commemoration*, 23.

9. *Proceedings Connected with the Semi-Centennial Commemoration*, 27–28.

10. *Proceedings Connected with the Semi-Centennial Commemoration*, 46.

11. *Proceedings Connected with the Semi-Centennial Commemoration*, 52.

12. *Proceedings Connected with the Semi-Centennial Commemoration*, 52.

13. LCH, 528.

14. LCH, 608.
15. LCH, 608.
16. LCH, 535–536.
17. Charles Hodge to John Johns, Princeton, Mar. 4, 1873, CHP, Box 16, Folder 67.

Chapter 56: Science and Darwinism

1. The best general overview and history of the Evangelical Alliance is Philip D. Jordan, *The Evangelical Alliance for the United States of America, 1847–1900: Ecumenism, Identity and the Religion of the Republic* (Lewiston, N.Y.: Edwin Mellen, 1982).
2. Jordan, *Evangelical Alliance*, 93.
3. A copy of Hodge's address can be found in Philip Schaff and S. Irenaeus Prime, eds., *History, Essays, Orations, and Other Documents of the Sixth General Conference of the Evangelical Alliance Held in New York, October 2–12, 1873* (New York: Harper, 1874), 139–144. For the response to the address, see Jordan, *Evangelical Alliance*, 96.
4. Schaff and Prime, *History, Essays, Orations*, 318.
5. Charles Hodge to Caspar René Gregory, Princeton, Apr. 21, 1874, CHM, Box 28, Folder 44.
6. ST, 2:14–24.
7. Charles Hodge, "The Testimony of Modern Science to the Unity of Mankind," BRPR 31:1 (Jan. 1859): 107; Hunter Dupree, *Science in the Federal Government: A History of Policies and Activities*, rev. ed. (Baltimore, Md.: Johns Hopkins University Press, 1986), 82. Hodge wholeheartedly agreed with his fellow Presbyterian Abner A. Porter who wrote in the *Southern Presbyterian Review*, "no *fact* in any department of human knowledge has yet been discovered even in appearance contradictory of any of the statements of the Bible. It is the *reasoning* of men on facts which conflicts with it." Abner A. Porter, "The Unity of the Human Race," SPR 4:3 (Jan. 1851): 367.
8. Charles Hodge, "Scripture and Science," NYO, Mar. 26, 1863, 98–99.
9. John W. Stewart, "Mediating the Center: Charles Hodge on American Science, Language, Literature, and Politics," *Studies in Reformed Theology and History* 3:1 (Winter 1995): 28.
10. "Quarterly Scientific Intelligence," BRPR 24:2 (Apr. 1852): 350–356; "Quarterly Scientific Intelligence," BRPR 24:3 (July 1852): 526–531.
11. WID, 131.
12. Ronald L. Numbers, "Charles Hodge and the Beauties and Deformities of Science," CHR, 88.
13. David N. Livingstone, *Darwin's Forgotten Defenders* (Grand Rapids, Mich.: William B. Eerdmans Publishing, 1987), 13.
14. Ronald L. Numbers, *Creation by Natural Law: Laplace's Nebular Hypothesis in American Thought* (Seattle: University of Washington Press, 1977), 91–100.
15. ST, 1:550–552; 556–558; 573–574.
16. Charles Hodge, "The Testimony of Modern Science to the Unity of Mankind," BRPR 31:1 (Jan. 1859): 104.
17. WID, 142.
18. Hodge, "Testimony of Modern Science," 105.
19. Hodge, "Testimony of Modern Science," 105.
20. WID, 22.
21. An insightful discussion of Hodge's growing tension with the men of science of his age can be found in Numbers, "Charles Hodge and the Beauties and Deformities of Science," 79–81; 101.

22. WID, 1.

23. WID, 177.

24. WID, 48.

25. WID, 2.

26. William Paley published the first edition of his *Natural Theology* in 1802. William Paley, *Natural Theology; or, Evidences of the Existence and Attributes of the Deity, Collected from the Appearances of Nature* (New York: Evert Duyckinck, 1820), 2–29. See also Livingstone, *Darwin's Forgotten Defenders*, 3–7.

27. WID, 56.

28. WID, 40–41. See also Livingstone, *Darwin's Forgotten Defenders*, 36–37.

29. WID, 64.

30. WID, 48.

31. WID, 48.

32. WID, 46.

33. Mark A. Noll and David N. Livingstone, eds., *What is Darwinism?* by Charles Hodge (Grand Rapids, Mich.: Baker Books, 1994), 12.

34. WID, 3–4.

35. WID, 60.

36. Numbers, "Charles Hodge and the Beauties and Deformities of Science," 90–91.

37. For insight into Asa Gray's sympathetic position on Darwinism, see Livingstone, *Darwin's Forgotten Defenders*, 57–64 and Asa Gray, Review of *What is Darwinism?* in NAT 465 (May 28, 1874): 348–353.

38. WID, 39.

39. WID, 64.

40. WID, 141. Jonathan Wells has argued that Hodge was so committed to his Confessional faith that he proved unable to entertain arguments from natural theology that ran counter to his theological convictions. While Hodge undoubtedly weighted all his conclusions in favor of scripture, Wells underestimates just how seriously Hodge did take into account evidence found in nature—and upon occasion adjusted his scriptural interpretations to fit such evidence. Jonathan Wells, *Charles Hodge's Critique of Darwinism: An Historical-Critical Analysis of Concepts Basic to the 19th Century Debate* (Lewiston, N.Y.: Edwin Mellen Press, 1988). A particularly good discussion of Hodge's engagement with Darwinian thought can be found in John Bradley Gundlach, "The Evolution Question at Princeton, 1845–1929" (Ph.D. diss., University of Rochester, N.Y., 1995), 132–144.

41. WID, 141.

42. At the age of sixteen, William Berryman Scott helped Hodge correct the printer's proofs for *What is Darwinism?* and agreed with Hodge's stand on Darwinism. William Berryman Scott, *Some Memories of a Palaeontologist* (Princeton, N.J.: Princeton University Press, 1939), 49. Later, Scott became a staunch advocate of theistic evolution. He collaborated with James McCosh on *The Religious Aspect of Evolution* (1888). After Hodge's death, A. A. Hodge favorably reviewed Asa Gray's *Natural Science and Religion*, in which Gray argued for the teleological nature of Darwin's work. A. A. Hodge, Review of *Natural Science and Religion* by Asa Gray, PR 1 (1880): 586–589.

43. Scott, *Some Memories of a Palaeontologist*, 75. It is unclear what book of Darwin's Hodge was actually reading: *Journal of a Naturalist* or *Voyage of the Beagle*. Darwin has no book titled *Voyage of a Naturalist*.

Chapter 57: "O Death, Where is Thy Sting?"

1. Charles Hodge to Hugh Hodge, Princeton, Oct. 15, 1851, CHP, Box 12, Folder 1.
2. David B. Calhoun, *Princeton Seminary* (Carlisle, Pa.: Banner of Truth Trust, 1996), 2:55.
3. Archibald Alexander Hodge, *Outlines in Theology* (New York: Robert Carter & Bros., 1879); Archibald Alexander Hodge, *The Atonement* (New York: T. Nelson & Sons, 1868); and Archibald Alexander Hodge, *Popular Lectures on Theological Themes* (Philadelphia, Pa.: Presbyterian Board of Publication, 1887).
4. Francis Landey Patton, *A Discourse in Memory of Archibald Alexander Hodge* (Philadelphia, Pa.: Times Printing House, 1887), 47. For a fuller discussion of A. A. Hodge's teaching at Princeton Theological Seminary, see Charles A. Salmond, *Princetonia: Charles and A. A. Hodge with Class and Table Talk of Hodge the Younger* (New York: Scribner & Welford, 1888), 104–110; Calhoun, *Princeton Seminary*, 2:68; 101.
5. "O Death where is they Sting?" Apr. 11, 1875, CHM, Box 26, Folder 62.
6. "Death," Mar. 28, 1875, CHM, Box 26, Folder 61; "Follow me," Jan. 28, 1875, CHM, Box 26, Folder 60; "No Man having put his hand to the plow, and looking back," Dec. 5, 1875, CHM, Box 26, Folder 65; "Loyalty to Christ," Dec. 12, 1875, CHM, Box 26, Folder 66; "Dying Unto Sin," Sept. 10, 1876, CHM, Box 26, Folder 69; "Love not the World," Jan. 16, 1876, CHM, Box 26, Folder 67; "What must I do to be saved?" July 1877, CHM, Box 26, Folder 70.
7. A good account of the spectacle of Henry's funeral can be found in Albert E. Moyer, *Joseph Henry* (Washington D.C.: Smithsonian Institution Press, 1997), 1–8.
8. LCH, 579.
9. *Memorial of Joseph Henry* (Washington D.C.: Smithsonian Institution, Government Printing Office, 1880), 13; 14.
10. LCH, 580.
11. "Last Will and Testament," June 10, 1878, CHM, Box 31, Folder 11.
12. William Henry Green, "Dr. Charles Hodge," CU (July 3, 1878): 4.
13. LCH, 586
14. "Death of Dr. Charles Hodge," *Messenger* (June 26, 1878): 4; "The Late Dr. Hodge," *New York Observer and Chronicle* (July 4, 1878): 211.
15. "Religious," *National Repository* 4 (Sept. 1878): 277.
16. Henry A. Buttz, "Rev. Charles Hodge, D.D., LL.D.," *National Repository* 5 (Jan. 1879): 60.
17. "Dr. Charles Hodge," CU (June 26, 1878): 530.
18. Green, "Dr. Charles Hodge," 4.
19. "Death of Dr. Charles Hodge," 4.
20. Green, "Dr. Charles Hodge," 4.
21. As quoted in Calhoun, *Princeton Seminary*, 2:28.
22. Buttz, "Rev. Charles Hodge," 66.
23. "Religious," 277.

Epilogue

1. "Dr. Charles Hodge," CU (June 26, 1878): 530.
2. Lefferts A. Loetscher, *The Broadening Church: A Study of Theological Issues in the Presbyterian Church since 1869* (Philadelphia: University of Pennsylvania Press, 1954), 11.
3. LAA, 605–606.

4. *Benjamin B. Warfield, Shorter Writings*, ed. John E. Meeter, 2 vols. (Phillipsburg, N.J.: Presbyterian and Reformed, 1970, 1973), 1:389.

5. James H. Moorhead, "Afterword," CHR, 328–329.

6. Archibald Alexander Hodge and Benjamin B. Warfield, "Inspiration," PR 2:6 (Apr. 1881): 225–260.

7. Charles Hodge, "The Inspiration of Holy Scripture," BRPR 29:4 (Oct. 1857): 662.

8. Hodge and Warfield, "Inspiration," 242; 245. See also Benjamin B. Warfield, "The Inerrancy of the Original Autographs," in *Benjamin B. Warfield, Shorter Writings*, ed. Meter, 2:580–587; Benjamin B. Warfield, "St. Paul & Inspiration," PRR 4:13 (Jan. 1893): 1–24; Benjamin B. Warfield, "The Real Problem of Inspiration," PRR 4:14 (Apr. 1893): 177–221; Loetscher, *Broadening Church*, 31.

9. Harold Lindsell, *Battle for the Bible* (Grand Rapids, Mich.: Zondervan, 1976); see also Harold Lindsell, *Bible in the Balance: A Further Look at the Battle for the Bible* (Grand Rapids, Mich.: Zondervan, 1979).

10. Ernest R. Sandeen, "The Princeton Theology: One Source of Biblical Literalism in American Protestantism," CH 31:3 (Sept. 1962): 307; Joel A. Carpenter, *Revive Us Again: The Reawakening of American Fundamentalism* (New York: Oxford University Press, 1997), 70.

11. "Evangelical" is a highly vexed term. For my purposes here, I include American Fundamentalists under the umbrella term "Evangelical," noting that both groups are defined by: 1) the importance they place on the Bible; 2) a stress on the personal need to experience God's grace; 3) the belief that Jesus is the only way to attain an eternal life with God. For thoughtful treatments of American Evangelicalism, see George Marsden, ed., *Evangelicalism and Modern America* (Grand Rapids, Mich.: William B. Eerdmans Publishing, 1984); George Marsden, *Understanding Fundamentalism and Evangelicalism* (Grand Rapids, Mich.: William B. Eerdmans, 1991); and James Davison Hunter, *Evangelicalism: The Coming Generation* (Chicago: University of Chicago Press, 1987).

12. R. C. Sproul, *Essential Truths of the Christian Faith* (Wheaton, Ill.: Tyndale House Publishers, 1998), 251; John F. MacArthur, *Nothing but the Truth: Upholding the Gospel in a Doubting Age* (Wheaton, Ill.: Crossway Books, 1999), 52; John Piper, *Counted Righteous in Christ: Should We Abandon the Imputation of Christ's Righteousness* (Wheaton, Ill.: Crossway Books, 2002), 81.

13. Josh McDowell, *Evidence that Demands a Verdict: Historical Evidence for the Christ Faith* (San Bernardino, Calif.: Campus Crusade for Christ, 1972); Mark A. Noll, "Common Sense Traditions and American Evangelical Thought," AQ 37:2 (Summer 1985): 227.

14. ST, 1:1.

15. A good overview of American Dispensationalism can be found in Norman C. Kraus, *Dispensationalism in America: its Rise and Development* (Richmond, Va.: John Knox, 1958).

16. Lewis Sperry Chafer, *Systematic Theology*, 8 vols. (Dallas, Tex.: Dallas Seminary Press, 1947), 1:5.

17. Noll, "Common Sense Traditions and American Evangelical Thought," 227.

18. Carpenter, *Revive Us Again*, 69.

19. ST, 1:152.

20. *Proceedings Connected with the Semi-Centennial Commemoration of the Professorship of Rev. Charles Hodge* (New York: Anson D. F. Randolph, 1872), 54.

21. Charles Hodge, "The State of the Country," BRPR 33:1 (Jan. 1861): 1.

SELECT BIBLIOGRAPHY

Nineteenth-Century Journals, Periodicals, and Newspapers

The American Church Review
The American Presbyterian Review
Baptist Quarterly Review
Biblical Repertory
Biblical Repertory and Princeton Review
Biblical Repertory and Theological Review
Bibliotheca Sacra
Boston Daily Advertiser
Boston Quarterly Review
Boston Recorder
British Quarterly Review
Christian Advocate
Christian Review
Christian Union
The Congregational Quarterly
Mercersburg Review
Messenger
Methodist Quarterly Review
The Nation
National Repository
New Englander
New York Observer
New York Observer and Chronicle
New York Times
North American
Pennsylvania Gazette
Presbyterian
The Presbyterian Quarterly and Princeton Review
Presbyterian Review
Quarterly Christian Spectator
The Quarterly Review of the Evangelical Lutheran Church
Southern Presbyterian Review

Works Cited

Addresses and Proceedings at the Celebration of the One Hundredth Anniversary of the Founding of the American Whig Society of the College of New Jersey. Princeton, N.J.: Stelle & Smith Publishers, 1871.

Ahlstrom, Sydney E. *A Religious History of the American People.* New Haven, Conn.: Yale University Press, 1972.

———. "Theology in America: A Historical Survey." In *The Shaping of American Religion*, ed. James Ward Smith and A. Leland Jamison, 232–321. Princeton, N.J.: Princeton University Press, 1961.

Alexander, Archibald. *Biographical Sketches of the Founder and Principal Alumni of the Log College.* Philadelphia, Pa.: Presbyterian Board of Publication, 1851.

———. *The Canon of the Old and New Testaments Ascertained.* New York: A.D. Borrenstein for G. & C. Carvill, 1826.

———. "The Doctrine of Original Sin as held by the Church, Both Before and After the Reformation." *Biblical Repertory and Theological Review* 2:4 (Oct. 1830): 481–503.

———. "The Early History of Pelagianism." *Biblical Repertory and Theological Review* 2:1 (Jan. 1830): 77–113.

———. "Hints for Young Men in the Choice of a Wife." N.d.: n.p.; copy found in the Special Collections of Princeton Theological Seminary Library.

———. *A History of Colonization of the Western Coast of Africa.* Philadelphia, Pa.: William S. Martien, 1846.

———. "An Inquiry into that Inability under which the Sinner Labours, and Whether It Furnishes Any Excuse for His Neglect of Duty." *Biblical Repertory and Theological Review* 3:3 (July 1831): 360–383.

———. *A Sermon Delivered at the Opening of the General Assembly of the Presbyterian Church in the United States, May, 1808.* Philadelphia, Pa.: Hopkins & Earle, 1808.

Alexander, Henry C. *The Life of Joseph Addison Alexander.* 2 vols. New York: Charles Scribner, 1870.

Alexander, James Waddel. "Institutio Theologiae Elencticae." *Biblical Repertory and Princeton Review* 20:3 (July 1848): 452–463.

———. *The Life of Archibald Alexander, D.D.* New York: Charles Scribner, 1854.

———. *Princeton—Old and New: Recollections of Undergraduate Life.* New York: Charles Scribner's Sons, 1898.

Alexander, Joseph Addison, "A Cyclopedia of Biblical Literature." *Biblical Repertory and Princeton Review* 18:4 (Oct. 1846): 554–568.

The American Annual Cyclopædia and Register of Important Events of the Year 1867. Vol. 7. New York: D. Appleton, 1869.

Anbinder, Tyler. *Nativism and Slavery: The Northern Know Nothings and the Politics of the 1850s.* New York: Oxford University Press, 1992.

Anderson, Courtney, et al. *Heroic Colonial Christians.* Philadelphia, Pa.: J.B. Lippincott, 1966.

Atwater, Lyman H. *A Discourse Commemorative of the Late Dr. Charles Hodge.* Princeton, N.J.: Charles S. Robinson, 1878.

Baird, Robert. *Religion in the United States of America.* Glasgow and Edinburgh, Scotland: Blackie & Son, 1844.

Baird, Samuel. *A History of the New School.* Lansing: University of Michigan Library, 2006.

Barnes, Albert. "The Way of Salvation." Morris-Town, N.J.: Jacob Mann, 1830.

———. *An Inquiry into the Scriptural Views of Slavery.* Philadelphia, Pa.: Perkins & Purves, 1846.

Barth, Karl. *Protestant Theology in the Nineteenth Century: Its Background and History.* London: SCM Press, 1972.

Beadle, E. R. *The Old and the New, 1743–1876.* N.p., 1876.

Beam, Jacob N. "Charles Hodge's Student Years in Germany." *The Princeton University Library Chronicle* 8:3 (Apr. 1947): 103–114.

Beaman, Robert S. "Alexander Hall at the Princeton Theological Seminary: Construction of a Building and the Establishment of an Institution." *Princeton History* 2 (1977): 43–58.

Beecher, Henry Ward. *Sermons, Preached in Plymouth Church, Brooklyn, New York.* London: Richard D. Dickinson, 1871.

Beecher, Lyman. *A Plea for the West.* Cincinnati, Truman & Smith; New York, Leavitt, Lord, 1835.

Bell, John. *On Baths and Mineral Waters.* Philadelphia, Pa.: Henry H. Porter, 1831.

Bell, Whitfield J., Jr., "Addenda to Watson's Annals of Philadelphia." *The Pennsylvania Magazine of History and Biography* 98:2 (Apr. 1974): 131–170.

Beyan, Amos. *The American Colonization Society and the Creation of the Liberian State.* Lanham, Md.: University Press of America, 1991.

Billington, Ray Allen. *The Protestant Crusade, 1800–1860.* New York: Macmillan Company, 1938.

Bishop, Robert H. *An Outline of the History of the Church in the State of Kentucky, During a Period of Forty Years: Containing the Memoirs of Rev. David Rice.* Lexington, Ky.: T. T. Skillman, 1824.

Botting, Douglas. *Humboldt and the Cosmos.* New York: Harper & Row, 1973.

Bozeman, Theodore Dwight. *Protestants in an Age of Science: The Baconian Ideal and Antebellum American Religious Thought.* Chapel Hill: University of North Carolina Press, 1977.

Breckinridge, Robert. *The Knowledge of God Objectively Considered.* New York: Robert Carter and Brothers, 1858.

———. *The Knowledge of God Subjectively Considered Considered.* New York: Robert Carter and Brothers, 1859.

———. "A Plain Statement." *Presbyterian* 5:16 (Apr. 16, 1835): 1.

Broadus, John Albert. *A Gentleman and a Scholar: Memoir of James P. Boyce.* New York: A.C. Armstrong & Son, 1893.

Broderick, Francis L. "Pulpit, Physics, and Politics: The Curriculum of the College of New Jersey, 1746–1794." *William and Mary Quarterly* 6:1 (Jan. 1949): 42–68.

Brown, Isaac Van Arsdale. *A Historical Vindication of the Abrogation of the Plan of Union.* Philadelphia, Pa.: Wm. S. & Alfred Martien, 1855.

Brown, Jerry Wayne. *The Rise of Biblical Criticism in America, 1800–1870.* Middletown, Conn.: Wesleyan University Press, 1969.

Brownson, Orestes. "Review of *Two Articles from the Princeton Review.*" *Boston Quarterly Review* 3:3 (July 1840): 265–277.

Brumberg, Joan. *Mission for Life: The Judson Family and American Evangelical Culture.* New York: New York University Press, 1984.

Burin, Eric. *Slavery and the Peculiar Solution: A History of the American Colonization Society.* Gainesville: University Press of Florida, 2005.

Bushnell, Horace. *God in Christ.* New York: Charles Scribner's Sons, 1876.

Butterfield, L. H. *John Witherspoon Comes to America: A Documentary Account Based Largely on New Material.* Princeton, N.J.: Princeton University Library, 1953.

———. *Letters of Benjamin Rush.* 2 vols. Princeton, N.J.: Princeton University Press, 1951.

Buttz, Henry A. "Rev. Charles Hodge, D.D., LL.D." *The National Repository* 5 (Jan. 1879): 60–66.

Calhoun, David. "The Last Command: Princeton Theological Seminary and Missions (1812–1862)." Ph.D. diss., Princeton Theological Seminary, 1983.

———. *Princeton Seminary*. 2 vols. Carlisle, Pa.: Banner of Truth Trust, 1994 and 1996.

Carpenter, Joel A. *Revive Us Again: The Reawakening of American Fundamentalism*. New York: Oxford University Press, 1997.

Carwardine, Richard J. "The Politics of Charles Hodge." In *Charles Hodge Revisited: A Critical Appraisal of His Life and Work*, ed. John W. Stewart and James H. Moorhead, 247–297. Grand Rapids, Mich.: William B. Eerdmans, 2002.

———. "The Second Great Awakening in the Urban Centers: An Examination of Methodism and the 'New Measures.'" *Journal of American History* 59:2 (Sept. 1972): 327–340.

"Case of the Rev. Mr. Barnes." *The Quarterly Christian Spectator* 3:2 (June 1831): 292–336.

Cashdollar, Charles D. "The Pursuit of Piety: Charles Hodge's Diary, 1819–1820." *Journal of Presbyterian History* 55 (1977): 267–274.

Catalogue of the Honorary and Graduate Members of the American Whig Society, Instituted in the College of New Jersey, in 1769. Princeton, N.J.: John Bogart, 1837.

Chafer, Lewis Sperry. *Systematic Theology*. 8 vols. Dallas, Tex.: Dallas Seminary Press, 1947.

Cheeseman, Lewis. *Differences between Old and New School Presbyterians*. Rochester, N.Y.: Erastus Darrow, 1848.

Chepesiuk, Ron. *The Scotch-Irish: From the North of Ireland to the Making of America*. Jefferson, N.C.: McFarland & Co., 2000.

Clark, Grace, Jessie Havens, and Stewart Hoagland. *Somerset County, 1688–1938: A Chronology with Tales from the Past*. Somerville, N.J.: Somerset Press, 1976.

Clemmer, Robert. "Historical Transcendentalism in Pennsylvania." *Journal of the History of Ideas* 30:4 (Oct.–Dec. 1969): 579–592.

Clinton, Robert J. *The Making of a Leader*. Colorado Springs, Colo.: Navpress, 1988.

Coalter, Milton, J. *Gilbert Tennent, A Son of Thunder: A Case Study of Continental Pietism's Impact on the First Great Awakening in the Middle Colonies*. Westport, Conn.: Greenwood Press, 1986.

Collins, Varnum Lansing. *President Witherspoon, A Biography*. 2 vols. Princeton, N.J.: Princeton University Press, 1925.

Conser, Walter H., Jr. *Church and Confession: Conservative Theologians in Germany, England, and America, 1815–1866*. Macon, Ga.: Mercer University Press, 1984.

———. *God and the Natural World: Religion and Science in Antebellum America*. Columbia: University of South Carolina Press, 1993.

Cremin, Lawrence. *American Education: The Colonial Experience 1607–1783*. New York: Harper & Row, 1970.

———. *American Education: The National Experience 1783–1876*. New York: Harper & Row, 1980.

Dabney, Robert L. *Systematic Theology*. Carlisle, PA: Banner of Truth, 1985.

Danhof, Ralph J. *Charles Hodge as Dogmatician*. Goes, the Netherlands: Osterbaan and le Cointre, 1929.

Davidson, Cathy N. *Revolution and the Word: The Rise of the Novel in America*. New York: Oxford University Press, 1986.

"Death of Dr. Charles Hodge." *Messenger* (June 26, 1878): 4.

Dick, John. *Lectures on Theology*. 2 vols. Philadelphia, Pa.: F. W. Greenough, 1838.

Dickinson, Jonathan. *The True Scripture-Doctrine Concerning Some Important Points of Christian Faith*. Boston, Mass.: D. Fowle, 1741.

A Digest Compiled from the Records of the General Assembly of the Presbyterian Church in the United States. Philadelphia, Pa.: R. P. M'Colloh, 1820.

Dod, Albert B. "Lectures on Revivals of Religion." *Biblical Repertory and Theological Review* 7:3 (July 1835): 482–529.

——. "Lectures on Revivals of Religion." *Biblical Repertory and Theological Review* 7:4 (Oct. 1835): 626–675.

——, and James W. Alexander, "Elements of Psychology." *Biblical Repertory and Princeton Review* 11:1 (Jan. 1839): 37–101.

Dorrien, Gary. *The Making of American Liberal Theology: Imagining Progressive Religion, 1805–1900.* Louisville, Ky.: Westminster John Knox Press, 2001.

"Dr. Hodge's Commentary on Romans in French." *Presbyterian* 11 (March 27, 1841): 50.

Drescher, Seymour. *Capitalism and Antislavery: British Mobilization in Comparative Perspective.* New York: Oxford University Press, 1987.

Dunaway, Wayland Fuller. *The Scotch-Irish of Colonial Pennsylvania.* Chapel Hill: University of North Carolina Press, 1944.

Dupree, Hunter. *Science in the Federal Government: A History of Policies and Activities.* Rev. ed. Baltimore, Md.: Johns Hopkins University Press, 1986.

Dwight, Timothy. *A Sermon Preached at the Opening of the Theological Institution in Andover.* Boston, Mass.: n.p., 1808.

Elkins, Stanley, and Eric McKitrick. *The Age of Federalism.* New York: Oxford University Press, 1993.

Ells, Robert J. *Forgotten Saint: The Life of Theodore Frelinghuysen; A Case Study of Christian Leadership.* Lanham, Md.: University Press of America, 1987.

Farmer, James Oscar, Jr. *The Metaphysical Confederacy: James Henley Thornwell and the Synthesis of Southern Values.* Macon, Ga.: Mercer University Press, 1986.

Faust, Drew Gilpin. *The Ideology of Slavery: Proslavery Thought in the Antebellum South, 1830–1860.* Baton Rouge: Louisiana State University Press, 1981.

——. *This Republic of Suffering: Death and the American Civil War.* New York: Alfred A. Knopf, 2008.

Fiering, Norman. *Moral Philosophy at Seventeenth-Century Harvard: A Discipline in Transition.* Chapel Hill: University of North Carolina Press, 1981.

Finke, Roger, and Rodney Stark. *The Churching of America 1776–1990.* New Brunswick, N.J.: Rutgers University Press, 1992.

Finley, Samuel. *The Successful Minister of Christ Distinguished in Glory.* Philadelphia, Pa.: William Bradford, 1764.

Finney, Charles Grandison. *Lectures on Revivals of Religion.* New York: Leavitt, Lord & Company, 1835.

——. *Lectures on Systematic Theology.* Oberlin, Ohio: James M. Fitch, 1846.

Fornieri, Joseph R., ed. *The Language of Liberty.* Washington, D.C.: Regnery Publishing, 2009.

Fox-Genovese, Elizabeth, and Eugene D. Genovese. *The Mind of the Master Class: History and Faith in the Southern Slaveholders' Worldview.* New York: Cambridge University Press, 2005.

Freehling, William W. *The Road to Disunion: Secessionists at Bay.* New York: Oxford University Press, 1990.

Frothingham, Octavius Brooks. *Recollections and Impressions, 1822–1890.* New York: G. P. Putnam's Sons, 1891.

Gapp, Kenneth S. "The Princeton Review Series and the Contribution of Princeton Theological Seminary to Presbyterian Quarterly Magazines." Princeton, N.J.: 1943. Typescript in the Special Collections of Princeton Theological Seminary Library.

Gardiner, Richard. "Princeton and Paris: An Early Nineteenth Century Bond of Mission." Senior Thesis, History Department, Princeton Theological Seminary, 1994.

Garretson, James M. *Princeton and Preaching: Archibald Alexander and the Christian Ministry.* Carlisle, Pa.: Banner of Truth Trust, 2005.

Gillet, Ezra Hall. *History of the Presbyterian Church in the United States of America.* 2 vols. Philadelphia, Pa.: Presbyterian Publication Committee, 1964.

Gillingham, Harrold E. "Some Colonial Ships Built in Philadelphia." *The Pennsylvania Magazine of History and Biography* 56:2 (1932): 156–186.

Giltner, John H. *Moses Stuart: The Father of Biblical Science in America.* Atlanta, Ga.: Scholars Press, 1988.

Gray, Asa. Review of *What is Darwinism? The Nation* 465 (May 28, 1874): 348–353.

Green, Ashbel. *An Address to the Students of the College of New Jersey: Delivered May 6th 1802.* Trenton, N.J.: Sherman & Mershon, 1802.

———. "The Christian Duty of Christian Women." Princeton, N.J.: Princeton Press, 1825.

———. "Extracts from the Minutes of the General Assembly of 1834" *Christian Advocate* (July 1834): 322–329.

———. *A Historical Sketch or Compendious View of Domestic and Foreign Missions in the Presbyterian Church of the United States of America.* Philadelphia, Pa.: William S. Martien, 1838.

———. *The Life of Ashbel Green, V.D.M. Begun to be Written by Himself in his Eighty-Second Year and Continued to his Eighty-Fourth. Prepared for the Press at the Author's Request by Joseph H. Jones.* New York: Robert Carter & Brothers, 1849.

———. *The Life of the Revd. John Witherspoon.* Princeton, N.J.: Princeton University Press, 1973.

———. "Proceedings of the General Assembly of the Presbyterian Church in May and June, 1834" *Christian Advocate* (Aug. 1834): 362–369.

———. "Proceedings of the General Assembly of the Presbyterian Church in May and June, 1834" *Christian Advocate* (Sept. 1834): 410–418.

———. "Proceedings of the General Assembly of the Presbyterian Church in May and June, 1834" *Christian Advocate* (Oct. 1834): 459–467.

———. "Proceedings of the General Assembly of the Presbyterian Church in May and June, 1834" *Christian Advocate* (Nov. 1834): 503–512.

———. "Proceedings of the General Assembly of the Presbyterian Church in May and June, 1834" *Christian Advocate* (Dec. 1834): 556–561.

———. *A Report to the Trustees of the College of New Jersey Relative to a Revival of Religion Among the Students of Said College.* Philadelphia, Pa.: William Fry, Printer, 1815.

———. *A Sermon Occasioned by the Death of the Rev. James Sproat, D.D.* Philadelphia, Pa.: William Young, 1794.

———. "A Solemn Warning to the Presbyterian Church." *Christian Advocate* (Feb. 1834): 63–69.

Green, William Henry. "Dr. Charles Hodge." *Christian Union* (July 3, 1878): 4.

Griffin, Patrick. *The People with No Name: Ireland's Ulster Scots, America's Scots Irish, and the Creation of a British Atlantic World, 1689–1764.* Princeton, N.J.: Princeton University Press, 2001.

Grodzins, Dean. *American Heretic: Theodore Parker and Transcendentalism.* Chapel Hill: University of North Carolina Press, 2002.

Guder, Darrell Guder. "The History of Belles Lettres at Princeton." Ph.D. diss., University of Hamburg, 1964.

Guelzo, Allen C. "Charles Hodge's Antislavery Moment." In *Charles Hodge Revisited: A Critical Appraisal of His Life and Work,* ed. John W. Stewart and James H. Moorhead. Grand Rapids, Mich.: William B. Eerdmans, 2002.

Gundlach, John Bradley. "The Evolution Question at Princeton, 1845–1929." Ph.D. diss., University of Rochester, New York.

Gura, Philip F. *American Transcendentalism: A History*. New York: Hill & Wang, 2007.

———. *The Wisdom of Words: Language, Theology and Literature in the New England Renaissance*. Middletown, Conn.: Wesleyan University Press, 1981.

Gutjahr, Paul C. *An American Bible: A History of the Good Book in the United States, 1777–1880*. Stanford, Calif.: Stanford University Press, 1999.

———. "'Hundreds of Souls in the Balance': An Eastern Congregational Minister Ponders Moving West to Iowa." *Palimpsest* 74:2 (Summer 1993): 54–61.

Hageman, John F. *The History of Princeton and Its Institutions*. 2nd ed. 2 vols. Philadelphia, Pa.: J. B. Lippincott, 1879.

Hall, James, ed. *Forty Years' Familiar Letters of James W. Alexander, D.D.* 2 vols. New York: Charles Scribner, 1860.

Handy, Robert T. *A History of Union Theological Seminary in New York*. New York: Columbia University Press, 1987.

Hardman, Keith J. *Charles Grandison Finney, 1792–1875: Revivalist and Reformer*. Grand Rapids, Mich.: Baker Book House, 1987.

Harrison, Richard A. *Princetonians, 1769–1775*. Princeton, N.J.: Princeton University Press, 1980.

Hart, D. G. "Divided between Heart and Mind: The Critical Period for Protestant Thought in America." *Journal of Ecclesiastical History* 38 (Apr. 1987): 254–270.

———. *John Williamson Nevin: High Church Calvinist*. Phillipsburg, N.J.: P&R Publishing, 2005.

———. "Poems, Propositions, and Dogma: The Controversy over Religious Language in American Learning." *Church History* 57 (Sept. 1988): 310–321.

Hatch, Nathan O. *The Democratization of American Christianity*. New Haven, Conn.: Yale University Press, 1989.

———. "Elias Smith and the Rise of Religious Journalism." In *Printing and Society in Early America*, by William L. Joyce, et al. Worcester, Mass.: American Antiquarian Society, 1983.

———, and Mark A. Noll, eds. *The Bible in America: Essays in Cultural History*. New York: Oxford University Press, 1982.

Haviland, John. *The Builder's Assistant, Containing Five Orders of Architecture*. Vol. 1. Philadelphia, Pa.: John Bioren, 1818.

Herbst, Jurgen. *The German Historical School in American Scholarship*. Ithaca, N.Y.: Cornell University Press, 1965.

Higginson, Thomas Wentworth. *The Sympathy of Religions*. Boston, Mass.: Reprinted from the Radical, 1871.

Hill, George. *Lectures on Divinity*. Philadelphia, Pa.: Herman Hooker, 1844.

"Historic Philadelphia from the Founding until the Early Nineteenth Century." *Transactions of the American Philosophical Society*, n.s., 43:1 (1953): 1–331.

Hitt, Russell T., ed. *Heroic Colonial Christians*. Philadelphia: J. B. Lippincott, 1966.

Hochschild, Adam. *Bury the Chains: Prophets and Rebels in the Fight to Free an Empire's Slaves*. New York: Houghton Mifflin, 2005.

Hodge, Archibald Alexander. *The Atonement*. New York: T. Nelson & Sons, 1868.

———. *The Life of Charles Hodge*. New York: Charles Scribner's Sons, 1880.

———. *Outlines in Theology*. New York: Robert Carter & Bros., 1879.

———. *Popular Lectures on Theological Themes*. Philadelphia, Pa.: Presbyterian Board of Publication, 1887.

———. Review of *Natural Science and Religion* by Asa Gray. *The Presbyterian Review* 1 (1880): 586–589.

———, and Benjamin B. Warfield. "Inspiration." *The Presbyterian Review* 2:6 (Apr. 1881): 225–260.

Hodge, Charles. "An Account of the Present State of the Island of Puerto Rico." *Biblical Repertory and Princeton Review* 10:4 (Oct. 1838): 602–644.

———. "The Act and Testimony." *Biblical Repertory and Theological Review* (Oct. 1834): 505–522.

———. "The Act and Testimony." *Biblical Repertory and Theological Review* (Jan. 1835): 110–134.

———. *Adequate Support of the Ministry: Sustentation Fund.* Princeton, N.J.: Blanchard, 1866.

———. "Adoption of the Confession of Faith." *Biblical Repertory and Princeton Review* 30:4 (Oct. 1858): 669–692.

———. "American Board of Commissioners." *Biblical Repertory and Princeton Review* 21:1 (Jan. 1849): 1–42.

———. "The *American Quarterly Review* on Sunday Mails." *Biblical Repertory and Theological Review* 3:1 (Jan. 1831): 86–134.

———. "Anniversary Address: American Home Missionary Society." *The Home Missionary* 2:2 (June 1, 1829): 3, 18–20.

———. "Barnes on the Epistle of the Romans." *Biblical Repertory and Theological Review* 7:2 (Apr. 1835): 285–340.

———. "Christ, the Only Sacrifice." *Biblical Repertory and Princeton Review* 17:1 (Jan. 1845): 84–138.

———. "The Christian Spectator on the Doctrine of Imputation." *Biblical Repertory and Theological Review* 3:3 (July 1831): 407–443.

———. "The Church and the Country." *Biblical Repertory and Princeton Review* 33:2 (Apr. 1861): 322–376.

———. "The Church—Its Perpetuity." *Biblical Repertory and Princeton Review* 28:4 (Oct. 1856): 689–715.

———. *A Commentary on the Epistle to the Ephesians.* New York: Robert Carter & Brothers, 1858.

———. *A Commentary on the Epistle to the Romans.* Philadelphia, Pa.: Grigg & Elliot, 1835.

———. *Conference Papers.* New York: Charles Scribner's Sons, 1879.

———. "Conscience and the Constitution." *Biblical Repertory and Princeton Review* 23:1 (Jan. 1851): 125–158.

———. *The Constitutional History of the Presbyterian Church in the United States of America.* 2 vols. Philadelphia, Pa.: Presbyterian Board of Publication, 1851.

———. *A Discourse Delivered at the Re-Opening of the Chapel, September 27, 1874.* Princeton, N.J.: Chas. S. Robinson, 1874.

———. "Discourses on Christian Nurture." *Biblical Repertory and Princeton Review* 19:4 (Oct. 1847): 502–539.

———. "A Discourse on the Latest Form of Infidelity." *Biblical Repertory and Princeton Review* 12:1 (Jan. 1840): 31–71.

———. *Discussions in Church Polity.* New York: Charles Scribner's Sons, 1878.

———. *A Dissertation on the Importance of Biblical Literature.* Trenton, N.J.: George Sherman, 1822.

———. "The Elements of Psychology." *Biblical Repertory and Princeton Review* 28:2 (Apr. 1856): 331–387.

———. "England and America." *Biblical Repertory and Princeton Review* 34:1 (Jan. 1862): 147–177.

———. "Essays in the Presbyterian by Theophilus on the Question: Is Baptism in the Church of Rome Valid." *Biblical Repertory and Princeton Review* 18:2 (Apr. 1846): 320–344.

———. "Eutaxia; or, the Presbyterian Liturgies." *Biblical Repertory and Princeton Review* 27:3 (July 1855): 445–467.

———. "Examination of some Reasonings against the Unity of Mankind." *Biblical Repertory and Princeton Review* 34:3 (July 1862): 435–464.

——. *An Exposition of the First Epistle to the Corinthians.* New York: Robert Carter & Brothers, 1857.

——. *An Exposition of the Second Epistle to the Corinthians.* New York: Robert Carter & Brothers, 1860.

——. "Finney's Lectures on Systematic Theology." *Biblical Repertory and Princeton Review* 19:2 (Apr. 1847): 237–277.

——. "The General Assembly of 1835." *Biblical Repertory and Theological Review* 7:3 (July 1835): 440–482.

——. "The General Assembly of 1836." *Biblical Repertory and Theological Review* 8:3 (July 1836): 415–476.

——. "The General Assembly of 1837." *Biblical Repertory and Princeton Review* 9:3 (July 1837): 407–485.

——. "The General Assembly of 1843." *Biblical Repertory and Princeton Review* 15:3 (July 1843): 407–472.

——. "The General Assembly of 1845." *Biblical Repertory and Princeton Review* 17:3 (July 1845): 428–471.

——. "The General Assembly of 1846." *Biblical Repertory and Princeton Review* 18:3 (July 1846): 418–456.

——. "General Assembly of 1860." *Biblical Repertory and Princeton Review* 32:3 (July 1860): 511–546.

——. "General Assembly of 1861." *Biblical Repertory and Princeton Review* 33:3 (July 1861): 511–568.

——. "The General Assembly of 1862." *Biblical Repertory and Princeton Review* 34:3 (July 1862): 464–524.

——. "General Assembly of 1863." *Biblical Repertory and Princeton Review* 35:3 (July 1863): 439–499.

——. "General Assembly of 1864." *Biblical Repertory and Princeton Review* 36:3 (July 1864): 506–574.

——. "The General Assembly of 1865." *Biblical Repertory and Princeton Review* 37:3 (July 1865): 458–514.

——. "God in Christ." *Biblical Repertory and Princeton Review* 21:2 (Apr. 1849): 259–298.

——. "History of the Apostolic Church." *Biblical Repertory and Princeton Review* 26:1 (Jan. 1854): 149–192.

——. "The Idea of the Church, Part I." *Biblical Repertory and Princeton Review* 25:2 (Apr. 1853): 249–291.

——. "The Idea of the Church, Part II." *Biblical Repertory and Princeton Review* 25:3 (July 1853): 349–389.

——. "The Inspiration of Holy Scripture." *Biblical Repertory and Princeton Review* 29:4 (Oct. 1857): 660–698.

——. "The Integrity of our National Union vs. Abolitionism." *Biblical Repertory and Princeton Review* 16:3 (Oct. 1844): 545–581.

——. "Lachmann's New Testament," *Biblical Repertory and Princeton Review* 6:2 (Apr. 1834): 269–281.

——. "Lecture Addressed to the Students of the Theological Seminary." *Biblical Repertory. A Journal of Biblical Literature and Theological Review* 1:1 (Jan. 1829): 75–98.

——. "The Life of Archibald Alexander." *Biblical Repertory and Princeton Review* 27:1 (Jan. 1855): 133–159.

———. "The Mystical Presence." *Biblical Repertory and Princeton Review* 20:2 (Apr. 1848): 227–278.

———. "A Narrative of the Visit to the American Churches." *Biblical Repertory and Theological Review* 7:4 (Oct. 1835): 598–626.

———. "The New Divinity Tried." *Biblical Repertory and Theological Review* 4:2 (Apr. 1832): 278–304.

———. "Notes, Explanatory and Practical, on the Epistle to the Romans, designed for Bible-Classes and Sunday Schools." *Biblical Repertory and Theological Review* 7:2 (Apr. 1835): 285–340.

———. "A Plea for Voluntary Societies." *Biblical Repertory and Princeton Review* 9:1 (Jan. 1837): 101–152.

———. "Presbyterian Reunion." *Biblical Repertory and Princeton Review* 40:1 (Jan. 1868): 53–83.

———. "Presbyterianism." *Biblical Repertory and Princeton Review* 32:1 (Jan. 1860): 546–567.

———. "President Lincoln." *Biblical Repertory and Princeton Review* 37:3 (July 1865): 435–458.

———. "The Princeton Review on the State of the Country and of the Church." *Biblical Repertory and Princeton Review* 37:4 (Oct. 1865): 627–657.

———. "Principle of Protestantism as Related to the Present State of the Church." *Biblical Repertory and Princeton Review* 7:4 (Oct. 1845): 626–636.

———. "Principles of Church Union, and the Reunion of the Old and New-school Presbyterians." *Biblical Repertory and Princeton Review* 37:2 (Apr. 1865): 271–313.

———. "Prof. Park's Remarks on the Princeton Review." *Biblical Repertory and Princeton Review* 23:2 (Apr. 1851): 306–347.

———. "Protest and Answer." *Biblical Repertory and Princeton Review* 40:3 (July 1868): 456–477.

———. *Questions on the Epistle to the Romans: Designed for Bible Classes and Sunday Schools.* Philadelphia: Grigg & Elliot, 1835.

———. "Relation of the Church and State." *Biblical Repertory and Princeton Review* 35:4 (Oct. 1863): 679–693.

———. "Retrospect of the History of the Princeton Review." *Biblical Repertory and Princeton Review*, Index Volume (1871): 1–39.

———. "Review of an Article in the June number of the *Christian Spectator*, entitled, 'Inquiries respecting the Doctrine of Imputation.'" *Biblical Repertory and Theological Review* 2:3 (July 1830): 425–472.

———. "Review of Sprague's *Lectures to Young People.*" *Biblical Repertory and Theological Review* 3:3 (July 1831): 295–306.

———. "The Revised Book of Discipline." *Biblical Repertory and Princeton Review* 30:4 (Oct. 1858): 692–721.

———. "Rights of Ruling Elders." *Biblical Repertory and Princeton Review* 15:2 (Apr. 1843): 293–332.

———. "Scripture and Science." *The New York Observer*, March 26, 1863, 98–99.

———. "Short Notices." *Biblical Repertory and Princeton Review* 17:1 (Jan. 1845): 190.

———. "Slavery." *Biblical Repertory and Theological Review* 8:2 (Apr. 1836): 268–305.

———. "The State of Religion in France." *Christian Advocate* (Oct.–Nov. 1827): 449–453, 499–502.

———. "The State of the Country." *Biblical Repertory and Princeton Review* 33:1 (Jan. 1861): 1–36.

———. "Stuart on Romans." *Biblical Repertory and Theological Review* 5:3 (July 1833): 381–416.

———. "Sunday Laws." *Biblical Repertory and Princeton Review* 31:4 (Oct. 1836): 733–767.

———. "Sustentation Fund." *Biblical Repertory and Princeton Review* 38:1 (Jan. 1866): 1–24.

———. "The Teaching Office of the Church." *The Foreign Missionary Chronicle* 16:6 (June 1848): 161–172.

———. "The Tecnobaptist." *Biblical Repertory and Princeton Review* 30:2 (April 1858): 347–389.

———. "The Testimony of Modern Science to the Unity of Mankind." *Biblical Repertory and Princeton Review* 31:1 (Jan. 1859): 103–149.

———. "The Theology of the Intellect and that of the Feelings." *Biblical Repertory and Princeton Review* 22:4 (Oct. 1850): 642–674.

———. "The Tracts of the Times." *Biblical Repertory and Princeton Review* 10:1 (Jan. 1838): 84–119.

———. "Unity and Diversities of Belief even on Imputed and Involuntary Sin." *Biblical Repertory and Princeton Review* 23:4 (Oct. 1851): 674–695.

———. "The Unity of the Church." *Biblical Repertory and Princeton Review* 18:1 (Jan. 1846): 137–158.

———. "The Vicarious Sacrifice." *Biblical Repertory and Princeton Review* 38:2 (Apr. 1866): 161–194.

———. "The Visibility of the Church." *Biblical Repertory and Princeton Review* 25:4 (Oct. 1853): 670–685.

———. "Voluntary Societies and Ecclesiastical Organizations." *Biblical Repertory and Princeton Review* 9:3 (Jan. 1837): 101–120.

———. "The War." *Biblical Repertory and Princeton Review* 35:1 (Jan. 1863): 140–169.

———. *The Way of Life.* Philadelphia, Pa.: American Sunday-School Union, 1841.

———. *What is Darwinism?* New York: Scribner, Armstrong, & Co., 1874.

———. *What is Presbyterianism?* Philadelphia, Pa.: Presbyterian Board of Publication, 1855.

Hodge, Hugh L. *Memoranda of Family History Dictated by Hugh L. Hodge M.D. LL.D.* N.p., 1903.

———. "Lecture on Cholera Morbus; on the Pathology and Therapeutics of Cholera Maligna." *American Journal of the Medical Sciences* 12 (1833): 293–306, 386–432.

Hodges, Graham Russell. *Slavery and Freedom in the Rural North: African Americans in Monmouth County, New Jersey, 1665–1865.* Madison, Wisc.: Madison House, 1997.

Hogeland, Ronald. "Charles Hodge, The Association of Gentlemen and Ornamental Womanhood: 1825–1855." *Journal of Presbyterian History* 53 (1975): 239–255.

Holifield, E. Brooks. "Mercersburg, Princeton, and the South: The Sacramental Controversy in the Nineteenth Century." *Journal of Presbyterian History* 54 (1976): 238–257.

———. *Theology in America: Christian Thought from the Age of the Puritans to the Civil War.* New Haven, Conn.: Yale University Press, 2003.

Holt, Michael F. *The Rise and Fall of the American Whig Party: Jacksonian Politics and the Onset of the Civil War.* New York: Oxford University Press, 1999.

Hopkins, Samuel. *Works of Samuel Hopkins.* 3 vols. Boston, Mass.: Doctrinal Tract & Book Society, 1854.

Horton, James Oliver, and Lois E. Horton. *Slavery and the Making of America.* New York: Oxford University Press, 2005.

Howe, Daniel Walker. *Making the American Self: Jonathan Edwards to Abraham Lincoln.* New York: Oxford University Press, 2009.

———. *The Political Culture of the American Whigs.* Chicago: University of Chicago Press, 1979.

———. *The Unitarian Conscience: Harvard Moral Philosophy, 1805–1861.* Middletown, Conn.: Wesleyan University Press, 1988.

———. *What Hath God Wrought: The Transformation of America, 1815–1848.* New York: Oxford University Press, 2007.

Humboldt, Alexander von. *Cosmos: A Sketch of a Physical Description of the Universe.* Translated by E. C. Otté. 5 vols. London: Henry G. Bohn, 1849, 1851, 1852, and 1870.

Hunter, James Davison. *Evangelicalism: The Coming Generation.* Chicago: University of Chicago Press, 1987.

"The Idea and Aims of the Presbyterian Review." *The Presbyterian Review* 1:1 (Jan. 1880): 3–7.

"*Index to Systematic Theology* by Charles Hodge." *Bibliotheca Sacra* 31 (Apr. 1874): 195–197.

Jackson, John P., Jr., and Nadine M. Weidman. *Race, Racism and Science: Social Impact and Interaction.* Santa Barbara, Calif.: ABC-CLIO, 2004.

Jarratt, Devereux. *The Life of the Reverend Devereux Jarratt.* Baltimore, Md.: n.p., 1806.

Johnson, Thomas Cary. *The Life and Letters of Benjamin Morgan Palmer.* Carlisle, Pa.: Banner of Truth Trust, 1906.

Johnston, Ruth Y. "American Privateers in French Ports, 1776–1778." *The Pennsylvania Magazine of History and Biography* 53:4 (1929): 352–374.

Jordan, Philip D. *The Evangelical Alliance for the United States of America, 1847–1900: Ecumenism, Identity and the Religion of the Republic.* Lewiston, N.Y.: Edwin Mellen, 1982.

Joyce, William L., et al. *Printing and Society in Early America.* Worcester, Mass.: American Antiquarian Society, 1983.

Kennedy, D. James, and Jerry Newcombe. *How Would Jesus Vote?* Colorado Springs, Colo.: Waterbrook Press, 2008.

Kerr, Hugh T., ed. *Sons of the Prophets: Leaders in Protestantism from Princeton Seminary.* Princeton, N.J.: Princeton University Press, 1963.

King, Lester S. *The Medical World of the Eighteenth Century.* Chicago: University of Chicago Press, 1958.

———. *Transformations in American Medicine: From Benjamin Rush to William Osler.* Baltimore, Md.: Johns Hopkins University Press, 1991.

Knapp, George Christian. *Lectures on Christian Theology.* New York: M. W. Dodd, 1850.

———. *Lectures on Christian Theology.* Trans. Leonard Woods Jr. New York: N. Tibbals, 1872.

Kraus, Norman C. *Dispensationalism in America: Its Rise and Development.* Richmond, Va.: John Knox, 1958.

Kull, Irving Stoddard. "Presbyterian Attitudes Toward Slavery." *Church History* 7:2 (June 1938): 101–114.

Labaree, Leonard W., ed. *The Papers of Benjamin Franklin.* Vol. 1. New Haven, Conn.: Yale University Press, 1959.

Lane, Belden C. "Miller and the Eldership: A Knickerbocker Goes to Nassau." *Princeton Seminary Bulletin* 6:3 (1985): 211–224.

"The Late Dr. Hodge." *New York Observer and Chronicle* (July 4, 1878): 211.

"The Late Mrs. Hodge." *The Presbyterian* 20 (Jan. 12, 1850): 6.

Laws of the College of New Jersey; Revised, Amended, and Adopted by the Board of Trustees, September 30, 1813. Trenton, N.J.: n.p., 1813.

Leach, Frank Willing. "The Philadelphia of our Ancestors." *The North American* (Sunday, June 14, 1908): 1, 7.

Lindsell, Harold. *Battle for the Bible.* Grand Rapids, Mich.: Zondervan, 1976.

———. *Bible in the Balance: A Further Look at the Battle for the Bible.* Grand Rapids, Mich.: Zondervan, 1979.

Livingstone, David N. *Darwin's Forgotten Defenders.* Grand Rapids, Mich.: William B. Eerdmans Publishing, 1987.

Loetscher, Lefferts A. *The Broadening Church: A Study of Theological Issues in the Presbyterian Church since 1869.* Philadelphia: University of Pennsylvania Press, 1954.

———. *Facing the Enlightenment and Pietism: Archibald Alexander and the Founding of Princeton Theological Seminary.* Westport, Conn.: Greenwood Press, 1983.

———. "The Problem of Christian Unity in Early Nineteenth-Century America." *Church History* 32:1 (Mar. 1963): 3–16.

MacArthur, John F. *Nothing but the Truth: Upholding the Gospel in a Doubting Age*. Wheaton, Ill.: Crossway Books, 1999.

MacCormac, Earl R. "Missions and the Presbyterian Schism of 1837." *Church History* 32:1 (March 1963): 32–45.

Maclean, John. *History of the College of New Jersey, From Its Origin in 1746 to the Commencement of 1854*. 2 vols. Philadelphia, Pa.: J. B. Lippincott, 1877.

Macleod, John. *Scottish Theology in Relation to Church History since the Reformation*. Carlisle, Pa.: Banner of Truth Trust, 1974.

Marsden, George M. *The Evangelical Mind and the New School Presbyterian Experience*. Eugene, Oreg.: Wipf & Stock, 2003.

———, ed. *Evangelicalism and Modern America*. Grand Rapids, Mich.: William B. Eerdmans, 1984.

———. *Fundamentalism and American Culture: The Shaping of Twentieth-Century Evangelicalism, 1870–1925*. New York: Oxford University Press, 1980.

———. *Understanding Fundamentalism and Evangelicalism*. Grand Rapids, Mich.: William B. Eerdmans, 1991.

Marsh, Charles. "Stuart's *Commentary on the Epistle to the Hebrews*." *Quarterly Christian Spectator* 1 (1829): 112–147.

Martin, Terence. *The Instructed Vision: Scottish Common Sense Philosophy and the Origins of American Fiction*. Indiana University Humanities Series 48. Bloomington: Indiana University Press, 1961.

Mason, Matthew. *Slavery and Politics in the Early American Republic*. New York: Oxford University Press, 2006.

McCosh, James. *The Religious Aspect of Evolution*. New York: G. P. Putnam's Sons, 1888.

McDowell, Josh. *Evidence that Demands a Verdict: Historical Evidence for the Christ Faith*. San Bernardino, Calif.: Campus Crusade for Christ, 1972.

McPherson, James M. *Battle Cry of Freedom: The Civil War Era*. New York: Oxford University Press, 1988.

"Meeting of the Presbyterian National Union Convention." *New York Times*, November 8, 1867, 5.

Memorial of Joseph Henry. Washington, D.C.: Smithsonian Institution, Government Printing Office, 1880.

Menand, Louis. *The Metaphysical Club: A Story of Ideas in America*. New York: Farrar, Straus, & Giroux, 2001.

Meranze, Michael. *Laboratories of Virtue: Punishment, Revolution, and Authority in Philadelphia, 1760–1835*. Chapel Hill, N.C.: Institute of Early American History and Culture, 1996.

Messler, Abraham. *Centennial History of Somerset County*. Somerville, N.J.: C. M. Jameson Publisher, 1878.

———. *First Things in Old Somerset, A Collection of Articles Relating to Somerset County, N.J.* Somerville, N.J.: Somerville Publishing Company, 1899.

Miller, Perry. "Jonathan Edwards to Emerson." *New England Quarterly* 13:4 (1940): 589–617.

———. *The Life of the Mind in America from the Revolution to the Civil War*. New York: Harcourt Brace Jovanovich, 1965.

Miller, Samuel. "*The Appropriate Duty and Ornament of the Female Sex*," A Sermon, Preached March 13, 1808. New York: Hopkins & Seymour, 1808.

———. *A Brief History of the Theological Seminary of the Presbyterian Church at Princeton New Jersey.* Princeton, N.J.: Printed by John Bogart, 1838.

———. *A Brief Retrospect of the Eighteenth Century.* 2 vols. New York: Burt Franklin, 1803.

———. *An Essay on the Warrant, Nature and Duties of the Office of The Ruling Elder in the Presbyterian Church.* Philadelphia, Pa.: Presbyterian Board of Publication, 1832.

———. "Letters to Presbyterians." *Christian Advocate* (April 1834): 78–86.

Miller, Samuel, Jr. *The Life of Samuel Miller.* 2 vols. Philadelphia, Pa.: Claxton, Remsen & Haffelfinger, 1869.

Minutes of the General Assembly of the Presbyterian Church in the United States. Philadelphia, Pa.: Presbyterian Board of Publication, 1847.

Minutes of the General Assembly of the Presbyterian Church in the United States of America. Philadelphia, Pa.: Stated Clerk of the General Assembly, 1789–1869.

Moorhead, James H. "The 'Restless Spirit of Radicalism': Old School Fears and the Schism of 1837." *The Journal of Presbyterian History* 78:1 (Spring 2000): 19–33.

Morgan, David. *Protestants and Pictures: Religion, Visual Culture, and the Age of American Mass Production.* New York: Oxford University Press, 1999.

Morison, Samuel Eliot. *Three Centuries of Harvard.* Cambridge, Mass.: Harvard University Press, 1936.

Moss, Roger W. *Historical Sacred Places of Philadelphia.* Philadelphia, Pa.: University of Pennsylvania Press, 2005.

Moyer, Albert E. *Joseph Henry: The Rise of an American Scientist.* Washington, D.C.: Smithsonian Institution Press, 1997.

Mullin, Robert Bruce. *The Puritan as Yankee: A Life of Horace Bushnell.* Grand Rapids, Mich.: William B. Eerdmans, 2002.

Murchie, David Neil. "Morality and Social Ethics in the Thought of Charles Hodge." Ph.D. diss., Drew University, 1980.

Murray, Andrew E. *Presbyterians and the Negro—A History.* Philadelphia, Pa.: Presbyterian Historical Society, 1966.

Myerson, Joel, ed. *Transcendentalism: A Reader.* New York: Oxford University Press, 2000.

Nash, Henry S. *The History of the Higher Criticism of the New Testament.* New York: Macmillan Company, 1900.

Nelson, John Oliver. "The Rise of the Princeton Theology: A Genetic History of American Presbyterianism until 1850." Ph.D. diss., Yale University, 1935.

"Neology." *The Quarterly Christian Spectator* 6:3 (Sept. 1834): 509–512.

Nettles, Thomas J. *James Petigru Boyce: A Southern Baptist Statesman.* Phillipsburg, N.J.: P&R Publishing, 2009.

Nevin, Alfred, ed. *Encyclopedia of the Presbyterian Church in the United States.* Philadelphia, Pa.: Presbyterian Publishing, 1884.

Nevin, John W. *The Mystical Presence and Other Writings on the Eucharist.* Philadelphia, Pa.: United Church Press, 1966.

Nichols, James Hastings, ed. *The Mercersburg Theology.* New York: Oxford University Press, 1966.

Noll, Mark A. *America's God: From Jonathan Edwards to Abraham Lincoln.* New York: Oxford University Press, 2002.

———. "Before the Storm: Life at Princeton College 1806–1807." *The Princeton University Library Chronicle* 42 (1981): 145–164.

———. "Charles Hodge." In *Reading Romans through the Centuries*, ed. Jeffrey P. Greenman and Timothy Larsen, 169–186. Grand Rapids, Mich.: Brazos Press, 2005.

———. *The Civil War as a Theological Crisis*. Chapel Hill: University of North Carolina Press, 2006).

———. "Common Sense Traditions and American Evangelical Thought." *American Quarterly* 37:2 (1985): 216–238.

———. "The Founding of Princeton Seminary." *The Westminster Theological Journal* 42 (Fall 1979): 72–110.

———. Introduction. In *The Way of Life*, by Charles Hodge. New York: Paulist Press, 1987.

———. *Princeton and the Republic, 1768–1822*. Princeton, N.J.: Princeton University Press, 1989.

———. "The Princeton Review: 1825–1929." *Westminster Theological Journal* 50 (Fall 1988): 283–304.

———, ed. *The Princeton Theology, 1812–1921*. Grand Rapids, Mich.: Baker Book House, 1983.

———. "The Response of Elias Boudinot to the Student Rebellion of 1807: Visions of Honor, Order, and Morality." *Princeton University Library Chronicle* 43 (August 1981): 1–22.

———, and David N. Livingstone, eds. *What is Darwinism?* by Charles Hodge. Grand Rapids, Mich.: Baker Books, 1994.

Nord, David P. *Faith in Reading: Religious Publishing and the Birth of Mass Media in America, 1790–1860*. New York: Oxford University Press, 2004.

Norton, Andrews. *A Discourse on the Latest Form of Infidelity*. Cambridge, Mass.: John Owen, 1839.

———. "The New School in Literature and Religion." *Boston Daily Advertiser* (Aug. 27, 1838): 2.

Novak, Steven J. *The Rights of Youth: American Colleges and Student Revolt, 1798–1815*. Cambridge, Mass.: Harvard University Press, 1977.

Numbers, Ronald L. *Creation by Natural Law: Laplace's Nebular Hypothesis in American Thought*. Seattle: University of Washington Press, 1977.

Oaks, Robert F. "Big Wheels in Philadelphia: Du Simitiere's List of Carriage Owners." *The Pennsylvania Magazine of History and Biography* 95:3 (July 1971): 351–362.

Oberdorfer, Don. *Princeton University: The First 250 Years*. Princeton, N.J.: Princeton University Press, 1995.

O'Connor, Thomas H. *Lords of the Loom: The Cotton Whigs and the Coming of the Civil War*. New York: Scribner, 1968.

Osen, James Lynn. "The Revival of the French Reformed Church, 1830–1852." Ph.D. diss., University of Wisconsin, 1966.

Paley, William. *Natural Theology; or, Evidences of the Existence and Attributes of the Deity, Collected from the Appearances of Nature*. New York: Evert Duyckinck, 1820.

Palmer, Benjamin Morgan. *The Life and Letters of James Henley Thornwell*. Richmond, Va.: Whittet & Shepperson, 1875.

Park, Edwards Amasa. "New England Theology." *Bibliotheca Sacra* 9:33 (1852): 170–220.

———. "Remarks on the Princeton Review." *Bibliotheca Sacra* 8:29 (1851): 135–180.

———. *Sketch of the Life and Character of Prof. Tholuck*. Edinburgh: Thomas Clark, 1840.

———. *The Theology of the Intellect and of the Feelings*. Andover: Warren F. Draper, 1850.

———. "Unity and Diversities of Belief even on Imputed and Involuntary Sin; with Comments on a Second Article in the Princeton Review." *Bibliotheca Sacra* 8:31 (1851): 594–667.

Patton, Francis Landey. *A Discourse in Memory of Archibald Alexander Hodge*. Philadelphia, Pa.: Times Printing House, 1887.

Piper, John. *Counted Righteous in Christ: Should We Abandon the Imputation of Christ's Righteousness?* Wheaton, Ill.: Crossway Books, 2002.

Pochmann, Henry A. *German Culture in America: Philosophical and Literary Influences: 1600–1900*. Madison: University of Wisconsin Press, 1957.

Pope, Earl A. "Albert Barnes, The Way of Salvation, and Theological Controversy." *Journal of Presbyterian History* 57:1 (Jan. 1979): 20–34.

———. "The Rise of the New Haven Theology." *The Journal of Presbyterian History* 44:1 (Jan. 1966): 24–44.

———. "The Rise of the New Haven Theology II." *The Journal of Presbyterian History* 44:2 (March 1966): 106–121.

Porter, Abner A. "The Unity of the Human Race." *Southern Presbyterian Review* 4:3 (Jan. 1851): 357–381.

Powell, John. *Bring Out Your Dead: The Great Plague of Yellow Fever in Philadelphia in 1793*. New York: Time, 1965.

Presbyterian Re-Union Memorial Volume. New York: De-Witt C. Lent, 1870.

Proceedings Connected with the Semi-Centennial Commemoration of the Professorship of Rev. Charles Hodge. New York: Anson D. F. Randolph, 1872.

Rainy, Robert, and James Mackenzie. *Life of William Cunningham, D.D.* London: T. Nelson & Sons, 1871.

Rapport, Mike. *1814: Year of Revolution*. New York: Basic Books, 2008.

Rawlyk, George A. *Ravished by the Spirit: Religious Revivals, Baptists, and Henry Alline*. Kingston, Ont.: McGill-Queen's University Press, 1984.

Raymond, Miner. *Systematic Theology*. 3 vols. New York: Phillips & Hunt, 1877–1879.

"Religious." *National Repository* 4 (Sept. 1878): 277.

Ripley, George. *Defence of "The Latest Form of Infidelity" Examined: A Second Letter to Mr. Andrews Norton*. Boston, Mass.: J. Munroe, 1839.

Robinson, James. *The Philadelphia Directory for 1805*. N.p.: Printed for the Publisher, 1805.

Rosenberg, Charles E. *The Cholera Years: The United States in 1832, 1849 and 1866*. Chicago: University of Chicago Press, 1987.

Rothe, Richard. *Theologische Ethik*. 5 vols. Wittenberg, Germany: Zimmermannsche Buchhandlung, 1867.

Rowe, Henry Kalloch. *History of Andover Theological Seminary*. Newton, Mass.: Thomas Todd, 1933.

Rush, Benjamin. *The Autobiography of Benjamin Rush: His "Travels Through Life" Together with His Commonplace Book for 1789 to 1813*. Princeton, N.J.: Princeton University Press, 1948.

Sachs, Aaron. *The Humboldt Current: Nineteenth-Century Exploration and the Roots of American Environmentalism*. New York: Viking, 2006.

Salmond, Charles A. *Princetonia: Charles and A. A. Hodge with Class and Table Talk of Hodge the Younger*. New York: Scribner & Welford, 1888.

Sandeen, Ernest R. "The Princeton Theology: One Source of Biblical Literalism in American Protestantism." *Church History* 31:3 (Sept. 1962): 307–321.

Savage, Henry Lyttleton. *Nassau Hall, 1756–1956*. Princeton, N.J.: Princeton University Press, 1956.

Sawtelle, William Otis. "Acadia: The Pre-Loyalist Migration and the Philadelphia Plantation." *Pennsylvania Magazine of History and Biography* 51 (1927): 244–288.

Schaff, Philip. *The Principle of Protestantism*. Philadelphia, Pa.: United Church Press, 1964.

Schaff, Philip, and S. Irenaeus Prime, eds., *History, Essays, Orations, and Other Documents of the Sixth General Conference of the Evangelical Alliance Held in New York, October 2–12, 1873*. New York: Harper, 1874.

Scharf, J. Thomas, and Thompson Westcott. *History of Philadelphia* 3 vols. Philadelphia: L. H. Everts, 1884.

Schleiermacher, Friedrich. *The Christian Faith*. 2 vols. New York: Harper Torch Books, 1962.

Schmidt, George P. *Princeton and Rutgers*. Princeton, N.J.: D. Van Nostrand Company, 1964.

Schmidt, Leigh Eric. *Restless Souls: The Making of American Spirituality from Emerson to Oprah*. San Francisco: HarperCollins, 2005.

Scott, Hugh Lenox. *Some Memories of a Soldier*. New York: The Century, 1928.

Scott, William Berryman. *Some Memories of a Palaeontologist*. Princeton, N.J.: Princeton University Press, 1939.

"The Scriptural View of Divine Influence as opposed to Pelagian and other Views." *The Quarterly Christian Spectator* 7:4 (Dec. 1835): 591–597.

Selden, William K. *Princeton Theological Seminary: A Narrative History, 1812–1992*. Princeton, N.J.: Princeton University Press, 1992.

Shedd, William G. T. *Dogmatic Theology*. 3 vols. New York: Charles Scribner's Sons, 1894.

Sherrill, Lewis Joseph. *Presbyterian Parochial Schools, 1846–1870*. New Haven, Conn.: Yale University Press, 1932.

Shumway, Daniel B. "The American Students of the University of Gottingen." *German American Annals* 8:5–6 (Sept.–Dec. 1910): 171–254.

Slocum, Stephen Elmer, Jr. "The American Tract Society: 1825–1975: An Evangelical Effort to Influence the Religious and Moral Life of the United States." Ph.D. diss., New York University, 1975.

Smith, Elwyn Allen. *The Presbyterian Ministry in American Culture: A Study in Changing Concepts, 1700–1900*. Philadelphia, Pa.: Westminster Press, 1962.

Smith, H. Shelton. "The Church and the Social Order in the Old South as Interpreted by James H. Thornwell." *Church History* 7:2 (June 1938): 115–124.

———, Robert T. Handy, and Lefferts A. Loestscher. *American Christianity: An Historical Interpretation with Representative Documents*. 2 vols. New York: Charles Scribner's Sons, 1963.

Smith, Helmut Walser, ed. *Protestants, Catholics and Jews in Germany, 1800–1914*. New York: Berg, 2001.

Smith, Henry Boynton, and Roswell D. Hitchcock. *The Life, Writings and Character of Edward Robinson*. New York: A. D. F. Randolph, 1863.

———. *System of Christian Theology*. New York: A.C. Armstrong and Son, 1884.

Smith, James Ward, and A. Leland Jamison, eds. *The Shaping of American Religion*. Princeton, N.J.: Princeton University Press, 1961.

Smith, Timothy L. *Revivalism and Social Reform in the Mid-Nineteenth-Century America*. New York: Abingdon Press, 1957.

Smith, Wilson. "William Paley's Theological Utilitarianism in America." *William and Mary Quarterly* 11:2 (Apr. 1954): 402–424.

Spann, Edward K. *The New Metropolis: New York City, 1840–1857*. New York: Columbia University Press, 1981.

Sprague, William. *Annals of the American Pulpit*, 9 vols. New York: Robert Carter & Brothers, 1857–1869.

Sproul, R. C. *Essential Truths of the Christian Faith*. Wheaton, Ill.: Tyndale House, 1998.

———, ed. *Soli Deo Gloria: Essays in Reformed Theology*. Nutley, N.J.: Presbyterian and Reformed Publishing, 1976.

Stampp, Kenneth M. *The Peculiar Institution: Slavery in the Ante-Bellum South*. New York: Vintage Books, 1989.

Staudenraus, P. J. *The African Colonization Movement 1816–1865*. New York: Columbia University Press, 1961.

Stein, Stephen J. "Stuart and Hodge on Romans 5:12–21: An Exegetical Controversy About Original Sin." *Journal of Presbyterian History* 47:4 (Dec. 1969): 340–358.

Stevenson, Louise L. "Charles Hodge, Womanly Women, and Manly Ministers." In *Charles
Hodge Revisited: A Critical Appraisal of His Life and Work*, ed. John W. Stewart and James H.
Moorhead, 159–179. Grand Rapids, Mich.: William B. Eerdmans, 2002.

Stewart, John W. "Mediating the Center: Charles Hodge on American Science, Language, Literature, and Politics." *Studies in Reformed Theology and History* 3:1 (Winter 1995): 1–114.

Stewart, John W., and James H. Moorhead, eds. *Charles Hodge Revisited: A Critical Appraisal of
His Life and Work*. Grand Rapids, Mich.: William B. Eerdmans, 2002.

Stewart, Kenneth J. *Restoring the Reformation: British Evangelicalism and the Francophone 'Réveil'
1816–1849*. Waynesboro, Ga.: Paternoster, 2006.

Stocker, Rhamanthus M. *Centennial History of Susquehanna County, Pennsylvania*. Philadelphia,
Pa.: R. T. Peck, 1887.

Stout, Harry S. *The Divine Dramatist: George Whitefield and the Rise of Modern Evangelicalism*.
Grand Rapids, Mich.: William B. Eerdmans, 1991.

Strong, Augustus H. *Systematic Theology*. 3 vols. Philadelphia, Pa.: Griffith & Rowland, 1907.

Stuart, Moses. "The *Biblical Repertory* on the Doctrine of Imputation." *The Quarterly Christian
Spectator* 3:3 (Sept. 1831): 497–512.

———. *A Commentary on the Epistle to the Romans*. 2nd ed. Andover, Mass.: Gould & Newman, 1835.

———. *A Commentary on the Epistle to the Romans*. 4nd ed. Glasgow, Scotland: Thomas Tegg &
Son, 1838.

———. *Conscience and the Constitution*. Boston, Mass.: Crocker & Brewster, 1850.

———. "On the Study of the German Language." *Christian Review* 6 (1841): 446–471.

———. "Remarks of a Protestant on the Biblical Repertory." *The Quarterly Christian Spectator* 3:1
(March 1831): 156–168.

Sweeney, Douglas A. *Nathaniel Taylor, New Haven Theology, and the Legacy of Jonathan Edwards*.
New York: Oxford University Press, 2003.

"*Systematic Theology*." *Mercersburg Review* 19 (April 1872): 318–321.

"*Systematic Theology* by Charles Hodge." *Mercersburg Review* 20 (Jan. 1873): 177–179.

Taylor, Nathaniel W. *Concio ad Clerum: A Sermon Delivered in the Chapel of Yale College, September 10, 1828*. New Haven, Conn.: Maltby & Homan Hallock, 1842.

———. "Spring on the Means of Regeneration." *Quarterly Christian Spectator* 1 (Mar. 1829): 1–40.

Thompson, Ernest Trice. *Presbyterians in the South*. 3 vols. Richmond, Va.: John Knox Press, 1963.

Thornwell, James H. *Collected Writings*. 4 vols. Richmond, Va.: Presbyterian Board of Publication, 1873.

———. "Dr. Thornwell on Ruling Elders." *Southern Presbyterian Review* 18:1 (July 1867): 30–46.

———. "The Elder Question." *Southern Presbyterian Review* 2:1 (June 1848): 1–67.

———. "The State of the Country." *Southern Presbyterian Review* 13:4 (Jan. 1861): 860–889.

Toner, J. M. *The Medical Men of the Revolution*. Philadelphia, Pa.: Collins, 1876.

Torbett, David. *Theology and Slavery: Charles Hodge and Horace Bushnell*. Macon, Ga.: Mercer
University Press, 2006.

Turner, James. *Without God, Without Creed: The Origins of Unbelief in America*. Baltimore, Md.:
Johns Hopkins University Press, 1985.

Turretin, Francis. *Institutes of Elenctic Theology*. 3 vols. Translated by George Musgrave Giger.
Edited by James T. Dennison Jr. Phillipsburg, N.J.: P&R Publishing, 1997.

Tuveson, Ernest Lee. *Redeemer Nation: The Idea of America's Millennial Role*. Chicago: University
of Chicago Press, 1968.

The Twelfth Annual Report of the American Society for Colonizing Free People of Colour of the United States. Georgetown D.C.: James C. Dunn, 1829.

Walker, Williston. *Ten New England Leaders.* New York: Silver, Burdett, 1901.

Ware, Henry, Jr. "The Personality of the Deity. A Sermon Preached in the Chapel of Harvard University, September 23, 1838." Boston, Mass.: n.p., 1838.

Warfield, Benjamin B. *Benjamin B. Warfield, Shorter Writings.* Edited by John E. Meeter. 2 vols. Phillipsburg, N.J.: Presbyterian and Reformed, 1970, 1973.

———. "The Real Problem of Inspiration." *Presbyterian and Reformed Review* 4:14 (Apr. 1893): 177–221.

———. "St. Paul & Inspiration." *Presbyterian and Reformed Review* 4:13 (Jan. 1893): 1–24.

Warner, Harriot W. *The Autobiography of Charles Caldwell, M.D.* Philadelphia, Pa.: Lippincott, Grambo & Co., 1855.

Watson, John F. *Annals of Philadelphia and Pennsylvania.* 3 vols. Philadelphia, Pa.: Edwin S. Stuart, 1884.

Webster's Speeches. Boston, Mass.: Ginn & Company Publishers, 1897.

Weigley, Russell F., et al,. *Philadelphia: A 300-Year History.* New York: W. W. Norton, 1982.

Wells, David F., ed. *Reformed Theology in America: A History of Its Modern Development.* Grand Rapids, Mich.: Baker Books, 1997.

Wells, Jonathan. *Charles Hodge's Critique of Darwinsim: An Historical-Critical Analysis of Concepts Basic to the 19th Century Debate.* Lewiston, N.Y.: Edwin Mellen Press, 1988.

Wertenbaker, Thomas Jefferson. *Princeton, 1746–1896.* Princeton, N.J.: Princeton University Press, 1946.

"What is the Real difference between the New-Haven Divines and those who oppose them?" *The Quarterly Christian Spectator* 5:4 (Dec. 1833): 657–672.

White, Henry Alexander. *Southern Presbyterian Leaders.* New York: Neale Publishing, 1911.

White, Ronald C., Jr. *Lincoln's Greatest Speech: The Second Inaugural.* New York: Simon & Schuster, 2002.

Wigger, John H. *Taking Heaven by Storm: Methodism and the Rise of Popular Christianity in America.* Urbana: University of Illinois Press, 1998.

Wilentz, Sean. *The Rise of American Democracy: Jefferson to Lincoln.* New York: W. W. Norton, 2005.

Williams, Charles Richard. *The Cliosophic Society, Princeton University.* Princeton, N.J.: Princeton University Press, 1916.

Wilson, James Grant. *Colonel John Bayard and the Bayard Family of America.* New York: Trow's Printing & Bookbinding, 1885.

Winsor, Justin, ed. *The Memorial History of Boston.* 4 vols. Boston, Mass.: J.R. Osgood, 1881.

Witmer, Andrew D. "'To Educate For Heaven': Charles Hodge and Religious Instruction in American Common Schools, 1825–1850." M.A. thesis, History Dept., University of Virginia, May 2002.

Woods, Leonard. *History of the Andover Theological Seminary.* Boston, Mass.: James R. Osgood, 1885.

Wosh, Peter J. *Spreading the Word: The Bible Business in Nineteenth-Century America.* Ithaca, N.Y.: Cornell University Press, 1994.

Wright, Scott Robert. "Regeneration and Redemptive History." Ph.D. diss., Westminster Theological Seminary, 1999.

Zilversmit, Arthur. *The First Emancipation of Slavery in the North.* Chicago: University of Chicago Press, 1967.

INDEX